TEST CRITIQUES: VOLUME VII

Daniel J. Keyser, Ph.D.

Richard C. Sweetland, Ph.D.

General Editors

TEST CRITIQUES
Volume VII

TEST CORPORATION OF AMERICA

LC 84-26895

ISBN 0-9611286-6-6 (v. 1)   ISBN 0-933701-14-4 (v. 1 softcover)
ISBN 0-9611286-7-4 (v. 2)   ISBN 0-933701-15-2 (v. 2 softcover)
ISBN 0-9611286-8-2 (v. 3)   ISBN 0-933701-16-0 (v. 3 softcover)
ISBN 0-933701-02-0 (v. 4)   ISBN 0-933701-17-9 (v. 4 softcover)
ISBN 0-933701-04-7 (v. 5)   ISBN 0-933701-18-7 (v. 5 softcover)
ISBN 0-933701-10-1 (v. 6)   ISBN 0-933701-19-5 (v. 6 softcover)
ISBN 0-933701-20-9 (v. 7)   ISBN 0-933701-21-7 (v. 7 softcover)
                             ISBN 0-933701-13-6 (softcover set)

Printed in the United States of America

CONTENTS

v

ACKNOWLEDGEMENTS

The editors wish to acknowledge the special contributions of our test reviewers. They have done an outstanding job. Our thanks extend from our deep pleasure and gratitude over their participation and the quality of their work. We know many of the contributing reviewers were as "caught up" in this project as we, and are now writing additional reviews for subsequent volumes. And, thanks also go to the test publishers themselves who released information to the reviewers in an expeditious manner.

We also wish to express thanks to the staff members at Test Corporation of America who are involved in this project: Jane Doyle Guthrie, Cheryl Morai Young, Kelly Scanlon, Barbara Cochrane, Frances Lucas, and Therese Wood. Eugene Strauss and Leonard Strauss, directors of Westport Publishers, Inc., have given freely and generously their support, encouragement, and business advice. Our indebtedness to both gentlemen is legion.

Finally, we want to express our warmest thanks to our readers. It is their use of *Test Critiques* that gives a final validity to this project. It is our sincerest desire that *Test Critiques* will have a true application for them.

INTRODUCTION

Test Critiques is a fulfillment of a goal of the editors and a continuation of a task begun with the publication of *Tests: A Comprehensive Reference for Assessments in Psychology, Education and Business* (1983), its *Supplement* (1984), and *Tests: Second Edition* (1986). With the *Test Critiques* series, we believe that we have moved into the final phase of this project—to include those vital parts that were not appropriate for our directory. With *Tests: Second Edition* and the *Test Critiques* series, the reader will have a full spectrum of current test information.

When *Tests* was published, a decision was made to leave out important psychometric information relating to reliability, validity, and normative development. Normative data and questions of reliability and validity were considered simply too complex to be reduced to the "quick-scanning" desk reference format desired. It was also apparent to the editors that a fair treatment of these topics would unnecessarily burden less sophisticated readers. More learned readers were familiar with other source books where such information could be obtained. The editors were aware, however, that a fuller treatment of each test was needed. These complex issues, along with other equally important aspects of tests, deserved scholarly treatment compatible with our full range of readers.

The selections for each volume were in no way arbitrarily made by the editors. The editorial staff researched what were considered to be the most frequently used psychological, educational, and business tests. In addition, questionnaires were sent to members of various professional organizations and their views were solicited as to which tests should be critiqued. After careful study of the survey results, the staff selected what was felt to be a good balance for each of the several volumes of critiques and selection lists were prepared for invited reviewers. Each reviewer chose the area and test to be critiqued and as can be noted in each volume's table of contents, some reviewers suggested new tests that had not been treated to extensive reviews. As test specialists, some reviewers chose to review tests that they had extensively researched or were familiar with as users; some chose to review instruments that they were interested in but had never had the opportunity to explore. Needless to say, the availability of writers, their timetables, and the matching of tests and writers were significant variables.

Though the reviewers were on their own in making their judgments, we felt that their work should be straightforward and readable as well as comprehensive. Each test critique would follow a simple plan or outline. Technical terms when used would be explained, so that each critique would be meaningful to all readers—professors, clinicians, and students alike. Furthermore, not only would the questions of reliability and validity along with other aspects of test construction be handled in depth, but each critique would be written to provide practical, helpful information not contained in other reference works. *Test Critiques* would be useful both as a library reference tool containing the best of scholarship but also useful as a practical, field-oriented book, valued as a reference for the desks of all professionals involved in human assessments.

It might be helpful to review for the reader the outline design for each critique contained in this series. However, it must be stressed that we communicated with each critique writer and urged that scholarship and professional creativity not be sacrificed through total compliance to the proposed structure. To each reviewer we wrote, ". . . the test(s) which you are reviewing may in fact require small to major modifications of the outline. The important point for you to bear in mind is that your critique will appear in what may well become a standard reference book on human assessment; therefore, your judgment regarding the quality of your critique always supercedes the outline. Be mindful of the spirit of the project, which is to make the critique practical, straightforward, and of value to all users—graduate students, undergraduates, teachers, attorneys, professional psychologists, educators, and others."

The editors' outline for the critiques consisted of three major divisions and numerous subdivisions. The major divisions were Introduction, Practical Applications/Uses, and Technical Aspects, followed by the Critique section. In the Introduction the test is described in detail with relevant developmental background, to place the instrument in an historical context as well as to provide student users the opportunity to absorb the patterns and standards of test development. Practical Applications/Uses gives the reader information from a "user" standpoint—setting(s) in which the test is used, appropriate as well as inappropriate subjects, and administration, scoring, and interpretation guidelines. The section on Technical Aspects cites validity and reliability studies, test and retest situations, as well as what other experts have said about the test. Each review closes with an overall critique.

The reader may note in studying the various critiques in each volume that some authors departed from the suggested outline rather freely. In so doing they complied with their need for congruence and creativity—as was the editors' desire. Some tests, particularly brief and/or highly specialized instruments, simply did not lend themselves easily to our outline.

Instituted in Volume III, an updated cumulative subject index has been included in this volume. Each test has been given a primary classification within the focused assessment area under the main sections of psychology, education, and business. The subject index has been keyed to correspond with *Tests: Second Edition.*

It is the editors' hope that this series will prove to be a vital component within the available array of test review resources—*The Mental Measurements Yearbooks,* the online computer services for the Buros Institute database, *Psychological Abstracts,* professional measurement journals, the forthcoming *A Consumer's Guide to Tests in Print* by Hammill, Brown, and Bryant, etc. To summarize the goals of the current volume, the editors had in mind the production of a comprehensive, scholarly reference volume that would have varied but practical uses. *Test Critiques* in content and scholarship represents the best of efforts of the reviewers, the editors, and the Test Corporation of America staff.

TEST CRITIQUES

Selma Hughes, Ph.D.
*Associate Professor of Psychology and Special Education, East Texas
State University, Commerce, Texas.*

ADAPTIVE BEHAVIOR INVENTORY

Linda L. Brown and James L. Leigh. Austin, Texas: PRO-ED.

Introduction

The Adaptive Behavior Inventory (ABI) is a norm-referenced test designed to evaluate the functional daily living skills of school-age children. The ABI assesses overall adaptive behavior and contains scales that appraise specific aspects of adaptive behavior such as self-care, communication, and social, academic, and occupational skills. The authors of the ABI are Linda L. Brown and James E. Leigh. Linda Brown, the senior author, has a distinguished background in test construction being the co-author of the Behavior Rating Profile (BRP; Brown & Hammill, 1978, 1983), and the Test of Early Socioemotional Development (TOESD; Hresko & Brown, 1984). The BRP makes use of an ecological approach to the assessment of disturbed behavior and is a standardized test that examines the home, school, and interpersonal environments of targeted students from different perspectives. The TOESD is a downward extension of the BRP and both tests deal with maladaptive behavior, the study of which contributes to an understanding of adaptive behavior.

The Adaptive Behavior Inventory, first published in 1986, has not been revised since its publication. No other forms of the test have been developed for special populations because the ABI, in its present form, already provides two sets of norms. One set of norms is based on students who are mentally retarded, and one set is based on students who have a full range of intelligence quotients (Brown & Leigh, 1986).

The test was developed in response to the current demand for measures of adaptive behavior as a complement to intelligence testing. Brown and Leigh point out in the test introduction that assessment of adaptive behavior started as a direct result of the Civil Rights Movement in the United States in the 1960s. Initially, there was concern over the increased numbers of minority students who were referred to classes for the mentally retarded. This concern led to the addition of measures of adaptive behavior into assessment procedures designed to determine eligibility for placement in special classes.

The Adaptive Behavior Inventory test materials consist of a manual, the ABI Profile and Response Sheet, and the ABI-Short Form Response Sheet. The ABI Response Sheet consists of five scales with approximately 30 or more items on each, which are rated according to four criteria. The Communication Skills scale has 32 items, the Occupational Skills scale has 28 items, and the Self-Care, Academic, and Social Skills scales each have 30 items. The response categories are 0, which indicates that the student being evaluated does not perform the skill; 1, which indicates that the student is beginning to perform the skill; 2, which indicates that the student performs the skill most of the time; and 3, which indicates that the student has mastered the skill.

The ABI-Short Form is an abbreviated form of the ABI and contains 50 items selected from the parent instrument. The ABI-Short Form includes every third item from each of the five scales. For example, from the Self-Care, Social, and Academic scales, items 3, 6, 9, 12, 15, 18, 21, 24, 27, and 30 are included. The response rating is the same 4-point Likert rating that is used for the ABI.

The examiner's function is to complete the rating for each item on the ABI or the ABI-Short Form based on either personal knowledge of the student being evaluated, or based on information from other professionals who have had regular contact with the student over a period of time. The student being evaluated is not involved directly in the testing unless the examiner chooses to set up situations to test the subject's mastery of those items that describe skills that the examiner (and other contributors) have not had a chance to observe.

The ABI and the ABI-Short Form are suitable for use with students ranging in age from 5–0 through 18–11 years. Within each scale the items are arranged in ascending order of difficulty so that basal and ceiling levels may be obtained in the administration of the test. The items are worded in clear, concise English and in simple, declarative statements, which do not permit ambiguity. In addition, the protocol sheets contain, on the cover page, a profile form of the results. Standard scores are plotted on a chart that shows the area bounded by one standard deviation above and below the mean. Scores beyond this range fall in a shaded area, which facilitates interpretation of the score. The cover pages of both the ABI and the ABI-Short Form also contain identifying data on the student being evaluated, the score summary, and the conditions under which the evaluation instrument was administered.

Practical Applications/Uses

Adaptive behavior assessment, or the evaluation of the daily performance of activities required for personal and social sufficiency, is receiving much attention from professionals who work with handicapped and nonhandicapped individuals in various settings (Harrison, 1987). Measures of adaptive behavior were not an integral part of assessment until the early 1970s, when the inclusion of adaptive behavior in the definition of mental retardation in 1973 led to the development of scales to assess adaptive behavior. According to Scheerenberger (1983), mental retardation and the concept of adaptive behavior have been intertwined in meaning and use throughout the history of special education. However, it was not until adaptive behavior was formally included in the definition that the need for scales to assess adaptive behavior became evident.

Handicaps other than mental retardation are now aided by the use of adaptive behavior scales. Meachem, Kline, and Stovall (1987) discuss the use of adaptive behavior scales with children who have hearing and visual impairments. They point out that the use of such scales is advantageous in academic and vocational areas for placement and programming. The degree of sensory impairment is not always the determining factor in placement, but rather, the student's functioning level of adaptive behavior skills. Similarly, for programming purposes it is often more desirable to increase the student's adaptive behavior skills than to work on developmental tasks previously perceived as necessary for students with sensory impairments.

Adaptive behavior scales also hold promise as a tool for the difficult task of differentiating autistic children from other low-functioning children who are not autistic (Volmar, Sparrow, Goudreau, Cicchetti, Paul, & Cohen, 1987). Sparrow and Cicchetti (1987) discuss the use of adaptive behavior scales in determining areas of greatest deficit in children with a variety of psychological disturbances. Findings from this and similar studies have implications for the clinical treatment of psychologically disturbed children, thus emphasizing the need for adequate measures of adaptive behavior.

In the field of learning disabilities, adaptive behavior scales are increasingly being suggested for use in distinguishing subtypes of learning disabilities. For example Weller, Strawser, and Buchanan (1985) use an adaptive behavior scale, which they developed to identify subtypes of learning disabilities. The scales are thus used as a designator of a continuum of severity in learning disabled individuals.

It is evident from this discussion that not all adaptive behavior scales are the same and that scales can be developed for different purposes and for different populations. Some adaptive behavior scales are designed to describe fairly typical development in the general population. Others are designed to prescribe detailed sequential items in handicapped population. The former are known as descriptive scales and the latter as prescriptive scales (Taylor, 1985). Descriptive scales are used primarily for classification and placement, while prescriptive scales are used generally for programming.

The ABI has the potential to be used for a variety of purposes in a variety of settings. The manual suggests that it may be used for psychological and school-based evaluations. The appropriate person to complete the ABI is a classroom teacher or another member of the professional school staff who has had regular, preferably daily contact with the student over a period of 4 to 6 weeks or more. In secondary schools or in other settings where more than one teacher has instructional responsibility for the student being rated, the examiner should capitalize on the situation by asking several instructors to contribute ratings (Brown & Leigh, 1986).

The test may also be used by school counselors and psychologists to determine the presence of maladaptive behaviors as well as the presence or absence of adaptive behaviors. The test is essentially a school-related instrument and may not be suitable for use in long-term institutional settings. It may be used in regular classrooms, self-contained classrooms, resource rooms, special day schools, and other community-based facilities. Students in institutional (24-hour care) settings and nonschool facilities constituted 7% of those included in the mentally retarded sample. It is debatable whether the ABI could be used with students whose experiences were entirely in long-term care facilities because their experiences would be different from those of students who had been in public schools while residing in community-based facilities. Therefore, the test is suitable for students in both regular and special education within the public schools.

Norms were developed for the ABI based on two different populations. One normative sample, the Normal Intelligence sample, is representative of school-age students nationally. The second group, the Mentally Retarded sample, is representative of mentally retarded students nationally. The standardization sample of mentally retarded students also included a small number of students with sensory impairments, so that the ABI could be used, in theory, with students who had visual and hearing impairments. However, in practice the Likert-type scale makes no provision for students who have had no opportunity to develop a particular skill because of their handicap. Absence of that skill is rated "0" and counts against that student. In scales like the Pyramid Scales (Cone, 1986), which are adapted specially for the handicapped, provision is made for rating categories such as "psychologically incapable" and "no opportunity to observe", which more accurately reflects the capabilities of students with disabilities.

The test manual provides specific guidance for administering the test. Guidelines for selecting the appropriate component are offered, which are very helpful in determining whether to use the ABI or the ABI-Short Form because the pros and cons of using each are stated. All that is required to complete the test is a protocol sheet and a pen or pencil. The directions printed at the top of each scale on the protocol sheet and also reproduced in the manual.

The items progress in order of difficulty on each scale. The first item is the easiest and the last is the most difficult. It is not necessary to score all items on the scales because the test establishes basal and ceiling levels to reduce testing time. At the basal level for the ABI and ABI-Short Form, the student must pass five consecutive items with a perfect rating whereas of the ceiling level the student earns no points on five consecutive items. Testing is terminated after the student reaches the ceiling level, and credit is given for all items below the basal level. The time required for completing the ratings should be no more than 20 to 25 minutes if all five scales are used. For the ABI-Short Form no more than 5 to 10 minutes are required.

The instructions for scoring the ABI are presented clearly. The manual provides several examples of hypothetical situations, several sample pages of completed protocol, and profile sheets as shown in the manual. The scoring procedures are uncomplicated and require simple arithmetic. The raw scores on the five scales are first converted to standard scores (SS) with a mean of 10 and a standard deviation of 3. The raw scores may also be converted to percentile ranks (PR) by using the appropriate tables in the appendix. Table A is used to convert raw scores to SS and PR using the Normal Intelligence standardization group as referent; Table B uses the Mentally Retarded standardization group as the referent.

Both Table A and Table B show the SS equivalent for raw scores at different chronological age levels for each of the five scales. If four or more of the scales are completed, the examiner can combine the obtained SS to determine the student's full scale percentile rank and Adaptive Behavior Quotient (ABQ-FS). The ABQ-FS is a composite quotient with a mean of 100 and a standard deviation of 15. Table C is used for this information and again provides comparison with both sets of norms.

The ABI-Short Form is scored in a similar manner to the ABI but only yields a PR and a deviation quotient (ABQ-SF) that has a mean of 100 and a standard deviation of 15. This score is obtained by using either Table D or Table E in the appendix. Table D is used to convert the raw scores to ABQ-SF and PR using the Normal Intelligence standardization group as referent, while Table E uses the Mentally Retarded standardization group as the referent.

The scores are objective and do not involve clinical judgment on the part of the examiner. The manual devotes a chapter to the interpretation of the ABI results and provides more than usual ancillary information to aid in the interpretation. Anyone with a modest background in testing would profit immeasurably from the information in this chapter. The purpose and use of percentile ranks, standard scores, and quotients are explained and general points on score interpretation are given.

Guidelines are provided for interpreting the standard scores and quotients from the ABI and the ABI-Short Form along with a table showing the significance of scores in terms of classifications such as Very Superior, Below Average, and so on. Table 2 helps the examiner determine the significance of differences between scores, while Table 3 compares the standard scores and quotients to other widely used score distributions (e.g., z-scores, T-scores, etc.). The chapter concludes with a schema for comparing measures of adaptive behavior with measures of intelligence and with a comprehensive discussion of the significance of the findings in the diagnosis of mental retardation. It is this reviewer's opinion that this is one of the most worthwhile features in the manual.

Technical Aspects

The test authors discuss several kinds of validity in the test manual. Validity is an empirical demonstration that a test measures what it says it measures. The most important kind of validity is construct validity, the extent to which a test measures the trait or ability it purports to measure. The authors approach the construct validity of the ABI by first identifying four underlying premises on which they consider adaptive behavior depends, and the authors provide data from correlational studies to support premises.

The first premise is that performance on the ABI should be positively related to intelligence; the second, that it should be positively linked to achievement; the third, that performance on the ABI should be positively related to age; and the fourth, that the components of the ABI should be positively correlated to each other. The correlational studies cited find a moderate correlation between measures of intelligence and performance on the ABI and the ABI Short-Form. These findings are similar to those generally reported in the literature (e.g., Harrison, 1987).

Data is provided to show moderate correlation between the ABI and tests of academic achievement. The correlation is of the order of .35, which the manual interprets as "positive but moderate." Harrison (1987) interpreted similar data to mean that there was a low relationship between adaptive behavior and school achievement. Harrison did however, concede that the effect of adaptive behavior on achievement may be greater than the correlations indicate and conceded that adaptive behavior in school may have a greater relationship on achievement than adaptive behavior outside school. Because the ABI assesses adaptive behavior in school, the test authors appear justified in interpreting their results to mean that there is a moderate relationship between the two.

The third premise is supported by coefficients ranging from .86 for the Occupational Skills scale to .96 for the ABQ-FS. Adaptive behavior is strongly related to age. There is also ample evidence presented to show that the scales of the ABI are interrelated to each other. The authors of the test have demonstrated that the test has good construct validity.

The second type of validity addressed is content validity, which refers to the inclusion of an adequate sampling of skills in the test. The manual points out that the items selected for inclusion were deemed appropriate by a panel of experts, which included practitioners and theoreticians. The items would therefore seem to be consistent with current theory and practice of what is known about adaptive behavior. In addition, the manual presents empirical data that confirm the high-item discrimination, and therefore, the content validity of the ABI. Considerable evidence is also presented of criterion-related validity (the extent to which the ABI is related to other measures of adaptive behavior). The ABI correlates moderately well with other adaptive behavior scales.

Reliability is the extent to which a test is stable and consistent. The ABI reports high measures of internal consistency and test-retest reliability. The test-retest reliability coefficients in particular provide strong evidence of the stability of the ABI scores when used with both normal students and students who are mentally retarded.

The ABI was standardized on two normative samples and the manual provides good descriptive data on each sample. The Normal Intelligence sample consisted of 1,298 students ranging from 5-0 to 18-11 years of age, and the Mentally Retarded sample consisted of 1,076 students ranging in age from 6-0 to 18-11 years. Data for the sample was gathered from 24 states, which provides a geographical balance, and there are almost equal numbers of males and females included in each sample. The demographic characteristics show that race and ethnic background was taken into account, as was the language status of the students. Socioeconomic status is not discussed, yet this may be a variable that influences adaptive behavior.

Critique

The Adaptive Behavior Inventory is a six-component norm-referenced battery designed to assess a student's performance of activities related to daily living. The ABI evaluates the student's ability to communicate with others, to interact socially, to perform academic tasks and those related to following an occupation, and to take care of oneself in general. Information on the test is obtained from observation by a professional who is familiar with the student being evaluated. The ABI is designed to supplement or complement other test data and is not intended to replace other kinds of testing. The fact that the mean and standard deviation of the individual scales corresponds to the subtest mean and standard deviation of the Wechsler Intelligence Scale for Children-Revised (WISC-R) and that the ABQ-FS is the same as the WISC-R Full Scale IQ adds to the usefulness of the test as a diagnostic instrument.

Although the test is called an inventory it is more of an adaptive behavior scale because normative data on two different populations, with which the student being tested may be compared, are provided. The ABI is, therefore, a highly useful instrument for both diagnosis and placement decision making, as well as an instrument for planning intervention and for documenting progress in programs.

References

Brown, L., & Hammill, D. (1978 & 1983). *Behavior Rating Profile*. Austin, TX: PRO-ED.

Brown, L., & Leigh, J. (1986). *Adaptive Behavior Inventory*. Austin, TX: PRO-ED.

Cone, J. D. (Ed.) (1986). *The pyramid system: Comprehensive assessment and programming for handicapped persons*. Morgantown, WV: Pyramid Press.

Harrison, P. (1987). Research with adaptive behavior scales. *Journal of Special Education, 21*(1), 37–68.

Hresko, W., & Brown, L. (1984). *Test of Early Social Emotional Development*. Austin, TX: PRO-ED.

Meacham, F., Kline, M., & Stovall, J. (1987). Adaptive behavior and low incidence handicaps: Hearing and visual impairments. *Journal of Special Education, 21*(1), 183–196.

Scheerenberger, R.C. (1983). *A history of mental retardation*. Baltimore: Paul H. Brooks.

Sparrow, S., & Cicchetti, D.V. (1987). Adaptive behavior and the psychologically disturbed child. *Journal of Special Education, 21*(1), 89–100.

Taylor, R.L. (1985). Measuring adaptive behavior: Issues and instruments. *Focus on Exceptional Children, 18*(2), 1–8.

Volmar, F. R., Sparrow, S., Goudreau, D., Cicchetti, D. V., Paul, R., & Cohen, D. J. (1987). Social deficits in autism: An operational approach using the Vinel and Adaptive Behavior Scale. *Journal of the American Academy of Child Psychiatry, 26*, 156–162.

Weller, C., & Strawser, S. (1981). *Weller Strawser Scales of Adaptive Behavior for the Learning Disabled*. Novato, CA: Academic Therapy Publications.

Weller, C., Strawser, S., & Buchanan, M. (1985). Adaptive behavior: Designator of a continuum of severity of learning disabled individuals. *Journal of Learning Disabilities, 18*(4), 205–212.

Michael K. Gardner, Ph.D.

Assistant Professor, Department of Educational Psychology, University of Utah, Salt Lake City, Utah.

ADMISSIONS TESTING PROGRAM: SCHOLASTIC APTITUDE TEST

The College Board. New York, New York: The College Board Publications.

Introduction

The Scholastic Aptitude Test (SAT) is a 135-item, multiple-choice test of developed verbal and mathematical abilities related to successful performance in college (College Entrance Examination Board, 1987d). The test was developed by a committee of the College Board, chaired by Carl C. Brigham, during 1925–26 as an alternative to the curriculum-based, essay-format college entrance examinations then in use by the board (Donlon, 1984). The SAT grew out of the U.S. Army intelligence testing movement of World War I, but its authors were careful to distinguish it from general intelligence tests (Brigham, Angier, MacPhail, Rogers, & Stone, 1926). The SAT has always been considered to be one datum, to be used in conjunction with other data (e.g., secondary school grade point average, extracurricular activities, recommendations, etc.) in the college admissions process.

Since its first administration to 8,040 students in June, 1926, the SAT has grown enormously and has evolved in the process. Over one million high school seniors from the class of 1987 took the SAT at some point during their academic careers (College Entrance Examination Board, 1987b). In 1929, it was decided to report two separate SAT scores: a verbal score and a mathematical score. This allowed colleges to weight verbal and mathematical ability differentially when making admissions decisions (Donlon, 1984). This aspect of the test remains today: a verbal score, based on two 30-minute verbal sections, and a mathematical score, based on two 30-minute mathematical sections, are reported. Since 1974, the verbal section of the test has also reported two subscores: a vocabulary subscore and a reading subscore.

The test contains two additional 30-minute sections: a research section used for test equating and item pretesting, and the Test of Standard Written English (TSWE). The TSWE assesses a student's ability to deal with the conventions of standard written English, and is used often by colleges (see Bauernfeind, 1987) to place students in freshman writing courses. The TSWE is administered as part of the SAT, though it is reported as a separate score. A student cannot elect to omit the TSWE when taking the SAT.

Although item types within each of the tests sections have varied over the 60-plus-year history of the test, these item types have been stable since 1975. The two verbal sections contain a total of 25 antonyms, 20 analogies, 15 sentence completion items, and 25 reading comprehension questions. Items of a given type are blocked together, and usually proceed from easiest to most difficult. However, the reading comprehensive questions are the one exception to this ordering; their order is determined by the logic and organization of the passage. The vocabulary subscore is based on the antonym and analogy items, while the reading subscore is based on the sentence completion and reading comprehension items. The two mathematical sections contain a total of 60 items, approximately two thirds being standard multiple-choice mathematics questions and approximately one third being quantitative comparison questions. Again, items are blocked by type and ordered in terms of increasing difficulty. The research section is made to look indistinguishable from other verbal and mathematical sections of the test. The TSWE contains 35 usage items, requiring the examinee to identify errors in English usage in presented sentences, and 15 sentence correction items, requiring the examinee to choose the best phrasing for a sentence segment from among presented alternatives.

Special forms of the SAT are available in large type, braille, and on cassette for students with documented visual, hearing, physical, and learning disabilities (College Entrance Examination Board, 1987c, 1987d; Packer, 1987). It is also possible for disabled students, who can use a regular type version but require extra time, to take the test during certain prespecified regular nationwide testing dates and receive additional time. Whether a special testing is needed or registration for a regular testing date with additional time, students should ask a counselor for a copy of the *Information for Students with Special Needs*. (This pamphlet is available from ATP Services for Handicapped Students, CN 6226, Princeton, NJ, 08541-6226.)

Practical Applications/Uses

The SAT is primarily used by college admissions officers who are making admissions decisions concerning prospective students. It is also used by guidance personnel and secondary school students in deciding which institutions best suit a student's educational goals and abilities. Finally, the SAT has been used to identify seventh- and eighth-graders with unusual academic talent, though it should be pointed out that this is not a primary use of the test. The test is most appropriate for secondary schools students, primarily those in their junior and senior years of high school. Many technical schools and colleges require the SAT (or some similar test such as the American College Testing Program's ACT admissions test) as part of their applications procedure.

Admissions officers, faced with the job of selecting applicants likely to succeed at their institutions, often find it difficult to compare high school transcripts of applicants directly because grading policies and curriculum vary from school to school. The SAT is valuable because it provides a uniform yardstick against which to measure applicants. Although it might seem tempting simply to base admissions decisions solely on the SAT, there is good reason not to (College Entrance Examination Board, 1988a). The SAT provides a very time-limited measure of behavior (i.e., 3 hours of administration time). The high school transcript (i.e., grade point average or class ranking) provides a measure based on a much longer observation interval, usually 4 years. This tremendous increase in observation period more than compensates for the lack of measurement precision in transcripts. With the above caution in mind, potential SAT users should realize that the test can and does provide unique information toward the prediction of success in college, over and above that which can be provided by high school transcript measures alone. It is for this reason that many admissions officers use the SAT as one component of the college admissions process.

Just as the SAT helps the admissions officers select successful students from the pool of applicants, the SAT can help secondary school students and their counselors to find a college that matches the student's academic strengths as measured by the SAT. A number of handbooks exist that give the median SAT scores of admitted freshman at colleges and universities across the United States (e.g., Barron's *Profiles of American Colleges* [Barron's Educational Services, 1986]). By comparing his or her SAT scores against the reported medians, a student can get some sense of his or her competitiveness in the admissions process. However, students must also keep in mind that 50% of students admitted to any given school had SAT scores below the reported median. Also, high school transcripts are usually counted more heavily than SAT score and other data (e.g., recommendations, extracurricular activities, work experience, and in some cases whether or not a student's parents were alumni of the school) play an important role.

The SAT is administered around the world on test dates designated by the College Board and Educational Testing Service (ETS), who administers the SAT program for the College Board. Typically, there are several testing dates a year; however, not all testing dates are applicable in all states and countries. For specific information on testing dates, one should consult the *Registration Bulletin: SAT and Achievement Tests* (College Entrance Examination Board, 1987d), which is published annually by the College Board. It is available at most high schools or from the College Board ATP, CN 6212, Princeton, New Jersey, 08541–6212. Administration is usually on a Saturday morning, but Sunday administrations are available for students who cannot take the test on Saturday for religious reasons. A letter from the student's cleric is required to be eligible for Sunday administration.

In 1987–88, the fee for taking the SAT was $12.00. If a student cannot afford the test fee and is a junior or senior, the student can apply for a fee waiver through her or his guidance counselor (College Entrance Examination Board, 1987a). Additional fees may be incurred for late registration and/or standby registration. Fee waivers do not cover these special fees. The registration fee covers scoring of the test and reporting of the test scores to up to four colleges or scholarship programs. Scores can be reported to additional institutions for an extra charge.

As part of the registration procedure, students are requested to fill out a questionnaire concerning their high school academic background, grades earned in courses, extracurricular and community activities, and the type of college they would be interested in attending. This questionnaire is known as the Student Descriptive Questionnaire (SDQ), and about 95% of all test takers fill out at least some portion of it (College Entrance Examination Board, 1987b). The SDQ has many purposes: a) student recruitment by colleges through the ETS's Student Search Service (students must agree to participate in this service, and SAT scores are not directly reported to participating institutions by ETS); b) research done by ETS and the College Board on the characteristics of the SAT as a function of variables compiled through the SDQ (e.g., Do suburban students score more highly on the SAT than rural and urban students?); and c) paperwork consolidation for colleges who receive reports containing not only a student's SAT scores, but also their courses, grades, and interests as reported through the SDQ. It is this last use that seems most worrisome. Despite the College Board's assurance that, overall, the SDQ is an accurate representation of students' accomplishments (College Entrance Examination Board, 1987c; Donlon, 1984), the user must remember that the SDQ is a self-report measure. Admissions officers should verify SDQ information against high school transcripts to assure its validity.

Actual administration of the SAT occurs at approximately 3,800 designated test centers. These centers are scattered throughout the United States, and about 500 are located in 100 foreign countries on six continents (Donlon, 1984). Testing is usually administered to groups in a classroom setting. The College Board provides test center supervisors with guidelines for the physical testing conditions that all designated test centers should meet (Educational Testing Service, 1987). The administration procedure and instructions to students are tightly controlled by ETS. Instructions to be read to students are printed in the *Supervisor's Manual* (Educational Testing Service, 1987), and any deviations from standard testing procedure (e.g., a mistake in timing a section) must be reported to ETS. ETS then investigates the situation and determines whether the deviation would require an adjustment to students' scores or whether a special make-up test is required. Should a make-up test be necessary, ETS pays the cost of the second examination.

Although the actual test is 3 hours long, total testing time (including instructions, seating students, etc.) lasts about 3½ hours. Students must present valid identification (i.e., a picture identification card) to be admitted to the test. ETS considers test security a vital issue, and is committed to preventing impostors from taking the test for other students.

Students can, for a fee, request the opportunity to verify their scores themselves. Two options for score verification are available: a) SAT Question-and-Answer Service and b) SAT Score Verification Service. The SAT Question-and-Answer Service is available only for certain testing dates. The service provides the student with a copy of her or his answer sheet, the answer key, the SAT test questions (but not the TSWE questions), and a conversion table for converting raw scores into scaled scores. The SAT Score Verification Service provides everything the Question-and-Answer Service does, except the actual SAT test question.

A variety of scores are reported, in slightly different formats, to students, high schools, and colleges. SAT verbal and mathematical scores are reported as scale scores on a scale ranging from 200 to 800. There was a time (from the test's inception until 1941) when each testing was normalized to have a mean of 500 and a standard deviation of 100. Since 1941, however, each new form of the test has been related back to the 1941 testing using a procedure known as test equating, which means that the 1941 testing population has served as a de facto standardization group. It also means that the verbal and mathematical test scores are no longer restrained to have a mean of 500 and a standard deviation of 100. The graduating high school class of 1987 had a verbal mean of 430 and a mathematical mean 476. There has been a trend over the past 25 years toward a decrease in mean verbal and mathematical SAT scores, though during the past few years this trend seems to have ended (College Entrance Examination Board, 1987b). This has led some to attack the American educational system and it also has led the College Board to examine the score decline in detail (College Entrance Examination Board, 1977). It is this reviewer's opinion that the score decline represents changes in the values of American society (e.g., the value and emphasis placed on reading) rather than a decline in America's educational institutions or the abilities of America's students.

Students receive their SAT verbal and SAT mathematical scores as both point estimates (single numbers determined by the criteria of best estimate) and interval estimates (intervals ranging from one standard error of estimate below the point estimate to one standard error of estimate above the point estimate). The use of interval estimates in addition to point estimates is admirable because it reduces the likelihood that students will interpret small differences in point estimates as being meaningful. In addition to these two methods of reporting SAT verbal and mathematical scores, students are given the percentiles corresponding to their scores for three different comparison groups: college-bound seniors nationally, college-bound seniors within the student's own state, and a national sample of all high school students. The percentiles allow the student to attach some meaning to the scale scores, even if they are not familiar with the SAT scoring system.

The SAT verbal score is also broken down into two subscores: reading and vocabulary. The verbal subscores are reported as point estimates on a scale from 20 to 80 (similar to the verbal and mathematical scales with the trailing zero dropped). No interval estimates or percentiles are reported for these subscores. Finally, the TSWE score is reported as a point estimate (no interval estimates are provided) on a scale ranging from 20 to 60+. This scale is similar to that used by the verbal subscores. Because the test was primarily designed to identify students with difficulties in using standard written English, the test does not discriminate among the most able groups of students (those whose abilities would fall in the 60 to 80 range). The College Board recommends the use of the English Composition Achievement Test to discriminate among these highly skilled students. The TSWE also reports percentiles corresponding to the student's scaled score compared against college-bound seniors nationally and college-bound seniors within the student's own state. No percentile rank for a national sample of high school students is provided.

When scores are reported, not only are scores from the current administration reported, but also scores from previous administrations (up to a total of six administrations). A student cannot choose to present only his or her best scores. This creates a problem for admissions officers using the SAT: Which scores should be used? There are many possibe answers: a) take the highest scores from among a student's testings, b) take the most recent scores, and c) take an average of the student's scores over her or his testings. No solution is without potential problems. Taking a student's highest scores will give an edge to students who have taken the test many times, but it will also allow a student to compensate for an off day. Taking the most recent scores gives the student credit for any cognitive growth that may have occurred since previous testings, but it is subject to the possibility of a single bad test performance. The final alternative reduces error through averaging, but does not give credit for cognitive growth over time. Because no algorithm is trouble free, professional judgment needs to be used. Admissions officers should be sensitive to individual situations such as a single score that is out of line with other scores.

Students often wonder whether special SAT preparation classes will improve their SAT scores, and whether a second testing will increase their SAT scores. The evidence on "coaching" shows a small but measurable gain due to participation in special preparation classes (about 14 points for the verbal score and about 15 points for the mathematical score [Messick & Jungeblut, 1981]). The gain seems related to the amount of time spent preparing, but a diminishing return law also operates: each additional hour spent accounts for a smaller increase in scores than the previous hour did. In an effort to provide all students with equal access to preparation for the test, the College Board has prepared some excellent test preparation materials. *Taking the SAT* (College Entrance Examination Board, 1987e) is provided free to students who register for the SAT, which contains a description of the test, test taking tips, sample questions of each type with answers and explanations, and a sample SAT (an actual previously used SAT including the TSWE) for students to take as practice. This publication is excellent and should be read by all prospective test takers. Students can also purchase *10 SATs* (College Entrance Examination Board, 1988b), which contains the same information as *Taking the SAT* plus 10 formerly used SATs with TSWEs to be used as practice tests. Because the College Board publications contain real SATs, it is unlikely that school-based or commercial coaching services could provide better preparation materials.

Retaking the SAT is a difficult issue and somewhat of a gamble. Data show that approximately 65% of those who retake the test achieve score increases, while 35% receive a lower score than their previous testing (College Entrance Examination Board, 1987d; Donlon, 1984). The average increase is 10 to 20 points for each of the two SAT scores (verbal and mathematical). Large score changes are rare. About 1 in 20 individuals experiences a gain of 100 points or more and about 1 in 100 individuals loses 100 points or more. The tendency to experience a score increase is also a function of an individual's initial SAT scores. Those who have high SAT scores on their initial testing are somewhat less likely to experience a score increase than those who have low SAT scores on their initial testing. This presumably reflects the effects of regression to the mean.

Broad interpretation of SAT scores is possible even for the nonexpert (i.e., student taking the test) with the help of a guidance counselor. Counselors should consult the *ATP Guide for High Schools and Colleges: SAT and Achievement Tests* (College Entrance Examination Board, 1987c), which provides a readable summary of the report formats used by ETS and the psychometric properties of the SAT and TSWE. Admissions officers will want to know more about the use of the SAT as a predictor of college performance at their institution. ETS provides free validity analysis through the Validity Study Service to help college administrators determine the best weighting of the SAT verbal and mathematical scores, along with other predictors, at their institution.

Technical Aspects

The SAT is a sound psychometric instrument. Internal consistency reliability of SAT verbal and mathematical scores range from .90 to .93 (the reliability of different forms of the test varies slightly). Earlier reliability estimates were based on Dressel's (1940) adaptation of the Kuder-Richardson Formula 20 for formula scoring (i.e., correction for guessing). Later reliability estimates were based on item response theory. Reliability was calculated as one minus the ratio of average squared standard errors of measurement to total score variance. Internal consistency reliabilities for the vocabulary and reading subscores range from .81 to .89. These numbers are consistent with the fact that each subscore is based on a smaller number of items than the full verbal score. The internal consistency of the TSWE is between .88 and .89. Test-retest reliability (for students who took the SAT in the spring of their junior year and autumn of their senior year) is .88 for both the verbal and mathematical scores (Donlon, 1984).

Another way to measure reliability is the standard error of measurement (SEM) of scaled scores. This is an index of the extent to which students' obtained scores over repeated testings differ from their "true scores" (College Entrance Examination Board, 1987d). The smaller the SEM, the more reliable the test. The SEM for the SAT verbal score is approximately 30, while the SEM for the SAT mathematical score is approximately 35. The SEMs for the vocabulary and reading subscores are about 4.5. The SEM for the TSWE is roughly 3.7. It must be remembered that the scale for the verbal and mathematical scores is 200 to 800, while the scale for the vocabulary and reading subscores and the TSWE is 20 to 80. Therefore the SEMs for the main SAT scores should be divided by 10 for comparison.

Another statistic of interest is the standard error of the difference (SED). This number (in units of the score scale) is an indication of how much variability one should expect between two testings of the same individual on the same test, or of two individuals with the same ability on a given test. The SED for the SAT verbal score is approximately 45, and the SED for the SAT mathematical score is approximately 50. The SED for the vocabulary subscore is about 6.4, and the SED for the reading subscore is about 6.2. The SED for the TSWE is close to 5.3. The College Board recommends that users do not consider two scores of a given type to indicate a true ability difference unless they are at least 1.5 SEDs apart (College Entrance Examination Board, 1987c).

The various scores provided by the SAT are not empirically independent of one another. The verbal and mathematical scores correlate .66. The TSWE correlates .79 with the SAT verbal score and .63 with the SAT mathematical score. The reading subscore correlates .94 with the verbal score, and the vocabulary subscore correlates .95 with the verbal score. It should be noted that the verbal score is based on the items which compose the two subscores; therefore, these correlations are artificially inflated.

Despite the fact that the SAT is a timed test, data show that it has only a small speed component (College Entrance Examination Board, 1987c; Donlon, 1984). Approximately 65 to 75% of students complete the last item in each 30-minute section of the test. Because this appears to indicate insufficient time, the test items are ordered by difficulty, and many students omit the last item by choice. A better indicator is the number of students completing the item three quarters of the way through a section. This item is much easier in difficulty than the last item, and approximately 99% of the students taking a test complete this item. The average number of questions not reached by students within any single 30-minute section of the test is between one and two. Thus, the SAT seems to be much more of a power test than a speed test.

The validity of greatest interest for users of the SAT is predictive validity: namely, the ability of the test to predict freshman grade point average (GPA) at a post-secondary institution. The College Board has compiled the results of validity studies carried out at 685 colleges by the Validity Study Service from 1964 to 1981 (Ramist, 1984) and found the following: a) the best single predictor of freshman GPA is high school record (either high school GPA or class rank), which had a median correlation .48 with the criterion across the colleges studied b) SAT verbal and mathematical scores taken together correlate with the criterion almost as well as high school record—median multiple correlation of .42 across the colleges studied, and c) SAT verbal and mathematical scores added to high school record improves the median correlation with the criterion to .55. Thus SAT scores do contribute unique variance to the prediction of success in college, over and above that which can be predicted on the basis on high school record alone.

Using a single prediction equation can cause overestimation of performance for some subgroups of individuals and overestimation of performance for other subgroups. For instance, use of a single regression equation tends to underpredict the performance of women in college and overpredict the performance of men (Linn, 1973; Wild, 1977). Also, the SAT may not predict the performance of minority students as well as it predicts the performance of white students. Breland (1979) found that the SAT did not predict college performance as well for black students at predominantly white colleges as it did for white students. However, the increment in correlation with the criterion due to SAT scores was greater for black students (.12) than for white students (.08). This indicated that although the SAT did not predict well for black students at predominantly white colleges, the high school record was an even poorer predictor for blacks than for whites. The message from these studies is that each college should perform its own validity studies, and should probably perform separate validity studies for different student subgroups (provided that a sufficient number of students of a given type exist to make the results meaningful). Given that the Validity Study Service is free through ETS, it is hard to understand why a college would not perform its own validity studies.

Critique

The SAT is a test with excellent psychometric properties. It has a long history in the college admissions testing area and will probably continue to be used by postsecondary institutions in the future. Critics of the SAT point out that the best predictor of college performance is the high school record, not the SAT (Chance, 1988; Crouse & Trusheim, 1988). They also note that the increment in predictability due to adding the SAT in prediction formulas is quite small. The rebuttal to such arguments is that without the SAT, there would be pressure to change grading policies to give students higher grades, thus increasing these students' chances of admission to the college of their choice. But this type of grade inflation would destroy the predictive validity of high school records. Once colleges realized that high school transcripts could no longer predict the ability to do successful work in college, they would move to other criteria. Many of these other criteria, such as whether a student went to high school in a wealthy community or a poor community, might predict success in college, but they would almost certainly be more discriminatory than any current critic of the SAT believes the SAT is.

When sorting large numbers of students, as most admissions officers do, even small increments in predictability are useful. The SAT is therefore a useful adjunct in the college admissions process. But students must keep in mind that predictability when dealing with large numbers of cases is not the same thing as predictability in a single case. Though SAT scores predict college success on the average, many low scorers will succeed in college, and many high scorers will not live up to their potential. Students and admissions officers both should keep in mind that the SAT is only one datum in the admissions process. It is a very useful datum, and this reviewer would recommend the SAT to potential users.

References

Barron's Educational Services. (1986). *Profiles of American colleges* (15th ed.). Woodbury, NY: Author.

Bauernfeind, R.H. (1987). Review of Test of Standard Written English. In D.J. Keyser & R.C. Sweetland (Eds.), *Test Critiques* (Vol. 6, pp. 609–614). Kansas City, MO: Test Corporation of America.

Breland, H.M. (1979). *Population validity and college entrance measures* (Research Rep. No. 79–08). New York: College Entrance Examination Board.

Brigham, C.C., Angier, R.P., MacPhail, A.H., Rogers, D.C., & Stone, C.L. (1926). The Scholastic Aptitude Test of the College Entrance Examination Board. In T.S. Fiske (Ed.), *The work of the College Entrance Examination Board 1901–1925* (pp. 44–63). New York: Ginn and Company.

Chance, P. (1988, May). Testing education. *Psychology Today,* pp. 20–21.

College Entrance Examination Board. (1977). *On further examination: Report of the advisory panel on the Scholastic Aptitude score decline.* (W. Wirtz, Chairman). New York: Author.

College Entrance Examination Board. (1987a). *Information for students with special needs.* New York: Author.

College Entrance Examination Board. (1987b). *1987 profile of SAT and Achievement Test takers.* New York: Author.

College Entrance Examination Board. (1987c). *1987–88 ATP guide for high schools and colleges: SAT and Achievement Tests.* New York: Author.

College Entrance Examination Board. (1987d). *Registration bulletin 1987-88: SAT and Achievement Tests.* New York: Author.

College Entrance Examination Board. (1987e). *Taking the SAT.* New York: Author.

College Entrance Examination Board. (1988a). *Guidelines on the uses of College Board test scores and related data.* New York: Author.

College Entrance Examination Board. (1988b). *10 SATs.* (3rd ed.). New York: Author.

Crouse, J., & Trusheim, D. (1988). *The case against the SAT.* Chicago: University of Chicago Press.

Donlon, T.F. (Ed.). (1984). *The College Board technical handbook for the Scholastic Aptitude Test and Achievement Tests.* New York: College Entrance Examination Board.

Dressel, P.L. (1940). Some remarks on the Kuder-Richardson reliability coefficient. *Psychometrika, 5,* 305–310.

Educational Testing Service. (1987). *Supervisor's manual—Instructions for administering: SAT and Test of Standard Written English and Achievement Tests.* Princeton, NJ: Author.

Linn, R.L. (1973). Fair test use in selection. *Review of Educational Research, 43,* 139–161.

Messick, S., & Jungeblut, A. (1981). Time and method in coaching for the SAT. *Psychological Bulletin, 89,* 191–216.

Packer, J. (1987). *SAT testing time for students with disabilities* (Research Rep. No. RR-87-36). Princeton, NJ: Educational Testing Service.

Ramist, L. (1984). *Predictive validity of the ATP tests.* In T.F. Donlon, (Ed.), *The College Board technical handbook for the Scholastic Aptitude Test and Achievement Tests* (pp. 141–170). New York: College Entrance Examination Board.

Wild, C.L. (1977). Statistical issues raised by Title IX requirements on admissions procedures. *Journal of the National Association of Women Deans, Administrators, and Counselors, 40,* 53–56.

Steven D. Brown, Ph.D.
Associate Professor of Counseling and Educational Psychology, Loyola University of Chicago, Chicago, Illinois.

James B. Rounds, Jr., Ph.D.
Associate Professor of Educational Psychology, University of Illinois, Champaign, Illinois.

ADULT CAREER CONCERNS INVENTORY

Donald E. Super, Albert S. Thompson, Richard H. Lindeman, R. A. Myers, and J. P. Jordaan. Palo Alto, California: Consulting Psychologists Press, Inc.

Introduction

The Adult Career Concerns Inventory (ACCI) is a 61-item questionnaire designed to measure career concerns of adults who are rethinking their careers and older adolescents who are about to enter the workforce. The ACCI assesses career concerns as they relate to the major stages and substages of career development: Exploration (substages: Crystallization, Specification, Implementation), Establishment (substages: Stabilizing, Consolidating, Advancing), Maintenance (substages: Holding, Updating, Innovating), and Disengagement (substages: Deceleration, Retirement Planning, Retirement Living). Thus, the ACCI provides a measure of the degree to which the respondent's career concerns lie within each stage and substage.

Donald E. Super is a professor emeritus at Teachers College, Columbia University and has held posts at the National Institute for Careers Education and Counseling, and Wolfson College, Cambridge, England. Dr. Super developed one of the first theories of career development (Super, 1953) and this, along with his publications from the Career Pattern Study, have made lasting contributions to vocational psychology and career counseling. He received a Distinguished Scientific Award for Applications of Psychology from the American Psychological Association in 1983.

Super's theoretical work parallels findings from his Career Pattern Study (CPS). His early research focused on the career development of adolescents and led to a model of career maturity that has had a widespread impact on career psychology. With the aging of the CPS subjects, Super shifted his focus from adolescent career maturity to the tasks confronting adults, finding that concepts developed from his study of adolescence were not applicable to adult career development (Super & Kidd, 1979). For example, the concept of life stages as applied to adults was modified to include minicycles of exploration, establishment, maintenance, and disengagement that result from career change. As applied to the ACCI, a 45-year-old worker changing careers, for example, would be in the Maintenance life stage according to chronological age, but could score high on the ACCI Exploration scale. Also, research on the adult CPS subjects led to the development of a model of career adaptability (Super & Knasel, 1979) that was proposed to be more relevant to understanding adult career development than was the earlier career maturity model. Career adaptability, defined as readiness to cope with changing work and working conditions (Super, Thompson, & Lindeman, 1988), directed the development of the ACCI.

The current version of the ACCI is the result of a long developmental history that is not specified clearly in the test manual (Super et al., 1988). The original form, developed from the dissertation research of Robin S. Zelkowitz (1974), was a 44-item version with 11 substage scales consisting of four items each. This work apparently led to the development of a longer 120-item form with 10 items for each of 12 substages that was followed by a shortened, 60-item form composed of 5 items in each of the 12 substages. These early forms were known as the Career Development Inventory, Adult Form (Super, 1977) and later as the Adult Career Development Inventory.

In the present version of the inventory, 60 items are grouped in sets of five according to the particular substages that they have been assigned. Thus, the first five items of the ACCI are "crystallization" items, while the final five are "retirement living" items. Two dissertation studies (Zelkowitz, 1974; Phillips, 1982) cited in the manual found this arrangement of items to be superior to a random ordering of items in terms of internal consistency estimates, factor structure, and validity evidence. Neither study is, however, well described nor are the actual results of the studies presented. The Zelkowitz dissertation employed the first 44-item version of the scale. It is not clear which version of the scale was employed by Phillips.

Item 61 is intended to provide information on the recycling aspect of adult career development. The item begins with a brief definition of career change as a shift in field of employment rather than a change of jobs within the same field and then asks respondents which of five choices best describes their current stage of career change (1 = not considering, 2 = considering a career change, 3 = planning a career change, 4 = implementing a career change, 5 = made a career change). The item is unscored and is intended to provide the user with information on the respondent's concern for career change. No information is provided in the manual on how the item is used other than to state that "It remains then up to the counselor to clarify meaning in an interview" (Super et al., 1988, p. 11).

Practical Applications/Uses

The ACCI is designed to be self-administering and can be completed individually or in groups. It is recommended that an examiner, familiar with career development theory, explain the purpose of the inventory and how it will be used prior to self-administration. In addition, when administered in groups, the manual recommends that one proctor be available for every 25 examinees. Self-administration time ranges from 15 to 30 minutes.

The items are contained on a single 8 ½" × 11" sheet with a separate 8 ½" × 11" answer sheet. Demographic information (sex, age, employment status, education, marital status, job satisfaction, career progress and prospects satisfaction, and career field) is also requested on the answer sheet. The directions accompanying the items are quite clear. Respondents are instructed to rate each statement, except Item 61, on a 5-point scale in terms of "how strong these concerns are at this point in your career" (1 = No Concern, 2 = Little Concern, 3 = Some Concern, 4 = Considerable Concern, 5 = Great Concern).

The ACCI can be self- or machine-scored. The back of the test page contains scoring instructions and a profile upon which raw scale and subscale scores and percentile equivalents can be plotted. The self-scoring directions appear to be somewhat complicated and technical. For example, scoring is accomplished by placing the number of items receiving each rating (i.e., 1, 2, 3, 4, 5) under each subscale, multiplying item frequencies by ratings, summing the resultant products, and dividing by 5 (the number of items in each subscale). The result is an average rating for each subscale with higher scores reflecting greater concern in that substage. However, respondents are instructed to 1) "enter the distribution of ratings for each group of five items in each substage" and 2) "then compute the average score for the substage by dividing the weighted sum by the number of items in the group." Although examples are provided after each set of instructions, one wonders how many respondents understand what "distribution of ratings" and "weighted sums" mean. Although no data are available on the frequency of scoring errors, the reviewers' guess is that it is substantial.

As indicated earlier, the ACCI is intended for adults and older adolescents. An eighth-grade reading level is reported in the manual. Thus, the reading level seems to be appropriate for the intended audience. Norms are provided for a sample of 373 adults (136 men and 225 women) divided into four major age groups (24 and under; 25-34; 35-44; 45 and older). However, there are no norms for persons who would be expected to be in the Disengagement stage (ages 60-65) nor for older adolescents. Reliability and validity studies appearing in the manual describe the use of the ACCI with respondents, ages 21 to 51, from academic and corporate settings. Education levels of respondents in the normative and psychometric samples seem to contain a disproportionate number of college and professionally educated people. Thus, the ACCI may be appropriate for use with college educated adults between the ages of 24 and 45. Its usefulness with older adolescents, retirement age persons, and non-college-educated persons remains to be demonstrated.

The ACCI was developed for use in career counseling and placement activities as a tool for the assessment of career concerns among workshop participants and counseling clients. A particular advantage of the self-scoring format for the ACCI was described in the manual as providing immediate feedback to participants career development workshops.

The manual further claims that the ACCI can be interpreted ipsatively and normatively. Ipsative interpretations (a bit of a misnomer, as scores, not interpretations, are usually described as ipsative) allow the user to compare an individual's score on any single subscale to his or her scores on the other subscales, yielding a rank ordering of the client's concerns with the tasks involved in each substage. Raw average subscale scores are used for this purpose. Thus, a person with an average score of 4.5 on the Specification subscale and an average score of 4.0 on the Implementation subscale would be seen as more concerned with the tasks of specification than with the tasks of implementation.

Such an interpretation should, however, only occur when the subscale scores are reliably different. The manual fails to point this out, treating all differences among scale and subscale scores as real (i.e., reliable). The manual does report standard errors of measurement for the scales and subscales that can be used to determine reliable differences among the scales. However, these errors of measurement are inappropriate for most counseling purposes because they are based on a small sample ($N = 68$) of academic professionals. Furthermore, these standard errors seem too large for a 5-point scale (i.e., career stage standard errors are greater than 2.5 and career substage standard errors are greater than 1.4). Before attempting to interpret differences among scale scores for an individual, the reviewers recommend that counselors use the appropriate standard deviations from the norm tables presented in Appendix B to calculate standard errors of measurement. Unfortunately, reliability coefficients are not reported for the norm sample. Thus, the user will need to rely cautiously on reliability coefficients reported for university professional staff ($N = 68$) and corporate employees ($N = 331$) to compute standard errors of measurement.

For normative interpretations, tables are provided in the manual for converting raw stage scores (but not substage scores) into percentiles. Separate tables are provided for the combined normative sample of 373 men and women, for females ($n = 225$), and for males ($n = 123$) broken down further into four age categories (under 25; 25–34; 35–44; 45 and over). The manual is quite clear about the limitations of this norm group in terms of its size, educational bias, and lack of sufficient number of older (60–65) and younger (18–22) subjects in the sample and wisely urges caution in normative interpretations.

Technical Aspects

Psychometric data on the current version of the ACCI are not extensive. The manual reports two reliability studies on the internal consistency of the ACCI scales and subscales. The first, with 68 professional staff from a Northeastern technical university, reported all Cronbach alpha coefficients for substages, with the exception of the Deceleration substage, to be in the .80s and for all major stages to be above .90. The other study employed a sample of 331 employees of a large international corporation and found internal consistency estimates for all substages and major stages to be above .90, with the exception of the Deceleration substage, which was .81. No data have been reported on the test-retest stability of the ACCI scales and subscales.

Studies exploring the validity of the ACCI are also few. One doctoral dissertation (Mahoney, 1986) reported that corporate employees who were classified on the basis of age and ACCI data as age-stage congruent reported higher levels of job satisfaction than did those classified as age-stage incongruent; differences were not found for career satisfaction.

In a study of the stage concerns of the norm group, the manual reported data inconsistent with career development theory (Super, 1957, 1980) for men. Specifically, when major scale scores were rank ordered in absolute value separately for males under 24, between 25–34, 35–44, and over 45, it was found that Establishment rather than Exploration was the dominant concern of the youngest age group. The older age groups showed dominant concerns that were consistent with developmental theory (i.e., 25–34, Establishment; 35–44, Maintenance; over 45, Disengagement). Interestingly, women's dominant career concerns appeared to be more consistent with career development theory, with each age group's highest ranked scale score being consistent with predictions of theory. Whether the former results are a function of problems with theory, the ACCI, inadequate statistical analyses (i.e., no tests for significant differences among the stage scores were reported), or all three, however, cannot be ascertained from the data presented. Further research on the ACCI and theoretically predicted career stage concerns seems particularly necessary.

Finally, the ACCI was developed as a hierarchically structured instrument with four major scales and 12 subscales (3 for each major scale). A factor analytic investigation of the structure of the ACCI in a sample of 393 corporate employees (Mahoney, 1986) failed to support a hierarchical structure. The results of this investigation, described too briefly in the manual, suggested that three factors, accounting for 59.6% of the total variance, best described the structure of the ACCI in the sample. The first factor combined the Establishment and Maintenance scales and subscales, while the second and third factors included the Exploration stages and substages and Disengagement scales, respectively. Although the authors of the manual attribute the merging of the Establishment and Maintenance scales to the homogeneous age, sex, and job security of the sample (not described in the manual), it should still be noted that the subscales did not emerge as distinct lower order factors as would be hypothesized by the hierarchical model of career development that guided the construction of the ACCI.

Critique

All in all, it appears that the ACCI is the result of an extensive evolutionary process of test construction that began in 1974 as part of the Career Pattern Study. However, evolution is not yet complete and the ACCI, in its present form, is still at a rudimentary stage. Norms are of inadequate size, especially in the younger (i.e., older adolescents) and older age groups. Evidence on the construct validity of the instrument is also lacking and what is available is often not consistent with the theory of adult career development.

The ACCI was developed to fulfill three functions: 1) to provide assessment in career intervention, 2) to assess needs of adult workers and students, and 3) to direct research on adult career development theory. The data to date are inadequate to suggest that the ACCI is useful for these purposes. Fundamental to all three uses is evidence of construct validity, for until we have some evidence that the ACCI is measuring what it is intended to measure, its use in counseling or in research is questionable. There also needs to be more evidence on whether its use in career interventions adds to outcome beyond current strategies of assessing adult stage concerns through counseling interviews.

The manual adequately describes the current norm group in terms of major demographics as well as ACCI scores, highlights the limitations of these norms, and cautions against inappropriate uses. Adult development theory upon which the ACCI is based is well described and the user is urged to become familiar with career development theory before employing the instrument. Sufficient references are provided in the manual to achieve adequate theoretical knowledge.

On the negative side, the manual does not adequately describe how the ACCI was developed except to note the names and briefly describe the number of items in previous measures. What is needed is a more detailed discussion of the evolution of the instrument, how items were selected, and the criteria used to retain and eliminate items for this version. This information would have been particularly useful in evaluating the ACCI in its current form because most reliability and validity studies reported in the manual were on earlier versions of the instrument. A clearer understanding of how the earlier instruments compared to the ACCI may have allowed for a more positive evaluation of the validity of the ACCI. More careful attention to descriptions of samples and sample selection procedures used in the validity studies is also needed.

The ACCI scores obviously signify the intensity of career concerns, but the manual, with the exception of giving broad descriptions of career stages, provides no description of what the various scales measure that could be used by counselors or clients to guide interpretation. For the major scales, the user will need to abstract ideas from general descriptions of career stages to provide an interpretation. For the subscales, the test authors tell the user to rely on item content for interpretation. Not discussed in the manual, however, are the meanings of high and low scores or how to ascertain when a score is of diagnostic importance.

Until adequate norms, understandable self-scoring procedures, counseling impact data, and further validity evidence are available, the ACCI should be used cautiously in counseling. Also, ipsative interpretations should not be attempted until adequate reliability estimates are available from appropriate norm groups for calculating standard errors of measurement. Because the ACCI is the only instrument (to the reviewers' knowledge) that is designed to assess adult career stage concerns, its use in research in adult development may be justified. However, investigators should keep in mind the lack of construct validity evidence on the ACCI when using it in research and interpreting results emanating from its use.

All in all, one must distinguish between potential and current status of an instrument (Tinsley, 1985). The ACCI may ultimately prove useful for its intended applied purposes. It is just that the current data are too meager to justify its use today.

References

Mahoney, D.J. (1986). *An exploration of the construct validity of a measure of adult vocational maturity.* Unpublished doctoral dissertation, Teachers College, Columbia University.

Phillips, R. (1982). *The relationship between the professional career development and the adult life cycle for women and men.* Unpublished doctoral dissertation, University of New Mexico, Albuquerque.

Super, D.E. (1953). A theory of vocational development. *American Psychologist, 8,* 185–190.

Super, D.E. (1957). *The psychology of careers.* New York: Harper & Row.

Super, D.E. (1977). Vocational maturity in mid-career. *Vocational Guidance Quarterly, 25,* 294–302.

Super, D.E. (1980). A life-span, life-space, approach to career development. *Journal of Vocational Behavior, 13,* 282–298.

Super, D.E., & Kidd, J.M. (1979). Vocational maturity in adulthood: Toward turning a model into a measure. *Journal of Vocational Behavior, 14,* 255–270.

Super, D.E., & Knasel, E. (1979). *Development of a model, specifications, and sample items for measuring career adaptability (vocational maturity) in young blue-collar workers.* Cambridge, United Kingdom: National Institute for Careers Education and Counseling.

Super, D.E., Thompson, A.S., & Lindeman, R.H. (1988). *Adult Career Concerns Inventory: Manual for research and exploratory uses in counseling.* Palo Alto, CA: Consulting Psychologists Press.

Tinsley, H.E.A. (1985). Review of My Vocational Situation. In D.J. Keyser & R.C. Sweetland (Eds.), *Test critiques* (Vol. 2; pp. 509–516). Kansas City, MO: Test Corporation of America.

Zelkowitz, R.S. (1974). *The construction and validation of a measure of vocational maturity for adults.* Unpublished doctoral dissertation, Teachers College, Columbia University.

Maxine B. Patterson, Ed.D.
Assistant Professor of Education, The University of Tennessee, Memphis, Tennessee.

AMERICAN ASSOCIATION OF TEACHERS OF SPANISH AND PORTUGUESE NATIONAL SPANISH EXAMINATIONS

American Association of Teachers of Spanish and Portuguese. Newark, Delaware: American Association of Teachers of Spanish and Portuguese.

Introduction

The National Spanish Examinations (NSE) serve as the basis for an annual competition among junior and senior high school students enrolled in Spanish classes. The examinations, which are produced in new forms each year, are designed to assess Spanish language knowledge and achievement at four achievement levels: Level I, Level II, Level III, and an Advanced Level. At each level, subtests are focused on the measurement of skills in four areas: listening comprehension, vocabulary, structure, and reading comprehension. The examinations include ". . . picture items, dialogs, vocabulary in context and structure items, rejoinders, error recognition items and reading passages" (McInnis & Guillermo, 1987, p. 2). Students at a given achievement level compete with others at the same level and in the same category of exposure to, or experience with, the Spanish language.

Three categories of exposure, or experience, are defined in the Guidelines for the 1987 National Spanish Examinations as 1) *Regular,* students with U.S. classroom experience only, 2) *Special,* students who have had exposure to and practice in Spanish in the home environment or during residence in a Spanish-speaking country for a period of 18 weeks or more, and 3) *Native,* students reared in a Spanish-speaking country who have attended for a period of 5 years or more schools where Spanish is the primary language of instruction. Students falling into the "native" category are eligible to compete in Level III or the Advanced Level examinations only.

Examiners and test centers are designated by local chapters or state coordinators of the American Association of Teachers of Spanish and Portuguese (AATSP), the sponsor and publisher of the NSE. Examinations are scheduled during a 3- or 4-week period in March of each year. Student winners of the competition at both the chapter and the national levels receive awards ranging from medals and books to college scholarships and study trips to Spain and Latin America (McInnis & Guillermo, 1987, p. 3). The names of winners, along with those of high-scoring non-winners, are published annually in the September issue of *Hispania,* the journal of the AATSP. The number of students completing the examinations in 1987 (the year for which information was provided to this reviewer) was estimated to be

66,041. They represented 2,470 teachers from 1,485 schools in 45 states, the District of Columbia, and the Virgin Islands (McInnis, 1987).

The AATSP was founded in 1917 for the purpose of promoting the teaching of Spanish and Portuguese. Its membership includes teachers of Spanish and Portuguese at all academic levels in the United States and Latin America. The AATSP initiated the development of the NSE in 1955 in response to ". . . a widespread demand in the early '50's with secondary school teacher members" (Charly, 1967, p. 857), who petitioned the organization to sponsor the development and distribution each year of printed and recorded tests for chapter and national competitions.

A committee appointed at the 1955 annual meeting of the AATSP was instructed to study other foreign language tests and examinations currently available and subsequently to prepare Spanish examinations for the second-, third-, and fourth-year secondary levels to be administered on a national scale. Working through the spring of 1956, the committee developed the initial forms of the NSE (Charly, 1967) that were administered for the first time on a national basis in March, 1957 (Kaulfers, 1972). The scope of the NSE remained unchanged for the first decade of its history. In 1967, however, the national NSE chairman reported that first- and fifth-year exams were made available for the first time (Charly, 1987, p. 858).

By 1978, dissatisfaction with some aspects of the NSE had been voiced by members of the AATSP. Responding to the criticism, the executive committee of the AATSP established a national committee to examine these national examinations and suggest revisions that would better reflect current classroom practices (Rose, 1978, p. 630). Designating 1980 as the target date for the first administration of the revised NSE, the executive committee also appointed several regional test-development committees to assemble the examinations at each level.

The need for revision of the NSE had been cited several years earlier by Kaulfers, who recommended the elimination of an auditory discrimination subtest and the addition of female voices to recordings used in listening comprehension subtests. Defining the auditory discrimination subtest as essentially a diagnostic test of aural acuity, Kaulfers (1972) suggested that it was inappropriate for inclusion in a functional test of actual ability to use Spanish in everyday life. Kaulfers further observed that the absence of female voices in recorded passages of the listening comprehension subtest could prove disadvantageous to students taught exclusively by females without exposure to Spanish spoken by male voices.

The unanticipated complexity of revising the NSE prevented the completion of the examinations in time for the 1980 competition. Thus, at its annual meeting in late 1979, the AATSP took the singular action of suspending the national Spanish contest for the following year. The revised NSE battery was first administered in 1981. It represented the work of four regional committees, who submitted a draft of the examinations. The final responsibility for the "new" NSE lay with a specifications committee. The final draft of the examinations had been pretested on a group of regular and native speakers from Colombia, Spain, and Puerto Rico (Hernandez & Guillermo, 1981).

Comparing the new version of the NSE to previous forms, the national NSE director, under whose leadership the revision was effected, stated that several changes had been made (Hernandez, 1980). The changes included the combining of Levels IV and V into a single Advanced Level and the assessment of a fee of (50¢)

per exam. The most significant change, according to the director, was the adoption of a policy limiting eligibility for participation in the NSE competition to students whose classroom teachers were members of the AATSP. That policy remained in effect until 1987, when eligibility was granted to students of nonmembers on the condition that the teacher pay a fee of $35.00 or the school pay a fee of $35.00 for *each* non-member teacher) (Guidelines for the 1987 National Spanish Examinations, 1987).

The organizational framework established in 1980 for the annual development of new NSE forms has remained in effect to the present. Thus, each of four regional committees, representing the South, East, Midwest and Southwest respectively, was responsible for drafting items for an assigned level of the 1987 NSE. The committees are composed of ". . . representative college professors and secondary school teachers, both English and native speakers, familiar with speech patterns from Latin America, Spain, and Spanish-speaking communities in the U.S." (McInnis, 1987, p. 856). Other teachers from the general AATSP membership are invited to participate in the test-development process by submitting items to the chairman of the appropriate committee. Final responsibility for the development of the examinations remains with a four-member specifications committee, which includes a specialist in tests and measurement.

Normative data, as typically defined, are not provided for the NSE. A statement issued by the national NSE office in 1974 explains that "new test forms are constructed annually, and although they are pretested on small population samples, no provisions are made for equating from level to level or from one year to another" (Turner & Charly, 1974, p. 540).

Test materials at each level of the 1987 version of the NSE include a 12-page examination booklet for the examinee and a cassette recording of spoken passages to be used by the examiner in the administration of the listening comprehension subtest. A printed answer key, along with a card-weight template for scoring are also provided. Stapled to the template is a note indicating that, due to a printing error, arrows on the template do not align properly with arrows on the answer sheet. Thus, the scorer is advised, the template must be adjusted to fit over the marks on the answer sheet. In lieu of a manual, the examiner is provided with a set of three color-coded documents (each with unnumbered pages) entitled, respectively, Guidelines for the Administration of the 1987 National Spanish Examinations (two pages), Directions for Administering the 1987 National Spanish Examinations (two pages), and Coordinator/Teacher Report (three pages).

The first three pages of test booklets for all levels are virtually identical. The first page, a perforated sheet, contains a Student Questionnaire for obtaining demographic data and a history of the examinee's exposure to the Spanish language. The second page (the reverse side of the first page) contains instructions and space for marking item responses, in addition to three enclosed areas. The first enclosed area is reserved for the entry of the examinee's name and category, and in the case of advanced students, the appropriate achievement level. The second area, for use by the testing center or school, provides space for the post-test entry of the examinee's raw score and rank in the examination; for indicating the name of the examinee's teacher; for specifying the status of the teacher with regard to AATSP membership; and, in the case of nonmember teachers, for noting payment or nonpayment of required fees. The third area, also for use by the testing center or school, contains blanks to be completed with the name, position, and AATSP chapter of the administrator and grader. Before beginning the examinations, examinees are instructed to remove the perforated sheet, which contains the answer sheet, to facilitate the marking of item responses. The third page of the test booklet is devoted to the identification of the director of the NSE, the specifications and test-development committees, and the individuals responsible for the recordings.

Examinations for all levels consist of 80 multiple-choice items. Items 1–30 constitute the listening comprehension subtest, and items 31–80 comprise the reading comprehension subtest. Within each subtest, items are grouped into alphabetically labeled parts. Varying in number from six in examinations for Levels I and III to seven in those for Level II and the Advanced Level, the parts function as organizers for groups of items with common response patterns.

Responsibility for all procedures in the testing process rests with the examiner or "coordinator." Upon receipt of the test materials, examiners are instructed to check the examinations and the accompanying cassettes, as well as to guard their security. Additional responsibilities include securing cassette recorders and proctors for each testing room at the test center, securing entrance and corridor signs to indicate room locations within the center, collecting and scoring all answer sheets, reporting test results to the national NSE office, collecting required fees for examinees whose teachers are not members of the AATSP, organizing a distribution of prizes, arranging newspaper publicity for winners and forwarding copies of resultant newspaper articles to the national office, and sending a list that summarizes results and student rankings to participating teachers.

Intended for use with junior and senior high school students, the NSE are designed to be difficult so that they will accommodate regular and special students at every level (McInnis, 1987, p. 856). Of the 187 respondents (based on an evaluation survey conducted among coordinators and teachers involved in the administration of the 1987 NSE), 29–48% rated the examinations as reasonably difficult (response rate varied from 45–60% among levels and subtests). A judgment of "too difficult" was made by 5–20% of the respondents. Their judgment appears to be corroborated by a drop in 1987 mean scores at Levels I and II, as compared to those of 1986 (McInnis, 1987).

Practical Applications/Uses

The NSE are designed to ". . . clearly discriminate student knowledge and achievement at each level [of junior and senior high school Spanish] on a national level" (Charly, 1977, p. 643). They are intended for use primarily in determining the recipients of prizes distributed annually by the AATSP to competing junior and senior high school students enrolled in Spanish classes. Because copies of the NSE are made commonly available after each annual competition, the examinations are also used as practice tests for students preparing for subsequent contests and as achievement tests in regular classroom settings. As a tool for measuring achievement in any case, the NSE are inappropriate for students who have had limited opportunity to develop aural comprehension skills. The examinations are likewise inappropriate for students taught solely by "conversational methods," without focus on grammatical structure or reading comprehension.

The NSE are specifically designed for administration on a large-group basis in testing centers. According to the AATSP, ". . . tests administered to students by qualified personnel other than their regular teachers of Spanish constitute an acceptable center situation" (Charly, 1976, p. 600). Typically, a separate testing room at each center is reserved for each respective level of the NSE. A coordinator, or teacher, appointed by the local or state AATSP affiliate is required for the administration of the examinations, in addition to one or two proctors per testing room.

Barring unanticipated problems with audiocassette players needed for the listening comprehension subtest, the NSE are administered easily. Instructions for administration are stated clearly and concisely in the two-page set of directions. At each level, the NSE are limited to 60 minutes. Fifteen minutes are devoted to the cassette-paced listening comprehension subtest and 45 minutes to the examiner-paced reading comprehension subtest.

Scoring of the NSE, the responsibility of the coordinator of the local testing center, may be done by hand or by computer. Center coordinators are encouraged by the national NSE office to ". . . institute Scantron or computer scoring if they have not already done so" (McInnis, 1987, p. 858). Apparently, the national office assumes no responsibility for payment of any charges attendant to computer scoring. Hand scoring of the 1987 NSE may be done with the printed answer key or with the hole-punched template included in the test materials. Scoring with the printed key requires 3 to 4 minutes per answer sheet. Use of the template would reduce scoring time substantially if the printed error mentioned previously were corrected. In its present configuration, however, the template subjects the scorer to error, as well as frustration.

Instructions to coordinators for reporting NSE results to the national office are confusing. On the one hand, coordinators who use computer-scoring procedures are directed to send to the national office the following data for each level and for each category within each level: number of students; mean, median, and mode scores; test reliability; and an item analysis. On the other hand, no mention is made of any types of similar data required of other coordinators. Presumably, statistical data on measures of central tendency, reliability, and item analysis are not expected from centers where the NSE are scored by hand. Nonetheless, a record of the number of students with hand-scored tests, as well as a full reporting of their raw scores, is critical to any further analysis of NSE results for the total population sample. This discrepancy raises questions about the derivation of national mean and median scores published in the report on the 1987 NSE (McInnis, 1987).

Technical Aspects

Scant information about the psychometric properties of the NSE are provided with the 1987 forms. The principal validity statistics accompanying the specimen copy of the examinations consist of means, medians, and standard deviations for all levels and for categories within levels, respectively, for the 1985-87 forms of the NSE. A single reliability coefficient is likewise included for each level and for each category within levels. The technique by which the values were derived is not identified, however. The reliability coefficients provided for the various levels and categories range from .77 to .93 for the 1987 NSE, from .86 to .91 for the 1986 version, and from .88 to .92 for the 1985 form.

As an instrument for assessing the attainment of objectives implied by the specifications published annually in *Hispania,* the NSE appear to have face validity. A semblance of content validity may be construed on the basis of the involvement of Spanish teachers in the development of the test battery and the control exercised by the specifications committee composed of content and testing experts.

Critique

In addition to its expressed purpose of measuring Spanish-language knowledge and achievement, the NSE battery is clearly a motivational tool for perpetuating the study and teaching of that language. In view of the fees attached to the participation of students of non-AATSP members in the NSE-based competition, it also appears to be a promotional tool for increasing membership in the association. Because it is the basis upon which awards, obviously perceived by examinees as valuable, are made to thousands of competing students in a national contest, it should, at the least, reflect psychometric soundness and scoring efficiency.

The absence of definitive statements about the technical aspects of the NSE renders suspect the psychometric soundness of the battery. Despite the obvious problems inherent in the gathering of relevant psychometric data on tests designed for a single administration, efforts should be made to ensure the validity and reliability of the NSE. With regard to reliability, for example, consideration should be given to the inclusion at each test level of a limited number of "anchor" items that would be repeated in the new forms of the NSE constructed annually. The use of anchor items in multiple annual forms would provide a database for equating tests from year to year and for evaluating the level of student achievement. In the event that anchor items were used in the NSE, the annual postadministration practice of releasing tests to interested teachers and students should probably be discontinued, and a standard set of "practice" tests should be constructed for distribution.

With regard to scoring efficiency, a centralized and systematic scoring mechanism is needed for the NSE. Such a mechanism would obviate the potential for scoring inconsistencies among testing centers and would lighten the heavy burden of responsibilities assigned to center coordinators, whose services are apparently provided without remuneration.

In addition to the psychometric and scoring aspects of the NSE, improvements should be made in some of the materials provided to examinees and examiners. Test items and answer sheets, judged on the basis of the 1987 forms, should be printed in larger, darker type to facilitate reading and hand scoring. Drawings used in the listening comprehension subtest should be sketched more clearly to ensure the probability of ready identification of the correct answer to a related question. Finally, the guidelines for the NSE should be rewritten for greater clarity of meaning, particularly with regard to scoring and reporting procedures.

The continued use for more than three decades of a technically flawed series of NSE batteries can be understood, perhaps, in the context of financial constraints within the AATSP and the apparent low priority assigned to the annual national competition. Despite its serious flaws, the NSE battery has the potential for being developed into an acceptable tool for measuring achievement of junior and senior high school students enrolled in Spanish classes. Its high-fidelity recordings are of excellent quality, its items are well constructed, and its content appears to sample adequately the content of Spanish courses at each of its respective levels.

References

Charly, H.T. (1967). History of the AATSP National Spanish Examination program. *Hispania, 50,* 857–859.

Charly, H.T. (1976). Announcement of the 1977 AATSP National Spanish Examinations. *Hispania, 59,* 600–601.

Charly, H.T. (1977). Report on the 1977 National Spanish Examinations. *Hispania, 60,* 642–643.

Guidelines for the 1987 National Spanish Examinations. (1987). Newark, DE: American Association of Teachers of Spanish and Portuguese (AATSP).

Hernandez, J.A. (1980). Announcement of the 1981 National Spanish Examinations. *Hispania, 63,* 634.

Hernandez, J.A., & Guillermo, T.R. (1981). Report on the 1981 National Spanish Examinations. *Hispania, 64,* 665–666.

Kaulfers, W.V. (1972). Review of the National Spanish Examination. In O.K. Buros (Ed.), *The seventh mental measurements yearbook* (pp. 600–601). Highland Park, NJ: Gryphon Press.

McInnis, J.B. (1987). Report on the 1987 National Spanish Examinations. *Hispania, 70,* 856–859.

McInnis, J.B. & Guillermo, T.R. (1987). *A.A.T.S.P.: The National Spanish Examinations.* Newark, DE: American Association of Teachers of Spanish and Portuguese (AATSP).

Rose, T. (1978). Report on the 1978 National Spanish Examinations. *Hispania, 61,* 629–630.

Turner, E.D., & Charly, H.T. (1974). Report on the 1974 National Spanish Examinations. *Hispania, 57,* 540–541.

Lucille B. Strain, Ph.D.
Professor of Education and Coordinator, Graduate Reading Education Program, Bowie State University, Bowie, Maryland.

ANALYTICAL READING INVENTORY
Mary Lynn Woods and Alden J. Moe. Columbus, Ohio: Charles E. Merrill Publishing Company.

Introduction

The Analytical Reading Inventory (ARI) is a test for individual administration designed to measure a constellation of skills and abilities believed to comprise total reading ability. Recommended primarily for use with students in Grades 2–9, the ARI is highly similar to informal reading inventories (IRIs) traditionally constructed by teachers and used in classroom settings. As in the case of teacher-constructed IRIs, the ARI contains graded word lists, graded passages, and questions for assessing comprehension of the passages. Specific behaviors that can be assessed by the ARI include word recognition, use of word-identification skills, oral and silent reading, reading comprehension, and reading levels of a student.

According to information provided in the introductory section of the ARI test booklet, the term *analytical* is used in the title of the ARI to indicate that the component parts of reading ability are assessed separately in relationship to an individual's total reading ability (Woods & Moe, 1985, p.3). It might be noted that this is essentially the same meaning implied by the term *inventory* in typical IRIs. The major difference between the ARI and teacher-constructed inventories probably lies in the attention to quality given it by its developers, its field testing, and its commercial availability.

The two authors of the ARI, Mary Lynn Woods and Alden J. Moe, are reading professionals. At the time of preparing the third edition of the ARI, Mary Lynn Woods was a reading specialist in the Orchard Day School in Indianapolis, Indiana. Alden J. Moe was associated with Louisiana State University. The test authors give credit in the test booklet to numerous persons who assisted in the field testing of the instrument. Special acknowledgments are made of the college and university students in reading education who tested the ARI in classroom and clinical settings (Woods & Moe, 1985, p. v).

The ARI was first published in 1977, a second edition was published in 1981, and the third edition was published in 1985. All editions have been published by Charles E. Merrill, a subsidiary of the Bell and Howell Company. The superiority of the third edition over the previous editions is claimed by the test authors to be the additional assistance provided for administering the inventory, interpreting its results, and recommendations for instruction.

According to the test authors, development of the third edition of the ARI took place over a period of 2 years and included writing, field testing, computer analyses, and several revisions of the 30 original paragraphs included in the test (Woods & Moe, 1985, p. 5). Content of the passages are original writings designed to be motivational for both girls and boys. The inventory is presented in three equivalent forms: Form A, Form B, and Form C. Each form of the ARI contains 7 graded word lists and 10 graded paragraphs for levels Primer through Grade 9. Questions for comprehension assessment are designed to be passage-dependent and to measure the reader's ability to 1) detect the main idea, 2) identify factual information, 3) define terminology, 4) distinguish between cause and effect, 5) make inferences, and 6) draw conclusions.

All materials essential for administering, scoring and interpreting results of the ARI are included in one spiral-bound booklet approximately 11" × 8". Specific parts of the booklet include: directions for administering the inventory, scoring, and interpreting the results; technical information related to development of the inventory; student booklets and teacher records for Form A, Form B and Form C; a Class Record Summary Sheet; and a selection of references. References are categorized as those related to diagnosis, correction, and remediation of reading difficulties; those related to common reading problems; and those utilized in development of the content of passages in the inventory.

Each student booklet for each form of the inventory contains graded word lists and graded paragraphs. The teacher record for each test form contains a Student Record Summary Sheet, a Qualitative Analysis Summary Sheet, reproductions of the graded word lists, and graded paragraphs contained in the student booklet. In addition, the teacher record contains comprehension questions and possible answers as well as provisions for counting miscues and scoring. Miscues are defined as the deviations from correct pronunciation that are made by a reader (Goodman & Burke, 1972).

Instructions are given in the test booklet on how to use the ARI. Prospective users are cautioned to read the test booklet in its entirety prior to attempting administration of the inventory. Included in the instructions section is the rationale for organization of the ARI, information related to its development and validation, information related to selection of content of the test paragraphs, and use of student and class record summary sheets. Equivalency of the three forms of the inventory enable the examiner to use any form independently of the other two.

Practical Applications/Uses

The ARI provides a systematic method for observing and recording details of an individual's reading behavior. Because of its nature, it is particularly suitable for use by persons involved in reading education. Classroom teachers, reading diagnosticians, and reading specialists are among those persons who will find the instrument efficient and effective for many of the purposes of reading diagnosis and instruction in their classrooms or clinics. Prospective teachers and other professionals in training will find the ARI convenient for many of the tasks associated with diagnosis of reading difficulties. Other professionals such as psychologists and researchers knowledgeable about reading can use the inventory to determine characteristics of individuals' reading behaviors. Although directions for using the ARI are relatively simple as compared with other instruments designed for similar purposes, it is essential that users have a basic knowledge of the nature of reading ability and its development for maximum effectiveness.

During the course of administering the ARI, the examiner is required to make many judgments that are facilitated if he or she is knowledgeable about reading ability. The examiner must observe the reader's miscues during oral reading and analyze these quantitatively and qualitatively. The examiner counts the miscues and also determines whether these alter the meaning of the text. Completion of the Student Record Summary Sheet and completion of the Qualitative Analysis Summary Sheet aids the examiner with these interpretations.

In some cases, where elected by the examiner, the reader may be asked to retell the content of a given passage or passages. This retelling provides information about the reader's knowledge of characters and the schematic structure of the plot. In lieu of retelling, or in addition to it, the reader may be asked to respond to questions about the passage. In these ways, the examiner acquires an understanding of the reader's ability to interpret the test author's message and/or understand the test author's language usage.

Technical Aspects

Passages in the ARI are original writings believed to have appeal for boys and girls in Grade 2 through Grade 9. To determine these interests, the test authors referred to several sources of information regarding children's reading interests. Sources cited in the test manual include *Children and Books* (Arbuthnot & Sutherland, 1972), *The New York Times Report on Teenage Reading Tastes and Habits* (Frieberger, 1973), *Reading Interests of Children and Young Adults* (Kujoth, 1970), and *Reading Children's Books and Our Pluralistic Society* (Tanyzer & Karl, 1972) (Woods & Moe, 1985, p. 5).Although passages do not represent a controlled vocabulary, selection of words used in the passages was influenced by reference to the graded word lists in *Basic Elementary Reading Vocabularies* by Harris and Jacobson (1972).

Readability formulas and computer analyses were used to validate grade levels of the passages and assure inclusion of appropriate grammatical constructions. The revised Spache formula was used to calculate reading-level estimates of primer through Grade 3 levels (Spache, 1974). Reading levels for Grades 4 through 9 were calculated with use of the Harris-Jacobson Formula 2 (Harris & Sipay, 1975). Computer analyses were used to provide specific information related to vocabulary variations and syntactic details of the language used in each passage. These procedures helped to ascertain that the passages in the test as a whole represented ascending levels of difficulty and that passages at a given grade level were comparable across all forms of the test.

Several tables pertaining to technical developments of the test are presented in the test booklet. Tables are included to show results of applications of both the Spache and the Harris-Jacobson formulas (Woods & Moe, 1985, Tables I and II, p. 7). Table III presents information pertaining to consistency within levels (Woods & Moe, 1985, p. 8). Table IV presents information about average sentence length and the longest sentence in each passage (Woods & Moe, 1985, p. 9).

The Analytical Reading Inventory was field tested by persons associated with its construction and development. Approximately 80 advanced students (students in their second course of reading instruction) tested use of the ARI by assessing the reading skills of 200 students in Grades 2 through 9. Comprehension questions were revised on the basis of results of the field tests (Woods & Moe, 1985, p. 9).

Criteria used for determining reading levels for individuals are those well established by time and long usage. Guidelines established first by Betts (1946) and later widely circulated in the work by Johnson and Kress (1976) are the bases for determining reading levels by use of the ARI (Beldin, 1970; Pikulski, 1974).

All criteria for determining reading levels are enumerated and explained in the test booklet of the ARI as are all scoring guides (Woods & Moe, 1985, pp. 12–19). Briefly, the independent level is determined on the ability of the reader to read a passage with no more than one uncorrected miscue in each 100 running words (99% correctly) with at least 90% comprehension. The instructional level permits no more than five uncorrected miscues (95%) and at least 75% comprehension. The frustration level occurs when the reader's miscues exceed 10% thus achieving less than 90% correctness in word recognition and only about 50% comprehension. The listening or capacity level (also called the hearing-comprehension level or the reading-potential level) is that level at which the individual comprehends 75% or more of material read orally by the examiner.

Critique

Concepts of the nature and uses of informal reading inventories are not novel. Most teachers and other professionals in reading and reading education are well acquainted with the purposes that can be served by an informal reading inventory. Teacher-constructed inventories have the advantage of being constructed from curriculum materials in use in a particular situation. When so developed, results of an IRI can be useful in placing students in materials (i.e., textbooks) suitable for their various levels of reading ability. The ARI, being typical of commercial IRIs does not provide so close a match between an individual's reading ability and a particular textbook. But, like other commercial IRIs, the ARI offers other advantages: 1) it is convenient to use, 2) it has been developed with a reasonable amount of care, 3) it has been field tested, 4) it provides directions for all aspects of its use, 5) it saves the examiner time and energy that would be expended in construction of an IRI that, likely, would not represent the quality characteristic of the ARI.

Users of the ARI, or any similar inventory, must keep in mind the purposes served by such an instrument. Results generally are not sufficient within themselves for providing a basis for major decisions to be made about a student. Results must be considered tentative and must be compared with results of other types of evaluation materials and procedures before they influence major decisions about students.

Michael C. McKenna (1983) reviewed some of the major important issues pertaining to IRIs and their uses. McKenna called attention to issues related to passage content and readability, choice of questions and passage dependency of questions, scoring criteria, and allowable miscues among other concerns. To their credit, the authors of the ARI offer rationales and describe procedures that comply reasonably with recommendations for improving the quality of inventories.

Woods and Moe (1985) are careful to assure readers that content (of the passages in the inventory) is based on topics reportedly of interest to children within the age groups and grade levels for which the inventory is designed. They cite specific sources and procedures used for ascertaining that content can be expected to appeal to many children in the given categories. Topics range from those appealing to the self-esteem of young children through various everyday, contemporary events to exotic stories of the far away for older readers.

To ascertain readability of the passages, two widely respected readability formulas were used. The revised Spache formula is highly appropriate for application to materials at the lower-grade levels. The Harris-Jacobson formula is suitable for application to materials at the upper-grade levels. Use of computer analyses to validate grade level suitability of materials represents the most efficient and effective procedures available for the task.

Comprehension questions designed to assess individuals' under standing of the passages in the ARI were selected in an effort to avoid providing the reader an opportunity to answer without reference to the passages. This appears to have been accomplished within reason. The number of questions seems appropriate and there is balance between factual and interpretive types.

Criteria for scoring to determine reading levels are based on time-tested and well-established guidelines. As pointed out by McKenna (1983), these guidelines have not been investigated thoroughly with regard to all aspects of their validity. These guidelines, however, remain practical in terms of major purposes for determining an individual's reading levels.

Unanswered questions still remain concerning the quantity and quality of miscues. Conflicting points of view can be found in the literature (Harris & Sipay, 1980; Ekwall, 1986). Procedures related to identifying and classifying miscues in the ARI seem to reflect reasonable approaches to this matter. In some instances, users of the ARI will have to determine the best procedure for their own purposes in their unique situations. This does not reflect negatively on the Analytical Reading Inventory. Rather, this is attributable to the nature of IRIs, generally. Users of IRIs must keep in mind that results are tentative and consist only of estimates, but can indicate direction for further diagnosis and measurement.

Woods and Moe have attempted to ease problems associated with having readers read orally at sight and the effect of this on the reader's comprehension. Users of the ARI are provided an alternative procedure that might be used when it is suspected that there is a significant gap between a reader's comprehension during oral and silent reading.

The format of the ARI makes it a convenient, practical, and portable instrument for the purposes it is designed to serve. It is compact and utilizes print the size and nature of which is appropriate for the respective levels of the test. It is this reviewer's opinion that among commercial informal reading inventories, the Analytical Reading Inventory can be recommended as one of the best available.

References

This list includes text citations and suggested additional reading

Bader, L. A. (1983). *Bader Reading and Language Inventory*. New York: Macmillan.
Beldin, H. O. (1970). Informal reading testing: Historical review and review of the research.

In W. Durr (Ed.), *Reading difficulties: Diagnosis, Correction and Remediation*. Newark, DE: International Reading Association.

Betts, E. A. (1946). *Foundations of reading instruction*. New York: American Book Company.

Burns, P. C., & Roe, B. D. (1985). *Informal Reading Inventory* (2nd ed.). Chicago, IL: Rand-McNally.

Ekwall, E. E. (1986). *Ekwall Reading Inventory* (2nd ed.). Newton, MA: Allyn & Bacon.

Ekwall, E. E., & Shanker, J. L. (1988) *Diagnosis and remediation of the disabled reader*. Needham Heights, MA: Allyn & Bacon.

Goodman, Y., & Burke, C. (1972). *Reading Miscue Inventory.* New York: Macmillan.

Harris, A. J., & Jacobson, M. D. (1972). *Basic elementary reading vocabularies* (The First R Series). New York: Macmillan.

Harris, A. J., & Sipay, E. R. (1980). *How to Increase Reading Ability* (6th ed.) New York: David McKay.

Johnson, M. S., & Kress, R. A. (1976) *Informal reading inventories*. Newark, DE: International Reading Association.

McKenna, M. C. (1983). Informal Reading Inventories: A Review of the Issues. *The Reading Teacher, 36,* 670–677.

Pikulski, J. N. (1974). A critical review: Informal reading inventories. *The Reading Teacher, 28,* 141–151.

Silvaroli, N. J. (1986). *Classroom Reading Inventory* (5th ed.). Dubuque, IA: William C. Brown.

Spache, G. D. (1974). *Good reading for poor readers*. Champaign, IL: Garrard Publishing Company.

Woods, M. L., & Moe, A. J. (1985). *Analytical Reading Inventory (Test Manual)* (3rd ed.). Columbus, OH: Charles E. Merrill Publishing Company.

Delwyn L. Harnisch, Ph.D.
Associate Professor of Educational Psychology, Institute for Research on Human Development, University of Illinois at Urbana-Champaign, Champaign, Illinois.

ASSESSMENT IN MATHEMATICS

R. W. Strong and Somerset Local Education Authority.
Basingstoke, Hampshire, England: Macmillan Education.

Introduction

Assessment in Mathematics (AIM) was developed by the Somerset Local Education Authority in Great Britain to provide a record of the mathematics progress of individual pupils. The individual tests comprising the assessment are criterion referenced, being keyed to a single set of Guidelines in Mathematics, which were produced by the Somerset Education Authority earlier. As such, they are not intended to be used in placing children in rank order of ability or of producing a norm-referenced set of scores. Rather, they are intended to be a set of subskill tests for identifying strengths and weaknesses. Although no firm criteria are delimited in the manual, the suggestion is made that the objectives are expected to be mastered by the top 20–25% of 11 year olds. The objectives measured in this battery would reflect mathematics typically offered in the United States from Kindergarten to Grade 7.

The AIM is designed for either group or individual administration by the classroom teacher. The 89 objectives measured in AIM are divided into five main areas: Number, Measure, Shape, Probability and Statistics, and Relations. To measure these objectives AIM provides a set of 87 photocopy-master pupil sheets, with one objective being measured for each sheet. Prior to testing the desired sheet is duplicated in sufficient quantities for the class. The copy serves then as both test and answer sheet. Scripts for supporting interviews as well as suggestions for further assessment are provided in the Teacher's Book. There are 44 pupil sheets designed to test number operations, 24 for measurement, 13 for shape, 4 for probability and statistics, and 4 for relation.

There is a great deal of flexibility in utilizing the AIM materials with the responsibility for determining the details of test administration, such as time limits, sequencing, mastery level, and amount of assistance offered left to the discretion of the assessment administrator. The manual suggests that teachers use the items only when the child has had a broad variety of classroom experiences. It is felt that this helps to avoid the pattern of high test scores with little fundamental understanding.

The following benefits of using the test are offered in the Teacher's Book (Somerset Local Educational Authority, 1987): 1) to provide a common record of mathematics learned during the primary and early secondary years; 2) to give continuity to the learning process; 3) to provide various modes of questioning ranging from straight computation to interview situations for problem situations; and 4) to allow for continuity in designing learning programs appropriate to the individual student's needs. The Teacher's Book was compiled under the direction of Richard W. Strong, County Inspector for Mathematics of the Somerset Local Educational Authority, with the assistance of K. Davey, J. Fox of Exeter University, R. Futrille, E. Harper of Bath University, Sister E. Hewlett, H. Joint, W. Nickels, A. West, J. West, and J. Worth.

The AIM was produced in partial response to public concern about accountability and monitoring standards of schools. The Somerset Local Education Authority had produced a set of Guidelines in Mathematics, aimed to provide a common content framework for mathematics while allowing local variations. AIM was designed to provide a commonly agreed upon record-keeping and assessment system to use based upon this earlier derived framework. According to the Teacher's Book, subsequent usage of the AIM materials did ensure that more meaningful information was being transferred from class to class and school to school within the Somerset Local Education Authority.

Practical Applications/Uses

The materials in AIM can be used to provide a general record showing an overview of the mathematics learned during the primary and early secondary years. It must be remembered that this record is quite broad, which means that the descriptions offered provide at best a very general assessment of pupil progress. Within this broad outline, however, it is possible to provide a common record keeping strategy to allow for continuity in designing individual student programs.

In addition to the 87 photocopy-master pupil sheets, other required materials for testing include individual student record cards and a variety of site provided manipulatives, such as chips, dot cards, balance beams, base 10 units similar to Dienes Multibase Arithmetic Blocks, strips, squares, and attribute blocks. It should be noted that efforts were made to keep the apparatus required for the assessments to a minimum and limited to items that in the view of the test authors should already be present in the schools. A listing of required items is included at the top of each sheet to aid in test administration.

An individual record card should be filled out with the school, name of pupil, date of birth, and date of entry for each student prior to any assessment. This form would then be kept as a part of the student's permanent record. Following each assessment session, the administrator would then record the child's performance on this card. Performance is indicated by placing a mark in one of two columns. A check in column A indicates that the child demonstrates some experience with the concepts assessed, while a check in column B shows that the child is reasonably competent. Levels of performance for each of these marks are left to the discretion of the administrator.

Although each assessment has specific instructions, there is a common pattern throughout the set. A typical assessment is divided into three sections, each measuring a different level of student competence. For example, the first section would consist of a child completing work with the teacher, often using manipulatives or other supportive materials; the second would require the child to work a provided set of problems independently, using manipulatives; and the final section would consist of an independent test in which manipulatives use is not allowed. This evaluation approach allows information on student performance to be gathered in a dynamic fashion and across a variety of situations.

Technical Aspects

The Assessment in Mathematics series was published by Macmillan Education, Ltd. on behalf of the Somerset Local Education Authority. Technical information was limited to the county's own preparation of the test, which was intended to be a set of subskill tests for identifying strengths and weaknesses rather than producing a norm-referenced set of scores. No attempts have been made to develop norms, define levels of success, or to check the reliability and validity of the instruments.

Critique

In reviewing the AIM, one must remember that this Assessment in Mathematics (AIM) is not intended to rank children in order of ability, to produce norm-referenced scores, or to be evaluated on the criteria of standardized tests. Rather, it must be viewed as a local educational system's attempt to assess individual student's strengths and weaknesses and to provide a record of the mathematics progress of individual pupils.

A major strength of AIM lies in the variety of assessment techniques utilized. Assessing the real level of a child's mathematical understanding is never an easy task, a fact that the Teacher's Book clearly recognizes. The variety of activities in the AIM goes far beyond the usual static testing measures commonly used and has the potential of addressing this important assessment issue. Depending upon the particular assessment in use, a student would be given the opportunity to demonstrate competency through physical manipulatives, sketches, and alternative forms of representation in addition to the more standard numeric abstractions and algorithms. AIM's use of concrete operations, interview techniques, and on line testing of applications provides a more dynamic method of assessment and should be recognized.

The worthy focus upon conceptual understanding of content material carries throughout the entire AIM. For example, when the suggested order of assessment is followed, each operation is tested conceptually prior to checking the ability of the pupil to use the related algorithm. One is even cautioned in the Teacher's Book that

> memory fades quickly without practice and revision, so that it is necessary to ensure that skills are maintained at a suitable level of competence. A high score on one assessment sheet does not mean that the particular objective can then be left forever. (Somerset Local Education Authority, p. 4).

The use of British spellings, monetary systems, decimal notation, and word usages limits the immediate use of the AIM outside of the British system. It should be remembered, however, that this program was designed by one local education system to meet their own internal needs. Other local systems could certainly benefit from using the carefully constructed and well-designed materials from the Assessment in Mathematics as a model for designing a similar program for themselves.

References

This list includes text citations and suggested additional reading.

Campione, J. C., Brown, A. L., & Connell, M. L. (in press). Metacognition: On the importance of knowing what you are doing. In R. I. Charles & E. Silver (Eds.), *Research agenda for mathematics education: Teaching and assessment of mathematical problem solving*. Hillsdale, NJ: Lawrence Erlbaum.

Nohda, N. (December, 1986). *Teaching and evaluation of problem solving using open approach in mathematics instruction*. Paper presented at National Council of Teachers of Mathematics, University of California at San Diego, California.

Peck, D. M., & Jencks, S. M. (1979). How can you tell? *The Elementary School Journal, 80*(4), 178–184.

Schoen, H. L. (1979). Using the individual interview to assess mathematics understanding. *Arithmetic Teacher, 27*(3), 34–38.

Somerset Local Education Authority. (1987). *Assessment in Mathematics Teacher's Book*. London: Macmillan Education, Ltd.

Angela Carrasquillo, Ph.D.
Associate Professor of Education, Graduate School of Education, Fordham University, New York, New York.

BILINGUAL SYNTAX MEASURE II TEST

Marina K. Burt, Heidi C. Dulay, and Eduardo Hernandez Chavez. San Antonio, Texas: The Psychological Corporation.

Introduction

The Bilingual Syntax Measure II (BSM II) is designed to assess oral proficiency in English and Spanish of students in Grades 3 to 12. The test is an extension of the Bilingual Syntax Measure (BSM I) developed for children in Grades K through 3. The test uses the natural speech of students as the basis for assessing their level of structural proficiency in either English or Spanish, or both. The focus of the test is on oral syntactical ability derived from student responses to colorful cartoon representations designed to stimulate the production of specific linguistic structures.

The BSM II identifies students at one of six proficiency levels. The higher the level, the more proficient the student appears to be. Comparable scores on both tests indicate that the student has comparable proficiency in both languages. Students who demonstrate comparable proficiency in two languages may be either equally proficient or equally limited in both languages. These levels of proficiency correspond to natural language learning sequences based on the developmental psycholinguistic theory that certain groups of syntactic structures are generally acquired together during the process of language acquisition, with some structures being acquired early, some later, and others very late.

Marina K. Burt, Heidi C. Dulay, and Eduardo Hernandez Chavez are the authors of the BSM II. The three authors have credentials in the fields of language development and language proficiency. In developing the BSM II, the authors chose a model of oral language proficiency that corresponds to the work of Brown (1973), Cazden (1972), Clark and Clark (1977), and Ervin-Tripp (1974), which presents the psycholinguistic theory that children acquire language through a process of creative construction. According to the authors of the BSM II, language structures follow an order that is common to children of diverse backgrounds, provided that natural communication tasks are used to elicit the structures. The authors' language theory is that children gradually reconstruct rules for the speech they hear, guided by innate mechanisms that cause them to use certain strategies to organize their linguistic input and develop proficiency. Children continually refine their "transitional" rules until there is a sufficient match between their language system and that of proficient native speakers. The authors also indicate that in the construct validation of BSM II language structures appeared in a systematic and orderly manner. For example, they found that the progressive marker *ing* is acquired before the past irregular verb form.

BSM II places students at one of six English or Spanish proficiency levels, measuring a student's range of basic linguistic syntactic structures used in spoken communication. The BSM II identifies students at one of the following six proficiency levels in each language:

Level 1—No English or Spanish. Students at this level are able to understand little or no English or Spanish.

Level 2—Receptive English/Spanish. Students are unable to use English/Spanish for communication, although they are able to produce words or phrases spontaneously.

Level 3—Survival English/Spanish. Students are able to communicate in English/ Spanish, but make many mistakes by omitting words or replacing important words.

Level 4—Intermediate English/Spanish. Students are able to communicate their ideas, but often make mistakes in using complex syntactical forms.

Level 5—Proficient English/Spanish I. Students demonstrate proficiency in the language, approaching native proficiency, but still manifest incomplete learning of some of the more advanced structures.

Level 6—Proficient English/Spanish II. Students demonstrate proficiency in the syntactic structures found in the speech of native speakers through high school age.

Syntactical structures are placed in hierarchical order developed from 25 preselected syntactic structures (each represented by one test item) based on a paired comparative analysis of these 25 syntactic structures. This hierarchy is used to assign students to one of the six proficiency levels described previously.

The BSM II field-testing sample consisted of 775 students in Grades 3 to 12 who were fairly geographically representative of the nation as a whole (i.e., 11 different places representing five different geographic areas in the United States) and included an even representation of males and females. The ethnic representation of the sample included: Mexican-American students (60%), other Hispanic students, including Cubans, Puerto Ricans, and others (12%), and students not of Hispanic origin (17%). All grades were represented, with 49% of the sample from Grades 3 to 5, 24% from Grade 6, and an additional 27% from Grades 7 to 12.

The sample was not a random one representing either language and socioeconomic variation or the national population of students for whom the test was designed. In developing the test, the authors did not see the need for randomization of the sample, arguing that "structural hierarchies should be robust across samples and do not require stratified random samples of population to which results must be generalized" (Burt, Dulay, Hernandez Chavez, & Taleporos, 1980, p. 6). Although the authors argue that a randomly selected sample was not essential to the construct validity of the sample of BSM II, this reviewer considers that the sample should be representative of the national population of students for whom the test was designed.

Practical Applications/Uses

The BSM II technical manual describes test administration, scoring, interpretation, and specific instructions for administering each test item. The BSM II consists of a 28-cartoon story booklet and a response booklet containing 26 questions. The test consists of a conversation between the administrator and the student in which the student answers questions based on one of the pictures in the cartoon booklet. The booklet contains all the necessary directions and questions for administering the test. The administrator uses the response booklet to record answers in colored circles provided on the test. The cartoon booklet contains simple, colorful drawings. The story and the cartoon-like pictures appear to be free of stereotypes.

BSM II is designed to be used in a variety of settings, but especially in bilingual education and English as a Second Language programs. It may be useful in prescribing appropriate language placement and instruction from the point of view of syntactical (structural) proficiency. It is also useful in evaluating individual structural language growth. The most practical uses of the test follow:

1) To assess the oral language proficiency of students whose primary language is not English (or Spanish) in order to determine whether children are stronger in the second language being tested (English or Spanish), their primary language, or comparably skilled in both languages;

2) To identify student strengths and weaknesses in a range of grammatical structures in English or Spanish;

3) To determine the level of second language instruction appropriate for the students and the level of first language development;

4) For determining language "readiness" and program exit. This is relevant mostly to bilingual students in determining English language proficiency as the basis for the students to exit from the program.

Although the test authors suggest that one of the test's uses is in language and speech therapy, so far its use in these settings has been very limited, perhaps due to the constraints of the test in putting all the emphasis on syntactical and grammatical structures.

Administration of the test requires a picture booklet, a student response booklet for each student to be tested, and a pen or pencil for the examiner's use. The questions to be answered are found in the student response booklet. Questions are to be asked exactly as they are printed. Each set of questions refers to one or more pictures in the picture booklet. Several items are asked before a response is scored, allowing the student time to warm up. Average testing time per child is 15 to 20 minutes.

Extensive experience in test administration is not required for this measure; administration of the BSM II is easy, and the manual is clear and explicit. However, knowledge of Spanish or English (depending on the language being tested) linguistics, morphology, and syntax is necessary. Under each item a specific procedure is described, including the exact words to be used by the examiner. Scoring criteria are stated for each item. In scoring the individual response to a particular question, the authors indicate that 1 point be given when the response contains no grammatical errors and is syntactically appropriate to the question and 0 points be given when the response is syntactically and grammatically incorrect. The examinee receives one point for each correct item, and no partial credit is given. This makes scoring a matter of recording the student's pass/fail performance on the scoring sheet and computing a raw score. The numerical scoring derives from a right or wrong basis.

The student's proficiency level is determined by summing the number of correct responses in the squares and circles in the student response booklet. The scoring requires the use of four scoring panels, working sequentially. The first two panels (A and B) assign students to Level 1 or Level 2, which are the non-speaking levels. If the student's language proficiency exceeds the criteria of panels A and B, the scorer proceeds to panels C and D. Scores and proficiency levels are scored in the student response booklet.

Technical Aspects

The technical manual provides information related to the development of the test, its validity, and its reliability. The reliability of the BSM II was established through the analysis of internal consistency coefficients and a study of test-retest scores. The reliability of scores of BSM II was established by administering both the English and the Spanish version to 85 students. The sample included 50 males and 35 females in Grades 4 to 8. Coefficients based on internal consistency scores of clusters and totals for English (.80 to .90) were higher than scores for Spanish (.71 to .82). Retest correlations varied from .82 to .96. Although there was a small number of students at each grade level, results indicate stability of the subcluster scores, the proficiency levels classification, and the relative classifications. Although it includes only a small sample at each grade level, the data do indicate positive test reliability.

The test manual addresses certain aspects of construct and content validity. There is sufficient theoretical foundation underlying the procedures employed in selecting and ordering items to determine item difficulty and to form clusters. However, a rationale and validation for the particular cutoff scores selected is not included. It would have been helpful if the technical manual had included a description of how parallel the difficulty levels are for the English and Spanish forms.

Critique

The BSM II is a well-prepared test with a substantive theoretical foundation and justification for its design and implementation. The BSM II is a relatively new instrument about which little has been written. The reviewer recommends it primarily as one of a battery of screening instruments to classify and group second language students (English or Spanish) to participate in instructional programs based on their language proficiency. The test is also useful as an initial language screening test to determine whether students are stronger in their primary language or English (or Spanish), or how they compare in both languages.

The results of the BSM II need to be interpreted with caution because its scoring is calculated on a pass/fail basis. Students' listening and vocabulary comprehension and isolated production of phrases might not have any language significance. An answer that is conceptually correct but grammatically incorrect receives no points because partial credit is not given on the test.

The reviewer agrees with Garcia (1985) and Shellengberger (1985) in their claim that the assessment of syntax alone to determine language proficiency presents a very narrow view of language, especially when the test is designed to be used with young adults. Garcia cautions the use of relying only on the BSM II to measure oral language proficiency when there are different approaches to measure oral language proficiency, especially in older children and young adults where social functions of language may overshadow strict syntactic abilities.

References

This list includes text citations and suggested additional reading.

Brown, R., (1973). *A first language.* Cambridge, MA: Harvard University Press.

Burt, M. Dulay, H.C., Hernandez Chavez, E., & Taleporos, E., (1980). *Technical handbook.* New York: Harcourt Brace Jovanovich.

Clark, H., & Clark, E. (1977). *Psychology of language.* New York: Harcourt Brace Jovanovich.

Cazden, C. (1972). *Child language and evaluation.* New York: Holt, Rinehart & Winston.

Ervin-Tripp, J. (1974). Is second language learning like the first? *TESOL Quarterly, 8,* (pp. 197–198).

Garcia, E., (1985). In O.K. Buros (Ed.), *The ninth mental measurements yearbook* (p. 197). Lincoln, NE: Buro Institute

Hayes-Brown, S. (1987). Bilingual Syntax Measure II. In J. C. Aldelson, K.J. Krahnke, & C.W. Standsfield (Eds.). *Review of English language proficiency tests.* Washington, DC: Teachers of English to Speakers of Other Languages.

Krashen, S.D. (1978). Is the natural order an artifact of the Bilingual Syntax Measure? *Language Learning, 28* (1), 187–191.

Shellengberger, S. (1985). Review of Bilingual Syntax Measure II. In O.K. Buros (Ed.), *The ninth mental measurements yearbook* (pp. 198–199). Lincoln, NE: Buros Institute.

John J. Venn, Ph.D.
Associate Professor of Special Education, University of North Florida, Jacksonville, Florida.

BIRTH TO THREE ASSESSMENT AND INTERVENTION SYSTEM

Tina E. Bangs and Susan Dodson. Allen, Texas: DLM Teaching Resources.

Introduction

The Birth to Three Assessment and Intervention System is a developmental scale and programming guide for infants and very young children. The system consists of the *Birth to Three Screening Test of Learning and Language Development* (Bangs & Dodson, 1986), the *Birth to Three Checklist of Learning and Language Behavior* (Bangs, 1986), and the *Birth to Three Intervention Manual* (Bangs, 1986). The Screening test is a norm-referenced measure for initial identification of children at high risk for developmental delay. The Checklist is a 240-item criterion-referenced developmental scale. The intervention manual provides instructions for developing learning objectives, sample lesson plans, and activities for home training. The system is designed for children from approximately 1 to 3 years of age who are developmentally delayed. It is also appropriate for children with developmental delays from 4 to 6 years of age who are functioning in the 1 to 3 age range.

The system can be used for initial screening, diagnostic assessment, and intervention programming. The intervention aspects of the system are especially useful in programming. Parent involvement, training, and home instruction are key features of the intervention program.

Tina E. Bangs, Ph.D., the senior author of the test, is Professor Emerita at the Speech and Hearing Institute of the University of Texas Health Science Center in Houston. The original Birth to Three Scale was written by Dr. Bangs and published in 1979. This criterion-referenced scale was designed to be used by teachers of very young children with developmental delays. The second edition of the scale is a revised and expanded version of the original. Improvements include revising the original criterion-referenced scale, adding a norm-referenced screening test, and revising the intervention manual. The original intervention manual was titled the *Birth to Three: Developmental Learning and the Handicapped Child* (Bangs, 1979a). The norm-referenced Screening Test was written with Susan Dodson, M.A., who is an instructor in the Speech and Hearing Clinic at the University of Tennessee in Knoxville.

The test consists of five parts: three spiral-bound books and two score sheets, all 8½" × 11". The spiral-bound books include a 105-page examiner's manual for the checklist, an 83-page examiner's manual for the screening test, and a 75-page intervention manual. The score sheet for the checklist is 11 pages long and the score sheet for the screening test is 4 pages long. The materials and equipment needed to

49

administer the scales are not provided. These include common toys and other items that are normally used with infants and preschoolers. The materials needed for the screening test and the checklist are described in the manuals, and these need to be gathered together by the examiner prior to testing.

Both of the tests have the same five subtests: Language Comprehension, Language Expression, Avenues to Learning, Social/Personal Development, and Motor Development. Avenues to Learning is the subtest that measures cognitive development. The emphasis of the item content in all of the subtests is language. Many of the test items require verbal responses.

The examiner participates directly in the testing process by administering most of the test items to the child. With some items, the examiner may need to have the parent or primary caregiver administer an item while the examiner observes. Other items that cannot be observed directly can be scored by report of the parent or primary caregiver. For example, the social/personal behavior of avoiding dangerous situations may be scored by report.

The test is intended for children whose functioning level is believed to be below the 3-year age level. The test is also appropriate for children who are chronologically older than 3 but who are functioning below 3 years developmentally. The tests are not appropriate for newborn infants because newborns were not included in the test development and standardization process.

The first page of the 4-page answer form for the screening test includes room to record identification information about the child, sensory and physical information, a summary of scores, comments based on observation of the child during testing, and recommendations. The three remaining pages list the test items by subtest. The child's performance on each item is recorded on these pages next to each item and summarized at the bottom of each page. The first page of the 11-page checklist answer form is used to record identification information about the child, the test results in the form of a developmental age profile across the subtests, developmental age scores for each subtest, and comments about the child's performance. The other 10 pages list the test items by subtest, and the child's performance on each item is recorded on these pages. The form has room to evaluate the child three times using the same form so that performance over time can be observed. The answer forms are well designed and easy to use.

Practical Applications/Uses

The screening test and checklist are designed to provide a screening, diagnostic, and intervention system for children at the preschool age level who are mildly and moderately handicapped. The screening test provides a brief sketch of overall development and a norm-referenced score for each of the subtests. The developmental checklist is a longer criterion-referenced measure of skill development. The intervention manual provides information to couple the assessment with programming.

The screening test can be given individually or with groups of children in clinics, large group screenings in the schools, and in day-care programs. The criterion-referenced checklist is an individually administered diagnostic tool and is not designed for group administration. The intervention manual is for use with individual children and their parents in the home or with groups of children who are enrolled in programs in public schools, private schools, health clinics, agencies, and speech and language clinics.

Professionals who use this system include preschool handicapped teachers, home intervention specialists, educational diagnosticians, Child Serve specialists, speech and language therapists, psychologists, pediatricians, and health-care professionals including pediatric nurses. The screening test can be used by trained volunteers and other support personnel under the direct supervision of a qualified professional.

The system can be used also as a training tool for paraprofessionals and parents. The intervention manual can serve as a resource manual and curriculum guide for program development.

The screening test is especially useful as a tool for identifying young children who are at high risk for handicaps. The system is also useful for young children who have speech and language delays, but who are otherwise normal. The tests are not appropriate for use with severely and profoundly handicapped children because the content does not include feeding, physical management, neuromotor development, and other similar learning areas. The system has not been specifically designed for use with the blind or the deaf, and methods of adapting it are not described.

According to the test manual, the system is designed for use by those who know how to observe the behaviors of young children and can follow the administration procedures described in the test manual. To be qualified to use the test, examiners need to carefully study the manuals and practice giving the test before actually using it with children. No requirements for experience with handicapped children or other prerequisites are listed in the manuals.

The administration procedures are written clearly and are easy to follow. Because the screening test is a norm-referenced scale, it is necessary to follow the specified procedures strictly. The sequence of the test cannot be altered. On the other hand, the Checklist of Language and Learning Behavior is a criterion-referenced scale. Specific procedures are provided for each item, and they should be followed when administering the test. Because the test is not normed, the sequence of the test and other procedures can be modified to meet the needs of individual children. Any modifications should be noted clearly on the score sheet.

The screening test consists of a small number of items and can be administered easily in one session. Although the time required to administer this test can vary, it normally takes approximately 20 to 45 minutes when given individually. The checklist is a longer test. It does not need to be completed in one session, but should be completed within a 1-week period in order to obtain accurate developmental age scores.

The scoring instructions are presented clearly with good examples and illustrations. Examiners who are familiar with developmental testing will find that it takes a short period of time to learn how to score this test. Once mastered, it takes a few minutes to score the screening test and several minutes to score the checklist. There are no difficulties in scoring. The scoring procedure involves recording the child's performance in all five of the subtests using three criteria: 1 = pass (the child performed the behavior as described); +/- = emerging (the child is just beginning to perform the behavior); and – = fail (the child did not perform the behavior as described). The scoring procedures are different for the screening test and the checklist.

When scoring the screening test, the raw scores are determined by entering the total number of items marked with a 1 for each subtest at the bottom of the appropriate page of the score sheet. The raw scores are then transferred to the score summary on the first page of the score sheet. The raw scores for each of the five subtests can be converted using the tables in the manual to one of three derived scores: a T-score, a percentile rank, or a stanine.

When scoring the checklist, the raw scores, which are the total number of items passed in each subtest, are entered at the bottom of each appropriate page of the score sheet. The raw scores are then converted to developmental age scores by multiplying the total raw score by .75. The developmental age scores are written on the bottom of the page and are then transferred to a developmental age profile on the front page of the score sheet. The score has spaces to record age scores from three separate evaluations so that progress over time can be measured and then illustrated on the profile. This test can only be scored by hand, but the procedure is not difficult to do or time-consuming.

Interpretation, which is based upon the objective scores obtained and clinical judgment, is not difficult. Three derived scores can be obtained from the screening test. One of these scores, the percentile, is widely used and well known, thus inter preting this score should be easy for most examiners. The other two derived scores, a T-score and a stanine, are less widely used and may not be familiar to those who do not have specific training in assessment. There are also some severe limitations on the use of scores derived from screening tests. These limitations are explained in the interpretation section of the test manual.

The checklist provides developmental age scores that are not difficult to interpret. The checklist manual, when used together with the intervention manual, provide good, basic information on how to link testing results to intervention. This process involves clinical judgment. The emphasis is on home-centered or home-based intervention and working together with parents. Those who are experienced in developmental assessment will find that the information provided in the manual makes it easy to interpret the test appropriately and adequately. Those without experience in developmental assessment will find it necessary to study the manuals carefully to interpret the results of the tests.

It is also interesting that although subtest scores are available for both the screening test and the checklist, no provision is made for obtaining a global score from the tests. Global scores provide an overall developmental age across all of the subtests and are misinterpreted easily. Because global scores are not available, evaluators are forced to look at specific strengths and weaknesses rather than simply labeling a child as developmentally delayed in general. This also facilitates identification of gaps in development and areas in need of remediation.

Technical Aspects

The test authors report that the standardization process incorporated the collection of validity and reliability data, but data analysis was not described. The only reliability data reported were derived from an interrater reliability study of the screening test. This briefly summarized study, used the senior author of the test, a speech pathologist, and a nurse as the raters. The interrater reliability coefficients ranged from .88 to .99. No evidence supporting the reliability of the checklist was provided. Likewise empirical evidence supporting the validity of the two tests was not provided.

The screening test was standardized on a group of 360 children aged 4 months to 36 months. The sample was selected from three states. The method of selecting the children was not described, but the sample was divided by gender and type of community, rural or urban. The test authors report that efforts were made to obtain a sample that was representative of various ethnic and socioeconomic backgrounds. Unfortunately, no data describing the success of this effort are supplied. In analyzing the data from the standardization sample, Bangs and Dodson found that there were not enough items from some of the age groups that met the criteria for inclusion in the test. Although the process is not clearly described, they determined that scores from the original data of the 1979 scale would be more useful than the data from the standardization sample. The children's performance from this original data was analyzed using an unspecific type of regression analysis. The norms were formulated from this data analysis. Information on the nature of the original data from the 1979 scale was not given. Likewise, not enough information was given to describe the actual data analysis procedures, although they are described in a general way.

The standardization of the screening test is clearly inadequate. The normative sample and the data analysis are both questionable. There is insufficient evidence to support the use of the screening test as a norm-referenced tool. Likewise the data presented by the authors do not demonstrate that either test has adequate reliability or validity. More study needs to be done to establish the effectiveness of these tests.

Critique

The Birth to Three Assessment and Intervention System provides a well-planned and easy-to-follow program for initial identification, follow-up diagnosis, and intervention with preschool children who have mild handicaps and are functioning in the 1- to 3-year-old age range. The system is designed to provide more than test scores—the intervention manual shows how to use test scores together with other information to design an individual program for the child and the family. The system represents a significant enhancement of the original Birth to Three Scale (Bangs, 1979b).

Although the system has a number of uses, it seems to be particularly useful for special educators and other specialists who serve mildly handicapped preschoolers in home intervention programs. Another strength of the system is the emphasis on language development as the major learning area in intervention programs. The major weaknesses of the system are the deficient reliability, validity, and norms. The system can be useful as a criterion-referenced assessment and curriculum guide, but it is not adequately developed for use as a norm-referenced tool. When used as a criterion-referenced tool, the system does not have as many items in as much depth as some of the other available instruments. Many professionals will find that some of these more comprehensive tests and scales are often necessary. However, the system is attractive when a brief screening test and a relatively short developmental checklist are needed.

References

Bangs, T.E. (1979a). *Birth to Three: Developmental Learning and the Handicapped Child.* Boston: Teaching Resources.

Bangs, T.E. (1979b). *Birth to Three Scale.* Boston: Teaching Resources.

Bangs, T.E. (1986a). *Birth to Three Checklist of Learning and Language Behavior.* Allen, TX: DLM Teaching Resources.

Bangs, T.E. (1986b). *Birth to Three intervention manual.* Allen, TX: DLM Teaching Resources.

Bangs, T.E., & Dodson, S. (1986). *Birth to Three Screening Test of Learning and Language Development.* Allen, TX: DLM Teaching Resources.

Mark Stone, Ed.D.
Professor of Psychology, Alfred Adler Institute, Chicago, Illinois.

CAIN-LEVINE SOCIAL COMPETENCY SCALE

Leo F. Cain, Samuel Levine, and Freeman F. Elzey. Palo Alto, California: Consulting Psychologists Press, Inc.

Introduction

The Cain-Levine Social Competency Scale (CLS) is designed to measure a narrow and circumscribed set of characteristics: the social competence of trainable mentally retarded children. The scale consists of 44 items divided into four subscales: self-help, initiative, social skills, and communication.

Item development sampled those behaviors important for measuring social competence of mentally retarded children. Normative tables are provided for chronological ages 5–13, permitting the examiner to determine percentile ranks by age group for each subscale and the total social competency score.

The methodological and substantive bases of the CLS are contained in the work of Doll (1953) and Kirk (1957). Cain et al. recognized a need for the measurement of social skills as identified by Doll (1953) and Kirk (1957) and capitalized upon their ideas for making such a scale. Initial item development for the scale began in 1961 and continued through several preliminary forms to the current edition first copyrighted in 1963. The four subscales of the CLS are composed as follows:

1) *Self-Help.* This scale consists of 14 items intended to evaluate the manipulative and motor skills of the child. The orientation of the items, however, is not about the application of these skills, but about whether the child initiates the activity as a measure of independence.

2) *Initiative.* This scale has 10 items that measure the amount of self-direction observed in the child for engaging in daily living skills such as dressing, toileting, caring for clothing, and so on.

3) *Social Skills.* This scale has 10 items that assess the degree to which the child initiates interpersonal relationships with other children and adults.

4) *Communication.* This scale has 10 items that measure the degree to which the child makes himself understood in communicating needs and wants.

The CLS test materials consist of an examiners manual and a consumable test form. The manual gives the test rationale and directions for test administration. Some psychometric information on validity and reliability is presented, but it is sparse.

Practical Applications/Uses

The CLS is administered through an interview designed to measure the typical performance of a child on each item in the scale. This procedure requires that the respondent have sufficient background about the child in order to provide the spe-

55

cific information required. The items were designed to measure social competency behaviors commonly seen in the home situation. They are also intended to represent behaviors observable in the development of the trainable retarded child irrespective of setting. At home, the parent is most likely to be the one with extensive information about the child. In residential settings the informant might be a child-care worker. Some of the CLS behaviors could also be observed in general classroom situations allowing a teacher to be the respondent. School psychologists conducting a complete case study should find the CLS useful for evaluating the social skills of a child. Other persons wishing to use the test should first obtain training and experience in assessment.

Each item consists of a 4- or 5-point rating scale with descriptive statements for each point on the scales of independent behavior and social competency. These statements were designed to be operational and focus attention on observable aspects of child behavior.

The CLS manual contains two small sections approximately one page in length dealing with basic considerations for interviewing in the interview procedure itself. There are simulated question and answer examples for 13 of the 44 items. These examples provide an introduction to the interviewing strategy required to appropriately use the instrument. The typical interview should be conducted in approximately 30 minutes.

The descriptive statements for each item are ordered by difficulty level and rank from 1–4 or 1–5 from the least independent level of social competence to the most independent level. Answers are recorded on a two-page answer form. A simple face sheet is provided for demographic information and for recording the sums of the raw scores. Five tables are given in the manual for converting the subscale and total score to percentile ranks, one table for each of the five age groups for which norms are available. This scoring procedure is relatively straightforward and easily accomplished.

Interpretation of the CLS requires substantial background for understanding the concepts of social competency. Supplemental reading is necessary if any reasonable interpretations are to be made because the manual provides little background in this area. For more information on social competency see Doll (1953) and Kirk (1957). Valid interpretation beyond the scores requires the examiner to be versed in child development and particularly mental retardation. Except for several references no information is provided in the manual.

Technical Aspects

The content validity of the items is justified, according the manual, because the items were drawn from curriculum guides for the mentally retarded, by consultation with experts, and through examination of existing scales. Unfortunately, except for references to Kirk (1957) and Doll (1953) no supportive information is given in the manual. Final item selection was determined by 70% agreement by each group of judges; however, the qualifications of judges and details of these procedures are not given. Following "further scale development and item analysis" the existing scale was constructed.

Odd/even correlation coefficients were computed for the subscales and total scale for each of the five age groups. The coefficients ranged from .82 to .91 for the total scale and .50 to .95 for the subscales.

Test/retest reliability was evaluated on 35 randomly selected subjects retested 3 weeks after initial testing. The total score reliability coefficient was .98 and coefficient for the five subscales range from .88 to .97. Correlation coefficients were computed between IQ and CLS. The coefficients were .22 and .25 for the total scale for males and females respectively. Cain et al. (1977) argue that these low correlations demonstrate the CLS is measuring a different variable from the IQ test. Information regarding this study is minimally addressed in the manual. For example, the IQ test used is not mentioned.

Norms were derived from 716 trainable mentally retarded children in the state of California between the ages of 5-0 and 13-11. The intelligence quotients of these children ranged from approximately 25 to 59. Means and standard deviations by age group and sex are provided in the manual. The majority of wage earners in the parental demographics were reported to be in lower occupational positions; however, specific information was not available.

Critique

According to the criteria of DSM III-R and the American Association of Mental Deficiency, a diagnosis of mental retardation requires that significant below-average functioning be determined for both intellectual levels and adaptive behavior. The Cain-Levine Social Competency Scale is an instrument designed to meet the requirement by evaluating the level of social competency in trainable mentally retarded children. There is a clear need for such measures in assessment and preparatory to training and instruction. Such an instrument should be efficient and useful. The CLS is easily administered and scored, which makes it useful, but the manual itself is only 17 pages long and provides only the barest information for such an important topic as the measurement of social competency. Of course, it is not the function of a test manual to provide extensive descriptions of social competency. Nevertheless, it is important that a manual provide sufficient information to ensure that the scale is properly administered, scored, and interpreted.

Given the simplicity of the scale itself, it might be argued that the manual provides the barest ingredients. Guidance for test administration is perhaps the most extensive aspect of the manual. Scoring, while simple, is adequately defined. The psychometric properties of the test are not demonstrated. There is no supportive research provided in the manual by which to infer that the reliability and validity coefficients are supported to the level reported in the manual. In essence there is no verification of these data. Replications are necessary but nonexistent. The copyright dates of 1963 and 1977 are sufficient to recommend that supportive literature be provided in the manual or in a supplement to give the test user more information. This instrument clearly serves an important enough area of concern in the issues of mental retardation as to warrant this supplemental material.

The normative sample is highly restrictive. Studies should be done to verify the normative data derived solely from a sampling made in the state of California. Application of the CLS to other settings strains the credibility conveyed by the limited data and information contained in the manual.

Social competency, as defined by Cain et al. (1977), is a very important measure. When mental competency is assessed it is important to evaluate the social skills of a person, sometimes mental retardation and social competency are both below average. At other times one is high and the other low. It is important to measure these competencies and not infer one from the other without evidence. Cain et al. have clearly defined a variable of importance for assessment in mental retardation and have established a good beginning in the development of this scale. What is needed now is to support the application of the scale in other school and agency settings with supportive data on the stability of the original data. When this is accomplished, a good beginning will have been made in an important area of mental retardation.

References

Cain, L.F., & Levine, S. (1961). *A study of the effects of community and institutional school classes for trainable mentally retarded children* (U.S. Office of Education, Department of Health, Education and Welfare, Contract No. SAE 8257). San Francisco, CA: San Francisco State University.

Cain, L.F., & Levine, S. (1963). *Effects of community and institutional school programs on trainable mentally retarded children* (CEC Research Monograph Series B, No. B-1). Washington, DC: Council for Exceptional Children.

Cain, L.F., Levine, S., & Elzey, F.F. (1977). *Cain-Levine Social Competency Scale.* Palo Alto: Consulting Psychologists Press, Inc.

Congdon, D. M. (1969). The Vineland and Cain-Levine: A correlational study and program evaluation. *American Journal of Mental Deficiency, 74,* 231–234.

Doll, E.A. (1953). *The measurement of social competence.* Minneapolis, MN: Educational Test Bureau.

Gunzberg, H.C. (1973). *Social competence and mental handicap: An introduction to social education* (2nd ed.). Baltimore, MD: Williams & Wilkins.

Kirk, S. (1957). *Public school provisions for severely retarded children.* Albany: New York State Interdepartmental Health Resources Board.

Levine, S., Elzey, F.F., Thormahlen, P., & Cain, L.F. (1968). *T.M.R. School Competency Scale.* New York: The Psychological Corporation.

Levine, S., & Elzey, F.F. (1968). *San Francisco Vocational Competency Scale.* New York: The Psychological Corporation.

Levine, S., Elzey, F.F., & Lewis, M. (1969). *California Preschool Social Competency Scale.* Palo Alto, CA: Consulting Psychologists Press.

Semmel, M.I. (1973). The relationship of pupil-teacher interactions in classrooms for the TMR to pupil gain in communication skills. *Mental Retardation, 11,* 7–13.

Virginia E. Kennedy, Ph.D.
Professor of Special Needs Faculty, Pacific Oaks College, Pasadena, California.

CALIFORNIA PRESCHOOL SOCIAL COMPETENCY SCALE

Samuel Levine, Freeman F. Elzey, and Mary Lewis. Palo Alto, California: Consulting Psychologists Press, Inc.

Introduction

The California Preschool Social Competency Scale (Levine, Elzey, & Lewis, 1969) was designed to assess preschool children's competency in interpersonal behaviors and the degree to which they exhibit social responsibility. According to the authors, performance in these areas provides an indication of personality and mental development. Used for children ages 2 years, 6 months through 5 years, 6 months, the scale is completed by adults who are familiar with children's behavior in social situations. Responding to the scale's items requires observations of a child's actual performance. No specific testing situation is necessary. Results are stated as percentiles according to sex, age, and parental occupational level, divided into two categories of high and low.

The CPSCS was developed in response to a perceived need for an instrument that could provide information about a preschool child's social growth to complement assessment instruments in other areas of development. Behaviors were selected in terms of common cultural expectations to represent basic competencies to be developed in the process of socialization. In so doing, the authors sought to avoid the "equal opportunity to learn" criticism directed at many assessment devices.

The initial decision to specify a preschool setting as the context for the observations was made because of the great increase in the number of children in preschool programs and because of the greater comparability of factors instigating social interaction within the preschool as compared with the home. The scale was standardized based on teacher ratings, which were assumed to be the most accurate ratings of children's characteristic performance in a wide range of social interaction situations.

Behaviors to be included were identified by 1) observations of children in a variety of preschools that used a variety of orientations and activities, 2) discussions with the preschool personnel in these sites, and 3) a review of available instruments and extant literature dealing with the social behavior of preschool behavior. Criteria for selection emphasized that the behaviors must be observable within the preschool setting, must be objective and minimize value judgments and reflections of particular cultural orientations, and must be judged by early childhood educators as important to the child's social competency development. In addition, each item had to permit scaling on at least four levels to permit fine discriminations in competence, and high rank order agreement in the ordering of the levels within each item was required.

Based on these criteria, a pool of items was written that then was evaluated by early childhood educators and, subsequently, systematically analyzed by teacher groups enrolled in graduate programs in early childhood education. These groups judged each item in terms of its importance to preschool children's social competence, its clarity, relevance for the preschool age group, and their agreement with the rank ordering of the levels within each item. Following these analyses, an initial form of the scale was written.

The initial form was pretested on 1,165 children randomly selected from the ages of 2–6 to 5–6 years. Teachers in the preschools involved were asked not to rate children with severe hearing, visual, motor, or emotional problems. The children in the selected programs came from homes representing a wide range of occupational levels, and males and females were approximately equally represented. The ratings were analyzed in terms of percentage of preschool children rated at each level for each item, interitem correlations, item-total score correlations, and item-chronological age correlations. Items that were determined to show appropriate statistical properties were retained. These properties are not reported, however.

The norming sample approximated the proportion of preschool children in the major urban centers for each geographic region of the United States, based on figures from the U.S. Census Bureau. However, information regarding the number of children enrolled in preschool programs and their age, sex, and parental occupational level distribution was not available. Therefore, the authors decided to obtain equal numbers of children from each of the resulting categories. The norming sample was based on ratings of 800 children, 50 within each of 16 norming groups for age, sex, and occupational level.

An analysis of variance was conducted on the norming sample to determine the effects of age, sex, and occupational level on scores. There were main effects for each variable, indicating that a child's membership in a particular group (e.g., boy or girl) had an effect on the score achieved. Chronological age had the largest effect. There were no interactions between variables.

This test has not been revised or restandardized since 1969, and according to the publisher and one author there are no plans to do so (F.F. Elzey, personal communication, July, 1988).

The scale consists of a 16-page manual and a 4-page answer sheet to be completed by an adult in a preschool setting. The rater need not be a teacher, but must be someone who has observed the child in a number of social situations. Each of the 30 items consists of four statements about a particular social behavior, with varying degrees of competence reflected from statement 1 (i.e., lowest degree of competence) to statement 4 (i.e., highest degree of competence). The four levels contained in the statements imply a developmental progression in these behaviors as the child ages.

The examiner does not set up a testing situation; rather, all items should be completed through observing the child over time. The examiner starts with question 1 and proceeds through to question 30, circling the statement for each item that most closely describes the degree of competence displayed by the child. Items are stated as observable behaviors.

The behaviors to be rated were selected as those representing critical behaviors in the social functioning of children ages 2 years, 6 months to 5 years, 6 months (who are in preschool settings) and do not reflect any one orientation to early childhood development. The behaviors include response to routine, response to the unfamiliar, following instructions, making explanations, sharing, initiating activities, reaction to frustration, and accepting limits.

The answer sheet contains personal information on the front, including sex, age norm (age grouping), and occupational level of the major wage earner (divided into high and low occupational level). This information is used for determining the correct set of norms when scoring. The two inside pages of the answer sheet contain all 30 items; the examiner circles the number of one of four statements per item. Items are labeled with the behavior described (e.g., "Response to unfamiliar adults"). The back page of the answer sheet is the profile sheet on which the rating for each item is recorded, resulting in a visual profile of relative strengths and weaknesses or more developed and less developed competencies.

Practical Applications/Uses

The CPSCS is intended to provide an indication of a young child's development in the ability to function effectively in group settings that contain adults and peers. The authors view social competence and its development as important in the study of young children and believe that knowledge of a child's development in this area provides insight into personality and mental development. The scale specifically is designed to measure the adequacy of young children's interpersonal behavior and the degree to which they perform the social behaviors required in a preschool setting. Children's abilities to follow adult directions, seek help when appropriate, cooperate, and play with others are assessed.

The test has many uses:

1) it provides a relative index of the child's social competence, permitting comparisons with children of the same age, sex, and socioeconomic status;

2) it permits investigations of the effects of environmental and characterological variables on the child's development at differing ages;

3) it can be useful in predictive studies of school achievement;

4) it can be helpful in the evaluation of deviant groups;

5) it can be useful as a criterion measure of the effectiveness of different interventions at the preschool level (Levine et al, 1969).

The scale can be used by teachers for intra-child comparisons of social competency compared to cognitive, physical, or other areas of development (i.e., informally because no standard scores are derived). This would be helpful in program planning. Although there are no subtest, cluster, or factor scores to be derived, analyses of individual items could provide an informal, nonstandardized indication of the adequacy of particular behaviors.

The ability to compare a child to age-mates could assist in the identification of children whose development is considerably slower than "normal." Preschool directors and program developers could find this scale helpful when evaluating curricula in terms of social competence outcomes.

A potential new use of the scale would be to monitor, on perhaps a yearly basis, the social functioning of children with mild developmental delay, those "at risk" for later learning disabilities, and other preschoolers with mild handicaps. As attention to early identification and remediation increases, curricula, teaching approaches, and effective practices in mainstreaming these children into preschool programs will need to be evaluated. The development of social competence is a major aspect of curriculum for this age group and is an important outcome of mainstreaming.

The CPSCS is appropriate for use with all children ages 2–6 through 5–6, although they must be in a group setting such as a preschool. It would be essential, however, that the examiner note on the profile sheet such information as length of time enrolled in preschool or other group settings, home language if different from the language used for instruction in the school, and any child variables that could affect social competence such as developmental delay, language or speech disorders, emotional difficulties, and physical or sensory impairments.

The scale is completed on one child at a time by one rater. Examiners are discouraged from setting up situations to observe the test behaviors; rather, knowledge of a child accumulated over time should be the primary basis for the ratings. The suggested rater is a teacher in a preschool, although anyone familiar with the child in the preschool setting can complete the scale. Persons with experience and knowledge in normal child development would provide more accurate ratings than persons new to the field because some items require judgment. For example, some items require a knowledge of age-appropriate language use.

The administration procedure as explained in the manual is for a rater who has had "considerable opportunity to observe the child" (Levine et al., 1969) to rate the child's competence in terms of his habitual or typical performance. Each item should be rated independently of ratings on previous items. Additional rating instructions for some items are given to clarify (e.g., knowing one's address requires only street number and name) or define terms (e.g., "instructions" apply to social competency behaviors, not academic tasks). The procedure is quite straightforward and unambiguous. The main problem that could be encountered would be in the interpretation of words used in the scale. Although the words are not technical, and the statements mainly describe overt behaviors rather than emotional or other nonobservable states, knowledge of typical behaviors at these ages is essential for reliable ratings. The sequence of items could be changed with no loss of application of the norms. To complete the scale takes approximately 15 minutes.

Scoring the scale is easy and explained clearly in the manual. Each item receives one rating of competence, from 1 (lowest) to 4 (highest). The rater then sums all the ratings for the 30 items. All items must be rated; thus, the total score ranges from 30 through 120. This score is the raw score, which the rater then converts to a percentile score by referring to the appropriate table of norms. Norms were developed for four age groups: 2–6 through 2–11, 3–0 through 3–11, 4–0 through 4–11, and 5–0 through 5–6. Within each table are percentiles for males and females and high and low occupational level. High occupational level is defined as skilled, semiprofessional, professional, and executive positions. Low occupational level includes the unemployed, welfare recipients, and unskilled and semiskilled laborers. No further explanation to help in determining the level is included in the manual. If the occupation of the major wage-earner is unknown, the percentiles for the total males or females is used.

Learning to score the scale can be accomplished quickly, especially if the rater has experience in reading percentile tables. Generally, scoring should take only 10–15 minutes. The only apparent difficulty in scoring might be in the selection of occupational level. Once the raw score and percentile are determined, the rater can complete the profile on the back page of the answer sheet if desired. This presents a graphic picture of the child's performance on individual items. The interpretation of scores is not addressed by the authors in the manual or answer sheet. This is apparently determined entirely by the rater.

Technical Aspects

Validity of the scale items was established by an overall review conducted by individuals in early childhood education. In addition, although not reported as a validity study, in the process of determining the final items for inclusion in the scale an item-by-item review was conducted by teacher groups enrolled in graduate programs in early childhood education. These teacher groups were asked to rate each item in terms of their importance to preschool children's social competence. The raters' experience and knowledge in early childhood education were not stated. No other validity studies were reported in the manual. Although one of the scale's stated contributions is its ability to help predict school achievement, apparently no studies of predictive validity were conducted.

Because the scale relies on observations for its ratings of children, a measure of interrater (between rater) reliability was necessary. Three studies were conducted on a total of 110 children in three states and eight programs. Reliability coefficients ranged from .75 to .79. The authors point out that these are conservative figures because since differences between raters on use of the scale and knowledge of the children were not taken into account. Therefore, there is a possibility of reaching different scores if more than one rater rates the same child, which reduces confidence in the scale.

A measure of internal consistency, an odd-even reliability, was applied. Internal consistency refers to the assumption that in tests designed to measure a single basic concept (in the CSPSC, social competence), "it is reasonable to assume that people who get one item right will be more likely to get other, similar items right" (Kubiszyn & Borich, 1987, p. 293). The scale was divided into two halves, one consisting of all odd-numbered items and the other all even-numbered items. The total score for each child on each half was determined and the correlation between the two computed. Children's scores on the two halves should be similar. These reliability coefficients were computed by age, sex, and occupational level, and ranged from .90 to .98 after correction by the Spearman-Brown formula. This formula adjusts the reliability coefficient upward to reflect the reliability the scale would have if each half were the full length of the scale (i.e., a test is usually more reliable if it is longer) (Kubiszyn & Borich, 1987).

A third study of reliability was conducted to determine the correlation between each item and the total score. Performance on each item should reflect total performance. These correlations were reported for sex by occupational level and ranged from .29 to .80. Of the 30 items, 21 had higher correlations for girls than for boys. In general, however, there was not a great range between all correlations. Over 80% of the items showed correlations of .50 or above with the total score. This indicates that high or low ratings on particular items should not be taken as good indicators of overall social competence.

The results of the reliability studies would suggest that all items are related to each other (i.e., they are rating the same concept, although ratings on individual items should not be considered to reflect total performance). The most troublesome reliability indicators are those for different observers, suggesting that an assurance of training in use of the scale and insistence on knowledge of the particular child being rated are necessary for accurate ratings.

Critique

The California Preschool Social Competency Scale addresses an area that has few other standardized testing instruments. It was more carefully developed than usual and successfully attempts to operationalize and make observable an often ill-defined and "internal" set of skills.

A few major cautions need to be stated. First, social competence seems to be a value-laden construct by its nature. The behaviors in this scale are those determined to be important by a group of teachers studying early childhood education who are unidentified as to cultural or economic background, as well as theoretical approach to early childhood. The items therefore reflect the values of an unknown group of teachers. As stated in the review by Calfee (1978),

> The social responsibility and independence items are the sort that fit the expectations of a typical preschool teacher, e.g., the child *nearly always* accepts it when an adult sets limits on his activity. One can imagine a group of well-adjusted preschoolers who do not necessarily conform to this particular set of expectations (p. 721).

Indeed, the norms reveal that boys and children from the low occupational level score lower than do girls and children from a high occupational level. Thus, these two lower scoring groups do not show as much of the behaviors deemed by this group of teachers to comprise social competence, merely by virtue of being a boy or from a lower occupational level. These children may be quite socially competent in other situations, or may be judged competent by teachers from a different orientation or experiential background.

A related point is that the scale items reflect social competence from an adult's perspective rather than from a child's. Presumably, one outcome of social competence is whether, in fact, a child is accepted or liked by other children, a point that is not addressed. An examination of each item shows that 14 of the 30 items concern primarily interactions with or responses to adults rather than children, with the highest degree of competence considered to be displayed by children who follow directions the first time they are given and show other such abilities. The total score in large part would certainly seem to indicate the child most liked by teachers who value compliance. It seems possible that a child could score well on this scale and still not have any friends because of a high number of other age-related behaviors such as teasing or threatening.

A third caution is that many items (15 of the 30) judge a child's ability to receive and express language. Following and remembering instructions, making suggestions for the direction of play, and seeking help are examples. Indeed, the item that is most highly correlated to the total social competence score is "Making explanation to other children," which requires a high degree of skill in referential communication. This language factor may help explain the superior scores on the scale for girls and children from higher occupational levels.

Although the behavioral wording of the items makes the scale less subjective as an observation instrument than many others, the observer must know the child well in order to detect emerging behaviors as well as those that are already established.

A final major caution when considering the use of this scale is that no information about interpretation is included. Decisions as to what the percentile score means in terms of normal versus atypical development and how to design educational programs to reflect the findings adequately are left to the rater (Proger, 1974). This lack greatly reduces the usefulness of the instrument.

The scale has limited value for individual use with children who seem to be functioning well socially. It can be helpful in examination of group skills, evaluation of curriculum goals, or analysis of group atmosphere or "ethos" (although it must be administered individually). Program goals and expectations must be consonant with those of the scale.

For children who appear to have difficulties in social areas or inconsistencies between social and other competencies, the scale could enable teachers to gain a detailed view of their social behaviors. Particular problems that could be remediated or particular competencies that might be overlooked could be identified.

In summary, the CPSCS is valid and reliable enough to use with confidence. As with any other assessment device, it should not be the only method used to assess a child's functioning in the area of social competence. Observations by more than one rater and systematic (recording of frequency or duration) observation of concomitant skills that are not on the scale, such as resistance to teasing, would add to its reliability.

References

Calfee, R.C. (1978). Review of the California Preschool Social Competency Scale. In O.K. Buros (Ed.), *The eighth mental measurements yearbook* (pp. 721–722). Highland Park, NJ: Gryphon Press.

Kubiszyn, T., & Borich, G. (1987). *Educational testing and measurement* (2nd ed.). Glenview, IL: Scott, Foresman and Company.

Levine, S., Elzey, F.F., & Lewis, M. (1969). *California Preschool Social Competency Scale.* Palo Alto, CA: Consulting Psychologists Press.

Proger, B.B. (1974). Review of the California Preschool Social Competency Scale. *Journal of Special Education, 8,*(4), 391–395.

Kenneth W. Wegner, Ed.D.
Professor of Education, Counseling Psychology, Boston College, Chestnut Hill, Massachusetts.

CALIFORNIA PSYCHOLOGICAL INVENTORY, 1987 REVISED EDITION

Harrison G. Gough. Palo Alto: Consulting Psychologists Press, Inc.

Introduction

The California Psychological Inventory (CPI) is a self-administered personality inventory developed for use with normal subjects. The original 1956 edition contained 18 standard scales designed to measure normal personality characteristics important in the prediction and understanding of individual behavior in social settings. The revised edition (Gough, 1987) added two standard scales plus three *vector* scales associated with the factorial structure of the inventory.

Harrison Gough never adopted a formal theoretical position according to Megargee (1972), thus his selection of the CPI scales is not based on an existing psychological theory. Gough is also skeptical of the validity of many theoretical positions in the interpretations of normal interpersonal behavior. His approach to selecting variables consists of "examining the setting in which the test is to be used and developing measurements based on the constructs already in operational usage there" (Megargee, 1972, p. 11). This practitioner's approach has general direct relevance and salience because it deals with concepts having already attained a degree of functional validity (Gough, 1968).

Concepts such as "responsibility" and "tolerance" that already exist in the realm of interpersonal behavior are the descriptive terms now applied by people to one another to describe their everyday behavior patterns and traits. Gough calls these *folk concepts*. "These 'folk concepts' must transcend a given era or a particular society" (Megargee, 1972, p. 12). The trait *dominance,* for example, was as relevant 2,000 years ago as it is today. Gough defines folk concepts as "aspects and attributes of interpersonal behavior that are to be found in all cultures and societies, and that possess a direct and integral relationship to all forms of social interaction" (1968, p. 57). He admits that there are probably other folk concepts that he has not included but the 20 scales in the CPI do correspond to the ways in which people describe themselves and others, and the way they can predict interpersonal behavior either alone or in combination.

There are 20 scales in the 1987 edition of the CPI. These scales are divided into four classes: Class I, 7 scales; Class II, 7 scales; Class III, 3 scales; and Class IV, 3 scales. Gough says that the scales based on his selected *folk concepts* have several important advantages: 1) immediate relevance for cross-cultural measurement; 2) variables that are meaningful and easily understood by the user;

and 3) scales that can validly forecast future behavior in the same context (Gough, 1968, p. 58).

Gough maintains that the CPl must be interpreted only by qualified professionals. He also believes that the use of terms other than folk concepts diminishes communication and causes loss of relevance. Cross-cultural research has been an essential part of the validation of the CPI in order to support these claims with data. Relationships found in United States samples have also been tested in many other countries. Most of these studies have found that this inventory predicts behavior abroad almost as well as it does here in the U.S.

Much of Gough's eclecticism stems from his joint education in sociology and psychology at the University of Minnesota. He graduated in 1942 as a sociology major and was excited by important social problems. He was exposed to psychologists such as Richard M. Elliot and Donald G. Patterson and gradually became convinced that psychological research methods had to be applied to socially significant problems identified by sociologists. His military service experience and postwar graduate education played a strong role in influencing the approach he would take.

Gough was at the University of Minnesota as a doctoral student in psychology while the Minnesota Multiphasic Personality Inventory (MMPI) was being developed and researched. Between 1946 and 1949 he took courses offered at the university by Meehl and Hathaway, who were the developers of the MMPl. He published articles about the application of the MMPI to the assessment of achievement, prejudice, social status, and delinquency. Gough published the CPI during his appointment at Berkeley, but much of it was researched and developed in Minnesota. The Minnesota approach placed a great deal of emphasis on the relationship between the criterion and the item. Being a pragmatist, Gough used different techniques for the derivation of various scales. Some variations were dictated by theory and some by expediency. (The two general methods used to develop the scales—internal consistency and external criterion—are described below). As a result the CPI is a heterogeneous instrument with each scale having its own characteristics. Because Gough placed primary emphasis on the prediction of behavior, he stressed convergent validity rather than discriminant validity. He used both the internal consistency and external criteria method to develop scales.

In the internal consistency method, the author decides which items should be included. This approach can be purely intuitive or partly empirical, where one is guided by data at some point. The latter approach was used in the derivation of 4 of the 20 scales. This is done by internal consistency analysis, where the test author intuitively selects a pool of items that appear to reflect the trait in question, administers the entire pool to a group of subjects, and then computes their scores on the test scale. Individuals with the highest scores and those with the lowest scores in the preliminary pool are identified. Analyses are then conducted to determine which of the items are differentiating most significantly between the two subsamples, and these, then, are retained for the final version of the scale. This rational approach is most likely to have high content validity. It usually reflects a consistent approach and can result in a scale closely related to a formal psychological theory. The validity of such a scale depends on the ability of the test authors to predict how people with the traits in question will respond to an item.

The Social Presence (Sp), Self-Acceptance (Sa), Self-Control (Sc) and Flexibility (Fx) scales of the CPI were all derived empirically using internal consistency analysis. Items that were related to the trait in question were selected and administered to a certain sample group. Item-total correlations were computed and those items with the highest correlations were selected for inclusion in the scale. The scale's validity was tested by correlating scale scores with measures of external behavior and other published personality scales.

The external criterion method is sometimes called the *empirical technique*. In this method, the criterion dimension to be measured is defined. Item selection is guided by the empirically determined relationship between the test item and a particular criterion measure. An initial item pool is first assembled and then given to groups of individuals who differ on the trait being assessed. Ideally, the two criterion groups are identical in every respect except for the trait being measured. Analysis is made of the item responses and the items that statistically differentiate the two groups are selected for the preliminary scale. The scale is first applied against the original criterion groups and, if the results are satisfactory, it is cross-validated on new samples. In using this method, discriminating items that are not obvious can be detected. A clinician who is aware of the lack of guilt of a sociopath would expect the item "Much of the time I feel I have done something wrong" to elicit a false answer when, in fact, it has been found that a true response is more characteristic.

This method of external criterion selection is used most often in tests that stress the practical prediction of various criteria as does the CPI. This method was used in the derivation of 13 of the 20 scales. In developing the CPI, Gough first studied the MMPI, but found that the items there were too oriented toward psychopathology for the folk concepts he wished to assess. Of the 480 items on the original CPI, 178 are almost identical to MMPI items and 35 others are very similar. The remaining 267 items were from the original scale.

After the initial item pool was selected, external criteria were chosen. The criteria used in the empirical derivation of the CPI scales varied from scale to scale. A common procedure was to ask a group of friends to nominate members of their group who were high or low on a trait in question. These people were provided with a description of the behavior patterns that related to the scale. The number of nominations received for each person would be tallied and group members were rank ordered on the trait. These rankings were used as criteria. Other scales used more objective criteria. The Femininity scale (Fm) was derived by contrasting responses of males with females. The Sociability scale (Sy) was based on the number of extracurricular activities in which a student participated. Gough used grades for other tests to select criterion groups for subsequent analyses for some scales (e.g., Intellectual Efficiency (Ie) had IQ scores as criteria). The other 10 scales developed in this fashion were: 1) Dominance (Do), 2) Capacity for Status (Cs), 3) independence (In), 4) Empathy (Em), 5) Responsibility (Re), 6) Socialization (So), 7) Tolerance (To), 8) Achievement via Conformance (Ac), 9) Achievement via Independence (Ai), and 10) Psychological-mindedness (Py).

A mixed strategy, not classified easily among the previously mentioned scales, was used to develop the Good Impression (Gi), Communality (Cm), and Well-being (Wb) scales. These were designed as validating scales to detect the general state of mind of the examinee.

The 1987 edition also contains three structural scales developed to capitalize on the underlying factorial structure of the inventory. This process involved selecting items that correlated highly with factorial axes and resulted in the development of vector scales: v.1, Internality; v.2, Norm-favoring; and v.3, Self-realization.

When the CPI was first published in 1956, it seemed desirable to have the scales arranged so that high scores on all 18 reflected positive behavior. Because the inventory emphasized factors contributing to interpersonal and social effectiveness, Gough also chose to rename some scales so that they reflected favorable dimensions. The Prejudice scale became the Tolerance scale, Impulsivity became Self-Control (SC), Dissimulation became Well-being (Wb), and Infrequency became Communality (Cm).

In addition to adding new scales in 1987, the items were also revised. Eighteen items of the original 480 were dropped (12 were repeated items) and 29 were changed in wording to make them more up-to-date, easier to understand, and free of undesirable phraseology. Items were deleted from 16 of the 18 original scales and items were added to 8 scales. The new scales, In and Em, were derived from existing items. Each scale now contains 28 to 42 items, and all of the original scales correlate .91 to .98 with their new versions using the normative sample of 1,000 males and 1,000 females. Although the rationale for changes in the original scales is not clear from the Administrator's Guide (Gough, 1987), they appear to have been made to improve the internal consistency and current relevancy of the scales.

The original CPI is available in French, German, Italian, and Spanish language versions; the 1987 edition is available in English only. Because it is entirely verbal in format, it may be administered orally to the visually impaired.

The materials used in administering the CPI include a 462-item reusable test booklet and an answer sheet that may be hand or machine scored (using a No. 2 pencil). Administration time is 45 minutes to 1 hour. With a slow reader or oral administration, several test sessions may be needed. The CPI may be "taken home" or mailed out and mailed back if necessary. The author indicates that age 13 (Grade 7) or above is an appropriate reading and maturity level for administering the CPI. The examiner may need to explain the meaning of a word or phrase, but should not attempt to explain the purpose or concept underlying an item. Answer sheets should be examined for items left blank because since too many omits may invalidate the profile.

The answer sheet is designed for computer or hand scoring. It has two sides with circular bubbles to record true or false responses. Hand scoring is a relatively simple clerical task using durable templates. Scoring is by total raw score for each scale. These scores are recorded on the answer sheet and at the bottom of the profile. There are separate profiles for the 1,000 male and 1,000 female normative samples. The profile is printed to allow conversion of raw to standard scores (mean score of 50 with standard deviation of 10) by marking the position of the raw score on the profile. The three vector raw scores are recorded on a graph on the back of the profile. Hand scoring and profiling will require 15 to 30 minutes per answer sheet.

Two types of computer scoring and interpretation are available from the publisher. The first produces the same profile information as hand scoring. The second adds a narrative interpretation of the profile plus several other special scales and indices (i.e., managerial potential and work orientation, social maturity, leadership, and creativity). Microcomputer software is also available for administration, scoring, and reporting at the testing location.

Perhaps the simplest method of describing the 20 folk concept scales of the CPI is to provide one high score and one low score descriptor of their intended implications. There are seven scales in Class I, which is designed to measure poise, ascendancy, self-assurance, and interpersonal adequacy. These include: Dominance (Do), confident versus unassuming; Capacity for Status (Cs), ambitious versus unsure of self; Sociability (Sy), sociable versus shy; Social Presence (Sp), self assured versus cautious; Self-acceptance (Sa), good opinion of self versus self-doubting; Independence (In), self-sufficient versus lacks self-confidence; and Empathy (Em), empathic versus unempathic.

Class II scales are designed to measure socialization, maturity, responsibility, and interpersonal structuring of values. These seven scales are: Responsibility (Re), responsible versus unconcerned; Socialization (So), conforming versus non-conforming; Self-control (Sc); controls emotions versus expresses strong feelings; Good Impression (Gi), pleases others versus being oneself; Communality (Cm), fits in easily versus being different; Well-being (Wb), feels good versus concerned about problems; and Tolerance (To), tolerant of other's values versus intolerant.

Class III scales are designed to measure achievement potential and intellectual efficiency. They are: 1) Achievement via Conformance (Ac), strong drive in structural settings versus difficulty with structured tasks; 2) Achievement via Independence (Ai) strong drive and initiative versus difficulty in vaguely defined tasks; and 3) Intellectual Efficiency (Ie), intellectually efficient and motivated versus slow starting.

The Class IV scales are a mixed group of measures of intellectual and interest modes. They include: 1) Psychological-mindedness (Py), feeling and thinking orientation versus the practical and concrete; 2) Flexibility (Fx), variety oriented versus well-organized; and 3) Femininity/Masculinity (F/M), sensitive versus action-oriented.

Three vector scores representing the factor structure are also reported: 1) Internality (v.I) measures introversion versus extraversion; 2) Norm-favoring (v.2) measures the tendency to follow or not follow rules; and 3) Self-Realization (v.3) reflects a sense of personal integration or attainment of goals. The graphic presentation of the v.1 and v.2 scores on the profile separates respondents into four types: *Alphas,* who are outgoing, dependable, and enterprising; *Betas,* who are moderate, responsible, and reserved; *Gammas,* who are pleasure-seeking, restless, and adventurous; and *Deltas,* who are disaffected, private, and withdrawn. The v.3 scores are independent of v.1 and v.2 and are used to develop a cuboid model providing seven levels of functioning (poor to superior integration) of the four types.

Practical Applications/Uses

Gough's goal in developing the CPI was to predict what a person will do in a particular context and/or to identlfy how they would be described by others. It was *not* designed to measure traits per se but to describe and predict behavior. Thus, the CPI is useful in both helping clients understand themselves and in making preditions for the future.

The CPI is intended for use with normal subjects, although some studies have been done on psychiatric cases. Through *The Ninth Mental Measurements Yearbook* (1985) there are 1,443 citations suggesting populations for which the CPI might be useful. These studies have investigated the relationship of the CPI scales to scholaotic achievomont, occupational groups, creativity, leadership marital adjustment, delinquency, smoking cessation, and many other phenomena. The 1987 revision of the CPI appears to be oriented more towards occupational settings. The Managerial Potential and the Work Orientation special scales may be useful in personnel selection. Also, persons in managerial occupations tend to be model *Alpha* types. However, the reader is cautioned that no research on the CPI or any other personality instrument has demonstrated a definitive relationship between personality and any specific occupation.

Megargee (1972) has emphasized the need for studies and normative data for minority groups, but these are not provided in the Administrator's Guide (Gough, 1987). There needs to be more research in cross-cultural uses and with special populations, such as the elderly and those with health problems or disabling conditions.

Although the CPI is designed for predicting behavior of normal people, it has been used in clinical settings. Generally, research indicates that mild problems, such as worriers and disciplinary proneness, can be identlfied using the CPI. Clinical studies indicate that scores of counseling clients are significantly different from non-clients on certain parts of the test.

Use of the CPI for diagnosing psychiatric problems, such as schizophrenia, has not been adequately tested. The lack of research can be attributed to the fact that the clinician has other tests, such as the MMPI, that better meet this purpose. The research that has been done is relatively unsophisticated. It has demonstrated a strong tendency for individuals whose life-styles are different to have the same type of profile. Studies attempting to use the test to measure treatment success have been inconclusive. The test has been most effective with people who have societal problems (i.e., delinquents, prisoners, etc.) rather than intrapsychic ones. Megargee (1972) suggests that the CPI might be useful for assessing candidates for sensitivity and encounter groups and also for estimating the probability that an individual will profit from vocational counseling or rehabilitation therapy, More research will have to be done before the test can be ruled out as a clinical instrument for use with severely disturbed individuals.

As described previously, the administration, scoring, and profiling of the CPI are quite simple (whether hand or computer processed). Directions for administration are clear and hand scoring and profiling are easy clerical tasks. Computer-processed answer sheets relieve the examiner of the latter clerical tasks and will also provide a computer generated narrative description of the client. These reports can be extremely helpful in assisting the individual clinician's judgment.

Like all other personality tests, structured or projective, the CPI must be interpreted by a skilled, well-trained psychologist who is thoroughiy familiar with the research literature. All interpretations should be made in the context of interview data if they are to approach accuracy at all. There is little empirical research dealing with the CPI as it is used in clinical practice. Most CPI investigations explore quantitative relationships between a single scale and some criterion measure, and generally exclude data from other CPI scales, insights by the interpreter, and relevant environmental factors. This suggests that in interpreting profiles, the clinician is funtioning in an area characterized by clinical folklore, speculation, and hypotheses. Much research needs to be done concerning the analysis and conceptualization of the individual case and such interpretations, as are done now, should be based not on the CPI alone but also on conditions under which it was administered, the respondent's basic characteristics (age, race, marital status, sex, education, etc.), and other relevant case history, interview, and test data. The meaning of test patterns varies as a function of the context.

The CPI appears simple and seems to offer a shortcut to personality assessment in contrast to instruments such as the Rorschach. However, if the interpreter is to interpret data accurately, he or she must learn the subtle meaning of the various scale configurations and their contraindications. He or she must develop a thorough understanding of the constructs each scale defines, study their construction as well as content, and read the validational literature and conceptual analyses. Some scales appear to have a nonlinear relationship with behavior. For example, a moderate elevation on the Self-control (Sc) scale can be taken as contraindicating aggressive acting out; however, an extremely high Sc score may indicate a potentially unstable conflict between strong aggressive impulses and rigid controls that could result in episodic flareups. Moderate elevations on Flexibility (Fx) indicate adaptability, T-scores over 80 seem to indicate a temperament that is too mercurial and volatile. In addition, the interpretation of some scales depends on the elevation of other scales. A person scoring high on the Dominance (Do) scale may be outgoing and concerned with leadership; a person who also scores high on the Good Impression (Gi) scale may exercise this leadership in a manner that demonstrates concern with and respect for others. However, a person scoring high on the Do scale and low on the Gi scale may be domineering, bossy, and egotistical. In general, more research should be done to demonstrate the validity of configural approaches to CPI interpretation.

Technical Aspects

The CPI is designed to measure a set of variables through the use of brief, accurate, and dependable subscales (Gough, 1987). The measurements are reported in descriptive concepts that possess broad personal and social relevance. Consequently, it is important that the test be valid on two levels: 1) its basic values and 2) how well the test meets the goals set for it.

The CPI's basic values have been criticized for two reasons. The first is that the test's variables describe character in value-loaded terms, which tends to encourage the idea that there is just one ideal personality. The second criticism is that there is an ethical overtone that suggests that low scores on some scales reflect faults rather than needs (Cronbach, 1959). A third criticism concerns the contradictions implicit in Gough's statements about uses for the test. On the one hand, he postulates that by measuring traits in terms of enduring folk concepts, cross-cultural use of the test should be possible. But he cautions against using the test with groups other than white students and young adults. It appears that the former is a hope of the author's while the latter is the practical reality, given the validation studies that have been done.

The second level of validity to examine is the degree to which the test meets the goals set for it, which is its construct validity. The goals stated in the Administrator's Guide are to: "1) to predict what people will say or do in specified contexts and 2) to identify individuals who will be evaluated and described in particular and interpersonally specific ways" (Gough, 1987, p. 4).

Gough chose the instrumental or pragmatic approach to validate the scales, in which the scales are evaluated in terms of how well they identify people who are described by others in terms of that trait. Typically this has been done by correlating scores with ratings on Q-sorts or adjective checklists completed by peers, spouses, or interviewers. One criticism of the CPI comes as a result of factor analytic research, which has demonstrated that six or less subscales would be sufficient to deal with most of the reliable variance. Thus the discriminant validity of the test is not very high, due to the high intercorrelations between scales. For example, the intercorrelations of the seven Class I scales range from .59 to .75 in the normative samples of 1,000 males and 1,000 females. To partially satisfy these criticisms Gough developed the v.1, v.2, and v.3 structural or vector scales. The v.1 scale measures introversion-extraversion, and is indexed to the F/M, Sc, and Gi scales at the introversion pole and Sa, Sy, Do, and Sp scales at the extraversion pole. The v.2 normative or rule following scale is indexed to Cm and So at one pole and Fx at the other. Self-realization (v.3) was indexed to the sum of the Wb, To, and Ie scales. Gough's factor analysis of the normative samples produced three factors (Extraversion, Consensuality and Flexibility) that seem related to v. 1 and v.2. A fourth factor (Control) appears somewhat related to v.3.

It is apparent then that convergent validity has been obtained at the expense of discriminant validity. Low discriminant validity results in redundancy and high correlations with measures of response bias and response set. Despite this, Gough has been reluctant to reduce the redundancy, lest it lower the convergent validity. Furthermore, Gough has refuted criticisms of the CPI relating to response bias and response set by pointing out the existence of scales within the test that measure random answering, malingering, and social desirability. Research evidence has further weakened these criticisms of the CPI (Megargee, 1972).

Megargee (1972) deals with the issue in his discussion of the development of the CPI:

> Gough's approach to test construction emphasized the building of scales for the purpose of predicting socially relevant behavior patterns. As a result, the development and validation of the CPI has aimed at maximizing predictive and concurrent validity even at the expense of other test attributes such as factorial purity and discriminant validity. The failure of some CPI scales to have the latter attributes is of more concern to personality researchers who wish to use the CPI for trait measurement than it is to those who wish to predict practical criteria, such as the likelihood a student will be graduated from high school (p. 33)

Gough emphasizes the predictive validity of the CPI more than its construct or trait validity. He states, "The purpose of each scale is to predict what an individual will do in a specified context and/or to identify individuals who will be described in a certain way" (Gough, 1968). In this respect, the CPI has been demonstrated to be capable of making long-range predictions, sometimes over a period of several years. It can, apparently, validly forecast such things as high school graduation and college matriculation, particularly when used in conjunction with other sources of data. Data from research on college students indicate that the CPI is more predictive of GPA than of leaving school (Megargee, 1972).

Concurrent validity has been tested, and the findings indicate that CPI data correlate highly with behavior observations, but not so well with other tests like the MMPI (Kelly, 1965).

In summary, the validity data seem to indicate that the goals of the test are fairly well met. Although most studies do not test the goals directly, high correlations with behavioral observations and the ability of the test to predict events several years away indicate that the CPI can be employed usefully to predict interpersonal behavior.

The following briefly outlines the stability amd internal consistency studies of the CPI as reported in the Administrator's Guide (Gough, 1987). It is worth noting here that the CPI has been criticized for the lack of split-half correlation studies to test its overall internal consistency. A third kind of reliability, equivalence, has been tested through correlation of different language forms of the test.

Stability, which is the amount of variation in scores over a period of time, has been examined in a number of studies of test-retest correlations. It is important that the CPI have a high long-term reliability coefficient because it is designed to measure enduring personality characteristics. The relevant studies show a long-term reliability, which is lower than it optimally should be, but high enough to indicate that the test is fairly stable. The Administrator's Guide (Gough, 1987) reports on two stability studies in detail. In the first, two high school junior classes took the CPI in the fall and again a year later as seniors. The median stability coefficient for 102 males was .68, ranging from .43 for Cm to .76 for both Sc and Wb; for 128 females the median was .71, ranging from .58 for Em and Ai, to a high of .79 for Ie. This is a modest correlation, which Gough suggests may represent the differing rates of maturation among these adolescents during the year between testings.

An equivalency study compared the French and English versions with high school students, using a 1-week interval. The students attended English-speaking schools, but came from French-speaking homes. For the 85 males the median correlation was .68, with a range of .50 to .83. For the 38 females, the median was .70, with a range of .42 to .83. Most of the students reported difficulty in reading the French form.

Alpha (internal consistency) coefficients are reported for random samples of 200 male and 200 female college students. The male median was .72, with a range of .45 on F/M to .85 for v.3. For females, the median was .73, with a range of .52 for Sa to .85 for v.3. This reviewer agrees with Gough in that these reliability coefficients are typical for self-report inventories.

Earlier studies of the reliability of the previous form of the CPI are generally in agreement with the findings summarized here. It appears that the CPI is a reliable test instrument, which may be used with confidence.

Critique

The reviews of the CPI since 1956 range from praise to severe criticism. Frequently they reflect the reviewer's attitude toward the "ideal" personality test. However, no such ideal has yet been developed. If the reviewer has a theoretical bent, the criticism is typically oriented against Gough's lack of definition of the basic constructs underlying the folk concepts. From a psychometric point of view, the CPI is attacked for its technical deficiencies. For example Eysenk (1985) criticizes the 1956 CPI for overlap of scales and suggests the CPI measures only two factors: neuroticism-stability and extraversion-introversion. Gough (1987) seems to have accepted this criticism by placing more emphasis on the factorial structure of the CPI and development of the vector scales in the 1987 edition.

On a positive note, the CPI has been praised for its extensive and careful development, sizeable samples, readable manual, and other good technical qualities. In fact, the 1987 Administrator's Guide could serve as a model for other personality tests. Gough appears to have corrected many of the criticisms such as appropriate normative samples and item content relevance. The CPI also ranks among the top personality tests in popularity of use with normal clients amd predicting group behavior with special populations. However, there is still much research to be done in the use of combinations of various scales in description and prediction of individual client behaviors.

All in all, the CPI has a long and substantial research base to support its usefulness. Gough and his colleagues have continued to heed advice of critics and improve the instrument. It is popular among both practitioners and researchers and it is likely that this popularity will continue in the future.

References

Cronbach, L.J. (1959). Review of the California Psychological Inventory. In O.K. Buros (Ed.), *The fifth mental measurements yearbook* (pp. 97–99). Highland Park, NJ: Gryphon Press.

Eysenek, H.J. (1985). California Psychological Inventory. In J.V. Mitchell, Jr. (Ed.), *The ninth mental measurements yearbook.* (pp. 252–253). Lincoln, NE: Buros Institute of mental measurement.

Gough, H.G. (1957). *California Psychological Inventory manual.* Palo Alto, CA: Consulting Psychologists Press, Inc.

Gough, H.G. (1968). An interpreter's syllabus for the California Psychological Inventory. Palo Alto, CA: Consulting Psychologists Press, Inc.

Gough, H.G. (1987). *California Psychological Inventory administrator's guide.* Palo Alto, CA: Consulting Psychologists Press, Inc.

Kelly, E.L. (1965). Review of the California Psychological Inventory. In O.K. Buros (Ed.), *The sixth mental measurements yearbook* (pp. 168–170). Highland Park, NJ: Gryphon Press.

Megargee, E. (1972). *The California Psychological Inventory handbook.* San Francisco: Jossey-Bass Inc.

Larry R. Cochran, Ph.D.
Associate Professor of Counseling Psychology, The University of British Columbia, Vancouver, British Columbia.

CAREER PROBLEM CHECK LIST

A. D. Crowley. Windsor, Great Britain: NFER-Nelson Publishing Company Ltd.

Introduction

Developed in Great Britain for use with secondary and college students, the Career Problem Check List (CPCL) is composed of 100 items that indicate career problems, three open-ended questions, and one question that allows students to indicate whether they would like to see a careers advisor. The open-ended questions ask students to describe other problems not recorded on the checklist, to describe the type of work they would like, and to record the number of items that particularly concern them, should they wish to join a discussion group. The 100 items are divided into seven problem areas concerned with 1) school or college, 2) decisions, 3) home, 4) a particular job, 5) applying for work or further education, 6) starting work, and 7) outside work.

Since receiving his Master of Philosophy in 1979 for a study of occupational interests, A.D. Crowley has shown particular concern for research problems of practical importance (1981a, 1983a). In part, Crowley's interest in developing the CPCL appears to have grown from one of his previous studies (1981b) that showed school personnel are not always aware of the needs of their students in planning career programs, providing activities that might be "irrelevant or meaningless whilst more pressing issues remain unresolved" (Crowley, 1983b, p. 2). The development of the CPCL is intended as a convenient instrument through which students can convey the kinds of problems or needs that are relevant to them.

The career problem items were constructed initially from lists of problems supplied by careers officers, teachers, and open-ended questionnaires completed by students. Trial checklists were developed and completed by several hundred secondary and college students, resulting in the refinement of items, deletions, and some additions. After three trials, the CPCL was shaped into its present form with 100 items grouped into seven areas. On the front cover, students are informed that the checklist provides a way to help indicate the problems they are experiencing in planning a career and that their responses will guide the efforts of careers officers and teachers to help them. Students are instructed to underline any item that describes the way they feel at the moment. When complete, they are to go back over the underlined items and circle the numbers of items that are of particular importance.

Norms of a sort were reported for a group of 510 Newcastle students, ranging in age from 14 to 16. The norms indicate the percentage of students who responded to each item. For example, 43% of the students worried about exams while only 2% worried about finding a place to live. Another kind of norm was based upon total

76

frequency of response across ages. Younger students reported more concerns than older students. Crowley refers to the norm tables as guides or samples rather than actual norms because responses were found to vary according to region, age, and whether or not students had completed a career education program. In short, the tables exemplify rather than establish a normative reference.

Testing materials include a small four-page booklet and a CPCL manual (Crowley, 1983b). On the front page of the booklet above the instructions, students record personal information, such as name and age. On the two inside pages the 100 items are grouped into seven areas, each set of items preceded by a stem such as, "I am having problems" or "I find that." On the back page are the three open-ended questions and the question of whether one would like an interview with a careers advisor.

Practical Applications/Uses

The CPCL is easy to administer, taking from 10 to 15 minutes. No special procedures are necessary for administration and no special qualifications are required for the administrator. Crowley recommends that groups should be limited to approximately 30 so that questions can be answered satisfactorily, but the CPCL could be easily administered in very large groups. Because the CPCL is not scored, but rather underlined items are tabulated, lay persons could also organize the results of testing.

Although the CPCL might be used in research, it is designed for practical use. Crowley envisioned five major ways that it might be helpful to counselors and teachers. First, the responses can be used to direct and focus individual counseling interviews. Attention is directed to problematic areas (e.g., applying for a job) and then focused upon particular items. Second, by identifying the needs of students, one can plan career programs that attempt to resolve frequently experienced problems. Third, there might be smaller groups of students with similar problems; if seen one by one, a counselor might use his or her time to inefficiently repeat, for instance, how one budgets finances. In this regard, the CPCL can be used to identify students for special groups. Fourth, by comparing student responses on two separate occasions, a counselor can monitor change and possibly the impact of career programs. Last, the items of the CPCL can be used as reminders of what to include in a well-balanced and comprehensive career education program.

While administration is unproblematic and its envisioned uses are clear, interpretation of the CPCL is more open and uncertain. Crowley suggests that a counselor examine the number, the kinds, and the unusualness of items underlined. However, there is no normative frame of reference for interpreting frequency, no frame for interpreting kinds, and no indication of what responses are unusual or what unusualness means in this context.

Technical Aspects

Evidence for reliability is based solely upon a single study of 45 14-year-old students who completed the CPCL twice with an interval of 10 days between test sessions. As a group, mean frequency of response did not differ significantly between the two sessions. For individual frequency, test-retest reliability was .82. A correlation between frequency of items underlined was .86, indicating that items received about the same number of underlinings 10 days later. Crowley also assessed the extent to which an item underlined on the first administration was underlined on the second administration. Across individuals, the average degree of agreement was 85%. In general, the reported reliabilities are supportive, but reported incompletely and inadequate for a confident judgment of reliability.

Evidence for validity rests upon concurrent and content validation. Concurrent validity was assessed first by counting the frequency of underlined responses for those who had and had not received help in career preparation. However, because help in career preparation varied systematically with age, no conclusion can be drawn clearly. Second, two different age groups showed different response rates for many items. According to Crowley, the different response rates "clearly reflect the kinds of concerns to be anticipated from these two different age groups." (1983b, p. 9). Third, in a more direct study, 497 students were asked if the CPCL allowed them to indicate or summarize their career concerns. All but eight found it to be acceptable. Content validity was assessed by asking 510 students, varying in age from 14 to 16, to list any career problems that concerned them but were not listed on the CPCL. Twelve students did list additional concerns, but these were apparently of a personal nature and not judged to be relevant as career problems.

No evidence for construct validity was reported. That is, response rates for the decision section were not correlated with a test of career indecision. Response rates generally were not correlated with tests of career maturity or career development, nor with any instrument that would validate the needs being evaluated. Because no evidence was reported, construct validity depends upon content validity at this time.

No evidence for predictive validity was reported. For example, are some needs more predictive of later career difficulties than others? Are some areas of more importance? Could one predict that students who expressed many concerns about applying for work experienced any more difficulty in finding work than those who expressed few concerns? Nothing of this sort was considered.

Of particular concern, no evidence was reported for the intended uses of the CPCL. As Vacc and Pickering (1985) noted in their review, "The CPCL's value within counseling programs has not been empirically documented" (p. 180). There is no evidence that time is saved, that needs are adequately assessed, that group formation is effective, that progress can be adequately monitored, and so on. All of the claims on behalf of the CPCL have yet to be demonstrated.

In general, the technical information reported in the manual is inadequate. Exact statistical tests, groups being tested, procedures, and the like, are often not reported or are vaguely summarized. The manual generally does not meet the standards of the American Psychological Association for tests. Evidence for reliability and validity is supportive, but much more is necessary. The lack of norm groups is troubling. Of particular significance, it is difficult to know how the items of the test were selected and what assurance there is that the items are a representative sample of career problems. It is this reviewer's opinion that there is not enough information in the manual to support or guide test use with any confidence.

Critique

Like the Mooney Problem Check List (Mooney & Gordon, 1950), the idea of a problem checklist for career counseling seems to be a useful one. Whether used in individual cases or group programs, the CPCL is intended to orient professionals to the concerns of their clients. However, in any instrument intended to *guide*, there is the danger of misguidance or superficial guidance, in general or for particular groups. The quality of the guidance offered by the CPCL is difficult to assess, given the information in the manual. However, there are some definite limitations and cautions that seem warranted.

As it is currently formed, the CPCL is culture bound to Great Britain. A North American youth would not be concerned with a National Insurance number card nor with paying National Insurance contributions. While these items are obvious, it supports the possibility that youths from other countries might have different career problems. Given Willis's (1977) study of British working-class youth making the transition from school to work, it seems doubtful that the CPCL would be useful even for all classes of youth in Great Britain. Examinees for whom the CPCL is applicable must be specified more sharply.

Unfortunately, interpretation is encouraged far beyond the bounds of intended use. One is to interpret the frequency, kinds, and unusualness of underlined items, but without any basis for doing so. There is no indication of what response rate means (i.e., anxiety, interest, pressure, conformity, class, etc.). There is no indication of what items mean, yet in one of the examples, a set of underlined items was taken to indicate uncertainty and despondency. Although there is no indication of what an unusual item is or means, this is offered as something to interpret or ask the person to explain. Interpretations of this nature require training in psychological testing, but no qualifications for test administrators were specified. Without such safeguards, any number of injudicious interpretations might be made of someone's responses, particularly given the lack of grounds for such interpretations. Upon what basis, for instance, would one judge despondency? And why would one judge despondency anyway from a test intended to convey career concerns? In over-interpreting responses beyond intended use and beyond that supported by evidence, the potential for misguidance is prominent.

The primary use of the CPCL is as a needs assessment instrument. In this regard, the CPCL lacks theory in the formulation of items. Neither Super (1957) nor Holland (1985) nor any theory of career development is an evident influence on item selection. This is important because youths may not be aware necessarily of what they need, any more than sailors at one time were aware that they needed fresh fruit to prevent scurvy. Knowing what one needs can be very confusing and uncertain, and for this reason, theories can be helpful. Much of the CPCL focuses upon externals, such as wages, proper attire, exams, but not upon more personal needs, such as clarifying values, resolving conflicting values or aspirations, evaluating options, setting priorities, gaining confidence, enhancing self-esteem, feeling more in control or able to affect outcomes, and just finding meaning in work, among other things. The lack of theory in the construction of the CPCL is conspicuous unfortunately by its absence.

But how serious is this lack of theory? Aside from the neglect of a number of relevant items, there is little system or organization evident in the CPCL. The 100 items are a collection of the significant and trivial, and do not rise above a collection. Along with significant items concerned with discovering abilities, interests, and an accurate view of self, there are items concerned with how to complain, having less money than friends, how to pass on messages, not being allowed out of the home much, being able to afford bus fares, and so on. The enduring and transient, general and particular, critical and superficial are laid out in no order with no informing vision of a career need. Is it really so important to know how to handle practical jokes played on newcomers, particularly because one is not a newcomer very long? This reviewer thinks not, and if this is the case, the CPCL suffers from a lack of a sure sense of what a genuine career need is.

Consider the situation in which the CPCL is to be used. A student reads the items and underlines what he or she thinks important at the moment. Do the underlined responses reflect the genuine needs of the student? In part, a checklist is an orientation to what a career problem is; it is not neutral. For this reason, an independent way of assessing needs is necessary to assess the value of the CPCL. For example, case studies of individuals might be compared with CPCL responses, or a rigorous needs assessment study of a group might be compared with group responses to the CPCL. In this way, one could judge how well the CPCL approximates what would be found from a much more time-consuming and in-depth investigation. Because this kind of study has not been done, it leaves the question open as to the adequacy of CPCL for needs assessment. For example, might not the CPCL distract students from genuine needs to more superficial concerns? Might it not camouflage a few salient needs with a greater number of peripheral needs? Whether the CPCL guides well or ill has yet to be determined.

In summary, the CPCL is a convenient instrument for assessing the career needs of a group or individual. However, at this time, it cannot be recommended for practical use. Evidence for reliability is restricted to a small group of 14-year-old students. Evidence for validity is insufficient as yet. Norm groups have not been established. Due to some item content, phrases, and lack of evidence, it is unsuitable for use outside of Great Britain. Perhaps of more importance, there is no clear conceptualization of what a career need is. For example, is a need a lack that will impair career functioning if not filled? Or is a need merely any concern one can think of, whether important or not? Or is a need simply a menu item for what one is prepared to offer in a career program? Whether an item is conceived one way or the other makes a great difference in how the CPCL would be interpreted. It also makes a difference in how such a test would be constructed. Given the information in the manual, it cannot be determined by what criteria items were selected, and consequently, what is really being assessed.

References

Crowley, A.D. (1981a). The content of interest inventories: Job titles or job activities. *Journal of Occupational Psychology, 54,* 135–140.

Crowley, A.D. (1981b). Evaluating the impact of a third year careers education programme. *British Journal of Guidance and Counselling, 9,* 207–213.

Crowley, A.D. (1983a). Predicting occupational entry: Measured versus expressed interests. *Journal of Occupational Psychology, 56,* 57–61.

Crowley, A.D. (1983b). *The Career Problem Check List manual.* Windsor, England: NFER-Nelson.

Holland, J. (1985). *Making vocational choices: A theory of careers.* Englewood Cliffs, NJ: Prentice-Hall.

Mooney, R., & Gordon, L. (1950). *Mooney Problem Check Lists.* San Antonio, TX: The Psychological Corporation.

Super, D. (1957). *The psychology of careers.* New York: Harper & Brothers.

Vacc, N., & Pickering, J. (1985). Review of the Career Problem Check List. In J.V. Mitchell, Jr. (Ed.), *The ninth mental measurement yearbook* (pp. 279–281). Lincoln, NE: The Buros Institute.

Willis, P. (1977). *Learning to labour.* Hampshire, England: Teakfield Limited.

Keith S. Dobson, Ph.D.

Associate Professor of Psychology, Department of Psychology, University of British Columbia, Vancouver, British Columbia, Canada.

CHILDREN'S DEPRESSION SCALE

Moshe Lang and Miriam Tisher. Hawthorn, Victoria, Australia: The Australian Council for Educational Research Limited.

Introduction

The Children's Depression Scale (CDS; Lang & Tisher, 1978) is a rationally designed severity scale that measures global depression. It contains several sub-scales that measure elements of depression and of pleasure and enjoyment. Developed in the latter part of the 1970s when scales to measure depression instruments for children and adolescents were virtually nonexistent, the CDS has retained considerable attention and use as a consequence of its early development and appearance. With the recent consensus that childhood depression is a legitimate and serious problem that can be assessed through the use of self-report scales (Kovacs, 1981), the CDS has an important role to play in the assessment of childhood and adolescent depression.

The CDS consists of two 66-item tests that are completed by the child and a significant other (e.g., parent) who knows the child well. In the child version of the CDS, the child reads each of the 66 statements and decides how self-descriptive each statement is based on a 5-point Likert-type scale of 1 (very wrong), 2 (wrong), 3 (don't know/not sure), 4 (right), or 5 (very right), and then deposits an index card containing the statement into one of five boxes corresponding to the rating scale. This mailbox type of format is innovative (although a bit clumsy for storage) and helps to hold the children's interest throughout the test. Although the CDS is intended for children aged 9 to 16 years, children at lower ranges (9–12) who cannot comprehend the statements may need an adult to administer the test orally (Lang & Tisher, 1978). The CDS Parent's Questionnaire (based on a 5-point scale) is in a paper-and-pencil format, in which the parent reads each statement and determines the degree to which each statement describes the child in question. This reviewer and his son completed the CDS within the 15-minute timeframe suggested by the authors (Lang & Tisher, 1978).

The CDS yields eight interpretable scale scores, six of which are oriented towards depression and two oriented towards a positive nature. The 48 depression statements are broken down into six scales: 1) Affective Response (AR; the affect or mood of the child); 2) Social Problems (SP; difficulties in social interaction, loneliness; and isolation); 3) Self-Esteem (SE; the child's sense of self-worth and value); 4) Preoccupation with Sickness and Death (SD; dreams and fantasies related to sickness and death); 5) Guilt (GI; self-blame and criticism); and 6) Total Depression (a composite of the five scales plus nine miscellaneous depression items). In addition, 18 positive statements from the CDS yield two other scales: 1) Pleasure and Enjoyment (PE; the presence of fun, enjoyment, and happiness, or the ability to experience pleasure and enjoyment) and 2) Total Pleasure (a composite of PE plus 10 miscellaneous positive items). AR, SP, SE, GI, and PE subscales contain eight statements each, and the SD subscale contains seven statements.

Practical Applications/Uses

Scoring the CDS is somewhat complicated due to the large number of scales. No scoring template is included and the examiner must use a key to find the items belonging to each scale and then compute scale totals by hand. Scale totals are then entered onto the record form as raw scores. The CDS could be easily enhanced by the development of a scoring routine for computer.

The CDS scores are interpreted by computing the decile score and comparing it to the norm tables provided on the record form. Separate norms are provided for the child and parent versions. For example, a raw score of 120 on the Total Depression scale places a child at the 5th decile. By contrasting the overall pattern of scale scores with the norms provided, a profile of the severity of the child's principal features of depression may be gained.

The normative group, upon which decile interpretations are based, is not very adequate (Rotundo & Hensley, 1985; Tonkin & Hudson, 1981); the subjects ($N = 37$) are described as "regular school attenders who had not missed more than ten school days during the year" (Lang & Tisher, 1983, p. 18), and no other information is given. Using this group's normative scores to determine the child's deciles may overestimate the severity of depression. In addition, because the normative deciles are based upon 37 children, each decile score is determined by about 4 children. The stability of such results is questionable.

The other contrast group used in the original development of the test is also problematic. The sample ($N = 40$) is described as a "group of relatively severe cases of school refusal" (Lang & Tisher, 1983, p. 18). Although depression may also be a feature of such children, the decile scores available for this normative group may well underestimate the scores for a truly depressed sample of children or adolescents. That clinically depressed children score higher than the normative school refusal group is supported by publisher literature (Lang & Tisher, 1983).

Scoring the CDS is somewhat complicated, although not obstructively so. Use of the decile score for interpretation, though straightforward, is problematic because of the size and nature of the normative samples.

Technical Aspects

Several studies of the reliability and validity of the CDS have been completed (Bath & Middleton, 1985; Lang & Tisher, 1983; Rotundo & Hensley, 1985; Tonkin & Hudson, 1981) and a number of technical aspects of the CDS have been investigated.

Internal reliability and consistency. Estimates of internal reliability and consistency have been reported several times. In the manual, Lang and Tisher (1978, 1983) report that the coefficient alpha for the total Depression score, based on 208 records, was .96. Other estimates of internal reliability, based upon the total CDS scores, range from .92 (Tonkin & Hudson, 1981) through .94 (Bath & Middleton, 1985) to .98 (Rotundo & Hensley, 1985). Although subscale reliabilities are lower than the total CDS scores (Tonkin & Hudson, 1981; Rotundo & Hensley, 1985), they are quite acceptable (all are above .50). The split-half reliability coefficient for the total CDS (Bath & Middleton, 1985) was reported to be .90. The general conclusion about the internal reliability of the CDS is that it is quite adequate.

Test-retest reliability. Very little data addressing the stability of CDS scores exists. Using an unstated sub-group of 60 school children, with a test-retest interval between 7 and 10 days, Tonkin and Hudson (1981) reported a test-retest reliability coefficient for the total Depression score of .74. These data are quite satisfactory for a measure of a fairly unstable construct such as depression.

Criterion-related validity. Several studies have been conducted contrasting various criterion groups. In the original validation of the CDS, Lang and Tisher (1978, 1983) were able to discriminate control from experimental (school-refusal children) with most of the scales of the CDS. The CDS scales that did not discriminate were the AR and SE. In a more comprehensive test of the ability of the CDS to discriminate groups, Rotundo and Hensley (1985) showed that the CDS could discriminate clinically depressed children who met the DMS-III criteria for depression from other psychiatric control subjects, who, in turn, could be discriminated from normal children. These data suggest that the scale has a strong potential for correctly differentiating depressed from nondepressed children.

Construct validity. Construct validity of the CDS has been investigated in several different ways. Some studies have looked at the correlations of the CDS scales with each other (Lang & Tisher, 1983; Rotundo & Hensley, 1985), some have examined the factor-analytic pattern of the CDS (Bath & Middleton, 1985; Lang & Tisher, 1983; Rotundo & Hensley, 1985; Tonkin & Hudson, 1981), and still others have correlated the CDS with related other instruments (Kovacs, 1981; Lang & Tisher, 1983; Rotundo & Hensley, 1985).

The high correlations reported among the CDS scales (Lang & Tisher, 1983; Rotundo & Hensley, 1985) suggest that the CDS scales are measuring some correlated construct or set of constructs.

Factor analyses of the CDS have lead to diversity in results. Although the CDS was rationally designed with six depressed and two positive scales, none of the various factor analyses has confirmed this system for interpretation. Lang and Tisher (1983) report one major factor accounting for 32% of the variance. Further reporting of their factor-analytic results is not presented. Tonkin and Hudson (1981), however, obtained three interpretable factors, accounting for 20.2%, 7.5%, and 5.2% of the variance. Bath and Middleton (1985) reported that a nine-factor solution was the best to account for their factor analysis of the CDS, while Rotundo and Hensley (1985) reported 13 factors in their unrotated factor analysis and a seven factor solution following a Varimax rotation. A stable factor analytic pattern does not emerge from the CDS; these results seriously question the utility of either the rationally designed scales of the CDS, or the use of current factor-analytically derived scales.

Correlations between the CDS and other scales have been reported by only a few investigators. Lang and Tisher (1983) report correlations with factors from the IPAT Anxiety scale. These correlations are generally significant and positive in direction, suggesting that the CDS is correlated with anxiety and its various factors. Of more importance, however, are data from Rotundo and Hensley (1985), who reported correlations of .84 between the CDS and the Children's Depression Inventory (Kovacs, 1981), showing very good convergent validity. Further, the correlation between the CDS and Piers-Harris Children's Self-Concept Scale was -.87, which is again indicative of good construct validity (Rotundo & Hensley, 1985).

In summary, although the data base for evaluating the validity of the CDS should be more developed to make a definitive statement, the existing data do suggest that the Total Depression score of the CDS measures some aspect of the negative affect associated with anxiety, low self-esteem, and depression. Although the overall Depression score may have utility, factor analyses clearly imply that stable factors cannot be found reliably. Interpretations of subscales of the CDS do not appear warranted at present.

Critique

The topic of childhood and adolescent depression is a recent development, and the authors of the CDS are to be congratulated for their efforts in producing a dimensional scale to assess the severity of such depression. The CDS does appear to produce a reliable and valid index of Total Depression that can differentiate clinical from nonclinical depression in children and adolescents. Although the CDS is not a diagnostic tool (i.e., the CDS does not yet have established cutoffs to define categories of depression), it can be used as an adjunct in the assessment of children and may be useful for indexing changes in levels of depression as a function of treatment or the passage of time.

As with most assessment tools, the CDS has limitations and could be improved in some areas. One of the strongest limitations of the CDS is the usefulness of the subscales. Although they may have rational grounds for existence, factor analyses fail to show that the subscales represent underlying factors. At this stage of development, these scales must be considered exploratory. Based upon the different factor-analytic solutions of the CDS, a major study of the factor structure and subsequent redefinition of scales is necessary.

Sex differences in the CDS scores have been mentioned briefly in the literature but need more complete explication. Lang and Tisher (1983) report data that suggest sex differences in the scores on the CDS, and other authors suggest that the existing sex differences warrant the consideration of different norms for male and female examinees (Bath & Middleton, 1985; Hollon, 1980; Tonkin & Hudson, 1981). Separate normative comparisons for boys and girls is a sound suggestion, in light of the known general sex differences in depression.

The test authors are continuing to research the CDS (Lang & Tisher, 1983; Tisher & Lang, 1981). Revisions to the scale or to the normative data may be needed to assess the severity of depression in this age range adequately. This reviewer suggests deleting the normative groups from the Record Form, and adding appendices in an expanded test manual of normative data, classified by sex, respondent (child vs. parent), and age. In this way, a better contrast between the child in question and the normative comparison group could be made. Although the CDS is a step in the right direction to assessing childhood and adolescent depression, it currently is conceived to be a research instrument. Further research is necessary before validated clinical interpretations can be made from this scale.

References

Bath, H.I., & Middleton, M. R. (1985). The Children's Depression Scale: Psychometric properties and factor structure. *Australian Journal of Psychology, 37*, 81–88.

Hollon, S. D. (1980). Test review: Children's Depression Scale. *Journal of Child Psychology and Psychiatry, 21*, 371–374.

Kovacs, M. (1981). Rating scales to assess depression in school-aged children. *Acta Paedopsychiatrica, 46*, 305–315.

Lang, M., & Tisher, M. (1978). *Children's Depression Scale (Research Edition)*. Hawthorn, Victoria, Australia: Australian Council for Education Research.

Lang, M., & Tisher, M. (1983). *Children's Depression Scale Manual Second Research Edition*. Hawthorn, Victoria, Australia: Australian Council for Education Research.

Rotundo, N., & Hensley, V. R. (1985). The Children's Depression Scale: A study of its validity. *Journal of Child Psychology and Psychiatry, 26*, 917–927

Tisher, M., & Lang, M. (1981). Comment on the Children's Depression Scale: Some further psychometric data. *Australian Council for Educational Research Bulletin, 30*, 19–20.

Tonkin, G., & Hudson, A. (1981). The Children's Depression Scale: Some further psychometric data. *Australian Council for Educational Research Bulletin, 30*, 11–18.

Ronald R. Morgan, Ph.D.
Associate Professor and Director, School Psychology Program, Loyola University of Chicago, Chicago, Illinois.

CHILDREN'S EMBEDDED FIGURES TEST

Stephen A. Karp and Norma Konstadt. Palo Alto, California: Consulting Psychologists Press, Inc.

Introduction

The Children's Embedded Figures Test (CEFT), a measure of personality, was designed to assess cognitive style in subjects aged 5–10. Cognitive styles generally are considered to be the broad, stylistic, perceptual-behavioral characteristics that are manifested with regard to a person's overall cognitive functioning and personality. Messick (1970) formally defines this quality as a preferred and typical mode of perceiving, remembering, thinking, and solving a problem.

Extensive research programs have led to the accumulation of a rich and varied data base related to cognitive styles (Goldstein & Blackman, 1977, 1978; Kogan, 1976; Messer, 1976; Witkin, 1978), and findings from numerous studies have indicated strong, consistent relationships between a person's attitudinal, motivational, and emotional characteristics and performance on cognitive and perceptual tasks (Anastasi, 1982). Of particular relevance to a review of the CEFT are early factor analytic studies, such as Pemberton's (1952) and Thurstone's (1944), that established relationships between the flexibility of closure factor and certain personality variables. To assess this flexibility of closure factor, tests such as the Gottschaldt figures were designed, requiring the identification of a figure embedded within the context of many distracting and confusing details.

Herman Witkin and his associates conceptualized this problem from a different perspective (Witkin, Lewis, Hertzman, Machover, Meissner, & Wapner, 1954/ 1972). They designed a research program that was aimed at identifying a person's ability to resist disruptive contextual cues. In a series of perceptual spatial orientation studies utilizing various perceptual tests (a tilting chair and room, a rod and frame that could be adjusted independently), these investigators demonstrated that people differed with respect to their degree of *field dependence* (i.e., the extent to which their perceptions were influenced by distracting environmental cues). With the accumulation of more research, field dependence came to be regarded as the perceptual component of a broader personality dimension, referred to as *global* versus *articulated* cognitive style or *psychological differentiation* (Witkin, Dyk, Faterson, Goodenough, & Karp, 1962).

The paper-and-pencil Embedded Figures Test (EFT) was developed by Witkin and his associates in the 1950s to measure field dependence, and considerable data indicate that the construct as assessed by the EFT is a stable variable (Anastasi, 1982). High odd-even and test-retest reliabilities, as well as significant intercorrelations among other tests of spatial orientation, have been noted. Relationships have been reported between measures of field dependence and interpersonal rela-

87

tions (Witkin & Goodenough, 1977), learning and memory (Goodenough, 1976), and achievement (Vaidya & Chansky, 1980). Although males tend to be more field independent than females, sex differences have not been found consistently before the age of 8 or in geriatric samples. Developmental studies indicate age-related changes in field dependence from birth to maturity to old age: field independence increases between 8 and 15 years, followed by a leveling off and a plateau period reached in young adulthood Witkin, Goodenough & Karp, 1967). Interestingly, old age samples appear to be field dependent (Comalli, 1965; Schwartz & Karp, 1967). It is important to note that the *field dependent* or *field independent* descriptor is not to be interpreted as necessarily desirable or undesirable.

To determine both the sources of individual differences in psychological differentiation during the growth years and the developmental changes in the extent of differentiation, it was necessary to assess field dependence in young children. Previous experience with the EFT indicated that it was too difficult for most children below the age of 9. Goodenough and Eagle (1963) developed a version (CHEF) that was easier and more appropriate for children in the 5-to-9-year age range. The structure of the complex figures used in the CHEF made disembedding easier than in the regular EFT. Furthermore, the modified test procedures of using the number of first correct choices made, rather than the time taken to find the simple form, minimized some of the difficulties (particularly the feeling of failure) that many young children reportedly experienced on the EFT.

As reported in the test manual (Witkin, Oltman, Raskin, & Karp, 1971), although the 1963 children's version proved to have adequate reliability and validity, it appeared to be cumbersome and impractical. The authors (Karp & Konstadt) of the current version of the CEFT have been involved since the 1960s with the evolving conception of the meaning of individual differences in performance on embedded figures tasks. In the development of the present (1971) CEFT, an initial pool of 72 complex stimulus figures representing recognizable objects (many of which were identical with the earlier Goodenough-Eagle stimuli) was used. These stimulus figures were administered to a representative sample consisting of 100 5- and 9-year-old children. The 27% highest and 27% lowest scorers in each age group formed the two criterion groups used in the development of two 25-item forms of the test, each of which discriminated significantly between the low and high criterion groups.

The manual clearly points out that the verbatim instructions presented are meant to serve merely as a guide for test users. Furthermore, it is noted that children often require "warm-up" and pretest training in order to obtain a reliable measure of test performance. The training-procedure section of the manual articulates discrimination training, practice, and demonstration procedures. The open-ended search time limit for finding the embedded stimulus figure (a tent or a house), however, appears to warrant empirical verification. Responses to the 25 stimulus figures are scored 1 (embedded figure is correctly identified) or 0, with a maximum score possible of 25.

Practical Applications/Uses

A systematic examination of the citation listings in *Psychological Abstracts*, ERIC, and the *Wilson Education Index* (which in fact yielded no citations) indicated four areas (assessment of cognitive styles, relationship to other measures, developmental uses, and cross-cultural assessment) in which much of the work is now taking place related to the technical adequacy and utility of the CEFT. The following subsections offer a selective review of findings within each of these four areas.

Assessment of cognitive styles. Burlingame, Eliot, and Hardy (1984) proposed a shortened version of the CEFT tent series as a possible predictor of early reading achievement. This 5-item version reportedly can be administered in approximately 10 minutes and addresses the problem encountered when some children are unable to complete the longer 25-item version. In another study (Hardy, Eliot, & Burlingame, 1984), indices of item difficulty were computed for both the tent and the house series from a sample of 240 children in Grades K–4. Results indicated that the failure rule should be reconsidered and the test shortened. Swyter and Michael (1982) administered a battery of tests including the Children's Embedded Figures Test and the Draw-A-Person Test to 160 third-graders. Results suggested the presence of a general trait of field dependence/field independence assessed across tests. Cromack and Stone (1980) described the development and concurrent validation of a group-administered measure of field dependence/independence designed for use with early elementary school children. The test was found to be reliable (alpha = .84) and significantly related to both the individually administered CEFT and the Portable Rod-and-Frame Test. This measure, designated the Children's Group Embedded Figures Test—Level 1, appears to provide a promising research instrument for assessing the cognitive style of young children.

As mentioned previously, sex differences before the age of 8 are consistently absent from CEFT research literature. Results of a study by Bowd (1972a) confirmed this observation with test data from a sample of 90 Canadian children in Grades K–2. In another study conducted by Bowd (1976b), levels of difficulty of individual CEFT items were calculated. Results indicated that item T4 was consistently more difficult than item T5, Bowd suggested that the order of their presentation be reversed. In an earlier study, Bowd (1974) had obtained data from a working-class kindergarten population and then retested 10 months later. The retest correlation between scores was found to be .80 ($p > .01$) and field dependence failed to correlate significantly with either sex or socioeconomic status. Dreyer, Nebelkopf, and Dreyer (1969) also reported positive test-retest data for 46 subjects tested in kindergarten and again in first grade. Scores on both administrations correlated .87, indicating stability of this cognitive-style measure for these young children over a 6-month period.

Relationship to other measures. Keogh and Tardo (1975) used three techniques to assess field dependence/independence with a sample of 63 third-graders: the Children's Embedded Figures Test and two rod and frame techniques, modified to make them portable. All three techniques were found to be appropriate for use with primary-grade children in a school setting. In a study by Keogh and Ryan (1971), pattern walking and drawing tasks, a modified Rod and Frame Test, and the CEFT were administered to 44 white middle-class 7-year-olds. Overall results indicated that the CEFT was not appropriate for children of this age. Boys were found to be more field independent than girls on the Rod and Frame Test and on pattern walking. With the exception of pattern drawing, moderate relationships were found among the measures. In a study designed to determine the relationship between the Conceptual Style Test (CST) and the CEFT, Stanes and Gordon (1973) conducted a study with a sample of 7- to 8-year old Australian boys and girls. Boys scored more analytic responses in the CST and located more embedded figures in the CEFT than did the girls, but the difference was significant only for the CST. Scores on the two tests did not correlate significantly.

In an interesting study with the CEFT as an anchor test, Saracho (1984) used the Goodenough-Harris Drawing Test (GHDT) to assess field dependence/independence in 240 first-graders and 240 third-graders and found that GHDT scores correlated with those on the CEFT. These findings were interpreted as supportive of the GHDT as a valid and reliable measure of field dependence/independence. Data presented by Dreyer, Dreyer, and Nebelkopf (1971) in another study using the CEFT as an anchor test related a portable version of the Rod and Frame Test to other measures of cognitive functioning for 300 kindergartners. A test-retest correlation of .96 was obtained over 1 month. Sex differences were found on both the portable Rod and Frame Test and the CEFT. Of particular interest were the high correlations found between these two measures for both boys (.61) and girls (.66), corroborating work done on global-analytic cognitive style with older age groups. Finally, Massari's (1975) study of 60 black first-graders and 54 black third-graders tested the hypotheses that reflective children would be more field dependent and more internal than their impulsive counterparts. Subjects were administered the Matching Familiar Figures Test, the Children's Embedded Figures Test, and the Locus of Control Interview (LCI). The first hypothesis was supported. Failure to find strong support for the second hypothesis was attributed to the generalized nature of the LCI.

Developmental uses. In a study of the developmental significance of selective perceptual activities, (Weisz, Quinlan, O'Neill, and O'Neill, 1978) administered the Rorschach and four structured tests of perception (CEFT, Gestalt Completion Test, Closure Speed Test, and Visual Recognition and Incomplete Objects) to five groups of children (CAs 6–12 years, MAs 6–12 years, IQs 99.92–123.67). The Rorschach was found to be significantly related to MA, as were all four of the structured tests. Interestingly, the Children's Embedded Figures Test was found to be the best predictor of MA; it accounted for 52% of the variance, while the six remaining measures yielded nonsignificant increments to a multiple regression equation. In a factor analysis, the four structured tests loaded on one factor (51% of total variance), while the three Rorschach variables loaded on a second (17%); MA loaded on both (.669 and .447; respectively). The hypothesis that level of development and not IQ determines cognitive competence received partial support from 13 of 14 statistical tests.

Ghuman (1977) explored the relationship among scores on Piagetian tests of conservation of weight, volume, and class inclusion, Raven's Standard Progressive Matrices, and the CEFT with 60 11- to 12-year-olds. The Children's Personality Questionnaire (CPQ) was also administered, and social class data were obtained. Significant correlations were found between CEFT scores (field dependence/independence) and the cognitive developmental variables, but not between the personality variables and CEFT scores. There was a significant difference reported between the two social classes: middle-class children performed better than working-class children, but no significant differences were noted across genders.

Weisz, O'Neill, and O'Neill (1975) administered the Peabody Vocabulary Test, the Rorschach, and the CEFT to 9- and 12-year-olds. A 2 X 2 factorial design was used to separate the effects of chronological age and mental age (MA, 9 and 12 years). Fifty-two percent of CEFT variance was accounted for by its correlation with MA, and the strength of the relationship between the Rorschach and field dependence was found to be derived largely from the mutual correlation of the variables with the cognitive developmental level reflected in MA.

A study conducted by Wagner (1978) in Morocco was designed to separate the effects of age and formal schooling in the development of cognitive style. A total of 384 males ages 6–22 were selected from urban/schooled, rural/schooled, urban/ nonschooled, and rural/nonschooled environmental backgrounds. Subjects were administered a shortened version of the CEFT. Results indicated that CA and schooling played major but independent roles in promoting perceptual development (and a field-dependent cognitive style), while general childhood environment appeared to have little effect. Wagner concluded that general statements relating cultural socialization practices to the development of a cognitive style should be carefully qualified by considering particular environmental experiences (e.g., formal schooling) that may differentially influence the development of a certain cognitive style. Finley, Solla, and Cowan (1977) conducted a developmental study by administering a battery of egocentrism and logical operations tasks to 52 second-graders who had scored as the 26 most field independent and 26 most field dependent on the CEFT. Results both supported previous work showing a positive relationship between field independence and conservation in young school-age children and extended these findings to show robust negative relationships between field independence and communication egocentrism, spatial egocentrism, and, to a lesser degree, role-taking egocentrism.

Riley and Denmark (1974) designed a study to ascertain the relationships among the CEFT, tests of verbal ability, and tests of general intelligence for lower-class blacks. Thirty-four pupils in Grades 1–2 and 53 in Grades 3–5 were given the CEFT, the Leiter International Performance Scale, and the WISC Vocabulary subscale. Contrary to the previous findings of Witkins et al., a correlational analysis revealed strong interrelationships between these tests. Grade level and sex were found to interact to produce different correlational structures for each condition. Interestingly, these findings raise questions related to the assertion that field independence varies independently of intelligence for all subjects regardless of age, sex, and social class.

In a study designed to examine the relationships among moral judgments, behavior, and cognitive style in young children, Schleifer and Douglas (1973) assessed level of moral maturity and administered a battery of tests, including the Children's Embedded Figures Test, to a sample of 3- to 7-year-olds. In the 6-year-old sample, level of moral maturity was found to be related to the cognitive styles of reflection/impulsivity and field dependence/independence, but not to verbal intelligence. Subjects characterized as immature in their moral judgments were found to be more impulsive and field dependent. Subjects with higher level moral judgments were also rated by their teachers as more attentive and reflective. In preschool samples, subjects highest on moral maturity were rated as less aggressive by their teachers, least impulsive in cognitive style, and, in the lower-class sample, more field independent.

Finally, Fleck (1972) investigated the relationship of field dependency and verbal mediation to Piagetian conservation behavior. It was hypothesized that the field-independent and the verbally mediating subjects would have grasped the principle of conservation to a significantly greater degree than field-dependent and non-mediating subjects. The main effect of field independence was found to be significant as hypothesized. Grade was also found to be significant, but neither the verbal mediation main effect nor any of the interactions were found to be significant.

Cross-cultural assessment. A few cross-cultural studies using the CEFT have been reported in the literature. In a study conducted by Kalyan (1985), 92 Indian students ages 12–15 from three income levels completed the CEFT, the WISC-R Block Design, and a series of tasks derived from Piagetian theory. Cognitive style was found to be significantly correlated with cognitive performance, and results from a factor analysis of the data indicated that a general cognitive factor appears to underlie cognitive restructuring and disembedding skills. Developmental differences by grade and performance differences across income levels, sex, and school type were also noted. These findings support the applicability of Piaget's and Witkin's theories for a non-Western sample.

Clark and Halford (1983) tested a sample of urban and rural aboriginal children (ages 7–12) and a sample of urban and rural Anglo-Australian children. These subjects were matched on reading and mathematics achievement, nonverbal intelligence, and three cognitive styles: reflection/impulsivity, field dependence/independence, and style of conceptualization. For the most part, previously observed cultural and location differences in school achievement were replicated. Urban subjects scored higher than rural subjects, and Anglo-Australians scored higher than aborigines. Both intelligence and cognitive style accounted for significant proportions of the variance shared by environmental (cultural and location) and scholastic achievement. However, intelligence was found to be a more powerful predictor of the effects of culture and location on school achievement than was cognitive style.

Lega (1981) administered a Colombian version of the Children's Embedded Figures Test to 135 kindergarten through second-grade Colombian children in two studies. Results indicated that the translated test has acceptable reliability ($r = .80$) and construct validity. Buriel (1978) attempted to relate three field-dependence measures to the reading and math achievement of Anglo-American and Mexican-American children. Previous studies relating field dependence to the superior academic achievement of Anglo-American children relative to Mexican-American children have relied almost exclusively on single-method approaches of measuring this cognitive style. Buriel's study attempted to make a more comprehensive test of the relationship between field dependence and achievement by comparing members of both cultural groups on three commonly used measures of field dependence in order to determine the consistency of cross-cultural differences, intercorrelations, and predictive validity of these measures across cultural groups. Mexican-American and Anglo-American subjects were administered the WISC Block Design, the CEFT, and the Portable Rod and Frame Test. Results indicated that a) Mexican-American children were not more field dependent than Anglo-American children, b) intercorrelations between the three field-dependence tests were not significant and comparable across cultural groups, and c) field dependence was not found to be of substantial differential importance to the school achievement of Anglo-American and Mexican-American children.

Technical Aspects

Only Form 1 of the Children's Embedded Figures Test has been standardized. The norming group used in the original standardization consisted of 160 children equally divided among four age groups (5–6, 7–8, 9–10, and 11–12 years), with an equal number of boys and girls selected across each age level. All children were administered Form 1, and those in the 9–10 and 11–12 year age categories also were given Form A of the EFT in order to obtain a criterion measure against which to check CEFT validity. The effects of age, sex, and the interaction between age and sex in CEFT performance were examined. Results indicated that the age effects were significant, performance becoming more field independent with age. In the standardization sample neither the sex nor interaction (age x sex) effects were found to be statistically significant. Given the small standardization sample, the limited normative data base reported in the manual can be considered tenuous at best. It is important to note that a number of studies (Elitcher, 1967; Mumbauer & Miller, 1970; Zimiles, 1970) cited in the manual have reported rather strong relations between CEFT performance and social class. Interestingly, a relationship between social class and EFT performance has not been consistently reported in the research literature.

Unfortunately, internal consistency reliability estimates are unavailable for the 5–6 year standardization subgroup because many children in this age group were not administered all 25 stimulus items. However, the internal consistency reliability estimates for all the other norming group age categories ranged from .83 to .90 and appear to be comparable to those obtained for the EFT. Incidentally, Dreyer, Nebelkopf, and Dreyer (1969) have reported a test-retest correlation of .87 in a separate study with a sample of 5- to 6-year-old children. All things considered, the CEFT appears to be a stable measure for use with children between 5 and 12 years of age.

Because many young children find the EFT too difficult, concurrent validation procedures attempting to relate CEFT scores to EFT scores have been performed for only the two older groups (9–10, 11–12) of the original standardization sample. The magnitude of these relations (.83 to .86) for the 11-year-olds appears to support the concurrent validity of the CEFT using the EFT as an anchor test. However, these concurrent validity coefficients were found to be considerably lower (.70 to .73) at age 9. As indicated in the manual, the drop in concurrent validity is probably the result of lowered reliability of the EFT at age 9 (.75 as compared with .90 at age 11). In addition, the test authors provide a brief review of studies in which criterion variables found to be related to EFT performance were also found to be related to CEFT performance for children at ages below 9. Overall, results of these studies indicated that CEFT performance improves with increasing age, is unrelated to gender, and is related to many of the same measures of psychological differentiation as the EFT.

Critique

Overall reliability of the Children's Embedded Figures Test appears adequate across most age levels but is considerably better at the higher age levels. Validity of the instrument appears more problematic. Some support for validity is offered, but additional research is required. Particularly encouraging are the results from the cross-cultural and developmental studies, and the research findings relating the CEFT results to other measures.

The effects of age, sex, and the interaction between the two in CEFT performance have been carefully examined. Results have indicated that the age effects are significant; performance becomes more field independent with age. In the standardization sample neither the sex or interaction (age x sex) effects were found to be statistically significant. Investigators have reported a consistent absence of sex differences before the age of 8, and questions have been raised as to the appropriateness of using the CEFT with children before age 7.

Cognitive style has been found to be significantly correlated with cognitive performance. CEFT performance appears to be a very good predictor of MA; however, the hypothesis that level of development and not IQ determines cognitive competence has received only partial support. Findings from a few studies in which age, sex, and social-class variables were controlled raise questions about the assertion that field independence and intelligence are not related.

Significant correlations have been found between CEFT scores and numerous cognitive developmental variables. Positive relationships have been reported between field independence and conservation in young school-age children. In addition, robust negative relationships have been reported between field independence and communication egocentrism, spatial egocentrism, and, to a lesser degree, role-taking egocentrism. Developmental differences in CEFT performance by grade and performance differences across income levels, sex, and school type have also been noted. Overall, these findings provide support for the applicability of Piaget's and Witkin's theories to an analysis of CEFT performance.

References

Anastasi, A. (1982). *Psychological testing* (5th ed.). New York: Macmillan.

Bowd, A. D. (1974). Retest reliability of the Children's Embedded Figures Test. *Perceptual and Motor Skills, 39*, 442.

Bowd, A. D. (1976a). Absence of sex differences on the Children's Embedded Figures Test. *Perceptual and Motor Skills, 43*, 729–730.

Bowd, A. D. (1976b). Item difficulty on the Children's Embedded Figures Test. *Perceptual and Motor Skills, 43*, 134.

Buriel, R. (1978). Relationship of three field-dependence measures to the reading and math achievement of Anglo-American and Mexican-American children. *Journal of Educational Psychology, 70*, 167–174.

Burlingame, K., Eliot, J., & Hardy, R. C. (1984). Revision of the tent series of the Children's Embedded Figures Test: A possible predictor of early reading achievement. *Perceptual and Motor Skills, 59*, 757–758.

Clark, L. A., & Halford, G. S. (1983). Does cognitive style account for cultural differences in scholastic achievement? *Journal of Cross-Cultural Psychology, 14*, 279–296.

Comalli, P. E. (1965, March). *Life span developmental studies in perception: Theoretical and meth-*

odological issues. Paper presented at the Eastern Psychological Association meetings, Atlantic City, NJ.

Cromack, T. R., & Stone, M. K. (1980). Validation of a group embedded figures test for young children. *Perceptual and Motor Skills, 51,* 483–486.

Dreyer, A. S., Dreyer, C. A., & Nebelkopf, E. B. (1971). Portable Rod-and-Frame Test as a measure of cognitive style in kindergarten children. *Perceptual and Motor Skills, 33,* 775–781.

Dreyer, A. S., Nebelkopf, E., & Dreyer, C. A. (1969). Note concerning stability of cognitive style measures in young children. *Perceptual and Motor Skills, 28,* 933–934.

Elitcher, H. (1967). *Children's causal thinking as a function of cognitive style and question wording.* Unpublished doctoral dissertation, New York University.

Fleck, J. R. (1972). Cognitive styles in children and performance on Piagetian conservation tasks. *Perceptual and Motor Skills, 35,* 747–756.

Finley, G. E., Solla, J., & Cowan, P. A. (1977). Field dependence-independence, egocentrism, and conservation in young children. *Journal of Genetic Psychology, 131,* 155–156.

Ghuman, P. A. (1977). An exploratory study of Witkin's dimension in relation to social class, personality factors and Piagetian tests. *Social Behavior and Personality, 5,* 87–91.

Goldstein, K. M., & Blackman, S. (1977). Assessment of cognitive style. In P. McReynolds (Ed.), *Advances in psychological assessment* (Vol. 4, pp.298–322). San Francisco: Jossey-Bass.

Goldstein, K. M., & Blackman, S. (1978). *Cognitive style: Five approaches and relevant research.* New York: Wiley-Interscience.

Goodenough, D. R. (1976). The role of individual differences in field dependence as a factor in learning and memory. *Psychological Bulletin, 83,* 675–694.

Goodenough, D. R., & Eagle, C. (1963). A modification of the Embedded-Figures Test for use with young children. *Journal of Genetic Psychology, 103,* 67–74.

Hardy, R. C., Eliot, J., & Burlingame, K. (1984). Children's Embedded Figures Test: An examination of item difficulty in grades K-4. *Perceptual and Motor Skills, 59,* 21–22.

Kalyan, M. V. (1985). Cognitive performance and cognitive style. *International Journal of Behavioral Development, 8,* 39–54.

Keogh, B. K. & Ryan, S. R. (1971). Use of three measures of field organization with young children. *Perceptual and Motor Skills, 33,* 466.

Keogh, B. K., & Tardo, K. (1975). Measurement of field independence-dependence in children: A methodological note. *Perceptual and Motor Skills, 40,* 743–746.

Kogan, N. (1976). *Cognitive styles in infancy and early childhood.* Hillsdale, NJ: Erlbaum.

Lega, L. I. (1981). A Colombian version of the Children's Embedded Figures Test. *Hispanic Journal of Behavioral Sciences, 3,* 415– 417.

Massari, D. J. (1975). The relation of reflection-impulsivity to field dependence-independence and internal-external control in children. *Journal of Genetic Psychology, 126,* 61–67.

Messer, S. B. (1976). Reflection-impulsivity: A review. *Psychological Bulletin, 83,* 1026–1052.

Messick, S. (1970). The criterion problem in the evaluation of instruction: Assessing possible, not just intended outcomes. In M. C. Wittrock & D. E. Wiley (Eds.), *The evaluation of instruction: Issues and problems* (pp. 183–202). New York: Holt, Rinehart & Winston.

Mumbauer, C. L., & Miller, J. D. (1970). Socioeconomic background and cognitive functioning in preschool children. *Child Development, 41,* 471–480.

Pemberton, C. L. (1952). The closure factors related to temperament. *Journal of Personality, 21,* 159–175.

Riley, R. T., & Denmark, F. L. (1974). Field independence and measures of intelligence: Some reconsiderations. *Social Behavior and Personality, 2,* 25–29.

Saracho, O. N. (1984). The Goodenough-Harris Drawing Test as a measure of field-dependence/independence. *Perceptual and Motor Skills, 59,* 887–892.

Schleifer, M., & Douglas, V. I. (1973). Moral judgments, behaviour and cognitive style in young children. *Canadian Journal of Behavioral Science, 5,* 133–144.

Schwartz, D. W., & Karp, S. A. (1967). Field dependence in a geriatric population. *Perceptual and Motor Skills, 24,* 495–504.

Stanes, D., & Gordon, A. (1973). Relationships between Conceptual Style Test and Children's Embedded Figures Test. *Journal of Personality, 41,* 185–191.

Swyter, L. J., & Michael, W. B. (1982). The interrelationships of four measures hypothesized to represent the field dependence-field independence construct. *Educational and Psychological Measurement, 42,* 877–888.

Thurstone, L. L. (1944). A factorial study of perception. *Psychometric Monographs, 4.*

Vaidya, S., & Chansky, N. (1980). Cognitive development and cognitive style in mathematics achievement. *Journal of Educational Psychology, 72,* 326–330.

Wagner, D. A. (1978). The effects of formal schooling on cognitive style. *Journal of Social Psychology, 106,* 145–151.

Weisz, J. R., O'Neill, P., & O'Neill, P. C. (1975). Field dependence-independence on the Children's Embedded Figures Test: Cognitive style or cognitive level? *Developmental Psychology, 11,* 539–540.

Weisz, J. R., Quinlan, D. M., O'Neill, P., & O'Neill, P. C. (1978). The Rorschach and structured tests of perception as indices of intellectual development in mentally retarded and nonretarded children. *Journal of Experimental Child Psychology, 25,* 326–336.

Witkin, H. A. (1978). *Cognitive styles in personal and cultural adaptation: Heinz Werner Lecture Series, Vol. 11, 1977.* Worcester, MA: Clark University Press.

Witkin, H. A., Dyk, R. B., Faterson, H. F., Goodenough, D. R., & Karp, S. A. (1962). *Psychological differentiation: Studies in development.* New York: Wiley.

Witkin, H. A., & Goodenough, D. R. (1977). Field dependence and interpersonal behavior. *Psychological Bulletin, 84,* 661–689.

Witkin, H. A., Goodenough, D. R., & Karp, S. A. (1967). Stability of cognitive style from childhood to young adulthood. *Journal of Personality and Social Psychology, 7,* 291–300.

Witkin, H. A., Oltman, P. K., Raskin, E., & Karp, S. A. (1971). *A manual for the Embedded Figures Tests.* Palo Alto, CA: Consulting Psychologists Press, Inc.

Witkin, H. A., Lewis, H. B., Hertzman, M., Machover, K., Meissner, P. B., & Wapner, S. (1972). *Personality through perception: An experimental and clinical study.* Westport, CT: Greenwood, (Original work published 1954)

Zimiles, H. (1970). Conceptual thinking in young children as a function of age and social class background. In J. Hellmuth (Ed.), *Cognitive studies* (pp. 230–241). New York: Brunner/Mazel.

Nancy A. Busch-Rossnagel, Ph.D.

Associate Professor of Psychology, Fordham University, Bronx, New York.

CHILDREN'S VERSION OF THE FAMILY ENVIRONMENT SCALE

Christopher J. Pino, Nancy Simons, and Mary Jane Slawinowski. East Aurora, New York: Slosson Educational Publications.

Introduction

The Children's Version of the Family Environment Scale (CVFES) assesses children's perceptions of family relationships. It is a downward extension of the Family Environment Scale (FES; Moos & Moos, 1981) for children ages 5 to 12 and examines the same 10 dimensions as the FES: 1) cohesion, 2) expressiveness, 3) conflict within the domain of relationships, 4) independence, 5) achievement orientation, 6) intellectual-cultural orientation, 7) active-recreational orientation, and 8) moral-religious emphasis within the domain of personal growth, 9) organization, and 10) control within the domain of system maintenance.

The 30 items of the CVFES (3 for each scale) were taken from the FES and converted into a pictorial, multiple-choice format. Each item has three choices or pictures, and each choice is a cartoon-like drawing of a family (usually a mother, father, son, and daughter). The three choices (pictures) vary along some dimension (e.g., body orientation or activity). In half of the items, the primary difference is in the verbalizations of the family member, which appear in "balloons" (similar to a comic strip). To complete the scale, the child is asked to indicate which of the three pictures "looks like your family." The scale may be administered individually or in a group; some individual assistance with reading of the verbalizations may be necessary, especially for children in the third grade or younger.

Christopher J. Pino, Ph.D. is a clinical psychologist with much of his experience focused on families. He is currently executive director of an out-patient psychiatric clinic. Nancy Simons, Ph.D. is a clinical psychologist with the VA and in private practice. Mary Jane Slawinowski is a guidance counselor for the Board of Cooperative Educational Services. The clinical background of all three authors is the key to the development of the CVFES. The need for children's views of the family was felt within the context of a family enrichment workshop (Pino, 1984), and thus the authors view the CVFES primarily as a clinical, rather than a research, tool.

The CVFES was standardized on a sample of 158 children (equal numbers of males and females) in Grades 1-6 in the Buffalo, New York, area. The manual (Pino, Simons, & Slawinowski, 1984) states that the children were mainly lower and middle SES, primarily Roman Catholic, and from a number of different nationalities. Pino believes that the sample may be representative of other urban areas "with similar demographics" (personal communication, June 9, 1988), but the lack of specific demographic information in the manual renders actual comparison of samples impossible. The authors of the CVFES urge caution in interpreting the results based on the limited normative samples. The results of the further standardization work mentioned as "in progress" in the 1984 manual were not available in 1988, so clinicians and researchers alike may need to develop their own norms for the populations of interest.

The materials for the CVFES consist of a manual, a student booklet, an individual answer form, and the examiner's worksheet (scoring key). The three choices for each item are presented on one page of the test booklet; children answer on the test booklet itself or on the individual answer form if the booklets are to be reused. Individual administration is required for children under third grade because the written material in the items is at the third-grade reading level. The profile obtained on the CVFES is identical to that from the FES with standard scores for each dimension graphed onto a chart.

Practical Applications/Uses

The CVFES is designed to measure children's perceptions of the 10 dimensions of the family environment detailed by Moos and Moos (1981). The test authors indicate that these perceptions can be most useful in the design and evaluation of family therapy and enrichment programs.

The subjects who will be able to most easily identify with the families in the items will be from a stereotyped family (e.g., two parents, one brother, one sister). In a content validity study (Pino, 1985), some children (the number or percent is not given) were unable to identify with the families pictured. Even though most children from single-parent families were able to respond, further work is needed in this area. Likewise, further work is needed to ascertain if black children have difficulty in identifying with the pictures (the families portrayed are white) and to develop a Spanish translation. The latter could be done spontaneously by bilingual users because the amount of written material is limited.

The authors developed the CVFES with the expectation that the clinician would individually administer the scale to the children due to their age. However, several studies referenced in the manual used group administration for older children. The manual does not provide specific instructions for the administration of the test, but four general thoughts should be covered with the child: 1) The CVFES is not a test. The fact that there is not one right answer for each item should be stressed to the child. 2) The family in the pictures may be different than the child's, but the child should pretend that each picture has his or her family in it. 3) The child should choose a picture that looks most like his or her family. 4) The child should answer on the booklet (or answer sheet if that method is used). For group administration, the method of answering should be detailed (e.g., the children should circle their choice). The time for administration is not stated in the manual. Younger children may need as long as 1 minute per item (a total of 30 minutes), but older children can probably finish in 10 to 15 minutes.

The scoring of the CVFES is easy because the items for each scale are presented together (e.g., Items 1, 2, and 3 for the Cohesion scale, etc.). A table in the manual and on the examiner's worksheet provides the weight (1, 2, or 3) for each choice, with a 3 indicating the highest level of the dimension. A 0 is given to questions not answered. The score for each scale is obtained by summing the weights of the choices for the three items and can range from 0 to 9.

The CVFES authors indicate several ways of interpreting the scores. First, scores may be compared to the norms, but the lack of criterion-related validity evidence implies that caution is needed in making evaluative statements based on the norms. A second interpretation is noted in a case study (Pino, 1984). The CVFES is completed in two ways: first, as the family really is and then as the child would like the family to be. The actual and the ideal then can be compared and used as the basis for a family treatment plan. This case study uses a "composite" FES profile, using scores from the CVFES for the children and from the FES for the parents. The details of obtaining the composite score are not provided, and several different methods might be used (e.g., an average of the family member's individual score or talking about the items and achieving a family consensus). The possible discrepancy in family member's scores on the CVFES and FES is the basis for the final interpretation suggested by the test authors. The match between the two scales is termed "clinically very good" (Pino, Simons, & Slawinowski, 1984, p. 7).

Given the possible limitations of the normative data noted above, the quality of the interpretations using any of these approaches will stem primarily from the clinical sophistication of the examiner. Although the norms and resulting standard scores for the FES are adequate (Busch-Rossnagel, 1985), standard scores based on the CVFES norms are of questionable usefulness. Thus, any composite score or match between the adult scores (on the FES) and children's scores is likely to be psychometrically flawed. The experienced clinician can use the information as one of several aids in diagnosis and treatment planning, but the CVFES scores (and any composite or match that includes them) should not be used by themselves.

Technical Aspects

The development of the CVFES relied on the items of the FES for its initial pool of items, and thus partial evidence for its validity comes from the development of the FES. The initial pool of FES items was obtained through interviews with families of diverse backgrounds, suggesting an initial concern with content coverage that carries over to the CVFES. The items from the FES were grouped in order so that the 30 items would tap the same content as the 90 original items. However, the authors give no indication as to the method used to select the grouped items, so it is difficult to evaluate the content coverage of the items.

In an initial evaluation of the validity of the scale, 16 children, ages 6 to 12, were asked to write a sentence describing what each picture said to them. Clinicians rated each picture for the agreement between the children's responses and the intent of the picture. The appendix in the manual presents the responses for one of the cohesiveness items, but no additional information is given about the results of the study.

Pino (1985) further investigated the "stimulus pull" of the pictures of the CVFES. The subjects were 26 third-graders and 30 seventh-graders from the same population as the normative sample. The children were asked to write the common meaning of the set of pictures, and raters once again evaluated whether the responses matched the subscale dimension. The results indicated that all 10 scales were correctly identified approximately 80% of the time by third-graders and 85% of the time by seventh-graders. Individual items for expressiveness and intellectual-cultural orientation showed an appreciable range (65% to 95%) in correct identification.

An examination of the items indicates why these scales might be less valid. For example, expressiveness seems to be equated with happiness in two of the items. That is, a weight of 3 is given to pictures where the parents are smiling to a child's verbalization of sorrow for a broken object and to the brother and sister talking or fighting (the behavior is not clear). The content of the items might be interpreted to mean that the parents do not express displeasure at the child's behavior of breaking an object or fighting. In the third item on this scale, a weight of 2 is given to the parents' ignoring a child's tears and a weight on 1 to the parents' saying "don't cry." (A similar commonsense problem in scoring the Independence items in an earlier printing of the manual and score sheet has been corrected.) One of the items for the Intellectual-Cultural scale shows a family watching TV; the content of the show varies among the choices. Although one show is obviously fiction (with caricature of a Martian and a spaceship), the content of the other choices is not clear. For example, the first might be a cheerleader, a gymnast, or a dancer.

Given that the authors see the CVFES as primarily a clinical tool, documentation of predictive or diagnostic utility would be most useful in evaluating the criterion-related validity of the CVFES. This is an area where the FES is weak (Busch-Rossnagel, 1985; Lambert, 1985), and the manual for the CVFES suffers from the same limitations. In a separate book, Pino (1988) has provided more information about the use of the CVFES in family therapy. It should be noted that many of the suggestions for clinical use of the CVFES require comparison and/or averaging of children's scores on the CVFES and parents' scores on the FES. Because the number of items on the two tests is different, such a comparison requires the use of standard scores. For the CVFES, these standard scores come from a normative sample within unknown demographics. The norms for the FES are presented separately for families with an older member, for black and Mexican-American families, for single-parent families, and for families of different sizes, so valid comparisons between parent and children will require similar breakdowns.

The 4-week test-retest reliability was .80 using the standardization sample. No range of reliabilities was given, so one might assume that this was the average reliability of the scale scores or that it was the reliability of the total score. Because the scoring is based on scales, not on the total score, separate reliabilities for the scales should be provided. Likewise, the internal consistency of the scales should be evaluated (e.g., with coefficient alpha). In looking at the internal consistency of the items, the test authors should also examine the corrected item-total correlations because several of the items appear to have almost identical content. For example, Item 1 and 3 on the Cohesion scale vary in the size of the pictures and facial expressions that are somewhat difficult to discriminate. Likewise, the parents' verbalizations in the Independence items are identical, so the only difference is in the content of the child's tasks. Such overlap in item content may cause a redundancy in the child's response that cannot be afforded, especially with 3-item scales.

Critique

Pino (1984, 1988) has presented evidence for the usefulness of the CVFES as a clinical tool. However, the valid use of this scale rests a great deal with the clinician's experience and use of other diagnostic and treatment planning tools because the validation evidence provided by the manual is not sufficient to guide the beginning practitioner. As such, the CVFES might best be evaluated as a subjective device.

The need to include children's perceptions of the family in both therapy and research, and the widespread use of the FES should compel the test authors both to revise the manual and to undertake further studies of the reliability and validity of the CVFES. In the revision of the manual, the authors should concentrate on making it easier to use, perhaps using standard headings such as purpose and rationale for development, test description, administration and scoring, reliability, validity, standardization, and interpretation. The reliability section should include test-retest information for the scales separately as well as information about the internal consistency of the scales. Details about the demographics of the standardization sample should be provided, along with an indication of what demographic factors were related significantly to CVFES scores (e.g., grade level, family size, etc.). The norms should be broken down by any demographics that were significant. Further work on the validation of the CVFES is recommended, possibly including revision of the Expressiveness and Intellectual-Cultural Orientation items. Studies focusing on the predictive and diagnostic utility of the test for different types of families also are necessary to make the test accessible to the beginning practitioner. Hopefully, the authors and others will undertake such studies to overcome the limitations of the CVFES because the current form of the CVFES is a promising start toward developing a much needed measure of children's perceptions of their families.

References

Busch-Rossnagel, N.A. (1985). Review of the Family Environment Scale. In J.V. Mitchell, Jr., (Ed.), *The ninth mental measurements yearbook* (pp. 407–408). Lincoln, NE: The Buros Institute.

Lambert, N.M. (1985). Review of the Family Environment Scale. In J.V. Mitchell, Jr., (Ed.), *The ninth mental measurements yearbook* (pp. 408–409). Lincoln, NE: The Buros Institute.

Moos, R.H., & Moos, B.S. (1981). *Family Environment Scale*. Palo Alto, CA: Consulting Psychologists Press.

Pino, C.J. (1984). Family diagnosis and treatment planning in multi-modal family therapy and personalized family enrichment. *Family Therapy, 11,* 175–183.

Pino, C.J., Simons, N., & Slawinowski, M.J. (1984). *Children's Version of the Family Environment Scale.* East Aurora, NY: Slosson Educational Publications, Inc.

Pino, C.J. (1985). A content validity study of the Children's Version of the Family Environment Scale. *Child Study Journal, 15,* 311–316.

Pino, C.J. (1988). *CVFES Sourcebook: Imagery in family diagnosis and therapy.* East Aurora, NY: United Educational Press.

S.E. Phillips, Ph.D.
Associate Professor of Measurement, College of Education, Michigan State University, East Lansing, Michigan.

CIRCUS

Educational Testing Service. Monterey, California: CTB/ McGraw-Hill.

Introduction

CIRCUS is a standardized achievement test battery for early childhood. The CIRCUS tests are an extension of the third edition of the Sequential Tests of Educational Progress (STEP III; Grades 3–12) into the primary and preprimary levels (preschool through early third grade). CIRCUS is designed to assess both the knowledge and the developmental skills of young children. It is organized around a circus theme with artwork and questions focused on circus animals and people. From a list of 15 measures at four levels (A–D), users may choose the combination of subtests to be administered based on the evaluation needs of their programs, curricular content and emphases, available testing time, and their philosophy of child development. The test publisher lists three uses for the test (program evaluation, individual assessment, and pretesting/posttesting) and provides both normative and criterion-referenced score interpretations.

The conceptualization of CIRCUS was based on Educational Testing Service (ETS) research in early childhood education and the review of curricular materials commonly used with young children. Its content was influenced by the following research studies by the ETS staff: The Longitudinal Study of Disadvantaged Young Children and Their First Experiences; The Evaluations of Sesame Street and the Electric Company; The School-Readiness Study; and Social Competency in Young Children. There are four levels of the CIRCUS test: 1) Level A, preschool to K.5; 2) Level B, K.5 to 1.5; 3) Level C, 1.5 to 2.5; and 4) Level D, 2.5 to 3.5. Each level is appropriate for approximately one year of development from the spring of one grade through the fall of the following grade. In deciding which subtests to include in the battery, ETS considered the range of developmental skills important to teachers and the potential effectiveness of classroom instruction. Several years of planning and pretesting preceeded the publication of each level of the CIRCUS test. Item and test bias and review procedures were used to develop tests suitable for heterogeneous populations; no separate tests are currently available for handicapped students, but it may be possible to test some of them individually. A Spanish edition, El Circo, is available for preschool and Grades K and 1.

Most of the subtests are designed for small group administration. Level A has no more than 2 items per page, Level B has no more than 3 items per page, and Levels C and D have 6 items per page. Children mark the picture in the test booklet that answers the question asked by the teacher (Levels A and B) or mark their answers in ovals below answer boxes of pictures, words, or numbers (Levels C and D). The test booklets are machine scorable but also can be hand scored.

The basic assessment subtests in the battery include Listening Comprehension (Levels A-D), Mathematics Computation/Concepts (Levels A-D), Pre-reading/ Reading Vocabulary/Comprehension (Levels B-D), and Writing Skills (Level D). Other measures include Phonics, General Knowledge, and Problem Solving (Levels A-D); Perceptual-Motor Coordination, Visual Memory, Visual Discrimination, and Letter/Numeral Recognition (Levels A-B); and Receptive Vocabulary, Auditory Discrimination, Functional Language, and Discrimination of Real World Sounds (Level A). Parallel forms are available for the basic assessment subtests for Levels C and D. CIRCUS also has the following measures for special purposes: Educational Environment Questionnaire, Say and Tell, Oral Reading, Things I Like, Make a Tree, and Activities Inventory. It is unlikely that any school would want to give all the subtests; administration of the basic assessment plus selection of those optional tests related to particular strengths or weaknesses of the educational program would probably serve most schools' assessment needs. Only the basic battery tests will be described in detail here; the reader is referred to the CIRCUS Manual and Technical Report (ETS, 1979) for descriptions of the other measures available in the CIRCUS battery.

Levels A and B include subtests entitled "Listen to the Story" and "How Much and How Many." Level B also includes the subtest "Word Puzzles (Pre-reading)." The "Listen to the Story" subtest requires the child to listen to sentence(s) read aloud by the teacher and indicate comprehension of the content by selecting the picture that fits the instructions given by the teacher. For example, the teacher might say that it rained the day of the circus and then ask the child to mark the picture (sunshine, snow, or rain) that shows what happened at the circus. These items measure basic comprehension including memory, sequence, functional language, interpretation, and vocabulary.

The "How Much and How Many" subtest measures understanding of number concepts. Included are concepts related to counting, one-to-one correspondence, ordination, comparison, simple additive notions, seriation, number-numeral correspondence, and simple spatial relationships. The procedure for marking answers is similar to that for the "Listen to the Story" subtest. Level B also includes paper-and-pencil items measuring readiness for addition and Piagetian conservation.

The "Word Puzzles" prereading subtest at Level B measures a child's understanding of structural and phonetic properties of words. Measured concepts include similarities and differences in word sounds, recognition of letter-sound correspondences, and blending of letter sounds into words.

Subtests for Level C and D include "Listening," "Mathematics," and "Reading." At Level D, there is also a "Writing Skills" subtest. The "Reading" subtest requires the child to read words, sentences, or short paragraphs and respond to a question by marking the box with the appropriate word, group of words, or picture. In addition to a total score, two domain scores are derived from the items in this subtest: vocabulary and comprehension. The content is similar to that found in primary level instructional materials but is not tied to any particular materials or vocabulary lists.

The "Mathematics" subtest includes computation, number concepts, and relational concepts. Part of the test is read aloud to the students by the teacher; on the remainder of the subtest, students work individually. One-to-one correspondence, order, place value, operations, ratios, fractions, number patterns, comparisons, shapes, graphs, open sentences, story problems, sums, differences, and products are covered in this subtest. Three domain scores are reported for this subtest: numerical and mathematical concepts, computation, and relational concepts.

The "Listening" subtest is an extension of the "Listen to the Story" concept in the lower level tests. Children are asked to respond to questions about parts of a circus story read aloud by the teacher. Questions include comprehension, understanding/interpreting events, sequencing, and vocabulary. The answer choices for this subtest are all pictures.

The "Writing Skills" subtest at Level D is a paper-and-pencil measure of spelling, word structure, capitalization, and punctuation. All items are multiple-choice; no actual production of writing is required.

The CIRCUS battery can be administered by the regular classroom teacher. No specific qualifications are required, but it is important that the teacher read and understand the directions thoroughly before beginning the test. Because so much of the test is administered orally by the teacher, the publisher recommends that it be given in small groups (ETS, 1979). Even so, there is a heavy burden on the teacher to keep track of many things simultaneously: the teacher must 1) read the item stem, 2) watch to be sure all the children are marking their answers in the right places, 3) judge how long to wait between items so that all children have adequate time, 4) keep the slow and bright students on task and motivated, 5) keep the children's attention, 6) keep children from blurting out answers aloud, 7) keep track of the place in the test and what needs to be read next, and 8) deal with any unexpected interruptions. This is a particularly demanding task with younger children who are not used to the testing materials or procedures and who may have short attention spans. Much of the validity of the test results and the appropriateness of the norms depends on the teacher maintaining standardized test administration procedures while still being sensitive to individual differences. Individual test administration might result in more reliable and valid data, but may not be cost-effective if all children are to be tested.

The publisher recommends that the test be presented to the children as a special classroom activity (ETS, 1979). Children should be tested when they are most alert, and it is recommended that no more than two subtests be given in any one day. Subtests should each be given in one sitting without interruption.

Identifying information for each child must be filled in on the cover of the test booklet before testing begins. Practice materials are also provided by the publisher and teachers are encouraged to use them ahead of time to prepare students for the task of marking answers in booklets. Most subtests also contain example items at the beginning of the test to introduce the students to item types and procedures for that subtest. The CIRCUS subtests are untimed; each subtest requires approximately 30 to 40 minutes to administer.

Scoring is based on the number of correct answers marked; there is no penalty for guessing, so children should be encouraged to answer every item even if they are unsure of the correct response. Detailed directions and forms for hand scoring are provided in the User's Guide for each level.

For the basic battery, the following scores are available for each subtest: raw score, standard score, percentile rank, percentile band, stanine, NCE, and grade level indicator (Levels C and D only). Because users can choose the combination of subtests to be administered, CIRCUS reports no total scores. For some CIRCUS subtests, domain scores based on subsets of items are also available. Reported domain scores include raw scores, percentile ranks, and stanines. The test manual appropriately warns users to interpret domain scores cautiously due to lower reliabilities with small numbers of items. Other normative data include sentence report tables that give verbal descriptions of ranges of test performance, national and local item *p*-values, and group norms tables. Individual growth expectancy tables for estimating CIRCUS performance on a test level from scores on a lower-level test are available in a separate publication. The same standard score scale for each subtest is common to all forms and levels of CIRCUS and is linked to the standard score scale for the STEP III test battery. Forms and directions for hand scoring are included in the User's Guide.

Practical Applications/Uses

As indicated previously, the CIRCUS test is designed for three major purposes: program evaluation, individual assessment, and pretesting/ posttesting. For these purposes, test results can be reported at the individual or group level for single items, groups of items, or an entire subtest. In addition, the teacher may gain valuable insights from observing the children while they work on the test exercises. For an expanded discussion of these purposes and their limitations, see the review of STEP III (Phillips, 1984), Practical Applications/Uses section.

National norming samples were used in the standardization of all levels of CIRCUS. The 1972–73 norming sample for Level A was drawn from all 4- and 5- year-olds attending preprimary education centers. Selected children represented a diversity of geographic regions, city sizes, and socioeconomic and ethnic backgrounds. A total of 1,006 preschool and 1,979 kindergarten children participated in the Level A norming.

The Level B 1975 norming sample consisted of first-graders in schools randomly sampled by strata (based on the same demographic variables listed above) from census data. A national sample of 6,394 children participated.

Levels C and D were normed in 1976–77. Approximately 5,000 second-grade children and 5,000 third-grade children, respectively for each of the two levels, participated in the norming in the fall and the spring of the school year. About half of the sample of schools participated in both the fall and spring administrations. In addition, Level B was administered to 4,753 kindergarten children in participating schools. Random sampling procedures similar to those for the original Level B norming were used to select the sample. Catholic schools were selected separately. Weighting was used to adjust the demographics of the norming sample to those of the national population. Stratification variables used for weighting included region, standard metropolitan statistical area, socioeconomic status, and proportion of minority enrollment.

Technical Aspects

The most important type of validity evidence for a standardized achievement test battery is what has traditionally been called content validity. Content validity evidence includes the care and thoroughness with which the test developer has constructed the blueprint, written items, reviewed items for match to the test blueprint, pretested the items, conducted bias reviews, and edited and assembled the items into the final forms. As other reviewers of CIRCUS and STEP III have noted (Aiken, 1985; Ligon, 1985), the manual describes these procedures in detail and indicates that appropriate procedures were followed at each step of the test development process.

Other validity evidence includes correlations with teacher ratings, intercorrelations among subtests, correlations of similar subtests across levels where two levels were administered to the same students, and factor analyses. Equated scores for the Cooperative Primary Tests are also reported for Levels C and D.

The intercorrelations among the basic assessment subtests at all levels suggest the presence of a general ability factor. This may be due in part to the common format of auditory presentation with pictorial responses across many of the subtests. In addition, all subtests require the children to listen carefully to oral directions in order to understand the requirements for each task. These common visual, auditory, and general cognitive skills interact with the specific content being measured and may explain in part why children who do well on one subtest also tend to do well on many others. Factor analyses confirm the presence of a general ability dimension as suggested by the subtest intercorrelations.

Correlations between subtests of the same subject matter for adjacent levels of CIRCUS are also high, ranging in the 60s and 70s for the basic assessments for Levels A/B, B/C, and C/D. Correlations with teacher ratings obtained prior to testing were a bit lower, ranging from the high 40s to low 60s. Teacher judgments of each skill for each child fell in one of four categories: very competent, generally competent, needing additional instruction, or lacking competence. The empirical performance of children in each of the four groups was used in the development of the verbal reports describing ranges of performance on each subtest.

For those children who took adjacent levels of CIRCUS in fall and spring of the same year, regression analyses were used to predict spring performance from fall test scores. Predicted scores were converted to ranges using ± 1 standard error.

The only other test scores available for comparison with CIRCUS scores came from the Cooperative Primary Tests. For Levels C and D of CIRCUS, equipercentile equating procedures were used to obtain equivalent standard/scaled scores on the two tests. No correlations between the scores on the two tests were reported.

Two types of reliability are reported for CIRCUS: parallel forms correlations and internal consistency KR_{20}s. The Levels C and D parallel forms subtest reliabilities ranged from .74 to .89 on the basic assessment subtests; reading was highest and listening was lowest at both levels. Internal consistency reliabilities on the basic assessment subtests ranged from .77-.87 for Level A; .85-.93 for Level B; .79-.94 for Level C; and .78-.93 for Level D. Similar to the results for the parallel forms reliabilities, the listening subtests tended to have the lowest internal consistency reliabilities while the reading subtests tended to have the highest internal consistency reliabilities.

Domain score reliabilities were significantly lower, in part because they included fewer items. They tended to be in the .60s and .70s for Levels A and B and in the .70s and .80s for Levels C and D. Reliabilities in these ranges are high enough to be suggestive, especially when stanine ranges (1–3 low, 4–6 average, and 7–9 high) are used, but are probably too low for individual decisions.

The common standard score scale for all CIRCUS levels was developed using Thurstonian scaling procedures. Parallel forms were linked by linear equating.

Critique

Considering the difficulties inherent in the measurement of preschool and primary children's skills, the CIRCUS tests are technically good instruments. The test development process was thorough and the norming samples reasonable given the limitations of sampling in these populations. The battery provides a wide variety of skills subtests. However, several limitations should be considered when interpreting results of the tests.

The manual suggests that one of the uses of the CIRCUS tests is student diagnosis. The manual probably says this because so many teachers and administrators want a single test to serve multiple functions. But a survey achievement test is *not* designed for this purpose. Achievement test items are samples of a much larger domain to which inferences can be made. They do not cover all skills children need nor do they contain enough items on any one skill to determine whether the child has mastered that skill or to diagnose why the child may be unable to do problems of that type. Even the domain level scores are typically not reliable enough for decisions at the student level. Achievement test scores can only be indicators of possible weaknesses suggesting areas that teachers might collect more information. Achievement tests are *not* intended to substitute for teacher judgment in determining the instruction appropriate for a particular child. However, the achievement test can provide a broad overview of relative strengths, weaknesses, and growth from year to year.

The test developers have tried to correct the misuse of grade equivalent (GE) scores by the use of a related measure called the grade level indicator (GLI). GLI scores are restricted in range to those grades in which norming data were actually collected. Pluses and minuses are used when a child's performance is above or below the empirically derived range. However, the limited range of norming grades for CIRCUS creates significant floor and ceiling effects that restrict the usefulness of the GLI scores. These scores are also anchored at three empirical testing points during the year, allowing for monitoring the possibility of differential growth in the fall.

While these changes are admirable and in the right direction, the textual material in the manual may be misleading. It leads the reader to believe that all those "nasty" properties of GEs are gone; but in fact the GLIs are similar in derivation to typical GE scales. In one section of the manual, the user is told that "GLIs for an individual student can be interpreted to mean that the student is capable of doing work at the grade indicated by the score" (ETS, 1975, p. 25). Although this statement is qualified later, on the surface it encourages the same kinds of misinterpretations for which the test developers fault GE scales. In addition, Hoover (1984) and Phillips and Clarizio (1988) have demonstrated that the "preferred" standard score scales of many achievement batteries have the same undesirable properties for which GE scales have been faulted. The reader is referred to these articles and to the companion STEP III review (Phillips, 1984) for further discussion of this issue.

Another note of caution is in order for longitudinal comparisons. The four levels of CIRCUS were normed at different times during the period 1972–77. Instructional changes during this period may result in misleading conclusions. Also, since attendance in preschool is noncompulsory, the norming samples at the lower levels may not be representative of the population of preschool-age children.

This reviewer cautions those who use this achievement test or any other in a pre/ post test design should be careful in interpreting the results. The high parallel forms reliabilities indicate large proportions of common variance that tend to result in low difference score reliabilities. At the subtest level, the Listening test should be interpreted cautiously, as reliabilities are a bit low for decisions at the individual student level. The verbal reports are very general and must be supplemented by additional data to provide instructional prescriptions. Also, to judge better the convergent/divergent validity of the test, it would be helpful to have comparisons of CIRCUS scores with other readiness tests, achievement test batteries, and ability measures. Finally, statements in the manual suggesting that students who maintain their percentile rank in the norm group over time are doing fine should not be accepted without question, especially for below-average students. Such students may actually be getting further and further behind each year (see Phillips & Clarizio, 1988, for an expanded discussion of this issue).

In summary, preschool and primary children are very difficult to measure accurately, especially with a paper-and-pencil test. All test results for such children need to be interpreted cautiously as suggestive rather than definitive. The willingness of the teachers to follow directions and to provide supplementary information about children's reactions to the test will have a significant impact on the validity of the interpretations of test performance. The design of the test for group administration is both a strength and a weakness; valid measurement of some children may require an individual administration. However, if used as an early warning indicator, it may be helpful in identifying children, classes, or schools that should receive additional resources and special attention. As Ligon (1985) observed in his review, the key question is whether the information obtained is worth the substantial time investment.

References

This list includes text citations and suggested additional reading.

Aiken, L.R. (1985). Review of CIRCUS. In J.V. Mitchell, Jr. (Ed.), *The ninth mental measurements yearbook* (pp. 326–328). Lincoln, NE: The Buros Institute.

Educational Testing Service. (1979). *CIRCUS manual and technical report*. Monterey, CA: CTB/ McGraw-Hill.

Hoover, H.D. (1984). The most appropriate scores for measuring educational development in the elementary schools: GEs. *Educational Measurement: Issues and Practice, 3*, 8–14.

Ligon, G. (1985). Review of CIRCUS. In J.V. Mitchell, Jr. (Ed.), *The ninth mental measurements yearbook* (pp. 328–329). Lincoln, NE: The Buros Institute.

Phillips, S.E. (1984). Review of STEP III. In D.J. Keyser & R.C. Sweetland (Eds.), *Test critiques: Volume I* (pp. 578–592). Kansas City, MO: Test Corporation of America.

Phillips, S.E., & Clarizio, H.F. (1988). Limitations of standard scores in individual achievement testing. *Educational Measurement: Issues and Practice, 7,* 8–15.

Snyder S.D., & Michael W.B. (1983). The relationship of performance on standardized tests in mathematics and reading to two measures of social intelligence and one of academic self-esteem for two samples of primary school children. *Educational and Psychological Measurement, 43,* 1141–1148.

Terry Cicchelli, Ph.D.
Associate Professor and Coordinator of Elementary Preservice Programs,
Fordham University, School of Education at Lincoln Center, New York,
New York.

CLASS ACTIVITIES QUESTIONNAIRE

Joe M. Steele. Mansfield Center, Connecticut: Creative Learning
Press, Inc.

Introduction

Lewin's (1936) theoretical formulation of life space as a dynamic field in which two interdependent vectors, person and environment, interact to affect behavior provides a broad framework for the study of classroom learning environments; that is, instructional climate as operationalized by Steele (1982) in the Class Activities Questionnaire (CAQ). Further, Murray's (1938) dual concept of needs and press suggests that learning environments may be viewed as a complex of personal needs that in turn may be related to a corresponding complex of environmental press. In a global way, Pace and Stern (1957) refer to needs as the notable characteristics of individuals, including drives, motives, and goals; similarly, press is regarded as a broad label for stimulus, treatment or process variables.

The author of the CAQ, Joe M. Steel, states in the CAQ manual that instructional climate (an aspect of environmental press) is defined by the characteristic demands of the classroom environment as perceived by students. Typically, this instructional climate includes perceived demands, norms of behavior, rewards, and a variety of other influences on learners (Steele, 1982, p. 1). As individuals' characteristic modes of responses infer needs decribing personality, so are the strengths and relationships of characteristic stresses, pressures, rewards, and other influences of the environment inferred in describing environmental press (p. 1).

Historically, the development of the environmental press concept as well as its instrumentation was undertaken initially by Stern, Stein, and Bloom (1956) within their assessment studies. These researchers demonstrated that an improvement in the prediction of performance was possible by defining the psychological demands of the situation in which the performance takes place. Using Murray's classification of needs as a model, Stern (1958) developed the Activities Index, a needs inventory. Subsequently, Pace and Stern (1957) developed a corresponding test for describing college environments or press, referred to as the College Characteristics Index. Later, in 1969, Sinclair developed the Elementary School Environment Survey, identifying varying aspects of environmental press in elementary school. During this same period, Walberg and Anderson (1969) found that measures of student perception of classroom environments could predict gains in cognitive, affective, and behavioral learning criteria, even after accounting for student achievement, interest in subject, and IQ.

This literature also interfaces with a series of work on teacher effects on classroom climate, such as Walberg (1969) showing the influences of teacher personality and attitude on classroom climate; Anderson and Walberg (1969) demonstrating relationships between some environmental characteristics and student achievement; and Gallagher and Jenne (1963) noting the central role of the teacher as initiator and determiner of classroom priorities and outcomes.

In their evaluation efforts with the Illinois Gifted Evaluation Project, Steele, House, and Kerins (1971) sought out in a range of classes common denominators for some comparable features of instructional climate that could be assessed and used to equate instructional programs. This search led to the identification of two domains:

1) *cognitive,* encompassing the levels of thinking called on in class activities and supported by the cognitive operations taxonomy developed by Bloom (1956) and others, and

2) *affective,* comprising the social and emotional conditions in the classroom and based on process variables derived from student observations of classroom environments (Ehman, 1970; Remmers, 1963). The decision was made to look at classroom transactions in these domains in order to determine what demands were being made upon students. Consequently, the original CAQ was developed to assess both domains of instructional climate on four major dimensions: 1) lower thought processes; 2) higher thought processes; 3) classroom focus; and 4) classroom climate, composed of 16 factors in the large scale evaluation effort of the Illinois gifted programs. A sample of 62 gifted classes was compared with 69 classes in Grades 6–12. These 131 classes represented 3,138 students and 93 teachers (41 males and 52 females). By use of the Horst (1949) formula for estimating reliability within and between class variance, estimates for each of the 4 dimensions and 16 factors of the CAQ indicated that 14 of 20 correlations were above .80 and 1 fell below .65. A pilot study ($N = 6$ classes; $S = 79$) yielded test-retest reliability coefficients for each dimension ranging from .59 to .91. In subsequent psychometric and evaluation studies, further testing of the original CAQ has resulted in the current form: a 27-item questionnaire composed of 5 dimensions and 21 factors (Steele, 1982).

The CAQ asks students to respond to statements describing general kinds of activities characterizing the class. Responses on the 4-point Likert-type scale range from "strongly agree" to "strongly disagree." The questionnaire is administered as a single instrument, but the cognitive scales are scored separately from those reflecting classroom conditions and students' attitude toward the class. In effect, the CAQ represents three separate instruments, assessing 1) cognitive emphasis, 2) classroom conditions (related to the affective and behavioral domains), and 3) strengths and weaknesses of the class. This structure is illustrated in Table 1 and described as follows.

Cognitive Emphasis. The CAQ cognitive scales, shown in Table 1 as factor 1-7, are keyed to the seven levels of Bloom's taxonomy: 1) memory, 2) translation, 3) interpretation, 4) application, 5) analysis, 6) synthesis, and 7) evaluation. These factors are considered hierarchical in nature, whereby each higher level requires and includes the use of lower level operations. Thus, the difference between lower and higher levels concerns complexity and not simply difficulty.

Note in Table 1 that for each of the seven cognitive levels, items are paired in

Table 1

Structure of the Class Activities Questionnaire

Dimension	Factor	Description	*r*	*Item No.*
LOWER THOUGHT PROCESSES	1. Memory	Activities calling for recall or recognition of information presented	.88	1, 10
	2. Translation	Activities calling for paraphrasing or expressing information in a different symbolic form.	.65	9, 21
	3. Interpretation	Activities calling for recognition of relationships and seeing implications of information	.86	6, 16
	4. Application	Activities calling for selection of appropriate methods and performance of operations required by problem situations	.83	3, 13
HIGHER THOUGHT PROCESS	5. Analysis	Activities calling for recognition of the structure of material, including the conditions that affect the way it fits together	.78	7, 12
	6. Synthesis	Activities calling for the generation of new ideas and solutions	.89	11, 23
	7. Evaluation	Activities calling for development and application of a set of standards for judging worth	.71	2, 20
CLASSROOM FOCUS	8. Discussion	Student opportunity for and involvement in class discussion	.58	5, 15
	9. Test/Grade Stress	High pressure to produce teacher-selected answers for a grade	.89	8, 22
	10. Lecture	Teacher role as information-giver with a passive, listening role for students	.82	4, 26
	11. Enthusiasm	Student excitement and involvement in class activities	.91	19

Continued

Table 1 (cont.)

Dimension	Factor	Description	r	Item No.
	12. Independence	Tolerance for and encouragement of student initiative	.85	14
CLASSROOM CLIMATE	13. Divergence	Tolerance for and encouragement of many solutions to problems	.70	17
	14. Humor	Allowance for joking and laughter in the classroom	.86	25
	15. Feelings Valued	Respect for the individual's personal feelings and ideas		18
	16. Ideas Valued	Student enjoyment of ideas studied in class		24
	17. Teacher Talk	Proportion of class time consumed by teacher talk	.94	26
	18. Homework	Weekly amount of outside preparation for class	.87	27
STUDENT OPINIONS	19. Qualities	Students' views of the best things about the class		
	20. Deficiencies	Students' view of things that need changing about the class		
	21. Comments	Students' comments regarding any aspect of the class		

order to determine consistency in responses. For a factor to be scored, two thirds of the class must show a consistent response to the pair of items (statements that express roughly the same category of teaching) concerned (Steele, 1982, p.8). The author adapted a criterion of 50% or more of student agreement or disagreement with both statements as an indication of a clear cut direction. Further, a second scoring system is based on a weighted point system from which mean student scores are computed, supporting the assumption that strong responses should be differentiated from moderate-to-low responses. As the values of 1 through 4 were assigned to scale positions, mean scores approaching 1.00 indicate positive attitudes towards statements and responses falling toward 4.00 indicate negative attitudes. A mean score approaching 2.50 or in the range of 2.25 to 2.75 is interpreted to indicate little emphasis on the course (Steele, 1982, p. 8). In interpreting scores, large differences between students' actual emphasis and teachers' intended emphasis should be examined item by item to determine plausible explanations for the existing discrepancy.

Classroom Conditions. Factors 8-18 in Table 1 comprise the 11 scales of classroom focus and affective climate. Factors 8, 9, and 10 are paired items scored in a similar way to those in the cognitive scales. Consistency and discretion of responses are determined and strength of responses is then found (Steele, 1982, p. 12). Factors 11–16 are assessed by a single item, and, again, the mean score of 2.5 with a range of 2.25 to 2.75 suggests a neutral zone or little emphasis for a scale. Factors 17 and 18 represent student estimates, and the median student response on these two items is used as a class estimate. Class mean scores are compared to a teacher's score.

Scores for each of the classroom conditions scales must be interpreted in light of the subject taught, the kind of pupils enrolled in the course, and the intent of the teacher. As before, contradictions between student and teacher scores need to be explored in order to provide reasons for differences in perceptions.

Strengths and weaknesses of the class. The open-ended section of the CAQ, shown as factors 19–21 in Table 1, provides students the opportunity to make any comments they wish regarding the classroom climate. One way of processing these responses is to apply a categorization system or a kind of content analysis. To be more subjective, one simply can consider the comments in the context of the other findings provided by the cognitive emphasis and classroom focus/affective climate scales.

While one way of analyzing students' perceptions to the environment is to use the student as the unit of analysis relative to identified and measured student characteristics (i.e., ability, performance on content, and perceived needs or responses to environments), another is to treat the classroom group as the unit of analysis relative to instructional climate. This approach, focused on the group's perception of reality in concert with the teacher's perception of intentionality, was taken in the design and development of the CAQ and its scoring. Based on measures of central tendency and content analysis, student responses are referred to as the *actual* emphasis of the instructor's practices; instructor's responses in turn are represented as an index of intended or *ideal* emphasis. Comparison of the student's Actual responses with the instructor's Ideal response provides a measure of congruence of the intent and practice of instruction (Steele, 1982, p. 8).

Cautiously, Stern (1970) points out the possibility of disparity between the perceived situation and the veridical one; however, for the students themselves the perception is the reality. No doubt the influence of the teacher and students on the instructional climate of the class needs further testing, but if social behavior, goals, attitudes, and interests are acquired through environmental conditioning, then it appears reasonable to identify the environmental press and structure the situation to be more congruent with the purpose of the classroom (Steele, 1982, p. 2).

Practical Applications/Uses

Students completing the CAQ report their perceived emphasis of the instructional setting with regard to the following conditions:

1) the high and low levels of thinking in class activities;
2) the focus of the teacher as information giver with students in a passive role or with students in an active role;

3) the degree of relaxation and openness in the classroom; and
4) the attitudes and feelings of students in relation to the activities they are engaged in.

In a similar way, teachers are asked to report their intended emphasis and predict what the students as a group will say. Thus, teachers can compare their "ideal" responses with the students' "actual" responses to examine their instructional purposes and better match their behaviors to these purposes (Steele, 1982, p. 4). As noted, a pattern of emphasis may depend on the subject being taught, academic and social characteristics of the students in the class, and purpose of the class.

Essentially, this instrument suggested for Grades 6 and above is a tool that may be used to improve instruction. It is possible to administer it 3 to 5 weeks after a course has begun for the purpose of formative evaluation or at the end of a course for a summative evaluation.

The CAQ may be completed in 20 to 30 minutes. A single question and answer sheet is available, along with clearly defined and easy-to-follow administration procedures under separate cover. The author conveniently suggests that completed questionnaires be scored at Northern Illinois University for a nominal fee. Results are provided in a detailed statistical printout.

Although the CAQ was designed initially to evaluate a program across classes and not a single class, it may be possible to use it in one as well as multiple classes. In particular, it does provide descriptions of patterns of emphases across classrooms. Evaluators and researchers may use the CAQ to characterize instructional climate focused on specific content areas, instructional strategies, special programs, and so on. While large-scale analyses of classroom environments pose no threat to individual teachers, single-class studies may do so.

Technical Aspects

By its very nature the CAQ operates to produce a low variance in a distribution of scores within a given classroom. Because students are expected to agree about the various characteristics in the classroom, the variance within classes is error variance (Steele, 1982, p. 18). As was noted, reliability coefficients for each dimension ranged from .59 to .91. However, a more relevant indicator of test reliability is the degree or percentage of consensus of responses to paired items, particularly because the CAQ promotes the class as the unit of analysis. In a study with a sample of 2,071 (Steele, 1971), six of the seven cognitive factors received consistent responses for approximately two thirds or more of the students. The percentages ranged from 43% to 70%. Only the Memory scale indicated a lower reliability. Further, the Steele (1982) states that approximately two thirds or more of the students showed consistency in their responses to the classroom conditions factors (p. 19). Unfortunately, the manual does not provide actual percentages to verify this statement.

The manual reports that content validity for the cognitive factors based on Bloom's taxonomy was tested in several studies, wherein 30 school teachers, 14 administrators, and 12 college professors classified items developed for the CAQ. Two thirds or more of the college professors agreed on the classification of 100% of the original items, and two thirds or more of the teachers and administrators agreed on the classification of 75% of the items, indicating substantial content validity for the activity descriptions or items in the CAQ.

While the noncognitive classroom activities are not based on a theoretical model, they are purported to represent a consensus of climate variables related to learning. The manual reports that teachers and students involved in the 4-year evaluation project of gifted programs in Illinois provided items that were extensively field tested (p. 16). The items were intercorrelated, and paired items in the affective factors showed relationships ranging from .43 to .96.

Construct validity was derived from several sources, including factor analysis of the instrument (Steele, 1971), cross-validation of factorial validity (Wahlstrom, 1971), and observational studies of classrooms. In the Steele (1971) study using 2,071 students in 72 gifted and 16 average classes, a principal-component analysis of items 1-25 yielded by varimax rotation 10 components accounting for 62% of the variance. Wahlstrom's (1971) cross-validation study used 1,831 students. Factor analysis showed factorial validation supporting Steele's work. Further, case studies of gifted programs using classroom observations (Hause, 1971) have provided data that tend to support the validity of factors in both cognitive and affective domains.

Critique

In support of the CAQ, student perceptions do provide a kind of snapshot of the classroom environment. Further, the perceptions called for in the CAQ appear to be of a low-inference nature. The reported test-retest reliability coefficients suggest that student responses on the CAQ are rather stable perceptions, resulting from accumulated class experiences in patterns of events rather than from responses to specific recent events. In addition, the validity of using students' observations for determining differential student reaction to teacher and classroom activities stems from the fact that, directly involved in classroom activities, students observe more of a teacher's typical behavior than is available to the outside observer (Goldberg, 1968). In short, student perceptions in a learning environment have been offered as useful for research (Anderson & Walberg, 1968; Anderson, Walberg, & Welsh, 1969; Rosenshine, 1970).

However, there are some shortcomings to be considered when using this instrument. One is the pooling of pupils' ratings without accounting for individual differences represented in all classrooms. Another is the use of a broad variable in the instrument (e.g., "liking the teacher"). Such variables do little to clarify the complexity of the classroom environment (Goldberg, 1968). Another consideration is the general notion that student perceptions may suggest somewhat unrealistic manifestations of feelings with a strong emotional bias (Randhawa & Fu, 1973).

In sum, the CAQ provides one realistic, economical, time-saving approach for collecting data on classroom learning environments. It appears that data generated from this questionnaire along with standard observations of students and teachers as well as findings of Aptitude Treatment Interaction (ATI) studies can produce a rich picture of a learning environment.

References

Anderson, G.J., Walberg, H.J., & Welsh, W.W. (1969). Curriculum effects on the social climate of learning. *American Educational Research Journal, 6*, 315-329.

Anderson, G.J., & Walberg, H.J. (1969). Classroom climate and group learning. *International Journal of the Educational Sciences, 2*, 175-180.

Bloom, B.S. (Ed.). (1956). *Taxonomy of educational objectives: The classification of educational goals.* New York: David McKay.

Ehman, L.H. (1970). *A comparison of three sources of classroom data: Teachers, students and systematic observation.* Paper presented at the annual meeting of the American Educational Research Association, Minneapolis.

Gallagher, J.J., & Jenne, W. (1963). *Productive thinking of gifted children* (Cooperative Research Project Number 965). Urbana, IL: University of Illinois, Institute for Research on Exceptional Children.

Goldberg, J. (1968). Influence of pupils' attitudes on perception of teachers' behaviors and on consequent school work. *Journal of Educational Psychology, 59*, 1-15.

Horst, P. (1949). A generalized expression for the reliability of measures. *Psychometrika, 14*, 21-31.

Hause, E. (1971). *Instructional climate in Illinois gifted classes. (Illinois Gifted Program Evaluation). Urbana, IL: University of Illinois, Center for Instructional Research and Curriculum Evaluation.*

Lewin, K. (1936). *Principles of topological psychology.* New York: McGraw-Hill.

Murray, H.A. (1938). *Explorations in personality.* New York: Oxford University Press.

Pace, C.R., & Stern, G.G. (1957). *College Characteristics Index, Form 457.* Syracuse, NY: Syracuse University, Psychological Research Center.

Randhawa, B., & Fu, L. (1973). Classroom environmental variable. *Review of Educational Research, 3*, 303-321.

Remmers, H.H. (1963). Rating methods in research on teaching. In N.L. Gage (Ed.), *Handbook on research on teaching.* Chicago: Rand McNally.

Rosenshine, B. (1970). Evaluation of classroom instruction. *Review of Educational Research, 40*, 279-300.

Sinclair, R.L. (April, 1969). *Measurement of educational press in elementary school environments.* Paper presented at the annual meeting of the American Educational Research Association, Los Angeles.

Steele, J. (1971). *Instructional climate in Illinois: Gifted classes.* (Illinois Gifted Program Evaluation). Urbana, IL: University of Illinois, Center for Instructional Research and Curriculum Evaluation.

Steele, J., Hause, E., & Kerins, T. (1971). An instrument for assessing instructional climate through low-inference student judgments. *American Educational Research Journal, 8*, 447-466.

Steele, J. (1982). *Assessing instructional climate: The Class Activities Questionnaire manual.* Mansfield Center, CT: Creative Learning Press.

Stern, G.G. (1958). *Preliminary manual: Activities Index and College Characteristics Index.* Syracuse, NY: Syracuse University, Psychological Research Center.

Stern, G. (1970). *People in context.* New York: John Wiley & Sons.

Stern, G.G., Stein, M.J., & Bloom, B.S. (1956). *Methods in personality assessment.* Glencoe, IL: Free Press.

Wahlstrom, M.W. (1971, April). *Factorial validation of the Class Activities Questionnaire.* Paper accepted for presentation at the annual meeting of the American Educational Research Association, New York.

Walberg, H.J. (1969). Teacher personality and classroom climate. *Psychology in the Schools, 5,* 163-169.

Walberg, H.J., & Anderson, G.J. (1969). Classroom climate and individual learning. *Journal of Educational Psychology, 59,* 414-419.

John A. Zarske, Ed.D.
Director, Northern Arizona Psychological Services, P.C., and Chairperson, Department of Neuropsychology, Flagstaff Medical Center, Flagstaff, Arizona.

COGNITIVE BEHAVIOR RATING SCALES
J. Michael Williams. Odessa, Florida. Psychological Assessment Resources, Inc.

Introduction

The Cognitive Behavior Rating Scales (CBRS; Williams, 1987) is a newly developed paper-and-pencil questionnaire designed to assess cognitive and behavioral deficits in brain-injured patients who cannot participate in standard examination procedures. The CBRS is intended specifically for use with patients who are either noncompliant with examination procedures or unable to offer reliable self-ratings of their cognitive and behavioral functioning. The CBRS represents a formal psychometric approach to structured interview and data gathering, allowing significant others to rate the presence and severity of cognitive impairment, behavioral deficits, and observable neurological signs in patients with possible brain impairment. As many brain-injured patients are difficult to evaluate, information provided by the Cognitive Behavior Rating Scales can be clinically rich and useful as an adjunct to a comprehensive neuropsychological examination.

The CBRS consists of nine scales: 1) Language Deficit, 2) Agitation, 3) Need for Routine, 4) Depression, 5) Higher Cognitive Deficits, 6) Memory Disorder, 7) Dementia, 8) Apraxia, and 9) Disorientation. The test is composed of 116 items that can be answered in less than 20 minutes and that provide information concerning family ratings of everyday behaviors. The test appears particularly useful in the examination of cognitive and behavioral sequelae following dementia.

The CBRS was intended as a research tool and is relevant to several areas of study. The test author intends the scale to be of heuristic value in facilitating future experimentation and research on such topics as dementia, closed head injury, neuropsychological outcome in cardiac surgery patients, the relationship between the Cognitive Behavior Rating Scales and other standardized neuropsychological and intellectual assessment procedures (e.g., the Halstead-Reitan Neuropsychological Test Battery and the Wechsler Intelligence Scales), discrimination and differential diagnosis of dementia from depression in the elderly, and interrater reliability and subtype analysis of dementing illnesses.

The test author, J. Michael Williams, Ph. D., has research interests in the assessment of memory complaints and abilities among depressed elderly adults and family observations of daily cognitive impairment in demented patients (Williams, Klein, Little, & Haban, 1986, Williams, Little, Scates, & Blockman, 1987). The initial item pool for the Cognitive Behavior Rating Scales was developed by collecting numerous descriptors of everyday/practical examples of cognitive impairment. Such items were selected from clinical interviews with family members of patients experiencing dementing illness, scientific literature addressing dementing illnesses and their diagnoses (Blessed, Tomlinson, & Roth, 1968; Hachinski et al., 1975; Wells, 1979), and guidebooks for families that describe behavioral aspects of cognitive impairments in everyday terms (Heston & White, 1983; Mace & Rabins, 1981). Items intended to assess depression were obtained through review of items from existing self-report inventories of depression. Additionally, a subset of demographic and personal history items were added to increase the utility of the CBRS in predicting premorbid intellectual functioning.

Using these methods, 200 initial items were generated. The item pool was reduced to 170 items by the removal of obviously redundant items. The current version of the test is a 116-item questionnaire requiring Likert-type ratings of the patient on a variety of scales. The test kit includes a manual (Williams, 1987) and 50 copies each of the Rating Booklet and Item Booklet. The respondent reads items from the Item Booklet and records ratings on a coding form on the inside cover of the Rating Booklet. Item Booklets are reusable. The Rating Booklet also contains 10 demographic/personal diagnostic questions regarding the patient and a scoring grid that allows the examiner to convert raw scores to percentile and T-scores.

The Item Booklet is separated into three sections. The first 92 items represent the nine scales and require the respondent to rate the degree to which the patient possesses a given skill or attribute using a scale of 1 (not at all like this person) to 5 (very much like this person). Items 93–104 tap only memory and intellectual ability and also employ a 5-point rating procedure. These items are not required for patients who are free of cognitive problems. A slightly different rating system is used for items 105–106. For these items, ratings range from 1 (person's ability is very low) to 5 (person's ability is very high).

The scale can be administered to and completed by a family member or another knowledgeable party in approximately 20 minutes. The examiner's level of participation in the testing procedure is minimal and the test forms are completed easily by any respondent capable of at least an eighth-grade reading level. A review of the protocol suggests the examiner will need to describe and display the two booklets and review the simple instructions briefly with the respondent.

No age range for the CBRS is reported in the manual though the initial normative sample ranged in age from 30–89 years. A review of the item wording suggests the test may be applicable for patients from young adulthood through late adulthood. The item content implies the patient was premorbidly capable of independent living and self-care. As such, the scale does not appear applicable for child or adolescent populations in its current form.

A brief description of the nine CBRS scales follows:

1) *Language Deficit* (LD). This scale consists of 10 items that assess the common consequences of language disorder. Item content focuses on conversational confusion, difficulty in following instructions, and problems in reading, spelling, and writing.

2) *Apraxia* (AP). This five-item scale assesses the coordinated planning and expression of motor and procedural sequences. The items focus on skills such as dressing and executing complex actions.

3) *Disorientation* (DO). The content of this five-item scale refers to the patient's

inability to attend to the environment and monitor everyday events, as shown in inattentiveness, confusion, and wandering.

4) *Agitation* (AG). Brain-damaged patients often express restlessness and poor impulse control. The six items on this scale focus on aggressive behavior, frustration tolerance, emotional distress, and restlessness.

5) *Need for Routine* (NR). Many brain-damaged patients with memory disorders are unable to tolerate contact with unfamiliar people or changes in routine activities. The overreliance on familiar settings often represents an attempt by the brain-injured person to manifest competence within familiar context. The seven items on this scale focus on the need for structure and routine.

6) *Depression* (DEP). This scale was included to allow evaluation of the degree to which depression contributes to the patient's pattern of impairment. The content of the 24 items focuses primarily on depressive symptoms, such as depressed mood, psychomotor retardation, and decreased motivation. A comparison of scores on this scale with scores on scales assessing cognitive functions helps to clarify the role of depression in the patient's overall clinical picture.

7) *Higher Cognitive Deficits* (HCD). The 12 items on this scale center on activities that require higher-order cognitive skills, such as memory, language, abstract reasoning, and motor execution. The items require the rater to scale global abilities, such as driving, managing money, and social judgment. Impairment of the activities implies that one or more of the component skills are impaired.

8) *Memory Disorder* (MD). Items that comprise the Memory Disorder scale reflect the common consequences of impairment in ability to recall and store information. The 21 items cover specific functions, such as remembering the names of friends, recalling phone numbers, and remembering to turn off household appliances.

9) *Dementia* (DEM). The 26 items that make up this scale represent common behavioral signs of diffuse brain damage or disease, such as nighttime wandering, suspiciousness, deterioration of personal habits, incontinence, loss of interest in hobbies, and decline in activities of daily living.

Practical Applications/Uses

Though the Cognitive Behavior Rating Scales is primarily a research tool, it provides a wealth of information regarding an individual's functional cognitive and behavioral capacities, making the test applicable to a variety of clinical concerns. The test is useful particularly in acute, inpatient rehabilitation settings, where initial residual skills are often primitive as patients evolve out of comatose states, or in intensive care situations. Often, such patients are combative and agitated and, therefore, difficult to examine. Similarly, severely brain-damaged people are often incapable of the prolonged attention to task that most standardized intellectual and neuropsychometric batteries require. In such instances, the CBRS can be a valuable addition to the examination process.

The CBRS also hold promise for applications in outpatient medical and forensic examination. Often, neuropsychologists are referred outpatients who are beyond the acute phase of recovery but who continue to display specific impairments in cognitive and social skills that limit their postinjury function. At times such deficits cause patients either to under- or overestimate their own levels of functioning. In such situations, clinicians often request interviews with persons knowledgeable of the patient's functioning to assure a reliable appraisal of presenting problems and complaints and to assist in the development of a well-rounded picture of the patient's functional strengths and weaknesses. The CBRS provides a well-organized structure for such interviews and has the advantage of yielding objective scores. Thus, the CBRS can serve as a model for structured interviews or as a means for objectifying information derived from clinical interview. Finally, the test may assist the examiner in "fine-tuning" interview and evaluative procedures to focus on specific areas of deficit. For example, a patient who rated low on the Depression scale may require more in the way of psychological interview and testing for affective disorder or personality change.

In completing the Cognitive Behavior Rating Scales, the respondent must read items from the Item Booklet and then record responses in a coded response grid on the inside cover of the Rating Booklet. This poses several problems. First, the instructions and examples of the rating system to be used by the respondent are provided only on page 1 of the Item Booklet; actual items are presented on pages 2–4 of the booklet. Such an arrangement would not be troublesome for most respondents, but some individuals may forget the numerical rankings and their behavioral anchors when not presented with a visual reminder of the ranking system. The Item Booklet could be improved by including the numerical rating system and appropriate anchors at the top of each page of the Item Booklet. An alternative solution would be to revise the Item Booklet so that each item was followed by a response grid, thus allowing the respondent to make responses directly in the Item Booklet.

Scoring can be completed by hand in 5–10 minutes by adding the rankings in the columns or rows that represent the different scales. Sums for each scale are totaled to obtain raw scores. The user then refers to tables in the appendix of the manual and on the last page of the Rating Booklet to obtain T-scores and percentile transformations for the raw scores. Raw scores can be entered on the last page of the Rating Booklet on a scoring grid, and a visual profile of T-scores and percentiles can be obtained by drawing connecting lines to each of the scale raw scores. T-scores have a mean of 100 and a standard deviation of 15. Increasing raw scores produce lower T-scores and percentiles. Low T-scores and percentiles signify low levels of ability or adjustment. The manual is well written and organized, providing a clear and concise section on scoring as well as sections on administration, interpretation, and test construction. Tables are easily understood and used.

The CBRS was normed on a sample of 688 volunteers ranging in age from 30–89 years, solicited from advertisements and announcements to the membership of a local Alzheimer's Disease and Related Disorders Association (ADRDA) and the American Association of Retired People (AARP). As such, the test is applicable for use with the general adult population. However, data supporting the validity of the CBRS is derived from a group of demented patients with moderate levels of impairment suggesting that results should be interpreted cautiously for more representative samples of brain-damaged individuals. As a research tool, the CBRS has potential use for comparison of different diagnostic groupings, correlational studies with standardized intellectual and neuropsychological assessment devices and for assessing differing levels of severity for specific disorders (e.g., mild vs. severe dementing illness).

Interpretation of the CBRS is relatively straightforward as scores are based on an objective scale as are most standardized intelligence tests. The T-score and percentile conversions allow easy comparison of the various scales with other neuropsychometric test results. Though the test could be administered by nursing staff, interpretation should be reserved for the doctoral-level psychologist/neuropsychologist with specific training in the assessment of brain-damaged individuals and the use of comprehensive neuropsychological test batteries. A considerable degree of sophistication and training would be required for the examiner to adequately and properly interpret this test. Additionally, training in the differential diagnosis of depression versus dementia in elderly patients would be helpful.

Technical Aspects

The 170 items in the CBRS are summarized using the nine scales. The validity of items placements was evaluated by 10 practicing neuropsychologists or "expert judges." The manual provides no demographic data regarding the judges, their specific backgrounds, or their knowledge of behavioral domains. An item was placed in a scale if eight raters agreed that the item belonged in a particular scale. This process resulted in a final item pool of 116 items.

The manual reports several reliability and validity studies on the CBRS. Data from three groups of subjects (30 demented patients, 30 matched normals, and a group of 400 normal subjects recruited from the membership of a local ADRDA). Test-retest reliability ranged from .61 to .94 for normal subjects. Internal consistency reliabilities from the sample of 400 normals yielded coefficients for the nine scales ranging from .78 to .92. Such studies suggest moderate to excellent reliability for the CBRS.

Concurrent validity studies of matched normals and demented patients revealed significantly lower ratings for demented patients on all but one of the nine scales (i.e., Depression). Non-stepwise discriminant function analysis was used to establish a classification rate for the rating scale. A canonical correlation coefficient of .91 resulted in correct classification of 100% of the demented and matched controls. Such findings suggest that family members employing the CBRS reliably rate demented patients. Also, because family members of matched normals did not rate depression items differently than families of demented patients, the scale may hold promise, as the author points out, in the differential diagnosis of depression and pseudodementia in the elderly.

The test author (Williams, 1987) appropriately points out several cautions in the use of the CBRS. First, he acknowledged the CBRS is not representative of general populations of brain-damaged individuals because its reliability studies were based on a demented population. Secondly, and more important, is the possibility that a "threshold" level of impairment may exist such that family members only become aware of deficits after impairment drops below a certain level. Thus, families may not be as accurate in appraising the cognitive and behavioral deficits of the mildly impaired individual. Likewise, the normative sample may not have sufficient numbers of mild cases for discrimination to be affected by such response tendencies. Williams's calls for more studies of patients with mild deficits to address the question of thresholds and respondent awareness of patient deficits (Williams, 1987).

Critique

This reviewer administered the CBRS to a patient referred for medical non-compliance secondary to stroke. The patient was a 68-year-old female inpatient with an admitting diagnosis of intercerebral hemorrhage. She was noncompliant with nursing and rehabilitation therapies and referred for behavioral assessment and intervention as well as assessment of higher cognitive functions. Though the examiner and patient had good rapport, she was dysphasic and difficult to converse with or to examine using traditional methods. She also had periods of emotional lability, frustration, and disorientation, causing her responses to be unreliable. Occasionally, she would purposefully answer questions erroneously, sarcastically, or otherwise sabotage her participation in rehabilitation interventions.

The CBRS was completed by the examiner, the patient's spouse, and a nurse familiar with the patient. The reviewer and nurse had considerable knowledge of the patient over 7 weeks of inpatient hospitalization with almost daily therapeutic contact and review of daily patient progress notes. The three separate ratings of the patient yielded profiles that were quite similar, especially in T-score and percentile ratings and relative elevations and surpressions of various scales. In no area did T-score ratings differ substantially from one rater to the next (3–5 points). Further, the general profile reflected in an objective sense the subjective impression of the rehabilitation team members that the patient suffered severe expressive language disturbance, memory impairment and impairment in higher cognitive functioning, and depression in addition to obvious features of organic brain syndrome.

The CBRS was a very welcome adjunct to the assessment of this individual and served as a cognitive-behavioral baseline for later comparisons. Also, as the patient became more responsive, she was able to participate more meaningfully in the rehabilitation treatment and neuropsychological assessment. Later intellectual and neuropsychological test scores reflected initial strengths and weaknesses as revealed in the Cognitive Behavior Rating Scales.

The CBRS is a brief and relatively simple paper-and-pencil questionnaire that holds considerable merit when included in the comprehensive neuropsychological assessment of brain-damaged patients. Used in conjunction with other tests and batteries, it can contribute rich clinical data regarding cognitive and behavioral functioning of the patient and augment more formal measures. It is especially useful with patients who, for one reason or another, find it difficult or impossible to participate in standardized examination procedures. This new test, currently in its first research edition, represents a significant advance in the development of structured interview technology for use with brain-damaged patients.

References

This list includes text citations and suggested additional reading.

Blessed, G., Tomlinson, B.E., & Roth, M. (1968). The association between quantitative measures of dementia and of senile change in the cerebral grey matter of elderly subjects. *British Journal of Psychiatry, 114,* 797–811.

Hachinskl, V.C., Linette, L.D., Zilhka, E., DuBoulay, G.H., McAllister, V.L., Marshall, J., Russell, R.W., & Symon, L. (1975). Cerebral blood flow in dementia. *Archive of Neurology, 32,* 632–637.

Heston, L.L., & White, J.A. (1983). *Dementia.* New York: W.H. Freeman and Company.

Mace, N.L., & Rabins, P.V. (1981). *The 36-hour day.* Baltimore: The Johns Hopkins Press.

Wells, C.E. (1979). Pseudodementia. *American Journal of Psychiatry, 136,* 895–900.

Williams, J.M., Klein, K., Little, M., & Haban, G. (1986). Family Observations of everyday cognitive impairment in dementia. *Archives of Clinical Neuropsychology 1,* 103–109.

Williams, J.M., Little, M., Scates, S., & Blockman, N. (1987). Memory complaints and abilities among depressed older adults. *Journal of Consulting and Clinical Psychology, 55,* 595-598.

Williams, J.M. (1987). *Cognitive Behavior Rating Scales.* Odessa, Florida: Psychological Assessment Resources, Inc.

Mary Ann Rafoth, Ph.D.
Assistant Professor of Educational Psychology, Indiana University of Pennsylvania, Indiana, Pennsylvania.

Gurmal Rattan, Ph.D.
Associate Professor of Educational Psychology and Director of Doctoral Studies, Indiana University of Pennsylvania, Indiana, Pennsylvania.

COGNITIVE SKILLS ASSESSMENT BATTERY

Ann E. Boehm and Barbara R. Slater. New York, New York: Teachers College Press.

Introduction

The Cognitive Skills Assessment Battery (CSAB) is an individually administered, instructional screening instrument intended for use by preschool and kindergarten teachers. The purpose of this measure is to assist instructors in making goal-referenced decisions concerning curriculum planning for a class or for individual students. The test provides teachers with information regarding a child's progress in cognitive and physical motor domains. Specifically, the five sections covered correspond to areas typical of kindergarten curricula: 1) orientation to one's environment, 2) discrimination of similarities and differences, 3) comprehension and concept formation, 4) coordination, and 5) immediate and delayed memory. The CSAB may be administered either at the beginning of the school year for screening and curriculum planning or at the end of the year for program evaluation. The resulting data can be used to highlight an individual's strengths or weaknesses or present a similar profile for a class. The test was developed to aid in evaluating young children's skills through a criterion-referenced rather than a norm-referenced model. However, the assessor's manual (Boehm & Slater, 1981) recommends evaluating a child's level of mastery by comparison with other children in the normative group. Although the test authors use the term "field sample" in contrast to "normative sample," the end results appear to be the same. That is, a norm-referenced model is used to interpret the data from the CSAB.

The test authors, Ann E. Boehm and Barbara R. Slater (Teachers College, Columbia University), are both well-known authors and researchers in the fields of early childhood education and early identification of learning problems. Boehm is also the author of a well-known and frequently used test of concepts for prekindergarten and kindergarten age children (Boehm Test of Basic Concepts-Revised, 1986).

The CSAB, first called the Inventory of Cognitive Skills and Visual-Motor Functioning, was designed to help teachers of prekindergarten children in evaluating program effectiveness. The initial test was started in 1966 and was field tested from 1968 to 1971. A kindergarten phase called the Kindergarten Assessment Battery was started in 1967 and field tested in 1969-71. To identify the skills assessed, the test authors engaged in a variety of activities, such as classroom observations and interviews with teachers, aides, and program developers in addition to field testing. A revision of the current test (Cognitive Skills Assessment Battery, 2nd ed.) was completed in 1981. The goals of the revision were to improve item presentation and to create a larger sampling of the behaviors tapped. As a result, 19 items were added and 7 items deleted from the original scale. However, the criteria used to add or delete items is not clearly stated. The CSAB is published in English only, but it may be appropriate for use with non-English speakers. In this case, the CSAB may be administered in both the child's native language and in English in order to obtain an accurate picture of the child's abilities.

Test materials provided include 1) a card easel, 2) an assessor's manual, 3) a protocol, and 4) a class record sheet that profiles both the child's and class's performance. The test kit requires, but does not provide, eight blocks of the same color, size, and shape and a watch with a sweep second hand. Primary-grade sized pencils and blank sheets of paper are to be provided by the examiner. A clipboard is also recommended to aid in recording responses. The test is individually administered usually taking between 20–25 minutes, although children experiencing cognitive and motor delays may take longer. Although administration of the test in one sitting is advisable, it may be given in two sittings when necessary. Two chairs, a large table to accommodate the card easel, and pupil response sheets are required.

The test may be administered by a teacher or by another professional familiar with general testing procedures. Although, the test is designed for prekindergarten and kindergarten age children, no specific age limits are specified. Children taking the test are likely to be between the ages of 4 and 6. A child's proximity to entering kindergarten or actual attendance in kindergarten will be the determining factor when deciding whether or not to use this test.

Difficulty level of the items varies to reflect developmental growth from prekindergarten to kindergarten. Some items receive partial points for completeness of response (i.e., labeling body parts on a picture receives more points than simple identification of such information), while other items are judged for accuracy and scored as a plus or minus. The resulting profile sheet purports to facilitate the modification of curriculum and/or instructional goals; however, the utility of such an approach is not clear.

Practical Applications/Uses

The CSAB could be used appropriately by school psychologists, classroom teachers, and practitioners to assess the functioning level of prekindergarten and kindergarten age children. Because many of the items on the CSAB are typical of general readiness tasks, this measure may yield information useful in making judgments regarding readiness for kindergarten. The test directions are clearly explained and easy to administer. A teacher's aide, who is carefully trained by an experienced assessor, could successfully give the test. Because the responses of young children are variable and influenced by situational factors, validity of the results obtained would be best made by someone with adequate training and knowledge of child development.

Although tasks on the CSAB are similar to content taught at the prekindergarten and kindergarten level, it is not clear how these tasks demonstrate measurement of specific skills (e.g., coordination, immediate and delayed memory). The test authors do not provide evidence that successful performance on the tasks of the CSAB are related to later academic success. Establishing concurrent validity with a known achievement measure may have addressed this issue.

The test is scored easily and quickly; a variety of potential responses (including black dialect) are given on verbal items to aid the examiner. However, interpretation of the test results may pose problems for teachers who may use the success/failure rates given in the test manual as norms. Because of these normative data, there may be a tendency to use the results of the CSAB to make decisions about readiness when this is not the stated intent of the test. There may also be a tendency to make generalizations about a child's abilities in the five goal areas based on performance on individual items, although the test authors state that information is not to be used in a summative fashion. In addition, Boehm and Slater (1981) do not address the role of clinical judgment regarding variables such as test anxiety and attentional problems that may adversely affect test validity in scoring and interpreting the CSAB.

Technical Aspects

As noted previously the CSAB is described as a criterion-referenced test designed to identify a child's cognitive strengths and weaknesses. However, no mastery levels are provided. Typically, mastery of a skill is established at 80% (Hopkins & Stanley, 1981) and enables the examiner to determine if the child is ready for instruction at the next level. Although this is the aim of the CSAB, lack of clear demarcations between different levels of task mastery (e.g., frustration, instructional, or mastery) makes it difficult to assess the efficacy of instructional techniques. Moreover, because a task such as writing one's name is not broken into component parts, failure to accomplish the task does not yield the type of instructional information typical of criterion-referenced tests. Instead, the test authors provide data from a normative group and use this information in an interpretive example in the manual.

It would appear that instead of utilizing an approach similar to traditional criterion-referenced tests, Boehm and Slater recommend that a child's cognitive deficiencies be identified by comparison with other children in the normative group. For example, the illustration on page 27 of the assessor's manual shows how Amy, a middle-class prekindergarten child, was one of 13% of children who could not identify the color red. Instruction for this child would then focus on developing a skill that most (87%) of the children in her normative group had acquired. It appears that while the CSAB was designed as a criterion-referenced test, the information taken from this measure is evaluated according to norm-referenced procedures. As a result, the utility of this measure is questionable.

According to the technical information provided in the manual (Boehm & Slater, 1981, Table 4, p. 30), 551 children in both prekindergarten and kindergarten participated in the fall administration of the CSAB while only 351 participated in the spring administration. Demographic information such as gender, ethnic background, language spoken at home, economic background, and average school income is well detailed. However, the criteria used in determining the family's socioeconomic status (SES) are not stated. Because SES is one of the major variables used in evaluating the child's performance, it is not clear what effect this would have in preparing instructional goals.

Reliability for the CSAB was established using a test-retest procedure involving a 2- to 3-week delay. Results were described in terms of the percentage of agreement between the two administrations. The sample size was somewhat limited, with only 16 children participating at the prekindergarten level and 32 at the kindergarten level. According to information presented in Table 7 of the manual (Boehm & Slater, 1981, p. 32), subtests involved in the memory area had the lowest levels of agreement for both groups of children. Curriculum decisions based on the children's performance on the memory tasks should therefore be made with caution.

Content evidence of validity was used to establish the meaningfulness of skills measured by the CSAB. To determine the extent to which the CSAB paralleled skills taught at prekindergarten and kindergarten levels, 51 teachers, aides, and student teachers were surveyed. Overall, slightly more than 85% of the skills taught at the prekindergarten level and 84% of the skills taught at the kindergarten level reported by the respondents were assessed by the CSAB. Results suggest that information assessed by the CSAB is consistent with information taught in school. However, the inclusion of student teachers and classroom aides whose judgment may be affected by lack of experience and familiarity with curricular goals might constitute a threat to validity.

In summary, the psychometric properties of the CSAB are less than desirable. For a criterion-referenced test, one would typically expect cutoff scores for performance at different levels of mastery. Because no such information is provided, it is difficult to determine the utility of the CSAB as a screening measure. Moreover, the practice of evaluating an individual's performance by comparison with that of peer-cohorts adds further to the confusion because the CSAB was not designed as a norm-referenced measure.

Critique

The CSAB was designed for prekindergarten and kindergarten teachers as an aid in setting curriculum goals. The test represents a compilation of items typical of readiness and screening measures such as number, letter and color identification, basic knowledge of name and address, and memory and visual-motor skills. However, its use as a readiness or screening test is hindered by the equivocal approach used to evaluate the results. Specifically, lack of mastery levels (e.g., frustration, instructional, and mastery) limits the potential usefulness of the instrument. Presentation in the test manual of an example interpreted from a norm-based perspective adds further to the confusion.

Although this measure has the potential for wide application at the prekindergarten and kindergarten level, its utility is hindered by problems of validity and a likelihood of misinterpretation by educators. In particular, the success/failure rate on individual items may be viewed in a cumulative fashion to make placement decisions. The tests might be helpful in individual goal setting (e.g., writing an Individual Educational Plan) or when in need of a quick assessment of the basic skills. However, caution should be exercised when using the measure to develop instructional goals.

References

Boehm, A.E., & Slater, B.R. (1981). *Cognitive Skills Assessment Battery Assessors manual.* (2nd ed.). New York: Teachers College Press.
Hopkins, K.D., & Stanley, J.C. (1981). *Educational and psychological measurement and evaluation.* Englewood Cliffs, NJ: Prentice Hall.

Michael J. Roszkowski, Ph.D.
Research Psychologist and Associate Professor of Psychology Research &
Evaluation Department, The American College, Bryn Mawr,
Pennsylvania.

Glenn E. Snelbecker, Ph.D.
Professor of Psychological Studies in Education, Temple University,
Philadelphia, Pennsylvania.

COMPUTER APTITUDE, LITERACY, AND INTEREST PROFILE

Mary S. Poplin, David E. Drew, and Robert S. Gable. Austin,
TX: PRO-ED.

Introduction

The Computer Aptitude, Literacy, and Interest Profile (CALIP) is an instrument designed to measure the three attributes indicated in its title. The CALIP was developed by Mary S. Poplin, David E. Drew, and Robert S. Gable, who are all scholars in the fields of psychology and education. The CALIP authors, all of whom hold academic posts at the Claremont Graduate School in Claremont, California, sought to develop a multipurpose instrument that would be appropriate for such diverse applications as vocational counseling, personnel selection, and training. As stated in the manual (Poplin, Drew, & Gable, 1984), the development of the CALIP was guided by an analysis and review of the sparse literature regarding abilities necessary for success in various computer-related occupations. The content of the Literacy portion of the battery was developed from "examination questions used in quantitative and computer science classes and from questions submitted by people practicing in various computer specialties (e.g., word processing, repair and sales)" (Poplin, Drew, & Gable, 1984, p. 7).

In the promotional material for the CALIP as well as in the CALIP manual itself, it is stated that the aim was to construct a scale 1) to provide assessments relevant for any computer-related occupation, not just programming, 2) to emphasize visual rather than verbal material in order to better gauge the abilities of minorities and linguistically handicapped individuals, 3) to be useful across a wide age span, and 4) to be comprehensive in nature, measuring the attributes believed critical to success in positions involving computer technology.

According to the manual, the CALIP was standardized in 1983 on a sample of 1,236 individuals whose characteristics are described in terms of geographical region of residence (from 22 states), rural versus urban setting (71% urban), sex (53% female), race (82% white), age (12 years to 60 years), and past and present occupation (approximately 60% were students in the seventh through twelfth grades, 21% were listed under an occupation, and the employment status of the remaining 19% is not indicated, although it would appear that they were college students). The test authors compared the relative distribution of the sample on these first four variables to the 1980 U.S. Census data and concluded that the sample is roughly representative of the United States population. Compared to the U.S. Census data, the CALIP sample has more Westerners and fewer Southerners in its ranks, and it is slightly more rural. Furthermore, it contains a slightly greater proportion of females, Asian-Americans, and American Indians and a lower proportion of blacks than the general population.

Also reported in the manual is the nature of the sample's experience with computers; although less than 4% of the members of this group were working as programmers, a much larger proportion had some sort of computer experience. The indices of exposure to computers that were collected are multiple and include level of experience (i.e., no experience, beginner, intermediate, advanced) in various computer-related activities. The activities are listed here in order of the percentage of the sample reporting at least beginner-level expertise: games (86%), user of packaged programs (54%), writing programs (43%), working as an operator with a mainframe (17%), repairing computers or video games (13%), managing computer personnel and systems (12%), computer hardware design (7%), and selling computers (6%). The extent of use by the sample of various types of programs is also reported (i.e., statistical packages, word processing, graphics, music, accounting/financial, engineering/architectural, agricultural, medical, and other). These ranged from a high of 44% (word processing) to a low of 4% (agricultural programs and medical programs). Slightly over 36% of these 1,236 persons had taken at least one computer course, approximately 40% reported having knowledge of the BASIC language, and 12% indicated that they knew LOGO, but their level of proficiency in these and in the other languages in the survey is uncertain. Close to half of the sample said that they currently used a computer at school or work, about 45% of the sample indicated "above average" interest in computers, and only 11% described their level of interest as "below average."

The CALIP consists of a 47-page Examiner's Manual, test booklets, and answer booklets. These materials may be purchased separately or as part of a complete kit consisting of 1 Examiner's Manual, 50 answer booklets, 10 test booklets, and a storage box. The only other materials needed to administer the scale are a stopwatch and a pencil. (The stopwatch is only required for one subtest.) The test itself consists of six discrete units titled Estimation, Graphic Patterns, Logical Structures, Series, Interest, and Literacy. The Estimation, Graphic Patterns, Logical Structures, and Series units form the Aptitude section of the battery, and as such, these four units can be appropriately considered as the subtests of the Aptitude domain of the CALIP, although the CALIP manual refers to all six units as subtests.

The following is a brief description of each of these six units constituting the CALIP.

1) *Estimation*. Under a time limit, the test-taker is required to estimate the number of darkened squares in an array containing both darkened and undarkened squares. The subtest contains 24 blocks (arrays) that vary in both size and pattern.

2) *Graphic Patterns*. This test consists of a set of 20 incomplete designs that have to be completed from the four or six alternatives offered for each one. The correct answer is based on implicit rules of patterning (i.e., matching, addition, subtrac-

tion, alternation, and progression of elements). These items were adapted from a test of nonverbal intelligence.

3) *Logical Structures.* This is a 20-item test requiring the person to find similarities (analogies) between different pairs or groups of numbers, letters, or words.

4) *Series.* Offered four options, the test-taker must determine which number or letter belongs in a particular sequence of items. There are 24 sequences to complete.

5) *Interest.* This scale is meant to measure affinity toward four types of "intellectual endeavors," namely people-oriented, things-oriented, numeric, and qualitative/emotional. Answers to these 20 questions are in a forced-choice format. The first 14 items require the individual to indicate whether he or she agrees or disagrees with a particular statement. The last six items are of a paired comparison type, asking the person to specify which of two activities he or she prefers. Only four of the items mention computers *explicitly*.

6) *Literacy.* Essentially a computer technology vocabulary test containing 30 items, this test covers such topics as programming, word processing, and computer-related electronics.

Although it is not listed as a subtest of the CALIP, there is a form called Experience Survey that is meant to assess the individual's exposure to (as opposed to what he or she has learned about) computer technology. According to the manual, consideration of the Experience Survey in conjunction with the Literacy test results should provide one with an "estimate of the degree or rate of learning about computer technology" (Poplin, Drew, & Gable, 1984, p. 7). This portion of the CALIP, however, is optional and does not translate into either raw scores or standard scores.

According to the authors of the CALIP, in all of the tests other than Interest, the items within each test are ordered by level of difficulty. The test-taker is encouraged to answer all the questions because there is no penalty for guessing in the scoring of the CALIP. Except for the Estimation subtest, the questions on the CALIP are of the multiple-choice variety. A scoring key is part of the manual (Appendix C), and if photocopied onto a transparency, it is easy to use as an overlay. Scoring is straightforward and simple. Only the Estimation subtest is timed (2 minutes). The rest of the battery has no imposed time restrictions, but, on average, about 1 hour is required to complete the battery. The CALIP can be group or individually administered (including self-administration).

According to the instructions in the manual, any adult who has read and becomes familiar with the administration and scoring section of the manual should be capable of giving this test; use is not restricted to psychologists or other licensed professionals. However, at the same time, the manual states (Poplin, Drew, & Gable, 1984, p. 35) that examiners should be familiar with the *Standards for Educational and Psychological Tests* (American Educational Research Association, American Psychological Association, & National Council on Measurement In Education, 1985). Detailed (step-by-step) instructions for group, individual, and self-administrations of the CALIP are provided. The manual indicates that individual administration is preferable in cases where test anxiety, test naivete, or reading difficulties are present.

Each of the six subtests results in a standard score that has a mean of 10 and a standard deviation of 3. These standard scores are simple linear transformations of the distribution of raw scores within each of four age groups, namely 12 through 14, 15 through 19, 20 through 29, and 30 through 60. To convert a raw score into a standard score, one merely consults the appropriate age-based table in the manual.

The decision to use only four age ranges was reached on the basis of an analysis of variance, searching for significant differences between the age ranges into which the standardization group was initially subdivided. If there was no significant difference between the raw scores of any two adjacent age ranges, these two age ranges were collapsed into one broader age grouping. (The original 10 groupings, in years of age, were 12–13, 14, 15, 16, 17, 18–19, 20–21, 22–24, 25–34, 35–60.)

In addition to the six scores described above, the standard scores from the four subtests measuring aptitude are summed into a composite that then is transformed into a Computer Aptitude Quotient (CAQ) having a mean of 100 and a standard deviation 15. The developers of the CALIP recommend (quite appropriately) that given the reliabilities of the individual aptitude subtests, one should use this composite rather than the individual subtest scores in determining an individual's aptitude, particularly when dealing with persons 12 to 14 years old.

A section on the interpretation of the results is included in the manual. It is stated therein that the Aptitude scores constitute the most important piece of information to be derived from the CALIP. The meaning of subtest standard scores is defined in nonstatistical terms by the manual as follows: 17–20 = superior; 14–16 = above average; 7–13 = average; 4–6 = below average, and 0–3 = poor.

Subtest or profile analysis is suggested as a further means for understanding the results. The manual states that any subtest score that is 3 standard score points above or below average may be indicative of a special strength or weakness. (Although it is not stated explicitly, the test authors appear to have 7–13 in mind rather than the 10 when speaking of an average score in this context. Thus, according to the test authors, any score above 16 or below 4 is significant.) Such a "profile analysis" of test scores, according to the creators of the CALIP, is not appropriate for 12- to 14-year-old subjects due to the instability of the aptitude and interest subtests within this age range. For individuals under 15, the manual states that the focus should be on the CAQ, not the individual subtests. Under this same interpretative scheme CAQ scores (the composite of the four aptitude subtests) of 131 to 145 are superior, 116–130 are above average, 85–115 are average, 70–84 are below average, and 55–69 are poor. The manual is vague, however, regarding how one is to treat significant discrepancies among the four aptitude subtest scores for persons who are *above* 15 years of age.

There was an "errata" sheet accompanying the manual listing corrections to the normative tables (Tables 20 and 21). Users of the CALIP are therefore urged to verify that they are scoring the CALIP in accordance with these modifications. Hopefully, future reprints of the manual will make these corrections in the tables themselves and will provide some indication as to whether the manuals are of the earlier or reprinted variety so as to avoid any potential confusion regarding which version users may have in their possession.

Practical Applications/Uses

It would appear that the CALIP is considered by the test authors to be appropriate for both educational and industrial settings. The manual discusses four specific applications for the CALIP: 1) to identify individuals who possess aptitudes for computer-related occupations, especially members of minority groups, women, reading disabled persons, and other individuals who may not otherwise be identified as being "talented" in this respect, 2) to generate information that allows a person to consider and make realistic career choices, 3) to provide an empirical basis for the allocation of an organization's resources (e.g., determination of the present level of ability and knowledge in an organization and the identification of needs), and 4) to evaluate the effectiveness of a training program.

Some specific examples are offered on how the CALIP may be applied to the solution of practical problems, such as identifying potential dropouts from computer courses and evaluating the effectiveness of a training program. With respect to the latter use, the authors of the CALIP indicate that they are planning to produce alternate (equivalent) forms of the CALIP (one of which can be used as a pretest and the other of which can be used as a posttest), thereby reducing the potential complications that come from testing with the same exact instrument on two occasions. The test authors point out that with just the one version currently available, using the CALIP as both a pretest and a posttest must be done with caution. Anyone considering using the CALIP for program evaluation should also be aware of a statement the CALIP authors make in another part of the manual, (namely)) that ". . .the normative data were collected in 1983 for the purpose of assessing individuals rather than groups, schools, programs, or organizations. Group means applied to nonlinear scales (such as percentile ranks derived from individuals) can yield misleading results" (Poplin, Drew, & Gable, 1984, p. 36).

The test authors also alert the potential user of the instrument about federal government regulations requiring "local" validation of employment procedures, including tests. It is noted within this context that the normative data for the CALIP are roughly representative of the population of the United States with regard to sex, race, ethnicity, and geographical area, but that ultimately, the responsibility for determining whether a test is appropriate for a particular case rests with the test user. A very important caution presented in the manual that a potential user should not overlook is found in the following statement:

> The CALIP has not been validated for making classification decisions because we have not yet gathered evidence sufficient to include regression equations that would differentially predict adult programmers, repair persons, sales personnel, product engineers and so forth. Therefore, a profile of a given individual, based solely on CALIP scores, should not be used for classification or selection purposes (Poplin, Drew, & Gable, 1984, p. 35)

The potential user of the CALIP is warned further that no experimental evidence exists documenting that any of the CALIP scores are subject to improvement through remediation, so "therefore the examiner should stress the tentative nature of any recommendations regarding remedial or enrichment methods and materials" (Poplin, Drew, & Gable, 1984, p. 36).

The manual recommends that the Literacy subtest be employed judiciously, emphasizing that it should not be used with young subjects or with individuals with limited computer exposure because the test is highly correlated to computer-related courses and experience. The examiner is instructed, however, to pay special attention to a low Literacy subtest score in the presence of a marked self-reported computer experience (from the Experience Survey), suggesting that it ". . . might justify thorough investigation of the examinee's past work and academic experience as on-the-job training might be required" (Poplin, Drew, & Gable, 1984, p. 34).

Technical Aspects

During the construction of the CALIP, the items forming it were subjected to both a qualitative and a quantitative item analysis. Under the qualitative item analysis, the items were examined to determine whether they 1) covered a representative sample of skills and 2) were free from confounding effects. The manual describes this process in general terms. Greater detail is provided about the quantitative analysis that consisted of an examination of each item's a) difficulty level and b) discriminating power (item-total score correlations). The scores from a random sample of 600 subjects drawn from the standardization population served as the basis for the quantitative analysis, and results regarding the retained items are reported at each of the four age intervals ($N = 1500$ at each age range) on which the norms were developed.

The medians as well as ranges of the percentages of difficulty for all six basic units (subtests) of the CALIP are reported in the manual. An average difficulty level of 50% across the six subtests and four age ranges is exhibited, with the 24 reported medians falling within the range of 18% to 84%. An inspection of the table listing the median levels of difficulty reveals that the Estimation subtest had the lowest median pass rate (highest difficulty level) in all four cohorts (31%), whereas Logical Structures showed the highest median pass rate (about 65%).

The median item-total correlations (discriminating power) for the Graphic Patterns, Logical Structures, Series, and Literacy subtests are presented at each of the four age ranges. These 16 median coefficients range from a low of .28 (Logical Structures at 12 to 14 years of age) to a high of .56 (Logical Structures at 15 to 19 years of age), the average being about .40. No data are presented on the item-total correlations in the Estimation subtest or on the Interest subtest, the explanation given for failing to do so being ". . . that correlational analysis of items on heterogeneous tests (such as Interest) and timed tests (such as Estimation) should not be expected to conform to normal standards" (Poplin, Drew, & Gable, 1984, p. 9). The decision not to report these coefficients may have been a last minute one because the table listing the item-total correlations (Table 2) indicates erroneously that data on all six subtests are to be found within it.

The reliability of the CALIP was investigated in terms of both internal consistency measures as well as measures of stability using the data from the entire standardization sample in both instances. To gauge internal consistency, two measures are employed, namely split-half reliabilities (adjusted by the Spearman-Brown formula) and Cronbach's alphas. These indices are available for the sample as a whole and for each of the four age-based cohorts on which the norms are developed. These internal consistency coefficients are not reported for the Estimation subtest, the Interest subtest, or for the Aptitude composite (i.e., CAQ score). The reasons for not presenting internal consistency data on the Interest and Estimation subtests is the same as for not reporting item-total correlations for these subtests (which were noted earlier). No rationale is offered for omitting an internal consistency analysis of the Computer Aptitude Quotient.

The CALIP manual reports the split-half coefficients and alpha coefficients for the Graphic Patterns, Logical Structures, Series, and Literacy subtests. These data are provided for the standardization sample overall (without regard to age) as well as for each of the four age intervals into which the sample was divided for norming purposes. The split-half coefficients and alpha coefficients were of approximately the same magnitude, falling within the narrow range of .89 to .92 for the sample in toto. Comparable split-half and alpha coefficients (high .80s-low .90s) were obtained within each of the three older groups, but at ages 12 to 14, these coefficients were somewhat lower in value, ranging from .75-.80 (split-half) and from .72-.78 (alpha).

The test-retest (temporal stability) reliability study discussed in the CALIP manual, based on a sample of 86 subjects drawn from all four normative age ranges, involves an analysis of all the sections of the instrument (except the Experience Survey). This study consisted of an administration of the CALIP on two occasions, 1 week apart, and the correlation of the two sets of scores. The results are presented in a table listing the values that were derived using raw scores as well as standard scores as input in the correlation procedure. The correlations computed using the raw scores yielded values almost identical to those obtained on the basis of standard scores. The correlations between standard scores on the two administrations of this inventory were .55 on Interest, .84 on Literacy, and .93 for the CAQ scores. The coefficients for the Aptitude section subtests ranged from .71 (Estimation) to .84 (Series). There is no breakdown in this table of the stability within each of the four age ranges. (The title of the table indicates that the reported coefficients reflect control for age.) However, there is mention in the narrative of differences in stability as a function of age. According to the manual, the test-retest reliability of the Interest subtest, when examined by age, had a value of .50 for those under 20 years old but equaled .88 for subjects who were 20 years old or older.

Under the discussion of the CALIP's reliability, the manual also presents the standard errors of measurement for all the scores available from this instrument (other than the Experience Survey). These were calculated using the alpha (for raw scores) and test-retest coefficients (for standardized scores) in the formula. The standard error of measurement is 4.0 for the CAQ, 1.2 for the standardized Literacy score, and 2.0 for the standardized Interest score.

Seven studies dealing with the CALIP's validity are abstracted in the manual. The first of these (which in the reviewers' opinion can be best viewed as a construct validation strategy) consists of an examination of the interrelationship between the subtests of the battery, using the entire standardization group as subjects and testing the hypothesis that the aptitude subtests will be "highly intercorrelated" because they all measure some aspect of computer aptitude. The resultant aptitude subtests correlation coefficients were .16 (Estimation with Logical Structures), .19

(Estimation with Series), .22 (Estimation with Graphic Patterns), .71 (Graphic Patterns with Series), .73 (Graphic Patterns with Logical Structures), and .89 (Logical Structures with Series). Despite the weak relationship of the Estimation subtest to the other three subtests, the developers of the CALIP indicate that this subtest has value because it can differentiate between groups that in theory should differ in computer aptitude (as described below). The intercorrelations between aptitude, literacy, and interest are also reported: Interest with CAQ = .22; Literacy with Interest = .37; Literacy with CAQ = .45.

The other six validity studies are criterion related in nature (concurrent validity to be specific) involving analysis of variance procedures to examine the relationship between CALIP scores and variables known to be related to computer skills and interest, namely age, sex, employment as an expert programmer, knowledge of computer languages, experience in writing programs, and number of computer courses taken. In general, the results were in the expected direction. For instance, raw scores on Aptitude and Literacy went up with age, whereas Interest did not. An analysis of covariance controlling for age showed that the CAQ scores of expert programmers are higher than a randomly selected sample. An intriguing finding was that females scored significantly lower than the males on Interest and Literacy but not in terms of Aptitude. In a sense these six studies also lend some support to the construct validity of the scale.

Because computer aptitude is related to mathematical skills, additional evidence for construct validity may be inferred from a journal article (Hearne, Poplin, & Lasley, 1986–87) showing that a moderate level of association ($r = .39 - .48$) exists between the Aptitude portion of the CALIP and the mathematics subscale of the Stanford Achievement Test in a sample of junior high school students.

The reviewers had the opportunity to use the CALIP in conjunction with a National Science Foundation-sponsored program designed to prepare teachers from various disciplines to teach computer science at the secondary level (Aiken & Snelbecker, 1985). The retraining program, approximately 11 months in duration, consisted of a course on structured BASIC, two courses on PASCAL, and a practicum on instructional design addressing BASIC and PASCAL. Course grades for each of the four courses were based on exams and individual projects. The 56 participants in this program were selected from 235 applicants and 42 of them went on to complete the entire sequence of courses. They took the CALIP at the start of the program (pretest) and then again at the end of it (posttest). Data gathered as part of the project (Snelbecker, Devlin, Roszkowski, & Aiken, 1986, 1987, 1988a; Roszkowski, Devlin, Snelbecker, Aiken, & Jacobsohn, in press) provide further information regarding the psychometric properties of the CALIP, namely 1) the temporal stability of the scores over the span of the program, 2) the correlation between the CALIP scores and grades in the courses that formed the program, 3) the relationship between the CALIP and the Computer Attitude Scale (CAS; Loyd & Gressard, 1984), and 4) the relationship among the CALIP domains and subdomains.

The 11-month stability coefficients, that is, the correlations between the pretest and posttest CALIP scores, were .76 (Interest), .65 (CAQ), .59 (Series), .52 (Graphic Patterns), .37 (Logical Structures), .35 (Literacy), and .31 (Estimation). The reviewers also correlated the pretest CALIP scores with the exam grade, project grade, and the final grade in each course. In each of the three computer language courses, the CALIP bore a stronger relationship with the exam grade than with the project grade. Notably, the CALIP failed to correlate with performance in the instructional design practicum, that required the teacher to exercise higher order skills to solve complex problems related to the teaching of BASIC and PASCAL. The relationship of the CALIP to the level of mastery in the three language courses (i.e., excluding the instructional design course) can be best captured by using an average of the three final grades as the criterion. These validity coefficients with the grade point average as the criterion were low to moderate, having the following values: .60 (Literacy), .52 (Logical Structures), .50 (CAQ), .43 (Series), .36 (Graphic Patterns), .31 (Interest), and .16 (Estimation). There were no statistically significant changes on any of the tests and subtests between the pretest and the posttest, including Literacy.

The absence of an increase in aptitude scores from pretest to posttest (after training in computer languages) can be seen as a desirable characteristic for a test purporting to measure this dimension because aptitude is supposed to be relatively immutable to short-term training, at least in the mind of the lay public. However, the reviewers were surprised to discover that there was no increase in the Literacy score, but close examination of the Literacy test items showed that this test did not reflect what was being taught in the program. The Literacy and the Interest scores from the CALIP bore a moderate degree of correlation with the total score from the CAS (a measure of attitude towards computers), the respective coefficients being .44 and .40. The Aptitude (CAQ)-CAS correlation ($r = .17$) was small and failed to reach statistical significance.

We also looked at the interdomain correlations of the CALIP on both the pretest and the posttest. The interdomain correlations from both administrations were small, the specific values being a) Interest with Aptitude $= -.08$ pretest and .10 posttest, b) Literacy with Aptitude $= .18$ pretest and .29 posttest, c) Interest with Literacy $= .25$ pretest and .34 posttest. (None of these coefficients was significantly different from those reported in the CALIP manual.) The intercorrelations among the subdomains forming the Aptitude section of the CALIP averaged .26 on the pretest and .45 on the posttest with the Estimation subtest being the one most weakly related to the others in both instances (average correlation equaling .20 and .34 on the pretest and posttest, respectively).

Critique

It was just in the recent past that computers and the skills needed to operate them were a very specialized technology falling within the province of only a few specialists. Increasingly, however, the computer (particularly the microcomputer) is encountered in everyday life, and today everyone is expected to be able to use the computer, at least to some extent. As of 1987, for example, a computer literacy course was a *required* part of the curriculum in 12 states (*Electronic Learning*, 1988) and this figure is probably already outdated.

Previously, psychological tests dealing with computer use were limited both in scope and number. That is, they were concerned primarily with measuring aptitude for computer programming, and such tests were intended primarily for use in the selection of personnel in industrial settings (e.g., the Computer Programmer Aptitude Battery mentioned in the CALIP manual). More recently, with the continuing influx of microcomputers into many spheres of life, a growing number of scales concerned with gauging attitudes towards computers, especially "computer anxiety," have been appearing in the literature. Generally, most of the computer attitude measures must still be viewed as research instruments, and only a few are being sold commercially at this point. An example of an attitude scale is the Computer Attitude Scale (Loyd & Gressard, 1984) mentioned earlier in connection with a discussion of the CALIP's validity.

The CALIP represents a very ambitious undertaking because it attempts to fill the contemporary need for an instrument that will provide a comprehensive assessment that takes into account multiple aspects, such as aptitude, literacy, and interest. In other words, unlike the other scales in the field, the CALIP tries to measure all three relevant attributes using a common standardization population. This eliminates the need for integrating information about an individual's standing on aptitude, literacy, and interest from different tests with possibly different characteristics. From this perspective a sounder logic thus exists for undertaking a profile analysis.

The CALIP manual presents a fairly comprehensive description of the standardization sample, although in view of the test's subject matter and its objectives, even greater detail would not be out of order. For instance, it would be of value to have more specific cross-tabulations of sample characteristics, such as knowledge of programming languages by age. A more detailed and elaborate account needs to be given on the actual process and steps involved in the selection of the standardization group, particularly regarding the nonstudents in the sample, including some statement on the size and characteristics of those who were contacted but who refused to participate. This type of information would allow for a better understanding of any potential bias that may be present in the current norms.

Presently, the norms for the CALIP are divided in terms of age (and on Interest, by sex as well). A key strength of the CALIP is the wide age range it covers. However, given that the CALIP is meant to serve as a device for measuring the skills of all computer-related professions, it is appropriate for the norms to be subdivided by specific professions as well (e.g., programmer, analysts, operator, repairperson, etc.). This provision would allow one to better gauge the relative standing of a particular person within the occupation he or she represents (or wishes to enter). The present standardization sample does not seem to include enough persons from any one profession to permit this type of norming.

The great amount of detail devoted to the description of the standardization group in this review was intentional because it is essential that the potential user be aware of the group that the person being tested is being compared against. This is especially true in the case of computer literacy and interest, which are subject to change quite rapidly over the next decade, perhaps even much earlier. Thus, in the future, the potential user of the CALIP must watch that the norms are not outdated. (There is less potential for this on the Aptitude portion of the CALIP.) It has already been reported that the incidence of computer anxiety has been declining over the last several years among college students (Turner, 1987). There is a similar danger that the test items themselves may become obsolete. For example, a question on the Literacy subtest dealing with the size of floppy discs was written before 3½" discs were available and does not allow for this answer.

The manual is written in a style that is easy to read and does a commendable job of explaining the technical terms necessary to understand the meaning of the reliability and validity data. (All statistical terms are defined so that individuals with limited knowledge of psychometrics can easily understand them.) However, the CALIP manual is somewhat inconsistent regarding the qualifications necessary to administer and interpret the scores. It is our opinion that this instrument can be easily misinterpreted or otherwise abused in the wrong hands, given the IQ-like properties of the CAQ. Therefore, the reviewers would recommend that it only be interpreted by persons who possess at least a "working knowledge" of test theory and vocational counseling. Interpretations by individuals with limited experience in these subjects need to be made cautiously, with the client being informed about these limitations in training.

The actual reliability and validity studies that are discussed in the manual are presented at a level of detail that is sufficient to allow one to judge their quality. Quite appropriately, the data are reported separately at different age levels (and sometimes by sex). Overall, the reliability of the CALIP is impressive. (The decision not to compute alpha coefficients for the Estimation subtest, which is a speed test, was correct because spuriously high reliability coefficients would have resulted.) The validity evidence reviewed in the manual deals mainly with the CALIP's applicability in relation to the measurement of programming skills, even though the 1988 catalog provided by the CALIP's publisher notes that "The CALIP not only measures aptitudes relevant to computer programming but also measures those aptitudes essential for a wide variety of computer-related uses (e.g., graphics, systems analysis, and repair)" (p. 43). The evidence for the CALIP's validity in applications other than programming still remains to be demonstrated (as the developers of the CALIP acknowledge). Therefore, pronouncements about the CALIP's appropriateness for varied uses need to be tempered until sufficient evidence supporting a particular application has been gathered, otherwise it may appear that the test publisher is shifting the burden of demonstrating validity to the consumer of the test, a growing practice that is causing concern in the field of measurement (Mervis, 1985). The reviewers' own study in the context of retraining teachers for the teaching of computer science at the secondary level lends support for the CALIP's use in the selection of appropriate candidates for such programs, although this instrument's lack of a relationship with performance in the instructional design practicum is quite disappointing and troubling, and warrants further study. It is hoped that other investigations will bear out the test authors' expectations for other as yet unvalidated uses.

To make proper use of the Literary section of the CALIP, one also needs to pay proper diligence to the concepts of content validity and curricular validity. (Content validity is the degree to which the items forming a test are representative of the domain that the test intends to measure. Curriculum validity, in turn, refers to the extent to which a given test reflects the content of a local curriculum.) The boundaries of the domain of computer literacy are very hard to define (Bowman, 1986), particularly because the definition of "computer literacy" is still evolving. Some schools are concerned solely with teaching programming languages, certain ones also teach computer electronics and robotics, while others have a focus on providing students with experience in using application programs like word processing, spreadsheets, and data base management (Hashway, 1987; Osgood, 1987).

The authors of the CALIP appear to have embraced an expansive as opposed to a restrictive definition of computer literacy, and thus, their test addresses a broad spectrum of knowledge that relates in some way to computer technology. The CALIP Literacy subtest samples topics ranging from basic electronics (i.e., soldering, integrated circuits, voltage) to the actual operation of a computer. The test items, which encompass both hardware and software questions, span the gamut from elementary to advanced. However, by trying to cover all aspects of the field in a reasonably short subtest, the Literacy portion can ask only a few questions from each content area. This creates a drawback if one is trying to evaluate the success of a computer literacy training program (a suggested use for the CALIP) in which the content of the training is narrower in focus (e.g., dealing with "software" rather than "hardware"). In such a situation, the Literacy subtest would lack curricular validity and consequently, it would not serve as an appropriate evaluation tool for this purpose. (The reviewers' use of the CALIP to measure the effects of a retraining program bears testimony to this point.) Scales like the Literacy subtest, which have "high bandwidth" (many topics covered) but with a "low fidelity" (each topic measured with only a few questions), are most suitable for "screening" purposes and not as a basis for making final irreversible decisions. A brief comment about the contemporary relevance of certain questions on the Literacy test is also in order. Some items (e.g., #6) are mainly of historical interest. Others (e.g., #4, #9) do not adequately take into account the nature of computers (especially microcomputers) as they are known and used today.

The prospective user of the CALIP should also be aware that the computer Interest scale on this instrument is rather unorthodox. Only 20% of the items on this short inventory ask questions about interest in computers per se. On the other items, the computer interest is inferred from knowledge of how people who participate in computer-related activities or have a self-professed interest in computers answered the particular question. The items forming this scale are said to tap interest for four types of endeavors—people oriented, things oriented, numerically oriented, and emotionally oriented. An interest in numeric- and things-oriented activities seems to be equated on this scale with interest in computers. In other words, the Interest scale taps the "correlates" of computer interest more so than the actual construct of computer interest. This may explain why the Interest scale is heterogeneous in nature. (One may recall that the developers of this instrument noted that internal consistency reliability was not computed for the Interest scale because it is heterogeneous in content.) Many psychometricians would question whether under such circumstances (i.e., absence of internal consistency/item homogeneity) one should summate the items into a total score, but this issue is nonetheless debatable.

In sum, the reviewers believe that the CALIP represents a pioneering effort into an important new area. The instrument seems to provide reliable information and may have potential for a number of different applications, but the prospective consumer needs to ascertain if in fact the available validity data already support the scale's application for the potential purpose one has in mind, or whether additional supporting evidence will need to be sought. Although the authors of the CALIP propose that it can be useful in a large variety of contexts and circumstances, the validity data to document the appropriateness for many of these uses still need to be developed. Moreover, in view of the ambiguities regarding the issue of what constitutes computer literacy for the population in general as well as for the different computer-related occupations, it is essential that the prospective user of the CALIP examine the actual test items to make sure that the operational definitions of the constructs measured by this test are consistent with those of the user.

References

Aiken, R.M., & Snelbecker, G.E. (1985). *Development of a model program for preparing computer science teachers at the secondary school level.* Project proposal funded by the National Science Foundation, Grant No. TEI-8550553.

American Educational Research Association, American Psychological Association, & National Council on Measurement in Education (1985). *Standards for Educational and Psychological Testing.* Washington, D.C.: American Psychological Association.

Bowman, R.F., Jr. (1986). Computer literacy: A strategy for cultivating consensus. *Technical Horizons in Education, 13*(10), 60–62.

Hashway, R.M. (1987). Computer education—What is it? *Proceedings of the Conference on Computers on Campus: Integrating Institutional Resources* (Vol. 1, p. 107–112). University of South Carolina, Columbia.

Hearne, J.D., Poplin, M.S., Lasley, J. (1986–87). Predicting mathematics achievement from measures of computer aptitude in junior high students. *Educational Research Quarterly, 10*(4), 18–24.

Loyd, B.H., & Gressard, C. (1984). Reliability and factorial validity of computer attitude scales. *Educational and Psychological Measurement, 44,* 501–505.

Mervis, J. (1985, November). Testing problems cited. *American Psychological Association Monitor,* p. 28.

One hundred and one things you want to know about educational technology: States that require students to take a computer literacy course (1988, May/June). *Electronic Learning,* p. 38.

Osgood, T. (1987, November). Computer literacy: The third generation. *Proceedings of the Conference on Computers on Campus: Integrating Institutional Resources* (Vol. 2, p. 45–47). University of South Carolina, Columbia.

Poplin, M.S., Drew, D.E., & Gable, R.S. (1984). *Computer Aptitude, Literacy, and Interest Profile (manual).* Austin, Texas: PRO-ED.

Roszkowski, M.J., Devlin, S.J., Snelbecker, G.E., Aiken, R.M., & Jacobsohn, H.G. (in press). Validity and temporal stability issues regarding two measures of computer aptitudes and attitudes. *Educational and Psychological Measurement.*

Snelbecker, G.E., Devlin, S.J., Roszkowski, M.J., & Aiken, R.M. (1987, April). *Aptitudes, attitudes and expectations of teachers "retraining" to teach computer science.* Paper presented at the meeting of the American Educational Research Association, Washington, D.C.

Snelbecker, G.E., Devlin, S.J., Roszkowski, M.J., & Aiken, R.M. (1988a, April). *Impact of computer courses on computer technology aptitudes and attitudes.* Paper presented at the meeting of the American Educational Research Association, New Orleans.

Snelbecker, G.E., Devlin, S.J., Roszkowski, M.J., & Aiken, R.M. (1988b, April). *Predicting achievement of teachers retraining to teach BASIC and PASCAL at the secondary level.* Paper presented at the meeting at the American Educational Research Association, New Orleans.

Turner, J.A. (1987, July 22). Familiarity with new technology breeds changes in computer-literacy courses. *The Chronicle of Higher Education,* p. 9, 12.

Betty E. Gridley, Ed.D.
*Assistant Professor of Educational Psychology, Ball State University,
Muncie, Indiana.*

COOPERATIVE PRESCHOOL INVENTORY-REVISED

*Bettye M. Caldwell and Judith H. Freund. Monterey, California:
CTB/McGraw-Hill.*

Introduction

The Cooperative Preschool Inventory-Revised (CPI) is a brief screening test intended for individual use with children ages 3 through 6. Designed to assess achievement in those areas necessary for school success, the current CPI is a revised and shortened form of the original Cooperative Preschool Inventory-Standardization Edition (see *The Seventh Mental Measurements Yearbook* [Buros, 1972] for description and reviews).

This inventory had its origins in the Head Start program in 1965. Dr. Bettye M. Caldwell conceived the idea for the first version of the instrument, for much of the item content, and for the supervision of data analysis of the original sample. Originally named the Preschool Achievement Test, the inventory was developed to enable an assessment of what a disadvantaged child knew prior to his or her introduction to Head Start. The desired outcome was an educational, rather than psychological, test that was easily administered, scored, and interpreted within existing time, space, and equipment constraints. The concern was not to develop a "culture fair test"; indeed, the goal was to display the disadvantage of differing cultural experiences. Caldwell's hypothesis was that, upon entering school, the child who came from a disadvantaged environment would show skill deficits when compared to nondisadvantaged youngsters.

The individual items were chosen on the basis of their match to the curriculum and the perceived importance of the assessed areas to functioning in a classroom environment. Based on her experience in a nursery school for disadvantaged children, Caldwell also included assessment areas that she judged to be especially problematic for these children. Seven subtests were designed to tap the various identified areas: information and vocabulary; number concepts and ordination; concepts of shape, motion, and color; concepts of time, object class, and social functions; visual motor performance; following instructions; and independence and self-help.

The first version of the inventory consisted of 161 items and was field tested in May 1965 by a number of trained examiners invited to participate by the Research and Evaluation Office of Head Start. With some changes, several versions of the scale were developed. Approximately 300 children from New York, Syracuse, Baltimore, Chicago, Los Angeles, a North Dakota Indian reservation, and rural Mississippi were examined using the scale.

After discussion of the results of this original pilot, many changes in format were instituted. The final order of item presentation was designed to maximize interest and reduce fatigue. The scoring system was refined by Donald Soule, who also analyzed data collected from national field testing. (In fact, some literature refers to one version as the Caldwell-Soule Inventory [Sontag, Sella, & Thorndike, 1969].) This new version was called the Preschool Inventory.

Original statistical analyses were performed on data collected from 389 children who participated in Head Start programs during the summer of 1965. Split-half reliabilities, correlations among the subtests, and factor analyses were done on the original 161 items. The researchers then shortened the instrument, eliminating items based on the factor analysis and intercorrelations with other items. Using the original standardization sample, the relationship between the original and the shortened version was .98; the split-half reliability, corrected by the Spearman-Brown method, was .95. The shortened inventory could be administered in 15 minutes.

This shortened form was shortened still further to an inventory of 64 items. Items eliminated were those not discriminating at different age levels. In 1969, the shortened version was distributed as the Preschool Inventory-Experimental Edition. Data from use of this edition are reported in the test manual *Handbook*. The experimental edition, with a few minor clarifying changes in directions for administration, became the Revised Edition in 1970. The placement of items was changed to conform to a more logical sequence, and with a few minor clarifications in scoring directions and the elimination of subtest scores, the instrument assumed its present form. A Spanish edition is listed in the test publisher's catalogue; however, no mention of its development was found in any of the supporting literature.

The CPI consists of an answer-recording leaflet, directions for administration and scoring, and the *Handbook*. (The publisher's catalogue still lists a *Monograph* among the CPI materials, which apparently discussed the development, psychometric characteristics, and uses of the inventory; however, this item is out of print and no longer available.) The authors state in the directions that the additional materials that examiners must supply have been kept to a minimum: a sheet of blank paper; three small metal cars, one each red, yellow, and blue; eight large crayons (jumbo washable Crayola crayons are strongly suggested); a box of checkers, of which only 10 of one color are used; and three cardboard boxes (directions for making these are supplied).

Examiners are given explicit instructions, along with suggestions for when cuing is appropriate (i.e., when the examiner is encouraging a reticent child to speak, when the child provides a vague and/or ambiguous answer, and when the child gives a marginally correct answer).

All 64 questions apparently are administered to all students; the manual offers no suggestions for basals or ceilings. Tasks for the child include copying common geometric shapes, answering general information questions, indicating ordination, recognizing simple quantitative concepts, analyzing social situations, and making comparisons. The examiner is supplied with the answers that were given during standardization and is prompted to provide verbal reinforcement for the child. For example, after the child completes a motor activity, the examiner is instructed to say "That's very good, now sit down in your chair."

The use of subtest scores is contraindicated by the failure of the revised edition items to "hold up" in terms of factor analyses of its constructs; hence, no profile is available. However, the subscales identified on the original instrument are listed in an appendix, which may be misleading if examiners do not carefully read the remainder of the information in the *Handbook*.

Practical Applications/Uses

While the CPI was designed originally for testing Head Start children, (Allerhand, 1967) little information is available on its actual use. The authors suggest that a strength of the instrument is that it is *not* considered "culture fair." It is intended to show the resultant effects of the opportunities lacking for children such as those eligible for Head Start.

The Cooperative Preschool Inventory is to be administered individually by a child's regular teacher. Individual item scoring is somewhat subjective, although sample answers are given. All items are scored as either right or wrong, with non-responses scored as incorrect. The total score is simply the number of correct answers, with a maximum possible of 64.

No guidelines are given for interpretation of scores; however, the *Handbook* provides normative data for various age groups. Raw scores may be converted to percentiles based on age and geographic location. Such normative interpretation seems straightforward and should be easily accomplished by teachers who administer the inventory. What this score indicates, however, is an entirely different matter. The *Handbook* suggests that the inventory measures the overall achievement that a child brings with him or her to the educational experience. If future accomplishments can be gauged by those of the past, the score could be construed as some sort of readiness or school preparedness indicator; however, percentile scores would seem to indicate where a child "stacks up" relative to peers at the beginning of the school experience. Apparently no predictive studies have been undertaken.

Technical Aspects

CPI norms were based on the responses of 1,531 children tested in over 150 Head Start classes throughout the United States in the Fall of 1969. Regional norms are also provided, for regions represented by at least 100 children. The *Handbook* breaks down the standardization sample by age, sex, and ethnic group. Children ages 3-0 to 6-5 were included, with the majority being between 4-0 and 5-5; 49% were boys and 51% girls. The sample was approximately 68% black, 17% white, 6% Mexican-American, and 9% other.

Two types of internal-consistency reliability coefficients were computed: Kuder-Richardson formula 20 and split-half (odd-even) corrected by means of the Spearman-Brown formula. These coefficients ranged from .84 to .92. Standard errors of measurement based on the reliability and standard deviation of a test ranged from 3.1 to 3.9 points. Mean biserial correlations of test items with the total score ranged from .45 to .56. The *Handbook* also provides tables of item difficulty.

Concurrent validity coefficients ranged from .39 to .65. These coefficients indicate the relationship between the Cooperative Preschool Inventory and the Stanford-Binet Intelligence Scale, based on 1,476 children in the standardization sample. Results of analyses of three additional samples also are found in the *Handbook*. Norms are given for 246 4-year-olds from Louisville, Kentucky; 133 children from a migrant opportunity program in Arizona; and 317 children from eight kindergarten centers in North Carolina.

Critique

A thorough literature search, by computer and by hand, failed to show any other studies examining the Cooperative Preschool Inventory. Most of the information is relatively old, (Robinson & Robinson, 1971) especially in light of events in the past 20 or so years. Although the inventory has had several updated copyrights, there is no indication that any revision or updating of norms has been done. Perhaps the lack of research means that the CPI is no longer in use. If so, perhaps it should be assigned to the archives; if not, users need to be cautioned about the outdated normative information.

The CPI has been touted as reflecting students' cultural differences, but the composition of the standardization sample does not indicate this is the case. All the available information is for groups of culturally different and/or disadvantaged youngsters. Therefore, comparisons are being made within a subpopulation rather than within the mainstream. That is, these norms allow the examiner to determine a child's relative position within a group of children who might be expected to be educationally disadvantaged. It certainly would not allow one to determine how these children are achieving when compared to "average" preschoolers.

The CPI format is fairly straightforward and easy to administer. However, other more recent and sophisticated instruments are available that would allow not only the kind of comparisons sought in the development of this instrument, but that also would enable the examiner to determine a great deal more diagnostic information. For example, tests from which subscale information can be used to determine specific domains of concern allow for more individualized interpretation than does a global score alone.

The lack of predictive validity information on the CPI is especially problematic. Why would one be interested in merely tapping preschool achievement if this achievement is not related in any way to future educational success? The use of this inventory in its present form cannot be recommended.

References

Allerhand, M. E. (1967). Effectiveness of parents of Head Start children as administrators of psychological tests. *Journal of Consulting Psychology. 31*, 286–290.

Buros, O. K. (Ed.). (1972). *The seventh mental measurements yearbook.* Highland Park, NJ: Gryphon Press.

Caldwell, B. M., & Freund, J. H. (1968, 1970, 1974, 1980). *Cooperative Preschool Inventory-Revised Edition.* Monterey, CA: CTB/McGraw-Hill.

Robinson, H. B., & Robinson, N. M. (1971). Longitudinal development of very young children in a comprehensive day care program: The first two years. *Child Development, 42,* 1673–1683.

Sontag, M., Sella, A. P., & Thorndike, R. L. (1969). The effect of Head Start training on the cognitive growth of disadvantaged children. *Journal of Educational Measurement, 62,* 387–389.

David Schuldberg, Ph.D.
Associate Professor of Psychology, University of Montana, Missoula, Montana.

CREATIVITY TESTS FOR CHILDREN

J. P. Guilford, Arthur Gershon, Sheldon Gardner, and Philip R. Merrifield. Orange, California: Sheridan Psychological Services.

Introduction

The Creativity Tests for Children (Guilford, 1971) comprise a set of 10 tests developed for use with elementary school-age children to measure a subset of the creativity facets of Guilford's (1967) structure-of-intellect model of intelligence. These tests represent a downward extension of the adult Guilford creativity tests.

In Guilford's famous structure of intellect parallelepiped of multiple primary mental abilities, a slab of 24 of the 120 cells in the model refers to Divergent-Production (DP) abilities. The 10 tests in the Creativity Tests for Children measure 11 of the 12 theoretically possible Divergent Production abilities in the Figural and Semantic content areas of the structure of intellect model; productions of Symbolic and Behavioral contents are not tested by the battery.

The Divergent Production slab in the structure of intellect model is formed by crossing four contents, Figural (F), Symbolic (S), Semantic (M), and Behavioral (B), with six products, Units (U), Classes (C), Relations (R), Systems (S), Transformations (T), and Implications (I). One cell, referring to Figural Relations (DFR), does not have a corresponding test in the Creativity Tests for Children and has not been demonstrated clearly as a factor in work with adults. Another cell, Semantic Transformations (DMT), is represented secondarily by one test in Form A, Names for Stories, primarily a test measuring Divergent Production of Semantic Units (DMU).

J.P Guilford (e.g., 1967) has provided an eloquent theoretical argument and empirical justification for the differentiation of the concept of intelligence, and he and his colleagues have engaged in a long-term research program to investigate the facets of intelligence. His systematic and finite theoretical model contains 120 discrete abilities. Guilford and his co-workers have developed tests and procedures to operationalize a large number of these facets. Using data gathered with these tests, they have embarked on a program of construct validation, relating test scores to criteria and attempting to demonstrate the facets of the structure-of-intellect model empirically, primarily through factor-analytic procedures. Up to 98 of the 120 cells in the model have been demonstrated, and Guilford (1971) states that these include 23 of the 24 Divergent Production abilities (DFR being the only exception). The structure of intellect model, and the measurement instruments based on it, have been criticized on both theoretical and empirical grounds (See, e.g., Vernon, 1979). In particular, questions have been raised about the number and the

---

The reviewer would like to thank George Camp for his very useful comments on this manuscript.

validity of the particular factors in the model, and concerning Guilford's use of "subjective" rotation methods to demonstrate them. Nevertheless, this model has been extremely influential, especially so in research on creativity.

Guilford's arguments for a multifaceted conception of intelligence have contributed to the distinction between traditionally measured intelligence (corresponding largely to the Convergent and Memory operations in the structure of intellect model) and creative aspects of intellect. Guilford posits the existence of 24 distinct aspects of creative productions (Divergent Productions). The construct of Divergent Productions or Divergent Thinking has played a central role in research on creativity in both adults and children, and the distinction between Divergent and Convergent thinking and the use of different tests and procedures to measure them is fairly well accepted by workers in the area of cognitive abilities. However, most researchers and theoreticians have focused on a more limited set of Divergent Production abilities than are present in Guilford's model. Divergent Thinking is often considered as a single variable, most commonly measured by an unusual uses test. This review will focus on the utility and the practicality of subdividing the Divergent Thinking construct for assessment purposes and will also describe some ways that the Creativity Tests for Children can be useful in this task.

The Creativity Tests for Children (1971) were developed by Guilford, A. Gershon, S. Gardner, and P. R. Merrifield (who share authorship of a number of the tests) to provide a downward extension of the well-known Adult Structure-of-Intellect Tests for use with a school-age population. Despite the importance of the structure-of-intellect theory and the widespread use of the adult tests based on the model, the Creativity Tests for Children have not caught on in the assessment of school-age populations and in creativity research and have generated little research outside of that of the Guilford group. The Torrance (1966) tests as well as tests from the Wallach and Kogan (1965), Getzels and Jackson (1962), and other studies are more commonly used in research. Seven of the Divergent Production abilities are measured by Meeker's (1982) tests.

Seven of the Creativity Tests for Children are based on adult tests, some with different instructions and items. Writing Sentences, Make Something Out of It, and Hidden Letters were developed specifically for the children's battery.

Normative data for the Creativity Tests for Children are provided in the manual (Guilford, 1971) based on research with close to 1,300 school children in California and Florida. This sample provided a modicum of ethnic diversity and was composed primarily of middle- to upper-middle class children, who also varied in whether they had been identified as gifted. The manual provides correlations of the Creativity Tests for Children with teachers' ratings of creativity and scores on several of the Torrance (1966) tests. The normative and validation research reported in the manual for the Creativity Tests for Children is preliminary and not rigorous and has been well criticized on methodological grounds by Yamamoto (1978).

Guilford et al. have made extensive use of a factor-analytic approach to construct validation. Earlier work isolated 16 of the 24 Divergent Production facets at the ninth-grade level and 7 at the sixth-grade level (see Dellas & Gaier, 1970). Guilford and Hoepfner (1971) refer to a factor-analytic study with sixth-grade children using five tests measuring Divergent Semantic abilities, including tests similar to or the same as a subset of the Creativity Tests for Children. But as Yamamoto

(1978) has stated, more research is needed to investigate both the validity and the psychometric properties of the Creativity Tests for Children.

The Creativity Tests for Children are intended primarily for use with elementary school-age children; the test manual (Guilford, 1971) provides norms for Grades 4–6. There is no theoretical upper-age limit for the tests; they overlap in content, items, and instructions with adult tests in the Guilford battery. Guilford (1975) notes that the tests could be used unchanged with adults, as the instructions and materials make no reference to "children." These instructions contrast those of the Torrance (1966) tests, which are directed towards the elementary school-age population, and make the Creativity Tests for Children potentially useful in studies of college-age populations or in longitudinal studies using two forms of the same tests.

Scoring and administration guides are provided for each test. There is also a B Form of the test, containing one additional semantic test, presumably Picture Writing, measuring DMT[1]. Names for Stories, primarily a measure of DMU, does not yield a sufficient number of clever responses when used with children to provide a reliable measure of DMT, and this test originally was considered to measure two abilities (DMU contaminated with DMT). The inclusion of Picture Writing in Form B relieves the test of being used as a measure of two abilities.

The Creativity Tests for Children are pencil-and-paper tests, administered in a group setting. The tests are carefully timed and use the format, familiar from the adult Guilford tests, of having separately timed parts (two, in the children's tests) running from 3 to 4 minutes each. The subject is allowed to work on only one of these parts at a time. Each test has its own answer booklet, and the subject marks his or her answer directly in the booklet. The tests take between 8 and 12 minutes, with 2 to 4 minutes required per test for instructions. The entire set of Creativity Tests for Children takes approximately 102 minutes. The test authors are flexible regarding the order of the tests within the battery, suggesting that an assessment begin with a test that will be perceived as easier and more interesting, (i.e., Make Something Out of It or Hidden Letters), and then alternate the administration of Figural and Semantic tests.

A friendly, relaxed, interested, and low-threat testing atmosphere is encouraged, and the children are told that the test results will have no effect on school grades, that they should enjoy the testing, and that it is similar to playing a game. One proctor is recommended per approximately 20 students to help with the instructions, to assist in starting and stopping students between tests and sections of tests, and to help children who have difficulty in beginning a test. The proctors can also ensure that subjects only work on one section of a test at a time. The instructions are read aloud while the subjects read silently. Guilford (1971) stresses the effect that "minor variations in conditions" can have on scores, and emphasizes the importance of standardized administration procedures and careful timing of the tests.

Subjects' scores on the tests are based on the number of different acceptable responses that they have produced. (Making Objects also scores the complexity of

---

[1]The reviewer presumes that the new test added to Form B is Picture Writing. However, this review is based only on an examination of Form B.

the designs produced.) For this reason, French (1978) has criticized the tests as measuring "glibness" or fluency rather than originality or cleverness. Training and experience with Divergent Thinking tests may be necessary for a scorer to be able to grasp the distinctions involved; the scoring guides for each test provide useful rules and examples.

Practical Applications/Uses

Potential applications of the Creativity Tests for Children include classroom creativity testing for educational planning, selection of youngsters for programs attempting to maintain or develop creative talent, and research with elementary school-age children. Consumers of this test are likely to be researchers, educators, and those planning or evaluating creativity-enhancing interventions.

The Creativity Tests for Children assess Divergent Production abilities in the Semantic-verbal and Figural-visual content areas (See Table 1). Of the 12 possible abilities in these areas, only DFR is not covered. Semantic units and transformations (DMU and DMT) are confounded in Form A, where they are both measured by Names for Stories.

The structure of intellect abilities measured by each of the Creativity Tests for Children, as well as the name of the corresponding adult test, if one exists, are listed in Table 1.

The 10 tests in the Creativity Tests for Children measure 11 Divergent Production abilities. As has been mentioned, Names for Stories taps Divergent Production of Semantic Units and transformations (DMU and DMT). Nonclever responses to this test represent operations on units, each title representing a unit of thought. A clever response to the test represents an operation on transformations for "it takes some shifting of ideas to be clever" (Guilford, 1971, p. 4). Clever titles occur only rarely in a school-age population, and clever and nonclever responses are combined in the scoring of the children's version of the test.

Divergent Production of Semantic Units has also been referred to as "Ideational Fluency" and "Originality." What to Do with It, based on the very popular adult test Alternate Uses, measures Divergent Production of Semantic Classes (DMC), also called "Spontaneous Flexibility." Thinking of unusual uses for common objects represents a shifting of classes to which the common object could belong. As has been noted, this is a frequently studied domain of Divergent Production, measured in different studies by one of a number of very similar tests.

Similar Meanings measures Divergent Production of Semantic Relations (DMR), sometimes called "Associational Fluency." The test requires that the subject provide synonyms, considered by the test authors to be related meanings or "related things."

Writing Sentences measures Divergent Production of Semantic Systems (DMS), also called "Expressional Fluency." The subject forms sentences of 2 or 3 words from a list of 5 words; the system that is being created is a "semantic system" or sentence.

Picture Writing is a newer test added in Form B and measures Divergent Production of Semantic Transformations (DMT). The subject is presented with a word having multiple meanings and is asked to make sketches that could represent these

Table 1

Creativity Tests for Children

Test	SOI Facet	Adult Form
SEMANTIC TESTS:		
Names for Stories	DMU; also DMT	Plot titles (adaptation)
What to Do with It	DMC	Alternate Uses (adaptation)
Similar Meanings	DMR	Associational Fluency (I) (adaptation)
Writing Sentences	DMS	
Picture Writing (Form B only)	DMT	Alternate Signs
Kinds of People	DMI	Possible Jobs (adaptation)
FIGURAL TESTS		
Make Something Out of It	DFU	Somewhat similar to Sketches
Different Letter Groups	DFC	Alternate Letter Groups
Making Objects	DFS	Making Objects (adaptation)
Hidden Letters	DFT	
Adding Decorations	DFI	Decorations

various meanings. Clearly, this test has a figural component despite the fact that it is a semantic test.

Kinds of People measures Divergent Production of Semantic Implications (DMI), also known as "Elaboration." In this case, the implication is a connection between an emblem and an occupation that might correspond to it. This task requires social comprehension and an ability to desymbolize the emblem, and also calls upon the subject to imagine a fictitious society in which novel emblems identify jobs.

In the area of figural contents, Make Something Out of It measures Divergent Production of Figural Units (DFU). The subject is asked to name objects that contain a particular shape, such as a triangle, which is presented pictorially. The test measures "the facile generation of ideas, where the ideas are units" (Guilford, 1971, p. 6). Here a semantic response is made to a figural stimulus.

Different Letter Groups measures the ability to generate a variety of Figural Classes or groupings (DFC). The groupings here consist of letters that have a particular common property, such as the use of slanting lines; note that this figural task also has a somewhat semantic content. Guilford (1971) notes that there has been little research on DFC.

Making Objects measures Divergent Production of Figural Systems (DFS), in this case the construction of different pictorial objects from elementary figures and lines.

Hidden Letters is a task that is similar to tests of perceptual disembedding (e.g., Witkin's Embedded Figures Test) and measures Divergent Production of Figural Transformations (DFT). It presents the task of finding letters of the alphabet in sets of identical complex figures. The transformation "lies in the act of making lines in the given figure play new roles as parts of letters" (Guilford, 1971, p. 7).

Adding Decorations asks the subject to draw decorations on line drawings of common objects and measures Divergent Production of Figural Implications (DFI). Generating these decorations represents the forming of visual-figural implications because "it is assumed that the lines that [the subject] adds are suggested either by the shapes of the objects or by [the subject's] knowledge of such objects that [the subject] has seen" (Guilford, 1971, p. 7). Note that one figural ability has not been demonstrated in Guilford and his colleagues' factorial studies. The Divergent Production of Figural Relationships (DFR) and the Creativity Tests for Children do not contain a test to measure this attribute.

Scoring guides for each test contain both general rules for scoring and specific examples. Scoring of subjects' responses on Divergent Production tests is a complex endeavor, and a certain amount of subjective judgment is called for. The manual emphasizes the importance of using experienced scores to score the tests, but does not report interrater scoring reliabilities. Although profile forms have been developed for each test, these were not examined for this review.

Technical Aspects

Arguments for the validity of the Creativity Tests for Children as measures of the abilities in the Divergent Production slab of Guilford's (1967) model of intelligence are largely based on arguments from research with the adult tests, and the actual functioning of the children's tests has been scantily studied, with the results not readily available. Different studies have also used different sets of tests as well as variants on the tests in the Creativity Tests for Children battery, making it difficult to compare test results across studies. For the three new tests developed specifically for the Creativity Tests for Children, Guilford states that "it was thought that if they proved to have fairly high reliabilities and low correlations with other tests, they could be assumed to measure their intended abilities" (Guilford, 1971, p. 8). This assumption, of course, is not a substitute for empirical work with the specific tests. The connection of the Creativity Tests for Children with the adult Guilford tests is not established, and the new tests are fit into the structure of intellect model largely on the basis of their "resemblance" to the adult tests or on conceptual grounds.

Moreover, the reliability and validity coefficients for the Creativity Tests for Children, including the three new tests, are variable and in some cases quite low. Regarding reliability coefficients, Guilford acknowledges, "tests of divergent-production abilities have not been noted for high reliability. Apparently, measures of the efficiency with which an individual can generate alternative items of information are dependent upon a number of irrelevant determining circumstances" (Guilford, 1971, p. 11). Correlations with teacher ratings of creativity are cited in Guilford and Hoepfner (1971) and range from -.04 to .54. The manual also reports correlations of the tests with IQ and with four of the Torrance (1966) tests.

As has been noted previously, Guilford was aware of the sensitivity of these and other Divergent Production tests to instructions and to motivational factors. Other research (e.g., Harrington, 1975) has indicated that variations in the instructions for Divergent Thinking tests can improve their performance as measures of the construct. This raises the question as to whether the instructions for the Creativity Tests for Children should be modified to include, for example, the instruction "Be Creative," and to give examples of the criteria for a creative response on each test. In addition, it is likely that examiners using these and other such tests need to pay greater attention to the techniques used to elicit cooperation from subjects, establish rapport, induce motivation to perform on the tests, and maintain a nonthreatening yet productive atmosphere.

Suggestions have also been made for the modification of scoring rules for Divergent Production tests (see Harrington, 1972). In general, "duplicates" or similar responses to an item are only scored once. The scorer, therefore, needs to develop rules to supplement those provided in the guides for determining what constitutes a "duplicate" response as opposed to a new idea. Responses that are excessively vague or general are also not scored, although for some of the tests the scorer is encouraged to be lenient in the sense of trying to tell what the subject had in mind. Additional lists of categories developed by other researchers (i.e., Harrington, 1972) have proven to be very useful in scoring the adult Structure of Intellect tests, and are likely to prove necessary in work with the Creativity Tests for Children. The scoring guides that come with the tests do provide both general rules and a series of examples, although they acknowledge that these usually cannot cover all possible situations.

The split-half reliabilities of Creativity Tests for Children tend to be higher than those of the corresponding adult forms, although estimated reliabilities for the individual tests range from only .42 to .97, suggesting, among other things, that the tests may be too brief. Guilford (1971) defends the use of short tests, pointing out that this allows for a wide sampling of the child's behavior through the use of multiple tests, adding that the examiner cannot rely on retaining a child's interest for a long period of time. However, one purpose of Form B was to allow lengthening of the individual tests to increase their reliabilities.

Research using the Creativity Tests for Children has mainly come from within the Guilford group. The use of individual tests in the battery has been unsystematic, with different versions and tests used in different studies. Very little research has used the entire battery in its present form. The criterion validity and factor-analytic studies reported in Guilford and Hoepfner (1971) have already been mentioned. These use only a partially overlapping set of tests. This subset of tests was also used in a study of personality traits and creativity test scores (also described in Guilford & Hoepfner, 1971). Research with the tests has also been reported in two articles on the distinction between traditionally measured intelligence and Divergent Production abilities.

Guilford and Hoepfner (1966) report correlations ranging between .13 and .50 for some of the Creativity Tests for Children and IQ as measured by the California Test of Mental Maturity. They note that when subjects' scores on the Divergent Production tests and IQ are plotted, the resultant scatter plots are triangular rather than elliptical in shape. Low IQ subjects show only low Divergent Production scores, whereas high IQ subjects receive a range of Divergent Production scores. The test authors use the shape of these scatter plots to argue for the distinctness of Divergent Production abilities and conventionally measured IQ. These data are reexamined for the individual creativity tests by Guilford and Christensen (1973). Reiss and Gold (1977) used one of the Creativity Tests for Children, Making Objects, as a measure of visual-figural problem-solving ability in a study of the relationship between rated creativity and the availability of a child's father. A nonstandard form of this test was used, modified for preschool children.

The Creativity Tests for Children manual presents correlations with several of the Torrance tests (see p. 15). Only four of the Torrance tests were used in this study, including Torrance Verbal tests 4 and 5 (Product Improvement and Unusual Uses, respectively). Guilford suggests that these two tests measure mainly DMI and DMT, because when combined they are correlated with Names for Stories ($r = $ .22) and Kinds of People ($r = $ .35). The low correlation of these Torrance Verbal tests, which included Unusual Uses, with What to Do with It is surprising, considering the similar content of the two tests.

Torrance Figural tests 1 and 2 were also used in this study. Torrance Figural test 1 is Picture Construction, and Figural test 2 is Picture Completion. Combined scores on these tests were correlated with Names for Stories (a measure of DMU and DMT; $r = $ .28). Guilford summarizes the disappointingly low correlations between these two sets of creativity tests by saying, "In general, the conclusion must be that the two test batteries measure mostly different Structure of Intellect abilities" (1971, p. 15). It is also likely that the fact that the subjects who took both the Torrance tests and the Creativity Tests for Children were in a gifted subsample led to low correlation coefficients due to a restricted range of (high) talent.

Critique

Primary advantages of the Creativity Tests for Children are that the tests are derived from an explicit theoretical model and allow relatively wide content sampling in the Divergent Production domain. The tests include the distinction between Verbal (Semantic) and Figural (Visual) productions, a distinction also observed in the Torrance (1966) tests.

Creativity researchers vary greatly in their selection of measures, due to the wide range of constructs included under the umbrella term *creativity* and the predominance of very different measurement methods to assess these abilities. At this time it is difficult to make assertions about which of these tests of putative abilities provide solid measures or markers of the creativity construct(s), or to decide which of these measures should be included in a creativity battery.

The overall Guilford project continues to point to the importance of studying different facets of Divergent Production abilities, and there seems to be a need for continued investigating of the factorial diversity of this construct. The continued utility of the Creativity Tests for Children is likely to be in construct validation studies of Divergent Production abilities. It will be useful for studies to utilize a large-scale battery composed of a variety of Divergent Thinking tests in factor analytic studies. In addition, the Creativity Tests for Children can be useful for longitudinal studies and the investigation of the structural invariance or instability of these abilities across development.

The Creativity Tests for Children do not tap Behavioral contents, and thus do not measure much of what could be considered creativity in the area of social intelligence. The assessment of individual differences in the area of social cognition is likely to be especially useful in studying the relationship of creative functioning to personality style, and in the study of creativity in relation to social desirability and psychopathology.

In comparing the Creativity Tests for Children with the Torrance (1966) Tests of Creative Thinking, this review has noted that both sets of tests contain the distinction between figural and verbal aspects of Divergent Thinking. Intercorrelations of the tests, as with creativity tests in general, have been found to be low, presenting a problem for the operationalization of the creativity construct as consisting of a set (or even several sets) of relatively homogenous abilities.

This reviewer will repeat Yamamoto's (1978) statement that the Creativity Tests for Children represent "a useful research instrument that awaits further exploration" and to echo the warning that the use of such a set of instruments can become "involutional in character" (p. 243). The time is ripe for an integration of a number of abilities, measured by a variety of tests, generated from different theoretical perspectives, and tapped by different measurement techniques. An exciting development would be a further integration of neuroscience and information processing approaches with psychometric methods for the study of abilities. The abilities represented by the Divergent Production slab of Guilford's model are likely to play an important role in such an integration. At the present time the Creativity Tests for Children are no longer commercially available. This review argues for their preservation and for their continued usefulness in studying the dimensionality of the Divergent Thinking construct.

References

This list includes text citations and suggested additional reading.

Davis, G.A. (1973). *Psychology of problem solving*. New York: Basic Books.
Dellas, M., & Gaier, E.L. (1970). Identification of creativity: The individual. *Psychological Bulletin, 73*, 55–73.
French, J.W. (1978). Review of the Creativity Tests for Children. In O.K. Buros (Ed.), *The eighth mental measurements yearbook* (Vol. 1, pp. 363–365). Highland Park, NJ:Gryphon Press.

Getzels, J.W., & Jackson, P.W. (1962). *Creativity and intelligence*. New York: Wiley.

Guilford, J.P. (1950). Creativity. *American Psychologist, 5,* 444–454.

Guilford, J.P. (1959). Three faces of intellect. *American Psychologist, 14,* 469–479.

Guilford, J.P. (1967). *The nature of human intelligence*. New York: McGraw-Hill.

Guilford, J.P (1971). *Creativity Tests for Children: A manual of interpretation*. Orange, CA: Sheridan Psychological Services.

Guilford, J.P. (1975). Varieties of creative giftedness, their measurement and development. *Gifted Child Quarterly, 19,* 107–121.

Guilford, J.P., & Christensen, P.R. (1973). The one-way relationship between creative potential and IQ. *Journal of Creative Behavior, 7,* 247–252.

Guilford, J.P., Gardner, S., Gershon, A., & Merrifield, P.R. (1971). *Creativity Tests for Children*. Orange, CA: Sheridan Psychological Services.

Guilford, J.P., & Hoepfner, R. (1966). Creative potential as related to measures of IQ and verbal comprehension. *Indian Journal of Psychology, 41,* 7–16.

Guilford, J.P., & Hoepfner, R. (1971). *The analysis of intelligence*. New York: McGraw Hill.

Harrington, D.M. (1972). *Effects of instructions to "be creative" on three tests of divergent thinking abilities*. Unpublished doctoral dissertation, University of California, Berkeley.

Harrington, D.M. (1975). Effects of explicit instructions to "be creative" on the psychological meaning of divergent thinking test scores. *Journal of Personality, 43,* 434–454.

Meeker, M. (1982). *SOI Creativity Test*. Vida, OR: SOI Systems.

Reis, M., & Gold, D. (1977). Relation of paternal availability to problem solving and sex-role orientation in young boys. *Psychological Reports, 40,* 823–829.

Torrance, E.P. (1966). *Torrance Tests of Creative Thinking: Norms-Technical manual*. Princeton, NJ: Personnel Press.

Wallach, M.A., & Kogan, N. (1965). *Modes of thinking in young children*. New York: Holt, Rinehart, & Winston.

Vernon, P.E. (1979). *Intelligence: Heredity and environment*. San Francisco: Freeman.

Yamamoto, K. (1978). Review of the Creativity Tests for Children. In O.K. Buros (Ed.), *The eighth mental measurements yearbook* (Vol. 1, pp. 365–367). Highland Park, NJ: Gryphon Press.

Ric Brown, Ed.D.

Professor of Education, California State University, Fresno, Fresno, California.

DECISION MAKING INVENTORY

Richard Johnson, William C. Coscarelli, and JaDean Johnson. Columbus, Ohio: Marathon Consulting and Press.

Introduction

The Decision Making Inventory (DMI) is designed to assess an individual's preferred style of decision making. It was developed as an aid to help people understand how they make their decisions.

The DMI is based on a theory of decision making developed by Johnson (1978a), who suggested that a particularly relevant individual difference was variously termed as cognitive style, learning style, or decision making style. These differences were said to reflect a preferred way of gathering, organizing, and processing information. He further noted that the understanding of these differences was important in interpersonal and professional relationships. Johnson suggested that two distinct dimensions are discernible in most decision-making situations: information gathering (systematic or spontaneous) and information analysis (internal or external).

The manual contains over 20 pages of description of the theoretical underpinnings of the theory. A framework is provided using vectors to present the concept of the multiple forces exerted on an individual in a decision-making situation. These forces are noted to have both direction and value, leading an individual to a decision.

Rich Johnson, a colleague of Coscarelli's, developed a theory to aid practicing counselors in understanding client decision-making style and to aid researchers in conducting research in the area. He adopted an inductive-deductive strategy (Carkhuff, Alexik, Anderson, 1967) that began with observation of behaviors, classification of behaviors, and validation of the model. Johnson (1978a) developed an initial version of the scale in 1978 with a second version completed prior to his death later that same year. A third version was developed in 1979 (Coscarelli & Stonewater, 1979) with a fourth and fifth version, Form G, developed by Coscarelli in 1980. He developed also Forms H and I, which are reported in a 1986 supplement to the original manual.

The DMI is printed on a sheet with clear directions at the top and a place for name and other optional information as necessary. Each of the 20 questions is followed by a series of six small circles. The first circle follows the word "never" and the sixth circle precedes the word "always." Students are instructed to rate each item as it pertains to behavior in their personal lives.

Practical Applications/Uses

Procedures for administration are briefly explained in the testing manual. While qualifications of the examiner are not covered, it is clear from other parts of the

159

manual that a counselor is needed for interpretation and discussion with the respondent. The clearly written directions are printed on the same page with the DMI questions and there is space for respondent identification if required. The examiner is informed not to offer explanations or interpretation of any question during the 10-minute administration time.

In a 1986 scoring supplement, procedures are explained for scoring the inventory depending on the group being assessed (e.g., Form H for high school and college students, Form I for working adults). The supplement as well as the original manual describe scoring the DMI as "a conceptually simple process, but [it] does seem to confuse many" (p. 3 of the supplement, p. 31 of the original manual). A grid is provided to make scoring easier, especially if respondents are to score their own DMI.

Four scores are obtained from the DMI representing the subscales of Spontaneous, Systematic, Internal and External.

The Systematic subscale reflects an individual's deliberate movement from goal to goal. Systematic individuals make a choice based on data and will stay with that choice until more data are collected. These individuals think logically and approach decisions in an analytical way. The Spontaneous subscale reflects a style characterized by easy movement from goal to goal. Spontaneous decision makers are said to personalize the alternatives before acting. They want to act quickly, and their reactions seem to be more extreme. The External subscale attempts to capture a style wherein an individual must talk about a decision. The greater the decision, the greater amount of discussion that is needed. In contrast, the Internal subscale reflects private processing of alternatives. Therefore, the two dimensions described form different types of decision-making styles: spontaneous-internal, spontaneous-external, systematic-internal, systematic-external.

While each respondent fills in one of only six circles next to each of the 20 questions, the scoring guide assigns the value 1 to "never" and 7 to "always." The test author leaves out the value of 4 and justifies the 6-point scale stating that many have a tendency to choose the middle "almost as instinct"; therefore, a decision one way or the other was forced. For each scale, for each form, the items comprising the scale are given. Scores for the subscales are then found by adding the responses for the given items. Although 20 items appear on the DMI, only 13 are used for Form H and 14 for Form I, with the others described as "fillers" by Coscarelli. On the subscales with three items, a top score of 21 is possible. On the four-item subscales, a weight is assigned to limit the top score to 21. Once a score is found for each scale, an individual style is described as the greater of the two scores on the spontaneous-systematic dimensions and the greater of the two scores on the internal. Therefore, one could be any of the potential four combinations (i.e., spontaneous-internal, etc.). In case of a tied score on spontaneous-systematic, systematic gets chosen as does external in cases of an internal-external tie.

Revisions since 1977 have led to two forms at the present time, Form H (previously Form G) for high school and college students and Form I for working adults. Data for Form G has come from college students (at Southern Illinois University exclusively) attending freshman orientation, required business courses, or chemistry classes (overall N was greater than 1,000). Its revision, Form H, has recent data from Ohio State University freshmen ($N = 137$) and Illinois gifted high school students ($N = 75$). For Form I, data are reported from special education teachers ($N = 80$), Illinois FHA bankers ($N = 62$), and national training professionals ($N = 30$).

Two examples are presented in the manual regarding use of the DMI and related theory in counseling settings. One example in a career counseling setting suggests that a counselor assess a client's decision-making style independent of the DMI, then use the DMI to help refine the style. Discussions of the individual's style may help them make career decision choices. The example given is one who might have a spontaneous style, getting excited about each new occupation encountered and uncertain as to which one is the best. The career counselor would encourage the client to use the style to sort through information while making multiple choices. While their mind may be changing frequently, the clients are actively involved in getting data.

In the group counseling example given, the test author notes that the group process is enhanced by each member having to consider a variety of styles. Understanding that an external individual will want to talk everything out while the spontaneous individual wants to get on with it may aid the group as it moves toward its goal.

Technical Aspects

Estimates of reliability for Form G (over the five revisions) are noted from seven samples. Test-retest coefficients are reported to range from .27 to .71 for the four scales. Alpha coefficients range from .23 to .73. In all reports, the Spontaneous scale is consistently the least reliable. The test author notes that the estimates reported for Form G are "acceptable" given only three items per scale.

More recently, reliability estimates are reported in a supplementary writing for Forms H and I. For Form H, alpha coefficients range from .30 to .69, and from .34 to .73 for Form I.

Starting in 1981 with Coscarelli's fifth revision of Form G of the DMI, three different factor-analytic studies report confirmation of four factors with variance extracted ranging from 54% to 60%. Intercorrelation of the factors range from positive and negatives near 0 to .81. While no correlations are reported for the DMI and other scales, a factor analysis was shown incorporating the DMI with Kolb's (1976) Learning Style Inventory and the Decision Making Style subscale (Harren, 1983). The analysis from the 13 scales with 67 undergraduate students at Ohio State University showed no overlap of the DMI with Kolb's scales, but the Systematic scale shared a factor with Harren's Rational and Intuitive scales and the Spontaneous scale shared a factor with Harren's Intuitive and Dependent scales. The Internal and External DMI scales formed one, bipolar factor.

In terms of norms, data are reported for the four classifications of decision-making styles for gender, high school percentile rank, college GPA and class grade, and ACT scores. No analysis was accomplished with the tables reporting only means and frequencies.

Critique

Johnson's original goal of developing a theoretical framework for practicing counselors for understanding client decision making and providing aid to research in the area has been partially met by the DMI. Counselors can use results of the DMI in conjunction with the theoretical underpinnings in the manual to guide discussions with clients. The emphasis is on "guide discussions" rather than substantiate individual styles because the technical aspects of the DMI are not extremely well developed.

While numerous reliability studies are presented, test-retest and alpha coefficients are generally low and not very stable across the studies. While the test author states that the reliabilities are "acceptable" given only three or four items per subscale, it is not clear why such occurred. The instrument contains 20 items, of which 8 are described as fillers and are not used. It would have seemed reasonable over the course of 10 years to increase the number of items per subscale while keeping the overall length of the scale at approximately 20 items. Reports from the factor analyses over the years seem to substantiate the four factors, although several of the factors are fairly highly correlated. No evidence of use of the DMI as a research instrument is reported.

In sum, the DMI may be most useful as an inventory in counseling settings on courses where individuals are exploring how they make decisions. Discussions centered on the four styles presented may offer some degree of insight into an individual's decision-making style.

References

This list includes text citations and suggested additional reading.

Carkhuff, R.R., Alexik, M., & Anderson, S. (1967). Do we have a theory of vocational choice? *Personnel and Guidance Journal, 46,* 335–345.

Coscarelli, W.C. (1983). Developing a decision making inventory to assess Johnson's decision making styles. *Measurement and Evaluation in Guidance, 16,* 149–160.

Coscarelli, W.C. (1983). Decision making styles and the group process. *Performance and Instruction, 22*(8), 22–25.

Coscarelli, W.C., & Gordon, V. (1983, April). *A unified theory of individual differences?* Paper presented at the annual meeting of the National Society for Performance and Instruction, Detroit.

Coscarelli, W.C., & Stonewater, J.K. (1979). *The Decision Making Inventory—Form C.* Unpublished manuscript.

Coscarelli, W.C., & Stonewater, J.K. (1980). Understanding psychological styles in instructional development consultation. *Journal of Instructional Development, 3*(2), 16–22.

Harren, V. (1983). *Assessment of Career Decision Making manual.* Los Angeles: Western Psychological Services.

Johnson, R.H. (1978a). Individual styles of decision making: A theoretical model for counseling. *The Personnel and Guidance Journal, 56,* 530–536.

Johnson, R.H. (1978b). *The Decision Making Inventory.* Unpublished manuscript.

Kolb, D. (1976). *Learning Style Inventory technical manual.* Boston: McBer Co.

Piper, R. (1978). *A comparative, factor-analytic study of the Jungian Type Survey and Johnson's Decision Making Inventory.* Unpublished doctoral dissertation, Southern Illinois University at Carbondale.

Stonewater, J.K. (1981, October). *Four conversations: The academic advisor and decision making theory.* Paper presented at the meeting of the National Association of Academic Advisors, Indianapolis.

Janet E. Spector, Ph.D.

Assistant Professor, College of Education, University of Maine, Orono, Maine.

DECODING SKILLS TEST

Ellis Richardson and Barbara DiBenedetto. Parkton, Maryland: York Press, Inc.

Introduction

The Decoding Skills Test (DST) is a criterion-referenced diagnostic test of word recognition. The test measures three basic skills within the decoding domain: a) knowledge of sight vocabulary, b) application of phonics patterns, and c) word recognition in context.

Ellis Richardson, Ph.D., and Barbara DiBenedetto, B.A. developed the test over a 3-year period (1978–81) under a contract with the National Institute of Child Health and Human Development (NICHD). Dr. Richardson is a psychologist in the child psychiatric division of the Nathan S. Kline Institute for Psychiatric Research and he teaches in the Department of Psychiatry at New York University Medical Center. He has published extensively in the field of developmental dyslexia. DiBenedetto is associated with the City University of New York. At the time the test was developed, she was a researcher at the Kline Institute for Psychiatric Research.

The DST was initially conceived as a research tool. According to Richardson (1985), the objective was to develop an instrument that would identify children with developmental dyslexia and permit testing specific hypotheses about developmental dyslexia. Since its publication in 1985, the test has become widely available as an educational tool for diagnosing and remediating reading difficulties.

The DST kit includes the manual of instructions, presentation book, basal/ceiling scoring key cards, scoring booklets, and phonics profile worksheets. A stopwatch (not included in the kit) is recommended for recording time on one of the subtests. The manual of instructions describes the test design, administration and scoring procedures, and technical characteristics of the test (i.e., reliability and validity). It also includes scoring examples and four interpretive case studies.

The test is individually administered. The spiral-bound presentation booklet sets up like an easel, with the instructions facing the examiner and the test items facing the child. Separate cards summarizing the decision-rules for stopping and starting, known as the basal/ceiling and passage scoring cards, facilitate movement through the test. Verbal instructions for each subtest are given in the presentation booklet, although the examiner is advised that they do not have to be read verbatim to the student. Instead, one is urged to adopt a style appropriate for each child.

The test was designed to assess word recognition skills through the fifth-grade level. More advanced word lists were not included because students generally have fully developed decoding skills if they can read beyond the fifth-reader level.

163

The DST comprises three subtests. Subtest I (Basal Vocabulary) assesses skill in reading aloud lists of words selected from 10 widely used basal reading programs. Each list corresponds to a reader level ranging from preprimer through the second half of Grade 5. The 11 lists of 10-words each are arranged in order of increasing difficulty.

Subtest II (Phonics Patterns) measures proficiency in reading lists of real words and nonsense words that exemplify the regularities of our spelling system. The items vary in four dimensions: consonant pattern (single or multiple), vowel pattern (short vowel, marked long vowel, and vowel digraph), syllable pattern (monosyllabic and polysyllabic) and meaning (real and nonsense words). From a total of 24 lists containing five items each, the lists are divided into four sections: monosyllabic real words, polysyllabic real words, monosyllabic nonsense words, and polysyllabic nonsense words. The six lists in each section represent the following phonics patterns: a) single consonant, short vowel (CVC); b) multiple consonant, short vowel (CCVC); c) single consonant, long vowel (CVCe); d) multiple consonant, long vowel (CCVCe); e) single consonant, vowel digraph (CVV); and f) multiple consonant, vowel digraph (CCVV).

The five real words in each list in Sections 1 and 2 are arranged by grade level according to the Harris and Jacobson (1972) graded vocabulary lists. The words were selected from the second-through sixth-grade lists. No first-grade words were chosen because "first grade words are often memorized as sight words and the subtest seeks to determine the degree to which phonics patterns are applied" (Richardson & DiBenedetto, 1985, p. 4). The items in Sections 3 and 4 (i.e., the nonsense words) were created by changing one or two letters in each real word in Sections 1 and 2.

Subtest III (Contextual Decoding) assesses ability to read words that are embedded in short passages. The 11 passages correspond to reader levels from preprimer through the second half of fifth grade. Each passage includes a sample of words that were tested in Subtests I and II. This feature permits comparison of word recognition performance with and without the support of context. More specifically, each passage comprises the 10 Subtest I words for a given reader level along with 6 words selected from Subtest II lists. The words selected from Subtest II are all above the grade level of the passage to decrease the likelihood that they will have been learned as sight words. All other words in the passages are below-grade-level words according to the Harris and Jacobson lists. A series of simple questions follows each passage to assess recall of basic passage information.

The DST begins with Subtest I. To locate the starting point for testing, the examiner asks the child to read the Basal Finder, which is a series of three-word lists. The three words on each list are actually the first three items on each of the main lists. On the basis of the child's performance, the examiner selects the appropriate main list for the child to read. Testing proceeds to determine basal and ceiling levels. Basal is defined as the highest level at which the child achieves at least 80% accuracy (i.e., 8 of 10 words on the list are read correctly). Ceiling is defined as the level at which accuracy is less than 50% (i.e., fewer than five words are read correctly).

When the child has missed more than five words on a list (or has read all the lists with greater than 50% accuracy), the examiner moves to Subtest II, Phonics Patterns. As mentioned above, Subtest II comprises four sections: monosyllabic real words, polysyllabic real words, monosyllabic nonsense words, and polysyllabic nonsense words. All students begin Subtest II with the first list in the first section. Testing continues until the child misses 10 consecutive words or until the last list of Section 4 has been read. Examiners are advised, however, that they may deviate from this decision rule for children who are unable to read even the first few words in Sections 3 or 4. In this case, testing can be discontinued before the child makes 10 consecutive errors.

The starting point for Subtest III, Contextual Decoding, is determined by performance on Subtest I. The examiner begins with the passage corresponding to the Subtest I basal level. Testing continues until the child misses more than five basal target words in a given passage or completes the last passage on the test.

During the test, the examiner records the child's responses on the scoring booklet. The booklet contains the lists of words for each subtest with spaces for the examiner to check off the words that are mispronounced. Additional spaces next to each item allow the examiner to transcribe the child's errors. On Subtest III, Contextual Decoding, the examiner also records the time taken to read each passage.

The DST is described by the authors as a criterion-referenced test. Each student's performance is compared to a well-defined domain of reading tasks rather than to the performance of others who have taken the same test. Grade equivalent scores are used to report performance on Subtests I (Basal Vocabulary) and III (Contextual Decoding). The authors are careful to distinguish between their use of grade equivalents and the use of grade equivalents on norm-referenced achievement tests. On a norm-referenced test, a grade equivalent score of 1.8, for example, means that the student's raw score was equivalent to that of the average end-of-first-grade student. It does not necessarily mean that the student would be able to read material typical of the end-of-first-grade curriculum. Grade-equivalent scores on the DST, on the other hand, are criterion-referenced; they reflect the student's skill in reading words that are likely to appear at a particular basal reader level.

On Subtests I and III, two grade-equivalent scores are reported: instructional level and frustration level. The instructional level is defined as the level at which the student would likely be placed in a basal reader series. Operationally, it is the highest level at which the student achieves 80% accuracy. The frustration level is the level at which the reader can read some words, but would likely encounter difficulty. Operationally, the frustration level is the level at which accuracy drops to less than 50%. Performance on Subtest II is reported primarily in terms of the degree of mastery of particular phonics patterns (i.e., vowel patterns, consonant patterns, and syllabic patterns). In addition, a Phonics Transfer Index (PTI) can be computed to assess ability to apply knowledge of letter-sounds patterns to read unfamiliar words.

Other scores, such as reading rate, error rate, comprehension, error type, and response strength can be obtained to suit the diagnostic needs of the tester (see Richardson, DiBenedetto, Adler, & Kochnower, 1981).

Practical Applications/Uses

One of the major obstacles in research on reading disabilities has been the lack of uniformity and precision in identifying disabled readers. Typical standardized tests of reading achievement generally yield single scores that represent the undifferentiated combination of many elements. Two readers who earn the same score on these tests do not necessarily share a common reading problem. One may score low, for example, because of difficulty in decoding unknown words. Another, in contrast, may receive the same low score because of difficulty in understanding the meanings of words. The DST was designed to overcome the limitations of existing instruments by providing a diagnostic profile of a child's decoding skills.

Since its development approximately 8 years ago, the DST has been used in a variety of research situations, such as studying differences between good and poor readers (DiBenedetto, Richardson, & Kochnower, 1983; Kochnower, Richardson, & DiBenedetto, 1983; Richardson, DiBenedetto, & Adler, 1982). The test has also been used as a dependent measure in assessing the effects of treatments on reading performance. Winsberg, Richardson, and Kupietz (1983), for example, used the DST to study the effects of Ritalin on the reading performance of hyperactive children.

Now that the test has been published, its use in research on reading disabilities is likely to increase. Potential applications include: a) analyses of the relationship between the three subtests to test hypotheses about the development of word recognition skills in good versus poor readers or in normally developing readers, b) selection of comparable samples of good and poor readers in studies conducted by different investigators, c) identification of readers who show particular decoding profiles or error patterns (i.e., identification of reader subtypes), and d) analyses of the effects of different instructional programs on decoding performance.

Although the DST was originally created as a research tool, the test has a variety of clinical and educational applications. According to the authors, many of the schools that participated in studies conducted during the development of the DST have continued to use the test to monitor their reading programs. The test manual describes use of the test in three contexts. First, in clinical settings, the test can be used as part of a psychoeducational battery to identify students with decoding deficits. Second, the test can assist resource-room teachers in forming instructional groups and making programming decisions for students already identified as having decoding deficits. In addition, the resource-room teacher can use the test to evaluate the effectiveness of instructional interventions. Third, selected portions of the test (e.g., Subtest I or II) can be administered routinely to larger groups of students (e.g., entire schools, grades, or classrooms) to monitor reading progress.

In practice, whether the DST can compete with group-administered reading tests in monitoring large groups of students remains to be seen. The nature of the test suggests that it will be more appealing to clinicians (e.g., reading specialists, special education consultants, and psychologists) and resource-room teachers than to administrators or classroom teachers.

The test is most appropriate for students with word-recognition skills ranging from preprimer (early first grade) through Grade 5. Older students who are reading at these levels, however, can be tested with the instrument. The test, instructionally, will be most relevant in basal reader programs. Like many individually administered, diagnostic tests, the administration procedures of the DST are fairly complex. This is due primarily to the number of contingencies that guide the student's passage through the test. Although at first glance the procedures may seem confusing, once the examiner has developed a "schema" for the structure of the test and for basal and ceiling requirements, the process is actually quite simple. The manual estimates that the examiner will need to spend several hours reviewing the procedures prior to administering the test for the first time.

The manual itself is well organized and clear with respect to administration procedures. The examiner does not have to refer to the manual when giving the test because the instructions for each subtest are listed on the examiner's side of the presentation booklet. Also, the testing kit includes a separate basal/ceiling scoring key card to facilitate moving from list to list. Although the manual does not specify special training requirements for the tester, familiarity and experience with reading diagnosis would be advantageous, particularly if one wants to record the child's responses verbatim. Similarly, the novice needs to be familiar with the alternate, acceptable responses to the nonsense words. According to the authors, the test takes approximately ½ hour to administer. The time will vary, however, depending on the configuration of decoding skills of the individual child and the expertise of the tester.

If the DST is administered correctly, and basal and ceiling levels are established for all subtests, scoring is easily accomplished. The tester converts the raw scores for each list or passage to grade-equivalent scores using a table in the back of the manual. For Subtest III, reading rate, error rate, and comprehension scores are also recorded. Tables in the back of the manual facilitate the computation of reading and error rate. Scoring procedures are somewhat more complex for the Phonics Pattern Profile, but are clearly described in the manual and ample scoring examples are provided. The authors recommend that the Phonics Pattern Profile be omitted for students who are able to decode few items on Subtest II (i.e., raw score less than 10) or for students who are successful on almost all Subtest II items (i.e., raw score greater than 110). A separate scoring sheet (the Phonics Profile Worksheet) is provided for completing the Phonics Pattern Profile.

The manual indicates that scoring for the entire test takes approximately 15 minutes. The novice will undoubtedly require more time, particularly if the Phonics Pattern Profile is used.

The manual includes a complete and interesting chapter on diagnostic interpretation. The discussion is organized by subtest and contains explicit guidelines for drawing conclusions from test results. The test is interpreted primarily from a criterion-referenced perspective. That is, the tester determines the level of curricular material that the student can handle and the types of phonics patterns that have been mastered. The interpretation of the child's profile across subtests is more difficult, but should not pose problems for a psychologist or educator trained in reading diagnosis. Case studies illustrating diagnostic interpretation are included in the manual.

Although criterion-referenced interpretation is stressed throughout the manual, the chapter on interpretation includes normative guidelines, such as typical reading rates, error rates, and Phonics Patterns scores. For example, the authors categorize reading rate at the instructional level as "too fast" (more than 120 words per minute), "excellent" (80–120 words per minute), "average" (50–80 words per minute), "slow" (30–50 words per minute), or "very slow" (less than 30 words per minute). Although these explicit guidelines simplify interpretation, the manual does not indicate their empirical basis. To apply these normative guidelines without knowing how they were derived is risky.

The four case studies illustrating interpretation also include instructional recommendations based on the results of the test. The authors caution, however, that the test assesses only word recognition (i.e., decoding): "A complete evaluation of the child's development in reading should synthesize information obtained from the DST and a variety of other instruments" (Richardson & DiBenedetto, 1985, p. 21). For diagnostic purposes, tests of comprehension and language development are necessary complements of the DST. The value of the interpretative cases would be enhanced if illustrative data from comprehension and language tests were integrated with the DST results. Inclusion of these data might serve also to prevent the overzealous user from interpreting the results in isolation.

Technical Aspects

The results of reliability and validity studies conducted by the authors and their associates are reported in the manual and in an article by Richardson (1985). These data were collected during the 3-year test development period and involved several data sets. The DST was administered twice to the entire student body (Grades 1 through 5) of a New York City school ($N = 238$). A shortened form of the test was administered to over 1,200 children distributed across six schools in Atlanta, Georgia.

Both the New York City and Atlanta schools had participated in Project Follow-Through, a large, national project studying the effects of different instructional models on the achievement of children from low-socioeconomic status (SES) neighborhoods. All the New York City children and approximately two thirds of the Atlanta children had received or were receiving instruction (during Kindergarten through Grade 3) under the same Follow-Through model (i.e., Fordham University, Interdependent Learning Model).

Test reliability was established primarily on the basis of internal consistency. In studies of the DST, estimates of internal consistency (split-half, Cronbach's alpha, and Guttman's lambda) for Subtests I and II were high, ranging from .97 to .99. Test-retest coefficients are also reported for the DST, although the authors acknowledge that their test-retest procedures were unconventional. Typically, test-retest reliability is estimated by administering a test twice to the same group and then correlating the results of the two administrations. The interval between the two tests commonly ranges from 2 to 4 weeks. As the same basal vocabulary items appear on both subtests I (Basal Vocabulary) and III (Contextual Decoding) of the DST, immediate test-retest reliability was estimated by correlating performance on the two subtests. The correlations for both raw scores and grade-equivalent scores were all greater than .97. Although this approach deviates from standard test-retest procedures, the results indicate that DST scores are stable across at least two testing contexts (i.e., reading words in isolation vs. words in context).

The stability of DST scores over time was estimated with a 5-month interval between administrations for the 238 students in the New York City sample. Partial correlations between pretest and posttest were computed for each subtest controlling for grade placement. The correlations ranged from .87 to .93. Correlations were also computed for each separate grade. Although the manual does not detail the results, the authors report that most of the coefficients were greater than .9, while the lowest coefficient was .79 (for first grade, Subtest II scores). Given the length of time between the two administrations, the authors justifiably regard these results as a conservative estimate of reliability. The results reflect favorably on the stability over occasions of the DST.

The manual presents evidence regarding content, criterion, and construct validity. All the validity studies were conducted by the authors during the test development period. The students involved in the studies were from urban elementary schools, many of which were in low-SES neighborhoods.

Content validity is particularly critical for the DST due to the emphasis on criterion-referenced interpretation. The authors build the case for content validity on the basis of their item selection procedures. To construct the Basal Vocabulary subtest, the authors pooled the words from six "meaning-emphasis" and four "code-emphasis" basal series. Next they selected the 15 words most commonly introduced at each reader level. On the basis of a field test, they narrowed each list to the 10 most discriminating items.

The Phonics Patterns subtest also reflects attention to content validity. The patterns represent the most commonly occurring letter-sound regularities and the items were selected to minimize the possibility that they would have been memorized as sight words by students at each grade level.

The passages included in Subtest III were written by the authors to control for vocabulary and other text features (e.g., sentence length, syntactic complexity). The intent was to produce a passage at each level that would be similar to a typical basal reader passage at that level. The authors were constrained, however, by the need to include all the basal vocabulary items at the same level (from Subtest I) and some Phonics Patterns above the designated grade level (from Subtest II). As a result, some of the passages appear contrived and unnatural. If the facilitating effects of context on word recognition are in large part due to semantic predictability and the redundancies in text, the passages on the DST may underestimate the degree to which word recognition is improved by context.

Evidence of criterion validity is provided by correlations between the DST and existing reading tests, and by correlations between the DST and basal reader placement. In the New York City study, 238 children in Grades 1 through 5 were administered the DST in October 1978 and in May 1979. These same children took the Iowa Tests of Basic Skills (ITBS) in May 1978 and in May 1979. The manual presents validity coefficients relating October 1978 DST scores to ITBS scores in May 1979.

The results are reported both across grades (zero-order correlation) and controlling for the effects of grade (i.e., partial correlation). Because of the strong developmental trend in achievement scores, the partial coefficients provide better evidence of validity than the zero-order coefficients. Although separate results are reported for each subtest, the results are similar across subtests. Correlations between the ITBS and the DST were highest ($r = .61$ to $.71$) for the most decoding-related subtests (i.e., ITBS Vocabulary and Language Use) and lowest ($r = .35$ to $.57$) for the least decoding-related subtests (i.e., Math Problems and Math Concepts).

The manual also reports concurrent validity coefficients for smaller samples of students. Among the tests used were the ITBS, the New York City-Wide Reading Test, the Gilmore Oral Reading Test, and the Gates-MacGinitie Reading Test. In all cases, correlations between DST subtests and other reading tests were substantial (i.e., greater than .5). In most cases, the coefficients ranged between .7 and .8 (although grade-partialled coefficients are not reported).

Given the DST's emphasis on criterion-referenced interpretation, the relationship between DST scores and basal reader placement provides another measure of concurrent validity. In the New York City study, program placement data were available for 135 children in Grades 1 through 3. Grade-partialled correlation coefficients, relating grade-equivalent scores on the DST to basal reader placement in the school curriculum, were found to be high across all subtests of the DST. The coefficients ranged from .8 (Subtest II, Phonics Patterns) to .9 (Subtests I and III). Similar correlations were found in a study that tested a preliminary version of the DST in a smaller group of first- through third-grade students in an urban elementary school. The manual presents evidence of construct validity in the form of a) the convergent-divergent trend in the correlations between DST scores and scores on existing tests and b) the results of studies contrasting the performance of good versus poor readers.

Given the purpose of the test (i.e., to assess word recognition skills) one would expect the DST to correlate more highly with reading than with nonreading tests. In addition, within the domain of reading, one would expect the DST to correlate more highly with vocabulary than with comprehension tests. In all the studies that have been conducted on the DST, the expected patterns of performance have been observed. The ability of the test to discriminate between good and poor readers provides another measure of construct validity. A number of good and poor reader studies are described by Richardson (1985), two of which are also discussed in the manual. The studies involved approximately 200 elementary students. Some of the students were drawn from an urban elementary school receiving Title I funding, and others were selected from several middle-income, urban schools. In these studies, existing standardized tests were used to identify good and poor readers. Both groups were then tested on the DST and their performance compared. The poor readers consistently scored lower than good readers on the DST and were characterized by several distinctive patterns of performance. These studies support the validity of the test for use in identifying readers with decoding deficits.

Validity is also reported for one of the DST-derived scores, the Phonics Transfer Index (PTI). According to the manual, the PTI assesses the child's ability to transfer knowledge of letter-sound patterns to novel items. The items, all from Subtest II, are phonetically regular real words and nonsense words that were created by changing one or two letters in each real word. Operationally, the PTI represents the probability that a nonsense word item is pronounced correctly given that its corresponding real word is pronounced correctly. Regression was used to determine the extent to which the PTI would predict academic gain over a 5-month period. Gain was assessed by posttest scores on ITBS, DST, and program placement (i.e., basal reader level). The results indicated that the PTI accounted for a significant portion of the variance in program placement and DST posttest performance beyond that accounted for by pretest performance, grade placement, or score on ITBS Math Problems. These results attest to the validity of the PTI as a measure of phonics transfer that is independent of grade placement and general educational development.

Critique

The DST has a number of important strengths that make it a valuable addition to the testing field. First, the test is easy use. The test manual is clear and complete and the presentation book is conveniently arranged to facilitate test administration. The relatively short administration and scoring time contribute to the practicality of the test. Second, interpretation of the results is straightforward relative to other diagnostic reading tests. The test design and item selection procedures permit a domain-referenced interpretation of the results that can stand on its own, regardless of the instructional program in which the student is enrolled. In addition, there is evidence that the results can be linked to the curriculum in at least some school programs that use basal readers. Although the test is primarily criterion-referenced, the manual includes some normative guidelines (e.g., typical reading rates, PTI scores) to facilitate interpretation of the results. The utility of the guidelines would be clear if users were informed about how they were derived. Third, the test yields more precise information about a student's strengths and weaknesses in the decoding domain than other published reading tests. The Phonics Transfer Index, in particular, is a unique feature of this test. The PTI shows considerable promise in research on reading disabilities and may eventually be of practical benefit in diagnosing reading disabilities subtypes.

Like all other tests, the DST is subject to a number of limitations. First, by design, the DST has a limited scope. That is, the test assesses one aspect of reading—decoding—that develops over a relatively short span in a child's school career. On the one hand, the test derives its strength from its narrow range. As Cronbach (1984) noted, tests can strive for either bandwidth (i.e., broad but shallow content and age-range coverage) or fidelity (i.e., in-depth, quality coverage of a narrow content and age domain); they can not achieve both characteristics simultaneously. To the extent that it is a precise and efficient instrument for assessing decoding skills in first- through fifth-graders, the DST has fidelity. On the other hand, readers whose difficulties fall outside of the decoding domain will not be diagnosed by the test. For diagnostic purposes, the test should be supplemented by other language and reading tests, particularly those that assess comprehension.

Second, the test is most instructionally relevant in programs that use basal readers (either meaning- or code-emphasis). The grade equivalent scores and the phonics profiles generated by the DST are not likely to be welcomed by advocates of whole-language approaches that de-emphasize direct instruction in decoding skills. Third, the vast majority of studies on the reliability and validity of the DST sampled a single population—urban children from predominantly low-SES neighborhoods. Most of the students attended schools that were participating in Project Follow-Through under the same instructional model. Additional studies on different populations and instructional programs would enhance the credibility of the test.

Finally, the authors recommend the test for making programming decisions. The manual contains case studies prescribing instructional strategies on the basis of test results. No evidence is presented, however, regarding the effectiveness of the instructional strategies prescribed. Indeed, users of the test in educational settings are apt to find the DST to be no more effective than other available diagnostic tests in identifying the most effective remediation strategy for a particular child. This shortcoming reflects not so much on the DST as on our lack of knowledge about the relationship between particular student characteristics and the effectiveness of specific instructional treatments.

In summary, the DST is a well-designed and useful test. The test has special promise in research on reading disabilities and in clinical settings as part of a psychoeducational battery. The results of studies on the DST suggest that the test can be used to a) measure decoding skill and b) identify readers with decoding deficits. There is also some evidence that the test can be used successfully to place students in basal reader programs and to predict future progress in a basal reader program. Additional reliability and validity studies on different populations will strengthen an already strong test.

References

Cronbach, L.J. (1984). *Essentials of psychological testing* (4th ed.). New York: Harper and Row.

DiBenedetto, B., Richardson, E., & Kochnower, J. (1983). Vowel generalizations in normal and learning disabled readers. *Journal of Educational Psychology, 75*, 576–582.

Harris, A.J., & Jacobson, M.D. (1972). *Basic elementary reading vocabularies*. New York: MacMillan.

Kochnower, J., Richardson, E., & DiBenedetto, B. (1983). A comparison of the phonic decoding ability of normal and learning disabled children. *Journal of Learning Disabilities, 16*, 348–351.

Richardson, E. (1985). The reliability, validity, and flexibility of the DST for reading research. In D.B. Gray & J.F. Kavanagh (Eds.). *Biobehavioral measures of dyslexia* (pp. 279–296). Parkton, MD: York Press.

Richardson, E., & DiBenedetto, B. (1985). *The Decoding Skills Test*. Parkton, MD: York Press.

Richardson, E., DiBenedetto, B., & Adler, A. (1982). Use of the Decoding Skills Test to study differences between good and poor readers. In K. Gadow & I. Bialer (Eds.). *Advances in learning and behavioral disabilities* (Vol. 1, pp. 25–74). Greenwich, CT: JAI Press.

Richardson, E., DiBenedetto, B., Adler, A., & Kochnower, J. (1981). *Final report: The Decoding Skills Test (DST) project* (NICHD Contract #NO1-HD-7-2837). Washington, DC: National Institute of Child Health and Human Behavior.

Winsberg, B.G., Richardson, E., & Kupietz, S. (1983). *Ritalin and reading achievement in reading disabled, hyperactive children* (Proposal Application #MRPR0727). Washington, DC: National Institute of Mental Health.

Stephen L. Franzoi, Ph.D.

Assistant Professor of Psychology, Marquette University, Milwaukee, Wisconsin.

DESCRIPTION OF BODY SCALE

Richard E. Carney. San Diego, California: Carney, Weedman and Associates.

Introduction

Description of Body Scale (DOBS) is a standardized 14-item questionnaire for rating body structure employing a unidimensional classification scheme of masculinity-femininity that Sheldon, Stevens, and Tucker (1940) had previously labeled *gynandromorphism*. The DOBS manual (Carney, 1980) states that the questionnaire has applications in such areas as self-understanding, marriage and/or sex-role counseling, drug abuse and delinquency programs, and general counseling.

Richard Carney, the developer of the DOBS, is president of Carney, Weedman and Associates, a cooperative venture of academic and clinical psychologists. Carney first developed the questionnaire over 25 years ago as a standardized method for rating gynandrophy and attitudes toward this trait. Earlier forms of the DOBS had present body ratings and direct ratings of body satisfaction. Observer ratings were also done using body ratings. During the past 10 years measures of ideal body and inconsistency and incongruence between present and ideal body were also developed. Although the DOBS was standardized using an undergraduate population, data have been collected using other samples.

As described in the manual, the DOBS has a very simple structure. The dimension of body masculinity-femininity is measured by relative standing on seven body characteristics, where respondents first indicate how they are now, and then, how they would like to be. In total, 14 items are completed by the respondent. Each item consists of a 6-point scale, with concise descriptions of one body aspect at each end of the scale (e.g., 1=narrow, square hips vs. 6=wide, rounded hips). For each of the seven items, respondents indicate how they would describe themselves at the present time on the front side of the questionnaire form, and then how they would ideally like to be on the back side of the form. The DOBS is scored so that a high score on each item indicates highest masculinity of body structure, while a low score indicates highest femininity. Measures of consistency of present ratings and incongruence between present and ideal ratings are also available.

When the DOBS is used for self-ratings, Carney believes that it simply can be distributed to the respondents for them to complete. He does stress, however, that it is essential that the purpose for giving the DOBS should be explained and a cooperative attitude be obtained from the respondents. When the DOBS is used to rate others, the rater should practice briefly to become acquainted with the form and assure that a consistent procedure is used for the ratings. Carney also states that, whenever possible, observations should be made where the person being rated is dressed in a minimum of clothing, such as swim suits, gym shorts and T shirts, or underclothing. He stresses that nudity is not necessary or desirable when ratings are obtained, and that same-sex observers or mixed-sex raters, which include at least one professional member, should always be used. When more than one rater is used, they should cross-check their ratings until in mutual agreement.

The age groups for which this questionnaire was intended are those beyond puberty. Carney (1980) states that for girls this may be as early as 11 or 12 years, but for most boys the earliest age for use is likely to be 13 or 14 years.

Practical Applications/Uses

As the developer himself states, attempts to relate body structure to personality and behavior have a somewhat checkered history (Carney, 1980). The most well-known work is that of Sheldon (e.g., Sheldon & Stevens, 1942; Sheldon et al., 1940), which contained a number of methodological flaws (e.g., rater bias). Other studies did find a relation between mesomorphic (masculine) body structure and criminal behavior (Glueck & Glueck, 1950; Parnell, 1958), and Carney contends that he has found a relation between gynandromorphism and such behaviors as smoking, achievement orientation, and delinquent behavior (Carney, 1967, 1971; Carney, Feldman, & Loh, 1969). Based on this research, Carney believes that it may be possible to better understand behaviors such as criminality and drug abuse from the perspective of body structure and personality. Specifically, Carney (1980) contends that persons who physically resemble the stereotypic masculine body structure are more likely to engage in these types of behaviors. To date, there is little evidence supporting such an assertion.

Technical Aspects

In the Description of Body Scale there are four scores available. The first is the Present Body Masculinity Self Ratings (SB), with a high score indicating greater body masculinity. This score is obtained simply by summing the seven body item responses on the front part of the DOBS. The Ideal Body Ratings (IB) is identical to the SB except that the respondent indicates desired status of body. Inconsistency of Present Body Perception (KB) represents the variation of the seven present ratings about the mean of all seven ratings. Finally, Incongruence of Present-Ideal Ratings (CB) indicates the discrepancy between the present and ideal body ratings.

In the manual, Dr. Carney states that the validity of the DOBS "is high in the sense of construct, concurrent, and predictive validity" (1980, p. 47). Yet a close reading of the studies' findings presented in the manual does not support this conclusion. One of the most serious problems is the manner in which the data were analyzed; a good deal was subjected to factor-analytic techniques. The type of statistical inference made in these analyses was incorrect. For example, in the DOBS manual (1980, p. 20), alpha levels are assigned to the factor loading values (e.g., face: .290, $p < .01$), as if the factor loading values were Pearson correlation coefficients. Yet there is no rationale for employing factor analysis in this manner. Factor analysis is a mathematical tool like calculus, and not necessarily a technique of statistical inference like the chi-square, the analysis of variance, and sequential analysis (Rummel, 1970). Unfortunately, this inappropriate usage of factor analysis is employed in much of the analyses (e.g., Tables 4, 8, 10, and 11 in the manual), and it seriously undercuts the assertion that the DOBS has a good deal of construct validity.

Another problem with the factor analyses were the number of variables analyzed versus the number of subjects tested. When the researcher's interest is in inference from sample results to universal factors, the number of cases to variables should be as large as practical. Cattell (1952) suggests a minimum ratio of 4:1 (40 cases for 10 variables). Yet in one of the data sets, the ratio for the male sample is less than 2:1 (41 subjects and 21 variables) and for the female sample it is less than 3:1 (53 subjects and 21 variables). No conclusions should be drawn from such samples.

Another peculiarity is that findings often appear to contradict one another. For example, Carney states (1980, p. 36) that "over all behaviors males higher in [body masculinity] were also high in socially approved behavior style." Yet in this same data set, body masculinity in males was also highly correlated with helping in abortion, drinking, and avoiding others. Carney explains this contradiction in the following manner: "In summary, men with high levels of present and ideal body masculinity tend to have higher potential for a wide range of adventurous behaviors, the net effect of which is to place them higher in overall socially approved behavior" (Carney, 1980, p. 36) The logic of this conclusion is lost on the present reviewer, yet such conclusions are regularly made in the manual.

Critique

There is little, if any, persuasive evidence provided in the DOBS manual that would lead this reviewer to conclude that this instrument would be a useful addition to the study of human behavior. This does not mean the DOBS is an invalid measure; rather, there is little evidence that it *is* a valid measure. Further, while there may be some basis for the development of a body measure to identify body type in terms of a unidimensional scale of masculinity-femininity, this reviewer fails to see what that basis might be. The assumptions underlying the construction of the DOBS appear to be out-of-step with the sex-role literature of the previous 15 years, where masculinity and femininity are viewed not as a unidimensional construct, but rather, as separate, unique dimensions (Bem, 1978; Spence & Helmreich, 1978). If, however, the DOBS is updated to include insights gained from the sex-role literature, it may prove to be of use in the study of body type. In its present form, there are too many questions surrounding its structure and validity.

References

Bem, S.L. (1978). *The Short Bem Sex-Role Inventory.* Palo Alto, CA: Consulting Psychologists Press.
Carney, R.E. (1967). Sex chromatin, body masculinity, achievement motivation, and smoking behavior. *Psychological Reports, 20,* 859866.
Carney, R.G. (1971). *Risk taking behavior.* Springfield, IL: Chas. C. Thomas.

Carney, R.E. (1980). *Description of Body Scale*. San Diego, CA: Carney, Weedman and Associates.

Carney, R.E., Feldman, H., & Loh, W.F. (1969). Sex chromatin body masculinity and smoking behavior. *Psychological Reports, 25,* 261-262.

Cattell, R. B. (1952). *Factor analysis: An introduction and manual for the psychologist and social scientist.* New York: Harper & Row.

Glueck, S., & Glueck, E. (1950). *Unraveling juvenile delinquency.* Cambridge, MA: Harvard University Press.

Parnell, R. W. (1958). *Behavior and physique.* London: Arnold.

Rummel, R.J. (1970). *Applied factor analysis.* Evanston, IL: Northwestern University Press.

Sheldon, W.H., & Stevens, S.S. (1942). *The varieties of temperament.* New York: Harper & Row.

Sheldon, W.H., Stevens, S.S., & Tucker, W.B. (1940). *The varieties of human physique.* New York: Harper & Row.

Spence, J.T., & Helmreich, R.L. (1980). Masculine instrumentality and feminine expressivity: Their relationships with sex role attitudes and behaviors. *Psychology of Woman Quarterly, 5,* 147-163.

Daniel W. Stuempfig, Ph.D.

Professor of Psychology, California State University, Chico, California.

DIAGNOSTIC ACHIEVEMENT TEST FOR ADOLESCENTS

Phyllis L. Newcomer and Brian R. Bryant. Austin, Texas: PRO-ED.

Introduction

The Diagnostic Achievement Test for Adolescents (DATA; Newcomer & Bryant, 1986) is an individually administered norm-referenced academic achievement test designed to assess skill development and knowledge commonly taught in schools at the secondary level. Assessment is conducted in the areas of reading, mathematics, writing, science, social studies, and reference skills. Two subtests are administered to assess each of the first three academic realms and one subtest is associated with each of the latter three. As a measure of school performance in six content domains, the DATA can be used to help identify students who perform poorly in one or more areas of school, to determine academic strengths and weaknesses, and to document student progress in school learning, The test may also serve as a measurement tool in studies of academic achievement of secondary students.

The authors of the DATA, Phyllis L. Newcomer and Brian R. Bryant, are both trained in special education. Newcomer received her doctorate in special education from Temple University and presently resides on the faculty of special education at Beaver College in Glenside, Pennsylvania. Dr. Bryant completed his graduate work in special education at the University of Texas at Austin and now is Director of Research at PRO-ED, publishers of the DATA, and a faculty member in special education at his alma mater, Both Newcomer and Bryant have co-authored other tests, including the Diagnostic Achievement Battery (Newcomer & Curtis, 1983), Detroit Tests of Learning Aptitude—Primary (Hammill & Bryant, 1986), and Gray Oral Reading Tests—Revised (Wiederholt & Bryant, 1986).

According to the DATA manual, the test was developed in response to the need to assess individually "the variety of achievement skills that are relevant at the secondary level" (Newcomer & Bryant, 1986, p, 4). Although individually administered achievement tests for adolescents had been developed for single academic subjects, none had attempted to assess in a relatively comprehensive fashion the various skill areas that are taught in secondary schools. An earlier achievement test co-authored by Newcomer, the Diagnostic Achievement Battery (DAB; Newcomer & Curtis, 1983), was designed to measure academic achievement across the major curriculum domains, but the skills assessed are taught primarily at the elementary and intermediate levels (ages 6–14). The DATA is basically an extension of the DAB into the secondary level and, therefore, not only contains items directed at a higher level than those in the DAB but also omits subtests related to listening and speaking and includes subtests in science, social studies, and use of references.

In developing the DATA, the test authors referred to the achievement categories outlined by Hammill, Brown, and Bryant (in press). They decided that all major categories generally found in the basic secondary curriculum should be assessed. Thus, categories selected for inclusion in the DATA were Overall Achievement, Science, Social Studies, Reference Skills, Mathematics, Reading, and Writing. Only two categories, Occupations and Daily Living, were omitted. Several subcategories of Reading and Writing were also excluded because the test authors did not believe they were particularly valuable additions to an assessment of achievement for most secondary students. In addition, a decision was made to use no more than two subtests in measuring achievement in each category.

The original pool of items for the subtests was assembled from various resources, including textbooks used in Grades 7 through 12 in mathematics, algebra, science, and social studies. Content specialists then rated each item for its relevance to the curriculum area and for wording. From the results of this procedure, an experimental version of the DATA was constructed and administered to intact classes of students in Grades 7 through 12 in a West Virginia school district during the 1984–85 school year. Only items that had an item discrimination index of at least .3 and a level of difficulty between 15% and 85% were retained for the DATA.

During the 1985–86 academic year, the DATA was standardized on 1,135 adolescents (ages 12–18) from 15 states. Sampling procedures resulted in a normative sample that was representative of the national population in terms of sex, urban-rural residence, geographic area, race, and ethnicity. The sample percentage in each category deviated from the national percentage by no more than three points.

An item analysis of 50 randomly selected protocols from the norm group at 1-year intervals demonstrated satisfactory item discrimination and difficulty level. The median item discrimination index of subtests at three different age groups ranged from .38 to .85, with discriminating powers in the .50s being most frequent. With one exception, the range of median item difficulties on the subtests extended from 20% to 80%. Although the middle value of these difficulty indexes was 55%, one third of them were in the 70–79% range.

The present version of the DATA was first published in 1986. Other forms of the test have not been developed.

Test materials include two booklets and two forms that are packaged in a sturdy box. In addition to the carefully written manual, there is a Student Booklet that contains items or stimulus materials for eight of the nine subtests, a Student Response Form on which the student records his or her response to items on four subtests and part of a fifth subtest, and a Profile/Examiner Record Form that the examiner uses to record identifying information and test scores and to mark whether student responses to items are correct or incorrect.

There is a total of nine subtests in the DATA, although subtests may be administered separately or in different combinations. On all but the Writing Composition subtest 45 items are included, and except for the Writing Composition and Reference Skills subtests, the items are arranged in easy to difficult order. Subtests are intended generally to be administered to individuals, but some subtests, such as Spelling and Writing Composition, could be administered to small groups. A brief description of each subtest follows:

Word Identification. The student reads aloud from the Student Booklet phonetically regular and irregular words in isolation.

Reading Comprehension. Short (less than one page) passages from the Student Booklet are read silently by the students. After each, he or she is to respond orally to six comprehension questions asked by the examiner without looking back at the passage. Most questions involve factual recall, but a few are inferential.

Math Calculation. A variety of general mathematics, algebra, or geometry (two items) calculation problems are presented in the Student Booklet. They are worked on scratch paper, and answers are recorded on the Student Response Form.

Math Problem Solving. Mathematics word problems are read by the examiner as the pupil follows along silently in the Student Booklet. The subject may use scratch paper in calculating the answer, which he or she enters on the Student Response Form.

Spelling. Phonetically regular and irregular words are presented by the test administrator in the common format of stating the word, using it in a sentence, and repeating it. The Student Response Form is used for writing the words.

Writing Composition. Examinees are directed to look at three stimulus pictures in the Student Booklet and to use them as a basis for a story that they will write. They are allowed up to 15 minutes to complete the story.

Science. Questions of fact and terminology that pertain primarily to earth science, biology, and physics are read aloud by the examiner while the pupil reads the item silently from the Student Booklet. The one- or two-word response is given orally.

Social Studies. The subtest is similar to the Science subtest except that the item content is drawn from economics, geography, world history, and civics.

Reference Skills. Six sections of seven or eight items are included in the subtest. In the first two sections, worked on the Student Response Form, the subject is asked to use guide words to indicate the page where words would be found and is directed to alphabetize two lists of words. For the remaining four sections, skills in the use of an encyclopedia, dictionary, library catalog, and table of contents are assessed. Students are to use samples of reference works in the Student Booklet to state answers to questions asked by the examiner or to tell where specified information can be located.

Practical Applications/Uses

The DATA was designed to assess achievement levels reached by secondary students in the content areas of reading, mathematics, writing, science, social studies, and reference skills. Knowledge about student performance gained from the test is employed in several ways. The first stated purpose is in identifying secondary students who perform significantly below their peers in the curriculum areas included in the DATA (Newcomer & Bryant, 1986). Information derived from the test can be used to document whether or not a learning problem exists. Because various skills are measured by the test, a second purpose for using it is to assess relative strengths and weaknesses in achievement. Such information could be helpful in planning a student's educational program. Another stated purpose of the test is to document student progress in school. Through periodic testing, success of specific interventions and programs can be demonstrated. A fourth use of the test is in research where a test is needed to assess effects of variables on a wide variety of academic skills.

The test was developed to be used primarily in special education contexts at the secondary level (ages 12–18). Persons tested would most likely be students who are suspected of having mild, as opposed to severe, learning handicaps. Test scores could be used when writing a pupil's individual education program to verify that an academic school performance problem was present and to measure progress in content areas. Its diagnostic role would be limited to displaying general areas of strength and weakness (e.g., average math calculation skills but poor performance in math problem solving). Diagnosis of specific learning problems would require more in-depth assessment information than that provided by the DATA.

Test administration is performed one-to-one. Although special training in the use of the DATA is not necessary, the examiner should be competent in basic understanding of test scores and achievement testing. Normally this person would be a school psychologist, resource teacher, or special education teacher.

Procedures for administering the test are simple and well described. Directions tell the examiner very clearly what he or she is to do and print in uppercase the words he or she will speak, including all items read to the student. Instructions for determining entry levels on subtests for different age groups and for establishing basal and ceiling levels are related clearly in the manual. Additional cues to help in locating appropriate entry points and to assist in applying the correct rules for basals and ceilings are given in the Profile/Examiner Record Form. Specific acceptable answers are printed both with the items in the manual and on the Record Form.

Administration of the DATA is generally completed in one session approximately 1 to 2 hours long, depending upon the response level and speed of the student. Because subtests may be given selectively, time for administration can be shortened considerably.

Finding the raw scores on subtests is a relatively simple matter, and little training is required to master the procedure. With the exception of the Writing Composition subtest, which is scored by counting the number of words containing seven or more letters, responses are scored correct or incorrect according to a specified scoring key. On all but one of the subtests, the raw score then is computed by totaling the number of items below the ceiling performed correctly and the number assumed to be correct by virtue of being below the basal. On the Reference Skills subtest, the raw score is simply the number correct because all items are administered.

Raw scores from subtests are converted easily to standard scores (mean = 10 and standard deviation = 3) and a percentile rank associated with each standard score by referring to the normative tables. The meaning of these test statistics is described clearly in the manual, and simple verbal descriptors (e.g., "Average," "Above Average," "Superior," "Very Superior," etc.) associated with seven intervals of standard scores are given, along with the percentage of scores in each interval.

Subtest scores also are combined to yield several composite scores. In the content areas of reading, mathematics, and writing, scores from two subtests appropriate to each area are added and converted by use of a table to the same standard score scale as the individual subtests. An Achievement Screener composite is formed by summing the standard scores from Word Identification, Math Calculation, and Spelling and transforming the result with the aid of a table to a standard score, called a "quotient," having a mean of 100 and standard deviation of 15. The Total Achievement composite is derived by using a table to convert the sum of the standard scores of Reading, Mathematics, Writing, Science, Social Studies, and Reference Skills to the same scale as the Achievement Screener. Verbal descriptors and percentage of scores also are assigned to seven score intervals on this scale. Computation of the composites is facilitated by a format printed on the Profile/ Examiner Record Form. The form provides space for a summary of the various test scores and contains a profile for charting areas of strength and weakness as exhibited by subtest scores and academic composites.

A program for use with Apple or IBM computers is also available through PRO-ED for scoring the DATA. All of the scores and profiles that are on the Profile/ Examiner Record Form are printed. In addition, all possible intraindividual comparisons between composite scores (including other scores that can be entered in the program) are calculated, and those significant at the .05 level are listed.

The manual offers both proper cautions to be observed when interpreting DATA scores as well as suggestions for further assessment procedures, including "testing the limits" (Sattler, 1982). Nevertheless, interpretation of test performance should be made only by persons who have formal training in the nature of achievement testing.

Technical Aspects

Evidence related to three estimates of reliability is reported by the test authors, but no independent studies of reliability are cited. The first area of reliability to be considered is interval consistency, which is the degree to which items measure the same construct. Coefficient alpha was the index employed to assess the internal consistency of all the subtests except Writing Composition, which cannot be examined by this method. Fifty protocols were randomly selected from the normative sample from each 1-year interval. Among three age groups (12/13, 14/15, and 16/17/18), coefficients ranged from .90 to .98, with a median value of .95. The mean internal consistency reliability estimates of all DATA composites except Writing were .96, .97, or .98. The Writing composite reliability at all age groups was .88. Thus, the internal reliability of the DATA seems to be generally very good.

The second reliability index was test-retest reliability, which estimates stability of student performance over time. Within a 1-week interval, two testings were conducted using 58 students ages 12 through 18 attending school in Texas. Coefficients were calculated on all subtest and composite standard scores. All coefficients were significant at the .001 level, with subtest values ranging from .71 in Writing Composition to .95 in Spelling, and composite reliabilities varying from .86 for Reading to .93 for the Achievement Screener. These values indicate the test has satisfactory stability over time.

A third measure of reliability reported in the manual was the standard error of measurement (SEM) computed at three-age levels for all subtests and composite scores. Except for the Writing Composition subtest, for which only test-retest reliability was estimated, calculations of SEM were performed using internal-consistency reliabilities. The SEM of the raw scores for all subtests except Writing Composition and for all age levels was either 2 or 3, and the SEM of all corresponding standard scores was 1. Values of SEM for Writing Composition were generally one point higher than for other subtests. The SEM of standard scores for all composites except Writing and at all ages was 3, with 5 being the corresponding SEM for the Writing composite.

From the above evidence presented in the manual, the random error associated with DATA scores appears to be relatively small. Additional studies of reliability should be performed to verify this conclusion.

The test authors report three types of validity for the DATA: content, criterion-related, and construct. For content validity, the reader of the manual is directed to examine the procedures employed in selecting and analyzing items. With the possible exception of the Word Identification and Spelling subtests, the description of the development of items is too general to permit the user to make a careful assessment of content validity. For example, the manual states only that various content area textbooks were used and that a study of the type of information high school graduates were required to know in major curriculum areas was conducted. On subtests like Math Calculations, Math Problem Solving, Science, and Social Studies a statement of specific categories of content and an identification of the items that represent these categories are needed (Anastasi, 1981).

The skills that the student performs on the Writing Composition subtest (i.e., writing a short story) appear to provide a direct means for assessing the area of writing. However, the method of scoring the writing sample calls only for counting the number of words that contain seven or more letters. Because of the way the subtest is scored, questions regarding its content validity arise. Only one aspect of the broad domain of writing is sampled. Although word length may be correlated generally with writing skills (Deno, Marston, & Mirkin, 1981; Page, 1968), the use of the single dimension of written expression over other measures of writing ability (Schumm, 1987) may diminish the content validity of the subtest.

To demonstrate criterion-related validity of the DATA, subtest and composite standard scores of 234 undefined students from the normative sample were correlated with standard scores from one of four other tests of academic achievement. These tests were the Stanford Diagnostic Reading Test (Karlsen, Madden, & Gardner, 1983; $n=33$); the Stanford Diagnostic Mathematics Test (Beatty, Madden, Gardner, & Karlsen, 1984; $n=38$); the Iowa Tests of Basic Skills (Hieronymus, Lindquist, & Hoover, 1982; $n=67$); and the Iowa Tests of Educational Development (Feldt, Forsyth, & Linquist, 1981; $n=96$).

A total of 376 correlations was computed between the DATA and the other achievement measures. Although 86% of the coefficients met or surpassed .35, they tended to vary widely in value, from non-significance to .85. The highest correlations tended to occur, as expected, between general achievement composites (in the .70s and .80s), but other strong, consistent patterns of correlation between subtests were not as clearly discernable. Yet, the overall picture is that the DATA is related clearly to other measures of achievement and possesses adequate criterion-related validity.

Support for good construct validity of the DATA was obtained from five sources. First, a general increase in achievement in all subjects across age levels was demonstrated. An increase in subtest raw scores from one year to the next was noted with only three exceptions in the age range of 13 through 17. In addition, all the same scores correlated significantly ($p < .05$) with age, with a median value of .05.

In the second method of exhibiting construct validity, the hypothesis that all abilities measured by the DATA relate to each other because they all measure academic achievement was supported. Based upon the performance of 58 secondary students (ages 12–18) from Texas, intercorrelations between all DATA subtest scores and composites were significant ($p < .05$).

Another way in which evidence for construct validity was garnered was by relating aptitude scores from 67 students in the normative sample to their DATA scores. Results of the study revealed that correlations between DATA scores and the Short Form Test of Academic Aptitude (Sullivan, Clark, & Tiegs, 1974) ranged from .31 to .73, with a median of .50. Thus, the hypothesis that the DATA measures abilities related to school aptitude was reinforced.

A fourth way of studying validity of the achievement construct was to determine whether DATA test scores would differentiate groups known to differ in academic performance. All the mean DATA scores of 37 learning disabled children were significantly and dramatically different (one to two standard deviations lower) from those obtained by the norm group. The conclusion from this information is that the DATA is able to distinguish between groups that differ in known levels of achievement and, thus, exhibits construct validity.

The final procedure that pointed to construct validity in the DATA was correlating performance on individual items with total subtest scores. The resulting index of item discrimination calculated during the analysis of items indicated median discriminating powers of items in DATA subtests at three age levels were very satisfactory (indexes most commonly in the .50s). Thus, items in each subtest did an effective job of measuring similar traits.

In general, the evidence for the DATA's validity is satisfactory, especially in regard to construct validity. As the instrument becomes more widely used, studies conducted by independent researchers should be added to the base of evidence for assessing validity of this test.

Critique

The DATA appears to be successful in meeting the need for a relatively comprehensive individually administered test of academic achievement designed for use at the secondary level. Although some aspects of the development of the specific content of the test may require further elaboration, the DATA has demonstrated adequate reliability and validity to be used effectively in assessing general levels of achievement in major academic areas. The test should be useful primarily among special education professionals who wish to establish formally a student's level of school performance and to demonstrate his or her progress in achieving general academic goals.

Although the test has "diagnostic" in its title, the user should be aware that the DATA functions like a survey instrument of general achievement and has limited usefulness in pinpointing specific learning problems. The test might better serve a diagnostic function if knowledge and skills measured by specific items were described. Examiners then could assess not only the general areas in which students have academic strengths and weaknesses but also the skills in which the student may be deficient.

The DATA is relatively new, and as yet little has been written about it. Nevertheless, the instrument exhibits evidence that it can be a useful tool in the formal assessment of achievement among junior and senior high school students, primar-7x316.7ily with those who may have mild learning problems. As the DATA is employed more widely, reports on its use in the schools should be made available to enable psychologists and educators to evaluate its utility more thoroughly.

References

Anastasi, A. (1981). *Psychological testing* (5th ed.). New York: Macmillan.

Beatty, L.S., Madden, R., Gardner, E.F., & Karlsen, B. (1984). *Stanford Diagnostic Mathematics Test*. San Antonio, TX: The Psychological Corporation.

Deno, S., Marston, D., & Mirkin, P. (1981). Valid measurement procedures for continuous evaluation of written expression. *Exceptional Children, 48*, 368–370.

Feldt, L.S., Forsyth, R.A., & Lindquist, E.F. (1981). *Iowa Tests of Educational Development*. Chicago: Science Research Associates.

Hammill, D., Brown, L., & Bryant, B.R. (in press). *A consumer's guide to tests in print*. Austin, TX: PRO-ED.

Hammill, D. & Bryant, B.R. (1986). *Detroit Tests of Learning Aptitude—Primary*. Austin, TX: PRO-ED.

Hieronymus, A.N., Lindquist, E.F., & Hoover, H.D. (1982). *Iowa Tests of Basic Skills*. Chicago: Riverside Publishing Company.

Karlsen, B., Madden, R., & Gardner, E.F. (1983). *Stanford Diagnostic Reading Test*. San Antonio, TX: The Psychological Corporation.

Newcomer, P.L. & Bryant, B.R. (1986). *Diagnostic Achievement Test for Adolescents*. Austin, TX: PRO-ED.

Newcomer, P.L., & Curtis, D. (1983). *Diagnostic Achievement Battery*. Austin, TX: PRO-ED.

Page, E.B. (1968). Use of the computer in analyzing student essays. *International Review of Education, 14*, 210–224.

Sattler, J. (1982). *Assessment of children's intelligence and special abilities* (2nd ed.). Boston: Allyn & Bacon.

Schumm, J.S. (1987). Test review: Diagnostic Achievement Test for Adolescents (DATA). *Journal of Reading, 31*, 186–189.

Sullivan, E.T., Clark, W.W., & Tiegs, E.W. (1974). *Short Form Test of Academic Aptitude*. Monterey, CA: CTB/McGraw-Hill.

Wiederholt, J.L., & Bryant, B.R. (1986). *Gray Oral Reading Tests—Revised*. Austin, TX: PRO-ED.

Eugene H. Foster, Ed.D.
Director, Tygart Valley Counseling Center, and Visiting Professor, Davis & Elkins College, Elkins, West Virginia.

Allan L. LaVoie, Ph.D.
Professor of Psychology, Davis & Elkins College, Elkins, West Virginia.

DIAGNOSTIC CHECKLIST FOR BEHAVIOR-DISTURBED CHILDREN: FORM E-2

Bernard Rimland. San Diego, California: Institute for Child Behavior Research.

Introduction

Form E-2 of the Diagnostic Checklist for Behavior-Disturbed Children is a 109-item questionnaire designed to be completed by parents of children suspected of or diagnosed as having Autistic Disorder or other types of severe emotional disturbance (Rimland, 1984). It is a research instrument intended for identifying and classifying subgroups of children who display behaviors associated with early infantile autism and is not designed to discriminate autistic children from normal children or children with other types of developmental disorder, such as mental retardation and learning disability (Rimland, 1984). The test author has been quite clear in his caveat that the Diagnostic Checklist should not be employed as an "assessment instrument" (Rimland, 1984, p. 343).

The instrument, which is available in several languages, is distributed on request by the Institute for Child Behavior Research (ICBR). The ICBR continually adds the data contained in the completed checklist to its data bank for the purpose of future research. Scoring is done at ICBR. Parents and professionals who elect to use this service receive diagnostic information about the child on whom the questionnaire is completed. Parents completing the Diagnostic Checklist are encouraged to supply additional information and pertinent medical/developmental history along with the completed form. Children on whom the checklist is being completed ideally will be between the ages of 3 to 5, reflecting the author's observation that autistic children over age 5 "lose many of the traits that characterize them" (Rimland, 1984, p. 219). Parents completing questionnaires on children over the age of 5 are encouraged to remember their child's behavior at age 5 as a criterion for responding.

As of 1984 over 8,000 completed forms and supporting data were on file at ICBR. In private conversation with Dr. Rimland, these reviewers learned that as of July, 1988, over 10,000 checklist results are entered into ICBR's data bank, representing cases from 45 countries throughout the world (B. Rimland, personal communication, July 6, 1988).

Despite challenges regarding the technical adequacy of the Diagnostic Checklist (Parks, 1983) and some problems in attempts to replicate Dr. Rimland's study in which platelet uptake and efflux of serotonin were found to be related to checklist scores (Boullin et al., 1982), this instrument remains in widespread use. Indeed, Teal and Wiebe (1986) found that the Diagnostic Checklist was being used for diagnostic purposes within the public school setting. The popularity of this instrument can be attributed to Rimland's reputation as a long-time researcher and advocate for the existence of a biological basis for early infantile autism as well as to its natural appeal to the medical community, whose members are in a position to interact with parents concerning the etiology, diagnosis, and treatment of their young behaviorally disturbed children.

Practical Applications/Uses

When used as intended, the Diagnostic Checklist for Behavior-Disturbed Children provides valuable information to be employed in the continued research in the nature and causes of Autistic Disorder. Its ability to extract systematically from parents a large amount of information regarding the medical, developmental, and behavioral history of a child make this instrument both unique and invaluable in the quest for knowledge that leads to treatment and prevention of autism. The quality and accuracy of the information is, of course, dependent on the motivation of a given parent to complete this lengthy questionnaire and the parent's ability to read, understand, and objectively respond to test items. The issue of observer/reporter bias also warrants consideration.

A possible problem arises when the Diagnostic Checklist is used for diagnostic, placement, or treatment purposes outside its clearly stated applications. Its use for school placement or educational program purposes, for example, is clearly unwarranted given the supportive information presently available. This instrument's continued contribution to etiologic research in the effort to better understand the biological precursors to autistic behavior can be anticipated and encouraged, but when clinical and educational programming decisions are being made, a growing number of alternative, more appropriate instruments should be considered. The reviewers would like to emphasize the warning stated by Teal and Wiebe (1986) that practitioners ensure that instruments employed be suited to their intended purposes.

Technical Aspects

The technical literature on the Diagnostic Checklist can be summarized easily and concisely: reliability remains unknown despite widespread use and over 20 years of existence; validity shows promise, but has by no means been established.

Reliability should certainly have received more thorough investigation by this time. For example, it would be helpful to the prospective user to know the extent to which two parents agree when independently completing the questionnaire on their child, whether they produce the same answer from one occasion to the next, and if the items are unidimensional. With over 10,000 completed checklists on file, it would seem reasonable to examine them for internal consistency. Answers to these questions would not only strengthen the instrument in its current application but might also increase its appeal for use in other applications.

Validity issues are more complex with an instrument such as this. This checklist is intended for differential diagnosis of one form of severe emotional disturbance, namely autism, and hence validity ultimately depends on its ability to distinguish that one form from any others. The biggest difficulty emerges when one attempts to set up the standard against which to judge the Diagnostic Checklist. Rimland (1984) points out that the clinical criteria are inadequate; which is why he created this instrument in the first place. Differentiating between autism and other disorders and normals also will not answer the validity question because Rimland's purpose is to provide a test for differentiating among forms of Autistic Disorder. Thus, the Teal and Wiebe (1986) study does not provide the right kind of information, though their data would certainly suggest that broadening the use of the instrument might be productive. Biological indicators had some promise for supporting distinctions among types of autism, but to date the data picture is clouded (see, e.g., Boullin et al., 1982; Rimland, 1976, 1984). The burden of proof, however, remains with the test author to seek independent criteria on which to establish validity. This has not yet been done.

Critique

The Diagnostic Checklist for Behavior-Disturbed Children is designed as a tool to promote ongoing research in the study of Autistic Disorder. Rimland clearly states that it is not an assessment instrument and should not be employed as such (1984); still, researchers in the field have found that it is being used for diagnostic purposes by schools and other agencies (Teal and Wiebe, 1986). Until further development of the instrument has taken place, such applications are discouraged.

Validity and reliability issues have been raised regarding this instrument and some debate appears in the literature during the early to mid-1980s. It is somewhat alarming to find that hard data resolving these issues remain unavailable as of this writing. Such resolution would clearly lend support to the continued use of the instrument by other research teams. Dr. Rimland does share that more recent development of the instrument is underway at the present time including scoring keys that can be used by others in the field (B. Rimland, personal communication, July 6, 1988). Unfortunately, this information is still in the developmental stages and was not available at the time of this writing. Individuals considering this instrument for use as part of their research effort are advised to contact Dr. Rimland at ICBR in San Diego, California. Issues surrounding reliability and validity should be given particular attention by prospective users.

References

Boullin, D., Freeman, B.J., Geller, E., Ritvo, E., Rutter, M. & Yuwiler, A. (1982). Towards the resolution of conflicting findings. *Journal of Autism and Childhood Schizophrenia, 12,* 97–98.

Parks, S.L. (1983). The assessment of autistic children: A selective review of available instruments. *Journal of Autism and Developmental Disorders, 13,* 255–267.

Rimland, B. (1964). *Infantile autism: The syndrome and its implications for a neural theory of behavior.* New York: Appleton-Century-Crofts.

Rimland, B. (1971). The differentiation of childhood psychoses: An analysis of checklists for 2,218 psychotic children. *Journal of Autism and Childhood Schizophrenia, 1,* 161–174.

Rimland, B. (1976). Platelet uptake and efflux of serotonin in subtypes of psychotic children. *Journal of Autism and Childhood Schizophrenia, 6,* 379–382.

Rimland, B. (1984). Diagnostic Checklist Form E-2: A reply to Parks. *Journal of Autism and Developmental Disorders, 14,* 343–345.

Teal, M.B., & Wiebe, M.J. (1986). A validity analysis of selected instruments used to assess autism. *Journal of Autism and Developmental Disorders, 16,* 485–494.

Delwyn L. Harnisch, Ph.D.

Associate Professor of Educational Psychology, Institute for Research on Human Development, University of Illinois at Urbana-Champaign, Champaign, Illinois.

DIAGNOSTIC TESTS AND SELF-HELPS IN ARITHMETIC

Leo F. Brueckner. Monterey, California: CTB/McGraw-Hill.

Introduction

The Diagnostic Tests and Self-Helps in Arithmetic were designed to provide initial screening and specific diagnosis of all basic operations involving whole numbers, common fractions, decimal fractions, percents, and measurement. The test is composed of three integrated sets of materials: 4 screening tests designed to enable quick determination of class or individual success or failure, 23 diagnostic tests of basic arithmetic skills keyed to the screening tests, and 23 self-helps found on the back of the diagnostic tests consisting of worked examples for student self-study. Five of the diagnostic tests and self-helps measure addition, five measure subtraction, four measure multiplication, six measure division, one measures changing forms of fractions, one measures percent, and one measures operations with measures.

Dr. Leo J. Brueckner is the author of several texts in education including *Diagnostic and Remedial Teaching of Arithmetic* (1930), *Diagnostic and Remedial Teaching* (with E.O. Malby, 1932), and *Making Arithmetic Meaningful* (1953) and has served as senior author for five basal mathematics textbooks. He has authored numerous articles on diagnosis and remedial arithmetic. Dr. Brueckner is the author of standard survey tests in arithmetic processes and problem solving, individual clinical diagnostic tests, and readiness tests for all major areas of arithmetic processes.

The following benefits of using the test are offered by Brueckner (1955) in the manual: 1) use of the tests provides a systematic method of checking student progress, 2) the materials may be used effectively with any series of textbooks, 3) the materials may be administered to individuals or groups at any time during the school year, 4) test results are closely geared to the California Arithmetic Tests, and 5) the self-helps provide a systematic series of practice exercises that may be used for upgrading or rebuilding basic arithmetic skills.

Required materials for testing include a copy of the desired test for each student, a pencil with eraser for each student, student record sheets, and a manual containing information on administering, scoring, and interpreting the subtests.

Practical Applications/Uses

Use of Diagnostic Tests and Self-Helps in Arithmetic provides information concerning student performance in operations with whole numbers, common fractions, and decimals as taught in Grades 3–8. The information from the tests could be used for either individual or group diagnosis of specific skills in mathematics. Due to the test's design, this information is particularly useful for diagnosing difficulties in a students algorithmic performance. Because this test is site processed, analysis and corrective actions may be taken without undue time delays.

In administering any section of the test, required materials include a test sheet for each student, individual student record sheets, the test manual, and a pencil with eraser. Student test sheets should be marked with the student's name, grade, age, school, teacher, room, and date prior to beginning testing. Scripts are provided for the administration of each subtest. As the tests are graded power tests, as opposed to speed tests, no time limits are suggested. Instructions for test administration vary slightly depending upon whether the test being given is a screening test, a diagnostic test of basic facts, or a standard diagnostic test.

Each of the four screening tests serve to provide a high level summary of class performance and to provide general information concerning individual student weakness. Although the manual states that the screening tests may be given at any grade level, the screening tests were specifically constructed for administration at the fourth-, fifth-, and sixth-grade levels. The first three screening tests evaluate basic operations with a specific number type: Test I for whole number operations, Test II for fractional operations, and Test III for decimal operations. Each of these tests follow a similar testing format with each skill tested using four examples ranging from comparatively simple to difficult. Test IV is intended to provide a general screening for students above Grade 6 and includes 33 examples for each of the four operations using whole numbers, common fractions, and decimal fractions.

The first 5 of the 23 diagnostic tests are designed to measure student ability in recalling basic facts. For these tests, the examiner reads the problem from the test paper while the students record their answers. Although the pacing of the test is at the prerogative of the administrator, the manual (Brueckner, 1955) suggests pacing the problems so that the testing session is "rapid enough to prevent the finding of answers by counting or the use of other 'crutches' that are indications of a lack of mastery of the number facts" (p. 3).

Each of the 18 diagnostic tests that follow deals with one operation and contains sets of problems arranged such that an additional level of complexity is presented with each successive problem. For each skill or combination of skills in a given test, there are three or more problems including similar skills to aid in making an evaluation of student performance.

Scoring is done manually by the administrator, with the option given of allowing student help in correcting tests. Although answers are provided, the manual suggests that the examiner take the tests without reference to the key to become acquainted with the format of the tests. In marking the items, the letter C is placed to the right of the item if it is correct, the letter X if the item is not correct, and the letter O if no answer is given. Care should be exercised so that correction symbols are not written over the example in the event of later rescoring. Test scores are recorded in a marked box of each test sheet for later transfer to the individual record sheet. In interpreting these scores, mastery is indicated by no errors in the problems comprising that section, with two or more errors indicating a persistent difficulty in the skills or combination of skills being evaluated.

Technical Aspects

The validity of the Diagnostic Tests and Self-Helps in Arithmetic is solely addressed in the manual (Brueckner, 1955) through a brief discussion of face validity, with no mention of predictive, concurrent, or construct validity. As this discussion appears to have been based solely on the test author's analysis, the objectives for each test should be carefully matched against the curriculum of any classroom or school district considering the use of this test.

The issue of test reliability is treated in a similar fashion, with the majority of the reliability discussion centering around a description of the strengths provided by the testing format (Brueckner, 1955). Apart from a verbal description concerning how such a format guarantees a reliable test, no supporting evidence is given. Although mention is made regarding high levels of test-retest reliability, no evidence is provided supporting this claim.

The Diagnostic Tests and Self-Helps in Arithmetic were designed as a series of subskill tests to use in identifying pupil strengths and weakness, rather than producing a set of norm references scores. No attempts were made to develop norms.

Critique

In using the Diagnostic Tests and Self-Helps in Arithmetic, it is important to realize that the tests operate under the assumption that understanding an algorithm implies understanding the underlying concept, an assumption that Davis (1986) demonstrates runs counter to recent research. Davis (1986) offers many examples showing the error of assuming that knowledge of, and ability to follow, an algorithm or procedure demonstrates understanding of the underlying concept. In each of the examples he offers, one notices that the students are lacking any type of justification system for the answers which they produce. This is most easily demonstrated in the self-help section. The remediation offered consists of examples from the test, which are solved using a standard algorithm followed by a summary of steps necessary to reach a solution. The students are instructed to study the examples and then rework the exercises in the test using the same method. For example, in the self-help for division of fractions section the instructions to invert and multiply are demonstrated without describing the underlying rationale. Furthermore, often the algorithm recommended in the self-help section no longer reflects current teaching procedures or is incomplete. For example, in the self-help for subtraction of unlike fractions the instructions are given to change 1/2 to 1/4, but no method is provided for the student to do so.

The idea that this approach adequately measures mathematical thinking and offers sufficient remediation is not current with present views of mathematical thinking. Indeed, Burns (1985) suggests that student facility with rote procedures as measured by the Diagnostic Tests and Self-Helps in Arithmetic actually serves to hide the lack of basic understandings.

The series of diagnostic tests serves a worthwhile purpose by identifying specific problems in a student's working procedure. But, this is true only to the extent that the student utilizes the same algorithm as presented in the test itself. This makes it important to check the congruency between the tested mathematics objectives and the instructional objectives and practices of the local curriculum before considering the use of this test. More importantly, however, the identification of such procedural knowledge is hardly all one would expect from a test describing itself as diagnostic. One would expect a diagnostic instrument to provide information regarding which procedures a student is using and the degree to which these used procedures have a conceptual base, not just information concerning student success in using a particular procedure. A diagnostic test should also provide information regarding strategies and selection patterns utilized by the child and how well the child can use the procedures flexibly to solve everyday problems. Basing instruction upon the type of measures the Diagnostic Tests and Self-Helps in Arithmetic offer could easily result in treatment of a series of symptoms, while not addressing underlying causes.

References

This list includes text citations and suggested additional reading.

Brueckner, L.J. (1955). *Manual: Diagnostic Tests and Self-Helps in Arithmetic*. Monterey, CA: CTB/McGraw-Hill.

Brown, J.S., & Burton, R.B. (1978). Diagnostic models for procedural bugs in basic mathematical skills. *Cognitive Science, 2,* 155–192.

Burns, M. (1985, April). Teaching "what to do" in arithmetic vs. teaching "what to do and why." *Educational Leadership,* pp. 34–38.

Campione, J.C., Brown, A.L., & Connell, M.L. (in press). Metacognition: On the importance of knowing what you are doing. In R.I. Charles & E. Silver (Eds.), *Research agenda for mathematics education: Teaching and assessment of mathematical problem solving*. Hillsdale, NJ: Lawrence Erlbaum.

Davis, R.B. (1986). *Learning mathematics: The cognitive science approach to mathematics education*. New Jersey: Ablex Publishing Co.

Jencks, S.M., & Peck, D.M. (1981). Conceptual issues in the teaching and learning of fractions. *Journal for Research in Mathematics Education, 12*(5), 339–34.

Schoenfeld, A.H. (1985). *Mathematical problem solving*. Orlando: Academic Press.

Ardelina Albano Baldonado, R.N., Ph.D.

Associate Professor of Nursing, Loyola University of Chicago, and Assistant Dean and Director, Undergraduate Nursing Program, Marcella Niehoff School of Nursing, Chicago, Illinois.

DRUG USE INDEX

Frazier M. Douglass and Khalil A. Khavari. Milwaukee, Wisconsin: Khalil A. Khavari, Ph.D.

Introduction

The Drug Use Index (DUI), also called the Wisconsin Substance Use Inventory (WSUI), was developed by Frazier M. Douglass and Khalil A. Khavari (1978) to measure polydrug use. Construction and cross-validation studies of the DUI were supported by a research grant from the National Institute on Drug Abuse and by funds from the College of Letters and Sciences and the Graduate School of the University of Wisconsin-Milwaukee. The index was based on the responses from 1,121 adults: 517 males and 604 females (median age = 23 years). Of the totals, 811 were college students and 310 were primarily males in the work force (Khavari & Douglass, 1981).

The DUI contains 19 licit and illicit drugs and drug categories. Included are almost all psychoactive drugs, commonly used nonpsychoactive drugs, and anti-infectious drugs. The index comprises eight usage frequency levels for each of the 19 drugs and categories. It profiles the occurrence and extent of drug use by the individual. The frequency usage levels are designated by the following values: 0 = never tried the drug; 1 = tried but not currently using; 2 = less often than monthly use; 3 = monthly use; 4 = weekly use; 5 = several times weekly use; 6 = daily use; and 7 = several times daily use. Peaks on a profile plot depict drugs preferred by the individual.

Practical Applications/Uses

The DUI has been used in the study of attitudinal predispositions and behavioral attributes to drug use. The instrument includes the 19 DUI items and 132 personality, attitude, and behavioral questions. This instrument was administered to 335 college students as one of the methods used to establish the psychometric properties of the DUI.

The test authors have also used the DUI in a modified and simplified version as a component of another survey questionnaire. This 50-item questionnaire, which includes the DUI, is used more frequently by Khavari (K.A. Khavari, personal communication, April, 1988).

The DUI can be administered to individuals with an eighth-grade education and takes approximately 10 minutes to complete. A Scantron answer sheet is used and a clear coding system accompanies the instruction for administration. The questions are written in English, but no information is provided on the availability of foreign language versions.

The DUI has also been used to identify a hierarchy of drug use and its relationship to the cost-benefit or risk-benefit characteristics of a particular drug (Khavari & Douglass, 1980). Additionally, Khavari and Douglass (1981) used the index to develop the Drug Use Profile. Subjects in the study comprised 3,984. The test authors claim that reported patterns of drug use were suitable for developing norms for the profile because they were highly similar to the findings in a national study by Abelson, Fishburne, and Cisin (1977) and other studies by Groves (1974) and Single, Kandel, and Faust (1974).

By itself, the DUI may be used by a counselor or a therapist during an interview to elicit information from the individual regarding his or her levels of drug use. This valuable information can be used as a guide for a therapeutic regime or for counseling purposes. The profile also depicts drug use by subgroup populations (i.e., females, males, non-white, and older respondents). Hence, it can provide information for social and policy decision. For example, the index could be administered to persons presumed to be at high-risk to evaluate drug use in an inner city (Khavari & Douglass, 1981).

Coding and scoring are clear and simple. The complete package, DUI questionnaire, instruction for administration, Scantron answer sheet and permission to reproduce the material, may be obtained from K.A. Khavari. Concisely, plotting the responses to the DUI provides a quick and simple visual estimate and a precise measurement of drug usage by an individual and groups. Information obtained can be used for individual counseling and/or therapy and on epidemiological and longitudinal studies on population subgroups.

Technical Aspects

The DUI was initially based upon the responses of 1,121 subjects who indicated their use of each of 19 drugs and drug categories using eight usage frequency levels of 0 (never tried) to 7 (using the drug several times a day). Construction of the DUP used 3,469 subjects who represented a very heterogeneous segment of an urban environment. Although 62% were students in a university setting, substantial number of subjects were professionals, hospital employees, jail inmates, military reservists and industrial workers. Patterns of drug use were extremely similar to drug usage reported in a national study by Abelson et al. (1977). Procedures used to develop drug categories were similar to procedures used in the construction of the MMPI (Khavari & Douglass, 1981). In concert with other inventories used by the test authors and other investigators, the instrument was subjected to psychometric methods (split-half and test-retest) and cross-validation designed to establish its validity and reliability. Content validation studies included using the DUI in the final construction of the Drug Use Profile, in the study of personality correlates of hallucinogenic drugs (Mabry & Khavari, 1986) and in the replicated cluster analysis of extreme drug users by F.M. Douglass and K.A. Khavari, 1980. Reported reliability of the instrument was .7492 (Khavari & Douglass, 1978) and .89 (K.A. Khavari, personal communication, April, 1988). Validity of the DUI is documented and has a reliability of.89 (K.A. Khavari, personal communication, April, 1988).

Critique

Development of the DUI was based on sound conceptualization of the need to develop an objective and valid instrument to measure polydrug usage and frequency levels of drug consumption. The DUI has been used in conjunction with personality, attitudinal, and behavioral questions in an attempt to identify correlates of drug use and/or abuse. It has also been used more frequently with other instruments in cross-validation studies. As a self-report instrument, it is subjected to the issues of validity and reliability of self-reports. Items in the DUI simply ask the respondent to indicate if he or she is currently using the drug and if so, at what frequency levels. The DUI, in isolation from other constructs or hypotheses on drug use or drug abuse, does not lend to a clear and generalizable conceptualization of the motivations for selective use of drug(s) and/or predictions of drug abuse.Hence, utility of the DUI for clinical research for treatment purposes and for prediction of drug abuse is limited. At best its utility and relevance is for a quick identification of preferred drugs and frequency levels of usage by the individual that, when plotted on a Drug Use Profile sheet, may depict addiction or potential dependency to the drug (Khavari & Douglass, 1981). Nonetheless, the quantitative scores and profile cannot be interpreted in isolation from contextual variables and other correlates of drug use behavior.

References

Abelson, H.I., Fishburne, P.M., & Cisin, L. (1977). *National survey on drug abuse.* Rockville, MD: National Institute on Drug Abuse.

Douglass, E.M., & Khavari, K.A. (1978). The Drug Use Index: A measure of the extent of polydrug usage. *International Journal of Addiction, 13,* 981-993.

Douglass, F.M., & Khavari, K.A. (1980). Three types of extreme drug users identified by a replicated cluster analysis. *Journal of Abnormal Psychology, 89*(2), 240-249.

Groves, W.E. (1974). Patterns of college student drug use and lifestyles. In E. Josephson & E.E. Carol (Eds.), *Drug use: Epidemiological and social approaches* (pp. 242-275). New York: Wiley.

Khavari, K.A., & Douglass, F.M. (1980). Empirically derived hierarchy of use for psychotropics: A cost-benefit index. *Journal on Drug Education, 10*(4), 325-330.

Khavari, K.A., & Douglass, F.M. (1981). The Drug Use Profile: An instrument for clinical and research evaluations for drug use patterns. *Drug and Alcohol Dependence, 8,* 119-130.

Mabry, E.A., & Khavari, K.A. (1986). Attitude and personality correlates of hallucinogenic drug use. *The International Journal of the Addictions, 21*(6), 691-699.

Single, E., Kandel, D., & Faust, R. (1974). Patterns of multiple drug use in high school. *Journal of Health and Social Behavior, 15,* 344-357.

Paul R. Hoffman, Ph.D.

Associate Professor of Communication Disorders, Louisiana State University, Baton Rouge, Louisiana.

ELICITED ARTICULATORY SYSTEM EVALUATION

Susie Finn Steed and William O. Haynes. Austin, Texas: PRO-ED.

Introduction

The Elicited Articulatory System Evaluation (EASE) is a test designed to assess articulation through a sentence repetition task. The sentences are portrayed in the actions and states represented in a series of line drawings and contain target words that are phonetically transcribed to produce the basic data for two analysis formats—a traditional speech sound in word- and syllable-context analysis and a phonological process analysis. This test was developed by Susie Finn Steed and William O. Haynes of Ohio State University. It incorporates aspects of Dr. Haynes' research regarding effects of elicited imitation (Haynes & Haynes, 1979) and phonetic context (Haynes, Haynes & Jackson, 1982) upon children's articulatory performance as well as judgment reliability in articulation testing (Haynes & Steed, 1987). This is the first version of the instrument. No normative population has been assessed at this time.

The test package contains a picture book, a supply of score sheets, a supply of analysis booklets for a traditional analysis of consonant and vowel articulation and/or a phonological process analysis, and a test manual.

The picture book contains 30 black-and-white line drawings, each used to elicit from one to four sentences. The line drawings are thematically grouped as "stories" that vary in length from one to four drawings. For example, the first four drawings follow a group of people from their entrance into a zoo past a variety of zoo exhibits. The sentences elicited are descriptive in nature (e.g., "The sheep is white," "The turkey has lost a feather"). Thus, while a common setting and characters are established in the sequential drawings, the elicited responses do not necessarily constitute a storyline with plot or continuous action of the characters. Each of the elicited utterances contains two target words that are scored for articulation of all their constituent phonemes.

The response form contains a grid with 65 rows corresponding to the sentences. Each row contains two separate word columns for analysis of the two target words. Each word column is subdivided into 15 numbered columns representing the word/syllabic shape positions of the phonemes targeted in that word. Target phonemes are listed in the appropriate column and row. Column assignments are as follows: C1—word-initial vowels, C2—word-initial consonants, C3—the second consonant of word-initial consonant clusters, C4—the vocalic nucleus of the first syllable, C5 through C8—consonants that end the first syllable and begin the second syllable if the word is multisyllabic, C9—the vocalic nucleus of the second syllable of multisyllabic words if there is a third syllable, C10 and C11—consonants that end a second syllable and begin a third syllable, C12—the vocalic nucleus of a third syllable, C13 and C14—consonants that end the word, C15—a word-final vowel.

The examiner shows each picture in order and prompts the child to repeat a sentence related to the picture. The child's productions of the phonemes in the two target words are scaled by the examiner. If a sound's production is judged to be normal, the provided transcription on the score sheet is maintained. If the examiner perceives an error production, a traditional scoring scale is suggested (i.e., omission, substitution, distortion or addition). Omissions are noted by crossing out those sounds that are not produced. Substitutions are phonemically transcribed in the row and column of the target speech sound. Distortions are noted using an X or a phonetic transcription diacritical marking. Additions are written into the grid where they occur.

The analysis booklet leads the examiner through two analysis procedures. The first is a traditional analysis of errors for each phoneme that results in a calculation of the percentage of incorrect productions for each phoneme and for each phoneme in individual word/syllable positions. The second analysis provides for the calculation of percentage occurrence for a variety of phonological process errors.

The first section of the analysis booklet is organized for the traditional analysis of each speech sound. Phonemes are organized using a "Manner of Articulation" classification. Consonants are analyzed followed by vowels. The consonant analysis is subdivided into Nasals, Plosives, Fricatives, Affricates, Liquids, and Glides. Vowels are divided into Front Vowels, Central Vowels, Back Vowels, and Diphthongs. Each of these subclasses is denoted on the scoring sheet with boxes (the intersections of the word/syllable position columns and individual word rows) of different colors. The Nasals are green, the Labial and Alveolar Plosives are blue, the Velar Plosives are red, and so forth.

Each consonant is scored individually on an analysis grid that shows the word and syllable positions for each sound corresponding to the notations on the scoring form. The occurrences of each phoneme are denoted by white squares on a gray field. The examiner transposes errors from the score sheet to the analysis form. The analysis sheet also provides an area for noting the number of errors for that sound. The analysis sheet supplies the total number of occurrences and the examiner calculates a percentage of errors for each sound. By scanning the analysis form for each error sound, the examiner can describe where errors occurred with respect to word/syllable position.

The phonological process analysis section provides for the calculation of percentage of occurrence of the following processes: Deletion of Final Consonants, Consonant Cluster Reduction, Deletion of Unstressed Syllables, Fronting of Velars, Fronting of Fricatives, Stopping of Fricatives, Stopping of Affricates, Affrication of Fricatives, Gliding of Liquids, Prevocalic Voicing, and Vocalization. Each process is subdivided into possibly affected phonemes using a "Manner of Articulation" classification. The analysis sheet notes the column of the score sheet that is analyzed at any particular point and the color of the affected phoneme on the score sheet. For each subdivision, the analysis sheet supplies an appropriate number of boxes to be checked related to the possible occurrences of each process. The examiner uses this information to calculate percentages of use of the error processes.

Practical Applications/Uses

The EASE was designed to be used by a speech-language pathologist who wants to describe a misarticulating child's pattern of speech sound errors. The two analysis procedures employed are applicable to two differing populations of misarticulating children: 1) elementary school-age children who misarticulate one or a few speech sounds and 2) preschool children who misarticulate a wide variety of phonemes.

Characterization of the speech errors of the child with one or two phoneme production errors can be made using the test's Traditional Analysis forms. Clinically useful measurements of the percentage of occurrence of these errors and their location with respect to word and syllable boundaries are derived in a straightforward manner. These measures may be repeated as useful indices of the child's progress in a treatment program. They also provide the clinician with information regarding the contexts in which acceptable approximations of the child's error phonemes are produced. The clinician can use these as models of correct productions of the error sound for practice and comparison exercises within traditional therapy programs (Van Riper, 1939; McDonald, 1964).

Characterization of the speech sound productions of younger children or those with more severely impaired articulatory ability can be made using the phonological process analysis provided in the EASE. Phonological processes identified may be targeted within therapy by providing specific exercises in the production and perception of minimal pairs that are neutralized by the context (Elbert & Geirut, 1986) or by targeting the individual phonemes affected by a particular phonological process (Hodson & Paden, 1983). Alternatively, the child's refinement of the phonological system during a more holistic approach to expressive language improvement can be measured using this instrument (Hoffman, Schuckers, & Danloff, 1988).

Optimally, the child taking this test should be able to repeat the sentences used as stimuli. However, the younger child who misarticulates many phonemes is also likely to demonstrate wide-ranging language impairments that would preclude this optimal performance. The clinician may have to adapt the administration procedures for such children to elicit constituent phrases or even single-word productions. Inasmuch as the analysis forms deal only with single-word productions, the elicitation of complete sentence productions is not crucial to the analysis. Research suggests that use of single word productions rather than sentence productions results in an overestimate of the child's articulatory ability in terms of percentage of consonants correctly produced (Haynes et al., 1982). However, identification of phonological process errors requiring remediation may remain fairly stable despite this manipulation (Andrews & Fey, 1986).

The EASE was designed as an individually administered test and should take approximately 15-20 minutes for the child to complete the required task. Because the scoring form is somewhat different from the more typical picture articulation test in which one or two sounds are targeted in each single-word production, the practiced clinician will find the scoring sheet format quite "user friendly." During administration, the clinician need only be concerned with transcription of error sounds in two words that are denoted clearly on the scoring form. In essence, the clinician is transcribing the child's word productions on a form that supplies most of that transcription; only changes in the usual production of a word need to be noted.

At first glance, the analysis forms are imposingly long. However, by supplying the information needed for a "worst case" analysis, the forms make analysis of a smaller number of errors quite straightforward. A traditional analysis for a child with one or two phoneme errors should take much less time than the manual's predicted 45 minutes. A phonological analysis for a child with many errors would probably take the predicted time of 35 minutes, but the combined time for administration and analysis should be less than alternative procedures that utilize spontaneous speech samples (Ingram, 1981; Shriberg & Kwiatkowski, 1980) or elicitation of many more responses in which each response represents a single process error (Weiner, 1979).

The clinician performing the analyses should be familiar with the use of both forms of analysis. The traditional analysis has been available in commercially available tests since the early 1960s and the phonological process format available since the late 1970s. All speech-language pathologists should find these two formats familiar.

Technical Aspects

The current form of the EASE provides an initial study of the test's reliability and validity. The test was administered to nine children between the ages of 4 and 7 years. All were enrolled in articulation therapy. An unspecified number of clinicians, including undergraduate students, graduate students, and a certified speech-language pathologist, administered the test in a test-retest study with an intertest period of 1 week. During the first test period, a spontaneous speech sample was also gathered. During the second test administration, a second judge participated in scoring responses.

Test-retest reliability coefficients are reported at a variety of analysis levels. For overall percentage correct scores, the reliability was .90, for the traditional analysis the reliability was .88, and for the phonological process analysis the reliability was .90. Predictably, there was a range of reliabilities for individual speech sounds and processes. In general, those sounds or processes that are always correct or always in error for an individual child are more reliably judged. Child error rates closer to 50% produce lower reliabilities, in part because the child's productions are more likely to be fluctuating on these and, in part, because the judge cannot rely upon a child's typical production in making each judgment. Those sounds with test-retest reliabilities below .80 were nasals /m/ and /n/. None of the phonological processes produced test-retest reliabilities below this level.

Interjudge reliability levels were similar. Totals for the overall score ($r = .90$), traditional analysis ($r = .88$), and process analysis ($r = .90$) were all relatively high for this type of judgment. Interjudge reliabilities fell below .80 for all of the nasals, approximants /r/ and /w/, a single stop /b/, and a single fricative /f/. Phonological processes falling below this level included Final Consonant Deletion, Gliding, and Vocalization.

Like most articulation tests, the EASE relies primarily upon its content for the establishment of validity. Each of the consonants and vowels of a standard English dialect are assessed in what are acknowledged to be useful contexts related to word and syllable positions. Inasmuch as there is no absolutely verified theoretical description of syllabic shapes and consonantal functioning in those shapes, the test authors' choices in this regard are as good as any other. In a similar vein, from a wide variety of possible phonological processes, the EASE authors have selected a group that is typical of many misarticulating children.

Unlike many other articulation test developers, the authors of the EASE sought to establish concurrent validity by comparing percentage correct production of consonants during test administration and measures of articulation in spontaneous speech. The correlation between the percentage of consonants correctly produced during administration of the EASE and the percentage of consonants correctly produced in a spontaneous speech sample was relatively high ($r = .80$), as was the correlation between the total percentage correct on the EASE and the percentage of words produced correctly in spontaneous speech ($r = .81$).

Critique

The elicitation procedure used in the EASE provides a rapid method for obtaining a well-balanced data base for analysis of children's speech production errors. This procedure results in arguably more natural productions than the single-word naming or repetition responses employed in most articulation tests. It is more time efficient than published procedures that rely upon uncontrolled conversational speech samples which may be inadvertently gathered at a variety of linguistic complexity levels, affecting the child's articulatory performance in an unpredictable manner. The scoring format is innovative and should become a standard in tests that target specific word elicitations. If used with appropriate clinical insight into a particular child's level of functioning, the analysis forms are time efficient. Unfortunately, the naive user may spend an inappropriate amount of time following the whole analysis procedure when only portions are required.

The current edition lacks normative data, which is a considerable handicap for the clinician who must document that a particular child's articulatory development is not within the normal range. In such situations, the clinician would be required to administer a normed test prior to use of this instrument. The clinician may find it more efficient to calculate percentages of phonological process use from responses to the normed test, using forms like those developed by Lowe (1986).

References

Andrews, N., & Fey, M. (1986). Analysis of speech of phonologically impaired children in two sampling conditions. *Language Speech and Hearing Services in the Schools, 17*, 187–198.

Elbert, M. & Geirut, J. (1986). *Handbook of clinical phonology: Approaches to assessment and treatment.* London: Taylor & Francis.

Haynes, W., & Haynes, M. (1979). Pragmatics and elicited imitation: Children's performance on discursively related and discursively unrelated sentences. *Journal of Communication Disorders, 12,* 471–479.

Haynes, W., Haynes, M., & Jackson, J. (1982). The effects of phonetic context and linguistic complexity on [s] misarticulation in children. *Journal of Communication Disorders, 15,* 287–297.

Haynes, W., & Steed, S. (1987). Multiphonemic scoring of articulation in imitative sentences: Some preliminary data. *Language Speech and Hearing Services in Schools, 18,* 4–14.

Hodson, B. & Paden, E. (1983). *Targeting intelligible speech.* San Diego: College-Hill.

Hoffman, P., Schuckers, G. & Daniloff, R. (1988). *Assessment and treatment of children's phonetic disorders.* San Diego: College-Hill.

Ingram, D. (1981). *Procedures for the phonological analysis of children's language.* Baltimore: University Park Press.

Lowe, R. (1986). Phonological process analysis using three position tests. *Language Speech and Hearing Services in Schools, 17,* 72–79.

McDonald, E. (1964). *Articulation testing and treatment.* Pittsburgh: Stanwix House.

Shriberg, L., & Kwiatkowski, J. (1980). *Natural process analysis.* New York: John Wiley.

Van Riper, C. (1939). *Speech correction: Principles and methods.* Englewood Cliffs, NJ: Prentice-Hall.

Weiner, F. (1979). *Phonological process analysis.* Baltimore: University Park Press.

Janet A. Norris, Ph.D.

Assistant Professor of Communication Disorders, Louisiana State University, Baton Rouge, Louisiana.

EVALUATING ACQUIRED SKILLS IN COMMUNICATION

Anita Marcott Riley. Tucson, Arizona: Communication Skill Builders, Inc.

Introduction

Evaluating Acquired Skills in Communication (EASIC) is intended to provide an informal, systematic tool for assessing communication skills. The five Informal Communication Skills Inventories that comprise the EASIC are organized into developmental levels, including a prelanguage, two receptive, and two expressive levels. These inventories examine communication behaviors in the areas of semantics, syntax, morphology, and pragmatics. The resulting Skills Profiles may be used with the correlated EASIC Goals and Objectives to select and teach communication skills.

The author of the test, Anita Marcott Riley, developed the EASIC while teaching in the Garden City (Michigan) Public Schools' Developmental Learning Program for the Autistic. Her background in speech and language pathology included enrollment in the Department of Speech Science and Audiology doctoral program at Michigan State University at the time of the test's publication. Riley developed the instrument as a result of her involvement with diagnosing, assessing, and programming for autistic and autistic-like students with cognitive and communicative abilities ranging from the 3- month to 8-year.

The development of the EASIC occurred over a 6-year period, initially resulting in an abbreviated form of the inventory. The test author reports that over 200 autistic students between the ages of 2–26 were included in the derivation of the communication levels and skills assessed. The cognitive abilities of these students ranged from near normal to severely mentally impaired. The abbreviated form of the EASIC reportedly has been used in centers for the mentally impaired, autistic, and preschool developmentally delayed throughout the United States and Canada since 1981.

Although the manual states that the instrument required 6 years to develop and involved over 200 students (Riley, 1984), no further information is provided concerning the procedures used in the selection of items, the organization of skills into a developmental sequence, the representativeness of test items, or other issues related to test construction. No specific information is provided about the 200 students, such as a delineation by age, sex, level of cognitive functioning, handicapping condition(s), educational setting and/or placement, geographic location, or socioeconomic status. Appropriately, therefore, neither norms nor age levels are assigned to test items or to overall performance on the EASIC.

The materials for the EASIC consist of five Skill Inventory booklets and correlated Skills Profiles forms. Each booklet corresponds to a different level of communication skills. A Stimulus Picture Book and supplementary picture cards are provided for assessing specific inventory items within the four higher Skill Inventory levels. Additional test items that must be purchased by the examiner include 26 categories of common objects and toys, such as a hat, hairbrush, cups, combs, plastic foods, crayons, several varieties of toys, blocks, balls, and cars. A set of Goals and Objectives cards that designate a behaviorally written objective suggest materials that can be used to teach the goal and briefly describe an instructional procedure for accomplishing the goal.

The five Skill Inventories arrange communicative behaviors along a continuum. The first level, Pre-Language, assesses prerequisites to meaningful speech. The 27 items at this level are arranged according to skill clusters, defined as Sensory Stimulation, Object Relations, Means-End Causality, Motor Imitation, Matching, Rejection-Negation-Affirmation, Communicative Gestures, Social Interactions, and Nonverbal Communication Functions. Each cluster assesses from one to six corresponding skills, such as responding to environmental sound or matching identical objects. Each skill is comprised of from 1 to 10 component items, so that a behavior, such as matching, requires response to four different sets of objects.

Successive levels of the inventory are constructed similarly. Receptive Level I and Expressive Level I assess communication skills at the stage of emerging language. Both levels respectively measure the comprehension and expression of Noun Labels, Actions and Verbs, Noun Locations and Prepositions, Adjectives and Attributes, Two-Word Phrases, Interrogatives, and other skill clusters. Representative skills within these clusters include identifying common objects by noun labels, identifying an object by its function, or expressing size/color adjectives and attributes. Receptive Level II and Expressive Level II assess somewhat higher stages of semantic, syntactic, morphologic, and pragmatic functioning within many of the same skill clusters. Level II skills include identifying spatial relations and prepositions in pictures, identifying opposite attributes, expressing comparatives and superlatives, or answering when, why, how, and what-if questions.

The Skills Inventories booklets specify each skill to be assessed, the materials needed to evaluate that skill, the instructions that are to be provided by the examiner, and the list of specific stimulus items. Because several stimulus items are used to assess each skill (e.g., six objects are identified within the noun labels skill area and nine action pictures are presented within the responding to verbs skill area), a grid for marking the type of response produced for each stimulus item is provided. Finally, a space to mark the examiner's judgment of skill mastery based upon the component item responses accompanies each skill assessed. The resulting overall performance level assigned to each skill then is transferred to the correlating Skills Profile form that provides a concise summary profile. The Skills Profile contains spaces for recording and comparing performance across five administrations of the EASIC, so that changes over time can be observed easily.

The pictures contained within the Stimulus Picture Book and supplementary picture cards are black-and-white line drawings. They generally depict isolated objects or single actions, displayed in a multiple-choice format of three pictures per page (i.e., the correct choice and two foils). Both the stimulus pictures and the accompanying instructions provided by the examiner are conducive to the elicitation of simple pointing responses and/or one-word expressive responses.

No total scores, standard scores, age equivalencies for total test performance or for individual items, or other type of scores are obtained as a result of administering the EASIC. Rather, each skill is judged for its level of mastery, and the resulting Skills Profile indicates which skills have been accomplished or are emerging and which skills have not developed. Any judgment of the age and/or ability appropriateness of the skills is left to the examiner.

Practical Applications/Uses

The examiner's manual accompanying the EASIC provides no information concerning its theoretical basis, test construction, or test development, and minimal information related to test administration and scoring. A brief introduction that primarily summarizes the components of the inventories is followed by a two-page administration, scoring, goal selection, and materials description section. One additional page provides suggestions for assessing autistic students. Following these pages, the remainder of the manual consists of an appendix that lists the behaviorally written goals and objectives that correlate with the assessment items.

The EASIC manual does not state for whom the inventory is appropriate. The only references to subjects occur in the introduction and in the recommendation page that provides suggestions for administering the inventory to autistic students (Riley, 1984). The introduction states that the instrument has been used with autistic, mentally impaired, and preschool developmentally delayed students, implying that its use may be appropriate for these populations. The author makes no further statements about its purposes. It does not claim to function as a diagnostic instrument that can be used to determine if a developmental delay is present, and its lack of norms or age equivalencies of any type precludes its use in this manner. The introduction does state that the inventory provides a systematic tool for assessing a student's communication skills and a means for translating this information into individualized goals and objectives. It is, in essence, an elaborated skills checklist.

No recommendations are given concerning who may administer the inventory. However, both test administration and test scoring instructions are highly subjective and open to interpretation. Test items assume that the examiner possesses an appropriate background in linguistics and child development. For example, skill 7 within the Pre-Language Level (i.e., object permanence) instructs the examiner to hide items partially or fully and to judge the student's ability to retrieve them. Without further instruction, an individual lacking knowledge of Piagetian tasks would be unlikely to understand the purpose, method, or significance of task elicitation and response. Similarly, more advanced levels of the EASIC require that the examiner make judgments about communication repairs, reciprocal turn taking, and semantic relations, such as agent + object, without defining these terms.

Performance is not scored as pass/fail, but rather along a continuum of six performance categories ranging from "wrong" through physically manipulated, imitated, and various levels of cued and spontaneously occurring response types. Although it is never stated, this scoring system implies that the examiner must be proficient at using behavioral techniques, such as physical manipulation, imitation, gestural cues, phonetic cues, or sign to administer the inventory. The examiner also should have knowledge of a developmentally appropriate response type and of behavioral response terminology in order to make appropriate response judgments. Many of the items call for subjective examiner decisions. For example, item 24 at the Pre-Language Level states that the examiner observes whether an appropriate distance or physical proximity is maintained throughout the interaction, while the student is playing and/or talking, without providing any guidelines concerning what might constitute an appropriate distance, duration of the interaction, or activity.

General guidelines are provided for administering and scoring the EASIC rather than specific standardized instructions. The examiner is instructed to begin administering the inventories at the level judged to be appropriate based upon knowledge of the student and to use clinical judgment when determining when to discontinue the assessment. Within each skill area the examiner is allowed to choose to advance to a new skill if a student responds spontaneously on three items or to discontinue assessing that skill if the student requires cuing on three items. It appears that any portion of the inventory may be administered, that the assessment can be conducted over several sessions, that responses can be cued and assisted, and that reinforcement can be given for communicative attempts, although specific feedback on performance items is not recommended.

Determination of whether a skill has been mastered is also somewhat subjective and dependent upon examiner interpretation. If the "majority" of the student's responses to the component items within a skill are elicited spontaneously, then the skill is judged as "accomplished." If the majority of responses are cued, the skill is "emerging," while primarily imitated or manipulated responses to items result in a "not yet developed" judgment. To a great extent, this scoring system is dependent as much upon the examiner's behaviors as it is the student's behaviors because the examiner chooses the level and type of prompting given for each item.

Once scoring is completed, the information on skill accomplishment levels then is transferred to the appropriate Skills Profiles. From these profiles, skills that fall within the emerging criteria are recommended for consideration within an intervention program. Once again, the examiner is asked to make judgments in selecting the most important skills to teach, based upon developmental appropriateness and relevance to the student's ability to function within the environment.

Technical Aspects

As noted previously, little information is available to the test user about the development of the EASIC. If the instrument is to be used to select instructional goals and objectives and/or to measure progress in communication development, then adequate validity is important. However, there is no substantiation that any type of validity was established, including content validity. The test author reports that the assessed skills are arranged in five developmental levels, but no information or data are provided to support the claim. Each skill is assessed through response to 1–10 items, but there is no indication whether all of the items are at the same developmental level or whether they become progressively more difficult. It is unclear whether the skills become more difficult as one progresses through the booklet. There is no indication how the skills were selected, how they were assigned to the various levels, or why these particular skills were included on the inventories and not others. The skills certainly do not constitute a comprehensive evaluation of a child's communication abilities, yet it is recommended that goals and objectives be selected and taught that directly correlate with items assessed.

No justification is provided for the criteria used to designate a skill "accomplished," "emerging," or "not yet developed." That is, there is no evidence that a skill performed in isolation on the test actually is used functionally by the student, or that "emerging" skills should be targeted for intervention. It is possible that skills designated as emerging by the stated criteria might continue to develop on their own, or that "accomplished" skills will fail to generalize. This is particularly troublesome given that there are no data or results provided for reliability estimates. It is in fact likely that two examiners would obtain differing results because of the latitude allowed in eliciting responses and in scoring. An examiner familiar with the student and the conditions typically required to elicit a response would be likely to obtain a very different profile than an unfamiliar examiner.

Critique

The EASIC is essentially an elaborated checklist of skills and not an instrument that can be used for diagnostic, screening, or placement purposes. It is elaborated in that most of the assessed skills are comprised of several component items, and because scoring is not judged as pass/fail but rather along a continuum of elicitation/response performance levels. These are positive features for skills assessment because they provide the examiner with more information than do one-trial, pass/fail evaluations of a skill. The checklist format offers considerable latitude in both the examiner's elicitation of a response and the observations that can be made relative to the student's response. Thus, the examiner can observe and note the process by which a student does a task as well as judging the accuracy of the response. Checklists further allow the assessment to occur over extended periods of time, at more than one administration, and with flexibility in terms of the number and type of skills that will be evaluated, because interpretation is not based upon a total test performance.

However, in order to be useful in making educational decisions, a checklist needs to have the same properties as other assessment instruments. There must be demonstrated validity and reliability in order for the examiner to have any faith in the results. As stated previously, no apparent attempt has been made to address either of these critical issues in the EASIC. The very flexibility that initially makes this checklist appealing only adds to these problems. Whenever examiner judgment is required in evaluating a response, it is of greater importance that the skills have well-defined categories of responses, that raters are trained in their use, and that procedures are well explained. None of this has been accomplished in the brief procedures section of the manual. To be useful at all, the instrument would require administration by a highly trained and experienced professional with an understanding of the linguistic and psychological constructs referred to throughout the inventory items, but no mention of this requirement is made.

The test author never really states the purpose of the EASIC, but one is led to believe that it is to be used to identify specific skills that a student has and has not acquired and then used to teach these skills. This conclusion is reached because for each skill assessed within the inventories, there are correlated goals and objectives. The examiner is instructed to select goals and objectives from the profile of "emerging" skills. The planning of a student's educational program is a critical task. With no description of the theoretical basis underlying the inventories, no indication of how the component skills were selected or how others were excluded, no explanation of why the skills are considered to be important, and no discussion of what other factors need to be considered in developing an intervention program, educational planning based upon performance on the EASIC cannot be recommended.

Both within the subtitle (i.e., "A Five-Level Informal Communication Skills Inventory for the Preschool Language Impaired, Mentally Impaired, and Autistic Student") and in vague references to appropriate subjects mentioned almost casually within the manual, one is led to conclude that the instrument is used appropriately with severely handicapped and/or low-functioning students. Yet the stimuli for a large number of the skills that are assessed are elicited through black-and-white line drawings that must be discriminated on a page. Many young children, especially young handicapped children, may not be able to relate to the symbolic level required by picture identification or perform tasks that require making discriminations. The inventories do make use of objects for many of the skills assessed, and the flexibility in administrating the order of the items allows for picture tasks to be interspersed with tasks that make use of more concrete objects.

In addition to the picture stimuli provided by the test as purchased, approximately 50+ objects are required for administration. Fortunately, most of the objects are items that would be found typically within a classroom for young or low-functioning students. If an examiner did not have access to these items or did not choose to reassemble the objects each time an evaluation was conducted, the cost of assembling a kit based upon prices at a national discount store would be approximately $80.

The greatest objection this reviewer has to the EASIC is its proposed use as a method for selecting and teaching communication behaviors. Although a cursory remark is made in the manual stating that "the implementation of these goals and objectives must be functional and integrated into the student's daily routine for learning and generalization to take place" (Riley, 1984, p. 3), the procedures recommended on the goals and objectives cards largely are isolated drills on discrete skills that do not incorporate the communication of any meaningful information to any other person. The procedures follow behavioristic principles in the mode of presenting a stimulus (often a picture), eliciting a response on cue, and repeating the task. "Integration" into the student's daily routine supposedly is accomplished by setting up the same type of adult initiated request and obedient response whenever a similar situation (e.g., naming noun items or asking wh-questions) occurs within the context of daily routines.

Both the assessment as it is conducted by the EASIC and the intervention as described within the recommended procedures fail to measure or promote communication or social interaction in real-life situations and therefore tell very little about the student's knowledge or use of language for communication purposes (Fey, 1986;

Hart, 1981; Spradlin & Siegel, 1982). This teach-to-test procedure has been shown to be ineffective, in that students demonstrate progress on tests but that the progress has little or no bearing on the way in which the person actually uses language in typical social interactions (Culatta & Horn, 1982; Mulac & Tomlinson, 1977). Lack of generalization is particularly prominent among the severely language impaired and low functioning populations referred to by this instrument (Bricker, 1986; Bricker & Bricker, 1974; Bricker & Carlson, 1981; Mahoney & Weller, 1980).

The test-and-teach procedure, furthermore, decimates the communicative nature of language. Communication is a social behavior in which the speaker shares information and regulates the behaviors of others using language or gestures (Bates, 1976; Hart, 1981; Hart & Rogers-Warren, 1978; Spradlin & Siegel, 1982). Labeling isolated words or practicing rote phrases in simulated activities in a noncommunicative setting creates neither the motivation or experience with communication that constitutes the very nature of language and language development (Bricker, 1986).

In sum, as a checklist the EASIC has some appealing features, but its lack of validity and reliability render it unsuitable for most uses. Stronger objections are raised relative to the test-and-teach method recommended by this instrument for developing communication skills in handicapped students.

References

Bates, E. (1976). Pragmatics and sociolinguistics in child language. In D. Morehead & A. Morehead (Eds.), *Normal and deficient child language*, (pp. 411–463). Baltimore: University Park Press.

Bricker, D.D. (1986). *Early education of at-risk and handicapped infants, todlers, and preschool children.* Glenview, IL: Scott, Forseman and Company.

Bricker, W., & Bricker, D. (1974). An early language training strategy. In R. Schiefelbusch and L. Lloyd (Eds.), *Language perspectives: Acquisition, retardation and intervention* (pp. 431–468). Baltimore: University Park Press.

Bricker, D., & Carlson, L. (1981). Issues in early language intervention. In R. Schiefelbusch & D. Bricker (1981), *Early language: Acquisition and intervention* (pp. 477–516). Baltimore: University Park Press.

Culatta, B., & Horn, D. (1982). A program for achieving generalization of grammatical rules to spontaneous discourse. *Journal of Speech and Hearing Disorders, 2,* 174–181.

Fey, M.E. (1986). *Language intervention with young children.* San Diego: College Hill.

Hart, B. (1981). Pragmatics: How language is used. *Analysis and Intervention in Developmental Disabilities, 1,* 299–313.

Hart, B., & Rogers-Warren, A. (1978). The milieu approach to teaching language. In R. Schiefelbusch (Ed.), *Language intervention strategies* (pp. 193–236). Baltimore: University Park Press.

Mahoney, G., & Weller, E. (1980). An ecological approach to language intervention. In D. Bricker (Ed.), *A resource book on language intervention with children* (pp. 17–32). San Francisco: Jossey-Bass.

Mulac, A., & Tomlinson, C. (1977). Generalization of an operant remediation program for syntax with language delayed children. *Journal of Communication Disorders, 10,* 231–243.

Riley, A. M. (1984). *Evaluating Acquired Skills in Communication manual.* Tucson: Communication Skill Builders.

Spradlin, J., & Siegel, G. (1982). Language training in natural and clinical environments. *Journal of Speech and Hearing Disorders, 47,* 2–6.

Kathleen A. Camara, Ph.D.

Associate Professor of Child Study, Eliot Pearson Department of Child Study, Tufts University, Medford, Massachusetts.

FAMILY ADAPTABILITY AND COHESION EVALUATION SCALES

David H. Olson, Joyce Portner, and Yoav Lavee. St. Paul, Minnesota: Family Social Science, University of Minnesota.

Introduction

The Family Adaptability and Cohesion Evaluation Scales (FACES III) is the third version of a self-report instrument developed by David Olson and his colleagues that is designed to assess family functioning. The measure is comprised of 20-item scales that are intended to assess how family members perceive their family system and how they describe their ideal family system. The FACES were developed to assess family cohesion and family adaptability, the two major dimensions of the circumplex model of marital and family interaction developed by David Olson and colleagues. A measure of family satisfaction is obtained by analyzing the discrepancies between scores on the perceived and ideal descriptions. FACES III was developed for both research purposes and clinical assessment and can be administered to parents and children aged 12 years or older. Separate versions of the FACES III scales are available for administration to couples without children and for clinicians wishing to use the instrument as a tool for clinical assessment of family functioning.

The design of the FACES instruments was based on the conceptual work of David H. Olson and his associates at the Family Social Science Center at the University of Minnesota (Olson, Russell, & Sprenkle, 1979, 1980, 1983). A comprehensive review of family theory and family therapy literature led Olson, Russell and Sprenkle to identify three dimensions that they considered central in describing family behavior: cohesion, adaptability, and communication. Using these dimensions as their primary concepts, they developed the circumplex model of family functioning.

The FACES instruments were specifically constructed to measure two of the major dimensions in the circumplex model: family cohesion and adaptability. Cohesion refers to the degree to which there is emotional bonding between and among family members. Adaptability refers to the extent to which the family system is flexible and able to change its roles and relationships in response to situational and developmental stress.

Within the circumplex model, the test authors have identified four levels of family cohesion (i.e., disengaged, separated, connected, and enmeshed) and four levels of family adaptability (i.e., rigid, structured, flexible, and chaotic). The two moderate levels of cohesion (separated and connected) and of adaptability (structured and flexible) represent balanced levels of family functioning and are hypoth-

209

esized to be most viable for healthy family functioning, while the extreme levels (disengaged and enmeshed, and rigid and chaotic) are seen as more problematic for families over time. The combination of the four levels of cohesion with the four levels of adaptability yield 16 types of family systems. FACES was designed to enable the researcher or clinician to place individual family members or groups of families within the circumplex model.

The original 111-item self-report FACES scale was developed by Portner (1981) and Bell (1982). Two populations were used to develop the instrument: 410 young adults were used to assess the empirical validity, and 35 marriage and family counselors were used to assess the clinical validity of the scale. The instrument then was used in a study of 210 parent-adolescent triads. The FACES instrument did appear to discriminate between problem families and nonsymptomatic families. More nonclinic families and nonproblem families fell into the balanced areas of the circumplex model on cohesion and adaptability, although the majority of high-risk families were of an extreme type.

During the development of the FACES instrument, an attempt was made to make the circumplex model culturally relevant to families with varied ethnic and cultural backgrounds by taking into consideration variations in family acceptance of extreme behaviors. A Family Satisfaction measure was developed based on the assumption that as long as all family members are satisfied with the expectations of their family, families will function well. Family members are asked to complete the FACES instrument twice—once in terms of how they perceive their family system, and second, for how they ideally would like it to be. The difference in scores between perceived and ideal family functioning is used to measure family satisfaction. Thus, the test authors conclude that the greater the perceived-ideal discrepancy, the greater the dissatisfaction with the present family system.

The second major revision of the FACES instrument was completed in the spring of 1981 . The revisions were designed to create a shorter instrument so that it could be used with children and with those with limited reading ability. In this revision, the number of double negative items was reduced and a 5-point response scale was provided. During the development of FACES II, 464 adults (average age = 30.5 years) were asked to respond to 90 items. On the basis of factor analysis and reliability analysis, the initial scale was reduced to 50 items. Further reduction of the number of items occurred after FACES II was administered to 2,412 individuals in a national survey of nonproblem families across the life cycle from young couples with no children to retired couples (Olson et al., 1983). The final version of FACES II contained a total of 30 items, of which there were 16 measures of cohesion and 14 measures of adaptability.

Despite the revisions, FACES II still had limitations that made it difficult to use with children, some adults, and with families representing diverse family forms (e.g., divorced, remarried, single-parent, cohabiting couples, and couples without children). The test authors' goals in developing FACES III were to improve the reliability, validity, and clinical utility of the scales and to overcome some of the limitations of FACES II. Further analysis of data collected from 2,412 individuals in the national survey was conducted. The total sample was split into two random and independent samples. Sample I consisted of 1,206 individuals and sample 2 consisted of 1,000 adults and 206 adolescents. The test authors report in the FACES

III manual that they used an iterative process based on factor analyses to add, eliminate, and replace items and to shorten the scale. In addition, negative items were eliminated so that the scales became easier to understand and to score. Directions to family members were written more clearly, and an attempt was made to develop items that were relevant for a variety of family forms (e.g., nuclear, remarried, single-parent) and couples (e.g., married, cohabiting) without children. In addition, the test authors identified specific norms for adults across the life cycle.

The final 20 item scale of FACES III consists of 10 items assessing family cohesion and 10 items assessing family adaptability. There are two items for each of the five concepts related to the cohesion dimension: 1) emotional bonding, 2) supportiveness, 3) family boundaries, 4) time and friends, and 5) interest in recreation. There are two items for each of the three concepts related to the adaptability dimension—leadership, control, and discipline—and four items for the combined concepts of roles and rules. Each of the items is stated in a sentence format. The respondent is asked to read each of the statements and, using a scale that ranges from 1 (almost never) to 5 (almost always), is asked to decide for each how frequently the described behavior occurs in his or her family.

The scales may be administered a second time to obtain a respondent's ideal description of his or her family system. The discrepancy between the individual's ratings of the ideal and perceived family system becomes an indirect measure of family satisfaction.

Practical Applications/Uses

FACES III provides data for assessments of family life for both research and clinical work. The test authors state that about 200 research projects are currently using earlier versions of the scales (FACES and FACES II); but data from these ongoing projects were not available for this review. Several studies have been completed by Olson and his colleagues that test the validity of the three versions of the FACES scales.

There have been several published clinical studies that have used FACES and FACES II to discriminate nonproblem families from 1) those with runaway children (Bell, 1982), 2) those experiencing parent-adolescent conflict (Portner, 1981), 3) high-risk families (Garbarino, Sebes, & Schellenbach, 1984), 4) schizophrenic and neurotic families (Clarke, 1984), 5) chemically dependent families (Olson & Killorin; 1985, Killorin & Olson, 1984), 6) families of sex offenders (Carnes, 1985), and 7) families with adolescent juvenile offenders (Rodick, Henggler, & Hanson, 1985). These studies were used primarily to test the hypothesis that those families falling into the balanced areas of the circumplex model are more functional than those falling into the extreme areas.

FACES has also been used to examine the effects of a treatment program on alcoholic families (Bonk, 1984). Bonk found no significant differences in the mean scores on cohesion or adaptability after family participation in the treatment program, but did find significant increases in family satisfaction scores.

Other applications to research might include the use of the instrument to compare family perceptions between males and females, or between different kinds of families (e.g., divorced father-custody, mother-custody and joint-custody families.) It might also be used in longitudinal studies focusing on the development of family systems. The test authors emphasize the notion that families are dynamic, and, as such, the assessments gathered in FACES III will change over time. To date, no longitudinal studies using FACES III have been conducted. As a research tool, the scales seem best suited as a method for clustering families to determine what kind of family life systems are associated with particular types of psychological, intellectual, social, and emotional behaviors of adults and children.

In their manual, the authors also suggest that the collection of data relating to perceived and ideal evaluations of family members provides a measure of family satisfaction that offers directions for future therapy. However, the instrument does not prescribe specific methods for intervention; nor does it specify the problem areas in which dissatisfaction among family members may occur. It provides only general information on individual and family similarities and differences in perceptions of family cohesion and adaptability and overall satisfaction with the current family system. Thus, the instrument can identify the individuals within a family who may be more or less satisfied with the family system and can identify whether the individual would prefer a less rigid or less chaotic style of functioning. This information might help families and therapists in setting possible directions for growth as preferred by each family member, but it does not specify the nature of the problems. Clinical assessment is necessary to clarify the sources of dissatisfaction and specific strategies for growth.

The FACES scales were developed for use with parents at any stage of the family life cycle, families with adolescents who are 12 years or older, and for young couples without children (Couples Form). The manual suggests that individuals should respond to the items based on their assessment of interaction among family members currently living in the home. Therefore, the assessment of family functioning obtained is based only on household membership. Although this offers some clarity for those rating the family system, it provides a very limited view of the family system, restricting the system only to those who live together. It could be argued that a child who has moved away from home, or a divorced parent who lives at a different residence, but who still remains in contact with the children, still can exert a great deal of influence on the family system and remain an integral part of that system.

The instructions for administration of FACES III are brief. The manual does not list any introductory remarks for the examiner, nor does it specify the type of appropriate settings for administration. It would appear that FACES III can be administered in any setting appropriate for clinical or research assessment. A quiet room with few distractions, and the provision of confidentiality and privacy to individual family members would probably be best. The instrument could be administered within the context of individual or family counseling or with others in such settings as classrooms.

The manual does not identify the need for specific credentials to administer the FACES instrument. No special technical skill is required of the administor other than the ability to build rapport with respondents completing a pencil-and-paper task. Paraprofessionals, psychological assistants or associates, teachers, social workers or clerical assistants with little training would be able to administer the instrument. The manual does not suggest that the examiner read the instructions aloud or give help in clarifying responses. However, it would be best administered by an individual who understands the test questions. The items are written at a seventh-grade level so that children as young as 12 years can understand the items. The instrument can be self-administered assuming there is a sufficient reading proficiency. However, an examiner should be present to clarify questions and to make sure the scales are properly completed. Because there are only 20 items in the FACES III version, test administrators encouraged to check each answer sheet as it is turned in to check for incomplete information. For those who are visually impaired or who do not possess reading competency, the items could be read aloud by an examiner.

The amount of time necessary for administration of FACES III is not indicated in the manual, but it is probably not more than approximately 20-30 minutes. Administration of the instrument should be in a relaxed, unhurried manner.

The ease and objectivity of scoring for an individual response sheet is a major strength of FACES III. To obtain the scores on the perceived family system, the examiner must tabulate the odd-numbered items to derive the individual's score on cohesion and the even-numbered items to derive the individual's score on adaptability. Each of these scores can be plotted on a graph and classified into the circumplex model in four ways: 1) 16 family types; 2) balanced, mid-range, or extreme areas of functioning; 3) the four quadrants (flexible-separated, flexible-connected, structured-separated, or structured-connected); or 4) balanced and quadrants. (Reader is referred to Figure 1, see, Olson, Portner, & Lavee, 1985 for a diagrammatic representation of the circumplex model.)

For the second part of FACES III, the measure of the ideal family system, the score is derived using the same method just described. Thus, two scores are calculated for ideal cohesion and ideal adaptability. The differences between the scores of perceived and ideal cohesion, and perceived and ideal adaptability will yield a family satisfaction score.

To obtain a family profile score, scores of individual members on perceived cohesion are averaged together to yield a family perceived cohesion score. The same procedure is used to compute a family perceived adaptability score. (Although it is not stated in the manual, it is assumed that a similar procedure would be used to compute the ideal cohesion and ideal adaptability score. The differences between the family perceived cohesion and family ideal cohesion score would yield a measure of family satisfaction for the whole family.) Formulae for calculating couple and family scores are indicated in Table 8 of the manual. The family scores can be plotted on the circumplex model graph to determine the classification of the family system.

The test authors recognize that this method of computing a family score has some limitations. Mean scores can represent a family's perceptions as a unit if each family member's scores are similar. However, if there is considerable disagreement among family members, a mean score may distort the accuracy of the variability of individual perceptions. For this reason, the test authors suggest the use of a discrepancy score. Formulae for computing couple and family mean scores and discrepancy scores are indicated in Table 8 of the manual. Discrepancy scores can be computed between all possible dyads in a family system.

For assessments of a small sample of families (less than 10), the scoring of FACES

III can be done manually. At this time, machine and computer scoring are not available. However, for larger samples, individual responses to each item on FACES III could be entered into data formats used in existing computer packages such as SPSS-X, BMPD or SAS. These packages offer statistical procedures that can be used for the calculation of scores and analysis of data. The use of computer analyses would greatly reduce the amount of time spent in scoring. Alternatively, a program easily could be written to generate the variety of scores described in the FACES III manual.

Once scores have been tabulated, clinicians or researchers may find it useful to present the results of a family profile graphically. Several examples of graphs of family profiles are provided within the manual.

The classification of families into the circumplex model is based solely on the analysis of the objective scores obtained in FACES III. These scores are compared to norms and cutting points for the four levels of cohesion and four levels of adaptability. The authors of FACES III present norms and cutting points that have been established for groups of adults, families with adolescents, and for young couples without children. The norms and cutting points are indicated in Table 6 and Figure 7 of the manual and are based on the compilation of data obtained in studies conducted by Olson et al. (1983) of 2,453 adults, 1,315 families with adolescents, and 242 young couples.

Families are categorized in one of 16 family types, or in balanced, mid-range, or extreme categories, or in one of the four quadrants of family functioning: flexible-separated, flexible-connected, structured-separated, and structured-connected. However, once the family has been categorized, no further interpretive information is provided by the authors. Because there are no normative data available on the normative changes that may take place in the development of the individual and of the family, one cannot determine from one administration of FACES III which categories are likely to be associated with unhealthy family functioning. The authors themselves state that it may be that in response to stress or to developmental crises, a family may become more enmeshed, and that this may be adaptive for a family in the midst of a crisis. Data derived from the scores on FACES III may not be sufficient to adequately describe competence in family functioning.

A sample graphic representation of discrepancy scores for individual family members' perceptions of their own and ideal family is included in the manual. However, the FACES III authors do not identify methods for interpreting discrepancy scores. For example, the norms or cutoff points for discrepancy scores that may place an individual or family system at risk. Nor do the authors describe what might be "healthy" or normal discrepancy scores. It would appear that interpretation of these scores would best be completed by trained clinicians and family therapists who gather additional information on family functioning to determine need and directions of individual or family therapy.

Technical Aspects

Numerous studies have been conducted by Olson and his colleagues to test the reliability and validity of the FACES instruments. Initial studies conducted by Portner (1981) and Bell (1982) were designed to assess the empirical validity of the scale and to determine the alpha reliability of the two constructs of cohesion and adaptation. In these studies the FACES instrument appeared to discriminate between problem and nonproblem families. The alpha reliabilities for the cohesion and adaptability constructs in the original 111-item scale were .83 and .75, respectively.

In a national survey conducted by Olson et al. (1983), higher levels of cohesion and change seemed to be associated with better family functioning in "normal families." Interestingly, in clinical samples, a curvilinear relationship was found between the dimensions of cohesion and adaptability and family functioning. Extreme values on both constructs were more likely to be associated with dysfunction in these clinical families.

Several revisions of the scale have been completed over the years. With each new revision, a series of studies were completed to assess the internal reliability (Cronbach's alpha) of the constructs of cohesion and adaptability. During the development of FACES II, 464 adults completed the scales. Internal reliability estimates (alpha) for the reduced scale of 50 items were .91 for cohesion and .80 for adaptability. In addition, a test-retest reliability study was conducted in the fall of 1981 using the 50-item version. One hundred twenty-four university and high school students (average age = 19.2 years) who were not currently enrolled in a family studies course were asked to describe their "family of origin." The test-retest correlation for the 50-item FACES II scale was .84; the alpha reliability estimates for cohesion and adaptability were .83 and .80, respectively.

The 50-item scale was then administered to 2,412 nonproblem families in a national survey (Olson et al., 1983). The sample was divided into two equal subgroups. The Cronbach alpha estimates of reliability for the total group were .87 for cohesion, .78 for adaptability, and .90 for the total scale.

Additional analyses of the national survey data led to further reduction of the number of items in the scale. In these subsequent analyses, the total sample was split into two random and independent samples. Sample 1 consisted of 1,206 individuals and sample 2 consisted of 1,000 adults and 206 adolescents. A factor analysis of FACES II items was conducted with sample 1. Factor analyses were used to add, eliminate, and replace items for the scale. Twenty items were selected, 10 for each dimension. These items were factor analyzed using data from sample 2. The same factor structure that emerged with sample 1 was found with sample 2.

In FACES III, the dimensions of cohesion and adaptability were developed as independent orthogonal measures; no correlation was found between the two dimensions ($r = .03$). The reliability for the 20-item scale was computed for each split sample and for the total sample. The results were .76, .75, and .77 for the cohesion scales on samples 1 and 2 and the total sample, respectively. The alpha estimates for adaptability were .58, .63, and .62 for samples 1 and 2 and the total sample, respectively. Alpha estimates for the total scale were .67, .67, and .68 for samples 1 and 2 and for the total sample, respectively.

It would appear that the reduction of the number of items for the FACES III version resulted in lower reliabilities for the two dimensions and for the total score. However, the alpha reliabilities of FACES III are still at a respectable level, given the state of measurement in this field. One could also argue that the shortened version of the instrument may lead to greater reliability in the response of individuals who will find the shorter version easier to complete.

The authors of FACES III have completed extensive testing to establish norms and cutting points for the instrument. Data from samples of 2,453 adults, 1,315 families with adolescents, and 242 young couples were used to generate norms for these groups on each of the four levels of cohesion and adaptability.

The results of extensive studies are presented by Olson and his colleagues on the internal reliability and test-retest reliability of FACES III. However, no studies have reported any information on the external validity of the constructs of cohesion and adaptability. For example, there are no studies reported in the manual that present correlations between the cohesion and adaptability dimensions on the FACES scale and other scales measuring cohesion and adaptability, or on behavioral measures of these constructs. Studies yielding such data on the constructs would greatly strengthen the external validity of the scales for clinical and research use.

Critique

FACES III was developed as a self-report measure designed to assess the family system on the dimensions of cohesion and adaptability. The scales form one of the few standardized instruments available in the field of family assessment. The researchers have provided a thorough description of the test construction, development, and research that was carried out to test the validity and reliability of the instrument. The theoretical, conceptual, methodological, and empirical bases for the development of the three versions of the FACES instrument have been described in detail in numerous books and articles written by Olson and his colleagues. The FACES scales were developed specifically to be used within the context of placing families within the circumplex model of marital and family interaction, a model developed by Olson et al. for the purpose of bridging family theory, research, and practice.

The strengths of the instrument include the use of objective techniques for assessment of cohesion and adaptation; the substantial information that is provided by the authors on studies conducted to test the internal validity and reliability of the instrument; the ease with which the scales can be administered to family members; the careful scientific approach used in developing the constructs of cohesion and adaptability within the instrument; and the use of multiple sources to gather data on the family system.

The review of the scales and of studies that have employed FACES III suggest that there are at least five issues that need to be considered by potential investigators and clinicians wishing to use FACES III. First, in order to conduct a comprehensive assessment of family interaction, it is recommended that the instrument be used in combination with methods of family assessment other than those relying solely on self-report. In an early paper written about research methodology for family research, Olson (1977) notes the value of multitrait, multimethod research strategies to obtain data on the complex questions about interpersonal relationships, and he recommends the use of both self-report and behavioral methods in studies. For both research and clinical applications of FACES III, the utility and validity of family assessments would be greatly enhanced by the use of behavioral assessment, clinical interview, or observational assessments of family interaction. These methods frequently elicit different types of information about families; no one assessment tool has yet been developed that offers an accurate and complete portrayal of the complexities of family life.

A second issue relates to the application of the test to a variety of ethnic, cultural, and family structural groups. The authors provide norms for the cohesion, adaptability, and total scale scores for groups of adults, adolescents, and parents and for young couples without children. However, no data are provided on the appropriateness of these norms to families of varied ethnic or cultural origin. Neither are norms provided for families who have experienced divorce or remarriage of parents.

Respondents are expected to rate the frequency of occurrence of the items based on the interactions among members of their household. However, it may be argued that family members, such as divorced parents, who are no longer part of the household may still exert a significant influence on family cohesion and adaptability. The authors do not rule out the use of the instrument to assess the total family system, including those members who are not part of the same household. However, the wording of the items in the scales is awkward for such an assessment because some of the items refer to activities that are household related (e.g., doing chores, assigning household responsibility, etc.).

A third issue relates to the focus of FACES III on the assessment of general family functioning. Respondents are asked to rate the frequency of occurrence for each item based on their overall perceptions of family members, parents or children. However, perceptions of each of the children or of mothers or fathers separately are not obtained. The respondent is asked to generalize about the entire family. This could present problems for respondents who perceive their relationships with one family member quite differently from relationships with another. For example, for the item asking whether parents and children discuss punishment together, in some families one parent may do so quite regularly while the other does not. In this case, what response would a child or parent give? The response may be "almost always" for one parent and "almost never" for another. The likely response to such an item under these circumstances might be "sometimes," with the individual "averaging" the responses of the two parents. However, one could argue that this family style is quite different from one in which both parents "sometimes" discuss punishment with the children. In the present form of FACES III, the scoring for both families would be the same. As a result, the scores on the cohesion and adaptability dimensions may disguise important differences within the family. The problem becomes more complicated when adolescents from remarried families are asked to complete the scales. Does one include stepparent and parent within the assessment? According to the manual, the child would be encouraged to consider family members living together in the same household; however, this may not offer a complete or valid assessment of the entire family system.

The authors emphasize the dynamic nature of family life and note that the scores on FACES III may change from time to time, depending on the stage in the life cycle, or on particular crisis events the family may be experiencing at the time of administration. Olson suggests that the more "extreme" styles of family interaction may be more functional at certain times of the family's life. This suggests the need for longitudinal studies to examine the changes in the family system. This approach would provide normative data on family cohesion and adaptability at different developmental levels of the individuals within the family and of the family system. As Beavers and Voeller (1983) note in their criticisms of the circumplex model, the model avoids acknowledgment that there are differences in the levels of competence shown by families. There is a need for developing a continuum on which such levels can be assessed.

The interpretation of the classifications of families resulting from the FACES III scores is no simple task, given the dynamic nature of the family system. For example, Killorin and Olson (1984) discussed families that move to a more rigid structure and at the end of treatment function more like a rigidly separated family. He states that this type of family system seemed to be more functional for the family at that time. The determination of what is functional for families is not easily interpreted from the scores on FACES III. It would appear that clinical judgment is necessary for making such assessments. In this regard, FACES III is not as useful in offering an objective assessment of the family system. It would appear that clinical expertise is necessary for appropriate interpretation of scores and placement of the family within the circumplex model.

FACES III is also limited in that, in its present form, it can only be applied to families with adolescent children or with no children. There are no versions of the instrument available for use with children younger than 12 years. The development of such a scale would require restructuring the items to take into account issues relating to the child's level of development, as well as a rewording of some items to improve the clarity for younger children.

The development of an standardized assessment tool for analyzing family systems is a worthy and challenging task. Olson and his colleagues have certainly made significant headway in developing such a tool. Further refinement of the model and the instrument may yield promising results. At present, FACES III does have some limited value for researchers and clinicians in its identification of general patterns of interaction within the family system. The instrument, used with other instruments, and with the interpretive expertise of a skilled clinician may offer some guidance in planning therapeutic interventions and for understanding the more general systems of interaction used by families.

References

Barnes, H.L., & Olson, D.H. (1985). Parent-adolescent communication and the circumplex model. *Child Development, 56,* 438–447.

Beavers, W.R., & Voeller, M.N. (1983). Family models: Comparing and contrasting the Olson circumplex model with the Beavers systems model. *Family Process, 22,* 85–98.

Bell, R. (1982). *Parent-adolescent interaction in runaway families.* Unpublished doctoral dissertation, University of Minnesota, St. Paul.

Bonk, J. (1984). *Perceptions of psychodynamics during a transitional period as reported by families affected by alcoholism.* Unpublished doctoral dissertation. University of Arizona, Tucson.

Carnes, P. (1985). *Counseling sexual abusers.* Minneapolis, MN: CompCare Publications.

Clarke, J. (1984). *The family types of schizophrenics, neurotics, and "normals."* Unpublished doctoral dissertation, Family Social Science, Univerity of Minnesota, St. Paul.

Garbarino, J., Sebes, J., & Schellenbach, C. (1984). Families at risk for destructive parent-child relations in adolescence. *Child Development, 55,* 174–183.

Killorin, E., & Olson, D.H. (1984). The chaotic flippers in treatment. In E. Kaufman (Ed.), *Power To change: Family case studies in the treatment of alcoholism* (pp. 99–129). New York: Gardner Press, Inc.

Olson, D.H. (1977). Insiders' and outsiders' views of relationships: Research strategies. In G. Levinger & H.L. Rausch (Eds.), *Close relationships: Perspectives on the meaning of intimacy* (pp. 115–135). Amherst, MA: University of Massachusetts Press.

Olson, D.H. (1985). Commentary: Struggling with congruence across theoretical models and methods. *Family Process, 24,* 203–207.

Olson, D.H. (1986). Circumplex model VII: Validation studies and FACES III. *Family Process, 25,* 337–351.

Olson, D.H., & Killorin, E. (1985). *Clinical rating scale for circumplex model.* St. Paul, MN: Family Social Science, University of Minnesota.

Olson, D.H., & McCubbin, H.I. (1982). Circumplex model of marital and family systems V: Application to family stress and crises intervention. In H.I. McCubbin, A.E. Cauble, & J.M. Patterson (Eds.), *Family stress, coping, and social support* (pp. 48–68). Springfield, IL: Charles C. Thomas Publishers.

Olson, D.H., McCubbin, H.I., Barnes, H.L., Larsen, A., Muxen, M.J., & Wilson, M. (1983). *Families: What makes them work.* Beverly Hills, CA: Sage Publications.

Olson, D.H., Portner, J., & Lavee, Y. (1985). *FACES III.* St. Paul, MN: Family Social Science, University of Minnesota.

Olson, D.H., Russell, C.S., & Sprenkle, D.H. (1979). Circumplex model of marital and family systems II: Empirical studies and clinical intervention (pp. 128–176). In J. Vincent (Ed.), *Advances in family intervention, assessment, and theory.* Greenwich, CT: JAI Press.

Olson, D.H., Russell, C.S., & Sprenkle, D.H. (1980). Marital and family therapy: A decade review. *Journal of Marriage and Family, 42,* 973–993.

Olson, D.H., Russell, C.S., & Sprenkle, D.H. (1983). Circumplex model of marital and family systems: VI. Theoretical update. *Family Process, 22,* 69–83.

Olson, D.H., Sprenkle, D.H., & Russell, C.S. (1979). Circumplex model of marital and family systems: I. Cohesion and adaptability dimensions, family types and clinical applications. *Family Process, 18,* 3–28.

Portner, J. (1981). *Parent-adolescent interaction of families in treatment.* Unpublished doctoral dissertation, University of Minnesota, St. Paul.

Rodick, J.D., Henggler, S.W., & Hanson (1986). An evaluation of Family Adaptability and Cohesion Evaluation Scales (FACES) and the circumplex model. *Journal of Abnormal Child Psychology, 14,* 77–87.

Russell, C.S. (1979). Circumplex model of marital and family systems: III. Empirical evaluation with families. *Family Process, 18,* 29–44.

James E. Jirsa, Ph.D.
School Psychologist, Madison Metropolitan School District, Madison, Wisconsin.

HAPTIC INTELLIGENCE SCALE FOR ADULT BLIND

Harriet C. Shurrager and Phil S. Shurrager. Chicago, Illinois: Stoelting Company.

Introduction

The Haptic Intelligence Scale for Adult Blind (HIS) is an individually administered performance scale for blind individuals ages 16 through 64. The scale was constructed to "measure abilities not adequately assessed either by verbal tests of intelligence or existing performance tests designed or adapted for the blind" (Shurrager & Shurrager, 1964, p. iii). It is assumed that the HIS will be used in conjunction with a verbal intelligence test, thereby resulting in a more complete and meaningful assessment of adult blind capabilities.

The authors of the HIS, Phil S. and Harriet C. Shurrager, were associated with the Illinois Institute of Technology (IIT) for many years. H.C. Shurrager was an Associate Professor of Psychology and P.S. Shurrager was a Professor of Psychology and chairman of the Department of Psychology and Education (1946–1973). He has been Professor Emeritus since 1973. P.S. Shurrager has also worked as a psychologist and has done consulting work with a wide range of clients in business and industry. He has contributed journal articles in the fields of biology and experimental psychology and has co-authored the Occupational Aptitude Test Series (i.e., an employment screening device used by P.S. Shurrager in his private consultations with business and industry). P.S. Shurrager was a co-discoverer of the biochemical and physiological changes paralleling dark and light adaptation in the vitreous humor of mammalian eyes and was also the originator of spinal conditioning and learning at a motor neurone synapse. P.S. Shurrager has been a member of the American Board of Professional Psychology, the Society for Experimental Biology and Medicine, the Academy of Sciences (life), and he has been a Fellow of the American Academy of Neurology.

H.C. Shurrager earned her doctorate from the University of Illinois. The topic of her dissertation was the measurement of memory on an absolute scale. Following positions at the University of Pennsylvania and St. Lawrence University, H.C. Shurrager accompanied P.S. Shurrager to the Illinois Institute of Technology in 1946. H.C. Shurrager was the principal investigator of the work that led to the development of the HIS. The Shurragers retired from IIT in 1973 and currently live in Cape Coral, Florida.

The impetus for the development of the HIS was the Shurragers' belief that an individual's ability to be accepted by society and to "fit in" was largely determined by the individual's reaction to his or her handicap. As a corollary to this position, it was further reasoned that if variations in the adjustment to blindness were to be explored fully, it would be important to somehow measure the abilities contributing to the individual's problem-solving capacity. A significant part of these problem-solving abilities, based on earlier investigations, was identified as a kinesthetic and orientation factor based on the sense of touch, the haptic sense, which was especially important for blind people. The primary objective then was to meet an identified need for a nonverbal intelligence test for blind persons.

In 1954, the Shurragers together with S. B. Watson, an IIT doctoral student at the time, began to develop a performance scale for adult blind. This process was guided by or based upon the Performance scale of the Wechsler-Bellevue Intelligence Scale (WBIS). An experimental form of the scale was administered to partially sighted and blind persons in the Chicago area; the results were reported in Watson's (1956) dissertation. Building on this experience, H. C. Shurrager prepared a proposal to the Office of Vocational Rehabilitation (Washington, D.C.) for sufficient funding to allow the further development and national standardization of the scale.

The original 1954 scale consisted of five tests, four that were analogous to the WBIS: 1) Digit Symbol, 2) Block Design, 3) Object Assembly, and 4) Object Completion (Picture Completion in the Wechsler framework). The fifth test, Plan-of-Search, represented an attempt to adapt the Ball and Field test from the Stanford-Binet. This test, known then as the Performance Scale for Adult Blind (PSAB) formed the basis of the subsequent Haptic Intelligence Scale (HIS). Because intercorrelations of these five tests indicated a dominant common factor, two additional tests, Bead Arithmetic and Pattern Board, were developed and included in the scale. It was thought that the new tests required less fine or specific tactile discrimination and manipulation skills. The term "common factor" (in reference to intelligence testing) refers to a general mental ability or energy. As Sattler (1982) indicates, "Any intellectual activity involves both a general factor, which it shares with all other intellectual activities, and a specific factor, which it shares with none" (p. 38). The research form of the HIS then consisted of seven subtests: 1) Digit Symbol, 2) Block Design, 3) Object Assembly, 4) Object Completion, 5) Plan-of-Search, 6) Bead Arithmetic, and 7) Pattern Board. The seven-test version of the HIS was administered to 399 blind subjects. The fifth test, Plan-of-Search, was found to correlate .37 with the total of HIS subtests and .22 with the Wechsler Adult Intelligence Scale (WAIS) Verbal score. Interscale correlations were uniformly low; .27 to .33. In addition, standard deviations were very large and test-retest reliability was .57. On the basis of these findings, Plan-of-Search was eliminated as a HIS subtest. The final version of the HIS, completed in 1964 and consisting of six of the original seven subtests, has not been revised or adapted for individuals younger than 16 years of age, nor are there any foreign language versions available.

The *Digit Symbol* subtest is presented in a wooden tray with two heat-formed rectangular plastic test boards. Formed into the smaller (12" × 3") test board are six different symbols (from top to bottom: horizontal rectangle, inverted triangle, vertical rectangle, circle, square), which are raised slightly so they are discernible and recognizable by touch. On the face of each of these symbols is a different number of raised dots. The remaining test board is larger (12" × 8") and consists of eight rows of five raised symbols each. These symbols contain no dots.

The test is introduced by guiding the subject's hand down the first test board of raised symbols, counting the dots so that familiarity with the forms and dot patterns is achieved. Similarly, the subject is introduced to the larger test board containing the 40 raised symbols without any dots. The subject's task then, following a 10-symbol practice run, is to tell the examiner how many dots each of the 40-symbols contains by tactilely matching symbols without dots to symbols with dots.

The *Block Design* subtest presents the subject with four identical wooden blocks approximately 1½" square on the wooden tray. Each block face is either completely smooth, completely rough, or diagonally divided between rough and smooth. Following a sample, the subject is required to use the blocks to construct eight sequentially presented designs that are modeled on ⅛th" thick pieces of pressboard. The smoothness and roughness of the designs on the model plates is not an exact tactile match with the block faces that could prove to be at least confusing to some subjects. Task complexity ranges from the first design that is all rough and smooth in whole-block units, to design eight that is constructed using only the diagonal block faces.

The *Object Assembly* subtest is a series of four increasingly difficult puzzles that are assembled by the subject on the tray after the pieces have been arranged by the examiner in a prescribed manner and the subject told how many pieces there are for the particular puzzle being worked on at the time.

The *Object Completion* subtest requires the subject to correctly identify a missing part in 15 examples of common household or play items. There is a difficulty progression from first to last item. One of the items, a woman's garter belt with missing button, would probably not be recognizable to either men or women today.

The *Pattern Board* subtest consists of a 7½" square piece of wood approximately .75" thick with five rows of five ½" holes drilled into it. There is a permanently installed peg in the middle of the board that serves as a reference point. For this subtest, the subject is required to reproduce a demonstrated design made with various numbers of pegs that fit in the holes on the board. The subject is allowed a specific time limit (30 seconds for the first pattern and 60 seconds for each remaining pattern) to study a particular peg board pattern and then the pegs are removed by the examiner and given to the subject with the instruction to put them back in the same holes. The patterns become progressively more difficult.

The *Bead Arithmetic* subtest consists of 14 abacus problems together with instruction and practice in using the abacus. The abacus is approximately 12" × 11" and the individual beads are about 1¼" in diameter. For the first six problems, the examiner puts a number into the abacus and the subject tells the examiner what the number is. The numbers are increasingly difficult. The next five problems require the subject to enter a number provided by the examiner using the fewest possible beads. The last three problems require the subject to add two 3-digit numbers and provide the examiner with the answer. An oral response is never given credit if the beads are not in the correct positions.

The record form for the six HIS subtests is a straightforward, four page, menu-type arrangement that provides identifying information, score summary, and a Scaled Score Equivalent table on the front page and a place for recording subtest performance on the remaining three pages. Recording information and responses in this format is simple and should provide no problems to anyone with a basic familiarity with individual test practice. The record form also provides sufficient white space to allow the examiner to make notes regarding significant behavioral or response observations directly on the form.

A remark about the quality of the HIS materials is appropriate. The individual test pieces are well designed and should provide good service for an extended period. The wooden items, especially the Pattern Board, the pieces for Object Assembly, and the abacus for Bead Arithmetic, are extraordinarily well made. They are aesthetically pleasing to the sighted and could be expected to be tactically warm and pleasant to the blind. An effort to provide test materials of such high quality is not experienced generally by test administrators; it is especially gratifying to observe it in an instance where visual appearance is not a prime consideration for the individuals responding to the items.

The HIS test materials are provided in a sturdy, two-latch-with-handle suitcase type container weighing almost eighteen pounds, measuring 14" × 22" × 6" deep, and costing almost $530. All materials are well packed with sufficient cushioning to prevent shipping damage. For the clinician, however, who would have need of the materials on a regular basis, repacking everything each time would quickly become tedious. What is needed is either a divided case with interior latches/snaps to secure individual test items or a two-layer foam cutout system which would accomplish that same objective. These comments, of course, are only pertinent to the individual clinician who must travel to different locations. If the clinician is fortunate enough to have a stable base of operations where all assessment materials may be conveniently stored and handy for use, then the safe transport of materials is not an issue.

There are no optional tests or alternate forms of the HIS, all subtests are administered, four require a wooden tray which is provided, and all tests are timed. Included with the test materials is a pair of opaque goggles, but no mention of how to use them is found in the manual (Shurrager & Shurrager, 1964).

Practical Applications/Uses

Although closely modeled on the Wechsler Performance scale, the HIS is thought to measure different abilities in the blind than the Wechsler Performance scale does in the sighted. To the extent that this is true, and to the extent that an individual works with blind people, the HIS would seem to be capable of providing a needed and valuable perspective. The lower end of the age range (16 years of age) for the HIS would correspond to the last 2 or, in some cases, 3 years of high school, suggesting the possibility of using the instrument in an educational setting in addition to clinics, counseling centers, and vocational agencies. HIS test results at the high school stage of education probably would not influence specific academic programming, but the findings could certainly be appropriately applied to planning postsecondary education and/or prevocational or vocational experiences. The areas of possible use for the HIS appear to be essentially unlimited. It could be used in any situation where a need has been established for a measure of intellectual potential that includes an assessment of the haptic factors addressed by the HIS.

Even though the HIS subtests have been found to contain a rather large common factor, there are also unique aspects contained in each. Jordan (1978) has identified the following measurement focus for each HIS subtest. 1) Digit Symbol seems to tap attention, short-term memory, and psychomotor speed and is a "measure of the ability to master a new and essentially alien task" (Jordan, 1978, p. 210). 2) Block Design measures a more holistic or haptic perception as well as organizational ability, tactile sensitivity, reasoning, nonverbal concept formation, and orientation in space. 3) Object Assembly assesses aspects of what Jordan refers to as the "Kinematic Principle" (Jordan, 1978, p. 212), which is associated with the importance of movement in problem solving in blind individuals. 4) Object Completion requires an active concentration, including movement, and the ability to critically analyze the object the subject is holding. According to Jordan (1978), it is at this point that the blind individual is then able to proceed to identify what is essential, what is not essential, and finally, what is missing on the object. 5) Pattern Board "investigates space perception . . . involving the immediate recall of spatial and directional characteristics as if these qualities were entities in themselves" (Jordan, 1978, p. 215). 6) Bead Arithmetic taps a number of sequential skills including attention/concentration, active manipulation, and the use of an abacus to solve progressively more difficult arithmetic problems.

In summary, the HIS appears to measure "the ability to use touch and kinesis without visual cues to indicate how a subject has compensated for the loss of sight, and the ability and flexibility in dealing with non-visual materials" (Jordan, 1978, pp. 221–222). The HIS was standardized on totally blind persons and consequently there are no norms for the partially sighted.

An administration of the HIS requires many of the same circumstances and characteristics associated with any other assessment process; that is, a clean, airy, comfortable, and quiet room with a table and chairs. The room does not need to be especially well lighted or free from visual distractions because the subject is blind, however, these factors might negatively influence the examiner.

The manual is clear with respect to directions for each subtest although the conciseness of the directions seems to assume a familiarity with intellectual evaluation. This is not necessarily a negative situation, as it is anticipated that the usual examiner would in fact be a psychologist who is well trained and experienced in the administration, scoring, and, interpretation of instruments of this general type.

The order of test administration is Digit Symbol (2 minutes), Block Design (21 minutes), Object Assembly (20 minutes), Object Completion (15 minutes), Pattern Board (19 minutes), and Bead Arithmetic (14–15 minutes). If a subject needs the full amount of time for each subtest, the total amount of time required for administration, including giving instructions and directions, can last up to 2 hours. Assuming 45 minutes to 1 hour for the Verbal portion of the Wechsler scale and 30 minutes for scoring, the total then might take up to 4 hours.

As with any new instrument, a prudent examiner would wish to become thoroughly familiar with the HIS before using it in an evaluation setting. Such a process should include at least two practice administrations because the HIS does present rather unique demands on the examiner in terms of materials manipulation. Practice would also improve the smoothness of presentation, which would enhance subject confidence and general relaxation.

Hand scoring, the only option, is a very straightforward process consisting of 1) *determining* a raw score for each subtest—the sum of points earned on the particular test; 2) *converting* each raw score to a Scaled Score via a table that is conveniently provided on the front page of the profile form and in the manual; 3) *summing* the Scaled Scores to determine the Full Scale Score; and 4) *consulting* a table to determine the subject's IQ by age and Full Scale Score.

There is an error in the manual that could confuse the scoring process: in the table of contents, an entry reads, "TABLE OF IQ EQUIVALENTS OF RAW SCORES." (Shurrager & Shurrrager, 1964, p.v.) This entry should read, "TABLE OF IQ EQUIVALENTS OF *SCALED* SCORES." If a test is either omitted or unusable for any number of reasons, instructions are provided for obtaining a Full Scale Score from the remaining subtests.

The interpretation of the HIS results, in terms of the IQ provided, is relatively simple because it reflects a mean of 100 and standard deviation of 15, which is standard in the field. In addition, a wide range of clinical cues and insights may be gained from observing how the subject approaches tasks requiring the application of various types of nonverbal problem-solving ability. Information can also be gained by examining the pattern of relative strengths and weaknesses suggested by the individual subtests Scaled Scores. However, caution and restraint seem to be the most advantageous approach when interpreting the Haptic Intelligence Scale. As Shurrager and Shurrager suggest,

> although a great deal of work has already been done with the HIS, it is not represented as a perfected test in its present form. While the reliability of the full scale is good, the tests which comprise it show relatively high intercorrelations and relatively large standard deviations which, in combination with moderate reliability coefficients, result in high standard errors of measurement. It should be administered and interpreted with caution, with much of its current value being in the clinical cues it provides the trained psychologist using it (1964, pp. 25–26).

An additional note of caution regarding interpretation is related to practice effect. The HIS subtests are unique with respect to the materials used to address a specific population. Because of this, the subtests may remain in the subject's memory longer than would analogous materials from the Wechsler scales for a sighted person. It is anticipated that this effect would be most pronounced in the Object Completion and Bead Arithmetic subtests. Possibly the only time the HIS will provide completely uncontaminated results is with the first administration for a particular individual.

Technical Aspects

The original proposal for HIS standardization included testing 900 subjects between the ages of 16 and 64 in the same seven age groupings as were used in the Wechsler scales. Two hundred subjects in the age groups 20–24 and 25–30 were to be tested because these subjects were to form a reference population on the assumption (based on Wechsler) that they would do best on the test. In the remaining five age groups, 100 subjects were tested.

Information regarding the totally blind population in this country was not adequate at the time to allow either simple or stratified random sampling. As a consequence, the 1950 Census was used to establish a quota sampling system stratified on the basis of region, race, and urban/rural residence. A total of 994 blind people were tested and 700 of these were selected as part of the normative sample. Sources of subjects included "Workshops belonging to the National Industries for the Blind, State Vocational rehabilitation agencies, companies employing the blind, agencies administering vending stands, and welfare agencies administering aid to the blind" (Shurrager & Shurrager, 1964, p.11). Subjects were recruited from these cooperating agencies and by asking subjects if they had blind friends or acquaintances who might be interested in participating in the standardization. When testing was completed, it was found that subjects in the 20–34 age range had the highest scores so the original plan to use these 200 subjects as the reference group was followed. Standardization research found that "beyond the age of thirty-four, mean test performance on the HIS begins to decline appreciably with age" (Shurrager & Shurrager, 1964, p. 19). In constructing IQ tables, it was determined that there were no significant sex differences in total mean HIS scores.

Subjects were selected for reliability studies because they were willing to cooperate and because they were accessible. Test-retest reliability for the sum of five HIS tests, excluding Bead Arithmetic, for 124 subjects was .91 with a minimum 6-month delay. Individual subtest correlations ranged from a high of .81 (Pattern Board) to a low of .70 (Object Assembly).

Odd-even reliabilities were calculated from the scores of 399 subjects in the 20–34 age range for five HIS tests and the Full Scale Score. Correlations were corrected for length via Spearman-Brown, which is the standard procedure. Digit Symbol, being a test of precision and speed, did not meet the criteria for the split-half technique and therefore was not included. Odd-even reliabilities ranged from .79 (Object Assembly) to .94 (Bead Arithmetic); HIS IQ reliability was .95.

Validity studies, in the form of correlations of HIS and Wechsler scale verbal and performance tests were done. These correlations were obtained from scores of 399 subjects in the 20–34 age range. HIS test intercorrelations suggested a relatively large common factor even though each of the six was unique to some extent.

In regard to Wechsler scale verbal tests, coefficients from the blind group were consistently higher when contrasted with those from the sighted group. Wechsler Performance scale correlations were usually greater for Wechsler Verbal (from .48 to .67) than were HIS tests with Wechsler Verbal (from .32 to .61). Wechsler Performance with Wechsler Verbal was .77; HIS Total with Wechsler Verbal was .65. In general, it may be concluded that Wechsler "Performance tests administered to sighted persons are better predictors of verbal performance than are HIS tests administered to blind persons" (Shurrager & Shurrager, 1964, p. 24).

Critique

The HIS represents a meaningful and worthwhile approach to the assessment of blind persons. As Jordan (1978) states, "it is a subtle and highly sophisticated method of assessing individual differences and capabilities" (p. 221). The HIS has problems with respect to representativeness issues in the standardization, but this is more a function of access to blind subjects than to a failure of design. Validity and reliability coefficients are adequate, and given the limits of the times, they probably represent the best attainable. The HIS has not been revised since inception; as the original norms are more than 20 years old, the scale could benefit from the time and effort that process would require. A downward extension of the scale would be useful but, as is pointed out by the Shurragers (1964), it is unlikely that individuals younger than 16 years of age would be able to perform satisfactorily on enough items to provide the required distribution of scores.

The HIS is a unique instrument and, even though modeled on the Wechsler scales, it is different enough and difficult enough to preclude rapid accommodation and use. A potential examiner needs to spend some time with the HIS materials and manual before attempting even a practice administration. Few psychologists have the experience, to say nothing of the training, to be immediately comfortable with the HIS or with the process of recognizing and responding appropriately to the clinical cues that a blind subject may be providing. Cues regarding problem-solving strategy, learning style, and information-processing capability from blind individuals are probably sufficiently different from the experience of most psychologists to require additional time before real competence is developed.

The HIS is one of those instruments that has probably developed a small but loyal following over the years. In general, it can be said that it deserves such support and wider use would certainly be appropriate as well.

References

This list includes text citations and suggested additional reading.

Avery, C.D., & Streitfeld, J.W. (1969). An abbreviation of the Haptic Intelligence Scale for clinical use. *Education of the Visually Handicapped, 1*(2), 37–40.

Jordan, S. (1978). Some clinical interpretations of the Haptic Intelligence Scale for adult blind. *Perceptual & Motor Skills, 47*(1), 203–222.

Miller, L.R. (1977). Abilities structure of congenitally blind persons: A factor analysis. *Journal of Visual Impairment & Blindness, 71*(4), 145–153.

Sattler, J.M. (1982). *Assessment of children's intelligence and special abilities* (2nd ed.). Boston: Allyn & Bacon, Inc.

Shurrager, H.C., & Shurrager, P.A. (1964). *Manual for the Haptic Intelligence Scale for adult blind*. Chicago: Psychology Research.

Streitfeld, J.W., & Avery, C.D. (1968). The WAIS and HIS tests as predictors of academic achievement in a residential school for the blind. *International Journal for the Education of the Blind, 18*(3), 73–77.

Watson, S.B. (1956). *Development and standardization of a performance scale for adult blind*. Unpublished doctoral dissertation, Illinois Institute of Technology, Chicago.

Elaine Clark, Ph.D.
Assistant Professor of Educational Psychology, University of Utah, Salt Lake City, Utah.

Michael K. Gardner, Ph.D.
Assistant Professor of Educational Psychology, University of Utah, Salt Lake City, Utah.

HENMON-NELSON TESTS OF MENTAL ABILITY

Joseph L. French, Tom A. Lamke, and Martin J. Nelson. Chicago: The Riverside Publishing Company.

Introduction

The Henmon-Nelson Tests of Mental Ability were designed to measure aspects of mental ability that are considered important for academic success. The tests were first published in 1931 by V.A.C. Henmon, Ph.D., then Chairman of the Department of Psychology at the University of Wisconsin, and Martin J. Nelson, Ph.D., then Dean of Faculty at Iowa State Teachers College. The tests were developed in response to a need for a standardized group test that could be scored quickly and reliably and that could have maximum predictive validity in terms of academic achievement. Although not tests of achievement, the Henmon-Nelson authors state that,

> high performance on the tests requires the efficient utilization of verbal and numerical symbols and the ability to acquire and retain information in common symbol form for use at later times in the solution of verbal, quantitative and abstract reasoning problems. (Lamke, Nelson, & French, 1973, p. 4)

The Henmon-Nelson tests have undergone two revisions and two age extensions since the original development. The nature and purpose of the tests, however, have remained basically the same. The first revision, completed in 1957, was similar to the original test, but consisted of three grade levels rather than two. Consequently, the match between item difficulty and the range of mental abilities assessed was improved. The second and most recent revision was completed in 1973 by Joseph L. French, Ed.D., of Pennsylvania State University. In this revision, the test coverage (verbal, quantitative, and concept formation), format (single-score), and the types and number of items (90 multiple-choice items arranged in order of increasing difficulty for each of three grade levels, 3–6, 6–9, and 9–12) remained the same as the previous edition. Fifty percent of the items, however, were replaced because they were obsolete, had inappropriate difficulty levels, or had poor discrimination. Furthermore, the 1973 revision was published as a one-form test rather than two-form.

A Primary Battery (Nelson & French, 1973) extended the test downward to the second half of kindergarten through Grade 2. The battery consists of three subtests (Listening, Picture Vocabulary, and Size and Number) that measure skills important in learning to read, following instructions, and understanding basic math concepts. The Listening subtest was designed to measure reasoning abilities, comprehension of abstract relationships, and general knowledge; the Picture Vocabulary subtest was constructed to assess word knowledge; and Size and Number subtest was developed to evaluate spatial relationships and the child's understanding of numerical concepts.

Practical Applications/Uses

When combined with tests of achievement, the Henmon-Nelson tests can be useful in identifying children who have potential learning difficulties. The norms are based on an apparently representative sample of school-age children across the United States; however, there are no indications that children with specific handicaps were included in the normative sample (e.g., vision and hearing impaired, learning disabled, and mentally retarded). The tests, in fact, require a fair degree of verbal comprehension, visual acuity, and fine motor-coordination.

The method for selecting the communities and schools from which the sample was drawn seems adequate, the weighting procedures used to compensate for missing or skewed data appear psychometrically sound, and the characteristics of the normative group correspond well to those children included in the 1970 U.S. Census. Comparable norms were derived for children in Grades K-12 because the Primary Battery was standardized conjointly with the 1973 revision of the Grades 3–12 form.

The Henmon-Nelson measure is not recommended to evaluate specific learning disabilities or intellectual handicaps, nor as a sole measure of intellectual ability. The tests serve best as a screening device to identify children in need of further, perhaps individual, psychoeducational assessment. As a group test, the Henmon-Nelson is subject to problems such as poor motivation, inattention, and distractibility. Nonetheless, educationally relevant information can be obtained at a relatively low cost to the schools, especially when compared to the cost of individual ability testing. Classroom teachers and other trained personnel can administer the test in a relatively short time. The Grades 3–12 form has a time limit of 30 minutes, and the Primary Battery takes approximately 45 minutes to administer. The Primary Battery requires greater examiner involvement because the children must be paced, item-by-item, through the test.

Directions for administering and scoring are clearly written and the actual test materials are printed on high quality paper. The size of the test stimuli is adequate; however, the response boxes on the carbon-backed answer booklets for children in Grades 3–12, are very small. Furthermore, these reviewers found that some of the impressions made on the carbon-backed booklets were light and difficult to read. Because the 3–12 test booklets are available in both a consumable and a reusable format, test users can decide which format they prefer. The tests can be scored either by hand or machine. A variety of computer programs is available for statistical analysis of the test data (e.g., IBM and Digitek). MRC scoring service is available through Houghton Mifflin and provides inexpensive, high-speed scoring for individual students, as well as a report of all student scores (e.g., number of items attempted, raw scores, deviation IQs, percentile ranks, and stanines).

Whereas the Primary Battery yields three scores, one for each of the subtests (Listening, Picture Vocabulary, Size and Number), the Grades 3–12 form follows an omnibus-cycle format that yields a single score. Because the 1973 revision consists primarily of verbal items, a single score may be the best descriptor. However, readers familiar with other mental ability tests undoubtedly recognize the advantages to separate subtest scores (e.g., verbal, quantitative, reasoning) for instructional purposes. Both age and grade norms are provided for interpretation of test scores. Age norms are presented in terms of normalized-deviation IQs, IQ percentiles, and stanines. In order to facilitate comparison of Henmon-Nelson test scores with those of individual intelligence scales, such as the Stanford-Binet, the IQs have a mean of 100 and a standard deviation of 16. Grade norms are also reported in terms of grade percentiles and stanines; however, the distributions by grade have not been normalized. While the test authors provide general precautions to users regarding the appropriate use and interpretation of mental ability test data, they do not warn of the problems associated with the use of normalized and non-normalized distributions. Although the Henmon-Nelson is categorized as Level B according to the American Psychological Association standards (e.g., technical knowledge of test construction and background in educational measurements, statistics, child growth and development, and guidance), this categorization is unlikely to prevent its misuse and misinterpretation. Those professionals administering the tests must make a number of decisions, including when a form other than the one designated by grade placement should be used (e.g., giving the Grades 6–9 form to a 10th-grader) or when to select a particular level when overlap occurs (e.g., giving the Grades 6–9 form to 9th-graders instead of the Grades 9–12 form). For instance, studies have demonstrated that Grades 6–9 and 9–12 have a correlation of .88 (a fairly substantial correlation) when given to a 9th-grade group, whereas the Primary Form and Grades 3–6 have a correlation of only .61 for 3rd-graders. Despite the authors' allowance for flexibility in administering the Grades K-2 form to low-ability groups in Grade 3, the surprisingly small degree of intercorrelation between the two forms may warrant against such a practice. In any event, test users need to make informed decisions as to which form or level to choose.

Technical Aspects

Item selection for the 1973 revision included administration of items from the two forms of the 1957 edition of the Henmon-Nelson to 1,200 students in Grades 2, 4, 6, 8, 9, 11, and 12. The students were selected from five communities across three geographic regions (Southeast, Midwest, and Northeast). The communities were selected on the basis of representative socioeconomic and urban/rural distributions (see Lamke, Nelson, & French, 1973, p. 36 for specific information). By combining items from the previous revision of the Henmon-Nelson with newly developed items, a pool of try-out items was generated. Preliminary try-outs resulted in the development of two experimental forms that were used for a final try-out and subsequent selection of items for Form 1 with comparable item difficulty and internal consistency with those in earlier editions. Items selected for inclusion had an increasingly greater percentage of students passing the item as they progressed from one grade level to the next. To ensure adequate test reliability, items in the 1973 revision had a statistically significant biserial correlation with the total test score. Items were eliminated if the biserial correlations were less than .30 (typical correlations ranged from .40 to .60). Because the criteria for item inclusion in the Primary Battery were the same as the criteria for the 1973 revision (e.g., biserial coefficients of at least .30) and the typical correlations for the primary items had a similar range as the 1973 revisions items, the *Examiner's Manual* for the Primary Battery does not present a detailed discussion on the procedures for item selection.

Odd-even reliability coefficients for each grade were computed and ranged from .87 to .96 for the Grades 3–12 form, and from .71 to .89 for the Primary form. The correlations presented for the Grades 3–12 form, however, may be spuriously high given the fact that the test may have been "speeded" for those who could not complete it within the 30-min time limit. Because the 1973 revision has only one form, alternate-form reliability obviously could not be computed. Unfortunately, no test-retest reliability studies were conducted; this is somewhat unexpected because the purpose of the test is to predict academic performance.

Studies pertaining to the content, construct, and criterion-related validity of the Henmon-Nelson are presented in the *Examiner's Manual;* however, the discussion centered primarily on studies of the 1957 edition rather than the 1973 revision. Comparisons of the 1973 revised Henmon-Nelson with other tests of mental ability such as the Lorge-Thorndike Intelligence Tests (LTML) and the Otis-Lennon (OL), however, yield respectable correlations (.78 to .83 for the LTML and .75 to .82 for the OL). One problem with these studies is that a considerable period of time passed between the administration of the Henmon-Nelson and the administration of the second test of mental ability (either the LTML or OL) to subjects. This procedure requires the additional assumption that uniform cognitive growth across subjects is the true test of concurrent validity. That the correlations are as high as they are is impressive; differences in cognitive growth rates tend to reduce the correlations. Thus, these correlations can be construed as a lower bound for concurrent validity.

A number of other validity studies have been conducted and provide support for the 1973 revision, particularly the Grades 9–12 form. For instance, the relationship between the Grades 9–12 test and the WAIS with hospitalized alcoholics was examined by Kling, Davis, and Knost (1978), and the comparability of the Henmon-Nelson and other group ability tests, as well as individual IQ tests, was studied by Watson and Klett (1975). A respectable correlation of .80 was obtained between the WAIS and Henmon-Nelson, however; when weighted in a linear regression model, there was an improved prediction of the WAIS Full Scale IQ using the Henmon-Nelson deviation IQ.

Evidence presented in the *Examiner's Manual* for criterion-related validity is strong, with correlations ranging from .60 to .86 between the Henmon-Nelson and the Iowa Tests of Basic Skill (ITBS) for various grades and achievement areas. Unfortunately, the evidence is limited to one study. Support for the validity of the Primary Battery is even more limited and weaker in terms of the correlation with other ability and achievement tests (e.g., Lorge-Thorndike, $r = .57$ [Grades K-2] and .58 [Grades 3–6]).

Critique

Although it is reasonable to expect that the 1973 revised Henmon-Nelson performs at a level comparable to its predecessors, the authors have provided little convincing evidence. The failure to provide test-retest reliability is an example. What empirical studies the authors do report are flawed at times by inappropriate procedures (e.g., the use of odd-even reliability with a potentially "speeded" test and the allowing of significant time delays between the administration of similar ability tests in studies of congruent validity). Fortunately, the situation is not as bad as it seems. Other researchers interested in finding measures of mental ability that are economical in terms of time and expense have studied the Henmon-Nelson. For instance, studies that have compared the Henmon-Nelson to the WAIS and WAIS-R have consistently shown that the Grades 9–12 form is a powerful predictor of the Full Scale IQ score, although the validity coefficients are not higher than those found with Wechsler short-forms. Such studies demonstrate that there are good reasons to use the Henmon-Nelson (at least the upper-level form).

Because so little information is known about the performance of the Primary Battery, a knowledgeable opinion cannot be rendered. The procedures used to develop it seem comparable to the sound methods used in constructing the Grades 3–12 form. This is a promising sign. One can only hope that researchers will show as great an interest in studying the Primary Battery as they have in studying the Grades 3–12 form. Otherwise, the Primary Battery may meet the same fate as the 1961 College Form which has since been discontinued.

In general, the Henmon-Nelson is a good test of mental ability, especially in the Grade 3 to 12 range. It compares favorably to its many competitors and has a long and venerable history. The authors have invested much time and effort in test development, and it shows. In future revisions, these reviewers hope that the authors' efforts will be extended to test reliability and validity concerns.

References

This list includes text citations and suggested additional readings.

Gardner, E.F., & Slocum, M.O. (1978). *Review of the Henmon-Nelson Tests of Mental Ability.* In O.K. Buros (Ed.), *The eighth mental measurements yearbook.* Highland Park, NJ: Gryphon Press.

Klett, W.G., & Watson, C.G. (1986). The Henmon-Nelson and Slosson tests as predictors of WAIS-R IQ. *Journal of Clinical Psychology, 42,* 343–347.

Kling, J.O., Davis, W.E., & Knost, E.K. (1978). Henmon-Nelson IQ scores as predictors of WAIS Full Scale IQ in alcoholics. *Journal of Clinical Psychology, 34,* 1001–1002.

Lamke, T.A., Nelson, M.J., & French, J.L. (1973). *The Henmon-Nelson Tests of Mental Ability, 1973 Revision.* Boston: Houghton Mifflin Company.

Nelson, M.J., & French, J.L. (1974). *The Henmon-Nelson Tests of Mental Ability, Primary Form 1.* Chicago: Riverside Publishers.

Watson, C.G., & Klett, W.G. (1973). Prediction of WAIS IQs from group ability tests. *Journal of Clinical Psychology, 29,* 46–49.

Watson, C.G., & Klett, W.G. (1975). The Henmon-Nelson, Cardall-Miles, Slosson, and Quick Tests as predictors of WAIS IQ. *Journal of Clinical Psychology, 31,* 310–313.

Watson, C.G., & Klett, W.G., Kucala, T., Nixon, C., Schaefer, A., & Gasser, B. (1981). Prediction of the WAIS scores from the 1973 Henmon-Nelson revision. *Journal of Clinical Psychology, 37*, 840–842.

Nancy A. Busch-Rossnagel, Ph.D.

Associate Professor of Psychology, Fordham University, Bronx, New York.

HOME SCREENING QUESTIONNAIRE

Cecilia E. Coons, Elizabeth C. Gay, Alma W. Fandal, Cynthia Ker, and William K. Frankenburg. Denver, Colorado: Denver Developmental Materials, Inc.

Introduction

The Home Screening Questionnaire (HSQ) is a parent-completed questionnaire designed to screen the home environments of young children for factors related to later developmental delays, particularly of a cognitive nature. Two forms of the HSQ have been developed. The one for children from birth to 3 years of age includes 30 questions and a toy checklist of 50 items. The form for 3- to 6-year-old children includes 34 questions and the toy checklist. The questions are varied in nature—multiple-choice, fill-in-the-blank, and yes-no—and written at the 3rd- or 4th-grade reading level. The content for the items was taken from the Home Observation for Measurement of the Environment (HOME, Caldwell & Bradley, 1978), an assessment of home environments that is completed by a trained interviewer after observing the examinee for approximately an hour in the home setting. As a screening device, the HSQ is designed to identify those home environments that should be assessed in more depth.

The two primary test authors are Cecilia E. Coons, M.A., and William K. Frankenberg, M.D. Coons is a counselor at Fort Logan Mental Health Center in Denver, Colorado. Frankenburg is a pediatrician who completed a fellowship in child development at Yale University. He currently is Professor of Pediatrics and Preventive Medicine, University of Colorado Health Sciences Center. In addition to the HSQ, Dr. Frankenburg has developed numerous other screening tests, including the Denver Developmental Screening Test (DDST; Frankenberg & Dodds, 1967; reviewed by Walker, Bonner, & Milling, 1984) and the Prescreening Developmental Questionnaire (PDQ; Frankenburg, van Doorninck, Liddell, & Dick, 1976). Through these efforts and associated training materials, Dr. Frankenburg and his colleagues have sought to develop a comprehensive, practical protocol to facilitate screening for handicaps and delays in children from birth to age six. Thus, the HSQ is designed to screen home environments that might contribute to developmental delays, with the goal of early intervention to ameliorate environmentally based delays.

The rationale for the development of the HSQ is based on the impact of the environment on development. The possible negative effects of economically disadvantaged environments are seen in school-aged children: 50 percent of children residing in such environments experience school problems (van Doorninck, 1978). In a longitudinal follow-up of children whose home environments had been assessed when the children were 12-months-old, van Doorninck, Caldwell, Wright, and Frankenburg (1981) used scores from the HOME scale to predict elementary school problems. The scores correctly classified 68% of the children from low-income families and significantly reduced the error rate from blanket or random predictions.

In spite of the growing awareness of the impact of the environment on children's development, there are few standardized instruments designed to assess the environment of young children. Parental "status" variables, such as income, education, and IQ have been related negatively to children's intelligence and psychological adjustment. While the status variables are measured easily, they are of limited utility both in predicting school performance and in developing effective preventive programs as a result of several factors. Status variables account for only a small proportion of the variance in performance, and they obscure large within-status variability in environmental characteristics (Procidano, 1985). In contrast, the HOME inventory was designed to be a measure of environmental "process"; that is, of patterns of care giving and stimulation within the home that had been related empirically to child development (Caldwell & Bradley, 1984). Environmental processes included on the HOME inventory include parent-child interactions, emotional climate of the home, physical home environment, and discipline techniques.

While viewing the HOME in a positive light, Coons et al. highlighted the fact that it is not a screening instrument. HOME administration requires observation in the child's home by a trained observer for approximately an hour. Thus, the widespread use of the HOME to screen low-income environments clearly is not feasible. The HSQ was designed to meet the need for a screening device "by being quick, economical, easy to administer, and accurate in identifying a majority of children whose home environments are substandard " (Coons et al., 1981, p. 2).

To develop the HSQ, items from the HOME inventory were written in a question format. The agreement between the HSQ and the HOME then was refined in a three-phase pilot study. The subjects for this study were recruited from a public health clinic serving primarily low-income families in Denver, Colorado.During each phase, 50 parents completed the HSQ and were visited in their homes approximately 3 weeks later for the purpose of completing the HOME inventory. After each phase, agreement between the HSQ and the HOME was examined, and items were rewritten to limit the rates of over- and underestimation. At the end of the three phases, any item not meeting the criteria of 10% overestimation (a pass on the HSQ item and a fail on the associated HOME item) and 30% underestimation (a fail on the HSQ and a pass on the HOME) were eliminated from the HSQ. At the end of the pilot study, the correlations between the final HSQ and HOME inventory total scores were .71 for 61 children aged 0–3 and .81 for 58 children aged 3–6.

Cutoff scores for the HSQ were selected in a second study in which 799 (505 younger and 294 older) children were screened with the HSQ and followed-up with the HOME. The demographic characteristics of this sample, detailed in the HSQ manual, clearly indicate that the sample was low income. The ethnic breakdown of the 0- to 3-year-old group and the 3- to 6-year-old group, respectively, was as follows: 62% and 41%, Anglo; 4% and 8%, Black; 25% and 43%, Hispanic; and

9% and 8%, other. The test authors note that these ethnic proportions differ from those found in other parts of the United States. The sample had a somewhat higher level of education than might be expected in a lower SES population (e.g., 15% of the mothers and 26% of the fathers of the 0- to 3-year-olds had at least some college), a fact that might be explained by the requirement that parents had to be able to read the HSQ in English, which is likely to eliminate Hispanics with lower levels of education.

The materials for the HSQ consist of a reference manual and two 4-page questionnaires, one on blue paper for 0- to 3-year-olds and one on white paper for 3-to 6-year-olds. The parent answers the questions by checking an appropriate space or writing on the questionnaire itself. To complete the toy checklist, the parent checks which of 50 types of toys are in the home for the child's play. Completion of the HSQ takes from 15 to 20 minutes. Because the HSQ is a parent-report measure, the examiner's responsibilities are limited to providing the material and checking to see that it is properly completed (e.g., that the parent has not forgotten to complete the toy checklist, which is on the back of the form for the 3- to 6-year-olds.)

In addition to psychometric and scoring information pertaining to the HSQ, the manual contains valuable information about the process of screening. Thus, false positives and false negatives are identified, and the consequences of over- or underreferral for screening procedures are discussed.

Practical Applications/Uses

The HSQ was designed as a screening measure of the home environments of low-SES children. As such, when the HSQ is used, follow-up evaluations should be completed for those families whose HSQ result is suspect. In addition, intervention programs should be available to those families if the follow-up evaluation indicates a poor prognosis. As the authors emphasize, screening procedures "will only produce anxiety if there is no system for adequate follow-up" (Coons et al., 1981, p. 7). As a screening device, the HSQ does not diagnose specific family problems nor does it predict later development: "It is merely intended to screen for factors which may a depress a child's development" (Coons et al., 1981, p. 7). The HSQ can be useful to the multiplicity of disciplines concerned with promoting the optimal development of low-SES children. Two examples of settings in which the HSQ might be useful are public health clinics and the Head Start Program. Because the HSQ focuses on environmental factors, the test authors suggest the simultaneous use of a measure designed to screen for delays resulting from biological or genetic factors, such as the DDST. They also recommend periodic screening (twice during each of the two age periods at 18-month intervals) because possible environmental changes may occur.

The HSQ is used appropriately with children 0- to 6-years-old from low-SES populations. Because the parent instrument, the HOME inventory, does not discriminate environmental risk factors in middle- to upper-income populations, the HSQ is not recommended for use with these groups. In addition to the social class specificity, the material on the HSQ is culture bound; therefore, its efficacy in different cultures probably is limited.

Section II of the manual provides detailed scoring information for each question on the HSQ form for 0- to 3-year-olds, while Section III provides similar information for the form for older children. Scoring focuses on assigning points (usually 0 or 1) to each answer. Sometimes the scoring information seems overly detailed (e.g., "there is no penalty for marking other items" is indicated on several questions), but such precision helps to ensure accuracy in scoring. Scoring the toy checklist is more complicated (e.g. "one point if item 23 and any one of the following items is checked: 34, 39, or 40"), but the scoring is not difficult. The total score on the HSQ is the sum of the points from the question section and the toy checklist.

Interpretation of the scores is based on the cutoff scores identified by Coons et al. The criteria for the cutoff scores were identifying a majority of low (i.e., below the median) HOME scores and keeping the rate of false positive errors low. HSQ scores that fall at or below the cutoff scores are interpreted as being "suspect," indicating that the home environment of the child should be evaluated more extensively. Referrals for intervention should be made on the basis of the follow-up evaluation.

Technical Aspects

Reliability estimates for the HSQ were obtained from approximately 1,500 children (of which 799 were the standardization sample). Kuder-Richardson Formula 20 (K-R 20) estimates of the internal consistency were .74 (0-3 years, $n = 911$) and .80 (3-6 years, $n = 590$). Test-retest reliabilities over a 1-to 4-month period were .62 ($n = 30$) for the younger children and .86 ($n = 24$) for the older children. The HSQ has lower reliability for children younger than 1 year of age. The test-retest coefficient was .82 ($n = 17$) for 1- to 3-year-old children.

Validity evidence for the HSQ is of two types. First, HSQ items were adapted from the HOME inventory, so the validity of the HSQ rests, in part, on the validity of the HOME. Procidano (1985) reviewed the evidence for the validity of the HOME inventory (including correlations and multiple regressions with SES and mental test scores, classification analysis with discriminant functions, and cross-lagged correlations of HOME scores and Mental Scale scores from the Bayley Scales of Infant Development [Bayley, 1969])and concluded that "the validity of the instrument appears to be widely accepted" (p. 345).

Second, for their presentation of validity evidence in the HSQ manual, Coons et al. analyzed the relationship of HSQ scores to HOME scores from the standardization sample. These data also are presented in Frankenburg and Coons, 1986. Several measures of accuracy yielded the following results for the younger and older children, respectively:

1. *Percent agreement* (the overall rate of agreement between the HSQ and HOME results) was 74% and 71%.

2. *Co-positivity* (accuracy in predicting low HOME scores) was 81% and 86%.

3. *Co-negativity* (accuracy in predicting high HOME scores) was 66% and 55%.

4. *Predictive value of positive screening results* (accurate "suspect" HSQ scores compared with total "suspect" HSQ scores) was 77% and 68%.

5. *Rates of overreferral* were 14% and 21%.

6. *Underreferral rates* were 11% and 7%.

The low co-negativity percents and the high overreferral rates are based on the authors' assumption that "it is more desirable for a screening instrument to have high co-positivity [i.e., not to miss any children in need of further evaluation] than for it to have high co-negativity [i.e., identifying children not in need of follow-up]" (Coons et al., 1981, p. 6).

In this standardization sample, 62% of the 0- to 3-year-olds and 66% of the 3- to 6-year-olds would be referred for further evaluation. Coons et al. suggest that these rates "are reasonable considering the high rate of after school problems in these populations (approximately 50 percent)" (p. 6). However, not all the children with school problems have difficulties resulting from their familial environments, and rates that eliminate only one third of low-SES families from in-depth evaluation may be not be cost efficient.

Critique

An overall evaluation of the HSQ clearly must recognize it as a screening device. It was developed from an inventory with recognized validity, and the reliability estimates from the standardization sample are good, especially for children over 1 year of age. As acknowledged by the test authors, the standardization sample for the HSQ cutoff scores may be limited in generalizability. However, this limit need not curtail the use of the HSQ because the HOME inventory, on which the HSQ is based, has had widespread use. In the absence of additional standardization work by the test authors, large-scale users of the HSQ should be encouraged to use the detailed information in the HSQ manual to examine the reliability and accuracy of the HSQ cutoff scores for their particular populations. The authors themselves should be encouraged to develop a Spanish translation of the HSQ (as they have done with the parental-report PDQ), so that the Spanish-speaking low-income population that is placed at risk by language barriers also may be screened.

While a referral rate of two thirds is not desirable, more basic research into the causes of school problems by half of low-SES children is needed before environmental screening instruments can become more precise and efficiently intervening in low-SES environments. In the absence of such information, the authors of the HSQ have provided us with a richly detailed manual. It presents their biases about screening (e.g., keeping the rate of underreferrals low) and the limitations of the instruments. Most importantly, the manual makes it easy to use the HSQ in the prescribed manner.

References

Bayley, N. (1967). *Bayley Scales of Infant Development*. New York: The Psychological Corporation.

Caldwell, B.M., & Bradley, R.H. (1978). *Home Observation for Measurement of the Environment*. Little Rock: University of Arkansas, Center for Child Development and Education.

Caldwell, B.M., & Bradley, R.H. (1984). *Home Observation for Measurement of the Environment*. Little Rock: University of Arkansas, Center for Child Development and Education.

Coons, C.E., Gay, E.C., Fandal, A.W., Ker, C., & Frankenburg, W.K. (1981). *The Home Screening Questionnaire, reference manual*. Denver, CO: Denver Developmental Materials.

Frankenburg, W.K., & Coons, C.E. (1986). Home Screening Questionnaire: Its validity in assessing home environment. *Journal of Pediatrics, 108*, 624–626.

Frankenburg, W.K., & Dodds, J.B. (1967). *Denver Developmental Screening Test*. Denver, CO: Denver Developmental Materials.

Frankenburg, W.K., van Doorninck, W.J., Liddell,T., & Dick, N. (1976). *Prescreening Developmental Questionnaire*. Denver, CO: Denver Developmental Materials.

Procidano, M.E. (1985). Home Observation for Measurement of the Environment. In D. J. Keyser & R.C. Sweetland (Eds.), *Test critiques* (Vol II, pp. 337–346). Kansas City, MO: Test Corporation of America.

van Doorninck, W.J. (1978). *Prediction of school performance from infant and preschool developmental screening*. Paper presented at the Second International Conference on Developmental Screening, Santa Fe, NM.

van Doorninck, W.J., Caldwell, B.M., Wright, C., & Frankenburg, W.K. (1981). The relationship between twelve-month home stimulation and school achievement. *Child Development, 52*, 1080–1083.

Walker, C.E., Bonner, F., & Milling, L.S. (1984). Denver Developmental Screening Test. In D.J. Keyser and R.C. Sweetland (Eds.), *Test critiques* (Vol. I, pp. 239–251). Kansas City, MO: Test Corporation of America.

Brian Bolton, Ph.D.
Professor, Arkansas Research and Training Center in Vocational Rehabilitation, University of Arkansas, Fayetteville, Arkansas.

INTEREST CHECK LIST

U.S. Employment Service. Washington, D.C.: United States Department of Labor.

Introduction

The Interest Check List (ICL; U.S. Department of Labor [DOL], 1979c) is a vocational counseling tool that was developed expressly for use in conjunction with the *Guide for Occupational Exploration (GOE;* U.S. DOL, 1979a). The ICL consists of 210 job tasks to which the respondent indicates interest or disinterest. The 210 job activities are keyed directly to 66 Work Groups that comprise the major ability dimension of the *GOE's* occupational organization. The ICL provides vocational counselors with an alternative to the United States Employment Service Interest Inventory (USES-II; U.S. DOL, 1981); however, the two instruments are not interchangeable (see Bolton, 1985). An overview of the complete USES testing program is given by Droege (1987).

The ICL was developed by the staff of the Test Research Field Center of the California Employment Development Department, with general guidance from the Testing Division of the U.S. Employment Service. The U.S. DOL has published an Interest Check List for use by Employment Service counselors for more than 30 years. The 1967 edition of the ICL was keyed to the Worker Trait Groups and Occupational Group Arrangement of Volume II of the third edition of the *Dictionary of Occupational Titles (DOT;* U.S. DOL, 1965). Because Volume II of the *DOT* was difficult to use, the 1967 edition of the ICL was of negligible value to counselors.

Ongoing research by the U.S. Employment Service led to the development of a hierarchical occupational structure for organizing all jobs in the American economy, consisting of three major dimensions of classification: 12 Interest Areas, 66 Work Groups, and 348 Work Subgroups. The 1979 revision of the ICL was undertaken to incorporate the new occupational framework, which had been adopted as the basis of the *GOE.* Consequently, the ICL's only legitimate application is in conjunction with the GOE.

In comparison to the USES Interest Inventory, the ICL's advantage for vocational exploratory purposes is that it identifies respondents' interests at the level of the 66 Work Groups, instead of the 12 Interest Areas. The Work Groups are homogeneous occupational categories with respect to educational and aptitude requirements and the nature of job duties involved (Droege & Boese, 1982).

Results from the General Aptitude Test Battery (GATB) or Nonreading Aptitude Test Battery (NATB) are compared to minimum-ability requirements for each of the 66 Work Groups. These essential abilities for Work Groups are called Occupational Aptitude Patterns (OAPs). The rationale for choosing the ICL as an alternative to the USES-II, then, is that the ICL enables respondents to

240

express their vocational interest preferences at the same level that occupational ability requirements are assessed.

The 210 job activities that comprise the ICL are contained on a 4-page, single-fold form. The first page gives very brief directions to the respondent; the 210 job tasks are listed in double-column format on pages 2, 3, and 4. Spaces are provided for the respondent to check one of three options for each item: L (Like), ? (Uncertain), or D (Dislike). Each item is a short phrase, typically four to six words in length, that describes job tasks that most American adults are familiar with. Examples include. "Design and paint signs," "Guard inmates in a prison," "Sort fruit according to size," "Sell automobiles," "Manage a hotel or motel," and "Referee sporting events." The items appear to require about a fifth-grade reading capability.

The 210 ICL items are presented in 66 sets corresponding to the Work Groups and in the order of the Work Group codes (i.e., from WG 01.01 to WG 12.02). The first two digits identify the Interest Area and the next two digits refer to the Work Group within the Interest Area. For example, Work Group 07.05 is Records Processing in the seventh Interest Area, Business Detail, and Work Group 11.09 is Promotion in the eleventh Interest Area, Leading-Influencing. The number of Work Groups within Interest Areas ranges from two in Physical Performing to 12 in Mechanical.

The Work Group codes are printed in small type vertically along the left margin of each block of job activities. (Every Work Group is represented by a minimum of three job activities.) Thus, the link between the respondent's expressed interests and information in the *GOE* is conveniently available to counselor and counselee.

Practical Applications/Uses

The ICL was designed for use by U.S. Employment Service interviewers and counselors to assist them in their work with securing employment for individuals. However, the instrument may also be used by vocational counselors in high schools, job training organizations, rehabilitation agencies, and similar settings. Specifically, the ICL is "especially useful with counselees who have no definite, stated work interests or who are not aware of the variety of jobs and occupational fields that exist" (U.S. DOL, 1979c).

The client population for which the ICL may be used appropriately includes almost all adults aged 16 years and above. For counselees with severe physical handicaps, or with seriously deficient reading skills, the ICL could easily be administered by audiocassette. The only response required would be selecting one of three alternatives that indicate interest (or lack of interest) in the 210 job activities.

The ICL is essentially self-administering for the vast majority of counselees. It can be completed individually or in small or even fairly large groups. As with all assessment devices, regardless of how straightforward the procedure involved may be, the administrator should give a standard orientation. With the ICL, this introduction should include explaining that the ICL is not a "test," that there are no right or wrong answers, and that, while there is no time limit, responses should be made fairly quickly. After counselees have read through the directions on page 1, any questions that they have should be answered.

It is important to note that the ICL response format requires the counselee to mark one of three alternatives (L, ?, or D) for each of the 210 job tasks—not just to "check" only those job activities that are of interest. This should encourage respondents to read and consider each item more carefully. After completing the initial identification of job activities that seem interesting, the respondent is instructed to "go back and double check at least five activities that you would most like to do."

Because the ICL is a checklist and not a psychometric instrument, the counselee's responses, are not "scored," (i.e., the job activities preferred are not combined into summative scores). Rather, the ICL is an exploratory device that counselor and counselee can use to investigate further the counselee's vocational interests. The suggestions provided in the ICL instructions (U.S. DOL, 1979b) for interpreting results are helpful, such as looking for concentrations of interests within Work Groups and Interest Areas, ascertaining whether the counselee has relevant experience and/or training related to the "liked" activities, and investigating through discussion in consistencies and commonalities across diverse preferred job activities.

Administration of the ICL can be accomplished by a trained aide. Completion of the 210 items takes the typical counselee about 25 minutes. However, interpretation of ICL protocols requires professional training in vocational counseling and occupational psychology. The recommended strategy involves joint counselor-counselee exploration of the specific responses and patterns of vocational preferences recorded on the ICL in relation to the relevant information presented in the *GOE*.

Technical Aspects

The initial sampling plan for the 1979 revision of the ICL stipulated that each of the 66 Work Groups be represented by three work activity statements. It was subsequently determined that four Work Groups could not be adequately represented by just three items, because of the wide range of occupations within them. Therefore, the decision was made to include six items for WG 05.03 (Engineering Technology), WG 05.05 (Craft Technology), WG 06.02 (Production Work), and WG 06.04 (Elemental Work: Industrial). This expansion brought the total number of work activities in the ICL to 210.

Construction of the ICL involved four distinct phases (U.S. DOL, 1982a):

1. The first step involved identification of Subgroups within the 66 Work Groups to be represented by work activity items. For each of the four Work Groups listed above, six Subgroups were selected; three Subgroups were identified for the other 62 Work Groups. The choice of Subgroups for inclusion in the ICL was based on a variety of criteria, such as how representative the Subgroup was of jobs in the national labor market and how well the Subgroup represented the Work Group.

2. After 210 Subgroups were selected, the approximately 1,000 interests items that had been previously developed for various experimental editions of the USES Interest Inventory were reviewed for possible inclusion in the ICL. Details about construction of the USES-II are contained in the *Manual* (U.S. DOL, 1982b). Those items judged to be good matches for occupations in any of the 210 Subgroups were incorporated into the ICL without alteration.

3. New job activity statements were written for the remaining Subgroups by

choosing representative occupations within the Subgroups and then adapting definitions of the selected occupations given in the fourth edition of the *Dictionary of Occupational Titles (DOT;* U.S. DOL, 1977). The main criteria followed in preparing new ICL items were elimination of technical and esoteric terms and focus on work activities (i.e., description of actual job duties).

4. After preliminary items were selected or written for the 210 Subgroups, an extensive process of review and refinement was undertaken. The goal was to assure that each item would be a valid indicator of respondents' vocational interests. Criteria applied at this stage included: use of commonly understood words and phrases, elimination of overly prestigious connotations, exclusion of activities associated with predominantly male or female occupations, and verification of the major duties of the specific occupation for which the item was derived.

The careful design and implementation of a sampling plan for accurately representing the DOL's occupational structure constitutes strong evidence for the content validity of the ICL. In other words, the procedures followed in constructing the ICL essentially guaranteed that the range of occupations covered by the 66 Work Groups in the *GOE* are adequately reflected in the 210 work activity items comprising the ICL. In contrast, no studies of the ICL's reliability have been conducted. Nor have data about response frequencies been reported. Comments about these omissions are contained in the next section.

Critique

The 1979 version of the Interest Check List (ICL) was designed as an entry vehicle for the *Guide for Occupational Exploration* (GOE; U.S. DOL, 1979a). The publisher describes the ICL appropriately as a "nonscored interviewing aid." The primary advantage of the ICL, in contrast to the USES Interest Inventory, is that the 210 job tasks are keyed directly to the 66 homogeneous Work Groups in the *GOE*. Therefore, ICL results enable counselor and counselee to discuss the counselee's vocational interests at the same level that tested abilities are translated into minimum occupational performance requirements (i.e., the Occupational Aptitude Patterns, OAPs).

The ICL can be used as a vocational counseling tool with almost all adults 16 years and older who are not severely intellectually handicapped. The short (2-page) instructional sheet (U.S. DOL, 1979b) that accompanies the ICL provides a succinct overview of the rationale and development of the instrument, as well as directions for administration and suggestions for using ICL results in counseling. In fact, the ICL materials seem to be a model for concise, yet helpful, presentations of information about vocational counseling tools. In other words, the ICL is "user friendly."

And while the careful construction of the ICL establishes a strong case for its content validity, additional data about the checklist would be desirable. For example, information about the number of job activities "liked" by the typical respondent would be useful in understanding counselees' protocols. All that would be required are frequency distributions of the total number of items checked "like," as well as response distributions for the number of items preferred within Interest Areas and Work Groups, for representative samples of respondents.

Likewise, basic data pertaining to the reliability of the ICL could be collected easily. By readministering the ICL to a sample of counselees 2 weeks after the initial administration, it would be possible to calculate reliability coefficients for individual items, as well as for "scores" (totals of "liked" job activities) calculated within Work Groups and Interest Areas. Joint vocational exploration by counselor and counselee using the *GOE* assumes that the counselee's indication of interest in certain job activities is more than a superficial, transitory expression of vocational preferences. Favorable findings from a small reliability study would increase counselors' confidence in the ICL.

The primary psychometric problem with the ICL is one that is common to all checklist instruments. By interpreting endorsements of single items, or even preferences for two or three activities representing a Work Group, counselor and counselee may be putting unwarranted confidence in ICL results. Of course, this issue only serves to emphasize the importance of reliability studies of the ICL. In the absence of relevant evidence, counselors should regard ICL results as a preliminary indicator of the counselee's vocational interests, contingent on verification by independent information.

The ICL is a potentially helpful counseling tool when used in conjunction with the *GOE* to stimulate vocational exploration by adult job seekers. Unlike most other DOL instruments that are restricted for use by authorized agents, the ICL is available for sale to the public by the U.S. Superintendent of Documents.

References

Bolton, B. (1985). The United States Employment Service Interest Inventory. In D.J. Keyser & R.C. Sweetland (Eds.), *Test critiques* (Vol. 3, pp. 673–681). Kansas City, MO: Test Corporation of America.

Droege, R.C. (1987). The USES testing program. In B. Bolton (Ed.), *Handbook of measurement and evaluation in rehabilitation* (2nd ed., pp. 169–182). Baltimore, MD: Paul Brookes.

Droege, R.C., & Boese, R. (1982). Development of a new occupational aptitude pattern structure with comprehensive occupational coverage. *Vocational Guidance Quarterly, 30,* 219-229.

U.S. Department of Labor. (1965). *Dictionary of occupational titles* (3rd ed.). Washington, DC: U.S. Government Printing Office.

U.S. Department of Labor. (1977). *Dictionary of occupational titles* (4th ed.). Washington, DC: U.S. Government Printing Office.

U.S. Department of Labor. (1979a). *Guide for occupational exploration.* Washington, DC: U.S. Government Printing Office.

U.S. Department of Labor. (1979b). *Instructions for administering and using the Interest Check List.* Washington, DC: U.S. Government Printing Office.

U.S. Department of Labor. (1979c). *Interest Check List.* Washington, DC: U.S. Government Printing Office.

U.S. Department of Labor. (1982a). *Development of 1979 revision of the Interest Check List* (USES Test Research Report No. 36). Washington, DC: Author.

U.S. Department of Labor. (1982b). *Manual for the USES Interest Inventory.* Minneapolis: Intran Corporation.

Wyman E. Fisher, Ph.D.
Professor of Psychology and Chair, Department of Educational Psychology, Ball State University, Muncie, Indiana.

INTERMEDIATE BOOKLET CATEGORY TEST

Paul B. Byrd. Odessa, Florida: Psychological Assessment Resources, Inc.

Introduction

The Intermediate Booklet Category Test (IBCT) is among the latest in a series of revisions and adaptations of a neuropsychological test originally developed in the early 1930s by Dr. Ward Halstead at the University of Chicago (Halstead, 1947). This neuropsychological test, generically referred to as the Category Test and purported to be a measure of abstract reasoning and concept formation, was subsequently modified by Dr. Ralph Reitan and cast into separate forms for adults and older children ages 9 through 14 (Reitan, 1969). The instrument is still viewed as among the most important of the subtests of the Halstead-Reitan Neuropsychological Test batteries (children and adults) because of its sensitivity in identifying the neurologically impaired (Golden, 1979). Additional descriptions of the structure of the Category Test and the various constructs it purports to measure are contained in previous reviews published in *Test Critiques* (Dean & Rattan, 1984; Fischer, 1987).

The original and still widely used version of the Category Test requires the use of a projection box apparatus for presenting a series of stimulus figures on a milk glass screen. After the stimulus is projected by the examiner via a manual switching device, the examinee must match the stimulus with one of four keys to obtain a correct answer. The older children's version of the test, under consideration in this review, comprises six subtests and a total of 168 stimulus items. In order to score within the acceptable range, the subject must be able to discern predetermined underlying principles and apply them consistently throughout all subtests.

Because the projection box Category Test is expensive, mechanically fragile, and difficult to transport, in cases where it is inconvenient or infeasible to bring the patient to the laboratory, the author of the IBCT, Dr. Paul B. Byrd, a psychologist with the Community Counseling Services, Huron, South Dakota, felt the need for a portable substitute that would match the original in validity and reliability. A similar substitute Category Test for adults, the Booklet Category Test (BCT), was developed in 1979 (DeFilippis & McCampbell, 1979) and served as the model for the IBCT.

The IBCT is a booklet version adaptation of the projection box Category Test included as part of the Halstead-Reitan Neuropsychological Battery for Children (HRNB-C; Reitan, 1969). The kit for the IBCT includes two volumes (loose-leaf binders) of stimulus figures, a cardboard response strip, a manual, and a package of 50 scoring forms. The kit may be purchased from Psychological Assessment Resources, Inc. at a cost of $165.00 at the time of this writing.

The stimulus figures for subtests 1 to 3 are contained in volume 1 and subtests 3 to 6 in volume 2. These stimulus figures (the same in number and design as those in the projection box version) were reproduced on 8½" × 11" cardboard plates with the figures appearing in white on a black background. The plates are assembled in loose-leaf binders so that the figures can be presented easily to the examinee one at a time.

The manual for the IBCT is relatively brief. It provides a description of the test and relates it to previous versions of the Category Test. The administration and scoring section provides explicit directions for the examiner and includes exact wording in heavy dark print, identical except for minor variations to that of the projection box version. The cardboard response strip, containing numbers 1 through 4, is used in place of the response keys of the projection box version. The examiner, when using the IBCT, provides verbal feedback (i.e., "correct" or "incorrect") after each response in place of the bell or buzzer feedback signal provided by the projection box version.

Other than a reference to appropriate cutoff scores, the manual provides little interpretative guidance. The test author, however, cautions users to familiarize themselves with previous research conducted on the Category Test and provides several references for this. Two concurrent validity studies, comparing the IBCT with the projection box Category Test, are reported in the manual (Byrd, 1987). The first compared learning disabled children with regular education children while the second compared behaviorally disordered with regular education children. Validity coefficients together with error score means and standard deviations are reported for both studies.

The IBCT scoring form provides space for background information and recording of error scores for the total test and each of the six subtests. Each of the stimulus figures for the 168 items are reproduced in miniature with an accompanying space allowing the examiner to record the actual examinee response for each item.

Practical ApplicationsUses

The Halstead-Reitan Neuropsychological Test Battery continues to be the most widely used and researched comprehensive measure in neuropsychological assessment (Dean, 1985a). Within this battery, the subtest that has received the most attention by both clinicians and researchers is the Category Test. It is viewed as the most valid measure of diffuse cerebral dysfunction within the test battery (Golden, 1978, 1979). However, negatives such as the lack of portability, high cost, mechanical fragility, and sheer cumbersomeness of the projection box version have caused some to discontinue using it altogether (Swiercinsky, 1978) and others to find ways to shorten it (Gregory, Paul, & Morrison, 1979; Kilpatrick & Spreen, 1973) or modify it to limit some of its less desirable characteristics (Kimura, 1981; Hill & McLeod, 1984; DeFilippis & McCampbell, 1979; Slay, 1984).

The IBCT incorporates positive features for clinical use and research and, if its validity is substantiated by additional studies, may prove of considerable value to the neuropsychologist working with children. Its bargain price, as compared to its projection box counterpart, will make it more readily available to small clinics and university research centers with limited budgets. Its portability will allow bedside testing not readily accomplished with the projection box Category Test. Its lack of mechanico-electrical components and general simplicity of construction should reduce technician training time and lessen examiner errors even among experienced technicians. Even though booklet versions of the Category Test may not replace the projection box or the computerized versions presently appearing on the scene, it is anticipated that they will become the instrument of choice where portability is either necessary or highly desirable.

Because the IBCT is simple to administer and score (tasks that can be mastered by a technician in a short period of time), there is a danger that professionals not trained in neuropsychology may be tempted to administer and interpret it in their practices. As Dean (1985b) and Reynolds (1983) indicated, the Category Test, as part of the Halstead-Reitan Neuropsychological Test Battery, is a sophisticated instrument, requiring a firm grounding in neuropsychological theory for proper interpretation. This warning is particularly applicable when attempting statements about cortical dysfunction in children.

Technical Aspects

Because the IBCT is suggested as a possible alternate for the projection box Category Test for older children ages 9 to 14, the establishment of concurrent validity and score equivalency between the two forms is crucial. Of less immediate but of long-range concern is the question of equivalency of forms when used with a variety of pathological groups. To date, two studies equating the IBCT and the projection box Category Test have appeared in the literature and are summarized in the manual (Byrd, 1987).

Byrd and Warner (1986) compared samples of 24 9-to 14-year-old learning-disabled children and the same number of regular education children with the IBCT and the Category Test. Administration order was counterbalanced randomly. Concurrent validity coefficients for single age groups with the two samples combined (very small samples) ranged from .80 to .97. It is doubtful, however, whether these single age group correlations have any meaning because, on the average, they were computed on a maximum of eight students each. The correlation for all subjects combined between the IBCT and the Category Test was .89, a more than adequate concurrent validity coefficient. The reliability coefficient for the IBCT using a split-half analysis was reported as .91. Byrd and Warner (1986) report significant differences ($p < .001$) in error scores between the two groups on both the IBCT and Category Test. However, no significance tests were reported for mean error scores obtained by the two groups on the two forms of the test. Without such data, error score equivalency between forms (IBCT and Category Test) can not be claimed and the applicability of previous norms established for the projection box Category Test, as suggested by Byrd (1987), is questionable.

Byrd and Ingram (1988) conducted a second study in which they administered both the Category Test and the IBCT to 30 behaviorally disordered and 30 regular education students in randomized counterbalanced order. Both groups were reported to have average intelligence but no significance tests or covariance techniques were applied to determine if the groups actually differed in intelligence. The concurrent validity coefficients for all subjects combined and groups analyzed individually were in the low to middle .90s. These correlations are consistent with those obtained in the first study. The split-half reliability coefficient for the IBCT was found to be .92, but no information as to the specific procedure employed in the split-half analysis was reported. Byrd and Ingram (1988) report that mean error scores obtained from the two orders of administration (CT-IBCT or IBCT-CT) did not differ significantly but that the behaviorally disordered group scored significantly below the regular education group on both the IBCT and the Category Test. They concluded that the IBCT was an effective discriminator between these groups. The significance of this conclusion, however, is open to question because previous studies (Lansdell & Donnelly, 1977; Cullum, Steinman, & Bigler, 1984; Telzrow & Harr, 1987) have shown at least a moderate relationship between the Category Test and measures of intelligence. No statistical or experimental controls for the effects of intelligence were applied in this study. Error scores for both groups on both forms of the test (IBCT and Category Test) were reported, but statistical data supporting error score equivalency, again, were not included.

The author of the IBCT did not provide norms or a cutoff score differentiating normal from impaired performance; instead, Byrd referred the user to the cutoff (error score > 50) proposed by Reitan (1969) for adults or the classification of Category Test error scores for children developed by Selz and Reitan (1979). As indicated earlier, in reference to the first study, this is a questionable practice without firm data supporting equivalency of error scores between forms, particularly because the Selz and Reitan norms were based on research with the projection box Category Test.

Critique

The IBCT is a well-constructed portable adaptation of the projection box Category Test. The 168 stimulus figures are produced on heavy cardboard plates attractively bound in two durable plastic loose-leaf binders. The manual, though brief, is adequate in providing directions for administration and scoring, particularly if one assumes that the examiner is trained in the proper administration of the Halstead-Reitan Neuropsychological Test Battery. The scoring form, with its miniature reproductions of the stimulus figures, is an improvement over the one provided with the projection box Category Test and should aid in the reduction of administration and scoring errors.

Like its predecessor, the Booklet Category Test (BCT) for adults, the IBCT should find wide acceptance by clinicians and researchers in need of a portable form for use with children. However, additional large sample validity studies with both normal and diverse pathological groups are needed to establish firmly its equivalency with the time-honored projection box Category Test.

References

Byrd, P.B. (1987). *Manual for the Intermediate Booklet Category Test*. Odessa, FL: Psychological Assessment Resources.

Byrd, P. B., & Ingram, C. F. (1988). A comparative study of the Intermediate Booklet Category Test with the Halstead Category Test using behaviorally disordered and normal subjects. *The International Journal of Clinical Neuropsychology, 10*, 23–24.

Byrd, P.B., & Warner, P.D. (1986). Development of a booklet version of the Halstead Category Test for children age nine through fourteen years: Preliminary validation with normal and learning disabled subjects. *International Journal of Clinical Neuropsychology, 8*, 80–82.

Cullum, C.M., Steinman, D.R., & Bigler, E.D. (1984). Relationship between fluid and crystallized cognitive functions using Category Test and WAIS scores. *International Journal of Clinical Neuropsychology, 6*, 172–174.

Dean, R.S. (1985a). Neuropsychological assessment. In J.D. Cavenar & S.B. Guze (Eds.), *Psychiatry* (Vol. 1, pp. 1–17). Philadelphia: J.B. Lippincott.

Dean, R.S. (1985b). Review of the Halstead-Reitan Neuropsychological Test Battery. In J.V. Mitchell, Jr. (Ed.), *The ninth mental measurements yearbook* (pp. 644–646). Lincoln, NE: The Buros Institute.

Dean, R.S., & Rattan, G. (1984). The Booklet Category Test. In D.J. Keyser & R.C. Sweetland (Eds.), *Test critiques* (Vol. 1, pp. 113–116). Kansas City, MO: Test Corporation of America.

DeFilippis, N.A., & McCampbell, E. (1979). *The Booklet Category Test: Research and Clinical Form*. Odessa, FL: Psychological Assessment Resources.

Fischer, W.E. (1987). Halstead Category Test. In D.J. Keyser & R.C. Sweetland (Eds.), *Test critiques* (Vol. 6, pp. 208–215). Kansas City, MO: Test Corporation of America.

Golden, C.J. (1978). *Diagnosis and rehabilitation in clinical neuropsychology.* Springfield, IL: Charles C. Thomas.

Golden, C.J. (1979). *Clinical interpretation of objective psychological tests.* New York: Grune & Stratton.

Gregory, R.J., Paul, J.J., & Morrison, M.W. (1979). A short form of the Category Test for adults. *Journal of Clinical Psychology, 35*, 795–798.

Halstead, W.C. (1947). *Brain and intelligence: A quantitative study of the frontal lobes.* Chicago: The University of Chicago Press.

Hill, M., & McLeod, N. (1984). *Halstead Category Test: A computer version.* Jacksonville, FL: Precision People.

Kilpatrick, D.L., & Spreen, O. (1973). A revision of the Halstead Category Test for children aged 9 to 15. *Psychology in the Schools, 10*, 101–106.

Kimura, S.D. (1981). A card form of the Reitan-Modified Halstead Category Test. *Journal of Consulting and Clinical Psychology, 49*, 145–146.

Landsdell, H., & Donnelly, E.F. (1977). Factor analysis of the Wechsler Adult Intelligence Scale subtests and the Halstead-Reitan Category and Tapping tests. *Journal of Consulting and Clinical Psychology, 45*, 412–416.

Reitan, R.M. (1969). *Manual for administration of neuropsychological test batteries for adults and children.* Indianapolis: Author.

Reynolds, C.R. (1983). Booklet Category Test. *School Psychology Review, 12*, 487–488.

Selz, D., & Reitan, R.M. (1979). Rules for neuropsychological diagnosis: Classification of brain function in older children. *Journal of Consulting and Clinical Psychology, 47*, 258–264.

Slay, D.K. (1984). A portable Halstead-Reitan Category Test. *Journal of Clinical Psychology, 40*, 1023–1027.

Swiercinsky, D.P. (1978). *Manual for the Adult Neuropsychological Evaluation.* Springfield, IL: Charles C. Thomas.

Telzrow C.F., & Harr, G.A. (1987). Common variance among three measures of nonverbal cognitive ability: WISC-R Performance Scale, WJPB TCA reasoning cluster, and Halstead Category Test. *Journal of School Psychology, 25*, 93–95.

Brandon Davis, Ph.D.
Research Fellow in Neuropsychology, Neuropsychology Laboratory, Ball State University, Muncie, Indiana.

Raymond S. Dean, Ph.D.
Distinguished Professor of Neuropsychology, Ball State University, Muncie, Indiana, and Indiana University School of Medicine, Indianapolis, Indiana.

INTERNATIONAL VERSION OF THE MENTAL STATUS QUESTIONNAIRE

T. L. Brink. San Carlos, California: T. L. Brink, Ph.D.

Introduction

The International Version of the Mental Status Questionnaire(IVMSQ; Brink, 1979) was designed as a brief test for screening "senile confusion." The measure is intended to be individually administered in an interview. T.L. Brink, author of the IVMSQ, is presently on the faculty of the Western Graduate School of Medicine. He is also a member of the clinical faculty of Stanford University's Psychiatry Department in their School of Medicine. He has authored over 200 reviews and articles for medical and psychological journals. Dr. Brink is presently serving as editor of *Clinical Gerontologist.*

The number of older adults in the Western world is growing geometrically. Botwinick (1978), citing Census Bureau statistics, suggests that the percentage of people over age 65 constitutes up to 10% of the American population and that within the next 50 years, this proportion should increase to 15%. Related to this fact, the National Center for Health Statistics estimates that some 58% of nursing-home residents are confused and presumed to be suffering from forms of dementia (Poon, 1980). From a psychological point of view, the need for psychometrically sound assessment devices for use with the aged has become critical. Clearly, the identification of cognitive impairment has become a significant part of the ongoing psychological assessment needs of elderly patients.

A problem with assessing the cognitive functions of the aged relates to the fact that although the aged may demonstrate average performance relative to age peers, their scores often place them in the impaired range using our present norms. Such age-related decrements in functioning of older adults has become a significant area of research (Benton & Sivan, 1984; Botwinick, 1977, 1981; Price, Fein, & Feinberg, 1980; Simpson & Vega, 1971). Recent research of the morphological and physiological changes in the brain, and the concomitant cognitive correlates has begun to provide a biological understanding of the aging processes (Milsa, Marttila, & Rinne, 1984: Wu, Schenkenberg, Wing, & Osborn, 1981). However, few measures exist that allow us to apply this knowledge in the clinical setting.

While concern for appropriate assessment procedures has gained momentum,

Hoffman (1982) found that the admitting procedures by physicians neglected the even basic consideration of neurologic and psychologic functioning (e.g., dementia and delirium) with elderly patients. More recently, McCartney and Palmateer (1985), considered the initial assessment of newly admitted elderly patients to a medical center. In the 394 admissions, a mental status exam was administered only four times. Of these, in only two cases was a mental status exam of more than three items used. It seems clear from these data that gaining an understanding of the mental processes (e.g., dementia, confusion, etc.) of elderly persons admitted to hospitals is a neglected component of the medical workup.

The IVMSQ, designed to screen senile confusion, is a version of the Mental Status Questionnaire (MSQ; Kahn, Goldfarb, Pollack, & Peck, 1960) and is purported to be a refinement of the MSQ. However, the IVMSQ has no accompanying manual, and Brink offers no other documentation that details its development. Nor does he offer an extensive rationale for the present 10 items of the IVMSQ.

Apparently the original MSQ (Kahn et al., 1960) was presented as part of a series of 31 questions. From these items, 10 were selected on the basis of their utility in differentiating confused from alert patients. How the development of the MSQ relates to the construction of the IVMSQ is not provided by the author. The distinction between the MSQ and the IVMSQ also is not addressed by Brink (1979). However, it appears that the IVMSQ and the MSQ contain a very similar set of 10 questions. Given that, to some degree, there are distinctions between the IVMSQ and the MSQ, it is both confusing and psychometrically questionable to use the two tests interchangeably. Problems also exist in that Brink quotes psychometric data for the IVMSQ when, in fact, these investigations pertain to the MSQ. Unlike MSQ, the IVMSQ has two "forms" that differ only in regard to the last three items, which focus on either institutional or community-based patients. Such alternate forms add to further psychometric confusion.

Practical Applications/Uses

The test author cautions in the very brief introduction presented prior to the items that the IVMSQ is a test for assessing confusion, not organicity. Brink seems to feel that a very practical function of the measure is distinguishing patients with dementia from those coming from a deprived environment. However, the author offers no data to support this use of the IVMSQ. In order to pursue the distinction between individuals who suffer from dementia and those who reflect environmental deprivation, Brink recommends that the test be administered twice, with the examiner providing corrective feedback during the first administration. If the patient remembers the corrections on the second administration, Brink suggests that the initial errors were not due to dementia but to an information-deprived background.

Again, although Brink suggests that the purpose of the IVMSQ is to assess mental confusion, not organicity, an operational definition of confusion as distinct from organicity is not presented. As the term 'confusion' also has implications for organicity, it is unfortunate that Brink has chosen to use this term in reference to a concept supposedly distinct from issues of organicity. Alternatively, McCartney and Palmateer (1985) have suggested that although the patient who is in the primary stages of organic brain dysfunction may not appear grossly confused, a diagnosis of dementia may in fact be valid. It is quite possible, therefore, that the distinction that Brink proposes would not be sufficient to distinguish between organicity and confusion, even as he uses the term.

Further, the memory processes in the elderly should be a prime consideration in the development of a test such as the IVMSQ. However, there is no mention made of the significant concerns of memory processes and how memorial tasks in the aged are affected by various attentional dysfunctions (Craik & Byrd, 1981).

The IVMSQ is presented on a single sheet of paper. Brink offers two sentences on how the test might be administered to a person from a deprived environment and a brief one-paragraph statement outlining the scoring procedures and interpretation. Beyond that, no formal guidelines for administration or scoring are provided. Further, there are no age norms available; nor is there anything to suggest the range of ages for which the IVMSQ was intended.

Technical Aspects

Little data exist on the validity or reliability of either the scoring or interpretation of the IVMSQ. It would seem that, at the very least, some investigation of the utility of the measure in predicting dementia and/or confusion should be made available. Brink does suggest that the interrater reliability of the IVMSQ is .80 from previous research (Brink, Janakes, & Martinez, 1981). However, the actual article quoted in support of this reliability figure does not use the IVMSQ as published. Instead, it considers the construction of the Hypochondriasis Scale for Institutional Geriatric Patients (HSIG; Brink, Janakes, & Martinz, 1981). In a similar fashion, Brink cites a study of test-retest reliability of the IVMSQ (Brink et. al., 1986) when, in fact, the article referenced is a study of the MSQ.

Critique

Use of the IVMSQ should be considered with caution because of the lack of basic psychometric information as required by the *Standards for Educational and Psychological Testing* (American Educational Research Association, American Psychological Association, & National Council on Measurement in Education, 1985). Given that there are no data relating specifically to norms, reliability, and validity of the IVMSQ, its use seems tenuous. Further, the lack of structure in administration, scoring, and interpretation suggests little more than a clinical procedure of questionable utility. Until a more substantial attempt has been made to address the various psychometric questions, the use of this instrument can not be recommended. The IVMSQ may be best valued as a device directed towards the general structuring of an informal intake interview of an aged person. However, for professionals intent on dealing with a comprehensive overview of instruments and diagnostic concerns of elderly persons, numerous articles are available (Freeman, 1976; Kapoor, Karpf, Wienand, Peterson, Levey, 1983; Lawton, 1971; Miller, 1980; Smith & Kiloh, 1981). As well, Poon (1980) has provided an edited text that surveys many of the issues confronting the elderly in our population.

In summary, it is not sufficient for Brink to cite support for the IVMSQ based on data from another instrument, the MSQ. Nor can a purely rational basis for accepting the measure be justified in place of psychometric support. The overriding effect of the paucity of substantive test development procedures (i.e., standardization and norming) severely reduces the clinical utility of this instrument with aged persons. In the final analysis, there is little to justify its use with the population it is intended to serve.

References

This list includes text citations and suggested additional reading.

American Educational Research Association, American Psychological Association, & National Council on Measurement in Education (1985). *Standards for educational and psychological testing.* Washington, DC: American Psychological Association.

Benton, A.L., & Sivan, A.B. (1984). Problems and conceptual issues in neuropsychological research in aging and dementia. *Journal of Clinical Neuropsychology, 6,* 57–63.

Botwinick, J. (1977). Intellectual abilities. In J.E. Birren & K.W. Schaie (Eds.), *Handbook of the psychology of aging.* New York: Van Nostrand Reinhold.

Botwinick, J. (1978). *Aging and behavior* (2nd ed.). New York: Springer.

Botwinick, J. (1981). Neuropsychology of aging. In S.B. Filskov & T.J. Boll (Eds.), *Handbook of clinical neuropsychology.* New York: Wiley-Interscience.

Brink, T.L. (1979). *International Version of the Mental Status Questionnaire.* San Carlos, CA: T.L. Brink.

Brink, T.L., Janakes, C., & Martinez, N. (1981). Geriatric hypochondrias: Situational factors. *Journal of the American Geriatrics Society, 29,* 37–39.

Brink, T.L., Curran, M.L., Dorr, M.L., Janson, E., McNulty, U., & Messina, M. (1986). The set test for dementia and depression. *Clinical Gerontologist 4,* 69–72.

Craik, F.I.M., & Byrd, M. (1981). Aging and cognitive deficits: The role of attentional resources. In F.I.M. Craik & S.E. Trehub (Eds.), *Aging and cognitive processes.* New York: Plenum Press.

Freeman, F.R. (1976). Evaluation of patients with progressive intellectual deterioration. *Archives of Neurology, 37,* 658–659.

Hoffman, R.S. (1982). Diagnostic errors in the evaluation of behavioral disorders. *Journal of the American Medical Association, 248,* 964–967.

Kahn, R.L., Goldfarb, A.I., Pollack, M., & Peck, A. (1980). Brief objective measures for the determination of mental states in the aged. *American Journal of Psychiatry, 117,* 326–328.

Kapoor W.N. Karpf, M., Wienand, S., Peterson, J.R., & Levey G.S. (1983). Prospective evaluation and follow-up of patients with syncope. *New England Journal of Medicine, 309,* 197–207.

Lawton, M.P. (1971). The functional assessment of elderly people. *Journal of the American Geriatrics Society, 19,* 465–481.

Lezak, M.D. (1983). *Neuropsychological assessment* (2nd ed.). New York: Oxford University Press.

McCartney, J.R., & Palmateer, L.M. (1985). Assessment of cognitive deficit in geriatric patients: A study of physicians behavior. *Journal of the American Geriatrics Society, 33,* 467–471.

Miller, E. (1980). Cognitive assessment of the older adult. In J. Birren & R.B. Sloane (Eds.), *Handbook of Aging and Mental Health.* Englewood Cliffs, NJ: Prentice Hall.

Milsa, P.K., Marttila, R.J., & Rinne, U.K. (1984). Extrapyramidal signs in Alzheimer's disease. *Neurology, 34,* 1114–1116.

Poon, L.W. (Ed.). (1980). *Aging in the 1980s; Psychological issues.* Washington, DC: American Psychological Association.

Price, L.J., Fein, G., & Feinberg, I. (1980). Neuropsychology assessment of cognitive function in the elderly. In L.W. Poon (Ed.), *Aging in the 1980s.* Washington, DC: American Psychology Association.

Simpson, C.D., & Vega, A. (1971). Unilateral brain damage and patterns of age-corrected WAIS subtest scores. *Journal of Clinical Psychology, 27,* 204–208.

Smith, J.S., & Kiloh, L.G. (1981). The investigation of dementia: Results of 200 consecutive admissions. *Lancet, 1,* 824–827.

Wu, S., Schenkenberg, T., Wing, S.D., & Osborn, A.G. (1981). Cognitive correlates of diffuse cerebral atrophy determined computed tomography. *Neurology, 31,* 1180–1184.

Robert H. Bauernfeind, Ph.D.
Professor of Education, Northern Illinois University, DeKalb, Illinois.

IOWA TESTS OF EDUCATIONAL DEVELOPMENT—FORMS X-8 and Y-8

Leonard S. Feldt, Robert A. Forsyth, and Stephanie D. Alnot.
Chicago, Illinois: The Riverside Publishing Company.

Introduction

The Iowa Tests of Educational Development (ITED) are tests of general educational development for students in Grades 9-12. These are *not* course-oriented tests of school achievement. While they draw on school education, they also draw on learnings occurring elsewhere, in scouts, in part-time jobs, in reading newspapers and magazines, everywhere one has a chance to add to his or her skills in handling problems in everyday life.

Researchers working with general educational development tests have adopted the following definition.

A test of "general educational development" is a test of cognitive skills, given periodically, to measure student growth toward effective adult behavior.

ITED was the first test of general educational development designed for use with high school students. The first forms, X-1 and Y-1, were published at the University of Iowa in 1942. The current Forms X-8 and Y-8 became available in 1987. Thus, part of the history of the ITED is that the tests have been revised and/or updated approximately every 6 or 7 years.

The history of the ITED (Forms 1 through 7) has been traced by Peterson (1983) and by Craig (1984). E.F. Lindquist, the man who conceived and guided these tests for many years, died in 1978, but his influence is clearly manifest in these most recent forms. In 1987, after several years of philosophical differences between authors and publisher, ITED was dropped by Science Research Associates, Inc. (SRA) and was purchased by the Riverside Publishing Company. (Riverside is also the publisher of the Iowa Tests of Basic Skills for elementary schools.)

Table 1 presents a facts chart for reference throughout this critique. It shows that there are seven separate tests in the ITED program, a Composite score summarizing the seven separate tests, and a Reading Total score derived from the reading comprehension materials in three of the seven tests. The total testing time is 250 minutes, but the total administration time will run close to 300 minutes (5 hours).

There is one booklet containing all of the subtests for Form X-8 and a parallel booklet containing all of the subtests for Form Y-8. Each subtest is presented in two levels: Level I presents the first two thirds of the items and is recommended for Grades 9 and 10; Level II presents the last two thirds of the items and is recommended for Grades 11 and 12. There is one answer sheet for all of Level I and a different answer sheet for all of Level II. These same answer sheets can be used with either Form X-8 or Form Y-8.

Table 1

Facts Chart for ITED Forms X-8 and Y-8

Title	Emphases	Testing Time (minutes)	No. of Items	Median Raw*	KR_{20}*
TESTS					
Expression	Editing for grammar, style (54 items); spelling (15 items)	35	69	36	.92
Quantitative	Everyday measurements, formulas, graphs, geometrics	50	40	17	.87
Social Studies	Judgments, advertisements, cartoons (24 items); reading Social Studies passages (36 items)	45	60	32-33	.91
Natural Sciences	Developing hypotheses, recognizing facts (24 items); interpreting experimental research (36 items)	45	60	27-28	.91
Literary Materials	Interpreting stories, essays, poems	35	46	25-26	.89
Vocabulary	Synonyms for fairly common words in our society	15	40	16-17	.91
Sources of Information	Library references, other sources of information	25	46	28	.89
SCORES					
Composite	Total of the seven scale scores, converted to the same score scale as each test	250	361	—	.97
Reading Total	Total of reading comprehension items from Test 3, Test 4, and Test 5	—	118	59-62	.95

*Median raw and KR_{20} data are for mid-year 10th-graders on Form Y-8 in the national norms studies.

The directions in the test manuals are clear, ITED Directions for Administration, ITED Norms Booklet, ITED Teacher, Administrator, and Counselor Manual (Feldt, Forsyth, & Alnot, 1988a; 1988b; 1988c), although Level I and Level II directions are perforce awkward. The tests are group administered. All students are assembled in a central location (e.g., the lunchroom) with one administrator and perhaps one proctor for every 30 students. Alternatively, the tests can be administered to classroom groups by using the school's intercom system. One can argue for either approach; the positive aspect of both is that any administrative mistakes will apply equally to all of the students taking the tests.

Each test score is converted to a scale score that runs from a low of 1 to a high of 36. The all-students mean is approximately 15. The top of the scale was originally 30, but because of increasing raw scores in the 1950s and early 1960s, the scale was extended to a top of 36. This 1-to-36 scale is used mostly for growth and other research studies. National and local percentile-rank scores are provided for other score interpretations.

Riverside offers a great variety of scoring and data-processing services. The many computer services available are described and pictured in the Riverside Test Catalog. Samples of the printouts are shown on pages 120-126 of the 1988 catalog (Riverside, 1988). The publisher also offers an excellent manual for teachers, administrators, and counselors (Feldt, Forsyth, & Alnot, 1988b) providing a great variety of suggestions for using the test results.

Practical Applications/Uses

For the benefit of teachers, administrators, school board members, and newspaper reporters, it is productive to discuss the uses (and misuses) of these kinds of tests as seen through the eyes of E. F. Lindquist. In the 1930s and early 1940s, the state of Iowa was a leader in testing for school achievement at the high school level. That testing program, coordinated at the University of Iowa, provided end-of-the-year tests in such areas as English Mechanics, English and American Literature, World History, American History, Algebra, Plane Geometry, General Science, Physics, American Government, and Economics (Peterson, 1983). The program was successful in Iowa and it enjoyed an excellent national reputation, but, in 1942 Lindquist discontinued its use.

Peterson (1983) cited a number of political reasons for Lindquist developing an alternate program for Iowa high schools. But, beyond those reasons, it is clear that Lindquist was not pleased with his own subject-matter tests. One, he was convinced that students who would become effective adults in Iowa (and elsewhere) knew a great deal more about life than was found in those subject-matter tests, and he wanted to "tap into" those out-of-school learnings. Two, he was concerned about student *growth* (i.e., Which students are growing? Which are not?), and he needed repeated measures *in the same skill areas* to measure student growth (*A New Testing Service*, 1942).

A large part of Lindquist's thinking seems to have stemmed from a growing dissatisfaction with conventional subject-matter achievement tests. In 1941 he wrote:

The selection of content of the tests used (to date) has been based on an analysis of the things now being taught in the school subjects, not on our or anyone else's notion of what *ought* to be taught in these subjects. These tests have indicated to the schools to what extent they are attaining certain of the immediate objectives of instruction in individual school subjects, but have not indicated whether or not these objectives are valid in relation to ultimate objectives. Test scores, for example, might indicate how much a pupil has learned of what is now being taught in ninth grade algebra, but they will not indicate how much the teaching of algebra has contributed to his general ability to do quantitative thinking in situations met in life outside of school. (cited in Peterson, 1983, p. 53)

And, in an extraordinary document published in the spring of 1942, Lindquist cited 11 values of his proposed ITED testing program:

1) The tests used should measure as directly as possible the attainment of the ultimate objectives of the entire school program.

2) All of the tests should be administered, under standard conditions, to the entire student body.

3) The program must provide for the measurement of growth.

4) The tests used should measure the more permanent of the changes produced in the pupils.

5) The test results should not be usable in the rating of individual teachers.

6) The description of the pupils' educational development provided by the tests must be expressed in readily interpretable form.

7) The test profile for each individual pupil must be readily available at all times to each of his teachers and counselors.

8) The measures derived must be highly comparable from test to test.

9) Each of the tests must yield highly reliable measures of the abilities of the individual pupil.

10) The testing program ideally should impose no clerical or statistical burdens whatever upon teachers and administrators, and in all other respects should involve the minimum of administrative inconvenience.

11) The total cost of the services of the program must be within the reach of the majority of the public schools (*A New Testing Service*, 1942, pp. 9-16).

In this 1942 document Lindquist focuses on student growth toward effective adult behavior, insists that such tests not be used to rate individual teachers, and shows an early concern with machine data processing, a concern that led to his 1955 completion of the first electronic scoring machine (Peterson, 1983).

Again today, one *must* see these tests as focusing on life skills that may or may not have been taught in specific school courses. This reviewer offers four points that may help to clarify and reinforce this concept:

1) In the early years of the Iowa testing programs, Lindquist included a test of trends in current affairs titled The Test of Understanding of Contemporary Affairs. When, in 1942, he reluctantly withdrew this test from the Iowa testing programs, he wrote that "high school pupils in general are very seriously uninformed about contemporary affairs, and . . . a very large proportion of them know practically nothing about what is going on in the world today" (cited in Peterson, 1983, p. 20).

2) Through all of his years with the ITED program, Lindquist included current

events in the social studies tests, principles of health and safety in the science tests, and problems of consumerism in the mathematics tests.

3) In the early years of the ITED program, Lindquist required Iowa high schools to give the tests during the first 3 weeks of September:

> Each school will decide on what dates to give the tests, but each school is very strongly urged to administer the tests as soon as possible after school opens. The earlier the tests are administered, the less is the danger [sic] that they will be influenced by the temporary or immediate results of current instruction, and the greater is the likelihood that they will measure only the relatively permanent acquisitions of the pupil. (*A New Testing Service*, 1942, p. 26)

While this requirement was impossible to maintain (hot weather, teacher-pupil relations, etc.), this reviewer is overwhelmed by the unrelenting logic of Lindquist's thinking: If educators want to learn what students really know and what they can achieve and learn when away from the classroom setting, then educators must determine when the best time in the school year would be to gather such information.

4) At a sales conference at SRA headquarters in Chicago (attended by this reviewer), a new salesman raised his hand: "Dr. Lindquist, could I then tell my customers that you are trying to test what remains after the facts have been forgotten?" And Lindquist eagerly replied that that was exactly what he was trying to do.

Of course, there have been many types of criticisms of the ITED program: the tests are too long, they require too much reading, they are too expensive, they aren't fair, they don't test what is being taught during the school year.

Among professional specialists in measurement, two were especially displeased with the ITED program. Oscar Buros (1977) wrote:

> It was not surprising that the new [ITED] battery appeared to many of us to be essentially a reading and scholastic aptitude test. . . . It is hard to imagine a more drastic change than this 1942 shift from the Iowa subject-centered tests to the ITED reading-aptitude battery. . . . I think it unfortunate that so much attention is being paid to predicting success at the next higher level, while less and less attention is being given to determining what was learned at earlier levels. (p. 11)

A.G. Wesman (1965) saw the ITED program as making too much money, based on too little research, using tests with unnecessarily high intercorrelations.

It should be noted that Lindquist's notion of "general educational development" gained wide acceptance among junior and senior high school counselors and administrators; similar tests were soon developed elsewhere (i.e., the Sequential Tests of Educational Progress [STEP], the Tests of Achievement and Proficiency [TAP], and the Comprehensive Tests of Basic Skills [CTBS] by test programmers who wanted to compete with Lindquist.

Technical Aspects

As mentioned previously, each test score is converted to a scale score that runs from a low of 1 to a high of 36. The all-students mean is approximately 15, but the scale is then extended upward to reach a high of 36 while reaching a low of only 1.

The ITED scale thus is not a "Standard Score Scale" although it is sometimes called by that name in the literature.

The national norms for the X-8 and Y-8 tests were developed by equating ITED raw scores with the national norms scores of the Iowa Tests of Basic Skills (ITBS) and especially the Tests of Achievement and Proficiency (TAP). (See ITED Norms Booklet, Feldt, Forsyth, & Alnot, 1988b, pp. 6-8.) This reviewer endorses the work, because it should provide smooth growth curves and comparable norms scores for schools giving any combination of Riverside's ITBS, TAP, or ITED. Even if the norms are not exactly "on target" nationally, the norms from these three testing programs should be consistent with each other.

New national norms studies for ITED are currently in development, and it is expected that the new norms will be operational in the fall of 1989. What if these new national norms are appreciably different from those of ITBS and TAP? This question is troublesome for the project directors at Riverside and at the University of Iowa.

The reliability data shown in Table 1 are fairly representative and certainly more than satisfactory. Most of the medians are near 50% correct. The Quantitative, Natural Sciences, and Vocabulary tests show medians somewhat under 50% correct; the Sources of Information test shows a median notably higher than 50% correct.

The user's manual (Feldt, Forsyth, & Alnot, 1988c) provides a wealth of data for the X-8 and Y-8 tests. The data clearly show that most students are able to finish these tests in the time allowed, and that few score below chance raw scores (p. 83). The data also show that the ITED scores are highly intercorrelated, ranging from a low of .64 to a high of .85, with a median of .76 across four studies (p. 72). That median of .76 represents 58% common variance between scores.

The matter of ITED predictive validity in schools is very well established, and this reviewer sees no need for further studies using the Form 8 tests. A summary of correlations between the ITED Composite Score and grades in high schools and colleges has been provided for test users in a University of Iowa publication (*Manual for Teachers, Counselors, and Examiners*, ITED, 1980, pp. 45–46). As expected, these correlations typically run in the .40s, .50s, and .60s.

A much more productive line of research would involve patterns and levels of ITED performance of those students who eventually became established lawyers, physicians, journalists, and so on. With the great amounts of ITED data for Iowa students, are the test authors not near the point of attaining such data? For example, a statement such as "This was the mean ITED profile of high school students who eventually became lawyers here in the state of Iowa" could add a whole new dimension to the ITED testing program.

In the meanwhile, there is the matter of content validity. Several colleagues have studied the X-8 and Y-8 forms, and all enthusiastically endorsed the tests save one. This reviewer especially endorses Test 7, Sources of Information, and Test 2, Quantitative Thinking. The latter is totally free of the brutal "modern math" period. Rather, it is full of real-life problems such as, "How much money will you need?" "How much time will you need?" "How much paint will you need?" However, Table 1 shows that American students are not doing very well in solving these kinds of problems.

Test 1, Expression, is not endorsed by this reviewer. For example, the student's first task is to read a fairly long article, and then to go back through the article editing it for grammar, syntax, and *style*, with multiple choices for underlined segments. It is this reviewer's opinion that editing for *style* is a skill needed in professional publishing houses, and not one that is needed in everyday life in Iowa or elsewhere. In planning their Form 9 tests, it is this reviewer's suggestion that the ITED authors take an in-depth look look at the College Board's Test of Standard Written English for alternate (and faster) approaches to measuring editing skills

Critique

This reviewer has focused on Lindquist's thinking for two reasons. First, educators are struck by the logic of the man's thinking and by his 11-point checklist for a dynamic testing program for high school students. Second, there are educators that would take us back to Iowa, circa 1940, with narrow subject-matter achievement tests with which to "evaluate" our curricula, textbooks, and teachers. This reviewer asks those educators please to consider a testing program that checks for student growth in handling life problems, based in part—but only in part—on the courses they have been taking. Such a testing program need not involve ITED; it could use the TAP, STEP, CTBS, or any other test battery that is true to the notion of "general educational development."

The X-8 and Y-8 tests reviewed here are clearly consistent with Lindquist's notion of "general educational development." The test items seem mature, realistic, measuring skills that will be needed by "effective adults." One can quibble with items here or there, but the overall thrust is surely in the direction of what students will need to be able to do as effective adults in American society.

As for O.K. Buros's (1977) criticism of these kinds of tests as repeatedly measuring "scholastic aptitude," that assumption is partially true (i.e., students who are strong in reading and mathematics are well placed for advanced schooling). But Lindquist also tested for current events, health and safety, and consumerism. One could ask which test is better designed for college-bound students, a test of world history, algebra, and physics, or a test of health, safety, and consumerism? Some educators would agree that the latter test is better designed for all sorts of high school students.

As for Wesman's (1965) criticisms of Lindquist's work, it is true that correlations among tests of "general educational development" run quite high, approximately .76 in ITED X-8 and Y-8. Thus, such tests are not especially efficient statistically. But, in this reviewer's opinion, the test questions are the *heart* of any testing program. For example, suppose that these two questions correlate .90 with each other.

If your clothing catches on fire, you should run for a
   A) window.
   B) blanket.
   C) telephone.
   D) fire station.
If you see a serious automobile accident, you should *first*
   A) call a doctor.
   B) call the police.

C) call a tow-truck.
D) try to administer first aid.

If these two items correlate .90 with each other, the testing program lacks statistical efficiency, one item or the other can be removed from the test with no great loss in reliability (in rank ordering students). But, if educators think about "effective adult behavior," they will probably keep both items. This is a point that Wesman (1965) and other researchers seem to have missed: If the questions are important in the lives of students, educators won't be overly concerned about statistical redundancies. Lindquist stated this point forcefully in the following publication:

> There is no better way to judge the validity of these tests than to put yourself in the student's place and to take the tests yourself. In this way, decide for yourself what the tests really measure and what abilities are required from the student. Then make up your own mind whether or not these abilities represent the desirable outcomes of a program of general education. There is no statistical substitute for a common-sense evaluation of this kind. (1960, p. 19)

Using that criterion, this reviewer endorses most of the items in ITED Forms X-8 and Y-8 and the test author's work in the establishment of general national norms. Yet, three aspects of the X-8 and Y-8 materials should be noted: 1) The test gets off to a very slow start with the English editing test. This reviewer feels that Form 9 of ITED should begin with the Vocabulary test, using very simple words such as *friendly* or *true*. 2) The entire test booklet may be a deterrent to some students. The vertical spacing is fine, but the reading passages are long and cramped. Where are the short stories, the short essays, the short poems? Where is the color? The ITED booklets are printed in black and a second color. This reviewer suggests that a brighter, more attractive color might motivate students. 3) There is little justification for the Level I–Level II treatment at the high school level. Such treatment is confusing and perhaps unnecessary, as shown by the flat growth curves for the item data. Except for the Vocabulary test, few p values increase more than 20% between Grade 9 and Grade 12 (Feldt et al., 1988b). One needs to recall that much of that limited growth is a function of the fact that drop-outs are not represented in the data for Grades 11 and 12.

After studying the data in Table 1, this reviewer recommends Level I for every student in near-average schools and Level II for every student in schools with a highly-talented, college-bound population. With that plan in operation, all of the item data would apply to all of the students in a given school.

In summary, ITED Form 8 has satisfactory national norms, satisfactory reliabilities, and excellent content validity. Its scores can be used to track student growth across the high school years and to show students their unusual strengths and weaknesses on national norms. So, this reviewer endorses use of the Form 8 batteries, but also looks forward to Form 9 for the reasons cited previously.

References

This list includes text citations and suggested additional readings.

Buros, O.K. (1977 July–August). Fifty years in testing: Some reminiscences, criticisms, and suggestions. *Educational Researcher*, p. 11.

Craig, R.C. (1984). Review of the Iowa Tests of Educational Development. In D.J. Keyser & R.C. Sweetland (Eds.), *Test critiques* (Vol. I, pp. 365–367). Kansas City, MO: Test Corporation of America.

Feldt, L.S., Forsyth, R.A., & Alnot, S.D. (1988a). *ITED Directions for Administration*. Chicago, IL: Riverside Publishing Company.

Feldt, L.S., Forsyth, R.A., & Alnot, S.D. (1988b). *ITED Norms booklet*. Chicago, IL: Riverside Publishing Company.

Feldt, L.S., Forsyth, R.A., & Alnot, S. D. (1988c). *ITED Teacher, Administrator, and Counselor manual*. Chicago, IL: Riverside Publishing Company.

Kifer, E. (1985). Review of the Iowa Tests of Educational Development (Seventh Edition). In J.V. Mitchell Jr. (Ed.), *The ninth mental measurements yearbook* (pp. 723–725). Lincoln, NE: Buros Institute.

Lindquist, E.F. (1960). *Manual for the school administrator: Manual for the Iowa Tests of Educational Development*. Chicago, IL: Science Research Associates.

Manual for teachers, counselors, and examiners—ITED. (1980). Iowa City: The University of Iowa.

A new testing service. (1942). Iowa City: University of Iowa.

Peterson, J.J. (1983). *The Iowa testing programs*. Iowa City: University of Iowa Press.

Riverside Publishing Company. (1988). *Test resource catalog—1988*. Chicago, IL: Author.

Wardrop, J.L. (1985). Review of the Iowa Tests of Educational Development (Seventh Edition). In J. V. Mitchell Jr. (Ed.), *The ninth mental measurements yearbook* (pp. 725–727). Lincoln, NE: Buros Institute.

Wesman, A.G. (1965). Review of the Iowa Tests of Educational Development. In O.K. Buros (Ed.), *The sixth mental measurements yearbook* (pp. 51–55) Highland Park, NJ: Gryphon Press.

G. Cynthia Fekken, Ph.D.
Assistant Professor of Psychology, Queen's University, Kingston, Canada.

Ronald R. Holden, Ph.D.
Assistant Professor of Psychology, Queen's University, Kingston, Canada.

JENKINS ACTIVITY SURVEY

C. David Jenkins, Stephen J. Zyzanski, and Ray H. Rosenman.
San Antonio, Texas: The Psychological Corporation.

Introduction

The Jenkins Activity Survey (JAS; Jenkins, Zyzanski, & Rosenman, 1979) is a self-report, multiple-choice inventory designed to assess the coronary-prone behavior pattern known as Type A behavior. Type A behavior has been implicated as an independent risk factor in the etiology of coronary heart disease, including both myocardial infarction and coronary atherosclerosis. Thus, the JAS potentially offers objective data on a behavior pattern that is pertinent to various cardiovascular disorders.

Drs. C. David Jenkins and Stephen J. Zyzanski, both psychologists, collaborated extensively with Dr. Ray H. Rosenman, a cardiologist, to developed the JAS so that health care professionals (e.g., physicians) and industrial and clinical practitioners and researchers (e.g., epidemiologists) would have an instrument for evaluating an individual's Type A behavior that was easy to master, administer, score, and interpret. Initially, Type A behavior was clinically assessed through the Structured Interview (Roseman et al., 1964). This Structured Interview measured not only the content of an individual's responses, but also verbal style and nonverbal patterns in responses when the individual was exposed to mild stress. Such characteristics were used clinically to differentiate between patients with coronary disease and patients with other illnesses. However, because the Structured Interview required detailed training, practice, and guidance under a qualified instructor, an objective measure was sought. The JAS represents a psychometric attempt to duplicate the Structured Interview.

Construction of the JAS emphasized empirical, clinical, and theoretical considerations. Initial test items were based on the protocol of the Structured Interview, the clinical observations of Jenkins, and a review of Type A theory. From these, an experimental version of the survey, consisting of 64 items, was developed in 1964. Item selection was based upon the ability of items to differentiate statistically between men who had been classified as either Type A or Type B (i.e., lack of Type A characteristics) using the Structured Interview. Forty items passed this selection procedure and, in combination with 21 new test items, comprised the first published edition of the JAS in 1965. In 1966, the second published version (57 items) of the JAS emerged. This version omitted items from the 1965 version that were redun-

264

dant or psychometrically inferior in distinguishing between Type A and Type B men. Additionally, a number of new items were added. At this stage, three additional scales, derived through factor analysis, also became part of the JAS: Speed and Impatience, Job Involvement, and Hard-Driving and Competitive. The third edition (64 items) of the JAS was published in 1969. This version retained only those items from the 1966 edition that maximally discriminated between Type A and Type B men as classified by *both* previous editions of the JAS. Further, some new items were added to strengthen the assessment of JAS factor scales and to evaluate some recent clinical hypotheses. Form B of the JAS (54 items) was published in 1972. This form dropped 12 items not providing independent information regarding status on the Type A or factor dimensions, added two new experimental items, and reworded other items so that they would be appropriate for both men and women. In Form C (52 items), the two experimental items from Form B were deleted and the format of the survey was modified for administrative and scoring purposes. Form C represents the current adult version of the JAS. The survey yields an overall Type A score based on 21 items as well as scores on three factor scales.

Factor scales consist of Speed and Impatience (21 items), Job Involvement (24 items), and Hard-Driving and Competitive (20 items) dimensions. The Speed and Impatience factor evaluates time urgency as expressed in the behavioral style of the Type A person. The Job Involvement scale assesses the commitment of an individual to his or her occupation. Finally, the Hard-Driving and Competitive dimension measures the intensity and effort a person puts forth in various activities.

Other versions of the JAS also exist, perhaps the best known of which is the student version, Form T (Glass, 1977; Krantz, Glass, & Snyder, 1974). The JAS Form T consists of 44 items and represents a modification of Form B; test items related to income and occupation were either deleted or changed. As a consequence, this version does not have a Job Involvement factor scale. In addition to the student form, Form N is gaining some popularity. A shortened form of Form C, it consists of only those 39 items needed to score the overall Type A scale plus the three factor scales. Yarnold, Bryant, and Grimm's (1987) comparison of long and short versions of Form T supported the strategy of culling JAS items from the larger context by demonstrating that the psychometric properties of the items and scales are not affected substantially. The JAS has been translated or modified for use in at least the following languages: Dutch (Appels, Jenkins, & Rosenman, 1982); Flemish (Kittel et al., 1978); French (Kittel et al., 1978); East Slovakian (Stancak, Kollar, Mrinak, & Skorodensky, 1983); German (Myrtek & Greenlee, 1984); Italian (Caracciolo & Molinari, 1986); and Spanish (de Flores, Llorente, Valdés, & Torrubia, 1985). As well, an English version adapted for use in Britain has been developed (O'Looney & Harding, 1985).

The standard JAS is a 4-page, nonreusable booklet containing 52 multiple-choice questions. Respondents' answers are written on the actual question booklet. The JAS (Forms C and N) is applicable for use with employed persons between 25 and 65 years of age. In the manual (Jenkins et al., 1979), it is suggested that respondents have at least an eighth-grade level reading ability. JAS Form T is appropriate for university students. For all JAS forms, testing may involve either group or individual assessment.

Practical Applications/Uses

The JAS was designed to provide a standardized, objective measure of the coronary-prone behavior pattern. Medical practitioners may find the JAS to be an important component of a larger assessment battery that includes the evaluation of other coronary heart disease risk factors such as blood pressure, serum cholesterol level, smoking, obesity, prior history, diabetes, and family history. Researchers in various medical, psychological, and organizational and industrial fields also may find the JAS to be a useful measure of Type A behavior.

The JAS requires approximately 15 to 20 minutes to complete. Test administration requires minimal instruction and responsible proctor should be capable of adequately supervising the testing procedure. Although the manual suggests that the JAS may be completed without supervision, such a procedure may engender careless responding or inappropriate discussions with others. When administering the test, no reference to heart disease should be made. Although respondents may be permitted to omit an item under some circumstances, they should be encouraged to answer all questions. Further, queries regarding the content of a particular test item should not be discussed beyond the level of providing dictionary-equivalent definitions of unfamiliar words.

Because items and item responses are each differentially weighted, scoring the JAS is a complex task. Hand scoring is prone to error and takes approximately 25 minutes per protocol. Further, the manual does not supply the appropriate weights for scoring the test; these coefficients are supplied separately by the publisher. Exactly how the weights were derived for scoring the three factor scales is presented neither in the manual nor the source article describing the original factor analyses (i.e., Zyzanski & Jenkins, 1970). To facilitate scoring, the test publisher offers a computerized service that scores the four scales on the JAS and presents them in various norm-based formats on a profile sheet.

Interpretation of the JAS is based on objective scores for each of the four scales. The computerized scoring of the survey presents the four scale scores in four formats. First, raw scores that are not immediately interpretable are presented. Next, standard scores are presented. These scores have a mean of zero and a standard deviation of 10 and represent an individual's raw scores after they have been standardized using the test's normative data. The normative sample comprises 2,588 men who completed the JAS in 1969 and who were aged 48 to 65 years old and employed in middle- or upper-level jobs. The third format presents scores as percentile ranks representing the percentage of persons in the normative group that scored below the respondent. Finally, standard scores are presented in a graphic form.

Although interpretation may be assisted by the use of the computerized summary, the manual cautions that other relevant factors need to be examined. For example, the appropriateness of the JAS norms for the particular respondent must be considered. This point should be emphasized because the Scoring Service Fact Sheet, JAS test booklet, and manual are unclear about what normative sample will be used by the computerized scoring service. If the respondent is not represented by the normative group, other norms, supplied in the manual, should be sought. Normative data for various groups are supplied in the manual. The manual further suggests that, clinically, JAS results should not be interpreted in isolation; results should be evaluated in combination with other pertinent risk factors for coronary heart disease.

Technical Aspects

Two types of reliability, test-retest and internal consistency, have been evaluated for the JAS. Retest reliabilities are reported in the manual for intervals ranging from 4 months to 4 years. Three sets of data derived from the Western Collaborative Group Study (WCGS), each representing over 2,300 participants, showed that the retest reliabilities of the Type A and the three factor scales range from .56 to .74. Jenkins et al. (1979) pointed out that the JAS was still evolving during the period when these retest data were being collected. For example, the two JAS versions used in the 4-year retest had only four items in common. Perhaps these data also could represent parallel forms reliability. A fourth retest study described in the manual reported slightly higher reliabilities (.65 to .82) for a 4 to 6 month interval using a 1966 JAS version ($N = 92$ men) only. Similarly, Johnston and Shaper (1983) reported a .79 retest reliability with a sample of British men over both 17 and 34 weeks for the Type A scale only. An East Slovakian version of the JAS had a retest reliability of .72 for a sample of 320 men (Stancak et al., 1983). For Form T, 1-week retest reliabilities of about .90 were reported from all three scales using 30 university students (Holden & Hickman, 1987). For a computerized version of Form T, the 1-week retest reliability of the Type A scale was .80, whereas the other two scales had reliabilities over .90 (Holden & Hickman, 1987). Finally, a German version of the student JAS showed a .61 correlation for the Type A scale over a 1-year interval (Myrtek & Greenlee, 1984).

Calculation of the internal consistency for the JAS is not entirely straightforward because the scale scores are based on differentially weighted item responses. Jenkins et al. (1979) reported internal consistencies based on a modification of coefficient alpha that requires estimated item reliabilities. Internal consistency for the Type A scale is approximately .84. Similar estimates for the other three scales range from .73 to .83. However, Mayes, Sime, and Ganster (1984) countered that coefficient alpha is the correct reliability index because JAS total scale scores are based on summed item responses. Citing Nunnally's personal communication as support, Mayes et al. argued that Jenkins et al. (1979) misinterpreted Nunnally's (1967) discussion of reliability and that the internal consistency estimates reported in the manual are inflated. Mayes et al. (1984) calculated coefficients alpha for the four JAS scales based on a sample of 63 female public employees. Internal consistencies were found to be unacceptably low: .29, .38, .24 and .56 for the Type A, Speed and Impatience, Hard-Driving and Competitive, and Job Involvement scales, respectively.

Whereas Mayes et al. (1984) used standardized item scores to correct for differential item variances due to the weighting system, Shipper, Kreitner, Reif, and Lewis (1986) used the weighted item responses when determining alpha. Presumably the rationale for the latter approach is that coefficient alpha applies to the total score, which is itself based on items having unequal variances and, hence, unequal contributions to the total. Shipper et al. (1986) presented an alpha of .52 for the Type A scale extracted from the complete Form C. To circumvent the item weighting difficulties, Ray and Bozek (1980) recast the JAS to a Likert format and calculated a coefficient alpha of .76 across all 54 items for a sample of 122 adults.

In contrast to Form C, no disagreement exists on how to evaluate internal consistency for the Type A scale of Form T because unit weights are used for scoring this scale. Palladino and Tryon (1980) reported a coefficient alpha of .70 for a sample of 208 college students (104 men, 104 women). For groups of 30 college men, Holden and Hickman (1987) showed coefficients alpha of approximately .50 for the Type A scale under both standard paper-and-pencil and computerized administration conditions. Corresponding coefficients alpha for the Hard-Driving and Competitive and the Speed and Impatience scales were approximately .65 and .70, respectively.

The original factor analysis of the JAS was undertaken to determine if the Type A behavior pattern was best conceptualized as a single, unified set of behavior and characteristics or as a loosely constructed group of relatively distinct behavior and characteristics. Zyzanski and Jenkins (1970) performed a principal axes factor analysis of the dichotomized responses of two independent samples of WCGS men to a 61-item version (1965) and to a 57-item version (1966) of the JAS. Three factors, Speed and Impatience, Hard-Driving and Competitive, and Job-Involved, were judged to be replicable across men designated as Type A or Type B using the Structured Interview within each sample. Thus, Zyzanski and Jenkins (1970) used this replication as evidence that Type A behavior is not a unitary construct. For Form T of the JAS (on which work-related items have been modified or deleted), Glass (1977) reported some support for the Speed and Impatience and the Hard-Driving and Competitive factors. Subsequent factor analyses have found some evidence for the replicability of the original three factors in the adult JAS (Begley & Boyd, 1985; Waldron, Zyzanski, Shekelle, Jenkins, & Tannenbaum, 1977) and of the two relevant factors in the student JAS (Fekken, Jackson, & Holden, 1985; Yarnold et al., 1987). Nevertheless, researchers generally agree that the dimensionality of the JAS is underrepresented by three factors (Begley, & Boyd, 1985; O'Looney & Harding, 1985; Shipper et al., 1986) or two factors, in the case of Form T (Fekken et al., 1985; Yarnold et al., 1987). Furthermore, the dimensionality of the items representing only the Type A scale (O'Looney & Harding, 1985; Yarnold et al., 1987) or a single-factor scale (O'Looney & Harding, 1985) is much better described by a number of factors rather than a single factor. Finally, the three-factor structure of Zyzanski and Jenkins (1970) may not hold across various ethnic groups. For example, Waldron and her colleagues (1977) found that a three-factor solution could be derived for samples of black men and women; however, the particular constellation of items loading each of the factors suggested alternate factor names and interpretations. A study of Japanese-American men (Cohen, Syme, Jenkins, Kagan, & Zyzanski, 1979) again yielded three new factors. Such factor structures may reflect different sociocultural influences on the behavior patterns associated with Type A behavior.

The JAS was originally developed to maximize prediction of the Structured Interview. Logically, the first aspect of validity that should be examined is the predictive validity of the JAS for the interview. In the manual, the percentage of similar typological classifications are estimated at 73% for the original WCGS cross-validation sample and 70% for a sample of 563 men participating in a Belgian study using French and Flemish versions of the instruments (Jenkins et al., 1979). Further research establishes empirically that the JAS typically has 60 to 70% classification accuracy for the Structured Interview (e.g., Bortner & Rosenman, 1967; Herbertt, 1983; Matthews, Krantz, Dembroski, & MacDougall, 1982; Young & Barboriak, 1982). This accuracy rate also generalizes from employed men to male college students (MacDougall, Dembroski, & Musante, 1979; Matthews et al., 1982) and to female college students (MacDougall et al., 1979, Musante, MacDougall, Dembroski, & Van Horn, 1983). A notable exception to the general pattern of findings is a study by Byrne, Rosenman, Schiller, and Chesney (1985). They found that, for a group of 582 employed men, the JAS misclassified about 67% of those designated Type A by the Structured Interview and 27% of those designated Type B.

Even accepting the 60 to 70% classification accuracy rate does not give strong support for the JAS's predictive validity for the Structured Interview. First, Matthews (1982) argues that a 60 to 70% overlap between the JAS and the interview constitutes only a 10 to 20% improvement over chance levels, because approximately 50% of the population may be designated Type A. Second, the Pearson product moment correlations between the Type A scale scores and interview categorization range from .20 to .40 across male adult samples (Chesney, Black, Chadwick, & Rosenman, 1981; Matthews et al., 1982), male undergraduate samples (Matthews et al., 1982) and female undergraduate samples (Musante et al., 1983). Recent investigations of the JAS and its subscales and the Structured Interview and its components have shown that the JAS and the interview do have some common variance, especially associated with pressured drive and judgments of hostility, competitiveness, and energy level. On the other hand, the interview has unique variance associated with speech behavior and the JAS has unique variance associated with time pressure (Matthews et al., 1982; Musante et al., 1983). Within the Type A literature, the consensus is emerging that the JAS and the Structured Interview are not measuring identical components of coronary behavior and are not interchangeable (Chesney et al., 1981; Matthews, 1982; Matthews et al., 1982; Musante et al., 1983).

Predicting Type A designation with the Structured Interview is only an intermediate step. The real purpose for assessing Type A behavior is to predict coronary heart disease. How well does the JAS predict this criterion? A prospective study with men participating in the Western Collaborative Group Study demonstrated that higher JAS scores were related to a higher risk of developing coronary heart disease. Specifically, the annual rates per 1,000 of developing heart disease were 8.0, 10.7, and 14.3 for individuals scoring in the bottom-, middle-, and upper-third, of the JAS score distribution, respectively. (Jenkins, Rosenman, & Zyzanski, 1974). A subsequent study of men in the WCGS who had suffered heart attacks found that the JAS Type A score was the single strongest predictor of recurrent heart attacks (Jenkins et al., 1979). These studies provide clear evidence for the predictive validity of the JAS. However, these two studies are the only prospective studies linking the JAS to coronary heart disease and they are based on the sample on which the JAS was developed (Matthews, 1982). Generalization of the JAS's predictive success to alternate samples is needed.

Nevertheless, retrospective studies that have found an association between the

JAS and coronary heart disease have been conducted with both the WCGS and other populations. For example, WCGS men who had suffered a heart attack before taking the JAS scored significantly higher than a control group of randomly selected men (Jenkins, Zyzanski, Rosenman, & Cleveland, 1971). This finding held up for another sample even when traditional risk factors were taken into account (Shekelle, Schoenberger, & Stamler, 1976). Hospitalized coronary patients scored significantly higher on the Type A and the Hard-Driving and Competitive scale than patients hospitalized with other diseases (Glass, 1977; Kenigsberg, Zyzanski, Jenkins, Wardwell, & Licciardello, 1974). In Hawaii, Japanese-American men who had adopted a Western life-style showed a higher prevalence of coronary heart disease that was in proportion to their Type A behavior (Cohen et al., 1979). O'Looney (1984) reported on five retrospective studies using non-English language versions of the JAS to predict either myocardial infarction or angina pectoris. O'Looney cites two Dutch studies, a Lithuanian study, and a Polish study that demonstrated a significant predictive relationship between the presence of coronary heart disease and JAS scores (Appels, Jenkins, & Rosenman, 1982, as cited in O'Looney, 1984; Appels, Jenkins, Gostautsas, & Nijhuis, 1981, as cited in O'Looney, 1984; Verhagen, Nass, Appels, van Bastelaar, & Winnubst, 1980, as cited in O'Looney, 1984; Zyzanski, Wrzesniewski, & Jenkins, 1979, as cited in O'Looney, 1984). In a cited Finnish study, however, no relationship between the JAS and coronary heart disease emerged (Hanses, Reunanen, Maatela, Impivaara, & Aromaa, 1982, as cited in O'Looney, 1984).

Finally, various studies have reported on the association of the JAS to coronary atherosclerosis. Jenkins et al. (1979) reported on the results of a double-blind study in which men with severe atherosclerosis scored higher on all four JAS scales than men diagnosed as having less severe atherosclerosis. These significant results maintained even when they were controlled statistically for age, previous heart attacks, and degree of self-reported angina pain. Although a second study mentioned in the manual found no JAS-coronary artery disease link, Jenkins et al. (1979) interpret the overall findings as evidence for the pathophysiological mechanism linking Type A behavior and coronary heart disease. The literature presents some support for this interpretation (see Krantz & Durel, 1983), but the findings are inconsistent. For example, Caracciolo and Molinari (1986) reported that the mean scores on the Type A, Speed and Impatience, and Hard-Driving and Competitive scales were elevated to the 70th percentile for a group of 23 Italian patients suffering from coronary artery disease. On the other hand, Blumenthal et al. (1985) reported no significant relationship between the JAS scales and severity of coronary artery disease as documented by coronary angiography.

Evidence for the concurrent validity of the JAS for other measures of Type A behavior is modest at best. Of particular interest is the relationship of the JAS to the Framingham scale, the only other prospectively validated measure of Type A characteristics (Haynes et al., 1978). The Framingham scale is made up of 10 items reflecting global Type A behavior that were administered in the Framingham study of risk for coronary heart disease. Lee, King and King (1987) reported a correlation of .54 between the Type A scale of Form N and the Framingham scale for a large sample of students. Byrne et al. (1985) found a similar correlation for a nonstudent sample as did Holden and Hickman (1987) for a student sample responding to Form T. Harding and O'Looney (1986) reported slightly lower correlations between the JAS Type A scale and the Framingham scales for both Type A and Type B. Restriction of range was no doubt a contributing factor. Correlations of the Speed and Impatience and the Hard-Driving and Competitive scales with the Framingham were similar (Byrne et al., 1985; Holden & Hickman, 1987); however, the Job-Involvement scale was weakly related (Byrne et al., 1985). The 14-item Bortner scale has been related to coronary heart disease in a retrospective context (Bortner, 1969). The JAS Type A and Speed and Impatience scales correlate .40 to .60 with the Bortner scales whereas the Job Involvement and Hard-Driving and Competitive scales correlate .30 or less (Byrne et al., 1985; Herbertt, 1983; Mayes et al., 1984). The JAS scales also have been correlated with other, less studied measures of Type A behavior such as the Vickers scale (e.g., Byrne et al., 1985; Herbertt, 1983), the Thurstone Type A Scale (Byrne et al., 1985; Lee et al., 1987; Mayes et al., 1984) and a bipolar Adjective scale (Byrne et al., 1985; Caracciolo & Molinari, 1986; Lee et al., 1987). In general, the Type A and the Speed and Impatience scales correlate from .40 to .60 with these alternate measures; the Job Involvement and Hard-Driving and Competitive scales correlate from .10 to .30.

One strategy for elucidating the Type A construct as assessed by the JAS has been to evaluate the convergence and discrimination of the JAS for other psychological measures. Generally, the JAS correlates with theoretically relevant constructs such as assertiveness and interpersonal confidence (Byrne et al., 1985; Chesney et al. 1981; Irvine, Lyle, & Allon, 1982; Jenkins et al., 1979; Musante et al., 1983; Ray & Bozek, 1980), and activity and lack of self-control (Chesney et al., 1981; Jenkins et al., 1979). Matthews (1982) reviewed the evidence linking the JAS to achievement-striving and concluded that not only did the JAS correlate with other measures of achievement (e.g., Matthews & Saal, 1978), but also it correlated with numerous consistent constructs such as occupational aspirations, grade-point average, number of hours worked, and so on. The JAS did not appear to be correlated with anxiety (Nielson & Dobson, 1980) nor with psychological distress (Chesney et al., 1981), although in some studies it was moderately associated with neuroticism (Byrne et al., 1985; Irvine et al., 1982). The JAS scales also were not confounded by social desirability (Fekken & Jakubowski, 1988; Ray & Bozek, 1980). The foregoing generalities tend to apply to both adult and student populations, although they may be somewhat more accurate for men than women. For example, Musante and her colleagues (1983) obtained a theoretically meaningful constellation of trait-JAS relationships for men but virtually no significant relationships for women. This finding is contrary to other research (e.g., Waldron et al., 1977) that showed similar JAS psychometric properties for (Caucasion) men and women.

Following the assumption that Type A behavior is related to coronary heart disease via various physiological mechanisms, one type of research that evaluated the construct validity of the JAS related JAS scores to physiological reactivity. Type A individuals are not necessarily expected to have higher resting heart rates or blood pressure than Type B individuals. Rather, Type As are presumed to overreact physiologically (and behaviorally) to perceived threat in some situations. Thus, the situation is central in eliciting not only the Type A behavior pattern, but also the sympathetic neuroendocrine responses that may affect the cardiovascular system. Evidence linking the JAS to physiological hyperactivity is weak (Contrada, Wright,

& Glass, 1985; Krantz & Durel, 1983; Linden, 1987; Mayes et al., 1984). At best, the JAS may be related moderately to changes in systolic blood pressure, as concluded in two reviews (Contrada et al., 1985; Matthews, 1982). Matthews (1982) found some evidence relating JAS scores to physiological responses reflecting sympathetic activation other than heart rate and blood pressure (e.g., adrenalin or cortisol secretions); however, as others have concluded (Contrada et al., 1985; Krantz & Durel, 1983; Linden, 1987), Matthews concluded that the JAS tended to be markedly weaker than the Structured Interview. Further, Mayes et al. (1984) argued that most studies linking the JAS to hyperactivity were conducted in the laboratory under contrived stress conditions. Little evidence exists that Type A individuals, as defined by the JAS, overreact physiologically to actual job or life stressors.

A second type of research that examined the construct validity of the JAS has yielded considerably more positive evidence. Generally, the differential performance of JAS-defined Type A and Type B individuals has been evaluated under stressful laboratory conditions. The majority of these studies have been conducted with undergraduate students. Stressful situations have been operationalized in terms of failure, fatigue, external distractions, competition, difficulty, and requiring slow responding. Glass (1977) was among the first to demonstrate that Type A individuals show exaggerated achievement strivings, impatience with delays, and aggressiveness when provoked interpersonally. A subsequent review (Matthews, 1982) summarized further evidence that Type A individuals outperform Type B individuals in difficult situations that require persistence and endurance. Yet other studies show that a Type A person performs more poorly than a Type B on tasks requiring a slow pace. Matthews (1982) interpreted these findings as consistent with the achievement-striving and speed and impatience aspects of Type A behavior. Some studies have shown that Type A individuals are more aggressive than Type B individuals, for example, in the context of the Prisoner's Dilemma (Van Egeren, 1979). However, Matthews (1982) argued that alternative interpretations of such results precluded firm statements on any Type A-aggressiveness association.

Critique

The JAS does a relatively poor job of living up to its original purpose, namely, to predict the Structured Interview. General agreement is found in the Type A literature that the Structured Interview and JAS are not interchangeable and that the Structured Interview is the better measure. The performance of the JAS is often explained by noting that the original conceptualization of the JAS emphasized the interview content at the expense of the interview's sensitivity to various behavioral stylistics exhibited under mild stress. Concern over the initial conceptualization of the JAS would appear to be a recurrent theme when addressing a wide variety of problems related to the JAS.

The comparability of various JAS versions needs systematic investigation. The empirical item selection strategy and the evolving Type A construct (in terms of the three factor components) resulted in dropping and adding items. Changing the composition of items on the JAS has implications for the Type A construct. Moreover, research on the construct validity has overwhelmingly employed the student version of the JAS whereas research relating coronary heart disease to the JAS has exclusively used adult versions. Despite lack of empirical demonstration of the equivalence of these forms, the literature tends to treat different JAS versions equally. Such a tack may be obscuring the meaning of the construct that the JAS was intended to measure.

The interpretation of individual differences in JAS scale scores needs to be approached cautiously. JAS scales are not especially homogeneous. The internal consistencies are reportedly modest or even low. Furthermore, various factor analytic studies show that the content of the entire JAS or even of its three factor scales is quite heterogeneous. Jenkins and Zyzanski (1982) have argued that concern with individual differences is largely irrelevant because the Type A-Type B distinction should be viewed as a typology not a continuum. However, many researchers and the computer-scored test protocols provided by the test publishers treat JAS scores as reflecting relatively homogeneous dimensions. The meaningfulness of evaluating individual differences in JAS scores should be considered in light of the low internal consistency and diffuse content of the JAS scales.

Finally, the validity of the JAS for predicting criteria other than the Structured Interview bears mention. The relationship between the JAS Type A scale and coronary heart disease has given major impetus to research on Type A behavior. Concurrent validity studies have helped to elucidate the construct underlying the JAS as tapping achievement-striving and impatience with delays. Whether the JAS adequately assesses aggression or hostility, now believed to be an important feature of coronary-proneness, is much less clear. Similarly, the dimensions measured by the factor scales, especially Job-Involvement, appear to be peripheral to the recent elaborations of the Type A construct. How the JAS-defined Type A behavior mediates coronary heart disease is still a key research issue. Although the JAS is a weak predictor of physiological hyperreactivity in a stressful situation, it is a strong predictor of behavioral overreactivity. What may be lacking is a comprehensive theoretical model relating situational parameters to the cognitive and affective reactions of coronary-prone individuals and their resultant physiological and behavioral reactions.

References

Appels, A., Jenkins, C.D., & Rosenman, R.H. (1982). Coronary-prone behavior in the Netherlands: A cross-cultural validation study. *Journal of Behavioral Medicine, 5*, 83-90.

Begley, T.M., & Boyd, D.P. (1985). The relationship of the Jenkins Activity Survey to Type A behavior among business executives. *Journal of Vocational Behavior, 27*, 316-328.

Blumenthal, J.A., Herman, S., O'Toole, L.C., Hanley, T.L., Williams, R.B., Jr., & Barefoot, J.C. (1985). Development of a brief self-report measure of the Type A (coronary prone) behavior pattern. *Journal of Psychosomatic Research, 29*, 265-274.

Bortner, R.W. (1969). A short rating scale as a potential measure of pattern A behavior. *Journal of Chronic Diseases, 22*, 87-91.

Bortner, R.W., & Rosenman, R.H. (1967). The measurement of Pattern A behavior. *Journal of Chronic Diseases, 20*, 525-533.

Byrne, D.G., Rosenman, R.H., Schiller, E., & Chesney, M.A. (1985). Consistency and variation among instruments purporting to measure the Type A behavior pattern. *Psychosomatic Medicine, 47*, 242-261.

Caracciolo, S., & Molinari, S. (1986). Convergent validity of self-reported Type A behavior pattern of patients with coronary artery disease. *Psychological Reports, 58,* 831-838.

Chesney, M.A., Black, G.W., Chadwick, J.H., & Rosenman, R.H. (1981). Psychological correlates of the Type A behavior pattern. *Journal of Behavioral Medicine, 4,* 217-229.

Cohen, J.B., Syme, S.L., Jenkins, C.D., Kagan, A., & Zyzanski, S.J. (1979). Cultural context of Type A behavior and risk for CHD: A study of Japanese American males. *Journal of Behavioral Medicine, 2,* 375-384.

Contrada, R.J., Wright, R.A., & Glass, D.C. (1985). Psychophysiologic correlates of Type A behavior: Comments on Houston (1983) and Holmes (1983). *Journal of Research in Personality, 19,* 12-30.

de Flores, T., Llorente, M., Valdés, M., & Torrubia, R. (1985). Psychometric analysis of behavior pattern A in the Spanish population and its relationship with personality variables. *Activitas Nervosa Superior, 27,* 73-80.

Fekken, G.C., Jackson, D.N., & Holden, R.R. (1985). The Jenkins Activity Survey (Form T): Is a two-factor solution appropriate? *Canadian Journal of Behavioral Science, 17,* 74-78.

Fekken, G.C., & Jakubowski, I. (1988). *Occupational striving and general health in the Type A university student.* Manuscript submitted for publication.

Glass, D.C. (1977). *Behavior patterns, stress and coronary disease.* Hillsdale, NJ: Erlbaum.

Harding, C.M., & O'Looney, B.A. (1986). A note on the Jenkins Activity Survey. *Personality and Individual Differences, 7,* 409-414.

Haynes, S.G., Levine, S., Scotch, N., Feinleib, M., & Kannel, W.B. (1978). The relationship of psychosocial factors to coronary heart disease in the Framingham Study: methods and risk factors. *American Journal of Epidemiology, 107,* 362-383.

Herbertt, R.M. (1983). A critical evaluation of some commonly-employed methods for the assessment of Type A coronary-prone behavior. *Personality and Individual Differences, 4,* 451-456.

Holden, R.R., & Hickman, D. (1987). Computerized versus standard administration of the JAS (Form T). *Journal of Human Stress, 13,* 175-179.

Irvine, J., Lyle, R. C., & Allon, R. (1982). Type A personality as psychopathology: Personality correlates and an abbreviated scoring system. *Journal of Psychosomatic Research, 26,* 183-189.

Jenkins, C.D., Rosenman, R.H., & Zyzanski, S.J. (1974). Prediction of clinical coronary heart disease by a test for the coronary-prone behavior pattern. *The New England Journal of Medicine, 290,* 1271-1275.

Jenkins, C.D., & Zyzanski, S.J. (1982). The Type A behavior pattern is alive and well—when not dissected: A reply. *British Journal of Medical Psychology, 55,* 219-233.

Jenkins, C.D., Zyzanski, S.J., & Rosenman, R.H. (1979). *Jenkins Activity Survey manual.* New York: Psychological Corporation.

Jenkins, C.D., Zyzanski, S.J., Rosenman, R.H., & Cleveland, G.L. (1971). Association of coronary-prone behavior pattern scores with recurrence of coronary heart disease. *Journal of Chronic Diseases, 24,* 601-611.

Johnston, D.W., & Shaper, A.G. (1983). Type A behavior in British men: Reliability and intercorrelation of two measures. *Journal of Chronic Diseases, 36,* 203-207.

Kenigsberg, D., Zyzanski, S.J., Jenkins, C.D., Wardwell, W.I., & Licciardello, A.T. (1974). The coronary-prone behavior pattern in hospitalized patients with and without coronary heart disease. *Psychosomatic Medicine, 36,* 344-351.

Kittel F., Kornitzer, M., Zyzanski, S.J., Jenkins, C.D., Rustin, R.M., & Degré, C. (1978). Two methods of assessing the Type A coronary-prone behavior pattern in Belgium. *Journal of Chronic Diseases, 31,* 147-155.

Krantz, D.S., & Durel, L.A. (1983). Psychological substrates of the Type A behavior pattern. *Health Psychology, 2,* 393-411.

Krantz, D. S., Glass, D.C., & Snyder, M.L. (1974). Helplessness, stress level, and the coronary-prone behavior pattern. *Journal of Experimental Social Psychology, 10,* 284-300.

Lee, D., King, D., & King, L. (1987). Measurement of the Type A behavior pattern by self-report questionnaires: Several perspectives on validity. *Educational and Psychological Measurement, 47,* 409-423.

Linden, W. (1987). On the impending death of the Type A construct: Or is there a phoenix rising from the ashes? *Canadian Journal of Behavioral Science, 19,* 177-190.

MacDougall, J.M., Dembroski, T.M., & Musante, L. (1979). The structured interview and questionnaire methods of assessing coronary-prone behavior in male and female college students. *Journal of Behavioral Medicine, 2,* 71-83.

Matthews, K.A. (1982). Psychological perspectives on the Type A behavior pattern. *Psychological Bulletin, 91,* 293-323.

Matthews, K.A., Krantz, D.S., Dembroski, T. M., & MacDougall, J.M. (1982). Unique and common variance in structured interview and Jenkins Activity Survey measures of the Type A behavior pattern. *Journal of Personality and Social Psychology, 42,* 303-313.

Matthews, K.A., & Saal, F.E. (1978). Relationship of the Type A coronary-prone behavior pattern to achievement, power, and affiliation motives. *Psychosomatic Medicine, 40,* 631-636.

Mayes, B.T., Sime, W.E., & Ganster, D.C. (1984). Convergent validity of Type A behavior pattern scales and their ability to predict psychological responsiveness in a sample of female employees. *Journal of Behavioral Medicine, 7,* 83-108.

Musante, L., MacDougall, J.M., Dembroski, T.M., & Van Horn, A.E. (1983). Component analysis of the Type A coronary-prone behavior pattern in male and female college students. *Journal of Personality and Social Psychology, 45,* 1104-1117.

Myrtek, M., & Greenlee, M.W. (1984). Psychophysiology of Type A behavior pattern: A critical analysis. *Journal of Psychosomatic Research, 28,* 455-466.

Nielson, W.R., & Dobson, K.S. (1980). The coronary-prone behavior pattern and trait anxiety: Evidence for discriminant validity. *Journal of Consulting and Clinical Psychology, 48,* 546-547.

Nunnally, J.C. (1967). *Psychometric theory.* New York: McGraw-Hill.

O'Looney, B.A. (1984). The assessment of Type A behavior and the prediction of coronary heart disease: A review. *Current Psychological Research and Reviews, 3,* 63-84.

O'Looney, B.A., & Harding, C.M. (1985). A psychometric investigation of two measures of Type A behavior in a British sample. *Journal of Chronic Disorders, 38,* 841-848.

Palladino, J.J., & Tryon, G. (1980). Study of the Jenkins Activity Survey. *Psychological Reports, 46,* 1030.

Ray, J.J., & Bozek, R. (1980). Dissecting the A-B personality type. *British Journal of Medical Psychology, 53,* 181-186.

Rosenman, R.H., Friedman, M., Strauss, R., Wurm, M., Kositchek, R., Hahn, W., & Werthessen, N.T. (1964). A predictive study of coronary heart disease: The Western Colloborative Group Study. *Journal of the American Medical Association, 189,* 15-22.

Shekelle, R.B., Schoenberger, J.A., & Stamler, J. (1976). Correlates of the JAS Type A behavior pattern score. *Journal of Chronic Diseases, 29,* 381-394.

Shipper, F., Kreitner, R., Reif, W.E., & Lewis, K.E. (1986). A study of four psychometric properties of the Jenkins Activity Survey Type A scale with suggested modifications and validation. *Educational and Psychological Measurement, 46,* 551-564.

Stancak, A., Kollar, J., Mrinak, J., & Skorodensky, M. (1983). Validity and test-retest reliability of Jenkins Activity Survey for East Slovakia population. *Activitas Nervosa Superior, 25,* 100-101.

Van Egeren, L.F. (1979). Social interactions, communications, and the coronary-prone behavior pattern: A psychophysiological study. *Psychosomatic Medicine, 41,* 2-18.

Waldron, I., Zyzanski, S., Shekelle, R.B., Jenkins, C.D., & Tannenbaum, S. (1977). The coronary-prone behavior pattern in employed men and women. *Journal of Human Stress, 3,* 2-18.

Yarnold, P.R., Bryant, F.B., & Grimm, L.G. (1987). Comparing the long and short forms of the student version of the Jenkins Activity Survey. *Journal of Behavioral Medicine, 10,* 75-90.

Young, D., & Barboriak, J.J. (1982). Reliability of a brief scale for assessment of coronary-prone behavior and standard measures of type A behavior. *Perceptual and Motor Skills, 55,* 1039-1042.

Zyzanski, S.J., & Jenkins, C.D. (1970). Basic dimensions within the coronary-prone behavior pattern. *Journal of Chronic Diseases, 22,* 781-795.

Delwyn L. Harnisch, Ph.D.

Associate Professor of Educational Psychology, Institute for Research on Human Development, University of Illinois at Urbana-Champaign, Champaign, Illinois.

KERBY LEARNING MODALITY TEST, REVISED 1980

Maude L. Kerby. Los Angeles, California: Western Psychological Services.

Introduction

The Kerby Learning Modality Test (KLMT) is designed to serve as a group screening test of perceptional modality functioning. It is based on the premise that there are three independent channels or modalities through which learning may take place (vision, hearing, and motor activity), mediated by the visual, auditory, and kinesthetic perceptual systems. The KLMT is a diagnostic test, not an achievement test. A low score on a subtest serves to indicate areas of weakness to be remediated so that improved performance may be achieved in the future. In the same manner, a high score serves to indicate strengths, which can be tapped for future instruction.

The KLMT is designed for group administration by the classroom teacher and consists of three forms suitable for different age levels: Kindergarten (age 5), Primary (ages 6–8), and Intermediate (ages 8–11). Each form contains subtests consisting of four visual and four auditory subtests designed to measure visual discrimination (VD), visual closure (VC), visual memory (VM), visual motor coordination (VMC), auditory discrimination (AD), auditory closure (AC), auditory memory (AM), and auditory motor coordination (AMC).

The actual test booklets range from 13 to 16 pages, depending upon the level. Total time for test administration is 45 minutes, 15 minutes of which is required for actual testing and the remaining time dedicated to distributing materials, giving instructions, and collecting materials. Test scoring is done using a scoring template and takes approximately 2 minutes per test.

The first version of the KLMT was administered at the J. B. Watkins Elementary School in Chesterfield County, Virginia, during February 1971 to Grades 3 through 6 ($N = 297$). The following year was devoted to refining the instrument and in February 1972, the revised KLMT was readministered in the same school. Selected subtests were then revised. The KLMT then was administered to the upper-grade students in two Richmond, Virginia, elementary schools. Primary and kindergarten versions of the KLMT were developed and field tested during the 1972–1973 time period, also in Virginia. Work since that time has centered upon the collection of norms and validity and reliability data.

The following benefits of using the test are offered by Kerby (1984) in the Teacher's Manual: 1) KLMT test results indicate children's modality preferences; 2) test results can be used to identify children with perceptual learning disabilities; 3) test results are highly correlated with actual classroom performance; and 4) interpretation of the test is quick and objective, permitting the classroom teacher to group students quickly according to their perceptual needs.

Required materials for testing include a copy of the test booklet for each student; student record sheets; a test manual containing information on administering, scoring, and interpreting the subtests; a cassette tape containing auditory subtests for the appropriate test levels; and, for the Intermediate subtest only, an answer sheet for each student to record their work.

Practical Applications/Uses

The KLMT provides normative information regarding children's modality preferences. The test's results are useful as a preliminary screen in identifying children with perceptual learning disabilities. Because information from this test is site processed, analysis and corrective actions may be taken without undue time delays.

In administering the KLMT, required materials include a test booklet for each student, individual student record sheets, the test manual, the appropriate cassette tape, an answer sheet (for the Intermediate level), crayons or pencil (depending upon the level given), a stopwatch, and a good quality cassette player.

Student test booklets or answer sheets should be marked with the student's name, school, grade, age, sex, date of test, and name of test administrator prior to beginning testing. Scripts are provided for the administration of each subtest, together with required timing. Total time required for the administration of the KLMT is 45 minutes, with 15 minutes required for actual testing and 30 minutes used for material handling and instructions.

For the primary and intermediate levels, scoring is done by hand with templates provided in the test manual. For the kindergarten test, it is necessary to construct a scoring key using a blank test booklet. Specific scoring criteria are provided for each of the subtests. Following the scoring of student answers, the raw scores are transferred to the record sheet. Percentile equivalents then are determined from the raw scores found in the tables of the test manual.

Technical Aspects

The question of face validity for the Kerby Learning Modality Test was initially addressed in an October 1972 study in which the KLMT was administered in two schools designated for children with learning problems. The results of the KLMT were in 93% agreement with decisions based upon the Slingerland Screening Tests for Identifying Children with Specific Language Disabilities (Slingerland, 1962), the Marianne Frostig Developmental Test of Visual Perception (Frostig, 1963), and a Psychoeducational Inventory of Basic Learning Abilities (Valett, 1968). Subsequently, a kindergarten version of the KLMT was given to approximately 100 students from J.B. Watkins Elementary School in Chesterfield County, Virginia. The test results were compared with teachers observations and found to agree in 92% of the cases.

Following these initial studies, the primary and intermediate test criteria were validated against diagnostic psychological data such as IQ tests, the Illinois Test of Psycholinguistic Abilities (ITPA), Wepman's Auditory Discrimination Test, Frostig's Developmental Test of Visual Perception, various reading tests (not named), and developmental scales (not named). Based upon a summary of these validating studies, the KLMT was in 69-100% agreement when compared with clinic or psychologist ratings, 50-100% agreement when compared with remedial reading placements, 81-89% agreement when compared with Title I placement, 67-94% agreement when compared with report card grades, and 64-69% agreement when compared with standardized achievement tests.

Because there were no comparable clinical or psychological data available for kindergarten, the KLMT was correlated with a slightly modified form of the Slingerland Screening tests (no information was provided concerning the nature of the modification). The following Spearman rank order correlations were obtained: .99 for the visual subtests, .99 for the auditory subtests, and .98 for the motor subtests. Although the test author argues that such high correlations are partly due to the fact that both tests attempt to measure the same phenomena and were normed on similar populations, one cannot help but wonder to what extent the modifications performed upon the Slingerland may have effected these correlations.

As the KLMT consists of brief, timed subtests, split-half reliability was not considered appropriate and was not computed. Test-retest reliability was calculated with values for the Spearman rank order correlation coefficients ranging from .83-.98 for the visual subtest, .87-.98 for the auditory subtest, and .88-.98 for the motor subtest. However, as the sample sizes were very small (18 to 34 subjects per each sex by age cell), one might question these figures. Alternate-form reliability was determined utilizing the overlapping coverage of the Primary and Intermediate test for the 8-year-olds. Spearman rank order correlations were found with values ranging from .86-.97 for the visual subtest, .69-.98 for the auditory subtest, and .72-.97 for the motor subtest. Comparisons between the Kindergarten test and the other forms were not possible as the Kindergarten test is designed for preliterate children.

The KLMT was standardized using 1,350 kindergarten through sixth-grade students from the J. B. Watkins Elementary School in Midlothian, Virginia. It should be noted that this standardization sample was entirely suburban, does not conform to the distribution for the United States as a whole, and did not include students with gross physical handicaps or students with below average IQs.

Critique

The underlying premise of the KLMT is that there are three independent channels or modalities through which learning may take place—vision, hearing, and motor activity—mediated by the visual, auditory, and kinesthetic perceptual systems. Evidence supporting the acceptance of this premise is present in the literature as evidenced by the work of Wepman (1971); Kirk, McCarthy, and Kirk (1968); and Barbe, Swassing, and Milone (1979). Further supporting evidence is shown in the Swassing-Barbe Modality Index (SBMI), which was based upon an identical set of beliefs.

A criticism of the KLMT lies in the discrepancies between levels of the required tasks used to measure the modalities. For example, the Kindergarten Auditory Motor Coordination test consists of following a series of verbal directions to create a diagram, while the Primary and Intermediate tests consist of copying a list of digits and letters as they are given—a simple auditory recognition and copying task. For this subtest, the kindergarten task is arguably more complex, involving on-line construction and interpretation of complex and potentially confusing directions. As an example, consider this audiocassette instruction from the kindergarten form: *"Put an X in the middle of the middle."* The cognitive demands required to interpret and follow such a set of directions are hardly in the same arena as writing a "7" when one hears it in a list of characters.

The first part of the Primary and Intermediate Auditory Closure tests requires the subject to listen to a set of paired nonsense words and judge whether they would have the same or different sound. The words for this task are initially presented phonetically, with each phoneme presented separately, and then as a whole word. Although the task seems quite reasonable when viewed on paper (i.e., F L E T — FLET), it takes on a totally different dimension upon hearing the audiotape; (i.e., EF EL EH TUH — FLET). One particular set of paired words, used in both Primary and Intermediate forms, consisted of five such phonemes and was undecipherable to this reviewer.

A helpful feature of the KLMT are the two sections of the manual dealing with specific recommendations for remediation strategies. These strategies are presented in two sections with the Primary and Intermediate forms discussed together and the Kindergarten form discussed separately. Detailed suggestions for supplanting observed difficulties or making use of perceived strengths in reading and mathematics instruction, particularly at the Primary and Intermediate levels, are offered, which can be used in the classroom by the classroom teacher. The focus of these suggestions are definitely in keeping with the goal of the KLMT as a classroom screening device.

Of less help is the section describing behavioral disorders associated with patterns of deficiencies as measure by the KLMT. Unlike the specific remediation strategies, which are firmly grounded in the literature, the comments made in describing behavioral disorders are based solely upon the test authors observations. While such observations are valuable, quite possibly correct, and worthy of being reported, it would have been helpful to see further justification for the conclusions reached and the suggestions offered. This is especially important as the casual reader could easily assume that these are equally grounded as the remediation strategies.

It is important that one not view the KLMT as a substitute for more formal testing and observational procedures. The KLMT, as the manual makes clear, was designed to serve as an initial classroom screening instrument, not as a final clinical diagnostic tool. As such, it is important to bear in mind that students whose scores indicate a potential disability should be given more intensive individual testing and observation prior to a specific diagnosis. Despite this, the KLMT remains a worthwhile tool for classroom use for identifying potential problems quickly for remediation, further testing and diagnosis, and instructional planning.

References

Barbe, W.B., Swassing, R.H., & Milone, M.N. (1979). *Teaching through modality strengths: Concepts and practices.* Columbus, OH: Zaner-Bloser, Inc.

Frostig, M. (1963). *The Marianne Frostig Developmental Test of Visual Perception.* Palo Alto, CA: Consulting Psychologists Press.

Kerby, M.I. (1984). *The Kerby Learning Modality Test manual.* Los Angeles, CA: Western Psychological Services.

Kirk, S.A., McCarthy, J.J., & Kirk, W.D. (1968). *Illinois Test of Psycholinguistic Abilities.* (rev. ed.) Urbana: University of Illinois Press.

Slingerland, B.A. (1962). *Slingerland Screening Tests for Identifying Children with Specific Language Disabilities.* Cambridge, MA: Educators Publishing Services.

Valett, R.E. (1968). *A Psychoeducational Inventory of Basic Learning Abilities.* Palo Alto, CA: Fearon Publishers, 1968.

Wepman, J.M. (1971). Modalities and learning. In H.M. Robinson (Ed.), *Coordinating reading instruction.* Glenview, IL: Scott Foresman.

Luella Sude Smitheimer, Ph.D
Speech and Language Pathologist, Port Washington Speech, Language and Hearing Center, Port Washington, New York.

LANGUAGE PROCESSING TEST

Gail J. Richard and Mary Anne Hanner. Moline, Illinois: LinguiSystems.

Introduction

The Language Processing Test (LPT) was developed to identify those students who experience difficulty in assigning meaning to auditory input and, consequently, have trouble organizing and retrieving information to formulate appropriate output. The two-fold purpose of the test is to provide diagnostic information and to generate remediation directions based on the responses of students.

The Language Processing Test was designed by Gail J. Richard and Mary Anne Hanner, speech and language pathologists. Each author holds a Master of Science degree from Eastern Illinois University, is certified by the American Speech, Language and Hearing Association, and is an Assistant Professor at Eastern Illinois University in the Department of Speech Pathology and Audiology.

Gail Richard received her bachelor's degree from Augustana College in Rock Island, Illinois. After earning her master's degree, she was employed in the Iowa public schools for 4 years as a speech and language pathologist. Her clinical area of concentration was with language-learning disabled and emotionally disturbed children. Currently, she is pursuing a doctoral degree at Southern Illinois University-Carbondale.

Mary Anne Hanner received her bachelor's degree from Eastern Illinois University. Like her colleague, Gail Richard, Ms. Hanner was employed as a speech-language pathologist in the public schools for 9 years. While functioning as a public school speech and language pathologist, she worked with many language and learning disabled children. As a result, she was able to apply her clinical knowledge to the design of the present tool.

As speech and language clinicians in the public schools, the authors felt there was a void in assessment and remediation materials for students diagnosed either as learning disabled, language disabled, or normal. The authors felt that traditional assessment materials did not provide enough information about the students they contacted. "We kept seeing children who could not retrieve information previously learned" (Richard & Hanner, 1985, p. 4). Thus, they designed a tool to identify students' language processing strengths and weaknesses in a hierarchical framework.

According to the authors, the theoretical hierarchy of tasks incorporated in the test battery is based on Luria's model of brain organization (Richard & Hanner, 1985). The Language Processing Test is based on the premise that observed behaviors are related to brain function and that for assessment purposes, these behaviors must be highly refined with controlled variables.

In the introduction to the manual, the authors provide an overview of Luria's model. For example, Luria defined three functional units in brain organization. The first functional unit is composed of the brain stem and the reticular activating system. This unit's primary responsibility is to activate the brain and ready the systems for input. The second functional unit consists of the parietal, occipital, and temporal lobes. This unit is the area in which received stimuli are organized, integrated, associated, stored, and retrieved. The third functional unit encompasses the frontal lobe. This unit is concerned with motor function as well as planning and management of behavior. Within each of the three units, there are specific levels of function called *zones*. The primary zone receives stimuli for that unit. The secondary zone attaches meaning to the stimuli received, and the third (tertiary) zone integrates information with other areas of the brain.

Within the temporal lobe (second functional unit), the primary zone includes the peripheral auditory nervous system and the central auditory tracts. These areas receive the auditory sensations. The secondary zone of the temporal lobe serves to analyze, organize, and associate the auditory stimuli. It is here that language processing occurs. The third (tertiary) zone of the temporal zone serves to integrate organized auditory stimuli with the third (tertiary) frontal lobe for speaking.

The authors of the Language Processing Test (LPT) state that the LPT evaluates behaviors mediated in the secondary zone of the temporal lobe. They suggest that prior to the administration of the LPT, primary zone dysfunction must first be eliminated as a possible factor. In fact, primary zone dysfunction can be identified through tests of hearing acuity and hearing discrimination. The LPT concentrates on the secondary zone, which functions as the major area of language processing. Here, analysis and organization of auditory stimuli can be delineated in a hierarchy of tasks. The tasks included in the LPT begin at a simple level and gradually increase in complexity. As a result, the demands placed on a student's language processing system progressively increase based on simple tasks to more complex ones.

The Language Processing Test consists of a 91-page (6" x 9") examiner's spiral bound manual and 20 separate test forms. The developers of the LPT selected eight categories or subtests to obtain information about the language processing abilities of children between 5 and 12 years of age. The categories are Labeling, Stating Functions, Associations, Categorization, Similarities, Differences, Multiple Meanings, and Attributes.

The design of this test is that of direct interaction with the subjects to be tested. Therefore, potential users of the LPT should be aware that of the eight subtests, seven are based solely on auditory input.

The LPT was developed to be administered to subjects 5 years of age and older. Test norms were established on students from ages 5 years, 0 months through 11 years, 11 months. The authors indicate that administering the LPT to students older than 12 years is appropriate if the examiner wished to determine the level of processing skills for an older child. However, they state that administration of the LPT to children younger than 5 years is not recommended.

This test was designed to increase in level of difficulty by beginning with a simple task and progressively increasing the demand placed on the student's language processing system. Because the test was developed to ascertain the language-processing capabilities of children thought to have language-processing disorders, the object of the LPT is to elicit specific behavioral characteristics that the authors had observed clinically with such children. These behavioral characteristics then serve as guidelines in identifying students who may need remediation for language-processing disorders. The behavioral characteristics are cited in the manual.

According to the manual, the eight LPT subtests were selected on the basis of being sound and acceptable clinical indicators of the ability to attach meaning to language and effectively formulate a response. Two of the subtests are actually pretests. A description of each subtest and required response types are presented below:

Pretest 1. The first subtest in the LPT battery is that of Labeling. There are 10 pictorial items. The examiner points to a picture and asks, "What is this?" A one-word naming response is required. This is a simple naming task. The most simple level of language processing is to attach an expressive label to an item. At this level, it is not necessary for the subject to apply any other language knowledge.

Pretest 2. The next subtest in the battery is that of Stating Functions. This pretest requires the student to name the function of the specific noun presented. The response must be an appropriate verb. The 10 items that are presented pictorially in Pretest 1 are given orally in Pretest 2. For each item, the examiner asks, "What do you do with (a) _____?"

Subtest A. This subtest, Associations, requires the student to name items that typically are associated with the 10 stimulus items given in Pretest 1. Using a question prompt for the 10 items, the examiner asks, "Now tell me what goes with a. . . . .?" At this level, the child must link an item with other related vocabulary. One-word responses are appropriate.

Subtest B. This subtest, Categorization, evaluates the student's ability to organize and retrieve items within groups. It requires recognition of broad similarities among items. In this subtest, the student must name three items that belong to the specific categories presented. For each item, the examiner says, "Name three _____," and should continue using that statement for the 10 items included in the subtest.

Subtest C. This subtest, Similarities, assesses the student's ability to compare like properties of two items. Ten stimulus items are presented and the student must identify the primary common aspects and describe how two objects are alike.

Subtest D. In this subtest, Differences, the student must address the contrast between the same 10 stimulus items used in Subtest C, Similarities. This level evaluates the student's ability to contrast two items. The subject must identify the primary aspects of item variance and describe how two objects are alike.

Subtest E. With this subtest, Multiple Meanings, the student must recognize and define a word in varying contexts. The student is required to state up to four definitions for each stimulus word. The examiner says, "I'll say a word. Then I'll put that word in a sentence. I want you to tell me what the word means. The word is _____. What does _____ mean?" Then, the examiner reads the next sentence and asks, "What does _____ mean now?" The ability to explain multiple meanings of the same word in different contexts is dependent on the student's use of synonyms and definitions. The appropriate meaning is determined from the context in which the word is used.

Subtest F. The final subtest, Attributes, evaluates the student's ability to apply processing strategies through item description. In order to generate attributes of words. There are eight possible attribute categories for Subtest F: function, components, color, accessories/necessities, size/shape, category, composition, and location/origin. To introduce the subtest, the examiner says, "Pretend I don't know what a car is. Tell me about a car; anything you can think of." As the child responds, the examiner can use prompts for attribute categories the student does not spontaneously generate. But the prompts are used only for training with the demonstration item; that is, the word *car.*

The test form that accompanies the LPT manual is an eight-page fold-out pamphlet used to record the student's responses for each of the eight categories. Pretests 1 and 2 as well as Subtest A (Associations) appear on one single page, Subtest B (Categorization) answers are recorded on a separate page, while Subtests C and D (Similarities and Differences) answers are recorded on the next two pages. Finally, Subtests E and F (Multiple Meanings and Attributes) have two separate recording pages. The first page of the test form provides space for the examiner to enter demographic information concerning the child (i.e., name, school, grade, date of administration, birthday, and chronological age). Space is available on the first page to enter the child's raw score for each of the eight subtests and age equivalency scores for Subtests B through F and the child's total test scores. Percentile scores and standard scores derived for Subtests A through F also can be entered. Finally, on the back page of the test form, the examiner will find two profiles formats. One profile provides graphic information for age equivalency, while the other gives a graphic display for standard scores achieved for each subtest and the total standard score. Although no age-equivalency scores are available for the Association subtest, they are included on the profile format.

Practical Applications/Uses

The LPT is designed to identify children with auditory deficiencies and corresponding language defects. Because it is designed to yield specific information about a student's language-processing abilities through an examiner's interpretation of a student's responses, the authors strongly state that the test should be administered by a trained professional. "Trained professionals" would include speech-language pathologists, psychologists, teachers of the learning disabled, and special-education consultants. Paraprofessionals would not be acceptable because they normally lack adequate training in administration, scoring, and interpretation of tests. However, the authors imply that paraprofessionals would be acceptable if they were to receive lengthy and detailed training.

The LPT is administered individually. Because the LPT is a test of auditory abilities, it is essential that the test setting be free of distracting noises or interruptions. The physical environment should be comfortable and the student put at ease prior to test administration. Therefore, the examiner should spend a few minutes speaking informally with the subject before the actual test situation.

The test is intended for children from 5 to 12 years of age. It can be used, however, with children older than 12 years to determine level of processing skills. The test can be used in schools, clinics, hospital settings, and by private practitioners.

Directions for administering the LPT are easy to understand and follow. Procedures for scoring, evaluating answers, and comparing performance on the subtests are presented in the manual. These procedures, however, are sometimes complex and require a good deal of individual judgment, even though examples of acceptable and unacceptable responses are included. Total administration time for each student should be approximately 30 minutes. To obtain optimal performance, the authors feel the test should be given in one session, particularly as the subtests are arranged in a hierarchical order of skill acquisition.

At first glance, the recording forms seem easy to use, requiring the rater to indicate correct (1) or incorrect (0) responses for seven of the subtests. For these subtests, the maximum score is 10. Scoring for Subtest F, however, is more complex because the examiner must register acceptable responses for each of eight possible attributes. Because there are 10 items and 1 point is given for every attribute category stated appropriately by the student, a maximum score of eight (8) is possible for each of the 10 items. Acknowledging the decisions on the correctness of an item that the scorer must make, the authors state that "in some subtests, there will be a need to record the actual response for comparison to the scoring standards" (Richard & Hanner, 1985, p. 14). This test is hand scored only. Neither machine nor computer scoring is available. Interpretation is based on internal clinical judgment. For each of the subtests included in the LPT, scoring standards are provided. For Pretest 1, Labeling, for instance, explicit scoring standards are given:

> the words listed below and on the Test Form are the only acceptable responses for which a student receives credit. The list of unacceptable responses does not include all possible responses, but serves as a reference for the examiner to determine appropriateness of responses. (Richard & Hanner, 1985, p. 18)

But for the remaining subtests, the instructions for scoring standards change to: "The responses that follow do not include all possible responses, but serve as a reference for the examiner to determine appropriateness of responses" (Richard & Hanner, 1985, pp. 20, 22, 25, 32, 39, 46). The publisher commented on this confusing scoring procedure during a telephone call by stating that clinical judgment is an appropriate approach to an analysis of a subject's answers because one cannot list every possible acceptable and unacceptable response (Jane Orman, personal communication, December 4, 1987).

Technical Aspects

The description of the standardization process, conducted in March and April of 1985, implies that the sample of students is fairly representative of normal language-developing children at all age levels. The final version of the LPT, including the two pretests (Labeling and Functions) and the six subtests (Associations, Categorization, Similarities, Differences, Multiple Meanings, and Attributes), was administered to random samples of subjects at yearly age intervals ranging from 5 through 11 years. The 970 subjects were selected randomly from 33 schools in Milwaukee, Wisconsin, and from 17 schools in Florida. For the standardization sample, there were 473 boys and 497 girls; approximately 68 boys and 71 girls were at each of the seven age levels. The standardization sample was limited to normal subjects. That is, children previously identified as having mental disabilities or language-learning disabilities or known hearing loss were excluded from the sample. The standardization sample was not restricted to any specific economic, intellectual, or racial group, but an attempt was made to ensure representation from minority populations in accordance with 1980 national census figures. As a result, 11% of the standardization was black, 5% Hispanic and 83% Caucasian. (The percentages in the chart on p. 66 add up to 99% rather than 100%.)

In the original construction of the LPT, there were seven subtests and an initial item pool of 140 items or 20 items per subtest. The original item pool was administered to random samples of school-age children, ranging in age from 5 through 11, and selected from the same schools used in the final standardization process. The item selection sample included 480 subjects from Milwaukee, Wisconsin, and 102 subjects from schools in Florida. The tests were administered and scored by trained speech and language clinicians. Each clinician evaluated six subjects randomly selected with consideration to race, sex, age, and school. Item difficulty indexes (percent passing each item) and item discrimination indexes (chi-square for high and low scores) were computed for each item at each of the seven yearly age levels. Ten items were then retained for each of the seven subtests from the original item pool to make up the final version. Items retained for each subtest were those that best met the criteria of demonstrating age progression in terms of percent passing and of demonstrating significant ability to discriminate between high and low scores on the subtests. On the basis of the item analysis data, two subtests (Labeling and Stating Functions) were deleted from the normative statistics but included in the battery as pretests to be administered to all students. The authors felt that these pretests should be given because the language processing skills involved are established by age 5.

Mean and median raw score values and standard deviations for each subtest at each of the seven age levels were computed and presented in the manual. The values given are for males and females combined. Male and female differences were tested for significance using *t*-tests for independent random samples. Only 4 of the 56 comparisons were significant, therefore, supporting the use of combined male-female norms.

For interpretation of test results, the authors include three types of scores: age equivalents, percentile norms, and standard scores. According to the manual, complete reporting of the LPT results should include all score types because each has unique strengths and limitations. The age-equivalent score is based on the premise that certain traits or skills will show progressive change as a result of the age factor. Age-equivalent scores are given for five of the eight subtests and the total test score. The total test score, however, is derived by adding the raw scores for six of the Subtests A through F. Age-equivalent scores are not given for the two pretests, Labeling and Stating Functions, or for Subtest A, Association. The authors provided specific rationales for two of the omissions. They stated that for the pretests, proficiency in these skills should be established by age 5; however no rationale was given for their inclusion in the battery of subtests. Age-equivalent scores are not reported for Subtest A, Associations, for two reasons: 1) the growth curve for this subtest is age-progressive but on a very gradual basis for children between 5 and 11 years, and 2) the range in scores for the youngest to the oldest age group (5 to 11 years) shows only limited change. For the LPT, age-equivalent scores were derived by plotting the median score values for each of the seven age levels and fitting a line to these points. Values falling on the line were the basis for the raw score or age-equivalent values. The authors added that age-equivalent values for the total test will not necessarily be the average of the subjects' Age-Equivalent score on the individual subtests.

The second type of score is that of percentile norms. While age-equivalent norms reflect the age level at which a subject performs on a test, percentile norms tell how the individual compares to others in his or her own age group. A percentile score indicates the percentage of students that will achieve below a particular score value. For example, if 25 % of the subjects in one age group score below 5 on a test, then the score of 5 is said to have a percentile rank of 25 for that age group. Raw scores and corresponding percentile norms are given for six subtests and for the total test at different age level. However, raw scores and corresponding percentile norms are not given for the 5- and 6-year-old age levels on Subtest F, Multiple Meanings. The reason given is that at these ages, the average score is less than 1, resulting in very limited raw score to percentile distributions for these two age levels.

The third type of score, standard score, provides the most important information for interpreting scores on the LPT (Richard & Hanner, 1985). Age-equivalent scores and percentile norms provide useful but incomplete information. Age-equivalent scores, for instance, do not indicate how extreme an individual's score may be or how it may compare to other subjects. An age equivalent of 7 years, 6 months may have very different implications for programming if achieved by an older subject as opposed to a younger one. The percentile score based on a raw score gives an indication of the relative standing of the score but percentiles have serious limitations for making comparisons between tests because of the inequality of their score units. Equal percentile differences do not represent equal differences in amount. To provide information about the relative standing of scores in units that have the same meaning throughout the entire range of values, standard scores were developed. The basic score unit in standard scores is the standard deviation of the reference group. An individual's score is expressed as the number of standard deviations above or below the mean of the reference group. For the purpose of reporting LPT results, standard score distributions with a mean of 50 and a standard deviation of 10 were established. The raw score to standard score conversions for the seven age levels and the total test score are presented in the manual. But due to the restricted range of scores either above or below the mean, standard score values greater than plus or minus 1 standard deviation could not always be reported for all subtests at all ages. The authors include a two-step formula to convert LPT test results from standard scores with a mean of 50 to standard scores with a mean of 100 and a standard deviation of 15.

Critique

There is much in the development and production of the LPT for which Richard and Hanner should be commended. An obvious need exists for standardized instruments such as this. However, the norms upon which the LPT profiles are determined are based on samples that are somewhat limited. The subtests should be restandardized on samples that are representative of a larger and more general population of normal language-developing children included in the seven age levels. In addition, LPT users need to know more about the composition of the population sample and the validity and reliability of the instrument in order to judge whether subjects were tested accurately; the reviewer used the LPT with 5 subjects and found clinical judgment to be a confusing and inaccurate method for determining a child's strengths and weaknesses.

This reviewer called the publisher of the LPT after reviewing the exceedingly sketchy information regarding the technical aspects of the test (Jane Orman, personal communication, December 4, 1987). Upon the reviewer's queries, it was determined that much information concerning validity and reliability was available as well as material related to the standardization process that had not been included in the 1985 manual. In this reviewer's opinion, the omitted information clarifies the procedures used to standardize the test and would help the uninitiated obtain a better understanding of test construction as well as scoring and interpretation procedures. Information about pretest construction and standardization process (e.g., the number of participating speech and language clinicians [100], the criteria regarding educational levels and training procedures) was given to the reviewer during a telephone interview (Jane Orman, personal communication, December 7, 1987). Information concerning test-retest reliability procedures also was provided.

From the telephone interview, this reviewer was given the impression that the faults found while using this test are not the responsibilities of the authors alone but apply primarily to the publisher. It is recommended, therefore, that the publisher create a new manual for this test and include all omissions concerning the technical aspects of the LPT. The LPT should be considered exploratory in nature and not a definitive diagnostic tool. When used, it should be included in a battery of other diagnostic instruments.

References

This list includes text citations and suggested additional reading.

Luria, A.R. (1976). *Cognitive development: Its cultural and social foundations.* Cambridge, MA: Harvard University Press.
Luria, A.R. (1982). *Language and cognition.* New York: John Wiley.
Richard, G.J., & Hanner, M.A. (1985). *Language Processing Test.* Moline, IL: LinguiSystems.
Salvia, J., & Ysseldyke, J.E. (1978). *Assessment in special and remedial education.* Boston: Houghton-Mifflin Company.

Jack S. Damico, Ph.D.

Assistant Professor, Interdisciplinary Linguistics Program and Division of Communication Disorders, Louisiana State University, Baton Rouge, Louisiana.

LANGUAGE SAMPLING AND ANALYSIS

Merlin J. Mecham and J. Dean Jones. Salt Lake City, Utah: Communication Research Associates, Inc.

Introduction

The Language Sampling and Analysis (LSA) procedure is a language assessment intended to describe various structural aspects of expressive language during an object/picture description activity. This oral language sampling consists of three stages: 1) language elicitation and recording, 2) transcription, and 3) analysis of the collected data utilizing frequency counts of traditional parts of speech and morphological inflections.

The authors of the LSA, Merlin J. Mecham, Ph.D., and J. Dean Jones, M.A., are speech-language pathologists with previous experience in test development and clinical language assessment. Dr. Mecham is Professor of Speech Pathology and Audiology at the University of Utah and has authored the Verbal Language Development Scale (1971) and co-authored the Utah Test of Language Development (UTLD; Mecham, Jex, & Jones, 1967). Mr. Jones is director of staff development and training at the Utah State Training School and is one of the co-authors of the UTLD.

The LSA manual was published in 1978 as a supplement to the UTLD. As such, it is applicable for use with the same populations as the UTLD (i.e., both normal and handicapped children between the ages of 9 months and 16 years). As a supplement, the LSA provides a more direct focus on the structural aspects of expressive language behavior (e.g., structural diversity, length, and fluency) than does the original UTLD. This is important, because a number of criticisms of the UTLD revolve around its poor face validity as a language assessment tool (cf. Naremore, 1979; Vaughn-Cooke, 1980). The LSA is considered a descriptive and domain-referenced tool to be used for comparison of a child's performances over time rather than for comparison with other children. Consequently, no effort to obtain normative data for the procedure has been reported. Since its publication, the LSA and its manual have not been revised, but the UTLD stimulus plates, which are used during the elicitation stage of the procedure, have been revised slightly and enlarged.

To utilize this language assessment procedure, the examiner must have access to the 21-page procedural manual *(UTLD-Supplement: Language Sampling and Analysis)*, two sets of stimuli (UTLD object kit and the plates from the UTLD test-plate booklet), the language sample stimuli instructions (Form A), two analysis forms (Forms B and C), and an audiotape recorder of good fidelity. The instructions for collecting, preparing, and analyzing expressive language data are sufficiently detailed in the procedural manual and can be divided into three stages: elicitation and recording, transcription, and analysis. Each will be briefly described.

Elicitation and recording. Once the child is brought into the data collection environment and the tape recorder is placed at a distance sufficient for clear recording, data elicitation may proceed. After turning on the recorder, the examiner, through the use of 71 stimulus items (10 objects and 61 line drawings), elicits expressive language by means of standardized questions and imperatives. The directions for this procedure are quite explicit, giving instructions regarding which stimulus item to introduce first based on the child's age and the examiner's impressions of the child's expected productions. For example, if the child is age 3 or older and appears to be producing three or more morphemes per utterance, the examiner should begin with item 27, which requests the child to describe a young boy eating. If less than 75 utterances are collected between the presentation of items 27 through 71, however, the examiner should move down from item 26 to item 1 (Mecham & Jones, 1978, p. 12). The visual stimuli (71 items) are each linked with four specific auditory stimuli options to aid in data elicitation. For example, item 41 shows a line drawing of a boxer, and the child is requested to "Tell me what's going on here"; if there is no response within 15 seconds, then the examiner may use one of three other auditory stimuli ("Tell me more," "What else?", and "Anything else?") (Mecham & Jones, 1978, p. 16). The data elicitation stage of the LSA is estimated to take approximately 30 minutes.

Transcription. The data that are collected must be transferred from the tape recorder to the Language Sample Data Sheet (Form B). The manual gives explicit instructions regarding orthographic transcription and the method utilized to segment the child's verbalizations into utterances. The segmentation method used, a modification of the procedure suggested by Barrie-Blackley, Musselwhite, and Rogister (1978), is clear and effective and requires little prior knowledge of language transcription on the part of the examiner. Transcription instructions not mentioned in the manual are provided on the Language Sample Data Sheet, which is designed to enable both the transcription of the utterances and the frequency counts of various parts of speech occuring side-by-side, thereby diminishing the chance of miscoding.

Analysis. The data analysis stage of the LSA provides some direction regarding which units (utterances) should and should not be analyzed due to unintelligibility or repetitiveness. This section also provides adequate instructions for conducting different analyses based on the occurrence of superficial aspects of language structure. These analyses result in four measures that the authors claim ". . . are considered to be fairly stable and general indicators of language change" (Mecham & Jones, 1978, p. 7). These measures—mean length of utterances (for words and morphemes), fluency of utterances, diversity of utterances, and completeness of utterances—are described in sufficient detail to derive accurate and consistent results. The analyses require little prior knowledge of linguistics or experience with grammatical analysis due to the explicit instructions provided both in the manual and on the two analysis sheets. The primary requirement for the examiner is an awareness of what constitutes a word and a morpheme and a working understanding of the traditional parts of speech (i.e., nouns, verbs, adjectives, and adverbs). The calculations required for deriving the four structural indices of language performance are straightforward and require little computational skill.

The forms utilized for the analysis stage, the Language Sample Data Sheet (Form B) and the Summary Analysis (Form C), are self-explanatory and provide a clear summary of the calculations described in the manual. The Summary Analysis Sheet provides a recapitulation section that enables a side-by-side comparison of all four analyses. This increases the ease of making a comparison between the four measures at one point in time and a over different data elicitation periods.

Practical Applications/Uses

It is important to stress that the Language Sampling Analysis should be considered more a procedure or approach to language description than a formal language test per se. It does not have many of the design characteristics usually required in a strong psychometric language tool (Simon, 1945; Meehl, 1954; Cronbach, 1971; McCauley & Swisher, 1984). According to the authors, the LSA manual ". . . is designed to provide a precise enough set of instructions as to enable comparable replication of measures and to insure reliability so that repeated measurements may serve as indices of change" (Mecham & Jones, 1978, p. 3). In keeping with this, the manual provides directions on the elicitation and audiotape recording of the examinee's responses to the description activity, directions on the segmentation and transcription of utterances, and specific directions regarding the analysis of the transcribed utterances. However, it does not provide for those behaviors or characteristics that are commonly seen in rigidly standardized language assessment measures. For example, there is no requirement for the immediate evaluation of observed behavior or detailed information on specific conditions of administration. Similarly, the instrument does not require simple and uniform responses to questions, nor does it provide any type of norm-referenced data in the form of age-related levels or normative tables that might be expected in standardized and norm-referenced language tests. According to the authors:

> Since the present language sampling approach is domain referenced (i.e., is not intended for comparing a child's performance to that of other children but rather is intended to assess certain characteristics of the child's language usage), inclusion of normative data for language sample comparisons is neither relevant nor practical. (p. 3)

This descriptive approach to language assessment—obtaining a sample of a client's expressive language and then analyzing it—is an appropriate tactic to take when attempting to comment on language ability or proficiency. Such language sampling is currently a preferred method of language assessment in speech-language pathology and has been utilized by numerous researchers and clinicians (Lee, 1974; Bloom & Lahey, 1978; Muma, 1978; Miller, 1981; Gallagher, 1983; Crystal, 1981; Damico, 1985). A basic advantage of language sampling is that it allows for the assessment of language as it actually functions in a real activity (e.g., object/picture description) rather than in an artificial task (e.g., labeling pictures or pointing to objects), which may have little relevance to language as communication. Indeed, various researchers have suggested that such techniques may be more valid and have greater clinical utility than do the traditional norm-referenced language assessment instruments (Prutting, 1979; Crystal, 1981; Muma, 1984, 1986).

Due to the LSA's language sampling design and its domain-referenced approach, there is generally (and appropriately) less concern over strict control of potential intervening variables in this procedure than one would expect in more norm referenced instruments (Muma, 1978; Crystal, 1981; Gallagher, 1983). Consequently, the administration of the LSA is fairly nonrestricted, and the manual does not attempt to standardize the data collection process rigidly.

A review of the administration information in the manual indicates that the LSA is an individually administered procedure with fairly strict control over the visual and auditory stimuli used but with little additional information specified for data collection. For example, there is no direct mention of the most appropriate physical setting for data collection, nor is there an explicit suggestion that one type of setting be used when collecting comparison samples over a period of time. Instead, the decision regarding the data collection setting and the need to control this variable over time is left to the examiner. Although there is one brief note on the need to control variables during repeated sampling, this clause does not specify any particular variables (see Mecham & Jones, 1978, p. 4). Given this lack of direction, it appears that the data may be collected in any setting that will allow the professional to collect a clear and uninterrupted language sample from the child—any setting relatively free from environmental distractions or noise that would distract the child from the task at hand (i.e., stimulus description) or that would interfere with the fidelity of the audio recording. This lack of direction regarding the setting may be problematic for users of the LSA because various research studies have indicated that the physical setting can have an effect on the quantity and quality of language obtained in language sampling (Scott & Taylor, 1978; Kramer, James, & Saxman, 1979). Specific effects on the LSA, however, have not been documented.

There is also plaucity of direction on the qualifications needed by an examiner to administer this procedure. This lack of specificity, however, is defensible given the design of the LSA. Because this procedure provides 1) very detailed instructions concerning which visual and auditory stimuli to present, 2) straightforward directions for transcription, and 3) analysis procedures that require little prior training (beyond a working knowledge of traditional grammar), examiners need not have extensive training. Consequently, the LSA may be used by a wide range of professionals (e.g., teachers, diagnosticians, special educators, speech-language pathologists) interested in making structural language comparisons in a given subject over time. One omission that might be problematic, however, is the failure to make recommendations regarding the control of examiner/child familiarity. It has been demonstrated (Scholtz & Ellis, 1975; Doyle, Connolly, & Revist, 1980; Tomasello, Farrar, & Dines, 1984) that subjects may utilize different language production during language sampling when the degree of familiarity with the examiner is varied (cf. Olswang & Carpenter, 1978). To control this potential variable, it would have been appropriate to specify that the same examiner be utilized to collect the sample and that this data collection occur only after some degree of familiarity with the examinee was achieved.

In reference to subject population, the manual makes no mention of the subjects for whom this tool is most appropriate. Although this information is implicitly available in the design of the procedure, it is not specified explicitly. As a supplement to the UTLD, the LSA can be considered appropriate for those populations for whom the UTLD was designed. This covers a wide range because the UTLD is intended for use with both normal and handicapped children and contains language-age scores ranging from 9 months to 16 years (Mecham, Jex, & Jones, 1967). Additionally, because the LSA is designed as a domain-referenced tool, it only compares a subject with him- or herself over time and, therefore, can be used appropriately with a wide range of subjects. The only subject populations for which it might be inappropriate would be those individuals unable to view or hear the stimuli (i.e., blind and deaf children).

In summary, although the administration instructions for the LSA are not sufficiently detailed in the manual, the inherent design of the procedure and its original development as a supplement to the UTLD do provide—at least implicitly—most of the information necessary for accurate and reliable use of the procedure. If additional attention is paid to the issues of physical setting, procedural replication during repeated samples, and awareness of the degree of familiarity between the subject and examiner, the administration procedures are adequate.

Clinical use of LSA suggests that the data collection takes approximately 30 minutes; the orthographic transcription requires approximately 45 minutes to 1½ hours; and the analyses require approximately 45 minutes to 1 hour each. Overall, the entire procedure will require from 2 to 3 hours to complete. This time requirement is not unusual when dealing with language sampling, and the 2 to 3 hours required by the LSA is less than the time required by some other language sampling procedures.

As previously noted, the LSA is designed to provide four measures of structural language performance. Each of these (mean length of utterance, fluency of utterances, diversity of utterances, and completeness of utterances) are sufficiently described in the manual to allow for the analyses and calculations. It is necessary, however, that the examiner have a basic working knowledge of, and an ability to identify, traditional parts of speech, morphemes, and various grammatical inflections because this knowledge is assumed, and no definition or explanation of these terms is provided.

The first measure, mean length of utterance (MLU), is a calculation of the average number of words and/or morphemes used per utterance. It is described using a modification of Brown's (1973) procedure and provides a number of rules for counting morphemes. The directions for the coding and computation of the MLU data for both words and morphemes on the Language Sample Data Sheet are clearly provided and require that the examiner have only an awareness of what constitutes a word and a morpheme. The calculations are clearly described and require little computational skill.

The second analysis procedure described in the manual involves what the authors term "fluency." This is an index of the amount of language produced over time (recommended time period of no less than 30 minutes), and it involves a simple calculation (division by 30) of the total number of words elicited in the first 30 minutes of the language sample. That is, it is a measure of words per minute during the stimuli description activities.

Diversity of language structures, used during the stimuli description activity, is the third measure obtained from the LSA. It focuses on the number of different words and/or word types and inflections used per utterance. That is, how many different words are used on average by the subject. There are three ways of computing diversity in the manual. The first divides the number of different content words per utterance into the number of nouns, verbs, adjectives, and adverbs per utterance. The second is a simple type-token ratio calculated by dividing the total number of words produced into the total number of different words. The last measure of diversity involves a simple type-token ratio of grammatical inflections. However, this last analysis of diversity is insufficiently described in the manual. There is only a statement that the computation ". . . can also be done for various grammatical inflections" (Mecham & Jones, 1978, p. 9), but no direction is given regarding which inflections to count.

The final structural language measure described in the manual involves the "completeness of utterances" (i.e., the number of utterances having the English subject-verb-complement grammatical configuration divided by the total number of utterances produced). Again, a basic knowledge of these three constituents is assumed, and, therefore, no information is provided in determining the identification of these grammatical elements.

Once the analyses are completed, the examiner should be given some direction regarding interpretation of the results. The LSA manual, however, does not provide interpretation information. Although Mecham and Jones suggest that other extended language sample protocols are more suited for diagnostic analysis and that the LSA is more appropriate for "assessing patterns [of change] over repeated measures" (1978, p. 10), exactly how this "assessing" of patterns should occur is unclear. The authors suggest that the measures can be effective 1) in monitoring change in the use of various language structures over time and 2) after an intervention period, but they provide no specific instructions or data on this interpretative aspect. The only information that appears directed toward interpretation of the procedural results involves two illustrations that simulate ". . . how an idea pattern would look for a child in a simple AB intervention design" (Mecham & Jones, 1978, p. 3) and in a multiple-base time-series design. For interpretative purposes, the examiner is required to make an assumption that an increase in the actual numerical value of the four structural measures is linked with increased language proficiency. This assumption is only implied by the authors, and no supporting evidence is supplied.

Technical Aspects

The Language Sampling Analysis manual provides little information concerning the reliability and validity of this procedure as a whole or of its various derived measures of language structure. Although a lack of concern over strict standardization of administration or an omission of norm-referenced data is understandable given the domain-referenced approach and its less structured language sampling design, the paucity of reliability and validity data is less defensible. No data are provided regarding the validity of this procedure as a measurement of language change or as an accurate index of improved language proficiency. Although such an instrument—focusing on various aspects of language structure—appears to have some face validity, this is not explicitly discussed by the authors, and no direct mention of validity is made in the manual.

Reliability is mentioned in the manual, but there are no extensive data reported. There are seven instances in which reliability is mentioned, but all seven deal only with the concept of interjudge or interobserver reliability. No mention is made of intrajudge reliability or temporal stability (test-retest reliability). Because the authors have suggested that the four measures derived from the analyses are indices of language proficiency at a given point in time, the concept of temporal reliability or stability is particularly important. Such measures need to be stable over short periods of time if they are to serve as valid indices of language proficiency.

The direct reference to interjudge reliability in the manual involves cautions to the examiner regarding reliable transcription and analysis. The authors suggest that if interjudge reliability of at least .85 is not achieved, then care should be taken when making comparisons. They also state that "A reliability index of below .70 should not be used even for making tentative judgments" (Mecham & Jones, 1978, p. 10). No supportive data for these statements are provided. Of particular concern are the demonstrations of interjudge reliability that the authors provide for each of the four measures. These reliability indices were not directly obtained by the authors for the LSA. Furthermore, most of the indices reported were obtained from a study focusing on other issues that simply reported interjudge reliabilities for a random sample of 15 utterances selected from three language samples (Olswang & Carpenter, 1978). Although these reliability data were sufficient for Olswang and Carpenter's study, they are inappropriate as a demonstration of interjudge reliability in a different and much more involved language assessment procedure. Overall, the reliability data provided in the manual are insufficient and, at times, misleading.

Critique

The Language Sampling and Analysis is described by its authors as a procedure that "provides a method for analyzing changes in certain variables felt to be important indicators of language growth or change" (Mecham & Jones, 1978, p. 10). Based on that statement, the authors have accomplished their objective. Through the domain-referenced approach, they have provided a way to determine changes in the four general variables they set out to measure. An evaluation of the adequacy of the LSA as a language assessment procedure (for diagnostic analysis or for measuring progress), however, involves more than just accomplishing the authors' objective. That objective must be carefully expanded. To have any value as a language assessment tool, the objective should read, "provides a *reliable* method for analyzing *stable* changes in certain variables that *are valid* indicators of language growth or change." The LSA does not accomplish this modified objective. It falls short of the mark due to its reliability and validity weaknesses.

An evaluation of the LSA's reliability as a language assessment tool suggests several problems. First, for an assessment instrument to be of some value, there must be an indication that the analyses can be accurately performed and that the same results can be obtained by different individuals (interjudge reliability) and by the same individual over time (intrajudge reliability). This has not been demonstrated for the LSA, and, in fact, there may be problems with these reliability issues. Due to the manual's lack of direction in categorizing parts of speech and its failure to provide explicit definitions for technical terms (e.g., morpheme), individuals may have difficulty with the classification of specific parts of speech (Bloom, 1967; Crystal, Fletcher, & Garman, 1976). Although it is possible that such difficulties would not be the case with the LSA, no data have been presented specifically on the procedure's interjudge and intrajudge reliabilities.

Second, for any assessment procedure to be reliable and valid, there must be a demonstration that the changes in the variables of interest occurring over time are systematic and linked to real changes in the underlying language proficiency rather than just due to random variation. That is, the procedure must have demonstrable temporal stability (test-retest reliability). This is an essential piece of information that actually reflects on the validity of the four variables measured by the LSA. If the four variables are truly indices of the child's underlying language proficiency, then the variables will be stable over short periods of time and will change only as the child's language proficiency changes (Carroll, 1968a; Cronbach, 1971). If this is not the case, then the measurement of these variables has no clinical or theoretical significance. The manual provides no data for the temporal stability of the variables under investigation.

Finally, the authors have not provided any information on the part-whole reliability of the measures recommended. There are no data supporting the stability of the measures as the length of the language sample changes. Based on a review of the literature, this could be problematic (Miron, 1981). For example, Hess, Sefton, and Landry (1986) studied the effects of language sample size on the stability of five different type-token-ratios in preschool children. They found that 1) type-token-ratios similar to those utilized in the LSA could not be directly comparable with samples containing different numbers of words; 2) the type-token-ratio scores between various segment sizes and the total scores of the same language samples were significantly different; and 3) the reliability coefficients for the type-token-ratios split into 50-word and 100-word segments ranged from .18 to .43. They estimated that sample sizes would have to be approximately 530 words in length to achieve reliabilities of .80; based on their data, that would be approximately 75 utterances. Although these results cannot be directly comparable to the LSA procedure, they must raise questions regarding its part-whole reliability.

Although the weakness of the reliability in the LSA *might* just be due to the lack of documentation, the procedure's validity problems appear more significant. As stated by Cronbach (1971), Messick (1980), and Muma (1984), construct validity is the major concern in the design, selection, and use of assessment instruments. Close analysis of the LSA suggests several difficulties that relate directly to the validity of the procedure as a language assessment tool. First, there is the question of the representativeness of the language data collected and analyzed. Numerous researchers have suggested that data collected in static object and/or picture description activities may tend to underestimate language proficiency (Longhurst &

File, 1977; Fokes & Konefal, 1981; Miller, 1981; Stalmaker & Creaghead, 1982). According to Oller (1979), this is due to the lack of meaningfulness and naturalness inherent in such activities. Children may or may not choose to respond to artificial, static picture and object description, and if they do not, it does not necessarily reflect their language proficiency.

Another potential validity problem involves the assumption made by the authors of the LSA that the four measures they utilize are "important indicators of language growth or change" (Mecham & Jones, 1978, p. 10). This has not been empirically demonstrated by the authors, and there is evidence to the contrary with some of these measures. For example, Carroll (1968b) has pointed out the fallacy of using simple type-token-ratio scores (i.e., diversity) as measures of language development. He suggests that such measures may yield decreased scores as one's language proficiency increases. This is due to the fact that even though more language might be used, many of the words will have already occurred. Consequently, the ratio score will decrease. The recent work of Hess, Sefton, and Landry (1986) supports this contention.

The use of Mean Length of Utterance (MLU) as a measurement of development may produce similar results. That is, contrary to assumptions of the authors, MLU may decrease as development increases. This may occur because there is no simple correlation between sentence length and sentence complexity (Crystal, 1981). It is possible that as one develops language one may become more efficient in conveying one's meaning and, therefore, may be more concise. It is also possible that MLU will vary due to variables other than language growth. Miller and Chapman (1981), for example, suggest that MLU is quite sensitive to contextual variables of all sorts and that, at times, changes in MLU may be due to these factors. Scores on the "completeness" measure that is utilized in the LSA may also increase or decrease due to factors other than language development. For example, a child may utilize ellipsis when responding to the LSA descriptive activities, but he or she may change over time due to familiarity with the task rather than improvement in language ability.

Thus, these four measures may vary greatly due to a host of factors, and their variation may seem inconsistent with the commonsense notion that as language develops scores on these measures rise. Although not explicitly stated in the LSA manual, this assumption that a rise in score parallels development is made implicitly, and it may not be valid.

An additional validity problem arises because the LSA focuses only on superficial aspects of language structure. The four measures are actually counts of traditional parts of speech and the simple relationships between these structural units. Because language is far more than just an ordered collection of these units (Crystal, 1981; Prutting, 1982), these measures may provide the examiner with inaccurate information about a child's language proficiency (Damico & Oller, 1980). This is particularly true when assessing minority populations (Damico, Oller, & Storey, 1983; Cummins, 1984). Because superficial aspects of language structure are more reflective of *where* one learned language than *how well* one learned it (Milroy & Milroy, 1985), LSA scores primarily reflect the ethnicity of minority students and not their language proficiency.

In summary, the Language Sampling and Analysis is a descriptive language assessment instrument that is based on undocumented assumptions regarding language growth and development and the ways such development might be quantified. Although the test manual is clearly written and the language sampling approach is appealing, the authors have not provided the necessary reliability and validity data to support the use of the procedure. Until data are made available to support the authors' contentions, clinicians are advised to utilize more fully developed language sampling procedures.

References

Barrie-Blackley, S., Musselwhite, C.R., & Rogister, S.H. (1978). *Clinical oral language sampling: A handbook for students and clinicians.* Danville, IL: Interstate Printers and Publishers.

Bloom, L. (1967). A comment on Lee's "Developmental Sentence Types: A method for comparing normal and deviant syntactic development." *Journal of Speech and Hearing Disorders, 32,* 294–296.

Bloom, L., & Lahey, M. (1978). *Language development and language disorders.* New York: John Wiley & Sons.

Brown, R. (1973). *A first language: The early stages.* Cambridge, MA: Harvard University Press.

Carroll, J.B. (1968a). The psychology of language testing. In A. Davies (Ed.), *Language testing symposium* (pp. 46–69). London: Oxford University Press.

Carroll, J.B. (1968b). Word frequency studies and the lognormal distribution. In E.M. Zale (Ed.), *Proceedings of the Conference of Language and Language Behavior* (pp. 213–235). New York: Appleton-Century-Crofts.

Cronbach, L.J. (1971). Test validation. In R. Thorndike (Ed.), *Educational measurement* (2nd ed., pp. 443–507). Washington, DC: American Council on Education.

Crystal, D. (1981). *Clinical linguistics.* New York: Springer-Verlag.

Crystal, D., Fletcher, P., & Garman, M. (1976). *The grammatical analysis of language disability.* London: Edward Arnold Publishers.

Cummins, J. (1984). *Bilingualism and special education: Issues in assessment and pedagogy.* San Diego: College-Hill Press.

Damico, J.S. (1985). Clinical discourse analysis: A functional approach to language assessment. In C.S. Simon (Ed.), *Communication skills and classroom success: Assessment of language-learning disabled students* (pp. 165–203). San Diego: College-Hill Press.

Damico, J.S., & Oller, J.W., Jr. (1980). Pragmatic versus morphological/syntactic criteria for language referrals. *Language, Speech, and Hearing Services in Schools, 11,* 85–94.

Damico, J.S., Oller, J.W., Jr., & Storey, M.E. (1983). The diagnosis of language disorders in bilingual children: Pragmatic and surface-oriented criteria. *Journal of Speech and Hearing Disorders, 48,* 285–294.

Doyle, A., Connolly, J., & Revist, L. (1980). The effect of playmate familiarity on the social interactions of young children. *Child Development, 51,* 217–223.

Fokes, J., & Konefal, J. (1981). Children's uses of four semantic cases in two conditions. *Journal of Communicative Disorders, 14,* 497–506.

Gallagher, T.A. (1983). Pre-assessment: A procedure for accommodating language use variability. In T.A. Gallagher & C.A. Prutting (Eds.), *Pragmatic assessment and intervention issues in language* (pp. 1–28). San Diego: College-Hill Press.

Hess, C.W., Sefton, K.M., & Landry, R.G. (1986). Sample size and type-token ratios for oral language of preschool children. *Journal of Speech and Hearing Research, 29,* 129–134.

Kramer, C., James, S., & Saxman, J. (1979). A comparison of language samples elicited at home and in the clinic. *Journal of Speech and Hearing Disorders, 44,* 321–330.

Lee, L. (1974). *Developmental Sentence Analysis: A grammatical assessment procedure for speech and language disorders.* Evanston, IL: Northwestern University Press.

Longhurst, T., & File, J. (1977). A comparison of developmental sentence scores from Head Start children collected in four conditions. *Language, Speech, and Hearing Services in Schools, 8,* 54–64.

McCauley, R.J., & Swisher, L. (1984). Psychometric review of language and articulation tests for preschool children. *Journal of Speech and Hearing Disorders, 49,* 34–42.

Mecham, M.J. (1971). *Verbal Language Development Scale.* Circles Pines, MN: American Guidance Service.

Mecham, J.M., Jex, J.L., & Jones, J.D. (1967). *Utah Test of Language Development.* Salt Lake City: Communication Research Associates.

Mecham, M.J., & Jones, J.D. (1978). *UTLD Supplement: Language Sampling and Analysis.* Salt Lake City: Communication Research Associates.

Meehl, P.E. (1954). *Clinical versus statistical prediction.* Minneapolis: University of Minnesota Press.

Messick, S. (1980). Test validity and the ethics of assessment. *American Psychologist, 30,* 1012–1027.

Miller, J. (1981). *Assessing language production in children.* Baltimore: University Park Press.

Miller, J., & Chapman, R. (1981). The relation between age and mean length of utterance in morphemes. *Journal of Speech and Hearing Research, 24,* 154–161.

Milroy, J., & Milroy, L. (1985). *Authority in language: Investigating language prescription and standardisation.* London: Routledge & Kegan Paul.

Miron, M.S. (1981). The resolution of disputed communication origins. *Speech and Language: Advances in Basic Research and Practice, 5,* 405–466.

Muma, J.R. (1978). *Language handbook: Concepts, assessment, intervention.* Englewood Cliffs, NJ: Prentice-Hall.

Muma, J.R. (1984). Semel and Wiig's CELF: Construct validity? [A letter to the editor]. *Journal of Speech and Hearing Disorders, 49,* 101–104.

Muma, J.R. (1986). *Language acquisition: A functionalistic perspective.* Austin, TX: PRO-ED.

Naremore, R.C. (1979). Review of "Utah Test of Language Development." In F. Darley (Ed.), *Evaluation of appraisal techniques in speech and language pathology* (pp. 78–81). Reading, MA: Addison-Wesley.

Oller, J.W., Jr. (1979). *Language tests at school.* London: Longman.

Olswang, L.B., & Carpenter, R.L. (1978). Elicitor effects on the language obtained from young language-impaired children. *Journal of Speech and Hearing Disorders, 43,* 76–88.

Prutting, C.A. (1979). Process /pras/ses/n: The action of moving forward from one point to another on the way to completion. *Journal of Speech and Hearing Disorders, 44,* 3–30.

Prutting, C.A. (1982). Pragmatics as social competence. *Journal of Speech and Hearing Disorders, 47,* 123–133.

Scholtz, G., & Ellis, M. (1975). Repeated exposure to objects and peers in a play setting. *Journal of Experimental Child Psychology, 19,* 448–455.

Scott, C.M., & Taylor, A.E. (1978). A comparison of home and clinic gathered language samples. *Journal of Speech and Hearing Disorders, 43,* 482–495.

Simon, C.T. (1945). Complexity and breakdown in speech situations. *Journal of Speech Disorders, 10,* 199–203.

Stalmaker, L., & Creaghead, N. (1982). An examination of language samples obtained under three experimental conditions. *Language, Speech, and Hearing Services in Schools, 13,* 121–128.

Tomasello, M., Farrar, M.J., & Dines, J. (1984). Children's speech revisions for a familiar and unfamiliar adult. *Journal of Speech and Hearing Research, 27,* 359–364.

Vaughn-Cooke, F.B. (1980). Evaluating the language of Black English speakers: Implications of the Ann Arbor decision. In M.F. Whiteman (Ed.), *Reactions to Ann Arbor: Vernacular Black English and education* (pp. 24–56). Washington, DC: Center for Applied Linguistics.

Joyce A. Eckart, Ed.D.
Assistant Professor of Education, Oakland University, Rochester, Michigan.

LEADERSHIP ABILITY EVALUATION
Russell N. Cassel and Edward J. Stancik. Los Angeles, California: Western Psychological Services.

Introduction

The Leadership Ability Evaluation (LAE) is a 50-item instrument designed "to assess the decision-making pattern of an individual when he or she functions as a leader"(Cassel & Stancik, 1981, p. 1). The LAE was first published in 1961 and revised in 1981.

The primary author of the test, Russell N. Cassel, received his doctorate in education from the University of Southern California in 1949. He was Professor of Educational Psychology at the University of Wisconsin at Milwaukee from 1967 to 1974. Dr. Cassel has been editor of *Education, College Student Journal* and *Reading Improvement* and has a long-standing interest in the dimensions of leadership. His article "Democratic Leadership" (Cassel, 1953) described basic principles necessary for effective leadership in a democratic society. As part of that paper, Cassel identified three patterns of leadership based on the work of Kurt Lewin (1939). In the LAE, the original three patterns of leadership have been refined and reflect Cassel's definition of leadership specifically in regard to decision patterns and social climate (Cassel & Stancik, 1981). Leadership in the revised LAE implies concern with influencing a person or group of people to support a leader's objectives. The LAE then is a measure of the following decision-making patterns:

1) *Laissez Faire (LF)*—a decision pattern centered on individual and independent group members. The leader exercises a minimum influence on the others but is always available to group members in the role of an advisor.

2) *Democratic-Cooperative (DC)*—a decision pattern centered on parliamentary procedure. The leader emphasizes the will of the group or the individual involved and retains the dual role of leader and group member.

3) *Autocratic-Submissive (AS)*—a decision pattern centered on a resource person, expert, or committee. The leader stresses the use of advisors and resource persons.

4) *Autocratic-Aggressive (AA)*—a decision pattern based on an ego-centered leader mode. The leader alone makes decisions; group members become aware of objectives and plans on a need-to-know basis (Cassel & Stancik, 1981).

In the LAE the examinee is presented with 50 situations and a four-alternative, multiple-choice response format for each. Each response is associated with one of the four patterns described above. The respondent chooses how he or she would typically act during a particular situation. Five scores are generated from the responses: four individual scores (LF, DC, AS, AA) and a Total Score. A characteristic decision-making pattern is provided by the Total Score.

The LAE is well organized and attractively packaged as an 8-page, 8½" × 11" expendable booklet. On the first page, the examinee fills in personal information and reads the directions. On the next six pages, situations are briefly presented in boldface type. The phrase "What would you do?" is repeated after each instance. Four choices of action are described. The examinee selects the action he or she would most likely follow by circling the letter (i.e., A, B, C, D) of the choice in columns to the left of the situation. These columns are labeled LF, DC, AS, and AA. The use of shaded horizontal bars helps to eliminate confusion in marking the choices. The last page of the booklet includes an LAE profile and a chart used to compute the Total Score.

The LAE may be group or individually administered. The manual suggests that persons with a sixth-grade reading level can complete the LAE. For those with a reading level below fifth grade, some assistance may be necessary. The directions should be read aloud in group testing situations. The test can be completed in 15 to 20 minutes. The examiner is free to answer any questions concerning the test short of answering the test questions.

The test manual directs the examiner to check each test to ensure that each situation has just one answer. If a total of four or more items are not answered or contain more than one response, the test should be considered invalid.

The LAE can be scored as a Total Score or as a profile. For the Total Score, the examinee counts the number of responses under each of the four decision-making mode columns and puts each raw score on the Total Score chart. Scores range between 0, no responses in that mode, to 50, all responses in that mode. Raw scores for each of the four patterns are entered into the chart, multiplied by the appropriate weighting factor, and summed for the Total Weighted Score. To find the Total Score, the Total Weighted Score is divided by 10. This score is used to determine the characteristic decision pattern of the individual. For the profile, raw scores for each decision-making mode and the Total Score are entered in the appropriate columns on the profile. The examinee compares his or her score with T-scores of typical individuals (i.e., T.I.) and of outstanding leaders (i.e., O.L.).

Interpreting the LAE can be done in three ways: Total Score analysis, profile analysis, and item response analysis. The Total Score represents the characteristic decision pattern of an individual. The manual provides tables of means and standard deviations on Total Scores and on the four decision modes for typical individuals, outstanding leaders, and eight comparison groups. If a profile analysis is needed, T-scores are provided for the decision modes and the Total Scores for typical individuals and outstanding leaders. Further explanation is provided to interpret the meaning of the tables for the four decision-making patterns. However, it is emphasized that the Total Score is the most important single indicator of acceptable or unacceptable leadership patterns. The LAE also can be analyzed with respect to item responses. The 50 items are categorized into life activities of the individual, including home and family life, work and vocational pursuits, play and avocational pursuits, school and educational pursuits, and community life. Responsibility for meanings associated with response patterns in life activities is left to the examiner's subjective interpretation.

Practical Applications/Uses

The test manual indicates that the LAE can be interpreted on three levels: Total Score analysis, profile analysis of each of the four modes of decision-making patterns, and item response analysis. The information provided from the profile helps the examinee to determine his or her typical decision-making pattern style. The individual compares his or her typical pattern to the pattern of various comparison groups supplied in the profile. T-scores on two groups are provided in the profile, typical individuals (T.I.) and outstanding leaders (O.L.). After individual scores have been tallied and have been recorded on the profile, the examinee can compare his or her score to the scores of T.I. and O.L. A Total Score of 11 or greater falls in the ineffective leadership range; a score of 10 or less falls in the effective leadership range. Based on the T-scores for each of the four decision-making modes, Cassel draws the following conclusions:

> LF—Raw scores above 13, or scores above 60T, suggest excessive dependence upon group members for arriving at decisions. Raw scores below 4, or scores below 40T, represent too little dependence upon group members for arriving at decisions.
> DC—Raw scores above 31, or scores above 60T, suggest excessive cooperation by the leader; raw scores below 20, or scores below 40T, suggest too little cooperation.
> AS—Raw scores above 11, or scores above 60T, represent excessive use of resource persons; raw scores below 5, or scores below 40T, indicate too little use of such persons.
> AA—Raw scores above 7, or scores above 60T, suggest excessive use of leader-dominated thinking; raw scores below 1, or scores below 40T, represent too little use of leader-dominated thinking. (Cassel & Stancik, 1981, pp. 4–5)

Although the test manual notes that the LAE can be interpreted as an item response analysis, there are no directions on how this could be done. This is unfortunate because information from an analysis of life activity situations is helpful when analyzing whether or not leadership decision-making patterns are situational specific.

Technical Aspects

No information is given in the manual about how items were selected for use nor how responses were categorized as LF, DC, AS, or AA. The manual does report that

> six research psychologists evaluated the four decision mode scores of the LAE against various social climate structures. There was agreement among all judges that the leadership patterns . . . were incorporated into the LAE as decision mode categories. (Cassel & Stancik, 1981, p. 6)

The test manual reports split-half reliability coefficients from a number of studies using the LAE instrument (Cassel, 1959; Cassel & Harriman, 1958; Cassel & Sanders, 1961). A table of reliability indices is provided for each decision-making mode and a Total Score on eight comparison groups ($N = 1,072$). Indices range from .341-.580 (LF); .537-.910 (DC); .286-.690 (AS); .341-.612 (AA); and .732-.911 (Total Score). Measures of AS appear least reliable while measures of Total Score are most reliable. The test manual reports that the analysis of discrimination between outstanding leaders ($N = 100$) and typical individuals ($N = 200$) based on the experiments of Cassel and Carp (1957) and Cassel and Haddox (1959). Intercorrelations range from .05 to -.72. A multiple regression analysis was performed to compute individual weights assigned to each decision-making mode (excluding AA). These weights are used to compute the Total Score. When age and intelligence were held constant, LF weighted 7, DC weighted 1, and AS weighted 4. Groups of outstanding leaders and above average ninth-grade students were used to analyze the Total Score. The manual reports

> the optimal cut off score of 10 or less predicted effective leadership in 68.5% of the cases. A score of 11 or greater falls in the ineffective leadership range; a score of 10 or less falls in the effective leadership range. (Cassel & Stancik, 1981, p. 8)

Pearson Correlations were reported between Total Score and several psychological measures (e.g., California Test of Mental Maturity, S-Form; Cooperative Reading [Comprehension] Test; Iowa Tests of Educational Development; Leadership Q-Sort Test; Goodenough Socio-Economic [Status] Scale) and chronological age ($n = 200$ male adults). Significant r's ranged from .45 for the Cooperative Reading [Comprehension] Test to -.14 for the Goodenough Socio-Economic [Status] Scale. Results indicated that there is no significant correlation between age and Total Score. Results of three studies are included in the revised edition of the LAE. Otte (1968) used the LAE as part of a study on school principals' personal and professional characteristics and their decision-making mode. Hill (1968) analyzed the commitment to persist in a doctoral program and decision-making patterns based on the LAE. Finally, Davies, Wyndham, and Binks (1969) used the LAE to trace change in decision-making patterns among 46 senior managers. After sensitivity training, AA and AS decreased significantly, DC increased significantly. No significant change was found in LS.

Critique

The Leadership Ability Evaluation, Revised Edition contains some major flaws that have not been corrected from the 1961 version (Black, 1965). First, the test booklet design could influence scores. Each page is headed LF, DC, AS, and AA, in the same order. Examinees could contrive scores by responding in a certain style following the column header. Next, items do not deal with relevant leadership positions. For example, in one situation, "Your mother shows favoritism toward you brother or sister. What do you do?", one does wonder if this is a relevant leadership situation for a diverse population of test takers. In scoring, importance is placed on a Total Score as the characteristic decision pattern of the individual, rather than scores on individual decision-making modes or an item analysis of the responses made by the individual in different life activity situations. The use of a Total Score is an oversimplification of the multifaceted dimensions of leadership. The use of multiple correlations that exclude AA are not explained. If one analyzes Total Score, a weighted factor of 0 for Autocratic Aggressive (AA) coupled with the cutoff score of 10 suggests that outstanding leaders respond to more situations in that mode; however, an ego-centered leader decision mode identified as Autocratic-Aggressive by Cassel and Stancik (1981) has been called a myth of leadership by Bennis and Nanus (1985). When interpreting scores, T-scores for typical and outstanding leaders are provided. However, the criteria for being classified as typical or outstanding is not included in the manual. The revised edition includes results of four studies that had not been reported in the 1961 manual, namely, Cassel (1961), Davies, Wyndham, and Binks (1969), Hill (1968), and Otte (1968). Information from these studies has not been used to revise norming tables. The inclusion of this information does not strengthen the study of validity, which Black (1965) had considered weak in the 1961 edition. Additionally, some of the information to be furnished by the examinee on the front page is not necessary for either scoring or interpreting the test. Finally, the test manual refers to the wrong tables to interpret the scores in the profile form (see p. 8 of the manual). In conclusion, the LAE is not a strong instrument for studying, identifying, or interpreting decision-making patterns typically exhibited by leaders.

References

This list includes text citations and suggested additional reading.

Bennis, W., & Nanus, B. (1985). *Leaders: The strategies for taking charge.* New York: Harper & Row.

Black, J.D. (1965). Review of Leadership Ability Evaluation. In O.K. Buros (Ed.), *The sixth mental measurements yearbook* (pp. 278–280). Highland Park, NJ: The Gryphon Press.

Cassel, R.N. (1953). Democratic leadership. *Educational Forum, 17,* 437–441.

Cassel, R.N. (1959). The Phoenix youth study proposal for delinquency reduction. *Journal of Educational Sociology, 33,* 67–72.

Cassel, R.N. (1961). A construct validity study on a leadership and a social insight test for 200 college freshman students. *Journal of Genetic Psychology, 99,* 165–170.

Cassel, R.N., & Carp, A. (1957). Combining criterion measures from R- and Q- methodologies for purpose of validation tests related to leadership. *American Psychologist, 12,* 408–409. (Abstract of a paper presented at the meeting of the American Psychological Association, New York, 1957).

Cassel, R.N., & Childers, R. (1963). A study of certain attributes of 45 high-school varsity football team members by use of psychological test scores. *Journal of Educational Research, 57,* 64–67.

Cassel, R.N., & Haddox, G., (1959). Comparative study of leadership test scores for gifted and typical high school students. *Psychological Reports, 5,* 713–717.

Cassel, R.N., & Harriman, B.L., (1958). Comparing pre- and post-training leadership test scores with norms for colonels and federal prisoners and with other test scores. *American Psychologist, 13,* 370. (Abstract of a paper presented at the meeting of the American Psychological Association, Washington, DC, 1958).

Cassel R.N., & Sanders, R.A., (1961). A comparative analysis of scores from two leadership tests for Apache Indians and Anglo American youth. *Journal of Educational Research, 55,* 19–23.

Cassel R.N. and Stancik, E.J. (1981). *The Leadership Ability Evaluation revised manual.* Los Angeles: Western Psychological Services.

Davies, E., Wyndham, J., & Binks, N. (1969). Psychological changes in sensitivity training. *Australian Psychologist, 3*(3), 171–176.

Hill, D.C. (1968). Leadership and test performance relationships as determinants of successful progress in doctoral level educational administration programs (Doctoral dissertation, University of Minnesota, 1968). *Dissertation Abstracts International, 29,* 4228A. (University Microfilms No. 69–6818).

Lewin, K. (1939). Field theory and experiment in social psychology. *American Journal of Sociology, 44,* 868–896.

Otte, A.W. (1968). Relationships between selected personal and professional characteristics of school principals and propensities toward group decision making (Doctoral dissertation, University of Minnesota, 1968). *Dissertation Abstract International, 29,* 1727A. (University Microfilms No. 68–17, 705).

John M. Bradley, Ed.D.

Associate Professor of Language, Reading, and Culture, University of Arizona, Tucson, Arizona.

LINGUISTIC AWARENESS IN READING READINESS

John Downing, Douglas Ayers, and Brian Schaefer. Windsor, Great Britain: NFER-Nelson Publishing Company Ltd.

Introduction

The Linguistic Awareness in Reading Readiness (LARR) is a group-administered test that is designed to assess knowledge about the functions and features of language that are related to reading and writing. The LARR was published by the NFER-Nelson Publishing Company in 1983. Two forms (Forms A and B) are available. According to the test manual (Downing, Ayers, & Schaefer, 1983), the purpose of the LARR is to determine ". . . the strengths and weaknesses of both individual pupils and the class as a whole with regard to their understanding of the linguistic concepts that they need for reasoning about the tasks of reading instruction" (p. 1).

This test consists of three parts: 1) Recognizing Literacy Behavior, a measure of awareness of the activities that are involved in reading and writing; 2) Understanding Literacy Functions, a measure of knowledge about the various purposes of reading and writing; and 3) Technical Language of Literacy, a measure of knowledge of the terminology associated with reading and writing instruction. A similar format is followed throughout the test in that the examiner reads aloud an item that involves the identification of some aspect of reading or writing, and the child listens and responds by drawing a circle around the aspect wherever it is located within a picture, a row of pictures, or a row of written symbols.

The LARR may be used by classroom teachers with groups of 10 to 15 kindergarten children. It is suggested that the LARR be given in three 20-minute sessions, with each session preferably occurring on a separate day. The test manual (Downing et al., 1983) provides some technical data about the LARR's reliability and validity obtained with two samples of kindergarten children. No normative data are available to the user for scoring and interpretation, but suggested standards of mastery are given to identify "below average" scores.

The authors of the LARR are John Downing, Douglas Ayers, and Brian Schaefer. John Downing earned a Ph.D. from the University of London in 1966 and was a professor of educational psychology at the University of Victoria, Victoria, British Columbia, until his death in 1987. He was a prolific writer and is best known for his research related to the initial teaching alphabet (i.t.a.) method of reading instruction. Downing's book, *Reading and Reasoning* (1979), contains a good review of the research on linguistic awareness up to that time. Douglas Ayers is a professor emeritus of education at the University of Victoria. Brian Schaefer was a graduate student in psychology at the University of Victoria at the time that the LARR was developed. He subsequently earned a Ph.D. in cognitive psychology from Oxford University and is currently in private business in the area of artificial intelligence and its application to instruction.

According to the test authors, the development of the LARR was stimulated by the theories of Jean Piaget and Lev Vygotsky and the research of Jessie Reid (1966) suggest that the learning of skills (e.g., reading and writing) is best accomplished when students understand the purpose of the skills and have internalized the concepts needed to think about how the skills are performed.

As part of a larger study of reading readiness in Canadian schools (Evanechko, Ollila, Downing & Braun, 1973), John Downing developed three tests of linguistic knowledge related to reading and writing similar to the three parts of the current LARR. The reliabilities of the three prototype tests were found to be low primarily because of inadequate test length. John Downing then collaborated with Douglas Ayers and Brian Schaefer in the revision and expansion of his prototype tests as a first step in the development of the LARR. The resulting revision was then administered to kindergarten students and 1 year later correlated with their reading achievement at the end of first grade. The results of this study revealed the LARR to have relatively good predictive validity in terms of reading achievement. The data from the predictive validity study were used to again revise the LARR tests to their present form. Although the test manual hints at forthcoming normative data, personal communication with one of the surviving authors reveals that no further development of the LARR is planned at this time (Brian Schaefer, personal communication, August 1, 1988).

Both Form A and Form B of the LARR have three separate student response booklets, one booklet for each part of the LARR. Part 1, Recognizing Literacy Behavior, has an 11-page student response booklet consisting of 22 items. Nine of the items consist of single pictures that contain either text or numbers. The child's task is to listen while the examiner reads the item and then to draw a circle around the part(s) of the corresponding picture in the response booklet that depict something that can be read. The remaining 13 items in Part 1 consist of rows of four pictures per item. The child's task for the last 13 items of Part 1 is to encircle the portions of one or more of the four pictures that relate to some aspect of reading or writing. For example, the child is asked to encircle something pictured that can be read (e.g., a note, sign, book, etc.), something that can be used for writing (e.g., a pencil, paper, etc.), someone pictured who is reading, or someone who is writing. Part 2, Understanding Literacy Functions, has an 8-page student response booklet consisting of 23 items. Each item consists of a row of four pictures of which one or more depict a function of reading or writing. The child's task is to encircle the portions of one or more of the pictures that show a literacy function such as reading to enjoy something, reading to find something out, writing to tell someone something, and so on. Part 3, Technical Language of Literacy, has a 7-page student response booklet consisting of 30 items. All 30 items show in the response booklet examples of writing ranging from rows containing letters or numbers to complete sentences. The child's task is to encircle the portion(s) of the item in the response booklet that relate(s) to the linguistic feature being tested (e.g., letters, capital letters, beginning letters in words, words, periods, top lines, etc.)

A 1-page class answer sheet is also provided for each of the three parts of the LARR. The three class answer sheets all have a similar format. Item numbers are listed across the top of the sheet together with the linguistic concept that they are intended to measure. A column of spaces are provided along the left-hand side of the sheet for the listing of the student names in a class. The result is a grid that can be used to record the responses of the students for each of the items. The resulting response grid is easy to use, requiring the examiner to record only correct responses in the boxes provided for each item. A raw score is determined for each part of the test, but no total LARR test score is computed. Columns are provided on the right-hand side of the response grid to record the raw scores and percentile or stanine scores. The columns for the percentile or stanine scores serve no purpose because there are no normative data available for those scores. However, the test user is encouraged to compute percent scores from the raw scores and enter them into the percentile/stanine answer sheet column. The class answer sheets are also designed to permit an item analysis by computing the proportion of the students getting an item correct against those attempting it. Because the answer sheet also provides the linguistic concept associated with each item, such an item analysis might be used to plan instruction.

A 32-page administrative manual (Downing et al., 1983) is also offered that gives a rationale for the development of the LARR, administration procedures, scoring keys for both forms, directions for scoring and interpretation, and some technical information. The administrative manual is readable, well organized, and provides relatively clear and complete information about how to prepare for testing, how to give the test, what to say when giving it, how to solve problems that might arise during testing, and how to score the test. Information regarding test interpretation is rather limited due to the lack of normative data.

Practical Applications/Uses

The LARR is designed for use by classroom teachers who wish to identify children who lack metalinguistic knowledge regarding certain aspects of reading and writing. There is general agreement that metalinguistic skills underlie learning to read (Hakes, 1982; Tunmer & Bowey, 1984). Recent research also supports the relationship between metalinguistic knowledge and reading (Kamhi, Lee, & Nelson, 1985; van Kleeck & Shuele, 1987). If used appropriately, the LARR should provide the practitioner with useful information about the reading and writing readiness of kindergarten children. Unfortunately, an appropriate use of the LARR involves the development of local norms, requiring an investment of substantial time and effort by the personnel of a school or school district.

The administrative manual (Downing et al., 1983) suggests the LARR is ". . . intended chiefly for young children in their first two grades in school. This is the beginning of the infants or first school in Britain or kindergarten and grade one in North America" (p. 1). This suggestion notwithstanding, there is no information provided concerning the use of the LARR with first-grade students. The available information suggests that the LARR is probably best suited to use with beginning-of-the-year kindergarten students. Although the LARR is still appropriate for use with end-of-the-year kindergarten students, it was found to be somewhat easy for them, and a ceiling effect was obtained with Part 1 that was especially pronounced on Form A. There is no information available concerning the use of the LARR with minority children or second-language children.

The LARR requires no special training to be given other than a careful reading of the administrative manual and student response booklets. The examiner is urged to monitor the students constantly while they are taking the LARR to make sure they are following directions and are working on the correct item. As a consequence of the need for constant monitoring, it is suggested that the size of the testing group be limited to no more than 15 students unless an aide can be used to help out. The administrative manual reports that each part of the LARR can be given in 20 to 25 minutes, resulting in a total of 60 to 75 minutes needed to give all three parts.

All scoring of the LARR must be done by hand. Scoring the three parts appears to be fairly uncomplicated; one only has to compare the student's responses in the response booklet to those depicted in the provided key. The test authors do warn that some of the responses of immature students may be ambiguous due to poor fine-motor coordination. Because some items require two or more responses, it is possible for a student to respond appropriately to only a part of an item. Credit is given for an item only when all parts of it are responded to correctly, and no credit is given for partial answers. No difference between the right/wrong system used on the LARR and a partial scoring system was found when both scoring systems were investigated with 300 kindergarten students.

Standards of mastery are provided to aid in the interpretation of the obtained percent scores. For example, scores of less than 50% on Parts 1 and 2 and less than 30% on Part 3 indicate "below average" performance for kindergarten students tested in November. The LARR administrative manual offers no explanation regarding the basis for the suggested standards of mastery. Although the class summary sheets for all three parts of the LARR are designed to facilitate pattern analyses in terms of items grouped by linguistic factors, the manual advises that the results of the LARR should be used ". . . as a guide to the general level of concept development in the individual child or the class" (Downing et al., 1983, p. 26).

Technical Aspects

Evidence for the LARR's reliability was limited to a measure of internal consistency, the Kuder-Richardson Formula 20 (KR20). The LARR tests were administered to approximately 330 kindergarten children during the fall and then again during the spring of the same school year. The six KR20's obtained during the fall testing ranged from .84 to .92, and the six obtained during the spring testing ranged from .76 to .91. The only KR20 falling below .82 was the .76 obtained during the spring testing with Form A of Part 1 (Ayers & Downing, 1982).

Even though the LARR is purported to have two "parallel" forms, no parallel form reliability data were reported. There is some evidence reported in the manual suggesting that the two forms may have differed in difficulty:

> in the May-June testing, the reliability of Part 1 (of the LARR) was considerably lowered because the test turned out to be somewhat easy, particularly Form A on which the average child got 84 percent of the items correct. (Downing et al., 1983, p. 29)

The manual reports that the LARR has good content validity. An analysis of the LARR test items reveals that they appear to be generally valid with the exception of several items on Parts 1 and 2. There are two items in Part 1 where the child is supposed to respond by circling a person who is "reading." Both items include pictures of people who are reading something that are keyed as being the answers. Both items also include pictures of people who are obviously writing, and a student circling those pictures will get the items wrong. The problem with these items is that when people write they also read to edit and guide their writing. Students who circle the "writing" pictures aren't really wrong, and they actually may be penalized for knowing too much. Part 2 has several items that may also present content validity problems. To conserve space, only one of the problem items will be addressed here. This item is similar to several others; the examiner asks the child to circle the picture(s) that show someone who is "telling" something. The pictures show people in a variety of activities, and the child is supposed to circle those pictures that depict a person writing something. The use of the word *telling* to represent the concept of writing is somewhat unusual. As the word *telling* is commonly used, it is associated more with speech than writing. One of the items is particularly misleading in this respect. It consists of four pictures, the keyed one showing a girl writing something. The other two pictures are obviously wrong, but the third picture shows a child standing while holding a picture of a boat. The picture looks very much like a child doing "show and tell" at school. Nonetheless, a child circling that picture would get the item wrong.

Some data regarding the predictive validity of the LARR are offered in the manual (Downing et al., 1983, p. 30). The LARR tests were given to 300 kindergarten children in a city in the province of British Columbia, Canada, near the end of the school year. The same sample of students was then tested for reading achievement with the Cooperative Primary Reading Test, Form 12A (Educational Testing Service, 1967) during the following year when they were finishing the first grade.

The manual provides incomplete data regarding the findings of this study. Six validity coefficients are possible across the LARR's two forms and three parts. However, only two of the six coefficients were reported; Form A of Part 3 yielded a validity coefficient of .48 and Form B of Part 3 yielded a coefficient of .60. In addition, the manual reports that a validity coefficient of .50 was obtained with Form A of Parts 1 and 3 combined. The reported validity coefficients of the LARR are respectable when compared with those obtained with other measures of reading readiness. Predictive validity data were reported for 12 classrooms. The class sizes ranged from 8 to 19 students. A table is given in the manual (Downing et al., 1983, p. 31) that provides Spearman rank order correlations of the LARR Parts 1, 2, and 3 with the CPR score for words and sentences and the total score. The validity coefficients for Parts 1 and 3 of both forms of the LARR ranged greatly across the classes (-0.26 to 0.78, with most of them around 0.30). The coefficients obtained with Part 3 of the LARR were more promising (-0.30 to 0.80 with 19 of the 24 coefficients falling above 0.50, 14 falling above 0.60, and 8 falling above 0.70). It appears from these data that Part 3 of the LARR offers a good predictor of reading achievement for most individual classrooms.

Critique

The LARR attempts to measure several important factors related to literacy: the awareness of the linguistic features, purposes, and functions of reading and writing. Especially in Part 3, Technical Language of Literacy, the test appears to hold promise as a valid way of predicting early success in learning to read. Unfortunately, the development of the LARR was never completed, and it appears that there is little chance that it ever will be. Little is known about the linguistic, racial, ethnic, and socioeconomic compositions of the samples of students with whom the LARR was used, other than they attended kindergarten in a city in British Columbia. Without well-described representative national norms, appropriate interpretation and use of LARR test scores requires the user to expend substantial effort constructing local norms, effort that most practitioners can't afford to give.

References

Ayers, D., & Downing, J. (1982). Testing children's concepts of reading. *Educational Research*, 24, 277–283.

Downing, J. (1979). *Reading and reasoning*. New York: Springer Verlag.

Downing, J., Ayers, D., & Schaefer, B. (1983). *Linguistic Awareness in Reading Readiness administrative manual*. Windsor, Great Britain: NFER-Nelson Publishing Company.

Evanechko, P., Ollila, L., Downing, J., & Braun, D. (1973). An investigation of the reading readiness domain. *Research in the Teaching of English, 7*, 61–78.

Hakes, D. (1982). The development of metalinguistic abilities: What develops? In S. Kuczaj (Ed.), *Language development: Language, thought, and culture* (Vol. 2, pp. 163–210). Hillsdale, NJ: Erlbaum.

Kamhi, A., Lee, R., & Nelson, L. (1985). Word, syllable, and sound awareness in language-disordered children. *Journal of Speech and Hearing Disorders, 50*, 207–212.

Reid, J. (1966). Learning to think about reading. *Educational Research, 9*, 56–62.

Tunmer, W., & Bowey, J. (1984). Metalinguistic awareness and reading acquisition. In W. Tunmer, C. Pratt, & M. Harriman (Eds.), *Metalinguistic awareness in children: Theory, research, and implications*. New York: Springer-Verlag.

van Kleeck, A., & Schuele, C. (1987). Precursors to literacy: Normal development. *Topics in Language Disorders, 7*, 13–31.

Julian Fabry, Ph.D.
*Counseling Psychologist, Meyer Children's Rehabilitation Institute,
Omaha, Nebraska.*

LURIA'S NEUROPSYCHOLOGICAL
INVESTIGATION

*Anne-Lise Christensen. Los Angeles, California: Western
Psychological Services.*

Introduction

The Luria Neuropsychological Investigation (Christensen, 1984b) is a method
designed to assess and evaluate various intact and deficient psychological functions in adults who have suffered some type of organic brain damage. It is organized and designed to gather information about patient's general state of arousal,
the degree to which they are oriented to their surroundings, and their individual
emotional response to their status and situation. Examinees are required further
1) to demonstrate their ability to accomplish selected sensorimotor and cognitive
tasks that include planning and carrying out simple and complex hand and mouth
movements, as well as 2) to ascertain their perceptions and their integration of
sensory feedback obtained from skin and muscles. Visual acuity, perceptions,
organization, and spatial orientation are assessed, and language expression and
comprehension of varying levels of complexity are tested. The person's ability to
read, write, and compute arithmetic equations is evaluated, as well as the ability to
demonstrate memory functions in learning and recall. Examinees are asked to
display their intellectual abilities of abstracting, forming concepts, and solving
problems. All of the information obtained is utilized to arrive at a qualitative diagnosis that serves as the foundation for the rehabilitation of deficits through intact
functions.

The method was first described by A. R. Luria (1947) in *Traumatic Aphasia,* which
publicized the results obtained in the Urals during the second World War. The
method was later presented more thoroughly in *Higher Cortical Functions in Man*
(1962), which was translated by Basil Haigh and published in 1966. A further revision and expansion was published by Basic Books in 1980.

A. R. Luria (1902–1977) was foremost a professor of psychology at Moscow University. After completing his medical degree, he became the leader of a research
laboratory at the Neurosurgical University named after the Russian neurosur-
geon, N. N. Bourdenko, who was in charge of the medical division of the Russian
Army. In the 1920s and 1930s, Luria was a member of the troika (along with Alexel
Leontiev and Lev Vygotsky) that maintained that complex behavioral processes
were not localized in particular parts of the brain, but rather were distributed
throughout the cortex in "functional systems." These systems were organized in a
hierarchical structure so that complex behavioral acts, such as writing or the pronunciation of words could be performed smoothly and precisely. These studies

314 Luria's Neuropsychological Investigation

promoted the investigation of higher cortical functions that they believed to be social in origin, while being mediated through conscious effort and language.

The Luria Neuropsychological Investigation was derived from Luria's *Higher Cortical Functions in Man* by Anne-Lise Christensen, a Danish psychologist at the Aarhus University Neurosurgical Clinic. Originally she had been asked to review the book for a Danish journal, but after reading and studying the method, she organized the tasks provided by Luria (1966) and translated the work into Danish. She then visited Luria's laboratory in 1970 and 1973. Luria advocated translating her work into English and offered Dr. Christensen an introductory chapter. (Later, the work was translated into Russian.) The second edition, second printing from Munksgaard became available in 1984.

The Luria method was used by Golden, Purisch, and Hammeke (1985) to develop the Luria-Dakota which later became the Luria-Nebraska Neuropsychological Battery. The qualitative approach advocated by Luria was supplanted by a more empirical one that stressed performance and compared an individual's accomplishment to a norm group of brain-injured adults. A profile was devised to illustrate a person's performance and aid in the interpretation of the results. The materials used in this adaption were those translated and developed by Christensen (1975) with some minor modifications. They were marketed by Spectrum Publications, Incorporated, New York. Subsequently, a children's version (1987) was developed for youngsters between ages 8 and 12. Western Psychological Services (Los Angeles, California) distributes this test and now publishes the Luria-Nebraska Neuropsychological Battery. A collaborative effort by the Finnish researcher Marit Korkman, working with Ursula Kirk, Teachers College, Columbia University, is currently underway to provide a children's version of the original Luria method (A.L. Christensen, personal communication, February 29, 1988). The Luria Neuropsychological Investigation was translated into Spanish in 1974 (first edition) and 1987 (second edition). It is also available in Finnish (1977), German (1979), Swedish (1984), Dutch, and Japanese. The German edition resembles the Luria-Nebraska Neuropsychological Battery because of its quantitative approach (A.L. Christensen, personal communication, February 29, 1988).

The Luria Neuropsychological Investigation test materials consist of a textbook (Christensen, 1984b) that provides certain theoretical perspectives as well as an assessment procedure for each function (e.g., motor) with explanations of behaviors manifested as a result of various lesions. It is suggested that a lesion in the frontal areas is identifiable when a patient who is sitting face to face with the investigator makes a mirror-image reversal of the movements he or she is asked to perform. Another section of the text describes the syndrome of disturbances for various regions (e.g., temporal) of the cortex, its accompanying behavior, and its location. This latter section was organized to adhere to the principle of double dissociation proposed by H. L Teuber (1959) to the effect that a focal brain lesion affects a common factor in a number of processes connected with the function of the affected area, whereas intact functions are not disturbed. The investigator can then check the reliability of the qualitative results. Four case studies are also furnished as examples in the use of the method.

A manual (Christensen, 1984a) is provided that guides the wording for the various tasks or tests administered. Furnished test cards are lettered and numbered to correspond to the different functions to be measured. For example, card G 29 is a drawing of a stack of blocks (Yerkes test) utilized to assess a person's intellectual operations in space, but more specifically spatial synthesis (Luria, 1980).

After a conversation with the examinee regarding his or her awareness of deficiencies, the examiner administers the tasks as part of the preliminary (i.e., testing the receptive analyzers) or selective (i.e., more complex mental functions) aspects of the investigation. The administration seeks to establish the qualitative features of the deficiencies and the intactness of the various functions. The investigation is intended to be used with adults suspected of organic brain damage, but it is so devised so that unaffected adults can accomplish the tasks. The person is assessed with regard to their 1) motor functions, 2) acousticomotor organization, 3) cutaneous and kinesthetic functions, 4) visual-perceptual functions, 5) expressive and impressive (receptive) speech, 6) reading, 7) writing, 8) arithmetic skills, 9) mnestic (memory) abilities, and 10) intellectual processes. An answer form is provided that helps to organize the investigation in gathering information from the preliminary conversation through the various aforementioned functions. The degree of disturbances in each of these areas beginning with motor functions can be rated on a 3-point scale ranging from no disturbance (0), a slight (mild) disturbance (1), to a severe disturbance (2). Another form is furnished and it provides space for the results of the learning experiment and some visual perceptual tasks. Finally, a diagram of five different sections of the cerebral cortex is provided for the plotting of the results and conclusions drawn from the investigation.

Practical Applications/Uses

Luria's Neuropsychological Investigation is not a traditional test (i.e., evaluates achievement performance), but rather a study of motor, sensory, and cognitive deficits in brain-damaged adults. Intact functions are also duly noted. From the onset, the examiner is concerned about how the person under assessment operates in relation to the three principal functional units of the cerebral cortex proposed by Luria. Composed of the reticular formation, higher regions of the brain stem, thalamic region, and the limbic system and its medial zones, the first functional unit is responsible for maintaining cortical tone, the waking state, and the regulation of these in accordance with demands place on them. The second functional unit is primarily responsible for obtaining, processing, and storing information. This unit is located in the lateral regions of the neocortex on the surface of the hemispheres and occupies the posterior regions, which include the auditory, general sensory, and visual areas. The third functional unit is responsible for programming, regulating and verifying mental activity and is located in the anterior regions of the hemispheres.

By conversing with the person being assessed, observing him or her, and then examining the visual, auditory, kinesthetic, and motor analyzers, the investigator can determine the deficits within the first and second functional units respectively. If difficulties are encountered, then more selective complex mental tasks are assessed. The aim is not to determine whether the person can solve the problem presented, but rather how it was solved or failed. The investigator must collaborate with the examinee by explaining the assessment, the problems encountered, and how these might affect his or her life on a daily basis. Hypotheses are generated about the pattern of deficits and further testing may be undertaken to discern the syndrome. After further analysis, a diagnosis is made and, if necessary, rehabilitation of the deficits then can be planned.

As previously mentioned, Golden (1987) and Golden, Purisch, and Hammeke (1985) have developed the method through quantitative means. A scored version was also developed at the Center for Rehabilitation of Brain Damage at the University of Copenhagen by Christensen (personal communication, February 29, 1988) for research purposes.

In addition to being used in clinical practice within a hospital, the Luria Neuropsychological Investigation could be used in rehabilitation (Christensen, 1986a, 1986b) and educational settings. By adapting the presentation of the method, it has been applied to the study of amateur boxers (Thomassen et al., 1979) and Turner's syndrome (Christensen & Nielsen, 1981). Presently, the method is being used by Rosenberg to study patients with conversion hysteria (Christensen, personal communication, February 29, 1988) and the potential exists for it to be used with other psychiatric disorders, such as schizophrenia, and other neurological groups, such as cri du chat syndrome. Research endeavors also need to be undertaken whereby severe and less affected individuals can be distinguished.

This assessment should be administered by individuals who have a background in the following areas: general psychological principles; human growth and development; neuroanatomy; neurophysiology; individual test administration; functions of measurement; clinical, counseling, educational, and school psychology; teaching methodology combined with principles of learning and rehabilitation. They must be sensitive, understanding, and gentle clinicians, who have learned from their own crises because they will encounter many brain-damaged people who are reevaluating their lives after being close to death. From diverse backgrounds and training in clinical, counseling, school, psychophysiological, or developmental psychology, special education, or neurology, users often have become specialized in neuropsychology. Selected parts of the investigation can be performed by speech pathologists, and occupational or physical therapists. Christensen (personal communication, February 29, 1988) has advocated, however, that these latter professionals should function in collaboration with a neuropsychologist.

The investigation is appropriate for assessing most adult individuals suffering from brain damage, with no other requirement necessary other than that the person be in a state of arousal in order to accomplish the tasks. Blind, deaf, and even severely affected individuals, such as aphasia, congenital microphalic mentally retarded adolescents, can be assessed. And it may even be used to differentiate severely depressed people from those suffering from some type of dementia. The investigation can be individually administered in an office or at a bedside. It is not an assessment to be administered to groups. As previously stated, the administrator should be highly qualified, as the conditions of testing vary from individual to individual. Luria would administer the investigation usually in the company of many other professionals studying the method, and the atmosphere was such that anyone could query the examinee. He required that students spend at least four years observing and administering the procedure, which usually begins by conversing with the examinee to ascertain his or her level of arousal, reactions to his or her dilemma, as well as his or her emotional response. An assessment of the visual, auditory, kinesthetic, and motor analyzers is then undertaken. From the accumulated evidence, more specific selected tasks are given to examine the person's expressive and impressive (receptive) speech, reading, writing, arithmetic skills, memory for learning and recall, as well as the intellectual processes abstracting, forming concepts, and problem solving.

Upon completion of the investigation, a clinical neuropsychological conclusion is formulated based on a comparative analysis of the results identifying the fundamental defects. Rehabilitation in the form of functional reorganization can then be planned and undertaken either intrasystemically (i.e., using either a more primitive, automatic level or a higher level of cortical processes) or intersystemically, which is primarily compensatory and relies on a different functional system either at the site of the lesion with unused synaptic receptors or through a larger unit that is intact (e.g., using the visual system to aid proprioception). In order to facilitate rehabilitation, the patient must recognize the defect, take an active part in the remediation, and make an effort to overcome the deficits (Christensen, 1986a, 1986b).

Scores are usually not given, but rather the results of the investigation are qualitatively described with the use of notes gathered during the assessment. Execution of the basic tests is so simple that anyone with at least a third-grade education without specific brain damage should be able to complete them. The textbook (Christensen, 1984b) can serve as a guide to the behaviors manifested during the investigation, but is not really sufficient when compared to the notes made during the assessment. It would appear that the adapted scored version (Christensen, personal communication, February 29, 1988) should be used primarily for research purposes. The interpretation and description of the results will vary according to the investigator's experience with the method, clinical acumen, and how complicated a picture the deficits present. Something is lost with the quantification of performance as well as its deviance from the principles set forth by Luria. A computerized analysis also may not yield as accurate as a picture (Christensen, personal communication, February 29, 1988).

Technical Aspects

Building on the work of Luria (1980), Christensen (1984a, 1984b) has organized and presented a somewhat holistic, phenomenological, individual, qualitative assessment that affords the investigator the opportunity to evaluate deficits in brain-damaged adults and subsequently plan for their rehabilitation. Each of the tasks, tests, or experiments seem to have been selected as a result of the breadth and depth of understanding of the human mind that Luria labored with for some 40 years. If there is any question regarding their "empirical" nature, a review of Luria (1980) would dispel this, because he went to such lengths in searching the neuropsychological literature to acquire what he believed to be the best approaches to studying the human mind and the brain.

Luria's method of investigating individuals with brain damage appeared Socratic in nature, and seemingly the results obtained by the examiner were subjected to scrutiny rather than the assessment method itself. This scrutiny (validation) was usually conducted via neurosurgery or post mortem autopsy. Currently some blood flow studies are being undertaken to investigate the theoretical postulates proposed by Luria regarding his "functional systems" position, although nothing has been published to date (Christensen, personal communication, February 29, 1988). No validity information is presented in the text or manual other than four case studies.

The reliability of the procedure rests with the "double dissociation" principle advocated by H. L. Teuber (1959). This notion contends that when a symptom (A) appears with a lesion in one structure, but not in another, and symptom (B) is found in yet another structure, it should not include symptom (A). If this principle is violated, then specificity or localization of dysfunction is also lacking. When general signs are present, they are usually linked to a unified syndrome (Christensen, 1984b). Other reliability data (e.g., test-retest, internal consistency) are absent from the manual. The adapted psychometric form (Golden, Purisch, & Hammeke, 1985; Golden, 1987) presents reliability and validation information for the method when subjected to statistical analysis and evaluation, although it deviates from the principles proposed by Luria and adhered to by Christensen.

Critique

The Luria Neuropsychological Investigation is a very comprehensive assessment of largely left-hemisphere functioning in brain-damaged adults. The merits of the investigation rest with the sociohistorical context perspective and systematic review and revision by its late author, A. R. Luria, and its proponent, Anne-Lise Christensen. The qualitative manner of the investigation provides valuable information regarding the deficient and intact abilities of the person being assessed that can be used in planning rehabilitation or retraining. This information would be difficult to obtain by purely quantitative means (Christensen, personal communication, February 29, 1988).

The administration and results are dependent on the clinical acumen and expertise of the examiner. To date, there is little training or education in the procedure available within the continental United States. Training in this method can be only obtained through studying with Christensen and her group at the Center of Rehabilitation for Brain Damage in Copenhagen, Denmark. To date, less than a dozen Americans such as Elkhonon Goldberg, Philadelphia, and David Ellis, Camden, New York, are trained in the method (A.L. Christensen, personal communication, February 29, 1988). The procedure requires intensive study and a broad educational background as well as experience and supervision. Golden never studied with Luria or Christensen and this fact raises some question regarding his administrative procedures, the results of each administration, and his research.

Some of the materials contained within the investigation on the accompanying cards are unusual or outdated and need to be replaced. The administration relies on language to mediate performance on the tasks and this may present some difficulties with severely compromised impressive-(receptively) speech-involved people. Again, the adequate evaluation of deficits would rely on the expertise of the administrator. Some revision is also clearly needed in light of recent advances with regard to various cognitive processes, including language.

However, the method is extremely flexible as evidenced by its many adaptions, although these may not be in keeping with Luria's aspirations. The systematic approach to evaluating the brain-damaged person provides recommendations for re-education of deficits that are organized around a theory of brain functioning that is amenable to scientific inquiry, evaluation, and validation.

References

This list includes text citations and suggested additional readings.

Christensen, A.-L. (1975). *Luria's Neurological Investigation* (1st ed.). New York: Spectrum Publications.

Christensen, A.-L. (1979). A practical application of the Luria methodology. *Journal of Clinical Neuropsychology, 1,* 241-247.

Christensen, A.-L. (1984a). *Luria's Neuropsychological Investigation manual* (2nd ed.). Copenhagen: Munksgaard.

Christensen, A.-L. (1984b). *Luria's Neuropsychological Investigation text* (2nd ed.). Copenhagen: Munksgaard.

Christensen, A.-L. (1984c). The Luria method of examination of the brain-impaired patient. In P.E. Logue & J.M. Schear (Eds.), *Neuropsychological rehabilitation* (pp. 5-28). Springfield, IL: Charles C. Thomas.

Christensen, A.-L. (1986). Applying Luria's theory to the rehabilitation process of brain damage. In B. Uzzell & Y. Gross (Eds.), *Clinical neuropsychology of intervention* (pp. 169-177). Boston: M. Nijhoff Publishers.

Christensen, A.-L., & Danielsen, U. (1987). Neuropsychological rehabilitation in Denmark. In M. Meier, L. Diller, & A. Benton (Eds.), *Neuropsychological rehabilitation* (pp. 381-385). New York: The Guilford Press.

Christensen, A.-L., Malmoos, R., & Townes, B. D. (1987). Rehabilitation planned in accordance with the Luria Neuropsychological Investigation: A case history of a patient with left sided aneurysm. *Neuropsychology , 1*(2), 45-48.

Christensen, A.-L., & Nielsen, J. (1981). A neuropsychological investigation of 17 women with Turner's syndrome—A.R. Luria's theory applied to Turner's syndrome. In W. Schmid & J. Nielsen (Eds.), *Human behavior and genetics* (pp. 151–166). Amsterdam: Elsevier/North-Holland Biomedical Press.

Golden, C.L. (1987). *Luria-Nebraska Neuropsychological Battery: Children's revision.* Los Angeles: Western Psychological Services.

Golden, C.L., Purisch, A.D., & Hammeke, T.A. (1985). *Luria-Nebraska Neuropsychological Battery: Forms I & II.* Los Angeles: Western Psychological Services.

Luria, A.R. (1947). *Traumatic aphasia.* Moscow: Moscow University Press. (English translation published in 1970 by Monton, The Hague)

Luria, A.R. (1966). *Higher cortical functions in man* (B. Haigh, Trans.). New York: Basic Books. (Original work published in 1962)

Luria, A.R. (1973). *The working brain: An introduction to neuropsychology* (B. Haigh, Trans.). New York: Basic Books.

Luria, A.R. (1980). *Higher cortical functions in man* (rev. ed., B. Haigh, Trans.). New York: Basic Books.

Reske-Nielsen, E., Christensen, A.-L., & Nielsen, J. (1982). A neuropathological and neuropsychological study of Turner's syndrome. *Cortex, 18,* 181–190.

Teuber, H.L. (1959). Some alterations in behavior after cortical lesion in man. In A.D. Bass (Ed.), *Evolution of nervous control*. Washington: American Association for the Advancement of Science.

Thomassen, A., Juul-Jensen, P., deFine Olivarius, B., Branier, J., & Christensen, A.-L. (1979). Neurological, electroencephalographic and neuropsychological examination of 53 former amateur boxers. *Acta Neurologica Scandinavica, 60*, 352-362.

Dan Zakay, Ph.D.

Senior Lecturer, Department of Psychology, Tel Aviv University, Ramat Aviv, Israel.

MANAGEMENT POSITION ANALYSIS TEST

W. J. Reddin. New Malden, Surrey, England: W. J. Reddin and Associates.

Introduction

The Management Position Analysis Test (MPAT) is a multiple-choice test designed to help a manager to adapt an effective managerial style to a specific managerial position. In order to achieve this purpose, the test was designed to measure both the demands a manager perceives as characterizing his or her particular managerial position and that manager's perception of his or her responses to these demands. It should be emphasized that the MPAT is not a personality test.

The MPAT is based on Reddin's (1967, 1970) 3-D theory of managerial effectiveness. The 3-D theory belongs to situational or contingency leadership theories that negate the conception held by trait theories, namely, that leadership is based on inherent personal characteristics and qualities of the leader. The contingency approach holds that leadership is "the process of influencing the activities of an individual or a group in efforts toward goal achievement in a given situation" (Hersey & Blanchard, 1977, p. 89). The focus in this approach is on observed behavior of leaders and their group members in various situations. This approach opened the door for training leaders because it was believed that "most people can increase their effectiveness in leadership roles through education, training and development" (Hersey & Blanchard, 1977, p. 89).

One of the basic assumptions of contingency theories is that there is not one best leadership style. Instead, leaders should be concerned with being effective in a specific situation by adapting their behavior to the needs of the situation and to their subordinates. Of course, effective leaders must also be aware of their own capabilities. Fiedler (1967) was one of the first to develop a leadership contingency model in which three major situational variables a leader should consider were defined.

Contingency models of leadership state that to be effective, a leader's style must be matched with the demands of the situation (Mitchell, 1984). The 3-D management style theory presented by Reddin was the first, however, to add an effectiveness dimension to leadership models. Reddin (1967) claimed that a useful theoretical model "must allow that a variety of styles may be effective or ineffective depending on the situation" (p. 93).

Recently Reddin (1983) presented a new typology of a leader's behavior. This eight-type typology is built on three independent dimensions: 1) Task Orientation (TO), the extent to which a leader directs his or her efforts, characterized by initiating, organizing, and directing; 2) Relationship Orientation (RO), the extent to which a leader has personal job relationships, characterized by listening, trusting, and encouraging; and 3) Leader Effectiveness (E); the extent to which the leader's

321

behavior is perceived as appropriate to the demands of the situation (Reddin, 1983, pp. 50–51). The possible combinations of being high or low on each one of the three dimensions yield eight types of leadership style:

1) *Separated*—(deserter): low TO, low RO, low E.
2) *Related*—(missionary): low TO, high RO, low E.
3) *Dedicated*—(autocrat): high TO, low RO, E.
4) *Integrated*—(compromiser): high TO, high RO, low E.
5) *Separated* + (bureaucrat): low TO, low RO, high E.
6) *Related* + (developer): low TO, high RO, high E.
7) *Dedicated* + (benevolent autocrat): high TO, low RO, high E.
8) *Integrated* + (executive): high TO, high RO, high E.

Clearly, this typology does not posit a single ideal leadership type. Any one of the four combinations of high and low on the behavior types of TO and RO can be either effective or ineffective, depending on the specific situation. This characteristic of the 3-D theory makes it distinctive from other leadership theories (e.g., McGregor, 1960; Blake & Mouton, 1964; Likert, 1977) that propose a single ideal leadership style. The MPAT scales are designed to enable a manager to gain greater insight into his or her leadership behavior in a specific managerial position in terms of this typology.

As noted, the eight leadership styles in the MPAT are based on the 3-D theory. The test's 20 situational elements were chosen to cover a wide range of situational elements in which a manager might use one or another behavior. A matrix composed of the 20 situational elements × the eight types was used for constructing the statements. A statement describing a typical behavior representing each one of the 160 combinations or an attitude towards it was constructed. Twelve experts and several hundred managers, studying the 3-D theory, evaluated the content validity of each statement and the criterion for the inclusion of a statement was a correct identification of the managerial type described by it by at least 50% of the judges.

Each of the 160 statements appears twice in the test, resulting in 80 sets of four statements. Each set of four statements pertains to either more effective or less effective managerial style, but the 20 situational elements are distributed so as to obtain maximum randomization. The reason each set of four statements is composed of either high or low effectiveness statements is to control for social desirability, "as it was assumed that the mixing of effectiveness levels could bring social desirability effects into play. The two out of four forced choice was used to increase the discrimination power of individual weak items and to further control for social desirability" (Reddin, 1983, p. 97). The test was developed on the basis of testing a core sample of 970 respondents consisting of 892 managers from 23 companies and 78 unrelated individuals who volunteered to participate in the study. The development of the test took place between 1970-1971, and included a test and a retest of the core sample as well as psychometric statistics, such as a factor analysis, which yielded the three factor scores. The norms that are used in the percentile conversion tables are also based on the core samples' scores.

It is claimed that the MPAT is reasonably culture free across the United Kingdom, Canada, and the U.S.

The MPAT consists of a questionnaire, an answer sheet, and an interpretation guide. A manager can self-administer the test, starting with answering the questionnaire and finishing with interpreting the results. On page 1 of the questionnaire, instructions for answering the questions are given. The MPAT consists of 80 sets, each composed of four statements. The respondent is asked to select two statements in each set that best describe what he or she does in the job currently held. In cases where none of the statements apply, the respondent is instructed to select the two statements that best describe what he or she would have done if it had been necessary to make a choice among the four statements. The selection is made by circling the numbers of the chosen statements. A total of 160 statements should be selected and the process should take about an hour.

After completing the questionnaire, the answer sheet, which has 320 consecutive numbers on it, is utilized. The numbers of the statements that were selected in the questionnaire are circled on the answer sheet, which is arranged as a matrix of 20 rows by eight columns. The number of circled numbers in each column, which corresponds to one of the eight leadership types, is counted. The more statements corresponding to a specific type are chosen, the more a manager is assumed to have a tendency to act in his or her position according to that type of leadership behavior. In order to find out these tendencies, the scores obtained in each type are converted to percentile scores. This is done by looking at a conversion table, presented on page 2 of the questionnaire. By following a few simple instructions, percentile scores for the two orientations of TO and RO can be contained also.

By following instructions provided on page 3 of the questionnaire, the number of selected statements in each row is computed to serve as a score for each one of the following situational demands: 1) Superior, 2) Co-workers, 3) Subordinates, 4) Staff Advisors, 5) Union, 6) Customers, 7) General Public, 8) Creativity, 9) Objectives, 10) Planning, 11) Change, 12) Implementation, 13) Controls, 14) Evaluation, 15) Productivity, 16) Communication, 17) Conflict, 18) Errors, 19) Meetings, and 20) Teamwork.

After completing all the calculations on the answer sheet, the respondent moves to the interpretation phase, which should take an additional hour. This is done with the aid of a booklet entitled Management Position Analysis. By following the instructions, three scores representing the following three factors are obtained: 1) Production Demands versus Employee Demands, 2) Team Orientation versus System Orientation, and 3) Independent versus Dependent. These three scores are converted into percentile scores by using the provided conversion table.

The next step calls for a graphic representation on a chart of the eight behavior types' percentile scores obtained from the answer sheet. Similar representations are made for the two orientation scores, the three factor scores, and the situational elements. To interpret his or her scores, the respondent refers to page G of the Management Position Analysis booklet, where each one of the obtained scores is defined briefly. Another booklet, entitled Interpretation Guide, presents the 3-D theory and describes in detail each one of the eight leadership types, the two orientations, the three factors, and the situational elements, as well as offering examples of interpreted profiles.

Practical Applications/Uses

The MPAT is an interesting instrument that can be used by organizational and managerial consultants in several ways: a) to analyze a new managerial position one is going to enter and to plan one's managerial style; b) to analyze a current managerial situation in order to gain insight into what should be changed in one's behavior or in the situational elements in order to increase managerial effectiveness; c) to aid in evaluating the level of fitness of a candidate for a specific managerial position; d) to aid in designing managerial jobs and in assigning managers to different positions within the context of an organizational development and as a training tool in general management training.

The MPAT is designed and offered as a "do it yourself" test. This method of application, however, is not recommended by this reviewer. It should be understood that the MPAT is not a diagnostic test with a known predictive and ecological validity. It can be a very helpful and thought-provoking tool when used by an expert for raising useful hypotheses. Self-scoring and interpretation by naive managers, however, might be misleading. Reddin (1983) himself indicates that

> The test seems to meet reasonable criteria for its use. The most cautious and general interpretation is that MPAT is a measure of self-perceived and self-reported attitudes, feelings, beliefs, and behaviors concerning aspects of the work situation. The bolder but reasonable interpretation is that MPAT is a test of ten types of behavior. (p. 116)

Reddin (1983) adds that "MPAT measures at least some of the types it claims to measure" (p. 111).

It should be made clear that the MPAT is mainly a test of behavior types and managerial orientations stemming from the 3-D theory. It is essential that any user of the MPAT be able to understand the theory before using the suggested interpretation. The acquaintance with the theory should be made after completing the questionnaire but before carrying out the interpretation.

Several problems that have to do with ecological validity should be taken into consideration while interpreting the MPAT.

1) The statements included in the MPAT were chosen arbitrarily, and it is not clear whether it represents the whole population of relevant managerial behaviors and situational elements.

2) As mentioned earlier, the MPAT's scores are not unequivocal.

3) The definition of a managerial position is not clear-cut, and the instructions given to respondents are not sufficient. This is an important point, because a complex managerial task can be divided into several specific managerial positions.

4) The norms on which the scoring is based were calculated on the basis of a sample of volunteers who responded by mail. This might be a biased sample, a problem of which Reddin himself is aware. It was presumed that the combination of the voluntary and confidential elements would increase the accuracy of the data collected, but the methodological problems involved with these two elements is well known.

5) It should be remembered that the MPAT is culture free only for North American and English managerial cultures. This should be taken into consideration while working with managers from related or foreign managerial cultures.

6) The norms are based on the core sample's scores collected around 1970. It is possible that these norms are no longer valid in the 1980s, even in the managerial culture represented by the core sample. The technological innovations that charac-

terize the work environment, such as automation, the introduction of computers, and the automated office, as well as fast computerized communication channels undoubtedly have changed many parameters of managerial effectiveness (Zakay, 1984). This topic should be examined and, perhaps, the MPAT should be adapted to the new technological era.

7) The scoring of the MPAT is quite complicated and tedious. It is advisable to develop a personal computer version that will compute the scores automatically.

Technical Aspects

An impressive empirical and psychometric effort was invested in order to assess the reliability and validity of the MPAT.

Test-retest reliabilities of 1-week to 3-month intervals were conducted and are reported to range between .56 to .85.

The content validity of the MPAT's statements was assessed by eight judges who were asked to sort the 160 statements according to leadership style. The percent right ranged between 59.3% for integrated + and 85% for separated –. In a second study, a high degree of agreement (64% to 100%) was achieved by 10 judges on whether a statement reflected greater or lesser effectiveness.

Scale intercorrelations, computed on the core sample's scores, range between –.76 to .73, and the correlations between the scores of each situational element and each leadership type are above .2 for 89% of the cases.

The construct validity of the MPAT was tested by correlating its scores with the following instruments measuring similar behaviors: 1) Least Preferred Co-workers (LPC) (Fiedler, 1967), 2) My Organization (MO) (Hall, 1961), 3) The Work Environment Preference Schedule (Gordon, 1970), and 4) Leadership Opinion Questionnaire (LQC) (Fleishman, 1969). This was carried out among a sample of 68 respondents and the obtained correlations, which ranged from –.41 to .43, were all significant and were found to be in the expected direction. No significant correlations were found in unexpected directions. This was not true, however, for the LPC, for which no significant correlations were found.

MPAT's validity was tested additionally against direct observations of managers' behaviors in a managerial effectiveness seminar. Seventy-seven managers were appraised and their behavioral scores were compared with their MPAT scores. In most cases, no significant differences were found.

In four other studies, it was found that the types of leadership behaviors were related to what was hypothesized for four independent variables including situational changes, birth order, personality traits as measured by the 16PF, and technology as measured by job function (Reddin, 1983, chapters 7–11).

It might be concluded that the reliability of the MPAT as measured by a test-retest process is intermediate, but it is still at the common level of reported reliabilities for similar tests. The content and construct validities of the MPAT, though not high, can be considered satisfactory. There are, however, some important considerations concerning the structure and psychometric characteristics of the MPAT that should be kept in mind.

1) It is not clear how the sets of four specific statements were constructed. It

might be that different combinations of statements might lead to different choice patterns. This point was not tested.

2) Reddin (1983) stated that the "He" rather than the "I" format was used for each statement in order to place the respondent in more objective frame of mind in considering his or her response to his or her situation. In the second edition of the MPAT the "I" form is used. No reference to the implications of this change is given in Reddin (1983).

3) A serious problem relates to the fact that each statement is replicated twice. This has two implications: a) it tenders all the correlational studies reported by Reddin (1983) somewhat problematic because of the internal dependency created within each respondent, and b) the scores are based on the number of items chosen that correspond to each behavior type. An assumption of a hierarchical scale is hidden here; namely, that if the same statement is chosen twice, the tendency toward the specific type is greater than in the case where the statement is chosen only once. One can argue, however, that the case where the same statement is chosen and not chosen in the same test has a completely different meaning, similar to an internal instability.

4) The factor analysis was conducted on 320 items and the sample of 970 subjects is too small for such an analysis (Nunnally, 1967). Moreover, the factor analysis was not validated. While conducting a factor analysis the first time, the obtained factors should be treated as hypotheses only and tested again on another independent sample.

Turning once again to the problem of validity, the ecological and predictive validity of the MPAT is not clear and should be treated cautiously.

Critique

In sum, the MPAT is an interesting and useful tool recommended for use by professionals. MPAT's users should be familiar with the 3-D theory on which the MPAT is based. The interpretation should be made with caution, bearing in mind all the reservations raised in the present review.

It is recommended that the MPAT be adapted to the technological environment that will characterize the late 1980s and the 1990s.

References

Blake, R.R., & Mouton, J.S. (1964). *The managerial grid*. Houston: Gulf.

Fiedler, E.F. (1967). *A theory of leadership effectiveness*. New York: McGraw-Hill.

Fleishman, E.A. (1969). *Manual for Leadership Opinion Questionnaire*. Chicago: Science Research Associates.

Gordon, L.V. (1970). Measurement of bureaucratic orientation. *Personnel Psychology, 23,* 1–11.

Hall, R. (1961). *An empirical study of bureaucratic dimensions*. Unpublished doctoral dissertation, Ohio State University, Columbus.

Hersey, P., & Blanchard, K.H. (1977). *Management of organizational behavior: Utilizing human resource*. Englewood Cliffs, NJ: Prentice Hall.

Likert, R. (1977). Management styles and the human component. *Management Review, 66,* 23–28, 43–35.

McGregor, D.V. (1960). *The human side of enterprise.* New York: McGraw-Hill.

Mitchell, T.R. (1984). *People in organizations.* New York: McGraw-Hill.

Nunnally, J.C. (1967). *Psychometric theory.* New York: McGraw-Hill.

Reddin, W.J. (1967, April). The 3-D management style theory. *Training and Development Journal,* pp. 8–17.

Reddin, W.J. (1970). *Managerial effectiveness.* New York: McGraw-Hill.

Reddin, W.J. (1983). *Management effectiveness & style—individual or situation.* Unpublished manuscript.

Zakay, D. (1984). Organizational human engineering: The design and implementation of computerized systems. In H.W. Hendrick & O. Brown (Eds.), *Human factors in organizational design and management* (pp. 575–579). Amsterdam: North Holland.

Edward E. Gotts, Ph.D.
Director of Psychology, Madison State Hospital, Madison, Indiana, and Principal Investigator, Appalachia Educational Laboratory (AEL), Inc., Charleston, West Virginia.

MARYLAND PARENT ATTITUDE SURVEY

Donald K. Pumroy. College Park, Maryland: Donald K. Pumroy, Ph.D.

Introduction

The Maryland Parent Attitude Survey (MPAS) examines four parental attitudes toward child rearing: disciplinarian, indulgent, protective, and rejecting. Although other procedures had been used before to measure these or closely related parent attitudes, the MPAS was designed to eliminate or reduce a problem shared by its predecessors. Specifically, previous child-rearing attitude measures could result in erroneous or invalid scores due to respondents answering the items in a "socially desirable" manner. That is, prior child-rearing attitude measures permitted respondents to answer on the basis of how they might wish to appear to others and/or to themselves in order to be well regarded. Thus, socially desirable responding might distort a respondent's measured attitudes. The MPAS was designed to reduce or eliminate this source of attitude measurement error.

Donald K. Pumroy, Ph.D., developer and publisher of the MPAS, is a clinical psychologist. He specializes in clinical child issues and practices behavior modification. He is Professor of Education and Psychology at the University of Maryland. Dr. Pumroy became interested during his graduate student days in the assessment of parents' child-rearing attitudes. At the same time he became aware of the need to control for social desirability responding. Cver the next 12 years he developed and tested the MPAS through a series of studies.

Since 1966, several researchers other than Dr. Pumroy have continued to use and study the MPAS. Thus, in order to understand the current status of the MPAS, it is necessary to review selected studies by other investigators. Together, these studies have generated meaningful knowledge about this instrument. Without the contributions of other researchers, the MPAS would have remained unchanged from Pumroy's (1966) original published description of it.

Pumroy has kept the MPAS active and available by supplying it for a nominal fee to those who request it. The MPAS packet contains the following: a research article on the MPAS (Pumroy, 1966), which serves as the manual; the MPAS booklet of attitude statements; scoring keys for the MPAS, used for assigning the statements to the four attitude scales; and standard scores (norms) for each of the four scales. Included with the packet is a cover letter that, among other things, grants the user permission to reproduce the materials. In this manner, Pumroy has encouraged research applications of this measure.

The norms, as published in the standard score table, are based on a relatively small sample (95 males, 93 females) of mostly young adults. The average age of the males was 20.8 years; the average age of the females was 18.5 years. The source of this particular sample of 188 is not identified in the table nor in Pumroy's (1966) journal article, but it can be inferred from other sources (e.g., Slough, Kogan, & Tyler, 1978) that the sample consisted of college students, most of whom likely were not parents. Brody (1965, 1969), however, used the MPAS with a group of mothers of preschool children prior to Pumroy's 1966 report—a fact of which Pumroy was aware as evidenced by his citing of Brody's work in his report. Yet, not until much later were a set of norms for parents published by Slough, Kogan, and Tyler (1978) Slough et al. reported means for 167 mothers of preschool children and compared their scores with those of a sample of 187 females mentioned in Pumroy (1966, Table 1) who were not the same sample as the females in Pumroy's published norm tables. These researchers (Slough et al., 1978, Table 3) also report scores obtained from small samples of parents of developmentally delayed children: 55 mothers and 38 fathers. To date, no other norms have been reported. Therefore, as with many experimental measures, the researcher must decide whether to apply the norms that exist or to develop his or her own. In any event, as Pumroy (1966) has acknowledged, the MPAS is strictly to be viewed as a research instrument and not a clinical tool, thereby rendering the issue of available norms considerably less important.

There is a single published version of the MPAS, although the present reviewer, as later reported below, and others (Brody, 1965; Willerman & Plomin, 1973) have used parts of the MPAS or made adaptations of it for use in their own studies. No information is available on the level of literacy or reading skill required of MPAS respondents. However, based on the reviewer's experience, most adults who read at an eighth-grade level or higher should have little difficulty comprehending the attitude statements. Oral administration to nonreaders would be difficult because the respondent would have to remember the two statements of each pair while comparing them in order to make some quite challenging personal value and performance discriminations—all without being able to review the actual statements by visual scanning as would a literate respondent.

The MPAS Booklet is a paper-and-pencil measure that can be written on directly, or the user could prepare a revised set of instruments for responding, so that answer choices would be registered on separate machine- or hand-scorable sheets. The MPAS booklet first instructs the respondent that its content focuses on parents' child-rearing attitudes by means of 95 pairs of attitude statements. The respondent is directed to select one of the two statements that most nearly resembles his or her attitude. It further admits that even though the choices may be difficult at times, the respondent should select the one most resembling his or her viewpoint or to select the initial reaction. The following example is suggested by Pumroy to illustrate how a typical pair of statements will be presented:

(A) Parents should like their children.
(B) Parents frequently find children a burden.

The 95 numbered pairs of statements immediately follow the preceding instructions.

It is understood that the respondent will read and answer each item without further instructions or assistance from the examiner. Hence, this instrument is suitable for administration to individuals or groups of literate adults who are capable of working on their own. Whereas the instrument is intended for use with parents, it is evident that it can be administered to adolescents or young adults who are not parents, if they otherwise can meet the instrument response demands.

No forms have been developed for displaying or reporting results back to respondents, nor has this typically been done in the MPAS studies reported.

Practical Applications/Uses

The MPAS is designed to measure four important attitudes toward child rearing. The following characteristics distill the essential ingredients of each of the MPAS core attitudes.

1. *Indulgent*—Parents having a relatively more indulgent attitude are basically child centered, generous, and loving. This is not to be confused with an indifferent, permissive, or laissez-faire attitude, because these latter attitudes do not include necessarily high expression of affection or emotional involvement. All of the foregoing attitudes, however, imply an unwillingness on the parents' part to set limits upon or regulate a child's behavior or to use consequences as a means of gaining compliance or promoting development. It would appear that indulgent parents seek the companionship of their children, cater to their needs and desires, lavish goods upon them, relieve them of unpleasant chores, and, of course, avoid restricting them.

2. *Rejecting*—These parents are obviously hostile toward their children. Their hostile feelings are easily and openly expressed in the disciplinary measures they use. That is, they are not so much oriented to changing a child's behavior as to inflicting punishment for some infraction or perceived shortcoming. These parents often arrange schedules and activities in ways that minimize the time they and their children will be together or will interact. They view children as being deliberately disobedient at times. The rejecting parent perceives children as reciprocating the hostile, negative feelings that the parent has toward them.

3. *Disciplinarian*—Parents expressing a high amount of this attitude value most highly the child's obedience and conformity to their expectations. Discipline is used freely, even generously. It is administered in a fair, consistent manner that is calculated to produce desired conformity. That is, these parents do not feel especially hostile toward their children, and hostile communication is not the objective of their discipline. Because they expect obedience, back-talk or argument is not welcome and may prompt additional discipline. One senses that these parents push their children, sometimes unreasonably, to demonstrate conformity to standards beyond their level of development. This suggests that they urgently want to see their children grow up and act like conforming adults. They measure their success or merit as parents by their children's obedience.

4. *Protective*—These parents are especially sensitive to the risks and dangers that their children face in growing up. That is, their children may be injured, fail, get into trouble, associate with improper companions, eat the wrong foods, make bad decisions, become upset, and so forth. Their view is that the world is a bit too much for children to handle, and the implication is that their concern or anxiety about this leads them to shelter their children, do things for them that they should be able

to do for themselves, monitor them closely, and insist that they know what is going on with them, including what they are thinking and feeling. The objective of this considerable intrusiveness and interference with development is that they shall succeed in protecting their children from harm.

The purpose of the MPAS is to measure the four preceding attitudes accurately by reducing the influence of social desirability upon the answers given. Having, then, a proper estimate of the four scores will suggest for an individual or a group the relative priority given to each attitude compared to the remaining three. In turn, the relative balance among the four attitudes will suggest a parent's preferred approach to child rearing and may indicate in part the style of parenting that will be followed.

Professionals and researchers who have an interest in these fundamental attitudes may be attracted to the MPAS as a research tool. The following suggested uses for the MPAS exceed the scope of applications currently supported in published reports. The MPAS could be used, for example, in prenatal classes, groups studying child abuse, family-life education, child development courses, child guidance centers, clinics offering child and family services, parent discussions sponsored by schools or community organizations, self-help groups, and so on. These contexts suggest that the applications may span secondary level and college students, young adults, more experienced parents, and those who are having special challenges or difficulties with child-rearing issues. The MPAS may be used in educational/ preventative, ameliorative/remedial, and to a more limited extent, corrective/therapeutic efforts. Potential applications include those for individuals, families, and groups. Measurement uses for which the MPAS may be suited include personal understanding or exploration, program evaluation, descriptions of participants or service-seekers, needs assessment, and monitoring of attitude change. Although the MPAS has potential in applications to psychological assessment and legal-forsenic matters such as child custody, further research would be needed to establish validity for specific types of inferences.

Practitioners and researchers from the following disciplines/professions may desire or need to measure the attitudes sampled by the MPAS: social work, counseling and guidance, school and clinical psychology, family-life education, child development, parent education, community mental health, program evaluation, family therapy, and psychiatry. Those with whom professionals would use the instrument are adolescents who could become parents and parents who are literate in English. Use with nonreaders would be difficult due to the respondents' need to shift attention back and forth in a self-paced manner between the two attitude statements of a pair, while deciding which one is most descriptive of their attitude.

Administration is comparable to that of all group-type instruments. Respondents are expected to work alone at their own pace. Upon completion, they return materials to the examiner. The examiner is present to distribute materials, give brief standard instructions, answer questions to clarify the procedure, and remain available to answer individual questions as they arise. It is the respondent's responsibility to identify issues for which he or she needs clarification. No special training is required to administer the MPAS. Estimates of the time required for administration have varied from 30 to 45 minutes.

Some years ago, this reviewer used the MPAS and several other instruments in a longitudinal study of how the child-rearing practices of rural and small-town parents related to their children's educational progress (Gotts, 1983; Gotts & Purnell, 1986). During a pilot study with 30 parents in 1978, a special administration problem occurred. The parents complained strongly about the forced choice (*A*- or *B*-statement) format. Moreover, they left about 10% of the items unanswered. Because this reaction had not been reported before, Dr. Pumroy was consulted. He had not encountered this reaction either and, furthermore, he no longer had information on how his subjects had responded to individual survey items. Because the use of item studies was impossible, the magnitude of the number of blanks in the pilot study and in Pumroy's published sample (Pumroy, 1966, Table 1) was analyzed. Whereas the mothers in the pilot study left about 10% of the items unanswered, less than 1% of the items in Pumroy's female sample were unanswered. No problems of this sort existed with the pilot study sample when they were presented items of other instruments that were not in a forced-choice format. The issue was not one of literacy. Consequently, a major format revision of the MPAS was developed before it could be used in the main study (Gotts & Purnell, 1986). This experience emphasizes the importance of pretesting an experimental measure like the MPAS whenever it will be administered to subjects who differ from those previously studied.

Scoring the MPAS is very straightforward and is a clerical-level activity. It takes perhaps 5 minutes. The first five items are not scored. Items 6 through 95 have both their A and B statements assigned to the four attitude scales, according to the key provided by Pumroy. No differential weights are assigned to item responses; instead, each item is given the value of 1 point. On this basis, an individual who answered all 90 items as instructed will receive a total of 90 points. These points are allocated among the four scales. No instructions are given for treating blank items or items with both choices marked, nor is the user told how to adjust scale scores if such improperly completed items are found in a record. Methods of handling missing data are reported in the psychometric literature, which should be consulted in the event that this question arises. For example, Dahlstrom, Welsh, and Dahlstrom (1972) discuss in a number of places the meaning and treatment of MMPI "cannot say" responses and provide a table (Appendix K) for adjusting scores based on the number of missing or "cannot say" items. A variety of possible treatments of such missing or absent responses is suggested by the "missing values" options available in SPSS (Hull & Nie, 1981). No scoring services are available, but the user easily could design a machine-scoring procedure if desired.

Because interpretation of the MPAS results is not considered in Pumroy's (1966) report, the four expanded attitude descriptions were presented previously to suggest what the respondent is saying about his or her attitudes. Generally, the user initially will focus interpretation on any score that is markedly higher than the others (each scale has a possible maximum score of 45). Often the contrasting lowest score will offer additional insight into the individual respondent's overall perspective. Considering the very tentative status of the present norms, it would be prudent to develop one's own norms, using descriptive statistics based on the sample(s) being studied. The user may develop additional perspectives on interpretation by weighing the collateral evidence for the MPAS's measurement properties carefully.

Technical Aspects

Split-half reliabilities were computed for the MPAS, using the Spearman-Brown formula to correct for attenuation due to decreased instrument length (Pumroy, 1966). The subjects for this study were 45 male and 45 female college students. The males' coefficients range from .675 to .758 for the four scales and the corresponding range for the females was from .666 to .843. It is interesting to note that the Indulgent score had the least split-half internal consistency of the four scales for males, while it had the highest internal consistency for the females. The least consistent scale for females was Rejecting. Pumroy (1966) also reports test-retest coefficients from .622 to .730 for another group of 30 males and 24 female college students. These test-retest coefficients are actually also stability coefficients, because the elapsed time between administrations was about 3 months. No other reliability studies were located.

One of Pumroy's (1966) central design objectives was to control for social desirability as a way of averting what Becker and Krug (1965) had noted was an essential source of response bias in the MPAS's predecessor, the Parent Attitude Research Instrument (PARI) (Schaeffer & Bell, 1958). Pumroy's method for accomplishing this was to subject the entire pool of attitude statements to a procedure intended to ascertain their social desirability values (Edwards, 1957). He had 178 subjects (including slightly more females than males, drawn about equally from among high school seniors, college students, and PTA parents) assume a response set to answer the items as a "good" parent would. They registered these judgments by indicating whether they thought a good parent would strongly agree (SA), agree (A), disagree (D), or strongly disagree (SD) with each statement. Later, using the computed percentages for the categories from SA through SD for each statement, Pumroy formed the pairs of statements that now appear together as items in the MPAS, so that the members of a pair were matched for social desirability, but belonged to two different attitude categories. He evaluated the extent to which this effort was successful in another study (Pumroy, 1966) by computing the relationship between each MPAS scale and a social desirability scale constructed by Edwards (1957). No details of this study are reported, except that the four correlations were quite small (–.17 to .19), thus confirming that the MPAS scales are relatively free of this influence (Pumroy, 1966). Tolor (1967) performed a similar study with two samples using the Marlowe-Crowne social desirability scale (Crowne & Marlowe, 1960) and once more found that the MPAS scales were not greatly influenced by a response set or bias of this type.

When constructing the MPAS, Pumroy (1966) enlisted nine psychologists to examine each attitude statement and assign it to one of five categories: the four previously discussed plus a fifth category, *Indifferent*. If six of the nine psychologists agreed on the placement ($p = .016$), then it was assigned to that category. Pumroy (1966) asserts that agreement at this level resulted in face validity. This method also produced scale content validity. The psychologists agreed on assignments to three categories but could not discriminate between Rejecting and Indifferent items. Consequently, Pumroy combined these items into a single category and labeled it Rejecting. The implication of assignment to four different categories is not that the attitudes are wholly independent—only that they are discriminable.

It is, thus, important to describe the extent to which the attitudes may be related to one another.

An inherent problem exists in the estimation of the foregoing relationships, however, because the scales are not statistically independent of one another. That is, the forced-choice format produces a measurement dependence among the scales; getting higher scores on some scales necessarily results in lower scores on others. These types of measurement-interdependent scales, of a series of qualities within an individual, are known as ipsative. Because of this statistical dependence, the assumptions are not met for the Pearson product-moment correlation. It is, nevertheless, sometimes used for descriptive purposes, with the understanding that it is not being used for inferential purposes.

Three published studies (Brody, 1965; Pumroy, 1966; Tolor, 1967) plus this reviewer's unpublished findings have involved estimations of the intercorrelations among the four MPAS scales. The consistency among the four sets of findings is impressive. In the following conclusions, the first two coefficients are for Tolor's (1967) two samples, the third for Pumroy's (1966), the fourth for Brody's (1965), and the fifth for the reviewer's findings from the study described in Gotts (1983). Indulgent and Disciplinarian attitudes are strongly negatively related (-.47, -74, -.69, -.75, -.57); Rejecting and Protective attitudes are strongly inversely related (-.56, -.53, -.55, -.62, -.47). Generally, much smaller relationships are found in the remaining comparisons. These suggest that Protective and Disciplinarian attitudes and Rejecting and Disciplinarian attitudes are both negatively correlated but at such minimal levels as to have little psychological meaning. Slightly larger negative relations appear between Rejecting and Indulgent attitudes (-.27, -.26, -.39, -.33, -.23) and Protective and Indulgent attitudes (-.34, -.07, -.20, -.11, -.31), but again, they are quite small relationships when compared to the first two noted above.

Brody (1965) studied the relationships between the four MPAS scales and the PARI's (Schaeffer & Bell, 1958) three scales (Authoritarian, Hostility-Rejection, and Democratic). All of these relationships are relatively modest, ranging from -.40 to .30. Four of 12 relationships reached statistical signficance: Rejecting and Democratic (-.40), Disciplinarian and Authoritarian (.30), Indulgent and Hostility-Rejection (-.30), and Indulgent and Democratic (.29). From these findings it is evident that the MPAS and PARI are measuring quite different attitudes.

Evidence for the construct validity of the scales has not been developed systematically, but there are some fragmentary results of interest. Pumroy (1966) found that males received higher Disciplinarian scores and females had higher Indulgent scores; older subjects had lower Disciplinarian and higher Rejecting scores, a finding that was replicated (Pumroy, 1966; Slough et al., 1978). Mothers of handicapped children had MPAS attitudes differing from those of other mothers (Slough et al., 1978). In an interactive play situation, Disciplinarian mothers were both more restricting and directing of their children; Rejecting mothers were more forbidding (Brody, 1965); and the PARI failed to predict parent behaviors in play situations. Pumroy (1966) observed that Rejecting parents had poorer attendance at discussion groups; Disciplinarian parents attended more consistently. The child-rearing attitudes of mothers and fathers were not significantly correlated for Indulgent and only modestly for Disciplinarian and Rejecting; these findings were comparable whether the attitudes pertained to sons or daughters (Willerman & Plomin, 1973). On the other hand, these same researchers learned that parents of boys had highly similar Protective attitudes ($r = .82$), while their Protective attitudes were not significantly similar if they had daughters.

An even smaller number of findings relate the MPAS attitudes of parents to their children's behavior. Using a brief, highly modified version of the MPAS, Willerman and Plomin (1973) found that parents whose scores were less Protective or less Indulgent had sons who were more active, but this relationship was not present for daughters. Indulgent and less Disciplinarian parents had children with an internality-externality orientation (or locus of control) similar to their own (Davis & Phares, 1969). These authors suggest that nurturing and accepting parent behavior may mediate the development of child-parent similarity. In a later phase of her data analysis, Brody (1969) found that high Disciplinarian mothers had children who used more "directing" behaviors toward their mothers during interactive play. She interpreted that these behaviors were due to a possible modeling effect. She further found that high Rejecting mothers' children less attentively observed their mothers, sought less information from them, spent more time playing independently as opposed to interactively, complied less frequently with mothers' requests, and sought more of their mothers' approval, praise, and attention. Brody did not explore relations between Indulgent and Protective attitudes and young children's behavior, so the absence of reporting on these was not due to a failure to find relationships.

These findings indicate that the MPAS does not measure merely interesting attitudes. Instead, the attitudes appear to have meaningful relationships to other parent and child characteristics and behaviors. Thus, the MPAS has the possibility of serving as a valid measure, with the extent of its applicability still remaining unknown. Considering the small number of studies that have used the MPAS compared to the PARI 12 (e.g., Becker & Krug, 1965), the MPAS has an impressive early record and the PARI a longer and disappointing one.

Critique

The development of the MPAS since 1966 has been largely a matter of chance, as Pumroy's responsibilities and interests have pulled him away from performing additional studies with it. Unfortunately, he has had neither an official nor an unofficial successor to be the instrument's advocate or repository. In the late 1960s, it appeared that Brody might exert the sustained imagination and empirical forcefulness required to move the instrument's development forward. This has not materialized, although her work with the MPAS has been among the best. In view of these circumstances, the continued interest shown in the MPAS has been encouragingly significant and disappointingly fragmented. In the area of parent attitude measures, it is difficult to think of another instrument that has produced so large a number of interpretable results from such a small volume of studies conducted in so piecemeal a fashion. This reviewer is impressed by that.

This reviewer is compelled to believe that the MPAS captured a worthwhile sample of variance that relates little to response bias and much to those aspects of attitude that correlate with other real behavior. Pumroy learned well what Allen

Edwards (1957) had earlier discovered about social desirability, including a methodology of item construction that substantially controls for this tendency.

Compared with the PARI (Schaeffer & Bell, 1958) the MPAS is a less theoretically sophisticated instrument, lacking the PARI's linkages to an intuitively appealing dimensionalized circumplex model. Yet in 1977, as the staff of the HOPE Follow-Up Study (Gotts, 1983) was selecting and adapting parent measures, the literature on the two measures suggested that the MPAS was the better instrument. The decision to use the MPAS was based to a certain extent on the early empirical promise it then showed, partly because the social desirability issue was fundamental and partly because its four identified child-rearing attitudes represented meaningful constructs to the staff and probably to parent respondents as well.

Judging that an instrument covers meaningful constructs is germane to the processes of establishing the construct validity of a measure. In 1977, the PARI constructs of Authoritarian and Democratic seemed too global and seemed to belong more in the personality rather than the child-rearing domain. Moreover, the PARI constructs were heavily loaded with meaning of an evaluative sort: good versus bad, close-minded versus enlightened, etc. They seemed to have less to do with how one behaves and more to do with issues of self-image. The latter perspective can be an occasion for impression management that is oriented to both self and others. Thus, the PARI constructs were flawed by the level at which they were conceptualized, with child-rearing being at another level. For this reason, the flaw probably could not be controlled by psychometric means for social desirability. The MPAS's constructs and the item contents representing them are tied more directly to intuitions and assumptions that readily surface in parents' thinking about what children are like, what they need or what is good for them, and what parents should do or are justified in doing. They represent the kinds of things that parents are going to think and do because they believe in them, and disagreement by others will not shake the parents' assumptions. Even if the child-rearing results are disappointing or counterproductive, these are the kinds of positions to which people hold fast. Furthermore, they represent attitudes that are embedded in interpersonal action systems that quite naturally lead to behavior more than to preoccupation with the self-image. Pumroy's selection of these particular palpable constructs (in contrast with the PARI's more global and remote constructs) could be traced to his personal intellectual history of a solid grounding in behavioral theory. This would have led him to seek child-rearing attitude constructs that were at appropriate levels to mesh with interpersonal action systems.

Now it can be made known that even the MPAS's fortuitously chosen constructs could be rendered at a more remote and abstract level, so that they would more properly mesh with global aspects of personality. For example, imagine that one hypotheorizes a "self-indulgent" personality type complete with propositions such as: child as a pampered extension of the parent's ego; gratuities dispensed to child as way of vicariously satisfying parent's own desire; parent unable to establish full separation from the child; and so forth. This example is not intended as a comment on personality theorizing as such; it only illustrates the issue of the level at which one construes a construct. Suppose now that one proceeds to prepare items on child rearing from a more fully developed version of "self-indulgent parent" as opposed to a "parent with an indulgent attitude toward child rearing."

Inevitably the items will be cast at different conceptual levels. The former will be more global and remote from actual child-rearing behavior.

It is for the foregoing reason that this reviewer closely restricted the descriptions of the four attitudes under "Practical Applications/Uses" to an action-system level. That is, this reviewer refrained from commenting upon other possibly interesting personality correlates of the four attitudes, except as these might have a more or less direct bearing on the actions of child rearing. With this "concept containment" strategy in mind, a user of the MPAS might justifiably proceed, as it were, to further fill up the four attitude containers with relevant descriptive, behavioral content—the more so as experience is gained in the use of the scales. However, if the concept containment strategy is followed, one should be wary not to extend the concepts' boundaries, and especially not unwittingly to shift the concepts to more abstract or personological levels. Herein lies part of the genius of Pumroy's work— that he selected interpersonal-action-system-compatible attitude constructs and that he populated them with item content representing feelings, assumptions, and actions inherent in child rearing.

References

Becker, W.C., & Krug, R.S. (1965). The Parental Attitude Research Inventory—a research review. *Child Development, 36,* 329–365.

Brody, G.F. (1965). Relationships between maternal attitudes and behavior. *Journal of Personality and Social Psychology, 2,* 317–323.

Brody, G.F. (1969). Maternal child-rearing attitudes and child behavior. *Developmental Psychology, 1,* 66.

Crowne, D.P., & Marlowe, D. (1960). A new scale of social desirability independent of psychopathology. *Journal of Consulting Psychology, 24,* 349–354.

Dahlstrom, W.G., Welsh, G.S., & Dahlstrom, L.E. (1972). An MMPI handbook: Vol. 1. Clinical interpretation. (rev. ed.). Minneapolis: University of Minnesota Press.

Davis, W.L., & Phares, E.S. (1969). Parental antecedents of internal-external control of reinforcement. *Psychological Reports, 24,* 427–436.

Edwards, A.L. (1957). *The social desirability variable in personality assessment and research.* New York: Dryden Press.

Gotts, E.E. (1983). Home-based early intervention. In A.W. Childs & G.B. Melton (Ed.), *Rural psychology* (pp. 337–358). New York: Plenum.

Gotts, E.E., & Purnell, R.F. (1986). Families and schools in rural Appalachia. *American Journal of Community Psychology, 14,* 499–520.

Hull, C.H., & Nie, N.H. (Eds.). (1981). *SPSS update 7–9. New procedures and facilities for releases 7–9.* New York: McGraw-Hill.

Pumroy, D.K. (1966). Maryland Parent Attitude Survey: A research instrument with social desirability controlled. *The Journal of Psychology, 64,* 73–78.

Schaeffer, E.S., & Bell, R.Q. (1958). Development of a parent attitude research instrument. *Child Development, 29,* 339–361.

Slough, N.M., Kogan, K.L., & Tyler, N.B. (1978). Derivation of parent norms for the Maryland Parent Attitude Survey: Application to parents of developmentally delayed children. *Psychological Reports, 42,* 183–189.

Tolor, A. (1967). An evaluation of the Maryland Parent Attitude Survey. *The Journal of Psychology, 67,* 69–74.

Willerman, L., & Plomin, R. (1973). Activity level in children and their parents. *Child Development, 44,* 854–858.

Leonard J. West, Ph.D.
Professor of Education, Baruch College, The City University of New York, New York, New York.

MINNESOTA CLERICAL TEST

The Psychological Corporation. San Antonio, Texas: The Psychological Corporation.

Introduction

The Minnesota Clerical Test (MCT), originally published in 1933 as the Minnesota Vocational Test for Clerical Workers, is intended for use in selecting people to fill a variety of clerical jobs. The content of the MCT has remained unchanged over the years; however, the test manual, published in 1979, replaces the earlier manual published in 1959. The authors of the revised manual (Dorothy M. Andrew, Donald G. Paterson, and Howard P. Longstaff) have established qualifications as psychometricians. The new manual provides updated information (normative, reliability, and validity data) for evaluating the test, based on testing by the publisher that was done mostly during the mid-1970s and on published studies of the MCT by others since the mid-1950s.

The MCT measures perceptual speed and accuracy in comparing pairs of names (of persons and companies) and pairs of numbers (ranging between 3 and 12 randomly sequenced digits). Of the 200 randomly sequenced pairs of each kind, 100 are identical, and the examinee is to identify by check mark the pairs that contain identical numbers. For the 15 minutes of testing (8 minutes for numbers and 7 for names), the score on each part is the number right minus the number wrong. A scoring template virtually guarantees error-free scoring.

Test content makes implicit that perceptual speed and accuracy in number and name comparisons is taken to be a major component of performance of clerical tasks. The clerical tasks judged to require perceptual speed and accuracy in name and number comparisons may be inferred to some extent from the types of examinees for whom the manual supplies the bulk of its data. Broadly classified, those examinees consist of applicants for clerical jobs; bank tellers and trainees; business machine operators; clerical trainees; clerks of many different kinds; clients for vocational rehabilitation; students in technical, business, and secretarial programs; and typists, stenographers, and secretaries. A nonclerical group, assemblers of electrical equipment, is also included, presumably to highlight the pertinence of the MCT to clerical positions as contrasted with a nonclerical occupation.

There are, of course, many "clerical" tests; some are aimed at factors presumed to be generic to clerical occupations, and others are more specifically targeted (e.g., at clerk-typists). This review, however, deals with the MCT on its own terms.

338

Practical Applications/Uses

The primary use of the Minnesota Clerical Test is for the selection or screening of job applicants. Its secondary use is as a vocational counseling instrument. If perceptual speed and accuracy in name and number comparisons is subject to improvement with practice or training, another use of the MCT could be to assess the effects of training on the skills measured by the test.

The MCT is short, reliable, and easy to administer. If one wished, only the names part or the numbers part of the test could be administered. The manual provides clear, nontechnical explanations of the concepts of norms, reliability, and validity. The deficiencies of employers' ratings as criterion measures are candidly stated. Additionally, nonsignificant as well as significant validity coefficients are reported (but not discussed).

Technical Aspects

The statistical data supplied in the manual as a basis for evaluating the MCT covers norms, reliability, correlations between the names and numbers scores, predictive validity, and correlations between MCT scores and scores on other tests (i.e., construct validity). With occasional exceptions, the tabled data are classified by sex and ethnic group (white, black, minority) and by job title, type of employer, and geographical area of employment.

Norms. Percentile norms are provided for 1) applicants for clerical jobs among five types of employers (utility company, bank, financial institutions, state university, and temporary employment agency); 2) employed bank tellers; 3) bank clerks and typists; 4) students enrolled in postsecondary technical or secretarial, or business programs; and 5) one group of nonclerical employees (electrical equipment assemblers).

Some idea of the applicability of the normative data to a prospective new user of the MCT can be gained from a breakdown of the 3,310 examinees (of whom all but 299 are females), distributed among 15 groups. Of the total 3,310 examinees, 2,006 were employed by or applied to banks (820 as tellers, 941 as clerks, 151 as typists, and 94 were applicants for clerical jobs). Applicants for clerical jobs with other employers numbered 689 (utility company, 107; financial institutions, 166; state university, 291; temporary agency, 125). The remainder consisted of 488 students and 127 nonclerical employees.

With a 200-point maximum score on each part of the MCT, the median, 50th-percentile score ranges from a low of 91–93 points for the comparison of names by female equipment assemblers to a high in the mid-130s for the comparison of both names and numbers by female applicants for a clerical job at a state university. Across all 15 groups covered by the table of norms, the median score centered at about 112–114 for both names and numbers—modestly above a chance score.

For 31 small groups of applicants, employees, and students classified by sex and ethnic group (Table 2 in the manual), means and standard deviations for both tasks are reported, with means more or less comparable to the median scores in the table of norms (Table 1).

Reliability. Test-retest reliability coefficients for an intertest interval of "approximately 4 days" were .81 and .83 for comparing numbers and .86 and .87 for company names for two groups of female students at private business schools. Stability coefficients, reflecting "the stability of the underlying trait or traits being measured rather than the simple reliability of the test instrument" (Andrew, Paterson, & Longstaff, 1979, p. 11), ranged between .56 and .81, with a median of .645, for three groups of bank employees (bookkeeping machine operators and two groups of clerks) over intertest intervals of 8 to 54 months.

Intratest Correlations. For eight groups "representative of those to whom the MCT is generally administered," (Andrew et al., 1979, p. 11) correlations between the names and numbers scores ranged from .58 to .73 with a median of .66, suggesting that "both parts of the test are measuring similar constructs [but] are sufficiently independent to permit meaningful interpretation of the separate scores" (Andrew et al., 1979, p. 11). For some clerical jobs, therefore, one might elect to administer only the numbers or only the names part of the MCT or to weight the two scores differentially.

Validity. The new manual provides three kinds of evidence for test validity, consisting of correlations of MCT scores with 1) measures of job or task performance, 2) measures of training outcomes, and 3) scores on other tests, some of which purport to measure abilities similar or related to those measured by the MCT. Examinees consisted of trainees, employees (including one nonclerical group), and students. Among the measures of job performance as criteria, employers' ratings or rankings overwhelmingly prevailed.

Validity coefficients that used job or training outcomes as criteria (Tables 6 and 7 in the manual) are based on 20 groups of examinees, 7 of which were involved in published studies by authors other than the test publisher.[1] Among 47 validity coefficients across the 20 groups (ranging from −.12 to .50), 21 were statistically significant (at .05 or .01 levels), ranging between .28 and .50. Among those 21, 5 involved an objective measure of performance, 2 used ratings of course success, and 1 used grade point average. The other 39 validity coefficients are afflicted by the low reliability of employers' ratings as criterion measures. The 21 statistically significant coefficients came from 12 of the 20 groups and, in all but three instances, apply to both names and numbers.

Construct validity, apart from the predictive validity reported previously, is evident in moderate to high correlations between MCT scores and scores on such tests as the Short Employment Tests, General Clerical Tests, and Personnel Tests for Industry. Finally, correlations between MCT scores and typing scores (words per minute) in straight copy work were significant for three groups of clerical applicants but not significant for three other groups (including one employed group). Straight copy typing, however, is an artificial task, absent from the realistic tasks of employed typists.

---

[1]Although eight independent studies are listed in the manual (Table 7), Haber (1959), is omitted from consideration here. Its outcomes are reported in a contradictory way—statistically significant validity coefficients are not starred as such (mere oversight by the test publisher). For the most part, those validity coefficients so far exceed the other 47 validity coefficients reported in Tables 6 and 7 as to strain their credibility. For 61 rehabilitation center clients whose level of functioning for clerical speed and quality was rated dichotomously (0 or 1) by two staff members, the four reported validity coefficients ranged from .67 to .88.

Critique

All in all, the Minnesota Clerical Test is a useful, if not uniformly powerful, test for its purposes. It is short, easy to administer, and reliable. The classification of its percentile norms by sex, ethnicity, type of job held or applied for, type of employer, and location of employment helps users to identify the most pertinent norms distribution for local purposes, as do the footnoted accompaniments of the data on validity.

In view of the vast variety of clerical job duties, however, catchall job descriptors such as "clerk" and "clerical" are not sufficiently discriminating. Differences in norms and in validity coefficients among groups with the same job title are unexplainable. Providing more explicit descriptions of examinees than catchall job titles does present some admittedly difficult problems in securing the necessary job-duties information and in determining a suitable level of detail for that information; however, the outcomes might be worth the effort and expense.

Similarly, replacing employers' ratings with more reliable, objective measures of job performance as criteria of test validity, although difficult and expensive, would supply a stronger basis for evaluating the MCT and all other tests that have heretofore relied on employers' ratings.

Finally, although the explanations of the concepts of norms, reliability, and validity are clear, those explanations stop short of providing a yardstick against which the reported validity outcomes can be judged by a nonspecialist. The fact that the distinction between statistical and practical significance is nowhere addressed is of great concern. For example, a validity coefficient of .28 ($N = 65$) is starred in the manual as statistically significant, but the accuracy of prediction from a correlation coefficient of that size is exceedingly modest. Test publishers might wish to consider including in their manuals tables of accuracy of prediction for selected values of the correlation coefficient (see Thorndike & Hagen, 1977, p. 68) and an explanation of the use of such tables.

References

Andrew, D.M., Paterson, D.G., & Longstaff, H.P. (1979). *Minnesota Clerical Test manual (1979 revision)*. San Antonio: The Psychological Corporation.

Thorndike, R.L., & Hagen, E. P. (1977). *Measurement and evaluation in psychology and education* (4th ed.). New York: Wiley.

Gene Schwarting, Ph.D.

Project Director, Preschool Handicapped Program, Omaha Public Schools, Omaha, Nebraska.

MISSOURI KINDERGARTEN INVENTORY OF DEVELOPMENTAL SKILLS

State Task Force on Early Childhood Screening. Columbia, Missouri: Center for Educational Assessment.

Introduction

The Missouri Kindergarten Inventory of Developmental Skills (KIDS) is an individually administered test designed to screen children entering kindergarten. It was developed by a Missouri state task force as a result of requests made by a number of school districts for such an instrument.

An experimental edition of KIDS was developed in 1975 and was administered to 200 children. The results were analyzed by the Missouri Testing and Evaluation Service at the University of Missouri in Columbia. Modifications were made, and the resulting instrument was field tested in the fall of 1975 with 1,175 children from across the state. Data were analyzed and slight changes were made in the test that was then administered in the spring of 1976 to an additional 3,000 children. The original norms group, therefore, consisted of more than 4,000 children from Missouri.

In 1978, feedback concerning the instrument was solicited from 50 representative Missouri school districts that consistently had utilized the instrument, and the original task force was reconvened. Additional items were developed then to extend the age range of the instrument for an alternate form, with field testing done in 1980. The norm group resulting was representative of school districts across the state and consisted of 4,709 children entering kindergarten in the fall of 1980. This group was equally divided by sex, with racial composition 85% white and 15% black.

KIDS is designed to survey six areas of development. On the original version of the test, these are number concepts, language, verbal concepts, paper-and-pencil skills, auditory and visual skills, and gross-motor skills. On the 1980 alternate version, these consisted of number concepts, auditory skills, language concepts, paper-and-pencil skills, visual skills, and gross-motor skills. The contents of both versions include an administration manual, a guidebook/statistical manual, a parent questionnaire, an individual student score sheet, and a variety of preprinted stimuli that require some preparation by the examiner. In addition, the examiner must provide primary pencils, a box with a lid, contact paper, chalk, an 8 ½" ball, an 8-foot balance beam, paper, coins, objects for counting, masking tape or chalk, and a watch for timing.

The test manual includes information on procedures for testing young children, general administration guidelines, item-by-item directions, and scoring information. The guidebook/technical manual provides information regarding the use of test results, suggestions for interpretation of scores, related learning activities, norms, and statistical information. Score sheets consist of four folded pages listing all the items next to boxes or circles for recording the scores, as well as a section for examiner observations regarding the child.

As indicated previously, KIDS is intended for use in screening kindergarten entrants. The 1978 edition is designed for ages 54–72 months and may be administered either in the spring or fall of the year of kindergarten enrollment. The 1981 version is appropriate for ages 48–72 months and may be administered any time during the year preceding kindergarten.

Both versions contain more than 90 items divided among the six sections, including a variety of tasks that will appear quite familiar to those accustomed to formal evaluation of young children. Skills measured include rote and rational counting, verbal responses to picture stimuli, similarities and differences, categorization of objects, drawing geometric figures, draw-a-person, letter and number recognition, visual and auditory discrimination, color identification, auditory memory, and various gross-motor tasks. The test manual references include Beery, Terman, and Merrill, and Harris and Goodenough, providing clues as to assessment instruments from which items were patterned.

As a result of the variety of items, the examiner must be actively involved in the evaluation process. This individual's role includes presenting stimuli, arranging materials, recording responses and scoring them based upon the instrument criteria, maintaining the interest and participation of the young child, and removing materials after they are presented. Scoring criteria vary according to the numerous type of activities presented, and range from being reasonably precise (e.g., letter identification) to quite subjective (e.g., walks a balance beam heel-to-toe with slight separation). There are no adaptations of the scale for individuals with handicaps or those for whom English is not the primary language.

Scores are recorded on the answer sheet next to each item, with response values varying from 0–4. These scores are summed for each of the six sections, and the results are converted by the age-norm tables (divided at 2- or 3-month intervals) into stanines and percentiles. The manual recommends that children whose performance on any of the subtests is at the 20th percentile or below should be referred for further evaluation. In addition to the age norms, a validity scale of 10 scattered items with a minimal level of difficulty is provided. Directions indicate that a score of six or less of these items should result in further evaluation. The test developers also provide a 24-item questionnaire for purposes of obtaining parent input.

Practical Applications/Uses

Because KIDS is designed for screening kindergarten entrants, it is of greatest use in a school setting. It is meant to be administered by kindergarten teachers, but could be given by others, including volunteers. Because the instrument is fairly complex and involves many items, practice and/or training is necessary. The manual recommends that districts develop their own in-service training program on the instrument and notes that an audiocassette is available at minimal cost for training purposes. The test developers project an average testing time of 35 minutes that includes scoring; this short time frame requires proficiency in testing and familiarity with the instrument.

General testing and scoring directions are presented in the administration manual, noting that the child should be given every item on the test, that second trials are possible only when indicated, and that the motor section may be administered out of sequence. In addition, general comments are made regarding the testing of young children as well as specific directions for the administration and scoring of each item. These item directions are clearly stated, and the manual is printed so as to provide easy access. These directions cover 35 pages.

In addition to its use as a screening instrument, KIDS may also be used for curriculum development. If class profiles are developed, those areas failed most often would indicate where emphasis should be placed in the instructional process. Also, individual profiles would indicate the need for intervention in specific areas with particular students.

Technical Aspects

As previously noted, the norm groups for both versions of KIDS were exclusively from cooperating school districts in Missouri. A review of the tables verifies that the sections of the instrument are developmentally based, as the average score for each age range is greater than at the age previous. Intercorrelations between the sections are significant (ranging from .28 to .66) but not so high as to indicate the sections are measuring the same traits. A factor analysis conducted with the 1981 edition (excluding the gross-motor section) found four consistent factors: visual-spatial relations, language development, recall of verbal material, and inferential-constructional skills. The validity of the instrument is based by its authors upon the developmental nature of its scores, content validity, and the factor analysis data; correlations with other instruments or with other criteria are not reported in the manual.

The reliability of KIDS is reported using Kuder-Richardson Formula 20 as a measure of internal consistency. These figures are reported for each subtest of both versions of the instrument and are extremely consistent, varying from .78 through .86. In addition, a test-retest reliability study involving 279 children with counterbalanced testing order and a 3-week interval was conducted. The results indicated reliability varying from .64 through .77 for all sections except gross motor, which was .41.

Critique

The Missouri Kindergarten Inventory of Developmental Skills appears to be a well-developed instrument that would be appropriate for its stated mission of screening children entering kindergarten. Items included provide measures of those skills found in early childhood education and often appear similar to items found in various other measurement tools used with this age range. A concern would be the applicability of the norms to children outside the state of Missouri, and the development of local norms would be recommended. It would also be a positive sign if the norms indicated the inclusion in the group of other ethnic groups and provided information as to socioeconomic status. Also, validation against another measure of development or against success in kindergarten would be recommended.

The major question regarding the use of the KIDS would involve the complexity of the instrument. The impression made is that it indeed would provide an excellent measure of kindergarten entrance skills. However, the instrument is lengthy, requiring familiarity and practice with the materials. To call it a screening instrument would a disservice; and those who elect to use KIDS should be aware of both the demands and the large amount of information that can be obtained.

References

This list includes text citations and suggested additional reading.

Ferguson, J.L., & Carlson, T.A. (1978). *Missouri Kindergarten Inventory of Developmental Skills (K.I.D.S.) technical report.* Columbia, MO: University of Missouri, Missouri Statewide Testing Service.

Manual of the Missouri Kindergarten Developmental Skills. (1976). Columbia, MO: University of Missouri, Center for Educational Assessment.

Manual of the Missouri Kindergarten Inventory of Developmental Skills, Alternate Form. (1980). Columbia, MO: University of Missouri, Center for Educational Assessment.

Wood, C., Powell, S., & Night, R.C. (1984). Predicting school readiness: The validity of developmental age. Journal of Learning Disabilities, 17, 8–11.

Michael Ryan, Ph.D.

Licensed Psychologist, Westside Family Mental Health Clinic,
Kalamazoo, Michigan.

MOTOR-FREE VISUAL PERCEPTION TEST

Ronald R. Colarusso and Donald D. Hammill. Novato, California:
Academic Therapy Publications.

Introduction

The Motor-Free Visual Perception Test (MVPT) purports to be a short and valid measure of global visual perception. Disenchanted with the major role subjects' fine-motor skills play in responding to items in other tests of visual perception, such as the Bender Visual Motor Gestalt Test or the Developmental Test of Visual-Motor Integration, the authors of the MVPT, Ronald P. Colarusso, Ed.D., and Donald D. Hammill, Ed.D., attempted to develop a test based on the work of Chalfant and Scheffelin (1969) that would eliminate or minimalize motor responses. During test development, the authors administered 105 items to 119 normal children. Using two criteria, item validity and level of difficulty, the test authors reduced the number of items to 36 for the final form. The MVPT was published first in 1972; there have been no revisions. Valid items had point biserial correlations between .30 and .80 with the total test score. Items that fell between the 15 and 90% level of difficulty at the different age ranges were considered as potential items for the MVPT.

The MVPT is a multiple-choice test (4 alternatives per item) using a flip-chart format. Each of the 36 items is presented on a separate page. Directions on other sections are similar but differ slightly. The test kit includes a manual, stimulus item book, and scoring sheets. The test consists of five sections: Spatial Relationships, Visual Discrimination, Visual Figure Ground, Visual Closure, and Visual Memory. The items are generally black and white geometric shapes, although there are a few alphanumeric figures.

Practical Applications/Uses

The test authors suggest that the Motor-Free Visual Perception Test was designed to be used by teachers, psychologists, educational specialists, and others who wish to obtain a quick, reliable estimate of a child's visual perceptual abilities. However, they are reticent to endorse its use as a school readiness tool because their validity studies found little correlation between the MVPT and measures of school achievement (Colarusso & Hammill, 1972). Perhaps its safest application would be research.

It is used most appropriately with children from 4 to 8 years of age. However, it is possible to administer the test to older individuals in order to obtain a perceptual age, which might be used cautiously to suggest the level at which an individual is

346

functioning. In other words, an older child with a perceptual age of 7 years theoretically would have the perceptual skills of a 8-year-old child.

The MVPT is administered individually, generally in less than 10 minutes. The directions are clear, and the materials are easy to administer. However, because the format is rather inflexible, it is unlikely that an examiner would choose to administer the five sections in an order different from the one prescribed. Each section has its own brief directions. For example, each item in one subtest consists of a stimulus figure with four multiple choice drawings beneath it. The examiner points to the stimulus item and says, "Look at this," then points to the answers and says, "Find it here."

The subject points to one of the four drawings to indicate his or her response. The examiner has only to circle the child's response on the scoring sheet. The correct response is printed in bold.

The raw score is obtained by counting the number of correct responses. Charts in the test manual then are used to convert the raw score into either a perceptual age or a perceptual quotient. The perceptual quotient, like an IQ score, has a mean of 100 and a standard deviation of 15.

The manual offers little discussion about interpreting test results, simply stating that any score below one standard deviation (perceptual quotient of 85) should be considered a deficit. A short list of references for remediation is provided. The authors never discuss the relationship between the perceptual quotient and the child's potential or IQ score.

Technical Aspects

The MVPT is a model of thorough and thoughtful test development. Item selection was researched thoroughly and carefully. Furthermore, the test has excellent reliability. Its test-retest reliability correlations varied from .77 to .82, and its split-half correlations ranged from .81 to .84. Finally, the Kuder-Richardson correlations ranged from .71 to .82. These data, which were obtained on a population of 881 normal subjects, demonstrate excellent consistency and reliability.

Unfortunately, the test's validity is more questionable. The authors maintain that the test contains content validity because of the way in which the items were selected. Although the content of the items and their method of selection suggest that the MVPT possesses content validity, the test's construct validity and criterion-related validity are more problematic.

The test authors attempt to demonstrate construct validity by correlating to other types of tests: visual-motor, school achievement or readiness, and intelligence tests. They maintain that high correlations between the MVPT and visual-motor tests and lower correlations with the achievement and intelligence tests would provide supportive evidence that the MVPT measures visual perception. The correlations with visual-motor tests such as the Frostig Developmental Test of Visual Perception and the Copying and Matching subtests from the Metropolitan Readiness Tests produced correlations of between .31 and .73. All but one correlation was significant at the .01 level. The highest correlation was with the total score of the Frostig test. When the MVPT was correlated with intelligence tests, the Slosson Intelligence Test (Slosson, 1963) and Pintner-Cunningham Primary Test

(Pintner & Cunningham, 1965), the correlations were .31 and .32. Finally, correlations with the Durell Analysis of Reading Difficulty, the Metropolitan Readiness Tests, and the Stanford Achievement Test produced correlation coefficients from .03 to .51, with a median of .38. The author concluded that the MVPT did, in fact, correlate higher with tests of visual-motor perception than with intelligence or school-related tests.

On the surface, these data appear impressive, particularly the correlation with the more accepted tests of visual perception, such as the Frostig Developmental Test of Visual Perception. However, closer examination of these validity studies reveals their flaws. Half of the studies used less than 50 subjects. Furthermore, in all of the studies, most of the subjects were lower-class, urban minorities. Consequently, the most that can be said for the MVPT is that it may be valid for this population. However, because the sample population is so narrow, it is possible that a third variable, such as exposure to a certain kind of preschool experience, is responsible for the results obtained.

Critique

The MVPT appears to be a beautifully developed psychometric instrument of questionable practical use. The authors should be commended for their careful and thorough item selection. Furthermore, the test is short and easy to administer and score. The instrument has good norms and excellent reliability.

However, the MVPT has questionable validity, and the construct it purports to measure has little utility. Although the authors have begun to perform the necessary validity studies, the populations being used are so narrow and restricted that the results cannot be generalized. Furthermore, the behaviors measured by the test items do not readily generalize to behaviors within the classroom. For example, the vast majority of stimulus items on the MVPT are nonlinguistic in nature. However, because of the emphasis on teaching reading in the early school years, the visual perception of linguistic figures are clearly the most critical. Furthermore, the Visual Memory subtest only measures recognition memory. Particularly as children become older, recognition memory is less important in school.

Another significant disadvantage of the MVPT is that it offers only one global score of visual perception. It may be that visual perception involves many discrete individual perceptual skills, such as visual memory, visual figure-ground, and so forth. The combination of all of these skills into one global score may result in information that is of little practical importance. If nothing else, one loses the ability to look at patterns and to assess strengths and weaknesses.

Finally, a number of researchers have challenged the appropriateness of perceptual training on both theoretical and empirical grounds (Cohen, 1969; Mann, 1970). In the manual, the test authors themselves disavow the applications and uses of the MVPT (Colarusso & Hammill, 1972, p. 14). They use their validity data to suggest that the construct that the MVPT measures may have little relationship to measures of school achievement and intelligence. Furthermore, Larsen and Hammill (1975) reviewed 60 studies and concluded that research suggests that the relationship between visual perception and academic success is not significant enough to be of use to teachers. Similarly, the use of visual perceptual training, based on such test results, has never been proven consistently to accentuate the teaching of reading and spelling (Jacobs, Wirthlin, & Miller, 1968; Wiederholt & Hammill, 1971).

In short, although the MVPT is a well-developed test, it offers little practical information to the clinician, school psychologist, or teacher. However, it may have some applications for the researcher.

References

Chalfant, J.C., & Scheffelin, M.A. (1969). *Central processing dysfunctions in children: A review of research*. Bethesda, MD: Department of Health, Education, and Welfare.

Cohen, S.A. (1969). Studies in visual perception and reading in disadvantaged children. *Journal of Learning Disabilities, 2,* 498–507.

Colarusso, R.P., & Hammill, D.D. (1972). *Motor-Free Visual Perception Test*. Novato, CA: Academic Therapy Publications.

Jacobs, J.N., Wirthlin, L.D., & Miller, C.B. (1968). A follow-up evaluation of the Frostig Visual-Perceptual Training Program. *Educational Leadership, Research Supplement, 4,* 169–175.

Larsen, S., & Hammill, D.D. (1975). The relationship of selected visual perceptual skills to academic abilities. *Journal of Special Education, 9,* 167–178.

Mann, L. (1970). Perceptual training: Misdirections and redirections. *American Journal of Orthopsychiatry, 40,* 30–38.

Pinter, R., & Cunningham, B.V. (1965). *Pinter-Cunningham Primary Test—Revised Edition*. New York: Harcourt, Brace & World.

Slosson, R.L. (1963). *Slosson Intelligence Test*. East Aurora, NY: Slosson Educational Publications.

Wiederholt, J.L., & Hammill, D.D. (1971). Use of the Frostig-Horne perception program in the urban school. *Psychology in the Schools, 8,* 268–274.

Jennifer Ryan Hsu, Ph.D.

Associate Professor of Communication Disorders, William Paterson College, Wayne, New Jersey.

MULTILEVEL INFORMAL LANGUAGE INVENTORY

Candace L. Goldsworthy. San Antonio, Texas: The Psychological Corporation.

Introduction

The Multilevel Informal Language Inventory (MILI) is an informal instrument for assessing a child's knowledge of specific syntactic constructions and semantic relations. The test, which contains two survey scenes, two survey stories, and 49 probes, yields a developmental profile of a child's strengths and weaknesses. The survey scenes and stories are used to determine structures that the child is producing. Forty-four of the probes assess knowledge of specific target constructions that are organized developmentally within eight grammatical categories. The responses to these probes may also be analyzed in terms of knowledge of specific semantic relations. Five additional probes, classified as "Associative Language," assess knowledge of word formation rules, word meanings, and idioms. Goldsworthy (1982) considers the test to be a "multilevel" approach to assessment. First, it uses three types of tasks (i.e., survey scenes, survey pictures, and probes) that are graduated in terms of difficulty and assess knowledge in different conversational formats. Second, the developmental ordering of the probes represents varying levels of difficulty. Third, the 44 syntactic probes assess knowledge at three different response levels: an evoked *spontaneous* response, in which a child generates an utterance in response to a picture; an *elicited* response, in which the child imitates the examiner's model; and a *receptive* response, in which the child selects an item named by the examiner. The three response levels are viewed by Goldsworthy (1982) as representing different levels of knowledge with the *spontaneous* the most advanced and the *receptive* the least. The MILI, which is intended to supplement results from other tests, may be used in diagnosis and ongoing assessment to determine therapy goals.

The MILI was developed by Dr. Candace L. Goldsworthy, a professor of speech/language pathology at California State University at Sacramento. Dr. Goldsworthy holds the Certificate of Clinical Competence in Speech/Language Pathology from the American Speech-Language-Hearing Association as well as the California State License in Speech Pathology. She has a Ph.D in Speech Pathology from Case Western Reserve University in Cleveland, Ohio. Dr. Goldsworthy has taught undergraduate and graduate courses in speech pathology and has provided clinical services for a number of years. She is a partner in the practice of Goldsworthy and Johnston and codirector of the Sacramento Scottish Rite Childhood Language Clinic.

According to Goldsworthy (1982), the MILI was developed to correct some deficiencies of language sampling procedures and standardized tests. Goldsworthy (1982) argues that language sampling procedures are a valuable source of assessment data but that they lack interrater reliability, fail to elicit structures the child is capable of producing, are difficult to administer, and are time-consuming to score. Although standardized tests correct some of these problems, Goldsworthy believes these tests have limited usefulness because test results do not translate more directly to therapy goals. The MILI was designed to include the desirable characteristics of language-sampling procedures. It was designed also to be easily administered, scored, and interpreted. In contrast to many standardized tests, the MILI was intended to provide information about a child's spontaneous production of specific syntactic structures and to yield results that will lead more directly to the formulation of therapy goals.

Goldsworthy (1982) reports that development of the MILI involved administering a draft to a sample of 45 children ranging from 4- to 12-years of age. Fifteen of the children were normal and 35 were language disordered. The responses of the children were used in revisions of the test items. Because the test is not a norm-referenced measure, no normative data are reported. There have been no revisions or special versions.

The MILI includes an examiner's manual, a picture manual, and record forms. The examiner's manual outlines the rationale for the development and use of the MILI. It also contains directions for administration and scoring as well as some general directions for developing therapy goals. There are four appendices in the manual. The first outlines the rules for calculating mean length of utterance. The second, which was written by Richard Kretschmer, provides a brief introduction to case grammar as well as a comprehensive listing of semantic cases. Two analyses that illustrate Kretschmer's semantic analysis are provided in the third and fourth appendices.

The picture manual contains the survey scenes, survey stories and 49 probes with pictures for 45 of the items. The survey scenes depict events from urban situations. One depicts activities at a construction site and the other a building fire. The survey stories depict events at a farm and a birthday party. The farm story, which involves a set of six pictures, is considered to be less complex and appropriate for younger or more disordered children. The birthday party has more events (i.e., eight frames) and is considered to require more complex language.

The 44 syntactic probes assess the ability to produce or comprehend constructions related to verb forms, nominals, modifiers, adverbs, prepositions, negation, interrogatives, coordination, and subordination. Each probe assesses a particular target construction through a set of stimulus items that involve responses at the evoked spontaneous, elicited, and receptive levels. The number of stimulus items per probe range from 3 to 18. An average probe contains three stimuli for the evoked spontaneous level, three for the elicited, and one for the receptive. The number of probes, the number of stimulus items and the types of constructions that are assessed within each syntactic category are summarized in Table 1.

Although most of the pictures for each probe depict people or animals engaged in some type of activity, some depict sets of objects. The pictures on a page may be a single scene or a set of separate scenes. A variety of formats are used for the

Table 1

Analysis of Stimulus Items Included in the MILI

Syntactic Category	Number of Probes	Constructions	Number of Stimulus Items
1. Verbs	11	Tense markers, present progressives, modals, infinitives, passives, participles, and gerunds	93
2. Nominals	12	Plural forms, possessive forms, articles, and pronominals	88
3. Modification	5	Early and late adjectives, adjective strings, and comparatives	37
4. Adverbs and Prepositions	6	Prepositions expressing location, instrument, and reason; adverbs expressing location, time, and manner	39
5. Negation	2	Article *no, hasn't, doesn't, dont,* and *can't*	18
6. Interrogatives	3	*Yes/no, who, what, where, when, why,* and *how*	23
7. Combining Propositions	5	Coordination of words and clauses; subordination with *if, because, before, after,* and relative clauses	45
Total	44		343

stimulus items within each probe. The evoked spontaneous level generally involves pointing to a picture and asking the child to "Tell me about this picture." Alternative formats include but are not limited to questions (e.g., "What's the matter with this _____?", "What do you think the _____ is saying?", "Why is the _____ happy?", etc.), instructions (e.g., "Tell me the rest of the story," "Tell me what happened," etc.), or guessing games (e.g., "You guess which one I am thinking of," etc.,). The same pictorial stimulus is used for the elicited and receptive levels for each target construction. The elicited level generally involves modeling the target response and then eliciting a similar response from the child while focusing on either another picture on the page or another item within the picture. At the receptive level, the child is asked to point to a part of the picture depicting some action, objective, or relationship named by the examiner. The target construction is embedded within a command such as "Show me _____" or "Point to the _____."

Each of the five "associative language" probes includes 10 stimulus items. The first probe assesses the ability to create compound words from individual words that are pictorially represented on a page. The second probe requires identification of synonyms and antonyms for a set of 10 words. The third and fourth probes assess knowledge of multiple meanings of words. In administering the third probe, the examiner reads a word and a sentence using the word. The examinee then is required to express a second meaning of the target word by constructing an alternate sentence with the word. For example, given the word *run*, the examiner reads a sentence such as "The team has one run." The examinee then must construct a second sentence such as "I like to run" that expresses an alternate meaning of *run*. The fourth probe requires the examinee to explain an absurdity resulting from the mismatch of a sentence context and a meaning of a word or phrase. The final probe assesses knowledge of figurative language by requesting the examinee to explain the meaning of 10 idioms presented in sentence contexts.

Responses to the survey scenes, survey pictures, and all probes are recorded on the Record Form. In addition, the Record Form contains three profiles and a cover page with space for listing any formal test results and informal clinical observations. One profile, entitled "Advance Checklist," is located on the cover page. The word "advance" in this case means "initial." That is, the Advance Checklist, which lists the syntactic constructions probed in the MILI, is intended to provide a record of the constructions that the child is known to produce prior to administration of the probes. Structures that are not present as indicated on the checklist and are expected given the child's age or MLU will become the targets for assessment via the probes.

The second profile, termed the "Syntax Profile," provides a summary of a child's performance on the syntactic probes that are selected for testing. The eight syntactic categories assessed by the MILI are listed vertically, and the probes within each category are listed horizontally. Placed at the top of the page are two horizontal bars that represent developmental continua in terms of MLU and age. The probes are located beneath the continua at points representing the approximate age and MLU when the structure is acquired. This acquisition information is based on research published during the 1970s and early 1980s. The Syntax Profile provides a summary of the sequence of acquisition for the target structures within each syntactic category. The developmental continuum for MLU ranges from 2.5 to 5.5 and the one for age ranges from 24 to 66 months. Because points within the ranges are not identified, the examiner must interpolate.

Performance on each probe item is summarized on the Syntax Profile by checking the level of correct responding (i.e., checking "s" for correct evoked spontaneous responses, "e" for correct elicited responses or "r" for correct receptive responses). Once the child's age or MLU is located on the developmental continua, the examiner will have a profile of performance that can be compared to structures that are expected for normal children at the same age or MLU. The Syntax Profile is then used to determine the appropriate sequence for presentation of syntactic structures in therapy.

A third profile, termed the Semantic Relations Profile, is located on page 3 of the Record Form. This profile permits analysis of the responses to the probes in terms of the semantic relations expressed in the utterances evoked by the stimulus items. The target constructions within each syntactic category are listed vertically on the left side of the page and the semantic relations within verb, nominal, adverbial, and modifier categories are listed horizontally at the top. A grid of dots is associated with each target construction and each semantic relation. Darkened dots indicate the semantic relations that are typically associated with the target responses and open circles indicate those relations that are not likely to occur. The examiner may analyze responses to each probe in terms of the semantic relations contained in the utterances. The child's actual profile of semantic relations then can be compared to the expected pattern indicated by the darkened dots. The semantic relations listed in the profile are defined in Table 4-1 of the examiner's manual. The categories are more general than those identified by Kretschmer in Appendix B.

Practical Applications/Uses

According to Goldsworthy (1982), the primary purpose of the MILI is to assess knowledge of specific constructions that have not been observed in a child's productions and to identify goals for an intervention program. The test can be used to supplement other tests in a diagnostic evaluation, to monitor progress during a therapy program, or to support other measures in verifying mastery at the end of the program (Goldsworthy, 1982). In addition, researchers may find that some of the probes can be used for purposes of data collection.

The MILI should be used after an impairment has been identified via standardized, norm-referenced tests. Although comparisons are made to the normal sequence of development, the MILI is not intended for diagnosis of a delay or disorder. The comparisons to normal language acquisition are for the purpose of goal selection. Initially, data collected from formal and informal procedures are used to determine structures that are part of the child's linguistic system and to identify questionable areas of performance. The MILI then is used to probe those structures that are expected given the child's age or MLU but have not been observed. The survey scenes and stories are intended to provide information on whether structures occur in a spontaneous description of a picture or a story-retelling task. The probe items, which evaluate the use of specific structures at different response levels, provide information on the mastery, emergence, or absence of the constructions. Once this information is obtained, emerging or absent structures are compared to developmental sequences outlined on the Syntax Profile and therapy goals are selected.

The MILI was developed for use in clinical settings. Goldsworthy (1982) states that users include speech/language pathologists and specialists in the field of learning disabilities. Other professionals who may find the test useful include teachers working with language impaired populations, such as the hearing impaired, mentally retarded, autistic, perceptually impaired, or neurologically impaired. Teachers working in communication-handicapped classrooms may also find the test useful.

According to Goldsworthy (1982), the MILI is designed to be used with 4- to 12-year-old children who have expressive language deficits. Goldsworthy (1982) describes the items as ranging "from those at the 'emerging semantic-syntactic' level to those at the 'associative language' level" (p. 1). This description is not very informative. The developmental continua suggest that some items included in the test could be given to a child with an MLU as low as 2.5 to 3.5. However, inspection of the probes placed at the youngest ages or lowest MLUs reveals that a child must be able to understand a command such as "Tell me about this one" or "Point to the _____ who is _____." In view of the verbal stimuli used to elicit responses at all levels (i.e., evoked spontaneous, elicited, or receptive), examinees must be able to understand 4- to 5-word commands and should be producing at least 2- to 3-word utterances with subjects and predicates. In addition, the test requires knowledge of vocabulary related to home, school, and playground activities. Some knowledge of animal names is also required. The associative language probes involve more advanced vocabulary. The instructions include words such as *synonyms* and *antonyms,* and the probes include words such as *frogman, horseradish,* and *chairman.* The associative language probes also involve tasks that will require advanced levels of linguistic and cognitive development. The examinees must be able to identify multiple meanings and construct sentences using specific words. They also must be able to detect and explain absurdities as well as explain the meaning of idioms.

The MILI is a flexible instrument with a unique format that permits a clinician to select specific probes depending on a child's level of functioning. Clinicians are encouraged to create additional items that are modeled on the probes. This flexibility does permit some adaptation of items to a child's level of functioning. As noted by Rueda (1988), the flexibility in administration is both a strength and a weakness. Although it permits adaptations that may facilitate performance, it also requires that examiners have good clinical skills and knowledge of language development (Rueda, 1988).

The MILI can be administered only on an individual basis. Inclusion of a duplicate set of the instructions in the examiner's manual (Goldsworthy, 1982) and the picture manual (Goldsworthy & Secord, 1982) provides the examiner with the option of standing the picture manual upright and reading the instructions from the back of each page or laying the manual down on a table and reading the instructions from the examiner's manual. The former option requires the examiner to sit across from the child, while the latter option requires the examiner to sit next to the child.

Speech/language pathologists, learning disabilities specialists, and teachers would be qualified to administer the MILI provided they have had training in language assessment. Examiners should read the directions carefully and administer the test in several practice sessions until they are familiar with the instructions for each item.

Administration of the survey scenes and stories is optional depending on whether prior information is available on the syntactic structures produced by the child. One survey scene and one survey story may be administered. The selection of the scene is based on the child's interest, and selection of the story is based on the child's level of linguistic functioning. The child is asked to talk about everything that is happening in the survey scene and to retell the survey story after it is narrated by the examiner.

Once the structures needing assessment are identified via previous test results and/or the survey scenes and stories, the appropriate probes are selected and administered. Probing a target structure should begin at the evoked spontaneous level, which Goldsworthy (1982) considers to be the most advanced response. If the child fails to manifest the target response, then probing proceeds to the less advanced levels (i.e., the elicited and receptive levels). All response levels may be given in cases where the child fails to manifest the target response. However, once a target response is obtained, subsequent response levels are not given.

In general, the instructions for administering each item are clear. However, there are several minor problems. One problem involves directions that refer to items on a page in terms of left, center, and right. These terms refer to items on a page when viewed from the front perspective. An examiner who chooses to administer the test by reading from the back of a page in the picture manual (an acceptable option according to the examiner's manual) will find that the directions "left", "center," and "right" must be reversed. However, this is not mentioned in the instructions. The mismatch between the pictures and directions could result in incorrect administration of all items with these directions.

A second problem relates to the design of the picture manual. Because the MILI is used to probe specific constructions, only selected items are administered to individual children. Locating items in the manual requires flipping through the pages, a time-consuming and inconvenient activity that may distract the child. The problem in locating items could be solved by placing tabs on the pictures. Because the instructions for each item are also included in the examiner's manual, tabs are needed in that manual as well.

The time required for administering the test varies depending on the number of items probed and whether the survey scene and pictures are administered. The test author recommends administering the survey scenes and pictures in one session. After the target probes are identified, they should be administered in a second session, that takes approximately 15 to 20 minutes. Administration of the survey scene takes approximately 8 to 10 minutes and the survey story 5 to 8 minutes.

Responses are scored on the Record Form. Responses to the survey scenes and stories must be transcribed before they can be scored. Key structures may be noted during elicitation of the language samples or the responses may be audiotaped for later transcription. The responses then are scored for the presence or absence of the syntactic constructions that are probed by the MILI. Structures observed in the survey scenes, the survey stories, and prior testing are recorded on the "Advance Checklist." Although the checklist provides a guide to the constructions probed by the MILI, scoring responses to the survey scenes and stories will require a sufficient level of grammatical knowledge to identify the target constructions in sentence contexts.

Scoring of the probe items may be done during administration of the test or later if the responses are audiotaped. The Record Form identifies each probe, provides space for transcribing responses to each stimulus item included in the probe, and identifies the target construction for each stimulus item. The target constructions are boldfaced and embedded within an utterance that is likely to be produced by a mature speaker. Adjacent to each target is a series of symbols that are marked to indicate for each stimulus item in the probe whether the target construction was produced at the evoked spontaneous, elicited, or receptive levels. The symbols are "s," "e," and "r," respectively. Scoring of this section is easy and straightforward.

Responses to the associative language probes only involve spontaneous productions. Space is provided on the Record Form to record the child's responses. There are no instructions for scoring errors and there is no summary profile for these items. Presumably, the responses would be examined to identify correct answers, incorrect answers, and the nature of any errors. However, no guidelines are provided for such an analysis.

All scoring is done by hand. The responses to the 44 syntactic probes are summarized on the Syntax Profile by checking "s," "e," or "r" for each target construction. Because each probe contains a number of stimulus items, the examiner must decide whether a child's responses are predominantly at the "s" (i.e., evoked spontaneous), "e" (i.e., elicited), or "r" (i.e., receptive) level. If the child's responses are consistent on all stimulus items within a probe, the decision will be straightforward. However, if the responses vary across levels, the decision will be difficult because there are no guidelines for identifying an overall response pattern in such cases. Furthermore, there are no criteria for deciding when a particular construction can be considered to be mastered at the spontaneous evoked level. It is possible that a child may produce the target at the spontaneous level for only some of the items. In these cases, decisions concerning mastery is a matter of clinical judgment. In general, further probing is recommended if an area is questionable. It is likely that in cases of variable performance, judgments regarding mastery will vary across clinicians. Unfortunately, no interrater reliability data are reported. Valid decisions concerning mastery will require knowledge of the issues related to such judgments and considerable clinical experience.

The responses to the 44 syntactic probes may also be scored in terms of semantic relations using the Semantic Relations Profile. Although the semantic relations listed on the profile are defined in Table 4-1 of the examiner's manual, no examples are given to illustrate the types of words and utterances that express the relations. Many of the relations are defined and illustrated in the extensive list provided in Appendix B. However, it would be more convenient if examples were included in Table 4-1. Furthermore, the inclusion of examples in the table would clarify instances where the categories identified in Table 4-1 don't completely match the categories identified in Appendix B. The scoring of the semantic relations will require some knowledge of current theories regarding case grammars and some practice in the analysis of semantic relations. Appendix B provides a brief introduction. However, Kretschmer and Kretschmer (1978) provide a more detailed discussion with additional examples in Tables 7, 8, and 9. Bloom and Lahey (1978), Miller (1981), and Stickler (1987) also discuss semantic relations and provide examples illustrating an analysis of productive language samples.

The instructions for scoring are included in the examiner's manual. The instructions for scoring the individual stimulus items of each probe are clear and easy to follow. If an examiner has the required knowledge of syntax and semantic relations, several practice sessions should be sufficient for learning to score the stimulus items of the probes. Those without the necessary background will require considerably more time and practice. The preceding discussion noted inherent problems in scoring the Syntax Profile, the Semantic Relations Profile, and the Associative Language Items. For these sections, it is not clear that either practice or careful reading of the instructions will eliminate interrater variation even among experienced and knowledgeable clinicians.

The length of time required for scoring the test will depend on which aspects of the test are administered. Transcribing and scoring should take approximately 15 to 20 minutes for the survey scenes and 10 to 15 minutes for the survey stories. If the responses are transcribed during administration of the test, the scoring time will be shortened. Scoring each probe item should take approximately 1 to 2 minutes. If the probes are administered and scored at the same time, then scoring of these items would be part of the 15 to 20 minutes recommended for the second testing session.

Because the data obtained from the MILI are used to determine therapy goals and/or constructions needing further probing, interpretation involves decisions regarding structures that are mastered, emerging, or absent. Such decisions are based on earlier scoring decisions whereby structures are entered on the Advance Checklist as present in spontaneous productions, or they are entered on the Syntax Profile as present at the spontaneous, elicited, or receptive levels. Structures that are spontaneously produced are ruled out as targets for therapy. In general, structures occurring at elicited levels should be taught first, and those with correct responses at the receptive level should be taught next.

Those that are produced at elicited levels are potential targets provided the failure to produce the target at the spontaneous level is attributable to lack of ability and not the nature of the stimulus item. Critical targets are selected on the basis of their order of acquisition as indicated on the Syntax Profile. The critical targets include constructions from different grammatical categories that appear at approximately the same point in development. Selection of goals from a set of potential targets should also be based on communicative need or the extent they contribute to communicative success (C. Goldsworthy, personal communication, June 23, 1988).

Although the ordering of goals within categories seem to be clear once the pattern of spontaneous, elicited, receptive, or absent responses are established, the ordering of goals across categories is not as clear. For example, it is difficult to determine the relative importance of targets from different categories that appear at approximately the same time. Clearly, there will be variation in clinical interpretations of the concept of communicative need or contribution to communicative success. The manual includes only one example of goals that are based on a student's Syntax Profile. The reason for including item AP-3 (adverbs of time) is unclear because it was scored as occurring at the spontaneous evoked level. Furthermore, the reason for ordering item V-9 (infinitives) prior to item AP-4 (adverbs of manner) is unclear because (according to the Syntax Profile), item AP-4 develops prior to item V-9. The rationale could involve communicative need. Additional examples would be helpful in clarifying how therapy goals can be derived from the test results. The examples should include a complete transcript of the child's responses, all scores, and the rationale for the selection and ordering of each goal. Without the examples, it is likely that clinicians will vary in goal selection for individual children. Data on interrater consistency in goal selection is needed.

The examiner's manual suggests that the Semantic Relations Profile may also be used to select therapy goals. This will require inspection of the Semantic Relations Profile. As a first step, the manual recommends scanning the columns under verb types for variety in verb usage. However, the manual does not indicate how this information should be translated into specific therapy goals. Next, the manual recommends scanning the profile for relations that were produced but not expected. Further probing is recommended to determine if the child is having difficulty expressing the expected relations. If difficulty is confirmed, then the manual suggests that activities should be developed that require expression of those relations. There are no recommendations concerning the relative ordering of semantic relations. Only one case is discussed and it is used to illustrate an example where there are syntactic deficits but no apparent semantic deficits. The inclusion of several case studies would help clarify the principles for identifying appropriate goals related to the expression of semantic relations. Without this clarification, interrater reliability is likely to be low.

Interpretation of the test results and selection of therapy goals requires a knowledge of language development. In particular, decisions regarding relative importance of various target structures will require a knowledge of the development of syntax, semantics, and pragmatics. Clinical experience also seems necessary for valid decisions. According to Goldsworthy (personal communication, June 23, 1988), the MILI should not be used by inexperienced clinicians.

Technical Aspects

Unfortunately, there appear to be virtually no reliability and validity data on the MILI. This is surprising, as Goldsworthy (1982) acknowledges that both formal and informal instruments are "subject to threats to reliability and validity" (p. 6). The examiner's manual comments on the content validity and reports field testing with a group of 15 normal and 30 language-impaired children. The results of the field test were used to develop a final draft of the test. As noted by Rueda (1988), there is no information on location or demographic characteristics of the subjects. The reported results indicate that the normal and disordered children perform "differently" on the probes. However, no supporting statistics are reported.

It is crucial that the reliability and validity of the test be established. Because the results of the test are used to develop a child's therapy program, it is important to know that a response is a stable indicator of a child's knowledge. In other words, it should be determined that the MILI has good test-retest and interrater reliability. Different examiners testing the same child should derive consistent performance profiles as well as consistent recommendations regarding goals. It is important to note that the former does not imply the latter. As noted previously, test results are likely to vary across examiners due to the lack of guidelines for goal selection and decisions regarding mastery of structures. In view of this, evidence of test-retest and interrater reliability should be obtained for at least experienced and knowledgeable examiners. Concurrent validity should also be determined. The assumption that the test can approximate the results of other language sampling procedures should be tested by determining the relation of data obtained with such procedures to data obtained with the MILI.

An assumption of the MILI is that the probes will elicit specific target constructions. Examiners are cautioned that failure to elicit a construction may not be due to lack of knowledge on the part of the examinee but failure of the stimulus item to elicit the intended response. Examiners are advised to probe further before deciding that such a failure is due to lack of knowledge. The likelihood that an item will elicit the intended response in an individual who has acquired a structure should be determined. Such data would contribute to the confidence an examiner places in decisions regarding mastery, emergence, or absence of structures at the evoked spontaneous level. The elicited level yields less ambiguous responses. Problems with the receptive level will be discussed later.

Goldsworthy (1982) argues that the MILI has content validity. Inspection of the items reveals a fairly broad sampling. However, the test does omit some constructions that develop during the acquisition period (i.e., 24–66 mos. and 2.5–5.5 MLU) specified for items that are included. For example, only one type of infinitive construction following only the main verb *is going* is included. However, other types of infinitive constructions appear by 66 months of age. Furthermore, the infinitives occur with several main verbs in addition to *go*. Several modals appear between 24 to 66 months. However, only two modals are included. The test does not assess past tense forms of the progressive aspect or of the copula *be*. *What doing* questions, *who-object* questions and *what* questions with verbs other than *happened* are omitted. Furthermore, there is only a limited sample of *yes/no* questions. Only the conjunction *and* and only a limited number of types of coordinate constructions are included. The subordinating conjunctions are limited to *if, because, before,* and *after. When* and *while,* which develop in the same age range, are omitted. Inspection of Lee's (1974) Developmental Sentence Scoring or Tyack and Gottsleben's (1974) protocol will reveal additional structures that are omitted from the MILI. In addition, the MILI does not identify various types of basic sentence structure. This is an important aspect of early language development that could be incorporated into some of the existing probes. Because the MILI is intended to assess only selected items depending on a child's level of functioning, the test could be expanded without affecting administration time. Such an expansion would increase the content validity and the adequacy of the test in describing the level of a child's production of specific syntactic structures.

The Semantic Relations Profile and the cases included in Appendix B provide an extensive list of semantic relations. Data is needed to determine if the probes and the survey items elicit the full range of relations listed in these sections.

Critique

The MILI has two features that add to the information obtained by available assessment methods. One is the inclusion of a systematic procedure for probing specific constructions. There are many situations in which probing is needed but no systematic procedures are available. For example, some formal tests recommend further probing if errors occur on specific items and some tests contain too few items in specific categories to permit decisions about level of mastery. In these cases, clinicians must develop their own procedures for probing. Although imitation or comprehension tasks provide a means for assessing knowledge of specific constructions, the MILI seems to be the first test that permits systematic evaluation of production of specific items at a "near" spontaneous level.

The second feature is the "multilevel" approach to testing. The inclusion of multiple tasks does enable comparison of performance in varying conditions. Structures that do not appear in response to the survey scene may appear in response to the survey stories. Furthermore, the three response levels of the probes provide important information regarding the level of development of a structure. Language sampling procedures do not provide information on whether individual children can imitate or understand specific structures that they cannot produce in a spontaneous situation. This information enables the ordering of goals for structures that may otherwise be considered to be completely absent in the child's linguistic system.

The MILI is one of the few tests that attempts to provide an intensive analysis of syntactic structures while looking at other aspects of language. It is important to determine that a child is expressing the full range of semantic relations as well as using specific syntactic structures. However, as noted in section II, the test needs clearer guidelines for the analysis of semantic relations and the determination of goals. The associative language section assesses some interesting aspects of language, such as the ability to create words. Unfortunately, there are no guidelines for determining goals for the associative language tasks. Although some of the tasks are interesting, it is not clear whether they are as important as other aspects of language that may be impaired. The rationale for inclusion of the items was based on the fact that the targets are frequently identified as goals in case reports (Goldsworthy, 1982). Thus, the items are intended to provide a means of systematic assessment (Goldsworthy, 1982). This is a weak rationale that does not address the issue of relative importance in overall communicative functioning. It is also important to note that some of the tasks require metalinguistic skills that are separate from linguistic knowledge. For example, knowledge of word meaning is separate from the ability to identify synonyms and antonyms. It is also separate from the ability to construct a sentence or explain a mismatch in word meaning and sentence context. Failure on an item may reflect either lack of knowledge or inability to perform the particular type of metalinguistic task. Identification of appropriate goals will require clinicians to analyze the reasons for failure. However, there are no guidelines for making these clinical judgments.

A goal in designing the MILI was to develop procedures that combine the desirable characteristics of language-sampling procedures and standardized tests. Based on the characteristics of standardized tests, the MILI was designed to be easily administered, scored, and interpreted. Aside from the problems of scoring and interpretation noted previously, the MILI delivers on its promise to be easy to administer.

A desirable characteristic of language-sampling procedures is the amount of information provided on a child's expressive language performance (Goldsworthy, 1982). Thus, the MILI was designed to yield information on syntactic and semantic structures that a child uses in spontaneous conversation. As noted earlier, the validity of this claim needs to be established through the appropriate comparative studies. However, informal observation suggests that the MILI provides information on the use of specific syntactic constructions that is similar to the results of language-sampling procedures. Furthermore, as noted by Goldsworthy (1982), the MILI is likely to provide information on a broader range of constructions than typically obtained in a language sample. However, it is important to note that normal conversation differs from the tasks included in the MILI in important ways that undoubtedly affect linguistic performance. For example, the ability to express specific syntactic constructions or semantic relations may vary as a function of pragmatic intents, communicative situation, or conversational participants. The format of the MILI limits the amount of information on the nature of these interactions.

In general, the probes are well designed and incorporate some creative ideas for eliciting target constructions. However, data are needed on the extent to which individual items elicit the intended targets in mature speakers. It seems likely that the elicited response level will yield the intended targets in children who have developed the structures. However, informal testing by this reviewer suggests that some items may not elicit the intended response at the evoked spontaneous response level. The test author recognizes this and cautions examiners to probe further before attributing omission to lack of knowledge of the structure. In particular, items V-2, V-3, V-5, V-10, N-3, N-11, M-4, AP-4, AP-5, and I-3 may not elicit the target structures. Children may also have some difficulty in giving the first response to item CP-4. With respect to the associative language items, some of the vocabulary included in items AL-1 and AL-2 may be difficult for even older normal children, and some of the idioms included in item AL-5 may not be familiar to all segments of the population.

At the receptive level, both correct and incorrect responses may provide ambiguous information regarding comprehension of the target construction. For example, there are several items that probe comprehension of verb forms through the use of commands involving relative clauses. This is illustrated by item V-1, which probes comprehension of the present progressive aspect by instructing "Point to the _____ who is climbing." Because relative clause forms are acquired after the present progressive aspect, failure on this item may be attributable to the relative clause rather than the present progressive aspect. There are several items of this type in which an incorrect response may not necessarily reflect lack of knowledge of the target form but lack of knowledge of other constructions which are also embedded in the command. The ambiguity of correct responses is illustrated by items V-1 and V-4, which assess the present progressive aspect and the third person present regular, respectively. Because the probes include pictures depicting different actions, recognition of the meaning of the verbs is sufficient for a correct response. That is, in item V-1, selection of the appropriate picture requires only knowledge of the meaning of *climb*. Unambiguous assessment of receptive knowledge of the present progressive or the third person singular would require a set of pictures differing only with respect to time of the action. Because the appropriate options are not included, correct responses on these items may reflect vocabulary knowledge rather than knowledge of the target structure. In general, both correct and incorrect responses at the receptive level will require additional probing and careful interpretation.

A basic assumption of the MILI is that the normal developmental sequence of structures should be used to determine goals for language-impaired children (see Carrow-Woolfolk, 1988, for some competing views). Although a developmental sequence is provided for target structures within each syntactic category, no sequence is provided for semantic relations or for the associative language items. Identification of goals for these areas is a matter of clinical judgment. The developmental sequences for the syntactic structures are based on research literature that was published during the 1970s and early 1980s. At that time, there was very little information about the relationship in the development of structures across syntactic categories. In view of the amount of research that has occurred since 1981, a review of recent research is needed with appropriate revisions in the developmental sequences. Finally, it should be noted that the developmental ordering of the negation items conflict with the sequence that has generally been accepted (see Lee, 1974; Tyack & Gottsleben, 1974; and Table 9.5 in Owens, 1988).

A positive characteristic of the MILI is the organization and attractiveness of the manuals and forms. The examiner's manual contains a discussion of language assessment that clinicians may find helpful. The manuals and forms seem to be carefully edited, although there are two typographical errors on page 31 of the examiner's manual. Also, items I-2 and I-3 are out-of-order in that manual (they are correctly ordered in both the picture manual and the scoring form). Rueda (1988) notes that the stimulus pictures are attractive and will probably interest children in the lowest age ranges for which the test was designed. The pictures also seem appropriate for children in the middle age range. In administering the test to a 7-year-old, this reviewer observed that the pictures for the probes maintained the child's interest for a period exceeding the recommended 20-minute time period. Although the survey story related to the farm also captured attention, the survey scene related to the construction site proved to be less interesting. Events depicted in the scene may not interest children from suburban settings. Both survey scenes include many small details which are somewhat difficult to see. The birthday party survey story is cluttered and visually overwhelming.

In conclusion, the MILI is a useful supplement to the set of tests clinicians use in diagnostic evaluations. It is also useful in monitoring progress of clients with syntactic deficits. It is one of the few instruments available that assesses semantic relations and perhaps the only one that systematically assesses specific syntactic constructions using multiple stimulus items and three response levels. However, there are several deficiencies of the test that need to be addressed before the test can be recommended: completion of the appropriate reliability and validity studies and additional guidelines for scoring and interpretation. The MILI has the potential for expansion, which will not increase administration time but will increase the options for probing. Such a revision would increase the test's usefulness.

References

This list includes text citations and suggested additional reading.

Bloom, L., & Lahey, M. (1978). *Language development and language disorders.* New York: John Wiley & Sons.

Carrow-Woolfolk, E. (1988). *Theory, assessment, and intervention in language disorders: An integrative approach.* Philadelphia: Grune & Stratton.

Goldsworthy, C. (1982). *Examiner's manual: Multilevel Informal Language Inventory.* San Antonio, TX: The Psychological Corporation.

Goldsworthy, C., & Secord, W. (1982). *Picture manual: Multilevel Informal Language Inventory.* San Antonio, TX: The Psychological Corporation.

Kretschmer, R. R., & Kretschmer, L. W. (1978). *Language development and intervention with the hearing impaired.* Baltimore: University Park Press.

Lee, L. (1974). *Developmental sentence analysis*. Evanston, IL: Northwestern University Press.

Miller, J. (1981). *Assessing language production in children: Experimental procedures*. Baltimore: University Park Press.

Owens, R. R. (1988). *Language development: An introduction* (2nd ed.). Columbus, OH: Charles E. Merrill Publishing Co.

Prather, E.M. (1988). Review of the Multilevel Informal Language Inventory. *Mental Measurements Yearbook*. (BSR file MMYD, Item AN 1004–151).

Rueda, R. (1988). Review of the Multilevel Informal Language Inventory. *Mental Measurements Yearbook*. (BSR file MMYD, Item AN 1004–151).

Stickler, K.R. (1987). *Guide to analysis of language transcripts*. Eau Claire, WI: Thinking Publications.

Tyack, D., & Gottsleben, R. (1974). *Language sampling, analysis of training: A handbook for teachers and clinicians*. Palo Alto, CA: Consulting Psychologists Press.

Sanford J. Cohn, Ph.D.
Associate Professor of Special Education and Learning and Instructional Technology, Arizona State University, Tempe, Arizona.

NEW JERSEY TEST OF REASONING SKILLS

Virginia Shipman. Upper Montclair, New Jersey: Institute for the Advancement of Philosophy for Children.

Introduction

The New Jersey Test of Reasoning Skills (NJTRS) is designed to measure elementary reasoning skills in language. The skills assessed by this criterion-referenced reasoning skills test correspond to elementary and essential operations in the domain of logic. (that is, *implication* is a logical operation; *inference* is a skill. One *infers* the conclusion that the premises of an argument *imply.*)

The NJTRS consists of 50 multiple-choice items in the form of syllogisms, representing 22 reasoning skill areas:
1) Converting statements
2) Translating into logical form
3) Inclusion/exclusion
4) Recognizing improper questions
5) Avoiding jumping to conclusions
6) Analogical reasoning
7) Detecting underlying assumptions
8) Eliminating alternatives
9) Inductive reasoning
10) Reasoning with relationships
11) Detecting ambiguities
12) Discerning causal relationships
13) Identifying good reasons
14) Recognizing symmetrical relationships
15) Syllogistic reasoning (categorical)
16) Distinguishing differences of kind and degree
17) Recognizing transitive relationships
18) Recognizing dubious authority
19) Reasoning with four-possibilities matrix
20) Contradicting statements
21) Whole-part and part-whole statements
22) Syllogistic reasoning (conditional)

The NJTRS was developed from 1976 through 1981 by Dr. Virginia C. Shipman, then senior research psychologist at the Educational Testing Service in Princeton, New Jersey, to evaluate the Philosophy for Children program (Lipman, 1976; Sternberg, 1984), created in 1969 by philosophy professor Matthew Lipman at Montclair (New Jersey) State College. Philosophy for Children was initiated to stimulate the development of reasoning skills in language by using techniques suggested by research performed by noted cognitive developmental psychologists and philosophers. The use of classroom dialogue as the key to sharpening reasoning, for example, emerged from the work of G.H. Mead *(Mind, Self, and Society)*, Vygotsky *(Thought and Language, Mind and Society)*, and Jerome Bruner *(The Process of Education)*. The choice of Grades 5 and 6 as appropriate for the introduction of logical skills was based upon Piaget's location of the formal stage of child development (cf. *Judgment and Reasoning in the Child*). Organizing materials to be learned into a story as opposed to a text came from Dewey *(The Child and the Curriculum)*, as did the notion that an educational session should begin with an experience upon which to reflect.[1]

The first step in the construction of the NJTRS centered on a survey of the logical competencies produced by language acquisition and the development of a taxonomy of logical operations performed in childhood (see Shipman, 1983). Once the detailed taxonomic domain was established, a representative sample of logical operations was selected, half inductive, half deductive. The content domain is suggested by the 22 skill areas listed previously.

The NJTRS has no norms per se, although the Institute for the Advancement of Philosophy for Children (IAPC) provides users with annual updates of national means for each grade level, so that comparisons can be made with means achieved locally. Fourteen studies have been performed with various populations, mostly heterogeneous by socioeconomic and ethnic considerations. Subjects of the studies were primarily third through eighth graders in mainstream classrooms in the United States public school system. Subjects of nine of the studies were fifth graders. The 1983–84 means for the NJTRS by grade are provided for Grades 2 through 13 (i.e., college freshmen). Average number of right answers out of 50 ranged from 22.71 for second-graders to 38.24 for college freshmen. The means for students from Grades 6 through 13 were quite level, suggesting that the test is inappropriate for students above Grade 5.

The NJTRS has attempted to attack the problem that most tests of reasoning skills require difficult reading levels. Inasmuch as the goals of the test makers was to test reasoning alone, the reading level was dropped as low as possible, posing few reading problems to students at the fifth-grade level and above. When children in lower grades are tested, the test is read to them, so as to avoid reading-reasoning contamination. In spite of these efforts, however, the NJTRS shows a correlation of .82 with tests of reading comprehension.

While IAPC promotes the use of the tests for both pre- and posttesting, they indicate that variant forms of the test are in preparation.

The NJTRS test booklet is 11 pages long with four to five multiple-choice items per page. Each item is presented in a syllogistic format with three answer options. No marks are to be made in the test booklet, as computer-scorable answer sheets

---

[1]Much of the descriptive material regarding the Philosophy for Children program and for the New Jersey Test of Reasoning Skills was drawn from a brochure, entitled "Philosophy for Children: Where Are We Now . . . ," received from the Institute for the Advancement of Philosophy for Children (IAPC), Montclair State College, Upper Montclair, New Jersey 07043 (201)893–4277. Dr. Matthew Lipman, Professor of Philosophy, is Director of IAPC; Dr. Ann Margaret Sharp, Professor of Education, is Associate Director.

are provided with lettered boxes to be filled in using a No. 2 pencil. An example of a test item follows:

> Dale is taller than Chris. Therefore,
> a. Chris is taller than Dale.
> b. You can't tell whether or not Chris and Dale are the same height.
> c. Chris is shorter than Dale.

Because the correct answer is *c*, one would pencil in *c* on the answer sheet. This item purports to assess proficiency in distinguishing symmetrical from asymmetrical relationships.

Most examinees take 30 to 45 minutes to complete this test. One is advised to administer the test under untimed conditions, although the test publishers claim that few individuals will find a 1-hour time limit a hardship. One form of the NJTRS, Form B, currently exists.

Answer sheets are provided, with each each item clearly numbered and separate from the others. The three choices for each item are shown inside a box as letters *a*, *b*, and *c*, the letter corresponding to the correct answer to be blackened in. There is also a bubble grid for the test taker's name, birthdate, and ID number.

No answer keys are furnished with the test. All scoring is done at the Institute for the Advancement of Philosophy for Children, Montclair State College, where the results become part of the IAPC Cognitive Skills Databank. For a single charge of $2.40 per test booklet, all scoring and analysis is included for up to four answer sheets per booklet. The booklets must be returned within a year or a new invoice will be sent to the customer.

A computer printout is provided for each class tested. The print-out includes: a) the Kuder-Richardson reliability index, b) the standard deviation data, c) the average (number correct out of 50) for each class as a whole, d) the percent of each class answering each question correctly.

In addition, each student receives a card indicating the number correct out of the number possible for each of the 22 skill areas. Information provided on this card includes the test taker's name, ID number, grade, total test score (i.e., number correct out of 50), percent correct, test date, and test form (IAPC). For each of the 22 skill areas, the number correct out of the number possible is shown. The maximum number of correct items for each reasoning skills category ranges from 1 to 4.

Minimal examiner participation is required when the test is given to fourth-graders and above. For test takers not familiar with the use of a separate answer sheet, some instruction may be required. For students who cannot read the test, the test is read to them.

The NJTRS clearly is geared for fourth- and fifth-graders. The test is simply and clearly written. The Flesch reading level is 4.5; the Fogg is 5.0. Many of the items are in dialogue form, so that children can examine the reasoning that occurs in their own speech, as well as in the discourse of adults.

Practical Applications/Uses

The New Jersey Test of Reasoning Skills is designed to measure elementary reasoning skills in language without contamination from *inert* sources, such as difficult vocabulary, reading levels, or items that draw from recollection of content, computation, or nonlinguistic skills. Because the NJTRS originally was conceived to evaluate a particular program, Philosophy for Children, which offers logic and reasoning to middle school children, the instrument is recommended by its publishers for use in other settings where reasoning and critical thinking skills represent the domain of content presented to students. The publishers also recommend its use as a criterion-referenced test for individual students to determine which areas of reasoning need remediation.

The NJTRS has been used mainly in middle school (i.e., fourth and fifth grade) classrooms in U.S. public schools in conjunction with the Philosophy for Children program. It is a relatively new instrument, so few other uses have evolved to date.

The restricted content domain of the NJTRS limits the potential for new applications of the test to situations that resemble closely the program of logic and critical thinking skills that it was originally created to evaluate.

While subjects from second grade through college freshmen have been given the NJTRS, it is clearly most useful with fourth- and fifth-graders. A ceiling effect seems to occur from Grade 6 on, and the test must be read to youths in Grades 3 or lower.

The test can be used with blind subjects simply by reading the items out loud, as for those too young to read it themselves. No other adaptations for handicapped or non-English-proficient subjects have been made to date.

The NJTRS is constructed ideally for administering to a large group in a typical classroom setting, as long as subjects are inhibited from seeing each other's work. No special requirements appear necessary for the examiner. A classroom teacher can easily administer the test.

No instruction manual exists. Directions for administration are extremely simple, involving a description of the item type and use of the separate answer sheet. The test is typically given under untimed conditions and generally takes 30 to 40 minutes to complete.

Interpretation of the NJTRS is based on objective scores, the number correct out of a possible 50. The test results seem best interpreted for a class as a whole taking the test. Perhaps this is due to the original purpose for which the instrument was developed.

The profile analysis for individual subjects seriously concerns this reviewer. The maximum number of items listed for each skill is four, with some skills having only one item comprising the subdomain. Such a limited number of items fails to provide a reliable profile for interpretation or analysis. For such purposes, the NJTRS is overambitious in its claims. The absence of substantial age norms also reduces the value of the test for individual interpretation.

Technical Aspects

Fifteen studies have been reported in which the New Jersey Test of Reasoning Skills was used (Burnes, 1981; Cinquins, 1981; Cummings, 1979; Curtis, 1979; Haas, 1976; Higa, 1980; Iorio, Weinstein, & Martin, 1984; Karras, 1979; Lipman, 1976; Reed & Henderson, 1981; Shipman, 1978; Shipman, 1983; Strohecker, 1985; Weinstein & Martin, 1982; Yeazell, 1981). Eleven of these studies are concerned with the impact of the Philosophy for Children program on reasoning ability: three with measuring changes in academic performance, five with the Philosophy for Children program's impact on creative thinking, and three with measuring changes in children's rational behavior. Subjects in these 15 studies are third- to eighth-graders, with nine of the studies focusing on fifth-graders. In all but one of the studies the subjects came from typical heterogeneous mainstream classrooms in the U.S. public school system; the other focused on academically talented children. Results are reported from high, middle, and low socioeconomic groups, as well as from diverse ethnic populations.

The NJTRS has been developed as a criterion-referenced test from an explicit and detailed domain (Shipman, 1983). The content validity is, therefore, quite good. The instrument has also shown sensitivity to subjects who have participated in the Philosophy for Children program, adding to its construct validity. In 11 of the 15 studies, for example, improved performance in reasoning ability (the dependent variable) was found to be significant.

Correlations of the NJTRS with the five subtests of the New Jersey College Basic Skills Placement Test were predominantly higher than, but certainly consistent with, correlations of two other similar tests of reasoning skills, the Cornell Critical Thinking Test and the Whimbey Analytical Skills Inventory, with the Basic Skills subtests (IAPC, 1986).

As mentioned in a previous section, the NJTRS claims to have removed "inert" confounders, such as vocabulary and difficult reading levels, from contaminating the measure of subjects' reasoning skills. The correlation of .82 with a test of reading comprehension undermines this allegation, however. The NJTRS runs the risk of being merely a test of reading comprehension, or at best a test of oral language comprehension in those situations in which the test must be read to subjects who cannot read the instrument themselves.

Critique

As a newly developed test, the NJTRS needs far more studies to create a construct validity that inspires confidence. Were one interested in the Philosophy for Children program, this reviewer would not think twice about recommending the use of the New Jersey Test of Reasoning Skills to evaluate the performance of classes of students in the program compared with other students of similar ability who did not take part in the program. This reviewer would not, however, recommend using the test to determine an individual's profile of developed reasoning skills, as the number of items per skill is far too small to yield reliable results. The absence of substantial norms, in spite of the Institute for the Advancement of Philosophy for Children's retention of all scores in its databank, further undermines the use of the test with individuals.

References

This list includes text citations and suggested additional reading.

Burnes, B. (1981). Harry Stottlemeier's discovery—the Minnesota experience. *Thinking, 3*(1), 8–11.

Cinquino, D. (1981). An evaluation of a philosophy program with 5th and 6th grade academically talented students. *Thinking, 2*(3/4), 8–11.

Cummings, N.P. (1979). Improving the logical skills of fifth graders: A study of philosophy as a teaching methodology in the elementary school. *Thinking, 1*(3/4), 90–92.

Curtis, B. (1979). Philosophy for Children in Hawaii. *Thinking, 1*(3/4), 52–59.

Haas, H.J. (1976). *Philosophical thinking in the elementary schools: An evaluation of the educational program, Philosophy for Children* (Unpublished report prepared for the National Endowment for the Humanities). Rutgers, NJ: Rutgers University, Institute for Cognitive Studies.

Higa, W.R. (1980). Philosophy for Children in Hawaii: A quantitative evaluation. *Thinking, 2*(1), 21– 31.

Institute for the Advancement of Philosophy for Children (1986). *Philosophy for Children: Where are we now* [Brochure]. Upper Montclair, NJ: Author.

Iorio, J., Weinstein, M., & Martin, J. (1984). A review of district 24's Philosophy for Children program. *Thinking, 5*(2), 28–36.

Karras, R.W. (1979). Final evaluation of the pilot program in philosophical reasoning in Lexington elementary schools 1978-79. *Thinking, 1*(3/4), 26–32.

Lipman, M. (1976). Philosophy for Children. *Metaphilosophy, 7*(1), 17–37.

Reed, R., & Henderson, A. (1981). Analytic thinking for children in Fort Worth elementary schools: Initial evaluation report, summer 1981. *Analytic Teaching, 2*(1), 5–12.

Shipman, V.C. (1978). *Philosophy for Children as a thinking skills program: An experimental report.* Unpublished manuscript. Princeton, NJ: Educational Testing Service.

Shipman, V.C. (1983). Evaluation replication of the Philosophy for Children program—Final report. *Thinking, 5*(1), 45–47.

Sternberg, R.J. (1984, September). Thinking skills in the curriculum. *Educational Leadership,* pp. 38–73.

Strohecker, M. (1985). Results of the 1983-1984 Philosophy for Children experiment in Lynbrook. *Thinking, 5*(2), 41–44.

Weinstein, M., & Martin, J. (1982). Philosophy for Children and the improvement of thinking skills in Queens, New York. *Thinking, 4*(2), 36.

Yeazell, M.I. (1981). A report on the first year of the Upshur County, West Virginia, Philosophy for Children project. *Thinking, 3*(1), 12–14.

Michael D. Franzen, Ph.D.
Associate Professor of Behavioral Medicine and Psychiatry, West Virginia University School of Medicine, Morgantown, West Virginia.

NON-LANGUAGE LEARNING TEST
Mary K. Bauman. Philadelphia, Pennsylvania: Associated Services for the Blind.

Introduction

The Non-Language Learning Test (NLLT) was designed to aid in the evaluation of intelligence of blind individuals. Prior to the development of the NLLT, most of the measures of intelligence in blind individuals relied heavily upon verbal information. Lightner Witmer, an early psychologist at the University of Pennsylvania, had been using a formboard to evaluate the blind, and this procedure was modified by Mary K. Bauman in 1947. The NLLT is not a test in the usual psychometric tradition; instead, it is a standard set of procedures by which the nonverbal problem-solving skills of blind subjects can be assessed. The information contained in the manual (Bauman, n.d.) is somewhat sparse, with the result that the test is probably best used by a clinician who has experience in working with the blind. The manual does suggest that the scores obtained from application of the NLLT may be less useful than an examination of the variations in scores across the three trials prescribed in the instructions.

The NLLT manual consists of the administration instructions, scoring suggestions, and interpretation suggestions. Additionally, the manual contains instructions for the construction of the test stimuli. The stimuli consist of an $11^{3/4}'' \times 8''$ formboard that has eight holes with four shapes cut out from the board. Into these holes fit blocks of different shapes, such as a diamond, a parallelogram, an elongated oval, and a six-sided figure that is shaped like a diamond with two extra parallel sides. Each of the four shapes is presented in the middle of the board and repeated along its periphery. Some of the blocks are one half the size of the cutouts, and some are one fourth the size of the cutouts. To the side of the formboard are four half-size blocks, cut lengthwise. In order to move the outside blocks into the inside holes, the one-fourth sized blocks must be moved to the peripheral holes.

The subject is instructed to move the smaller blocks into the peripheral holes and then move the blocks from the side of the formboard to the center holes. The shape and configuration of the board is demonstrated to the subject by guiding the subject's hands around the holes and the blocks and by providing verbal feedback. Then the examiner returns the blocks to their original places and asks the subject to repeat the task unaided. Following this trial, a second and third trial are administered. The score each time is the amount of time it takes the subject to finish the task. A limit of 5 minutes for each trial is suggested. The board is reversed following the first trial, and returned to the original position following the second trial.

Practical Applications/Uses

The Non-Language Learning Test appears to offer a unique approach to the evaluation of tactile recognition, manual dexterity, and nonverbal problem solving. This represents an increment over merely evaluating the verbal intelligence of a nonsighted individual. The manual also presents instructions for administering the procedure to sighted individuals. In these cases, there is no demonstration trial given because the subject should be able to see the shapes and the positions of the blocks and holes.

The manual suggests that the procedures can offer information regarding the ability of the subjects to learn from instruction as well as from experience. The NLLT is also said to allow evaluation of the subject's tactual discrimination, orientation in the work space, ability to derive information from the sense of touch, and the ability to deal with a complex whole.

The manual suggests four different patterns of performance with corresponding interpretations. For example, if the subject has a good first trial performance, a mediocre to poor second trial, and a good third trial, the manual suggests an interpretation of superficial memorizing without insight, and a prediction that such an individual would do well in familiar tasks, but would not be able to effectively problem solve independently. The interpretation of learning with insight is suggested when the subject does well on the first trial, improves his or her performance on each trial, and knows when a correct response has been made. The interpretation of an inability to deal with complexity is suggested when the subject has a poor first trial, significant disruption when the board is turned, and worse performance on the third trial. The interpretation of an inability to discriminate by touch is suggested when the subject verbalizes a correct understanding of the task but is unable to tell the holes apart.

Technical Aspects

There are no reliability data available on the NLLT. Because it is a problem-solving procedure, the NLLT might be hypothesized to show practice effects upon retest. The only available information related to NLLT validity is a concurrent validity study incompletely described in the manual. The scores of the three trials were correlated with the Wechsler Verbal IQ, and the score on the third trial was correlated with the score on the Pennsylvania Bi-Manual Assembly Test. The correlations were computed separately for a sample of 326 blind individuals and a sample of 353 sighted individuals. The correlations with Verbal IQ were small, ranging from $-.26$ to $-.39$. The correlation with the Pennsylvania Bi-Manual Assembly Test was approximately .50. Unfortunately, the characteristics of the sample, such as age, sex, and IQ range, were not described. Furthermore, the form of the Wechsler intelligence test was not stated. Because the NLLT was developed in the late 1940s, it is possible that the Wechsler-Bellevue Intelligence Scales were used, limiting the possible generalization to a more modern sample.

The manual also presents a table of percentile transformations of the raw scores at three different age groups for sighted and nonsighted individuals. The age groups are less than 26 years, between 26 and 39 years, and 40 years and older. The characteristics of the sample from which these percentiles were derived is not stated. It may be that some of the subjects in the correlational study described above may have been included in the normative sample. However, the totals are not equal. The total number of subjects in the normative sample is 331 (nonsighted) and 358 (sighted), while the total number of subjects in the correlational study is 326 (nonsighted) and 353 (sighted).

Critique

Although the NLLT is proposed as a nonlanguage measure of intelligence, a minimum of verbal intelligence is required to understand the task, as is true for most psychological tests. Despite its name, the NLLT actually is designed to be used with nonsighted individuals rather than with language-impaired individuals.

The utility of the NLLT is limited by the lack of reliability and validity data. This is particularly unfortunate because the NLLT appears to fill a gap in the available assessment procedures for blind individuals. As well as data relating the NLLT to other measures of general nonverbal intelligence, it would be useful to have data comparing performance on the NLLT to performance on manual tasks that are involved in job activities for blind individuals. Finally, the interpretation suggestions could be made more useful by empirical evaluations of the conclusions derived from an examination of score patterns.

References

Bauman, M.K. (n.d.). *The Non-Language Learning Test—Manual.* Philadelphia: Associated Services for the Blind.

Brian Bolton, Ph.D.

Professor, Research and Training Center in Vocational Rehabilitation, University of Arkansas, Fayetteville, Arkansas.

OBJECTIVE-ANALYTIC BATTERIES

Raymond B. Cattell and James M. Schuerger. Champaign, Illinois: Institute for Personality and Ability Testing, Inc.

Introduction

The Objective-Analytic Batteries (OA; Cattell & Schuerger, 1971) is the product of a half century of basic research on objective-analytic (O-A) personality tests by Raymond B. Cattell and his associates. The O-A Batteries, with the accompanying manual, *Personality Theory in Action* (Cattell & Schuerger, 1978), are unique among comprehensive, multitrait personality assessment procedures in that they consist entirely of objective tests, or what Cattell classifies as T-data. An objective test is one in which an examinee responds to a miniature situation, without knowing which personality trait is being evaluated. Unlike conventional personality measurement strategies which involve subjects' responses to questionnaires (Q-data) or observers' ratings of behavior (L-data), objective tests are not susceptible to self-report distortion or to the biases of judges.

The second term in the title of the O-A Batteries refers to the factor *analytic* statistical methodology by which the personality traits comprising the O-A Batteries were isolated, tentatively identified, replicated, and interpreted. After the functional unitary nature of the O-A traits was fully confirmed, validity studies were carried out to assess the relationships of the O-A factor measures to behavior in clinical, educational, and occupational applications. The O-A Batteries are in a kit consisting of 10 separate, single-factor instruments, each measuring a basic personality source trait of general relevance in professional psychology.

Raymond B. Cattell is a distinguished research professor emeritus at the University of Illinois where he directed the Laboratory of Personality and Group Behavior for 30 years. He has continued his research and writing in Hawaii since 1973. His 50 books and 450 scientific papers span the full range of human psychology, with special emphasis on personality measurement, multivariate statistics, learning theory, group dynamics, philosophy of science, and religious behavior. James M. Schuerger joined Cattell at the University of Illinois in 1988 to collaborate on the construction of a battery of objective-analytic tests that could be used by practicing psychologists in applied settings. Now a professor at Cleveland State University, Schuerger continues to conduct research on the O-A Batteries.

Programmatic research on personality measurement using objective test devices was initiated by Cattell in the early 1930s. The first systematic, comprehensive presentation of early work in this area was published in *Description and Measurement of Personality* (Cattell, 1948). The period of greatest activity in basic research on O-A measurement was the 1950s and 1960s. Among the several dozen publications generated by Cattell and his colleagues during this period, two are

374

especially prominent. *Personality Factors in Objective Test Devices* (Hundleby, Pawlik, & Cattell, 1965) summarized the factor analytic evidence from all existing investigations bearing on the verification of O-A source traits, while *Objective Personality and Motivation Tests* (Cattell & Warburton, 1967) is an encyclopedia of objective test procedures for use by personality researchers and test developers. Readers are referred to Schuerger (1988, pp. 287–289) for a useful overview of the history of objective personality assessment, including a chronological listing of major research publications.

Each of the 10 source traits contained in the O-A Batteries is measured with seven or eight separate tests that require a total testing time of about a half hour. All 78 tests were designed for administration to small groups of examinees, and the vast majority of tests involve reusable booklets with standard answer sheets, thus facilitating machine scoring for large-volume applications. Because the 10 O-A source-trait batteries are entirely self-contained, psychologists can select only those personality factors that they deem appropriate to their particular situations.

Brief descriptions of the 10 personality source traits measured by the O-A Batteries, with technical titles, U.I. (Universal Index) numbers, and three illustrative tests listed in parentheses, are as follows:

1) *Ego Standards* (U.I. 16)—Similar to being ego strength in the classical psychoanalytical sense, the traits have a stronger emphasis on self-assertion, achievement, boldness, and speed of action and decision. (Quicker Social Judgments; More Logical Assumptions Done; Greater Fluency on Objects)

2) *Independence vs. Subduedness* (U.I. 19)—This dimension is indicative of independence, criticalness, accuracy, capacity for intensive concentration, and perceptual field independence. (Better Immediate Memory; More Correct in Searching Task; Higher Index of Carefulness)

3) *Evasiveness* (U.I. 20)—This character trait is reflective of neurotic lack of objectivity, with some hostility and guilt proneness, but is sociable and dependent. (Greater Insecurity of Opinion; More Susceptibility to Annoyances; Greater Extremity of Response)

4) *Exuberance* (U.I. 21)—This temperamental predisposition manifests high spontaneity, fluency, imaginativeness, speed of social and perceptual judgment, and fast natural tempo. (Faster Marking Speed; More Garbled Words Guessed; Higher Frequency of Alternating Perspective)

5) *Capacity to Mobilize vs. Regression* (U.I. 23)—This personality factor is indicative of flexibility, general competence, emotional balance, and endurance of stress. (Higher Perceptual Coordination; Higher Ability to State Logical Assumptions; Fewer Threatening Objects Seen)

6) *Anxiety* (U.I. 24)—A well-established dimension of temperament, anxiety is evidenced by low ego strength, guilt proneness, ergic tension, suspicion, and poor self-concept. (More Common Frailties Admitted; More Emotionality of Comment; Less Willing Compliance in Unpleasant Tasks)

7) *Realism vs. Tensidia* (U.I. 25)—This personality trait is characterized by flexibility, sensitivity to reality, rejection of disturbing or imaginative intrusions, and a realistic orientation to tasks. (Lesser Pessimistic Insecurity; More Agreement with Homely Wisdom; Greater Accuracy of Ideomotor Performance)

8) *Asthenia vs. Self-Assurance* (U.I. 28)—This trait expresses ambivalence deriv-

ing from an unresolved conflict between demanding socialization and the need for self-realization, which results in resentful conformity. (Lower Severity and Guilt; More Cynical Pessimism; More Grudging Skepticism Regarding Success)

9) *Exvia vs. Invia* (U.I. 32)—The well-known extraversion-introversion dimension in personality theory is measured, with exviants being enthusiastic, uninhibited, and group-dependent. (Greater Willingness to Decide on Vague Data; More Fluency Concerning People's Characteristics; Lower Motor Rigidity)

10) *Discouragement vs. Sanguineness* (U.I. 33)—This trait reflects pessimism and discouragement of a lasting nature, with poor self-confidence and loss of objectivity. (Less Confidence in Unfamiliar Situations; Less Belief in Attainability of Goals; Greater Expectations of Unfavorable Consequences)

Practical Applications/Uses

The O-A Batteries can be used with normal populations in standard educational and occupational applications (e.g., prediction of academic achievement, vocational counseling, and personnel selection) and with clinical populations in rehabilitation, mental health, and psychiatric settings. Because the strongest validity evidence currently available pertains to psychiatric diagnosis, clinical applications of the O-A Batteries are especially appropriate. More generally, O-A source-trait measures should always be considered in the design of basic and applied psychological research.

All 76 tests comprising the O-A Batteries involve a regular paper-and-pencil response format and, therefore, can be group administered. Each test is individually timed, requiring from 1 to 6 minutes for completion; most tests take about 2 minutes. The seven or eight tests that compose each O-A source-trait scale require from 20 to 30 minutes of total testing time, with approximately half of the time subsumed by instructions and preparatory activity. The O-A Batteries can be administered in 5 hours, including two highly recommended 15-minute rest breaks. Administration of the O-A tests is made easier by the interesting and challenging nature of the task demands.

Because all instructions for administering the O-A Batteries are available on audiocassette tapes, the actual administration of the tests is not nearly as complicated as it first appears to be. Still, the properly qualified examiner will require considerable training and practice under the supervision of a professional psychologist before achieving an acceptable level of proficiency. The degree of skill necessary to administer the O-A Batteries is comparable to that needed for the typical individual intelligence test. An individual with a bachelor's degree in behavioral science and with training as a psychometric assistant can be trained to administer the O-A Batteries.

All but 12 of the 76 tests comprising the O-A Batteries involve reusable booklets and standard answer forms that are amenable to machine scoring. Eight of the 12 tests that require expendable booklets are used to assess Exuberance (U.I. 21), with the other 4 needed in the measurement of Capacity to Mobilize vs. Regression (U.I. 23) and Exvia vs. Invia (U.I. 32). Initial scoring of the 12 expendable booklets must be done by hand, but the procedure in every case is a straightforward, clerical task that can be accomplished quite easily.

The raw scores that result from the 76 tests may be the number of items completed or the number of items finished correctly, but the vast majority of the 76 raw scores are calculated as ratios of the above two simple scores, and these ratios may involve additional algebraic tranformations. For this reason, raw scores for O-A tests are referred to as *derived* raw scores.

Once the seven or eight derived raw scores for an O-A factor scale are calculated, they are entered onto a Score Summary Sheet. A sequence of arithmetic computations translates the vector of derived raw scores into a summative standard score in which the constituent O-A tests are differentially weighted in direct proportion to their factor analytically estimated contributions to the underlying personality source trait. The calculations outlined on the Score Summary Sheets could be programmed easily for microcomputer use. The normative sample on which the O-A Batteries are standardized consists of about 750 16- to 18-year-old high school students.

Interpretation of the O-A Batteries scale scores in personality assessment adheres to the same general principles that are followed with any other source trait instrument (e.g., multiple causation of behavior, pathology as quantitative deviation, and depth psychometry) (see Bolton, 1986, pp. 349–352). For interpretive purposes, the distinguishing characteristic of the O-A Batteries is that personality trait structure is assessed at a higher level of generality than through self-report and rating instruments (i.e., the O-A primary factors correspond to second stratum dimensions in Q- and L-data, such as Exvia, Anxiety, and Independence). Because the O-A source traits encompass both normal and abnormal personality dimensions, the O-A Batteries are is applicable in nonclinical as well as clinical settings. For a case example of O-A source trait interpretation in understanding normal adolescent development, see Bolton (1986, pp. 360–362).

Technical Aspects

The scientific foundation of the O-A Batteries combines two innovative features in modern personality assessment. The first is the use of objective tests that measure behavior in quasi-laboratory situations. Originally, many of the tests comprising the O-A Batteries were actually administered individually under strict laboratory conditions, but were eventually modified for group administration via paper-and-pencil format. Thirty years of inventing, developing, and refining objective devices culminated in publication of *Objective Personality and Motivation Tests* (Cattell & Warburton, 1967), a compendium of 400 objective testing situations.

Because the 400 miniature situations with their defined response possibilities can be scored in several different ways (e.g., completion, errors, and speed), the number of objective test variables exceeds the test situations. In fact, more than 2,000 response variables have been catalogued using the Master Index (M.I.) numbering scheme. It was through systematic investigation of this large population of objective measures of personality functioning that the source traits measured by the O-A Batteries were discovered.

The second innovation in personality measurement upon which the O-A Batteris are premised is the programmatic series of more than 20 factor analytic studies of carefully selected subsets of objective tests designed to identify replicable source-trait personality structures in T-data. The results of these statistical studies were collated and published in *Personality Factors in Objective Test Devices* (Hundleby et al., 1965). After the optimal factor batteries of objective tests were confirmed for the major O-A source traits, studies of criterion validity were undertaken, as well as analyses of age development trends, gender differences, and estimated trait heritabilities.

Basic psychometric properties of the O-A Batteries are presented in Table 1. Retest reliabilities (with an interval of less than 1 day) range from .62 to .93 with a median of .75, stability coefficients (over 3 to 6 weeks) range from .61 to .85 with a median of .71, and concept validities (correlations between trait scores and pure factors) range from .64 to .92 with a median of .76. These data indicate that the 10 O-A factor scales are highly stable measures of replicable personality source traits.

Table 1

Psychometric Characteristics of the O-A Batteries

Source Trait	Reliability	Stability	Validity
1. Ego Standards (U.I. 16)	.75	.61	.92
2. Independence (U. I. 19)	.75	.73	.79
3. Evasiveness (U. I. 20)	.74	.64	.68
4. Exuberance (U.I. 21)	.93	.78	.80
5. Mobilization (U.I. 23)	.71	.71	.76
6. Anxiety (U.I. 24)	.90	.85	.92
7. Realism (U.I. 25)	.62	.62	.74
8. Asthenia (U.I. 28)	.66	.58	.64
9. Exvia (U.I. 32)	.74	.67	.71
10. Discouragement (U.I. 33)	.81	.80	.85

The concept validities listed in Table 1, which indicate the degree to which the O-A measures align with the underlying source-trait factors, are primarily of *theoretical* import. Of much more value to practicing psychologists are the *concrete* relationships between O-A Batteries scale scores and important educational, occupational, and clinical criteria. A substantial body of evidence concerning the criterion relevance of the O-A Batteries is presented in *Personality Theory in Action* (Cattell & Schuerger, 1978); the interested reader should consult this volume for details.

However, because the largest and most impressive validity data pertain to the use of the O-A Batteries in psychiatric diagnosis, and because this area of application shows great promise for rapid advance, a brief summary of the relationships of O-A source traits to various clinical pathologies is appropriate. The diagnostic potential of the O-A source traits has been quantified in statistical discriminant functions that identified the following psychiatric groups, with proportions of agreement in parentheses (Cattell & Schuerger, 1978, p. 262): involutional depressives (67%), other psychotic depressives (64%), neurotic depressives (45%), schizophrenics (67%), manics (64%), anxiety neurotics (67%), and normal controls (94%).

Four O-A traits are common to most of the psychiatric diagnostic syndromes, thus comprising a "pathological core" with the following characteristics: more subdued (U.I. 19–), greater inhibition (U.I. 21–), more regressed (U.I. 23–), and poorer reality contact (U.I. 25–). In addition to lower scores on U.I. 19, U.I. 21, and U.I. 23, neurotics possess less ego strength (U.I. 16–) and much higher anxiety (U.I. 24+). Neurotics also deviate somewhat from normals on Evasiveness (U.I. 20+), Realism (U.I. 25–), and Exvia (U.I. 32–).

The primary diagnostic O-A source traits in differentiating schizophrenics from normals are U.I. 16–, U.I. 19–, U.I. 21–, U.I. 23–, U.I. 25–, U.I. 32–, and U.I. 33+. While most of these traits are shared with neurotics, there are several critical differences: the U.I. 21– difference for schizophrenics is less than neurotics, the U.I. 25– difference is greater for schizophrenics (more disturbed reality contact), U.I. 33+ (Discouragement) characterizes schizophrenia but not neurosis, and U.I. 24+ (Anxiety) is not a factor in the diagnosis of schizophrenia. For details regarding the differential diagnosis of the major psychiatric syndromes the reader is referred to the research summary in *Personality Theory in Action* (Cattell & Schuerger, 1978, pp. 252–256).

This review has focused entirely on the 10 best validated O-A source traits, measured with seven or eight tests, which are referred to collectively as the Main Kit. Two extensions of the Main Kit are available for use by professional psychologists and researchers. First, the authors provide lists of four or five supplementary tests, all of which are individually administered or require laboratory apparatus, for the 10 main O-A factors. The Supplementary Battery expands the coverage of the Main Kit factors, thus increasing the reliability and validity of the source-trait measurements (see Cattell & Schuerger, 1978, Appendix B).

The second supplement to the Main Kit, which is called the Extended Battery, consists of lists of recommended test procedures for assessing 10 additional, less-well confirmed O-A source-trait factors: Control (U.I. 17), Hypomanic Temperament (U.I. 18), Cortertia (U.I. 22), Narcism (U.I. 26), Apathetic Temperament (U.I. 27), Overreactivity (U.I. 29), Somindence vs. Dissofrustance (U.I. 30), Wariness vs. Impulsivity (U.I. 31), Inconautia vs. Practicalness (U.I. 34), and Stolparsomnia vs. Proneness to Excitement (U.I. 35). It should be emphasized that the O-A factors in the Extended Kit are only available on an experimental basis and require considerable effort by the investigator just to operationalize selected single-factor batteries (see Cattell & Schuerger, 1978, Appendix A).

Critique

Several features of the O-A Batteries Test Kit merit the attention of professional psychologists. Unquestionably, this represents a truly innovative approach to personality measurement and a major step in the direction of a scientific strategy for personality assessment practice and research. Because the O-A Batteries can be administered to small groups of examinees by an individual with bachelor's-level training or less, it is not as expensive or time-consuming as it might seem to be. The instructions for administration are available on audiocassettes and all but a few of the 76 tests use machine-scorable answer sheets.

The psychometric properties of the O-A source-trait scales are good and the criterion validity evidence is supportive of the usefulness of the O-A Battery, especially in clinical diagnosis and related tasks. The outstanding defect of the instrument is the limited normative sample for calculating standard scores. Performance data for high school students are sufficient for personality assessment of late adolescents and young adults, but any application beyond this range in the absence of additional standardization information requires caution. In conclusion, the O-A Batteries Test Kit comprises a valuable assessment technique for use by clinicians and researchers.

References

Bolton, B. (1986). Clinical diagnosis and psychotherapeutic monitoring. In R. B. Cattell & R. C. Johnson (Eds.), *Functional psychological testing: Principles and instruments* (pp. 348–376). New York: Brunner/Mazel.

Cattell, R.B. (1946). *Description and measurement of personality.* New York: World.

Cattell, R.B., & Schuerger, J.M. (1971). *O-A Battery Test Kit.* Champaign, IL: Institute for Personality and Ability Testing.

Cattell, R.B., & Schuerger, J.M. (1978). *Personality theory in action: Handbook for the Objective-Analytic Test Kit.* Champaign, IL: Institute for Personality and Ability Testing.

Cattell, R.B., & Warburton, F.W. (1967). *Objective personality and motivation tests: A theoretical introduction and practical compendium.* Champaign, IL: University of Illinois Press.

Hundleby, J.D., Pawlik, K., & Cattell, R.B. (1965). *Personality factors in objective test devices.* San Diego: R.R. Knapp.

Schuerger, J.M. (1986). Personality assessment by objective tests. In R. B. Cattell & R. C. Johnson (Eds.), *Functional psychological testing: Principles and instruments* (pp. 260–287). New York: Brunner/Mazel.

Ann H. Stoddard, Ed.D.

Professor of Education, University of North Florida, Jacksonville, Florida.

OPINIONS TOWARD ADOLESCENTS

William T. Martin. St. Louis, Missouri: Psychologists and Educators, Inc.

Introduction

Opinions Toward Adolescents (OTA) is an 89-item scale used to identify ideas and attitudes related to adolescence. It is divided into eight subscales that provide an interpretation of some personality characteristics that tend to affect interpersonal relations with adolescents. The author of the scale, Dr. William T. Martin, published a similar measure in 1969 entitled Self-Perception Inventory. The OTA was developed to look at compatibility between adults and adolescents. The major objective of the scale was to serve as an effective screening device for persons working with adolescents or seeking employment to work with adolescents. Persons scoring high on the negative continuum of the scale would appear to be incompetent candidates for job assignments with adolescents.

The OTA is a 4-point Likert-type scale composed of 89 statements to which the examinee responds from "Strongly Agree" to "Strongly Disagree." There is no neutral response offered. The items are divided into eight subscales: 16 conservative/liberal items, which measure prevailing flexibility of adult general attitudes; 10 permissive/punitive items, which measure self- and adolescent-defeating attitudes that tend to see adolescents as persons to control or to "work with;" 10 morally accepted/morally restrictive items, which measure traits that indicate both insensitivity to youth and rigid traditional values; 13 democratic/authoritarian items, which identify adult attitudes of superiority and point out adults who want to "control adolescents;" 10 trust/mistrust items, which identify adult attitudes that focus on suspicion and doubt toward adolescent behavior; 11 acceptance/prejudice items, which identify adult attitudes of antagonism toward adolescents that are gross negative generalizations without supporting evidence; 14 misunderstanding/understanding items, which measure compatibility between adults and adolescents, reflecting an understanding and acceptance between the two groups; and 5 sincerity/skepticism items, which manifest the examinee's apprehension about test-taking. This category does not concern adolescents, but rather relates to the manner in which the test taker responds to the other seven subscales.

The scale is intended to measure basic adult attitudes toward adolescents and is self-administering. The 89 statements are written on a fifth- or sixth-grade reading level. The answer form has demographic data, directions, and space for the responses. There is also space for the scorer to write in raw scores and percentile equivalents.

The profile sheet is two-sided. One side characterizes the interpretation of the profile sheet and the subscales as well as describes the norms for each subscale.

The other side of the profile sheet is a record of the profile itself. It uses T-scores and percentile equivalents to compare the examinee to the norm group. All subscales are plotted on two separate norm populations, college and adult, with an exception for the Sincerity/Skepticism scale. The two groups scored similarly, making it unnecessary for two separate norms.

Practical Applications/Uses

Designed as a basic scale to identify specific attitudes toward adolescents, the OTA scale serves as a screening instrument for persons who are seeking employment that specifies for adolescent interaction. It can also be used for a research tool and in staff development programs, particularly in the area of interpersonal skills and in settings that require adolescent treatment in-service training. Not only can the OTA be used with adults, but likewise with adolescents to evaluate themselves and to determine their own concept of adolescence. In the area of program evaluation, the OTA can be used additionally as an index of relationships among adolescent participants and personnel.

Personnel in educational settings will find the OTA scale useful, particularly when screening adults who will work directly with adolescents, such as counselors, teachers, social workers, and school nurses. Other settings where the OTA would be appropriately used are social agencies that extend their services to adolescents. With many services being provided to today's adolescents beyond the educational arena, the OTA has potential possibilities in every sector of society that interfaces with this age group.

Because of the specific terms used in the statements of the scale, the OTA is restricted to the use of ascertaining attitudes toward adolescents. If the scale is to be used with adults or adolescents who are non-English speaking, the OTA will have to be translated to the language needed. To adapt the scale for the visually handicapped, the print would need to be enlarged or the items read aloud to the examinee.

Inasmuch as the OTA scale is self-administering, it can be used in all types of settings: individually, small group, and large group. Monitoring or use of a proctor is not required because the scale measures an area in the affective domain and there are no right or wrong answers. The self-read directions request that no answers be changed. Erasures can be detected by the scorer or on a computer-scored answer sheet.

The time needed for administering the OTA scale is minimal, 15 to 20 minutes. Due to the middle value being eliminated from the response option, not only is bias and response reduced, but time needed to record responses is also reduced.

Scoring of the OTA is a relatively simple task. Scores for each subscale vary, and no total score is required. Separate cardboard template overlays are used for each separate subscale. If a computer-scored answer sheet is used, a printout can be provided for each subscale total. This procedure is possible because all statements of the scale are presented in a positive direction. The higher score indicates the right side of the continuum. Not all traits in this position are considered positive, however (e.g., "acceptance/prejudice" and "misunderstanding/understanding").

Concise directions for scoring are found on the cardboard templates. Scoring in its entirety should take approximately 5 minutes.

Interpretation of the OTA scores is comparatively easy. Total raw scores for each subscale are recorded on the answer sheet, as well as the percentile equivalents. One side of the profile sheet describes the interpretation procedures. Raw scores are converted to T-scores and percentile equivalents on the reverse side, adapting to two norm groups, college and adult. Individuals scoring within a 40-60 T-score area are considered to score similarly to the standardization sample. When an individual score is above 60 and below 40, it can be construed that the individual possesses the traits measured by the subscale. For example, a raw score of 14 on the Acceptance/Prejudice scale converts to a T-score of 70 and a percentile of 97 for the college group, and a T-score of 63 and a percentile of 92 for adults. On both norms, the individual would be considered to possess the trait of prejudice. Data can be plotted on either group to examine the 8-trait categories.

Technical Aspects

Content validity was carried out in conjunction with the scale development. The first pool of questions and open-ended statements were presented to several hundred adults who were educators, mental health workers, college students, student nurses, and other community persons. Items for the scale were cross-checked with the literature to generate item clusters. After the scale was constructed, it was administered to 100 undergraduate college students. Correlation coefficients ranged from $-.002$ to $+.222$, indicating that all scales appeared to be independent of each other.

Test-retest reliability for the OTA was based on 31 undergraduate college students (mean age $=$ 19). Reliability coefficients, ranging from .70 to .91 ($p = < .001$) on the eight subscales, indicated a substantial degree of stability.

There was no evidence in the OTA manual of any other type of validity being determined, such as concurrent validity. In addition, no standard error of measurement was reported. No studies using the OTA were found in the literature. Consequently, questions concerning other variables having an effect on its validity and reliability go unanswered. For example, do people of different racial, cultural, or socioeconomic groups hold different opinions toward adolescents than the normative sample?

Critique

The conceptualization of trying to identify specific opinions toward adolescents is good. Too often, personnel who are trained to work with youth do not necessarily have the appropriate attitudes toward them. A second reflection is that agencies and institutions generally require specific skills for employment, and applicants are usually tested for these skills, but too few of these establishments appraise attitudes.

The OTA may be used as a screening instrument with a pool of applicants who intend to work with adolescents, but the test author suggests that it be used as an adjunct to other testing and observation of behavior. The convenient format of the test booklet, answer sheet, and manual make the OTA easy to administer, score, and interpret. Clear concise information and directions assist in this process. The reading level is not difficult, making it possible to administer the OTA to a wide range of individuals. Clear concise information and directions assist in this process.

However, there are some problems with the OTA scale. First, the scale was not standardized on a large sample distributed across geographic areas. There also appears to be underrepresentation of minority groups, different age groups, and different levels of socioeconomic groups whose opinions about adolescents may differ greatly from the normative sample. Only 10 years separated the college and adult samples (mean ages = 20.00 and 30.12, respectively) whose opinions about adolescents may be very similar.

While reliability data for the OTA were impressive, the validity data presented are meager. Compensation for differences that occurred between the college and adult groups was to construct two separate profiles, a legitimate scheme. Nevertheless, the only standardization data offered among the three groups (two college and one adult) were the mean and the standard deviation for each subscale. There appeared to be no evidence of establishing criterion-related validity for the OTA. Consequently, there is no support to the allegation that the subscales measure what they profess to measure.

The OTA is not a newly constructed scale to identify opinions toward adolescents. The lack of studies or research using the OTA is disturbing. This reviewer located no investigations using the OTA on which to base some judgment or evaluation about its use, its effectiveness, or its shortcomings.

Of the three practical uses cited by the author, no studies were shown to determine its value. If school and agencies want to use the OTA as a screening stratagem, they should exercise prudence and use the OTA in conjunction with other methods of screening, including observation. Perhaps the best use of the scale presently is for research purposes. In that capacity, determination can be made about its worth before confirming that the OTA actually and accurately measures opinions toward adolescents. Further research should be conducted to provide evidence of criterion-related validity.

References

This list includes text citations and suggested additional reading.

Enright, R.D., Levy, V.M., Jr., Harris, D., & Lapsley, D.K. (1987). Do economic conditions influence how theorists view adolescents? *Journal of Youth and Adolescence, 16,* 541–559.

Galbo, J.J. (1987). An exploration of the effects of the relationship of adolescents and adults on learning in secondary schools. *High School Journal, 71,* 97–102.

Pomales, J., Clairborn, C.D., & LaFromboise, T.D. (1986). Effects of black students' racial identity on perceptions of white counselors varying in cultural sensitivity. *Journal of Counseling Psychology, 33,* 57–61.

Smith, D.C., Adelman, H.S., Nelson, P., Taylor, L., & Phares, V. (1986). Students' perception of control at school and problem behavior and attitudes. *Journal of School Psychology, 25,* 167–76.

Taylor, G.H., & Sayer, B. (1983). Attitudes of teachers towards the 9-13 middle school. *Educational Research, 25,* 71–74.

Vidoni, D.C. (1983). Behavior problems of children as perceived by teachers, mental health professionals, and children. *Psychology in the Schools, 20,* 93–98.

Martin, W.T. (1972). *Manual: Opinions Toward Adolescents.* St. Louis, MO: Psychologists and Educators.

Jerome Siegel, Ph.D.
Professor of Psychology, The City College of New York, New York, New York.

ORGANIZATION HEALTH SURVEY

William J. Reddin. Fredericton, New Brunswick: Organizational Tests (Canada) Ltd.

Introduction

The Organization Health Survey (OHS) was developed by P.T. Kehoe and W.J. Reddin, president of the company that publishes this test, and is designed to measure the "health" of an organization through respondents employed by organizations in a managerial capacity. The test consists of 80 "agree/disagree" questions designed to measure eight health dimensions: productivity, leadership, organization structure, communication, conflict management, human resource management, participation, and creativity. Scoring is accomplished through a built-in answer key upon which responses are recorded using carbon paper. There are 10 items for each scale; thus, scores can vary from 0 to 10 on each dimension. Norms are provided based upon 726 participants from nine organizations in terms of low, average, and high scores for each of the eight factors. The documentation supporting this instrument consists of a Fact Sheet and an Administrator's Manual. The OHS reportedly takes 15 to 20 minutes to administer; it is self-administered and self-scored.

Practical Applications/Uses

According to the authors, the Organization Health Survey can be used for a variety of purposes. It was originally designed to be used in government and industry by managers, administrators, and supervisors to determine the health and climate of an organization. It is suggested that sequential administrations are useful with a comparison of scores over time. The feedback to management can be helpful in problems dealing with increasing sensitivity to climate issues. It is also suggested that the OHS is useful as a management training instrument to promote discussion about organizational health; in fact, the manual provides a number of suggestions on how to use the OHS as a training instrument.

The administration (either self- or examiner administered) and scoring of this instrument are extremely simple and can be accomplished by a clerk. The OHS is scored by hand by counting the number of items answered for each of the factors. Interpretation of the OHS is difficult because the manual does not provide appropriate data for interpreting a profile of scores for the eight factors.

Technical Aspects

There are very little supportive data presented with the Organization Health Survey. The fact sheet contains simple norms ($N = 726$) consisting of a range of

386

scores ranked as High, Average, or Low for each of the eight dimensions measured. Low scores are generally less than 5; average scores are 5 to 7; and high scores are above 7. In the manual, these scores are further broken down into average scores for each factor for each of the nine organizations in the sample. (These organizations vary considerably, ranging from airline employees to workers in a mental hospital.) The percentage of the sample agreeing with each of the 80 items is then presented. There is no information regarding the interpretation of these data or how to interpret a profile of scores for an individual test.

Reliability data are provided based upon test-retest information on a sample of 88 participants retested 1 month after the original testing. The fact sheet reports coefficients ranging from .62 to .75. The manual reports additional data on the same sample of 88 (from two of the nine organizations) for each of the eight factors, with test-retest reliability coefficients ranging from .55 to .85 on split samples of 59 and 29 volunteer employees. No other information is given.

There are no validity data reported in the Fact Sheet or the test manual. Nor is there a simple discussion of face validity in any of the documents that were made available to this reviewer. The item validity is nowhere to be found in any of the supporting documents.

Critique

The Organization Health Survey was reviewed in *The Ninth Mental Measurements Yearbook* by Dey and Parsons (1985). Both reviews were extremely negative. The reviewers cited several other instruments as more appropriate for measuring perceived "health" and "climate" of an organization, such as the Organizational Climate Questionnaire (Litwin & Stringer, 1968) and Likert's Organizational Profile (1967). This reviewer would like to add the Survey of Organizations (Taylor & Bowers, 1972), which is published by the Institute of Social Research, University of Michigan.

There are major limitations with the OHS when the usual psychometric criteria are applied. There is no reported empirical or content validity. The authors expect the user to accept the face validity of 80 basic items without any justification. The reported reliability data are insufficient and inconclusive. Measures of internal consistency are not reported. Additionally, there is a failure to indicate standard errors of measurement for each of the reported coefficients in the manual. Therefore, an individual set of scores cannot be interpreted. The normative information provides no rationale on how scores are classified as high, average, and low, nor on how to interpret a profile of scores for each of the factors. In fact, the meanings of these factors are ambiguous because no rationale is given of how they were derived. A good deal of meaningless statistical information is given (e.g., how fast the quickest 10% of respondents completed the survey and how long it takes the slowest 10%).

In looking for something positive about the OHS, this reviewer decided to evaluate the fairly extensive bibliography presented at the end of the test manual. The latest reference given was dated 1972, a nd there were no reported studies using the OHS.

In this reviewer's opinion, the Organization Health Survey is a totally unacceptable instrument in terms of methodology, development, and reported statistical and technical data. It does not meet any of the psychometric standards common in the test industry and really seems to be totally inappropriate for usage in its present form. This reviewer would not recommend its use until validity studies are completed and appropriate reliability and normative information are developed. In the interest of professionalism, this reviewer would urge the publisher to remove it from the marketplace until satisfactory information can be documented and reported regarding its claims.

References

Dey, M.L. (1985). Organization Health Survey. In. J.V. Mitchell, Jr. (Ed.), *The ninth mental measurements yearbook* (pp. 1100–1101). Lincoln, NE: Buros Institute of Mental Measurements.

Litwin, G.H., & Stringer, R.A. (1968). *Motivation and organizational climate*. Boston, MA: Harvard University Press.

Likert, R.L. (1967). *The Human Organization*. New York, NY: McGraw-Hill

Parsons, C.K. (1985). Organization Health Survey. In J.V. Mitchell, Jr. (Ed.), *The ninth mental measurements yearbook* (pp. 1101–1102). Lincoln, NE: Buros Institute of Mental Measurements.

Reddin, W.J. (1981). *Organization Health Survey*. Fredericton, Canada: Organizational Tests Ltd.

Taylor, S.C., & Bowers, D.G. (1972). *Survey of Organizations*. Ann Arbor, MI: Institute for Social Research, University of Michigan.

Jerry Johnson, Ph.D.
Associate Professor of Mathematics, Western Washington University, Bellingham, Washington.

ORLEANS-HANNA ALGEBRA PROGNOSIS TEST

Gerald S. Hanna and Joseph B. Orleans. San Antonio, Texas: The Psychological Corporation.

Introduction

The Orleans-Hanna Algebra Prognosis Test is designed to predict the success of students in a first-year algebra course. As initially conceptualized, it is an algebra ability test that will "measure the pupil's ability to do the type of work to be learned in the way in which it is to be learned" (Orleans, 1934, p. 174). The test results can help teachers, counselors, administrators, and parents counsel students and make more accurate placements in a first-year algebra course. At issue is the identification of two contrasting groups of students, those who do not have the necessary skills or ability but would normally enroll in the algebra course and those who clearly have the necessary skills or ability but do not intend to enroll in the algebra course. Once identified, both student groups will benefit from placement in an appropriate mathematics course.

Joseph B. Orleans and Jacob S. Orleans developed the original version of the test in 1926. As chair of a mathematics department, Joseph B. Orleans was concerned with the problem of individual differences and its effect on student learning of mathematics. He developed prognosis tests for both algebra and geometry to identify the important individual differences, make correct course placements, and improve student success. Gerald S. Hanna, Professor of Educational Psychology and Measurement at Kansas State University and a former mathematics teacher, assisted in a major revision of the exam in 1968, the result being the Orleans-Hanna Algebra Prognosis Test.

Developed as a departmental exam by Joseph B. Orleans, the algebra prognosis test was first used in mimeographed form in 1926 with 300 students in the George Washington High School, New York City. The structure of the test was unusual in that it was composed of 11 brief instructional lessons, each explaining one small concept in algebra followed by a test based on the lesson. The intent was to measure the student's success at learning new algebraic content in a brief time period then use the results to predict the student's success at learning algebra over a full year. The success of Orleans's test, as measured by correlations with year-end measures, such as teacher ratings and an algebra achievement test, led to minor revisions, pilot testing in high schools throughout New York State, and eventual publication (Orleans, 1934). When made available nationally, the Orleans Algebra Prognosis Test retained its unique format. After numerous revisions, the current version of test contains nine miniature lessons complemented by self-report questions concerning the student's previous grades and a predicted algebra grade. A student's test score is a weighted combination of his or her success in the algebra lessons (60%) and the self-reported grades (40%).

The Orleans Algebra Prognosis Test was first published by the World Book Company in 1928. Though it received wide acceptance and use, the test was revised in 1950 to reflect changes in the mathematics curriculum. Assisted by Gerald S. Hanna, Joseph B. Orleans made a similar revision in his test in 1968, again motivated by curricular developments (i.e., the "New Math") and new research results relative to the use of different predictors for algebra prognosis (Hanna, Bligh, Lenke, & Orleans, 1969). Though the senior author is deceased, a final revision of the Orleans-Hanna Algebra Prognosis Test occurred in 1982 to incorporate new curricular and content emphases. Each test revision has required a new standardization procedure and validity testing. The use of the current version of the test is based on a normative population carefully selected to be representative of the national population of seventh- and eighth-grade students with respect to socioeconomic status, geographical region of the country, and size of school district.

The Orleans-Hanna Algebra Prognosis Test has 5 self-report questions and 60 questions involving algebra. The initial questions ask students to first report their most recent grades in mathematics, science, English, and social science/history and then predict the grade they would be most likely to receive if they took algebra. The 60 algebra questions are multiple-choice and are distributed among the nine miniature instructional lessons and a review test. The algebraic concepts covered include: 1) the substitution of numerical values in both monomials and binomials; 2) computations with signed numbers; 3) combining similar and dissimilar terms; 4) translating verbal expressions into literal expressions; 5) exponents; 6) simple equations and inequalities; and 7) functional notation.

The Orleans-Hanna Algebra Prognosis Test could be used to guide any student intending to enroll in an algebra course. However, reference-group norms are provided only for students who are completing mathematics courses at the seventh- or eighth-grade levels. Because of a verbal lesson-question format, reading difficulty is a recognized concern and should not confound the test's prognostic effort. Though undocumented, the vocabulary is claimed to not exceed (but averages well below) the sixth-grade level (Orleans & Hanna, 1982, p. 21).

Practical Applications/Uses

Designed primarily as a predictive instrument, the Orleans-Hanna Algebra Prognosis Test provides decision-making guidance information. The test authors' contend that this information must reflect the three variables most related to student success in a standard algebra course: 1) the ability to learn in situations similar to an algebra course; 2) the mastery and proficient application of necessary background skills/knowledge; and 3) interest/motivation factors, such as level of aspiration, study habits, and affective reaction to mathematics. Without intending to be a comprehensive measure of these three important factors, the test tries to measure selected aspects of each variable. In turn, the student's score is a weighted composite of information relative to tested abilities to learn algebra, recent course grades, and a student prediction of probable success in an algebra course. To have a maximal effect in the decision-making process, this score should be used in conjunction with other predictive information such as teacher recommendations.

Teachers, counselors, and parents could use the test results to help junior high students make realistic decisions, based on their probable success in an algebra course. Teachers also could use the test results on a group basis to plan an instructional program or adjust to the needs of students of different abilities. In schools that group by ability or have multilevel algebra programs, administrators could use the test results to help create uniform sections.

The Orleans-Hanna Algebra Prognosis Test can be administered and scored by any adult able to implement and follow the standard testing procedures. It can be used in either an individual or group setting. Approximately 15 minutes are required to complete the identifying information and five self-report questions, which must be completed carefully and fully because of the weighted scoring system. In the self-reporting of grades, possible problems could arise, such as students who claim that they have never taken one of the listed courses (e.g., social science), schools which do not use a letter-based grading system, or students who cannot remember previous course grades. Though the 1982 manual suggests possible solutions for these problems, considerable amounts of time could be required to ensure that each student has completed this section of the test. At no time is the examiner to use school records to verify or change student grades.

The algebra portion of the test has 60 questions and a time limit of 40 minutes. Students need to be encouraged to work at a rapid pace, as each of the nine instructional lessons must be read prior to the answering of their related questions. Slow readers are definitely at a disadvantage, regardless of their mathematical ability.

The scoring procedure is entirely objective; no special skills or knowledge are required. The method of scoring can be done either by hand, using a stencil key, or by machine, using NCS answer sheets. If a machine is used, it must be programmed to assign weights (i.e., $A=8$, $B=6$, etc.) for the student-reported grades. Each algebra question is worth 1 raw score point. The Total Raw Score is the sum of the five weighted self-reported grades (a maximum value of 40 points for all A's) and the 60 algebra questions (a maximum value of 60 points). Thus, the maximum Total Raw Score is 100 points.

Student test scores can be interpreted in several different ways, dictated by the intended use of the test. Students who can expect success or difficulty in an algebra course are identified using a rank ordering of the total raw scores. The rank ordering allows a teacher or school to group students into similar ability levels, thereby encouraging a differentiated instructional plan. From the rank ordering, a student gains a perspective of his or her ability relative to his or her local peers.

A two-way expectancy table (prognosis test score vs. final algebra grade) can be constructed to illustrate graphically the relationship between a predictive measure and a subsequent achievement measure. For example, based on the expectancy table provided in the 1982 test manual, a student with a raw score of 70 has the probability of getting these final grades in an algebra course: A (5%), B (19%), C (40%), D (25%), and F (11%). A student with this raw score can then make an enrollment decision, being sure to take into account other factors such as desired level of success. Each school is encouraged to develop their own expectancy table using only local data in order to account for special grading practices and curricular

Orleans-Hanna Algebra Prognosis Test

emphases. The study of extremes as individual cases (e.g., students with a raw score above 85 who fail algebra) may provide information important for a school's instructional plan.

Total Raw Scores can be converted into percentile ranks and stanines to help in the comparison of local groups with external reference norms. The gained information gives insight relative to the performance levels of local students and the strength of a school's instructional program. The 1982 test manual provides four tables involving standardization norms. Two of the tables represent eighth-grade students (N = 2,684) and a subset (n = 940) who were enrolled in algebra at the end of the following school year. The two remaining tables have a similar classification for a seventh-grade population (N = 1,195) and subset (n = 172). The national testing was done in 1980, involving 20 states at the eighth-grade level and 9 states at the seventh-grade level.

Finally, the Orleans-Hanna Algebra Prognosis Test includes a Student Report Form, designed to help students and their parents use the Total Raw Scores as useful information in the decision of whether or not to enroll in a beginning algebra course. The Report Form discusses important factors that affect success in learning algebra, then guides the student's interpretation of his or her raw score through the use of an expectancy table, percentile ranks, and stanines. Again, the availability of local data tables would be quite useful.

Technical Aspects

Throughout its lengthy history, the Orleans-Hanna Algebra Prognosis Test has been analyzed carefully relative to its predictive validity. A prognostic measure is of no value if it does not predict success effectively relative to a student's learning of algebra. After multiple longitudinal studies, the 1968 version of the test was shown to produce raw scores that correlated .73 with mid-year algebra achievement test scores, .72 with mid-year algebra grades, .83 with end-of-the-year algebra achievement test scores, and .72 with end-of-the-year algebra grades (Orleans & Hanna, 1968).

Because the 1982 version of the test did not involve major revisions, a limited research study was done to document the predictive validity of the current version, especially for the new population of seventh-grade students. In the spring of 1980, the Orleans-Hanna Algebra Prognosis Test was administered to seventh-grade students (N = 1,195) and eighth-grade students (N = 2,684), all enrolled in the sample of 21 schools used in the normed standardization procedure. These raw scores were not released to the schools until after the following spring, when end-of-the-year algebra grades were collected from population subgroups involving those seventh-grade students (n = 172) and eighth-grade students (n = 940) who took algebra. Once a standard correction formula was used to adjust for this restriction in the tested sample, the raw scores for the seventh- and eighth-grade students correlated .72 and .75 with end-of-the-year algebra grades respectively. Because these two values did not differ significantly at the .05 confidence level, the two populations were combined in the preparation of the expectancy table used in the test manual (Orleans & Hanna, 1982). It is important to note that the correlation values determined by the authors for the different versions over the past 60 years tend to exceed values obtained in other research studies using the same test as a predictor (Grover, 1932; Torgerson, 1933; Barnes & Asher, 1962; Bloland & Michael, 1984; Flexer, 1984).

In order to judge the test's ability to produce consistent scores, two types of reliability evidence were gathered. First, the internal consistency of the 60-item lesson-question portion of the test was estimated for the standardization sample using the Kuder-Richardson Formula 20. The KR-20 estimates were quite high, exceeding .95 for the seventh-grade population and .96 for the eighth-grade population. Second, to measure the reliability of the five self-report questions, a test-retest study was done using only three schools. After the 1968 and the 1982 versions of the Orleans-Hanna Algebra Prognosis Test were administered over a 2-week period, the questionnaire subtotals (using the weighted values) had a reliability value of .89 (Orleans & Hanna, 1982).

A final measure of reliability of the test lies in the discrimination indices produced by the item analysis of the 60 multiple-choice questions. First, the proportion of correct responses (or p-values) were calculated for each of the 60 items, using the data from the 2,684 eighth-grade students. Second, a point biserial correlation r-value was determined to indicate the raw score relationships between single items and the full 60-item test. The obtained r-values ranged from .39 to .67, with a mean of .59 and a median of .53. These values indicate the extend to which an item discriminates among students taking the test (Orleans & Hanna, 1982).

Evidence of concurrent validity for the Orleans-Hanna Algebra Prognosis Test would be determined by its correlation with a number of other established prognostic measures specific to algebra. The test authors offer no evidence of such correlations; unfortunately, only two research studies were found that included a check on concurrent validity. Torgerson (1933) reported a correlation of .76 between the 1928 version of the Orleans Algebra Prognosis Test with Lee's Algebraic Ability Test. Osburn and Melton (1963) showed that the Orleans-Hanna Algebra Prognosis Test and the Iowa Algebra Aptitude Test produced similar predictive validity correlations (.67 and .66, respectively) with an end-of-the-year algebra exam, but the two prognostic exams were not correlated directly.

In a discussion of the validity of the Orleans-Hanna Algebra Prognosis Test, two final aspects that need to be considered are 1) the use of student-reported grades, and 2) their assigned weights in the scoring of the test. Hanna, Sonnenschein, and Lenke (1983) concluded that the predictive validity of the lesson-question section alone was .49 and improved to a value of .60 when the weighted sum of the self-reported grades was included in the raw score. Also, the five self-reported grades had predictive validity coefficients ranging from a low of .39 for the expected algebra grade to a high of .45 for the science grade. Previously, Hanna, Bligh, and Lenke (1970) had demonstrated the equivalent validity of using the student-reported grades in contrast to the school-reported grades, which are more difficult to obtain. Finally, Lenke, Bligh, and Kane (1971) verified that the integral weights assigned to the self-reported grades were equivalent to the use of decimal-valued optimal weights obtained through multiple-correlation techniques.

Critique

In 1944, Guiler claimed that "more predictive research seems to have been done in elementary algebra than in any other learning field, the probable reason being the unusually high percentage of failures among beginners in the subject" (p. 25). Though Guiler's initial claim may not be true today, a great amount of similar research is being done currently and for the same reason given by Guiler. The basic goal is to use a predictive device such as the Orleans-Hanna Algebra Prognosis Test to help make adequate placement decisions, identifying and "weeding out" those students who lack the mathematical aptitude necessary to learn algebra successfully. Two important questions need to be raised, both involving the troublesome term *best*. Is a prognosis test the *best* approach given its financial expense? If yes, then which prognosis test is the *best* and how should it be used?

The Orleans-Hanna Algebra Prognosis Test is certainly a candidate for the best approach. Its validity as a predictor of success in algebra has been established. Yet, researchers differ in their opinions relative to the test's overall worth:

> The Orleans Algebra Prognosis Test did not detract from their [e.g., guidance counselors] prediction, but neither did it aid it much. It can be seen that it adds so little to the multiple correlation that it probably is not worth the expense nor the time involved in giving and correcting the test. The time might be better spent teaching an hour of algebra! (Barnes & Asher, 1962, p. 653)

> It might be inferred that despite the additional time and expense involved with administering such a test its use for purposes of selecting students for an eighth-grade algebra course is warranted. (Flexer, 1984, p. 358)

At the root of these differences in opinion is the distinction between being a *good predictor* and being the *best predictor* of success in algebra. Unfortunately, J.B. Orleans and G.S. Hanna do not address this question.

The necessary approach is the comparison of the ability of the Orleans-Hanna Algebra Prognosis Test to predict student success in algebra against other criteria. Using *r*-values and regression techniques, the majority of the relevant studies suggest that a student's previous mathematics grade is the best predictor of success in learning algebra, usually accounting for half of the variance (Layton, 1941; Duncan, 1960; Callicutt, 1961; Barnes & Asher, 1962; Ivanoff, De Wane, & Praem, 1965; Mogull & Rosengarten, 1972, 1974; Siglin & Edeburn, 1978). Thus, it is hard to justify the expense involved in using the Orleans-Hanna Algebra Prognosis Test when better results can be obtained using a single grade involving no expense. The one study with conflicting results is Flexer (1984), who concluded that the Orleans-Hanna Algebra Prognosis Test is the best overall predictor of success even when compared against previous grades. Though interesting, the difference between the results perhaps lies in the fact that Flexer worked with seventh-grade students, while the other researchers worked with eighth-grade students.

In the continuing search to find the optimal predictor, numerous other variables have been analyzed thoroughly, and they are generally outperformed by the Orleans-Hanna Algebra Prognosis Test. The more standard examples include chronological age, teacher predictions, IQ test results, grade-level achievement tests (especially mathematics subtests), reading scores, personality and interest measures, affective measures, and demographic variables related to parent educations and occupations (Taylor, Brown, & Michael, 1976).

An optimal use of the Orleans-Hanna Algebra Prognosis Test would be to include it as part of a prediction package, possibly as one variable in a regression equation. Begle's (1976) survey supports this approach by suggesting that different measures of specific abilities predict success in different aspects of algebra, though he argues that no set of measures will account for more than 50–70% of the variance in algebra achievement. The problem is to find the best combination involving four or less variables. Recent studies have tried to incorporate the predictive use of new measures, such as differential aptitude tests (Osburn & Melton, 1963), structure-of-intellect factor abilities (Holly & Michael, 1973), and indicators of Piagetian cognitive development levels (Bloland & Michael, 1984). Showing signs of progress, two studies have incorporated the Orleans-Hanna Algebra Prognosis Test into a discriminant function which correctly classified approximately 80% of the successful students and 80% of the unsuccessful students in an algebra course (Bloland & Michael, 1984; Flexer, 1984).

Researchers need to continue to analyze the use of the Orleans-Hanna Algebra Prognosis Test to clear up known anomalies. For example, Hanna and Sonnenschein (1985) concluded that the test is more successful in predicting success for girls than for boys, yet Flexer (1984) had found the reverse. Flexer also discovered that while the Orleans-Hanna Algebra Prognosis Test was the best predictor of end-of-the-year algebra grades, a standardized problem-solving test in mathematics was the best predictor relative to end-of-the-year algebra achievement test scores.

Local schools should use the Orleans-Hanna Algebra Prognosis Test to help make grade-placement decisions. Supported by Flexer (1984), Sabers and Feldt (1968) contend that parents and students will have "a more accepting attitude towards a placement system which employs a special aptitude test" (p. 907). Maximum benefit will be realized if each school would gradually build their own local norms, stanines, and grade expectancy tables for the interpretation of the total raw scores, possibly even using different weights for the two sections of the test. These local norms would improve the predictive validity of the Orleans-Hanna Algebra Prognosis Test by reflecting local grading practices, local teacher affects, and local curricular emphases. The establishing of arbitrary cutoff scores should be avoided, however, as research has clearly shown "a criterion stringent enough to prevent most of the potential failures is also likely to exclude a number of students who would succeed" (Flexer, 1984, p. 358).

References

This list includes text citations and suggested additional readings.

Barnes, W.E., & Asher, J.W. (1962). Predicting students' success in first-year algebra. *Mathematics Teacher, 55*, 651–654.

Begle, E.G. (1976). *Predicting success in beginning algebra: A review of the empirical literature (SMSG Working Paper #18)*. Stanford, CA: Stanford University.

Bloland, R.M., & Michael, W.B. (1984). A comparison of the relative validity of a measure of Piagetian cognitive development and a set of conventional prognostic measures in the prediction of the future success of ninth- and tenth-grade students in algebra. *Educational and Psychological Measurement, 44*, 925–943.

Callicutt, W. (1961). The problem of predicting success in algebra. *National Association of Secondary-School Principals Bulletin, 45*, 107–111.

Dinkel, R.E. (1959). Prognosis for studying algebra. *Arithmetic Teacher,* 6, 317–319.

Dunn, W.H. (1937). The influence of the teacher factor in predicting success in ninth grade algebra. *Journal of Educational Research,* 30, 577–582.

Duncan, R.L. (1960). *The prediction of success in eighth grade algebra.* Unpublished doctoral dissertation, University of Oklahoma, Norman.

Flexer, B.K. (1984). Predicting eighth-grade algebra achievement. *Journal for Research in Mathematics Education,* 15, 352–360.

Grover, C.G. (1932). Results of an experiment in predicting success in first year algebra in two Oakland Junior High Schools. *Journal of Educational Psychology,* 23, 309–314.

Guiler, W.S. (1944). Forecasting achievement in elementary algebra. *Journal of Educational Research,* 38, 25–33.

Hanna, G.S., Bligh, H.F., Lenke, J.M., & Orleans, J.B. (1969). Predicting algebra achievement with an algebra prognosis test, IQs, teacher predictions, and mathematics grades. *Educational and Psychological Measurement,* 29, 903–907.

Hanna, G.S., Bligh, H.F., & Lenke, J.M. (1970). Student-reported grades as predictors. *Personnel and Guidance Journal,* 48, 465–468.

Hanna, G.S., Sonnenschein, J.L., & Lenke, J.M. (1983). The contribution of work-sample test items, student-reported past grades, and student-predicted grades in forecasting achievement in first-year algebra. *Educational and Psychological Measurement,* 43, 243–249.

Hanna, G.S., & Sonnenschein, J.L. (1985). Relative validity of the Orleans-Hanna Algebra Prognosis Test in the prediction of girls' and boys' grades in first-year algebra. *Educational and Psychological Measurement,* 45, 361–367.

Holly, K.A., & Michael, W.B. (1973). Comparative validities and testing times for composites of structure-of-intellect tests and previous mathematics grades with composites of traditional standardized test measures and previous mathematics grades in prediction of success in high school modern algebra. *Educational and Psychological Measurement,* 33, 915–919.

Ivanoff, J.M., De Wane, E.T., & Praem, O. (1965). Use of discriminant analysis for selecting students for ninth-grade algebra or general mathematics. *Mathematics Teacher,* 58, 412–416.

Layton, R.B. (1941). A study of prognosis in high school algebra. *Journal of Educational Research,* 34, 601–605.

Lenke, J.M., Bligh, H.F., & Kane, B.H. (1971). Cross-validation of the Orleans-Hanna Algebra Prognosis Test and the Orleans-Hanna Geometry Prognosis Test. *Educational and Psychological Measurement,* 31, 521–523.

Mogull, R.G., & Rosengarten, W. (1972). Predicting student success in elementary algebra. *California Journal of Educational Research,* 23, 104–107.

Mogull, R.G., & Rosengarten, W. (1974). Predicting success in elementary algebra. *Alberta Journal of Educational Research,* 20, 34–38.

Orleans, J.B. (1934). A study of prognosis of probable success in algebra and geometry. *Mathematics Teacher,* 27, 165–180, 225–245.

Orleans, J.B., & Hanna, G.S. (1968). *Orleans-Hanna Algebra Prognosis Test manual.* New York: Harcourt Brace Jovanovich, Inc.

Orleans, J.B., & Hanna, G.S. (1982). *Orleans-Hanna Algebra Prognosis Test manual.* New York: Harcourt Brace Jovanovich, Inc.

Osburn, H.G., & Melton, R.S. (1963). Prediction of proficiency in a modern and traditional course in beginning algebra. *Educational and Psychological Measurement,* 23, 277–287.

Sabers, D.L., & Feldt, L.S. (1968). The predictive validity of the Iowa Algebra Aptitude Test for achievement in modern mathematics and algebra. *Educational and Psychological Measurement,* 28, 901–907.

Siglin, L., & Edeburn, C. (1978). *Predicting success of high school freshmen in Algebra I in the small rural school.* (ERIC Document Reproduction Service No. ED149 928)

Taylor, C.L., Brown, F.G., & Michael, W.B. (1976). The validity of cognitive, affective, and demographic variables in the prediction of achievement in high school algebra and geometry: Implications for the definition of mathematical aptitude. *Educational and Psychological Measurement, 36,* 971–982.

Torgerson, T.L. (1933). The validity of certain prognostic tests in predicting algebraic ability. *Journal of Experimental Education, 1,* 277–279.

Leslie J. Fyans, Jr., Ph.D.

Assessment Consultant, Illinois State Board of Education, Springfield, Illinois.

P-ACT PLUS

The American College Testing Program. Iowa City, Iowa: The American College Testing Programs.

Introduction

The P-ACT+ testing program has been designed to assess students at tenth grade to give them an indication of how the student will score on the actual ACT measure. Therefore, the P-ACT+ is designed to help the student systematically prepare for college and career. The P-ACT+ claims its genesis in the recent educational reform movement. This movement as described in reports from the Congressional Budget Office (Koretz, 1986, 1987) has focused upon a "serious reexamination of schooling in America . . ." with a concomitant ". . . increasing reliance on achievement tests as indicators of performance of students and school." (Koretz, 1986, p. xiii).

Thus, with all the energy of the educational excellence and reform movement one might expect test companies to show initiative in developing new ways to monitor and measure performance. Indeed, that may be the case with the new P-ACT+ program. Ostensibly it was designed from a systematic perspective with the goal of enabling "high school sophomores to get a good start on the complete task of making timely, productive plans for the future" and to provide those students with the information they need "to plan and prepare for future academic and career success." In actuality, what has been said of the field of psychology also may be cited for the P-ACT+: it may have a short history but a long past. That is, the P-ACT+ is a new instrument grounded firmly in its progenitor, the American College Test (ACT). The ACT has been researched, studied, and responded to by millions of students throughout the United States. Because the P-ACT+ can draw from such a strong testing tradition, it may not be surprising that it was developed so efficiently. In fact, upon initial examination, many may perceive the P-ACT+ to be a practice test for the ACT or, for that matter, a competitor to the Preliminary Scholastic Aptitude Test (PSAT). This practice-test supposedly is based upon a tenth grade curriculum level and upon the planning focus of the P-ACT+.

The P-ACT+ consists of four major component parts: 1) *academic tests,* 2) *an interest inventory,* 3) *study skills assessment,* and 4) *a student information section.* The following paragraphs will treat each of these in turn.

Advanced Tests. The developers of the P-ACT+ claim that its academic tests are based on a "major review" of curriculum and curricular experts following the educational reform movement. The focus was on the fundamental learning outcomes of students in Grades 8–10. The marketing material for the P-ACT+ even boasts that these academic tests will be the "only assessment instruments available focusing on college preparatory skills reflecting the 'reform-based curriculum' . . ." While that quote may speak more of its perceiver's singular specialty than of the statement's validity, it is necessary to review the content of the academic tests, which are remarkably similar to the ACT domain. These tests are the *writing skills* test (50 item's, 30 minutes) *mathematics* test (40 items, 40 minutes), *reading* test (25 items, 20 minutes), and *science reasoning* test (30 items, 25 minutes).

The *writing skills test* is aimed at the student's ability to analyze the conventions of standard written English, including punctuation, grammar, usage, and sentence structure. The format is relatively standard. Students are provided with several phrases and must select the most appropriate alternative. Unfortunately, this is the exact mode and format from which the assessment of writing is moving. More than 4 years ago, Quellmalz (1984) and Chapman, Fyans, and Kerins (1984) indicated that samples of real writing are required to evaluate student writing ability. This article was followed by a deluge of teaching and assessing of actual writing samples. Thus, the P-ACT+ writing test may lack some ecological validity as per the actual writing activities in the classroom.

The *mathematics test* focuses on the skills taught in first-year high school courses such as algebra and geometry. Formulas are not emphasized; quantitative reasoning is. Students obtain a total score, an algebra score, and a geometry score.

The *reading test* requires students 1) to *refer* to explicit statements and 2) to *reason* out implicit meanings from a reading comprehension passing. Again, unfortunately, the format and structure of these items do not reflect the direction of teaching and testing in the burgeoning field of reading. Experts such as Pearson (1986) and Krug and Linn (in press) of the University of Illinois have pressed for a "constructed meaning" and multiple-correct answers model for reading. This approach has been adopted by many teachers and districts. Thus, again the content of the P-ACT+ may be out of step (backwards) with the positive movement in reading instruction.

The *science reasoning* test is derived from the content of general science courses emphasizing the understanding of information in data, research summaries, and conflicting viewpoints. While these areas do deal with hypothesis generation and testing, they apparently are not process-oriented in fashion and may reflect more of a reading comprehension skill than a scientific reasoning skill. Furthermore, while the P-ACT+ brochure claims that minimal emphasis is placed on mathematical content, the sample items provided appear to require at least as much mathematical reasoning as the arithmetic test does.

Interest Inventory. In this section of the P-ACT+, students respond to 60 work-related activities in terms of their likes and dislikes. These responses are analyzed by the ACT's now familiar *World-of-Work* representation across the domains of Data, Ideas, Things, and People. The students also are given an idea of the preparation required for the vocations in which they exhibit the highest interest.

Study Skills Assessment. This section is provided to aid the student's effectiveness in study. Sixty questions survey the student in terms of managementof time and environment, reading, textbooks, taking class notes, using resources, preparing for tests, and taking tests.

Interestingly enough, the student is provided with a national percentile rank for his or her study skills. Although that may be important information, it may be less relevant than idiosyncratic data tailored to each student. In addition, the derivation of the "national percentile rank" may be somewhat suspect for study skills.

Student Information Section. Basic demographic data, student coursework, and curriculum planning are covered in this final section. These data are analyzed to provide guides or "clues for successful post-secondary planning . . ." The focus of this section is evaluating the *consistency* between the student's 1) educational plans and career goals, 2) selection of high school courses and post-high school education plans, 3) career plans and Interest Inventory results, and 4) self-reported needs for assistance, scores on academic testing, and study skills evaluation. However, the materials provided to the students and parents appear to be rather tabular. One might expect a more narrative, user-friendly format.

Materials provided for the P-ACT+ include a *Student/Parent Guide to Post-Secondary Planning and Preparation, Student Parent Guide to Using P-ACT+ Results, A Preliminary Technical Report,* and a P-ACT+ brochure. The student/parent guides are relatively readable and deal with the basic issues of score interpretation, but with a very heavy emphasis on *planning.* This latter focus is quite laudable. Students in their sophomore year of high school may not have concretized habits of planning and strategizing. The P-ACT+ materials give impetus to planning, especially when coupled with the student's report. These materials also introduce the student to the vocational theory behind the ACT program and even test-taking tips for doing well.

Practical Applications /Uses

The programmatic utility of the P-ACT+ is self-evident. It will potentially initiate in 10th-grade students the thoughtful planning and concentration necessary to reach their future goals. Against that backdrop, students receive information regarding four abilities that are very critical to their educational progress.

Perhaps an overlooked utility of the P-ACT+ is the way in which counselors and school principals apply the information it yields. Counselors can obtain, in one package, interest and ability information on students. Counselors then may give students the proper advice and counsel they need to meet their goals. Principals, too, profit from P-ACT+ information, particularly as it relates to perceived needs. Occasionally, it may be important for principals to know what the students perceive as their weaknesses. Additionally, principals may obtain, at an aggregate level, a perspective on overall student performance. From these two touchstones, the principal can provide leadership in mapping school and student improvement strategies. Parents also could be sensitized to student's career interests such that they then could provide the students with experiences or knowledge relevant to these career fields.

The administration of the P-ACT+ is similar to that of the ACT. That is, it is group administered and proctored. The results are submitted to the ACT offices for analysis and interpretation. They are then returned to the student and the school from the American College Testing Program.

Technical Aspects

At the outset of this discussion of the P-ACT+ technical aspects, it must be noted that only *preliminary* data are available as of the summer of 1988. The published results dated January 1988 are appropriately labeled *Preliminary Technical Manual*. This review of the results will include the following sections: 1) *norm development*, 2) *item difficulty*, 3) *item discrimination*, 3) *reliability*, and 5) *item scaling*.

Norm Development. Two alternative forms of the P-ACT+ were administered to a national sample of students in Grades 9, 10, and 11, during May 1987. The students were drawn in a stratified, random fashion from 35 schools nationwide. The actual sampling specification table is not delineated in the manual; however, such factors as public vs. private, urban vs. rural, and "various geographic locations" are listed. The test developers continue to indicate that they used school size and geographic regions to weight the student data. However, the weights and methods were not listed. The final norm sample included 4,419 9th-grade students, 1,599 10th-grade students, and 2,793 11th-grade students. Because the empirical norms are based on data from May 1987, the final norms are interpolated to arrive at fall norm estimates. Two norm groups were derived: national and college bound. The college-bound sample was obtained by desegregating the total sample according to responses to the demographic questions. The students' responses were scaled in terms of percentile ranks and scaled (1 through 32) along the conventionally known ACT scale. In terms of scaled scores, the interpolated 10th-grade means for college-bound students were 13.17 for writing ($SD = 7.39$), 13.49 for mathematics ($SD = 6.56$), 15.27 for reading ($SD = 5.34$), 15.54 for science reasoning ($SD = 4.93$), and 14.50 for the composites ($SD = 5.27$) on a 32-point scale. The corresponding means for the overall national group were 11.21, 11.70, 14.16, 14.54, and 13.03, respectively.

Item Difficulty. Items are analyzed in terms of the proportion of students who correctly answered each item. For all grades, a range of item difficulties were established ranging from .10 to .89. However, most items clustered from .30 to .69. For the spring 9th-grade sample, the most difficult area was science reasoning at .379; the easiest was writing skills at .494. For the spring 10th-grade sample, a similar pattern is found. Science reasoning, at .425, was most difficult, and writing skills, at .569, was easiest.

Item Discrimination. The discrimination indices of most of the P-ACT+ items are .30 or above. The mean-point biserial for the Grade 9 students range from .338 for science reasoning to .428 for writing skills. For 10th-grade students, the mean-point biserials range from .372 for science reasoning to .455 for writing skills.

Reliability. The reliability of the P-ACT+ is reported by Kuder-Richardson Formula 20 (K-R 20). This index portrays the relative homogeneity of items within each subtest. The lowest reliabilities are obtained in reading at .73 (9th grade) and .77 (10th grade) and science reasoning at .74 (9th grade) and .79 (10th grade). Estimates were .91 and .92 for writing and .87 and .90 for mathematics for 9th and 10th grades respectively. The composite reliabilities at the two grades are .94 and .95. The weakest of all reliabilities is for geometry (.67) for 9th-grade. However, this subtest contains only 18 items. The standard error of measurement (SEM), derived from the reliabilities, is given as 2.3 for writing skills, 2.3 for mathematics, 2.6 for reading, 2.4 for science reasoning, and 1.2 for the composite. These SEMs represent approximately one fifth of the mean for each subtest.

Correlational Structure. Factor-analytic results are not presented with the manual. However, the one matrix of intercorrelations that is given depicts relatively moderate correlational levels. For instance, the reading and writing subtests are correlated .73 at Grade 10 and .70 at Grade 9. Mathematics correlated .67 with science reasoning at Grade 10 and .65 at Grade 9. Reading and science reasoning correlated .66 at Grade 10, but only .61 at Grade 9.

The components comprising each of the subtests correlated noticeably higher. For example, rhetorical skills and usage/mechanics of the writing skills subtest correlated .84, and geometry and pre-algebra/algebra of the mathematics subtest correlated .72.

Item Scaling. As mentioned previously, the results of the national norming were calibrated for each test to the conventionally known ACT scale. The scale, adapted by the P-ACT+, ranges from a scale score of 1 to 32. The scales were developed for both college-bound students and the total national 10th-grade students. Following this scaling, the scale scores at the median for the college-bound students stands at approximately 12 to 13 for writing skills, and mathematics; between 14 to 15 for reading; and between 15 to 16 for science reasoning. The median for the composite falls between the scale scores of 13 to 14. As can be seen from the previous data, these scaled scores represent a slight skew to the distribution. The mean is just above the median of the distribution for all but science reasoning.

Critique

This critique of the P-ACT+ focuses first on conceptual marketing and second on technicality. In terms of marketing, the P-ACT+ is packaged as if it were the answer to a sophomore's dreams for planning a career. Indeed, the P-ACT+ offers a state-of-the-art approach to systematic exploration and integration of ideas and plans toward the future. Unfortunately, however, says the psychometric audience, for non-sophomores the P-ACT+ also appears to be a version of the conventionally known ACT, but for a younger population. In fact, the parallelism between the PSAT-SAT and P-ACT+-ACT cannot be overlooked. It may well be an important ethical consideration for the materials supplied by the P-ACT+ to be slightly less self-laudatory regarding its "uniqueness" and slightly more realistic regarding its ancestry.

The population the program serves is at a cognitive and motivational level that may have difficulty understanding the *need* for planning as well as the array of information contributed by the P-ACT+. The present materials may well communicate this to parents, educators, and counselors, but may miss the mark in touching 14- and 15-year-old students. Students may overlook the program's potential usefulness and simply take it as a trial run for the ACT.

Turning to the second focus of this critique, there may be some question regarding the technical base of the P-ACT+, although its psychometrics appear relatively substantial. Some of the reliabilities may well be considered rather low (e.g., .67 for geometry). Of course, that coefficient is based on only 18 items. However, should a test be structured to report individual student results on only 18 items? The *technical manual* discusses how students are expected to score on the ACT based on their performance on the P-ACT+. However, actual firm estimates could not be given. Naturally, these will become available as P-ACT+ research continues.

Nonetheless, two technical issues that will not disappear with future research involve the methods used to assess reading and writing skills. While the verbiage of the documents supplied with the P-ACT+ discuss its genesis from the educational reform movement, its reading and writing assessments belie this. In fact, its reading and writing components appear to be drawn not from recent reform, but from work that is several decades old. Reform-based assessment of reading might deal with multiple-correct answer passages to prefamiliarity and reading strategies, particularly with the latter if the results are to be used for vocational education planning. These bodies of assessment knowledge derived after heavy funding and research at the Center for the Study of Reading. Yet this new P-ACT+ assessment of reading does not even remain apparently mute on these components. Furthermore, the writing community, as represented by Quellmalz et al., have moved away from writing-as-editing-skills to writing-as-process-type models. Again, no analytic scoring of an actual essay is required of the student by the P-ACT+. On these two issues the P-ACT+ not only may appear to be unrepresentive of the basis of its item development but also be out of synchronization with the students it is testing if local teachers move to these more realistic and dynamic modes of teaching and assessing reading and writing. It may well be worth "going back to the drawing board" on these two facets of the P-ACT+ and instilling some of the spirit of reading and writing reform into the program to make it as valuable as its developers claim it is.

References

Chapman, C.W., Fyans, L.J., Jr., & Kernins, C.T., (1984). Writing assessment in Illinois. *Educational Measurement, Issues and Practice, 3*(1),24–26.

Koretz, D. (Ed.). (1986). *Trends in educational achievement.* Washington, DC: Congressional Budget Office.

Koretz, D. (Ed.). (1987). *Educational achievement: Explanations and implications of recent trends.* Washington, DC: Congressional Budget Office.

Krug, S., & Linn, R. (in press). Equating scores in reading comprehension: Rationale and results. In L.J. Fyans, Jr. (Ed.), *Multilevel designs in educational research.* Greenwich, CT: JAI Press.

Pearson, P.D. (1986). Comprehension revolution: Twenty years of research and practice in reading comprehension. In T. Raphael (Ed.), *Contexts of school based literacy* (pp. 41–64). New York: Random House.

Quellmalz, E.S. (1984). Towards successful large scale writing assessment: Where are we now? Where do we go from here? *Educational Measurement, Issues and Practice, 3*(1), 29–32.

David E. Levit, Psy.D.
Psychology Resident for Private Practice, Pittsburgh, Pennsylvania.

Grant Aram Killian, Ph.D.
Associate Professor of Psychology, Nova University, Fort Lauderdale, Florida.

Alan D. Katell, Ph.D.
Associate Professor of Psychology, Nova University, Fort Lauderdale, Florida.

PAIN APPERCEPTION TEST

Donald V. Petrovich. Los Angeles, California: Western Psychological Services.

Introduction

The Pain Apperception Test (PAT; Petrovich, 1957, 1973) is a projective test similar to the many other apperception tests available today, except that its stimulus is designed specifically to assess attitudes and interpretations related to the experience of pain. The Thematic Apperception Test (TAT; Murray, 1943) generally is considered to be the prototypical apperception test—the one after which most others are modeled, most notably the Children's Apperception Test (CAT; Bellak, 1975), the Senior Apperception Test (SAT; Bellak, 1975), the Object Relations Technique (ORT; Phillipson, 1973), and the PAT. Unlike most apperceptive tests, however, the PAT does not require or allow the subject to provide free responses or tell a story in response to the stimulus presented. Rather, all subjects respond to the same two questions ("How does the man feel?" and "How long will it hurt him?") on a 7-point scale after viewing each picture (Petrovich, 1973). The PAT, therefore, is a projective test that utilizes an objective scoring system.

As with all apperception tests, the PAT is based on the theory of apperceptive distortion. Bellak (1950) made the distinction between projection, which he sees as a more pathological defense mechanism, and apperception, in order to minimize confusion with other methods of psychological and physiological research. He defines apperception "as an organism's (dynamically) meaningful interpretation of a perception" (pp. 11–12). The manner in which we organize and interpret (or misinterpret) pure perception is referred to as apperceptive distortion. The term *distortion* is used because the perceptions we allow ourselves to become aware of, and the meanings we attribute to these perceptions, are influenced in varying degrees by internal forces such as past experiences and present needs (Abt, 1950). Murray (1943) utilized a similar concept of apperception and apperceptive distortion in devising his interpretation method for the TAT. He believed that humans are motivated by needs and environmental press and that the conscious and unconscious needs and presses of the subject would be reflected in the stories obtained by the TAT. The clinician needs to identify the hero in each story and the needs and presses of the hero to gain insight into the conscious and unconscious needs and presses of the subject. Perception, therefore, is a fusion of external (objective) and internal (subjective) stimulus. In order to gain a true understanding of any issue of perception related to human behavior, it is inadequate to focus solely on either objective or subjective stimulus.

Petrovich's conceptualization and construction of the PAT, which began in 1956 (Petrovich, 1973), was based on a doctoral dissertation submitted to the Department of Psychology of Washington University in St. Louis, Missouri, and researched at the Veterans Administration Hospital in Jefferson Barracks, Missouri (Petrovich, 1957, 1958a). The impetus for this research was the realization that pain is a complex concept and that the present methods of research focusing solely on physiological thresholds and tolerance levels were not producing a viable understanding of the experience of pain (Elton, Burrows, & Stanley, 1979; Petrovich, 1957, 1958a, 1960a; Reading, 1980). In order to understand why these research methods were not working, Reading (1980) asserted that pain has two main dimensions, sensory-discriminative and evaluative-emotional, and that current research methods failed to address the multidimensions of pain. Similarly, Petrovich (1960a) found that attempts to understand pain from a purely physical or neurological perspective were ineffective because they ignored the psychological context of the pain experience. That is, they focused purely on the sensory-discriminative dimension of pain and ignored the evaluative-emotional dimension. To gain a more complete understanding of pain, one had to account for or assess the psychological context (eg., prior experience, self-concept, attitudes, current needs, and current anxieties). It is these psychological dimensions that influence variable reactions to pain. The PAT was developed to initiate assessment of the psychological aspects of pain (Petrovich, 1960a) and to aid in the understanding of the intricate relationships involved in the pain experience (Petrovich, 1957).

According to Petrovich (1973), two major premises underlie the PAT:

1. Each person is predisposed to perceive pain in others in a characteristic and relatively constant manner, stemming from his personal, idiosyncratic experiences with, and reactions to, pain.
2. This characteristic perceptual response can be elicited by pictures of persons in pain which require a subject to judge intensity and duration of pain experienced by the depicted persons. (p. 1)

The pain situations depicted in the PAT were selected on the basis of a pain survey conducted by Petrovich (1958b). Students in introductory psychology classes at Washington University, 50 males and 50 females ranging in age from 18 to 33, were asked to list 10 situations that they associated with pain. Subjects also were asked to indicate which of these situations they actually had experienced and then to rank order the situations from 1 (most painful) to 10 (least painful). Petrovich then categorized these 1,000 responses into three categories: physical pain, psychological pain, and those that blend the two. Final selection of situations was based on "frequency, approximate position on a 'painfulness' continuum, bodily focus, and suitability for pictorial presentation" (Petrovich, 1973, p. 1).

Petrovich's (1958a) first experiment with the PAT was an attempt to prove that the responses to the PAT are not unique. Rather they are reflective of more stable characteristics of the individual and related to traits found to be influential in the pain experience by past psychological research and clinical observation. Specifically, 100 white male subjects from the medical and surgical wards of the V.A. Hospital in St. Louis were tested with the PAT, Eysenck's Medical Questionnaire (Eysenck, 1948) (to assess neuroticism), the Taylor Manifest Anxiety Scale (Taylor, 1953) (to assess manifest anxiety), and a pain experience questionnaire (to assess previous pain experiences). Significant positive correlations were found between the PAT and measures of neuroticism and manifest anxiety. Product-moment correlations, which were found to range from .31 to .43, were significant at the .01 and .001 confidence levels. No significant relationship was found between the PAT and measures of previous pain experiences. Split-half reliabilities ranged from .56 to .85 and were strong enough to suggest intrasubject consistency. Results of this experiment indicate that while the PAT does correlate positively with concepts considered influential in the pain experience—neuroticism and manifest anxiety—it does not correlate to actual pain experiences in the subjects tested. It seems that the PAT may assess the evaluative-emotional aspect of pain perception while ignoring the sensory-discriminative dimension. Moss and Waters (1960) also found the PAT to have a positive correlation to manifest anxiety (.30); however, due to small sample size, their correlation was not significant.

Examination of responses to individual cards in Petrovich's experiment resulted in the changing of three pictures and the interchanging of two pictures. These alterations were made because the pictures in question were not found to be discriminatory due to overly ambiguous situations depicted. For example, two pictures of a pricked finger, one in which the prick was inflicted by self and the other by another person, were replaced by pictures of two fly fisherman in which one fisherman was hooked in the neck, first by himself and then by the other man (Petrovich, 1958a). There have been no other revisions to the PAT.

No other forms of the PAT exist. However, due to problems that arose out of validity studies for the PAT, the Melbourne Pain Apperception Film was created as an alternative test (Elton, Quarry, Burrows, & Stanley, 1978). The Melbourne test was based directly on the PAT. It was felt by Elton et al. (1978) that the stimulus cards on the PAT were too ambiguous and contained too many extraneous cues. Therefore, the Melbourne Pain Apperception Film utilized a color film of a bare hand and forearm against a neutral background, depicting 10 situations of increasing painfulness. Responses were scored on the same two questions and with the same 7-point rating scale as that used on the PAT. The Melbourne Pain Apperception Film was found to correlate significantly to actual pain thresholds and tolerance levels while the PAT did not. Based on these results, the Melbourne test appears to be a more valuable tool than the PAT. However, further research needs to be conducted on the Melbourne test to see whether these results can be replicated.

Other methods of pain assessment that have gained more widespread use than the PAT involve either physiological thresholds and/or tolerance levels, rating scales, comparative performance on tasks to measure the effects of stimulation on the subject, and questionnaires. These methods are more widely used than the PAT because they have demonstrated valid and useful applications, whereas, the PAT has not.

Thresholds usually are tested by electrical stimulation of a finger. The point at which the stimulation first becomes painful is considered the threshold.

Tolerance levels are determined by continuing painful stimulation until the subject can not tolerate any more pain. The most popular form of this test, the Tourniquet Pain Test (Sternbach, Murphy, Timmermans, Greenhoot, & Akeson, 1974), uses a sphygmomanometer cuff (a device used to measure blood pressure) and hand exercise to induce ischemia pain (a blockage of the inflow of arterial blood) in the subject's nondominant hand.

Rating scales require the subject to rate stimuli or painful experiences on a fixed scale. These scales can assume various formats: 1) *numerical,* such as a 10-point scale (1–10) ranging from "no pain, to "can't stand pain" (Petrovich, 1973); 2) *continuums,* along which subjects mark their responses on a line that extends from "no pain" to "can't stand pain"; or 3) multiple-choice, where the subject selects the most appropriate descriptive word provided. The Pain Estimate, in which subjects rate their current pain levels on a scale of 1–100, is an example of this type of pain assessment technique.

Comparative performance tasks usually are carried out in a laboratory and are used to measure the effect of the stimulation provided on a particular task. The Kinesthetic After Effects Task (Petrie, 1967) is one such test. It requires the subject to select from a tapered block held in the left hand the spot that appropriately corresponds to the size of a standard block held in the right hand. This test indicates whether a subject augments or reduces incoming stimuli and then relates this information to the subject's ability to tolerate pain.

Along with physiological measures, questionnaires are the most popular method of assessing pain. The most popular questionnaire, based on a survey of the literature the most popular pain assessment tool, is the McGill Pain Questionnaire (MPQ; Melzack, 1975). The MPQ presents a number of word sets in which the subject is asked to select the most appropriate word. Although most of the word sets reflect sensory dimensions of pain, with less emphasis on affective and evaluative dimensions of pain, the MPQ does attempt to address the multidimensional aspects of pain. Research on the MPQ has shown the test to be reliable and valid when used correctly, which probably accounts for its wide spread use.

Three items make up the PAT packet: the PAT manual, the PAT protocol (answer form), and the PAT pictures. The PAT manual provides a description of the test, its development, and uses; normative data; reliability information; instructions for administration, scoring, and interpretation; and a brief discussion of validity. The PAT protocol consists of a brief demographic section that requests the test taker's name, age, sex, education level, occupation, marital status, and the date. This is followed by a listing of all PAT pictures by number (and letter where appropriate), and two multiple-choice questions for each picture. The examinee is asked the same two questions after viewing every picture, and for each picture, the two questions have the same seven possible responses from which the examinee may choose. The questions and their multiple-choice responses follow.

A. How does the man feel? (circle one)
 1. no pain
 2. hardly any pain

        3. some pain
        4. moderate amount of pain
        5. much pain
        6. very much pain
        7. can't stand pain
    B. How long will it hurt him? (circle one)
        1. not at all
        2. seconds
        3. minutes
        4. hours
        5. days
        6. weeks
        7. months (Petrovich, 1973)

Spaces are provided on the protocol for totaling scores for intensity (How does the man feel?), duration (How long will it hurt him?), and pain sensitivity (intensity and duration combined). The seven multiple-choice responses for intensity were established empirically from Edwards's method of successive intervals (Edwards, 1952), and the seven choices for duration were based on a logical temporal continuum (Petrovich, 1973).

There are 25 pictures in the PAT, all depicting a man in his thirties. Each picture differs as to the man's facial and body characteristics in order to facilitate projection into various pain situations (Petrovich, 1957, 1973). The depicted man's dress and comportment vary from picture to picture, depending on the activity and painfulness portrayed in each picture. If other people are required in the picture, only parts of their body are shown, again to facilitate projection (Petrovich, 1973).

All pictures were drawn in detail by William Howard French, a St. Louis artist, and then photographed, some with overlays to produce counterpart pictures (Petrovich, 1957). Each picture card is approximately the size of a TAT card. The 6″ × 7½″ pictures are presented on 8½″ × 11″ pieces of cardboard.

The 25 PAT pictures can be divided into three groups. Petrovich (1973) describes these three groups as follows. Series 1 consists of nine pictures, numbered 1–9, portraying situations of felt pain sensations. Series 2 consists of eight pictures, four counterpart pairs, reflecting anticipated pain vs. felt pain sensations. These cards are labeled 10-A, 10, 11-A, 11, 12-A, 12, 13-A, and 13. Pictures labeled A reflect that painful situations are about to happen, or are anticipated. Those numbered without an A reflect the same situations as the pictures labeled A, except that the situation *is* happening, therefore reflecting felt sensation. Any differences in response to these counterpart pictures is attributed to the emotional response to time and proximity (anticipation) of the painful stimulus. Series 3 consists of eight pictures, four counterpart pairs, concerned with the origin of the painful stimulus: self-inflicted vs. other inflicted. These pictures are labeled 14, 14-0, 15, 15-0, 16, 16-0, 17, 17-0. Those labeled without an 0 depict self-inflicted pain situations. Those labeled with an 0 are the same pain situations (within corresponding numbers), but the pain is being inflicted by someone else. Differences in the ratings of these counterpart pictures are attributed to perceived differences in other vs. self-inflicted pain.

The examiner's participation in the testing process is usually minimal, but varies according to which of two methods of administration is used. In general, the examiner may give the directions for taking the test, answer any questions the subject asks, and then leave the subject to self-administer the test. The second method usually is used with subjects who cannot read well. The examiner may need to read the questions and potential responses after each picture is presented, as well as mark the subject's appropriate response.

The PAT was not designed with any age group in mind. The relatively low difficulty level of the PAT allows it to be applied to a wide range of subjects. Anyone old enough to understand what they perceive and to verbalize a response to questions may take the PAT. The PAT has been administered successfully to children (Silverstein, 1963), adolescents (Moss & Waters, 1960; Notermans, & Tophoff, 1967), and adults (Blitz, Dinnerstein, & Lowenthal, 1968; Elton et al., 1979; Haase, Banks, & Lee, 1975; Notermans & Tophoff, 1967; Petrovich, 1958a, 1959, 1960a, 1960b; Silverstein & Owens, 1961; Ziesat, 1978). Because reading skills are not necessary, as indicated previously, the PAT may be administered to mentally retarded subjects. The examiner can read the questions to the subjects and record their responses (Silverstein & Owens, 1961). To date no studies have been performed to evaluate response differences arising from administrations in which subjects record their own responses vs. those in which the examiner records the responses.

The PAT does not have any subtests per se, and Petrovich does not utilize the concept of subtests. As discussed previously, the PAT *does* contain three series of cards assessing felt sensation, anticipated vs. felt sensation, and other vs. self-inflicted pain, respectively. All three series entail the exact same administration procedures. However, researchers do not always give all 25 pictures to all subjects. While all pictures within a series always are given, all three series are not always presented (Petrovich, 1957, 1960b, 1973; Silverstein & Owens, 1961; Ziesat & Gentry, 1978). The manual does not address whether all three series of cards should be used at all times, and no research has been done yet to assess the effects of a short form of the test.

As described earlier, the answer form for the PAT provides brief demographics of the subject, as well as the questions and multiple-choice responses to all pictures in all three series. The responses are numbered 1–7, yielding numerical profiles of the subject's responses. Scores for intensity, duration, and sensitivity to pain are obtained for each of the three series. A total score for sensitivity to pain also is obtained based on all three series.

Practical Applications/Uses

The PAT was designed to initiate investigations into the psychological context of pain in order to aid in the understanding of the experience of pain in humans. It is important to note that the goal of the PAT is increased understanding and *not* clinical prediction. It seems more appropriate, then, to use the PAT to compare scores between differing groups of people than to use it to compare one subject's score to a group. The manual, however, fails to make a distinction between group and individual scores and interpretations. Although the manual does not caution clinicians against making predictive statements based on an individual score, such caution is essential at this point in the development of the PAT. The use of the PAT should yield statements such as, "Diabetics' perception (or apperception) of pain is fundamentally different than normal subjects'," rather than, "Based on the PAT, this subject should experience less postsurgical pain than most people."

Three variables of the pain experience are assessed by the PAT, each in relation to the apperception of intensity, duration, and sensitivity to pain. These variables are reflected in the three series of cards: felt sensation, anticipation vs. felt sensation (where the effects of time and proximity are measured), and other vs. self-inflicted (where the effects of control and who inflicts the pain is measured). These three series of cards are designed to assess both the physical and psychological components of pain, although validity studies show no correlation between the PAT and actual pain experiences. Use of the PAT has raised questions as to other variables measured unintentionally. For example, in series 2, anticipated vs. felt sensation, the issue of avoidability of the pain may be influential in the apperception of the stimulus by different people (Petrovich, 1960b). Similarly, in series 3, other vs. self-inflicted pain, the issue of how beneficial the pain inflicted by others is going to be may influence subjects' responses (Petrovich, 1960b).

Petrovich (1973) states that the PAT was designed for research purposes in the psychological aspects of felt pain, anticipation of pain, and locus of control, which parallels the three series of cards in the PAT (felt sensation, anticipation vs. felt sensation, and self-inflicted vs. other-inflicted pain). However, he does suggest other applications that may be suitable. These other areas of possible investigation are perceptual defenses, pharmacology, amputation-prosthetics, sadism-masochism, attitudes and reactions to medical or dental situations, accident-proneness and prevention, and psychotherapy evaluation. Because the PAT has been correlated with measures of neuroticism and manifest anxiety, it has been used as a subtle measure of anxiety (Moss & Waters, 1960).

The PAT can be administered in any setting that affords the space, lighting, and lack of interfering stimuli necessary for the subject to see the cards, read the protocol sheet, and mark an answer (or hear the examiner read the questions and multiple-choice responses and verbalize an answer). Any well-lit, quiet room with a table and chair would be acceptable, whether it be an office, waiting room, or examining room. The PAT also can be given to the subject to take at home. No information is available on the effect of different settings on the PAT scores.

Because the PAT is designed for researching the pain experience, any profession researching pain could utilize the test, including psychology, psychiatry, medicine, dentistry, social work, the military, and sports. However, problems with validity have hampered the use of the PAT even within its designed application, and ideas and investigations into new applications of the PAT are at a virtual standstill.

The PAT can be readily administered to a wide range of subjects, both male and female (Petrovich, 1959). The relative ease of the task, the fact that reading and writing skills are not necessary, and that responses can be made by circling appropriate numbers or verbalized to an examiner are all factors allowing its administration to such a wide range of subjects. The only limiting factors for subjects would be blindness, a total inability to make sense of what one perceives, or an inability to respond to people or printed material. Other than blindness, the limiting factors for subjects reflect a person so regressed or retarded that testing of any kind would be impossible. The PAT has been used with mentally retarded (Silverstein & Owens, 1961) and schizophrenic (Petrovich, 1960b) subjects, again indicating that a subject would have to be severely regressed before being unable to take the PAT. It is unlikely that the problem of blindness will be overcome; thus, it seems extremely unlikely that the PAT will be adapted for use with blind subjects. Some minor modifications in administering the PAT have been employed with MR subjects (Silverstein & Owens, 1961) and also are advisable for children taking the test. One such modification is to ask the subject, after the test is completed, if he or she can describe what was going on in each picture in order to assure a basic understanding of the pain situation depicted. The other modification is to invert some of the multiple-choice response scales, again after the test has been administered properly, to see whether the subject is able to accurately use the rating scales.

The PAT can be administered individually, to groups, and independently (self-administered). If an examiner is used, he or she need not be highly trained. A basic knowledge of the instructions and materials is all that is needed. Administration procedures from the manual (Petrovich, 1973) are not specific, which hinders standardized presentation of the PAT. The examiner distributes the answer sheets to the subject(s) and requests that the identification information be filled out on the front of the sheet. The examiner then may read the instructions and go over them again if they are not clear to the subject. The manual does not specify whether the examiner must read the instructions aloud or whether the subject can read them on his or her own. The manual also does not indicate any limits as to the number of times instructions can be repeated if the subject does not understand them. There are no other instructions in the manual for administering the PAT. The manual does not specify whether the stimulus cards should be presented by the examiner or held by the subject. In the case of group administration, it is equally unclear whether each subject has his or her own set of pictures, the examiner holds up each picture (in which case all subjects would need to be close enough to the examiner to clearly see all aspects of the picture), or transparencies of the pictures are projected on a screen. The manual, then, leaves the test user to assume that, after the instructions are understood, those subjects that can are allowed to proceed at their own pace, controlling both pictures and protocol. Subjects unable to proceed on their own could be assisted by the examiner, who controls the protocol and perhaps the pictures as well. The amount of time required to administer an average PAT is approximately 15–20 minutes.

Obtaining raw scores from the PAT protocol sheet is as easy as adding. A complete protocol yields 10 raw scores, three for each series of cards and one overall pain sensitivity score. For each series of pictures, the scorer adds each column of the answer sheet vertically and then adds the totals for each column. Although not specified in the manual, "totals for each column" refers to total raw scores per series for intensity and duration scores. Thus, for each series of cards there is a raw score for intensity and duration. These two raw scores also are added together to obtain a third raw score for pain sensitivity in each series. The three pain sensitivity scores, one from each series of cards, can be added to yield the tenth raw score, an overall pain sensitivity score. Obtaining raw scores from the protocol sheet is rather self-explanatory upon inspection of the sheet and should not take more than a few minutes for the user to comprehend. It should take the scorer only a few minutes to calculate the raw scores on any protocol. Raw scores can be used as is to evaluate the protocol, or, as suggested by Petrovich (1973), raw scores can be converted to T-scores using the tables provided in the manual. Unfortunately, these tables are confusing in that some were printed incorrectly and supplemental tables were issued rather than reprinting the manual.

In spite of the suggestion to convert raw scores to T-scores, the interpretive scales presented in the manual are based on raw scores. Furthermore, they are only in reference to series 1 pictures (pictures 1–9). Interpretive scales are provided for intensity, duration, and overall pain sensitivity. Each scale is divided into very high, high, average, low, and very low, with separate raw score ranges for males and females provided for each division. Interpretations based on these scales seem rather useless, however, in that it is unknown how the categories obtained translate into human behavior. Interpretations can be made by comparing the subject's results, converted to T-scores, to several different populations whose norms are provided by tables in the manual. Normative data are provided for 100 male hospitalized veterans, 100 male chronic schizophrenics, 50 male hospital personnel, and 50 female hospital personnel. This type of interpretation would yield a general "fit" of a particular subject to one of the four normative groups cited. It seems, then, that a relatively low level of training is required to score the PAT and to interpret some of these scores based on the manual. However, because these interpretations are basically useless, it appears that a relatively high level of training is required to utilize the scores and interpretations in a meaningful fashion. Because a useful and valid system of interpretation does not exist for the PAT, it is left to the highly trained and creative researcher to develop a system for meaningful interpretation of the test results.

Technical Aspects

The test manual reports reliability scores for the four normative groups presented. These are in the form of split-half reliability scores. Test administration was divided into two parts, and the two sets of scores were correlated. These correlations, ranging from .56 to .89, indicate a reasonable level of intraindividual consistency. Unfortunately, the reliability data on the four normative groups were not obtained on the same cards, and none of the groups were administered the entire test. Moss and Waters (1960) administered the PAT to hospitalized juvenile patients four times over a 34-month period. They found the results of these four PAT administrations within the same individuals over time to be very consistent and the reliability correlations to be significant. It seems that whatever the PAT measures, it does so with an adequate degree of reliability.

The issue of validity for the PAT is not clear. Neither is it clear precisely what the PAT measures. Petrovich (1958a) alone reported significant positive correlations between the PAT and measures of neuroticism. However, Haase, Banks, and Lee (1975) and Moss and Waters (1960) were unable to replicate these findings.

Attempts at establishing concurrent validity (i.e., attempts to establish positive correlations between the PAT and other established measures of pain) have been unsuccessful. Several researchers have tried to correlate the PAT to physical tests of pain tolerance and pain thresholds (Blitz, Dinnerstein, &

Lowenthal, 1968; Elton, Quarry, Burrows, & Stanley, 1978; Ziesat, 1978). Subjects used were either pain patients or hospital staff, both male and female adults. None of these attempts yielded any significant correlations. Thus, it would seem that the PAT is not useful in predicting clinical pain or reactions to actual pain. Haase et al. (1975) attempted to find a correlation between the PAT and the Kinesthetic After Effects Task (KAE; Petrie, 1967), using both male and female students and staff of a university. The KAE measures whether the subject augments or reduces incoming stimulus. Augmentation-reduction has been demonstrated to relate significantly to pain tolerance. The PAT did not correlate significantly to the KAE. Ziesat's and Gentry's (1978) investigation into the PAT's concurrent validity was also unable to demonstrate the validity of the test. They administered the PAT, MMPI, the Health Index (Sternbach, Wolf, Murphy, & Akeson, 1973) (measures self-concept as an invalid, manifest depression, perceived impact of pain on daily activities, and the tendency to play pain games with medical personnel), Whitely Index (Pilowsky, 1967) (measures hypochondriasis), the Pain Estimate (self-report of actual current pain levels), and the Tourniquet Pain Test (Sternbach, Murphy, Timmermans, Greenhoot, & Akeson, 1974) (a test of actual pain tolerance) to patients on a pain ward of a VA hospital. Of the 528 correlations computed, between tests and subtests and subscales, only four significant correlations were found, about what would be expected by chance. Positive correlations were found between the PAT and the alcoholism and social introversion scales of the MMPI and the invalidism scale of the Health Index. A negative correlation was found between the PAT and the psychopathic deviate scale of the MMPI. The lack of positive correlations to established measures of pain beyond that expected by chance shows clearly that what the PAT measures is completely unknown. Until it is discovered precisely what it measures, other more established measures of pain should be used.

In the test manual, Petrovich (1973) states that the PAT reflects a high degree of face validity (i.e., that the pictures are obviously pictures of painful situations). However, the pictures are ambiguous enough to allow for many misinterpretations of the situations depicted, and some researchers argue that the PAT has no face validity (Haase et al., 1975). Petrovich also states in the test manual that questions regarding validity must wait until further research is conducted before being answered. The research available at the time of this review suggests that the PAT does not demonstrate any type of validity.

Critique

Because of its lack of validity and Petrovich's own assertion that it is a research tool to aid in the understanding of the pain experience, clinical application of the Pain Apperception Test is both unwise and unethical. the *Standards for Educational and Psychological Testing* (American Educational Research Association, American Psychological Association, & National Council on Measurement in Education, 1985), clearly places on the clinician and not the test publisher the responsibility for selecting valid tests and using them only under the circumstances for which the test is designed and normed:

When a test is to be used for a purpose for which it has not been previously validated, or for which there is no supported claim for validity, the user is responsible for providing evidence of validity. (APA, 1985, p. 42)

Because the PAT has failed to demonstrate any type of validity and exactly what construct it measures is unknown, no valid clinical inferences or interpretations can be made using it. Any clinician who chooses to use the PAT would be solely responsible for any negative consequences resulting from an invalid interpretation and could be held liable for such use. Some researchers go so far as to suggest a moratorium on the PAT (Silverstein, 1963; Spielberger, 1978). However, while the PAT is unsuited for clinical use, it does seem to measure *something* on a rather consistent basis. Unfortunately, it is unclear what this is. Further research may yield a better understanding of what the PAT measures, which then may lead to a valid clinical application of the PAT. While the projective approach, utilizing an objective scoring system, addresses reservations about the scorer's projection into the test's results (Killian, 1985), it may preclude the one avenue of clinical adaptation that is most apparent. That is, that the PAT could conceivably be used exactly like the TAT, requiring the subject to create a story based on the pictures, with its specific pull for issues involving pain perception. This approach has not been used or investigated in any of the available literature. This type of use would be subject to validity and reliability studies based on the new administration procedures. It is unlikely that the PAT will receive much further attention as there is little research being done on it, and the research that is being conducted is finding no validity. Probably one of the most striking examples of the PAT's inability to be recognized and to find its place in the field of pain research is its lack of inclusion in a 30-page overview of pain measurement offered by Chapman et al. (1985). It is evident that until researchers discover precisely what the PAT measures, it remains essentially unusable.

In spite of the lack of validity demonstrated by the PAT, it is readily available to clinicians through Western Psychological Services for $60.00 per kit. Clinicians should be cautioned, however, that the publisher's advertised claim that the PAT is a "valuable instrument for many settings where pain might be experienced or anticipated" (Western Psychological Services, 1988, p. 171) is unfounded and overstated. Correlations have not been found between PAT scores and actual experienced pain, and clinical use of the PAT in this manner may be unethical.

References

Abt, L.E. (1950). A theory of projective psychology. In L.E. Abt & L. Bellak (Eds.), *Projective psychology: Clinical approaches to the total personality* (p.3366). New York: Alfred A. Knopf.

American Educational Research Association, American Psychological Association, & National Council on Measurement in Education. (1985). *Standards for educational and psychological testing.* Washington, DC: American Psychological Association.

Bellak, L. (1950). On the problems of the concept of projection: A theory of apperceptive distortion. In L. E. Abt & L. Bellak (Eds.), *Projective psychology: Clinical approaches to the total personality* (pp. 7–32). New York: Alfred A. Knopf.

Bellak, L. (1975). *The T.A.T., C.A.T., and S.A.T. in clinical use* (3rd ed.). New York: Grune & Stratton.

Blitz, B., Dinnerstein, A.J., & Lowenthal, M. (1968). Performance on the pain apperception test and tolerance for experimental pain: A lack of relationship. *Journal of Clinical Psychology, 24,* 73.

Chapman, C.R., Casey, K.L., Dubner, R., Foley, K.M., Gracely, R.H., & Reading, A.E. (1985). Pain measurement: An overview. *Pain, 22,* 1-31.

Edwards, A.L. (1952). The scaling of stimuli by the method of successive intervals. *Journal of Applied Psychology, 36,* 118-122.

Elton, D., Burrows, G.D., & Stanley, G.V. (1979). The relationship between psychophysical and perceptual variables and chronic pain. *British Journal of Social and Clinical Psychology, 18,* 425-430.

Elton, D., Quarry P.R., Burrows, G.D., & Stanley, G.V. (1978). A new test of pain reactivity. *Perceptual and Motor Skills, 47,* 125-126.

Esysenck, H.J. (1948). *Dimensions of personality.* London: Rutledge Kegan Paul Ltd.

Haase, R.F., Banks, D.L., & Lee, D.Y. (1975). A validity study of the Pain Apperception Test. *Journal of Clinical Psychology, 31,* 747-751.

Killian, G.A. (1984). House-Tree-Person Technique. In D.J. Keyser & R.C. Sweetland (Eds.), *Test critiques* (Vol. 1, p. 338-353). Kansas City, Mo: Test Corporation of America.

Melzack, R. (1975). The McGill Pain Questionnaire: Major properties and scoring methods. *Pain, 1,* 277-299.

Moss, C.S., & Waters, T.J. (1960). Intensive longitudinal investigation of anxiety in hospitalized juvenile patients. *Psychological Reports, 7,* 379-380.

Murray, H.A. (1943). *Thematic Apperception Test manual.* Cambridge: Harvard University.

Notermans, S.L.H., & Tophoff, M.M.W.A. (1967). Sex differences in pain tolerance and pain apperception. *Psychiatria, Neurologia, Neurochirurgia, 70,* 23-29.

Petrie, A. (1967). *Individuality in pain and suffering.* Chicago: University of Chicago Press.

Petrovich, D.V. (1957). The Pain Apperception Test: A preliminary report. *The Journal of Psychology, 44,* 339-346.

Petrovich, D.V. (1958a). The Pain Apperception Test: Psychological correlates of pain perception. *Journal of Clinical Psychology, 14,* 367-374.

Petrovich, D.V. (1958b). A survey of painfulness concepts. *Journal of Clinical Psychology, 14,* 288-291.

Petrovich, D.V. (1959). The Pain Apperception Test: An application to sex differences. *Journal of Clinical Psychology, 15,* 412-414.

Petrovich, D.V. (1960a). The apperceptive study of psychological aspects of pain. *Perceptual and Motor Skills, 11,* 57.

Petrovich, D.V. (1960b). Pain apperception in chronic schizophrenics. *Journal of Projective Techniques, 24,* 21-27.

Petrovich, D.V. (1973). *Pain Apperception Test manual.* Los Angeles: Western Psychological Services.

Phillipson, H. (1973). *A short introduction to the Object Relations Technique: A projective method for the study of interpersonal relations.* Windsor, England: NFER-Nelson.

Pilowsky, I. (1967). Dimensions of hypochondriasis. *British Journal of Psychiatry, 113,* 80-93.

Reading, A.E. (1980). A comparison of pain rating scales. *Journal of Psychosomatic Research, 24,* 119-124.

Silverstein, A.B. (1963). Age differences in pain apperception. *Perceptual and Motor Skills, 16,* 169-170.

Silverstein, A.B., & Owens, E.P. (1961). Pain apperception in the mentally retarded. *Journal of Projective Techniques, 25,* 352-355.

Spielberger, C.D. (1978). Pain apperception test. In O. K. Buros (Ed.), *The eighth mental measurements yearbook* (pp. 990-991). Highland Park, NJ: Gryphon Press.

Sternbach, R.A., Murphy, R.W., Timmermans, G., Greenhoot, J.H., & Akeson, W.H. (1974).

Measuring the severity of clinical pain. In J.J. Bonica (Ed.), *Advances in Neurology* (Vol. 4, pp. 281–288).

Sternbach, R.A., Wolf, S.R., Murphy, R.W., & Akeson, W.H. (1973). Aspects of chronic low back pain. *Psychosomatics, 14*, 53–56.

Taylor, J.A. (1953). A personality scale of manifest anxiety. *Journal of Abnormal and Social Psychology, 48*, 285–290.

Western Psychological Services. (1988). *Western Psychological Services Catalog 1988–1989*. Los Angeles, CA: Author.

Ziesat, H.A., Jr. (1978). Correlates of the tourniquet ischemia pain ratio. *Perceptual and Motor Skills, 47*, 147–150.

Ziesat, H.A., Jr., & Gentry, W.D. (1978). The Pain Apperception Test: An investigation of concurrent validity. *Journal of Clinical Psychology, 34*, 786–789.

Peter Goldenthal, Ph.D.

Director, Psychotherapy Training Clinic, Bryn Mawr College Child Study Institute, Bryn Mawr, Pennsylvania.

PARENT-ADOLESCENT COMMUNICATION SCALE

Howard Barnes and David H. Olson. St. Paul, Minnesota: Family Social Science, University of Minnesota.

Introduction

The Parent-Adolescent Communication Scale is designed to reflect parents' and adolescents' perspectives of the quality of their interpersonal communication. In developing the scale, the authors, Howard L. Barnes and David H. Olson, were particularly interested in "issues such as the extent of openness or freedom to exchange ideas, information and concerns between generations; the trust or honesty experienced; and the tone or emotional tenor of the interaction" (Barnes & Olson, 1985, p. 57).

The Parent-Adolescent Communication Scale consists of three forms. The Adolescent and Mother Form and the Adolescent and Father Form are completed by the adolescent. The Parent Form is completed by each parent individually. Each form consists of 20 items reflecting interpersonal communication (e.g., showing affection, discussing problems, etc.). On the Parent Form the items reflect interacting with the child; on the Adolescent and Mother Form and on the Adolescent and Father Form the items reflect interacting with the respective parent. The items are otherwise identical on all three forms. Each form is printed on one side of a standard 8½" × 11" sheet. Items are numbered from 1 to 20. Adolescents complete both the mother and father forms, while parents individually complete the parent form as the items apply to their adolescent child. Respondents complete the forms by endorsing each of the 20 items using a 5-point Likert-type scale ranging from 1 (strongly disagree) to 5 (strongly agree). Respondents write the number reflecting the level of their endorsement of each item in the blanks appearing directly to the left of the items. No instructions appear on the forms.

The three forms comprising the Parent-Adolescent Communication Scale are scored on two subscales, Open Family Communication and Problems in Family Communication. Open Family Communication is intended to reflect the positive aspects of a free, natural, flexible, and satisfying exchange of both feelings and information. Problems in Family Communication is intended to reflect the negative side, primarily hesitancy, caution, and selectivity in the sharing of information and feelings. The Parent-Adolescent Communication Scale is presented and described in a manual that also includes other scales developed by Olson and his colleagues at the University of Minnesota for use in a large scale national survey (Olson, McCubbin, Barnes, Larsen, Muxen, & Wilson, 1985). The manual, which costs $45.00, contains the complete scale, administration instructions, scoring procedures, and a partial set of norms.

Howard L. Barnes is an asssistant professor in the Department of Human Development and Family Studies at Kansas State University. This scale arose from the work he did as a graduate student while working with David Olson in Minnesota. David Olson is a professor in the Family Social Science Department and director of the Family Inventories Project at the University of Minnesota. The Parent-Adolescent Communication Scale is one of nine self-report measures designed or revised by a research group at the University of Wisconsin for use in a large scale national survey of marital and family functioning (Olson et al., 1985).

The survey, which led to the development of the Parent-Adolescent Communication Scale and the other family inventories, was supported by the Aid Association for Lutherans (AAL), a fraternal life insurance company. The scale's norm subjects were primarily the Caucasian and Lutheran members of this association.

The sample consisted of 1,140 married couples of various ages and 412 adolescents. All policyholders from selected AAL branch office locations were listed, and then a stratified sample of families was selected randomly to represent seven life cycle stages: 1) young couples without children, 2) families with preschoolers, 3) families with school age children, 4) families with adolescents, 5) families in which the oldest child was 19, 6) empty nest families, and 7) retired couples. Of these, 261 families had a total of 350 adolescents living with them. Olson et al. (1985) also note that among the sample families only 4% of parents had ever been divorced, only 15% of adolescents reported any dislike of school, and only 8% of the respondents had ever received psychotherapy of any kind.

The scales are designed for group administration and require no involvement on the part of the person administering the scale other than handing it out and collecting it. The scale is designed to be comprehensible by individuals of average intelligence aged 12 or older. As far as this reviewer knows, the test has not been adapted for use with special populations or non-English speaking subjects.

Practical Applications/Uses

The large-scale study described previously used a group administration by group leaders. Family members were separated while filling out the scales. No particular training is needed to administer the scale as it is a simple pencil-and-paper self-report measure and could be as readily administered by a clerical person as by a professional. Details of the administration procedure are not spelled out in the manual that accompanies this scale (Olson et al. 1985). The scale can be completed in under 10 minutes.

The scale is scored by computing a total of endorsement values. Scoring is not difficult, but is awkward prone to clerical errors because of the need to manipulate the raw item scores in order to compute scores on the two subscales, Open Family Communication and Problems in Family Communication, and the total score. The examiner adds up the values from the 10 Open Family Communication items and then manipulates the 10 Problems in Family Communication item scores in one of three alternative ways: 1) by changing every 5 to a 1 and every 4 to a 2 on each of the 10 items, 2) by subtracting each score on the 10 items from 6, or 3) by adding up the 10 scores, subtracting the total from 60, and then adding the new value to the sum score from the other 10 items. This somewhat cumbersome hand-scoring procedure is the only one available at this time.

Interpretation of the scores involves consulting a table of total score norms based on the large Aid Association for Lutherans sample described previously. Total score norms, but not factor score norms, are included in the manual. Formal interpretation is mechanical and requires only clerical skill. Use of the scale to generate clinical hypotheses, of course, would require substantial clinical experience and sophistication and is not discussed in the manual.

Technical Aspects

Test items were generated based on a review of the literature on parent-adolescent communication (summarized in Olson et al., 1985). From this initial item pool, 35 items were chosen on the basis of both theoretical and practical considerations (i.e., being understandable to an average 12-year-old) for use in a pilot study.

Adolescents in the pilot study endorsed each item twice on a 5-point Likert-type scale (ranging from strongly agree to strongly disagree): endorsed once as it reflected their interactions with their mothers and endorsed once as it reflected their interactions with their fathers. There were 433 adolescent pilot subjects, of which 127 were high school students and 306 were college students. All adolescent pilot subjects were recruited from four schools and colleges in Minnesota and Wisconsin. Information regarding the ethnicity and socioeconomic status of these pilot subjects is not included in the manual. The parent form of the scale was not piloted.

Data from this pilot study were subjected to factor analysis, leading to the uncovering of three major factors: Open Family Communication, Problems in Family Communication, and Selective Family Communication. Based on the factor loadings, the item pool was reduced from 35 to 20. In developing their final instrument, the authors decided that the second and third factors, Problems in Family Communication and Selective Family Communication, were conceptually similar enough to be combined into one factor focusing on negative aspects of communication, a decision that the authors state was also made in response to practical considerations. The 20-item scale was administered to 1,841 subjects in the survey sample (1,140 families) who were divided into two groups ($n=925$ and $n=916$) for statistical analysis purposes in order to provide two samples for computation of internal consistency.

Internal consistency was computed using Cronbach's alpha for both samples. Internal consistency was adequate for both subscales. Cronbach's alpha reached .87 on both samples for Open Family Communication; .77 and .78 for Problems in Family Communication for the two samples; and .87 and .88 for the full scale for the two samples. No test-retest reliability figures are reported in the manual for the combined adult and adolescent sample.

The question of the validity of these scales involves two questions. 1) To what extent do the scales actually tap the nature and quality of communication between parents and their adolescent children? 2) Has the presence of two relatively discrete factors, one measuring positive aspects of communication and one measuring negative aspects, been demonstrated? The second question is somewhat easier to answer than the first. The results of the factor analytic studies are consistent with the authors' claim that two related but distinct phenomena are being measured. It should be pointed out, however, that the factor analytic studies are equally consistent with the presence of three factors, two negative and one positive.

The second question has been addressed by two empirical studies. Barnes and Olson (1985) analyzed questionnaire responses of a 426 family subsample of the original 1,140 family survey sample. In what was essentially a correlational study these researchers compared parents' and adolescents' responses on the Parent-Adolescent Communication Scales with their responses to other scales used in the survey: the family Adaptability and Cohesion Evaluation Scales (FACES II), a family satisfaction scale, a quality of life satisfaction scale, and a family inventory of life events. These scales are discussed in the manual (Olson et al., 1985), which includes the Parent-Adolescent Communication Scale. There are several important results to consider in evaluating the scale's validity with the sampled population. First, Barnes and Olson report that parents in families reporting a balance between family cohesion and family adaptability on FACES II ("Balanced Families") also tend to report more positive communications with their adolescent children than did parents in families that were more extreme on either adaptability or cohesion ("Extreme Families"). Adolescents in these same "Balanced Families," however, tended to report less positive communication, while those in "Extreme Families" reported more positive communication, the opposite of the result for adults and the opposite of the predicted results as well.

Discriminant analysis provides a means of determining the extent to which scores on one variable permit accurate sorting of subjects into classes, which will also be differentiated on several other variables of interest. Barnes and Olson (1985) report the results of a discriminant analysis of these data in which they treated families rather than individuals as the units of analysis. In this analysis, their interest was on differences among families, rather than on differences among family members within families. The results of their discriminant analysis show that dividing families based on family members mean communication scores permitted a discrimination among families mean scores on a number of other variables at the .0001 level, including family satisfaction, family cohesion, satisfaction with quality of life, and family adaptability.

Fisher (1987), in the only other published study using this scale with which this reviewer is familiar, failed to find a significant relationship between 95 college students' responses on the Parent-Adolescent Communication Scale and the extent of their discussion of sexual topics with their parents. In summary, then, these results are equivocal regarding the validity of this scale. There are strong indications that for parents there is a reasonably strong relationship between questionnaire responses and other family variables. Neither of these studies, however, found any significant relationship between adolescents' responses and the criterion variables.

Critique

The question of the quality of communication between parents and adolescents is of great importance to family research and to clinical practice with adolescents and their families. The scale's utilization of multiple perspectives on family communication gives it the potential to be useful in investigating this area. A researcher using this approach will benefit by being able to examine relationships between adolescents' perceptions and parents' perceptions as well as between mothers' and fathers' perceptions. Barnes and Olson (1985) argue persuasively that differences in responses between family members are most profitably viewed as real perceptual differences and not merely as measurement error.

Unfortunately, there is a difficulty in studying this potentially conflictual communication through the use of self-report measures. In order for such a self-report to be a veridical representation of actual attitudes, behaviors, and perceptions, it must rely on respondents' abilities and willingness to respond frankly and openly to questions. The procedure used by Barnes and Olson in which family members are separated during scale administration represents an excellent first step to reduce potential mutual influence. It is still likely that social desirability (Marlowe & Crowne, 1961) will be an important factor in how some individuals will respond to the scale. This is likely to be a problem for the researcher and the clinician alike.

Another problem arises because two changes were made to the scale *after* the initial investigation of its test-retest reliability and *before* it was cast into its final form. One change was that the test was reduced from 30 items to 20 so that the adult version could be completed in less time. The second change was that an adult form was added to the adolescent form. In addition, it is not clear that the adolescents who provided data for the computation of the test-retest reliability were representative of the sample of subjects who provided the data, which were later analyzed in terms of internal consistency or for the factor analytic study. To fully demonstrate the stability of scores over time, test-retest reliabilities using the final form of the scales should be computed for both parents and adolescents who are representative of the population for which the scale is intended to be used. In addition, more specific administration instructions and subscale norms should be included in the manual.

The homogeneity of the sample and the population from which it was drawn raises serious questions about its generalizability to other samples and families. The published norms are of very limited usefulness to any clinician or researcher whose sample is different from the unique and limited standardization sample. Norms based on research with families more representative of society as a whole, including ethnically diverse samples, clinical samples, divorced and remarried families, and so on are still needed. Finally, a problem arises from the fact that while the scale items certainly appear on the surface to tap issues involved in communication between parents and adolescents, there are at this time insufficient data to demonstrate its validity as a measure of communication for both parents and adolescents.

In summary, the Parent-Adolescent Communication Scale has the potential to be useful after considerably more work has been done to establish its reliability and validity. At this time its use as a formal assessment instrument would be premature. Until more research has been done with this scale, its most likely application will be as a tool to initiate family discussions.

References

Barnes, H.L., & Olson, D.H. (1985). Parent-adolescent communication and the circumplex model. *Child Development, 56,* 438–447.

Fisher, T.D. (1987). Family communication and the sexual behavior and attitudes of college students. *Journal of Youth and Adolescence, 16,* 481–495.

Marlowe, D., & Crowne, D.P. (1961). Social desirability and response to perceived situational demands. *Journal of Consulting Psychology, 25,* 109–115.

Olson, D.H., McCubbin, H.I., Barnes, H., Larsen, A., Muxen, M., & Wilson, M. (1985). *Family Inventories: Inventories used in a national survey of families across the family life cycle.* St. Paul, MN: Family Social Science, University of Minnesota.

Robert J. Drummond, Ed.D.

*Program Director, Counselor Education, University of North Florida,
Jacksonville, Florida.*

PARENT OPINION INVENTORY

*National Study of School Evaluation Staff. Falls Church, Virginia:
Nutlvnul Study of School Evuluuliun.*

Introduction

The Parent Opinion Inventory (POI) is a 55-item questionnaire designed to measure parents' opinions of their children's school and school programs. The inventory evaluates such areas as parent and school relations, instructional outcomes, school problems, program factors, student activities, support services, and psychosocial climate. The POI is one of four instruments in a series that also includes the Student Opinion Inventory, the Teacher Opinion Inventory, and the Community Opinion Inventory. The questionnaire contains 51 Likert-type attitude items and four open-ended questions. The four scales are used primarily in school evaluation and accreditation studies.

The Parent Opinion Inventory (POI) was developed by the National Study of School Evaluation to be a part of a complete school evaluation program. The scale has gone through a number of revisions. The initial development of the POI included three major phases. In phase one, the items for the questionnaire were developed from a review both of similar instruments and of the items used on the Student Opinion Inventory and the Teacher Opinion Inventory. A jury of experts was asked to evaluate and review the set of items. The experts consisted of doctoral students, professors in instruction and curriculum, school administration, and research. The items were then further reviewed by the Administrative Committee of the NSSE, parent teacher organizations, and other educators knowledgeable in the field. In phase two, the questionnaire was field tested in 17 communities characterized by different sizes, different socioeconomic composition, and school levels. The field-site supervisors were directed to ask parents taking the inventory to provide recommendations for improving the scale. In phase three, the scale was modified and the subscale reliability of the instrument and the internal consistency of the items was computed.

The 1988 Edition of the POI was revised to delete obsolete items. New items were developed to cover areas of omission. The wording of the items and the vocabulary used were evaluated carefully for clarity and focus. The POI was then field tested in three schools and the results factor analyzed. These data were used to select and revise the items on the scale. A new grouping of items to form subscales was developed based both on statistical and logical procedures. Item subscale correlations were computed and used as a criterion for inclusion on the inventory.

The Parent Opinion Inventory is comprised of Part A and Part B. There are 51 Likert-type attitude items in Part A, which assesses parents' attitudes on various

423

aspects of their children's school (e.g., The use of cocaine in our school is NOT a serious problem. A) Strongly Agree B) Agree C) Undecided D) Disagree and E) Strongly Disagree). Part B consists of four open-ended questions that allow parents to make recommendations for school improvement (e.g., Do you think that the school is offering the courses students need to face the problems of living today?).

The manual gives suggestions on how schools might go about determining what size sample of parents they would need to have reliable results and how to stimulate a high return.

Practical Applications/Uses

The POI is an instrument that can be used by school districts to help evaluate dimensions of the school program. The perceptions of parents certainly are important to school officials and provide an indicator of parental satisfaction with the schools their children attend. The opinions of parents can be compared with those of other citizens, teachers, and students. The instrument can be used alone or in conjunction with the Teacher Opinion Inventory, the Student Opinion Inventory, and the Community Opinion Inventory. The scale could be used for research purposes also.

The Parent Opinion Inventory was developed to accomplish three goals:

1) to assess parents' attitudes about the school and its programs,
2) to provide parents with an opportunity to make specific recommendations for improvement, and
3) to provide valuable data for school personnel in the decision making process relative to program development, policy formulation, administrative organization, faculty development and community relations (National Study of School Evaluation, 1988b, p. 3).

The test authors suggest that school districts follow systematic sampling procedures to get a sufficient number of responses from parents having students in the school system. In the previous edition, they stressed the necessity for representativeness instead of having a biased sample of parent opinion from groups such as parent-teacher organizations, pressure groups, and telephone feedback. The user is advised to follow good survey procedures such as sending a personal cover letter explaining the purposes of the survey, citing parental anonymity, stressing the importance of returning the instrument, indicating a suggested time by which they should return the instrument, and providing the parents with stamped return envelopes. The authors suggest further that the survey be publicized on TV and radio, in the newspaper, and in community meetings. Also it is suggested that a card be mailed to remind parents to return the survey close to the targeted date for completion.

POI directions are simple and easy for parents to understand. The inventory is untimed and can be completed in 15 to 25 minutes by parents. The inventory can be either hand scored or, if optical scan sheets are used, computer scored. The test authors suggest that the evaluator tally the number of responses and make a frequency distribution for every item. The frequencies then can be translated into cumulative percentages for each option in each item. After the simple statistics are computed, the evaluator can analyze the results. The four options can be assigned weights (e.g., 5= strongly agree, 4 = agree, etc.) and the means for each item computed. Scale means can also be computed.

The interpretation of Part A is made from the descriptive statistics computed for each item. No directions are given for how the responses from the open-ended items are to be interpreted. The interpretation of these comments would demand content analysis skills and no guidelines or references are included to help the user. No norms were reported in the manual. No case studies are provided in the manual on how the results could be interpreted.

Technical Aspects

The Parent Opinion Inventory appears to have face validity. The content of the questions is related to both the evaluative standards used by accreditation organizations and the important dimensions of the school program that would be of interest to parents. The consensus of experts and the feedback from school personnel and students were the criteria used by the test authors to select the items for the scale. Factor analytical studies were used to organize the items on scales in the instrument. No data are reported in the manual of the factor loadings of the items or the item scale correlations.

The POI reports the median reliability coefficient of .74 for the subscales. The coefficient alpha reliability of internal consistency for Part A is .94. No test-retest reliability coefficients were reported. The scale is used by many schools in evaluations studies, but little research has filtered on the scale into the professional literature.

Critique

The idea of having instruments to assess the attitudes and opinions of parents, teachers, community, and students is a good one. The information can be important to schools doing systematic studies of their program and preparing for accreditation visits. The present scale has little documentation of its research and theoretical background, and is not tied into research on effective schools. The items are very broad because they are designed to be answered both by parents of elementary students and of those in secondary schools. The scale could provide a generalized picture of the overall attitude of parents toward the school but not be valuable for providing attitude toward specific components and programs within the school.

The instrument is not attractively packaged. It would be tedious to tally from the answer sheet. Parents are also provided very limited space in which to write their responses to the open-ended questions in Part B. This reviewer found that the parent instrument was the least used instrument of the four in the series because it is normally mailed out and random sampling required is to get representative results. It is this reviewer's opinion that the manual needs to be revised and improved. More information needs to be included to aid the user in interpreting the test results. Case studies and norm information would be of help. More information on the validity and reliability of the scale is needed; no criterion-referenced or construct validity is presented, nor are studies or annotated bibliographies. The new revision has updated the items on the test and helped cover areas previously omitted. The concept has potential and the test could be very useful in evaluation and research studies if more effort was made for the test and test manual to conform to the guidelines for good educational and psychological tests.

References

National Study of School Evaluation. (1988a). *Community Opinion Inventory.* Falls Church, VA: Author.

National Study of School Evaluation. (1988b). *Parent Opinion Inventory.* Falls Church, VA: Author.

National Study of School Evaluation. (1988c). *Student Opinion Inventory.* Falls Church, VA: Author.

National Study of School Evaluation. (1988d). *Teacher Opinion Inventory.* Falls Church, VA: Author.

Delwyn L. Harnisch, Ph.D.
Associate Professor of Educational Psychology, Institute for Research on Human Development, University of Illinois at Urbana-Champaign, Champaign, Illinois.

PEABODY MATHEMATICS READINESS TEST

Otto C. Bassler, Morris I. Beers, Lloyd J. Richardson, and Richard L. Thurman. Bensenville, Illinois: Scholastic Testing Service, Inc.

Introduction

The Peabody Mathematics Readiness Test (PMRT) was developed to assess mathematics readiness skills and identify children who would be expected to experience difficulty in first-grade mathematics. The test consists of 30 items providing scores in five selected subscales of mathematical readiness skills, followed by a drawing test requiring student replication of five line figures.

The five subscales utilized in the test were viewed by the test authors as falling into a natural hierarchy of five dimensions. The dimensions making up this hierarchy in order of decreasing importance are Number, Containment, Size, Shape, and Configuration. In this context, Number refers to decisions based upon the number of objects; Containment refers to decisions based upon whether objects are inside or outside one another; Size refers to decisions based upon relative size of the line drawings; Shape refers to decisions based upon the arrangements of triangles, circles, or squares composing a figure; and Configuration refers to decisions made based upon reorientation, distortion, or missing or extended lines.

The PMRT is composed of two sections: a figure discrimination test and a figure drawing test. The discrimination test requires the student to mark which of three line drawings, constructed to vary along the earlier identified hierarchy, is the most different. Scoring is based upon a priori considerations of the dimensions composing the hierarchy and earlier analysis performed during preliminary testing. For example, suppose a question requires a student to make a choice between drawings varying along the Number and Containment dimensions. If the student selects according to the Number dimension, the student would be judged as operating at the higher level. There are 30 items of this type with each item comparing two of the five dimensions. Of these 30 questions, 8 are specifically identified as measuring Number, 6 measure Containment, 4 measure Size, 4 measure Shape, and 8 measure Configuration.

The drawing test requires the student to copy five simple line drawings. The rationale for including this section relies upon Kephart's (1970) description of the developmental stages a child needs to copy figures and the test authors' assertion that these developmental stages are also prerequisites for success in first-grade mathematics.

The following benefits of using the test are offered in the Administrator's Manual (Bassler, Beers, Richardson, & Thurman, 1979a): 1) identifying students early on who are likely to have difficulty in completing early mathematics, 2) providing a tool for use with the special populations of EMRs with a mental age of about 6 years and deaf children, and 3) enabling teachers to plan and implement a specific remedial program.

Materials required for testing include individual testing booklets used by the students in marking their responses, an individual performance record for each student tested, and an administrator's manual containing information on administering, scoring, and interpreting the subscales. For a given testing session, estimated at 20 minutes in the 1987–88 Scholastic Testing Service catalog, students would take both the discrimination and drawing subtests. Student responses are transferred into the individual performance record where they are scored, tabulated along the corresponding dimensions, and subscale scores plotted on a readiness profile. At this point suggestions for further remediation may be read from the readiness profile, with the options being additional readiness work needed, readiness work suggested, and no further readiness work needed.

Practical Applications/Uses

The Peabody Mathematics Readiness Tests are diagnostic tools designed to measure the ability of average children (4 to 6 years) and special education children (mental age of 4 to 6 years) to begin first-grade mathematics. The readiness factors of Number, Containment, Size, Shape, Configuration, and the skill of drawing are used to identify students who might be deficient in specific areas of early mathematics. An activity manual (Bassler, Beers, Richardson, & Thurman, 1979b) is provided, which contains example activities useful in supplementing areas of weakness identified in the PMRT.

In administering the PMRT suggested materials include a testing booklet, an individual performance record for each studen, extra booklets and records in event of damage, and an administration manual for the test administrator and proctors. Student testing booklets and individual performance records should be marked with the student's name, teacher, and date of test prior to beginning testing. Estimated time required for the administration of the PMRT consists of 20 minutes student time and 2–5 minutes for instructions.

The discrimination portion of the PMRT is scored using a three part process. First, the student's response is identified and the number corresponding to that response is circled on the individual performance record. Second, the number circled is transferred to the appropriate subscale column. Finally, the total scores for each subscale are computed by summing the individual scores and are then recorded on the individual performance record.

In scoring the drawing test, each item is independently scored with a correct drawing receiving 2 points, a partially correct drawing receiving 1 point, and an incorrect drawing receiving 0 points. Examples and short verbal descriptions are provided in the Administrator's Manual to aid in the scoring of each of the five items comprising this section. The administrator would then circle the score for each item on the individual performance record. The total score for this subscale is computed by summing the individual scores.

Should a student's score in any subscale or in the drawing test indicate that additional readiness work is needed, an activity manual is available to aid in planning remediation. This manual contains specific suggestions for further work in each of the five dimensions measured by the subscales and in the drawing test. These suggestions include items closely paralleling the test items themselves and mini-lessons teaching concepts such as larger-smaller, shape identification, and inside-outside.

Technical Aspects

Technical information is difficult to obtain for the PMRT. What is provided often suffers from reliance upon verbal assertions as opposed to more formal treatments. One would think that the question of face validity in a test such as this would be critical, yet there is no discussion of validity whatsoever. No correlations with other currently testing instruments are provided.

What little reliability information is provided is based upon Cronbach's alpha as adjusted by the Spearman-Brown Prophecy Formula for test length of 35. The coefficients range from a low of .40 to a high of .62. No information is given regarding test-retest reliability. Little information is provided on the norms. The test was normed using a sample of 898 subjects chosen from Louisiana, Missouri, New York, and Tennessee. No sample demographic characteristics are provided as well as how the norm sample compares with the United States as a whole.

The Technical Manual (Bassler, Beers, Richardson, & Thurman, 1979c) contains a single paragraph regarding factor analysis of the PMRT in which one is told that four weak factors emerged and that these did not replicate in another sample. It appears that the first factor analysis was based upon responses from 80 children to 41 items. The authors then report a second phase in which sample A was used to produce a new set of factors that were then replicated in sample B. Two of the factors in sample A seemed to replicate in sample B, the factors representing number and shape. This is all that is told concerning this phase of analysis. Nowhere is there presented evidence supporting either the five discrimination tasks or the claimed hierarchy of dimensions utilized in the PMRT.

Critique

Although a major weakness of the PMRT is its lack of technical information, perhaps the most significant weakness is the lack of any supporting evidence for the hierarchy of dimensions which serves as a foundation for the entire test. This lack of provided support substantially weakens the validity of the test due to the critical role such a hierarchy plays in the test construction and the importance this hierarchy plays in test scoring and interpretation. If we assume the five dimensions and their associated hierarchy, there remain additional complications with using the test.

Item scoring suffers from the scoring procedures used as well as dependence upon the proposed hierarchy of dimensions . For example, each item is designed to force a discrimination based upon two of the five dimensions. In scoring, a choice indicating that a child is discriminating based upon the higher of the two dimensions is awarded a score of 3, a choice indicating discrimination based upon the lower dimension is given a score of 2, and a choice indicating selection based on neither of the two dimensions is awarded a score of 1. In using this scoring procedure, the lower dimension is always awarded a score of 2, regardless of how many steps it might be removed from the higher dimension in the hierarchy. Because of this, scoring of the lower dimensions for any individual item more accurately reflects a mixture of lower dimensions and not a hierarchy.

Furthermore, the rationale behind the scoring of several items making up the test is difficult to comprehend. For example, one such item, purportedly measuring Number, consists of three sets of quarter circles joined in various manners. The first diagram consists of four of these quarters joined to form a single complete circle; the second is formed by joining two of these quarters, forming the top half of a circle, and then joining a third quarter immediately to the right (using a total of three quarters); the third is made from four quarters, as was drawn in the first diagram, arranged to form two top halves that are placed side by side. If one were truly discriminating on the basis of the number of sections present, one would expect the highest rating to be given to the second figure. Yet, this choice is given the lowest possible rating. Another item seems to introduce the dimension of perceived dimensionality. In this case, the most marked difference is that one of the three diagrams is rendered in such a fashion as to make it appear three dimensional. Not only is this not part of the supposed hierarchy, but by selecting this figure, which is a highly reasonable thing to do, one would receive the lowest possible score. Therefore, the distractor has a much stronger intuitive feel than the dimensions supposedly being measured.

An important potential use of the PMRT would be in profile analysis based upon the dimensions measured by the subtests themselves. But using the reliability information provided, with values ranging from .40 to a high of .62, scores on the subscales are not suited for profile analysis.

The Activity Manual contains very good activities, which would be worthwhile for inclusion into a young child's experiences. The importance of identifying larger and smaller, more and less, inside and outside, and so on are all worthy goals for early instruction. The primary purpose in many areas of the Activity Manual, however, seems to be to train the child in those skills viewed by the test authors as important to recognize for successful performance on the PMRT itself.

There is clearly a need for an instrument for the early identification of a student's degree of mathematical readiness. Such an instrument would truly aid in meeting the test authors' stated goals. Unfortunately, given the evidence provided, it is difficult to determine if the PMRT is such an instrument.

References

This list includes text citations and suggested additional reading.

Bassler, O.C., Beers, M.I., Richardson, L.I., & Thurman, R.L. (1979a). *Peabody Mathematics Readiness Test: Administrator's manual.* Bensenville, IL: Scholastic Testing Service, Inc.

Bassler, O.C., Beers, M.I., Richardson, L.I., & Thurman, R.L. (1979b). *Peabody Mathematics Readiness Test: Activity manual.* Bensenville, IL: Scholastic Testing Service, Inc.

Bassler, O.C., Beers, M.I., Richardson, L.I., & Thurman, R.L. (1979c). *Peabody Mathematics Readiness Test: Technical manual.* Bensenville, IL: Scholastic Testing Service, Inc.

Beers, M. I. (1973). *Diagnosis and remediation based upon a mathematics readiness test for entering first grade students* (Professional Paper Series No. 73–3). Nashville, TN: Institute on School Learning and Individual Differences, George Peabody College for Teachers.

Brashear, I.B. (1970). *An investigation of the development of mathematical concepts of children from four to six years of age* (Professional Paper Series No. 70-4). Nashville, TN: Institute on School Learning and Individual Differences, George Peabody College for Teachers.

Kephart, N. C. (1970). *The slow reader in the classroom.* Columbus, OH: Charles E. Merrill.

Andrew F. Newcomb, Ph.D.
Associate Professor of Psychology, University of Richmond, Richmond, Virginia.

PEER NOMINATION INVENTORY OF DEPRESSION

Monroe M. Lefkowitz and Edward P. Tesiny. Lenox, Massachusetts: Monroe M. Lefkowitz, Ph.D.

Introduction

The Peer Nomination Inventory of Depression (PNID) uses a peer nomination technique to assess the symptoms of depression among elementary school-aged children. The 19 items in the PNID are divided into three scales: Depression, which has 13 items designed to measure childhood depression; Happiness, which has 4 items to assess cheerfulness and contentment; and Popularity, which has 2 items to assess affiliation and friendship. A child's score on the PNID scales is based on peer group nominations obtained in a roster sociometric nomination procedure. The need for obtaining nominations from a stable peer group (e.g., children in a classroom) limits the clinical utility of the PNID. However, the excellent scale construction and sizable normative sample make the PNID a very promising research inventory.

The PNID was developed by Monroe M. Lefkowitz and Edward F. Tesiny, two scholars renowned for their epidemiological research with children. The development of the PNID originated with the selection of 29 items that were used in the clinical literature to describe the symptoms of depression (i.e., specifically affective, cognitive, motivational, and vegetative functioning). These items were reviewed by a panel of nine experts, and 16 were selected for inclusion in the inventory. Of these 16 items, 13 were thought to measure observable aspects of depression (e.g., "Who often cries?" or "Who often plays alone?"), and the remaining three were considered to index the mood of ebullience or happiness (e.g., "Who is often cheerful?"). After pilot testing on 82 fourth- and fifth-grade children, one depression item and one happiness item were added to the inventory along with two items to assess peer popularity (e.g., "Who would you like to sit next to in class?").

Although the PNID originally was validated as a 20-item scale (Lefkowitz & Tesiny, 1980), due to the results of item analyses more recent work with the instrument has eliminated one of the items ("Who thinks they are bad?") from the inventory. The psychometric properties of the PNID have been studied extensively with nearly 4,000 children (Lefkowitz & Tesiny, 1980, 1985), and the PNID is being adapted for use as a rating scale in which individual administration could be used (Lefkowitz, Tesiny, & Solodow, 1988). No other alternative forms for non-English-speaking or special populations have been developed.

A published test booklet for the PNID is not available because a unique booklet must be constructed for each test situation. The test authors provide a handout that guides the development of the test booklet and offers detailed administration instructions. In particular, the user develops a 23-page booklet that contains an identification page, three practice items, and the 19 items in the PNID. A single item is typed at the top of each page and below the item is the list of all children in the nominating group. In addition, "No Child" is typed at the bottom of each list to allow for nomination of no one from the peer group for a particular role. This booklet then serves as the answer form for the test. The user is advised to use colored pages in the booklet to assure that all children are on the same page in the group administration.

In an elementary school classroom setting, there is a clear need for at least one assistant during the testing process. After the completion of the identification item and the three practice items, each test item is read aloud to the children twice. The children then are instructed to draw a line through all names on the class roster that best fit the question (Lefkowitz & Tesiny, 1980). Although self-nomination is not permitted, the respondent may elect to nominate no one. During this process, the administrators' primary responsibilities are to read the test items, to help the children remain on the correct page, and to assure that the children are completing the test independently.

The PNID is most appropriate for use with children in third, fourth, and fifth grades. Sufficient normative data are available for interpretation (Lefkowitz & Tesiny, 1980, 1985), and with an administrator reading the items aloud, the children should have no difficulty with reading level. Although assessment of younger elementary school children is possible, normative data are not currently available and the children's reading level and understanding of test items complicates administration. The use of the PNID with older children is limited by the absence of normative data and the lack of a self-contained stable peer group because most older children are changing classrooms throughout the day.

Practical Applications/Uses

The PNID is designed as a research instrument for use in epidemiological and longitudinal studies of childhood depression. Although the test provides a measure of the symptoms of depression, the utility of the PNID to discriminate between children with depressive symptomatology as part of another psychiatric disorder and children with a depressive disorder has not yet been established. The PNID provides scores on the three variables of Depression, Happiness, and Popularity.

The use of the PNID requires the participation of a group of peers who know each other well. Administration of the test to individual children is not feasible (see Lefkowitz et al., 1988, for development of an individual rating scale). Although the instrument has exceptional research promise with groups of children, the limitation on administration to individual children precludes the use of the PNID as a practical clinical tool. Even in clinical settings in which a peer group may be present (i.e., residential care or inpatient psychiatric facilities), this peer group is unlikely to have a sufficiently stable history that would allow for comparable information among all of the children.

Administration of the PNID typically would take place in a group setting, most likely an elementary school classroom. The test is normed for third-, fourth-, and fifth-graders, and completion of the inventory is facilitated by the administrator reading the test items aloud to the children. The development of a color-coded test booklet allows for easy group administration with the aid of an assistant. Individual administration to all children within a stable peer group is, of course, possible, but unnecessary in populations of regular education children.

The manual (Lefkowitz & Tesiny, 1981) supplied by the test authors is straightforward and provides simple directives for the development of the test booklet and test administration. So long as the administrator and assistant have experience in the completion of group testing in the classroom, no special assessment skills are necessary. Although not stated in the administration manual, the test user should anticipate that group administration to 25 children should not take longer than 20 minutes.

The scoring system suggested for the PNID is relatively simple. The test authors propose that two kinds of scores be formulated for each child: a score on each test item and scores for the Depression, Happiness, and Popularity clusters. If a child is nominated for a test item, a 1 is given. The child's score on that item is the sum of the number of 1's received divided by the number of children present in the class. The user should be careful to remember that the divisor should be equal to the size of the nominating group (i.e., total class size minus 1 as self-nominations are not permitted). Cluster scores are equal to the sum of the adjusted item scores. In this procedure, a child's Depression score may range from 0, the result of being nominated by no peers, to 13, the result of being nominated by all peers on all items. The range for the Happiness cluster is 0–4 and the range for the Popularity cluster is 0–2.

As a practical matter, the complexity of scoring increases with the size of the nominating group. Although no computerized scoring of the instrument is described, a simple BASIC or PASCAL program would be a significant timesaver in cases of large samples. Alternatively, SPSS-X or SAS programs could also reduce computation time; however, this approach would not be as efficient because each child is likely to have multiple nominations for each item. Regardless, the user still will need to code the children's responses and key in the data set. For example, in a class of 25 students with each child making an average of three nominations on each of the 19 items, the scorer will need to handle initially over 1,400 data points. Hand scoring would be very tedious and susceptible to error.

The interpretation of the PNID is based on Lefkowitz and Tesiny's (1980, 1985) prior testing of 942 and 3,020 normal elementary school children. In their 1980 study, the test authors found that the standardization sample had a mean of 1.60 and a standard deviation of 1.16 on the 13-item Depression scale. When measurement error was accounted for, the 90% confidence interval for an elevated score in the upper 5% of true scores was calculated to have a mean of 3.51 and a standard error of measurement of .45. When a cutoff score of 4 was used, the positively skewed distribution of PNID resulted in 5.2% of the population being included as opposed to the 1.8% expected (with expected based on the cutoff score of 4 and being 2.1 standard deviations above the mean).

A practical interpretation of the use of a cutoff score of 4 is suggested by Lefkowitz and Tesiny (1985). The test authors offer two possible scenarios in which to receive a score of 4, a child would have to be nominated by all children on one third of Depression items or by one third of the children on all the Depression items. The data offered by Lefkowitz and Tesiny (1985) provide fairly convincing evidence that the cutoff score of 4 is an appropriate level for interpreting the presence of observable symptoms of depression. This database also provides separate normative information based on reading level, IQ, and income for third-, fourth-, and fifth-grade boys and girls. A qualified clinical psychologist or clinical researcher should have no difficulty interpreting the scores from the Depression scale of the PNID. Similar normative data do not appear to be available for the Happiness and Popularity clusters.

Technical Aspects

The reliability data for the PNID are based on a sample of 944 fourth- and fifth-graders drawn from 61 classrooms in 10 New York City elementary schools (Lefkowitz & Tesiny, 1980). These schools were located in three districts that represented a stratified cross-section of socioeconomic and ethnic households. Test-retest reliability was established by randomly selecting 35% of the children from the first six schools ($N = 177$) and retesting these children after approximately 2 months. The Depression scale items evidenced test-retest coefficients that ranged from .39 to .76 with a .79 coefficient for the total Depression score. Similarly, the test-retest correlations ranged from .52 to .70 for the Happiness scale items with an overall coefficient of .74 for the total Happiness score.

An assessment of homogeneity of the scales on the entire sample revealed that one of the original 14 depression items ("Who thinks they are bad?") did not demonstrate good internal consistency with the remaining items in the inventory. The removal of this item resulted in the coefficient alpha of .85 for the Depression scale. A coefficient alpha for the Happiness scale was reported as .88. In a further test of homogeneity each of the test items was correlated with the total corrected score. The range of item-total correlations was from .34 to .71 for the Depression scale and was from .63 to .78 for the Happiness scale.

The normative sample was assigned randomly to either a standardization or a cross-validation group ($N = 472$ in each group). In separate analyses, a varimax factor analysis was used to extract four factors from the 17 items in the Happiness and Depression scales. These four factors accounted for approximately 54% of the variance in each sample. Three of the factors were labeled Loneliness, Inadequacy, and Dejection, and each sample accounted for approximately 38% of the variance. The fourth factor in each sample was labeled Happiness and accounted for approximately 16% of the variance. The test authors reported that the criterion for simple structure was satisfied and that the factor structures for the two samples were isomorphic, reflecting acceptable cross-validation.

The test authors completed an interesting assessment of interrater agreement by first calculating the coefficient alpha for each of the 61 classes in their sample with the raters serving the same function as test items. An r to z transformation was completed for each of the 61 coefficients and the mean of these transformations resulted in a converted alpha of .75. The test authors concluded that this represented acceptable interrater agreement.

The content validity of the PNID was established by a panel of nine experts who reviewed the scale items as being indicative of the symptoms of childhood depression. Two self-report instruments, a modified version of the Children's Depression Inventory (Kovacs & Beck, 1977), a modified version of the Self-rating Depression Scale (Zung, 1965), and one teacher report single-item rating scale were used to assess concurrent validity. Although all correlations were significant, the resulting correlation coefficients were relatively small in magnitude, .23, .14, and .41, respectively.

The test authors assessed construct validity by examining the relationship between the subjects' scores on the PNID and their scores on a variety of measures that tapped the following domains: intellectual, social, self-perception, school, recreational activity, vegetative problems, and family income. A set of eight hypotheses regarding children with high PNID scores were examined; in the assessment of these hypotheses, significance is at $p < .001$ unless reported otherwise. 1) Support was found for depressed intellectual functioning—the correlations for standardized reading and math scores, figure drawing IQ, and teacher-rated achievement and work habits (both reverse scored) were -.23, -.27, -.10 ($p < .01$), .26, and .27, respectively. 2) Based on teacher (reverse scored) and peer ratings of social behavior, social functioning was negatively affected, $r = .22$ and -.27, respectively. 3) Happiness scale scores and self-report on the Coopersmith Self-Esteem Inventory (Coopersmith, 1967) indicated that peer-nominated depressed children were unhappy and had lower self-esteem, $r = -.24$ and -.12, respectively. 4) and 5) Children who were nominated by their peers as depressed had higher levels of external locus of control and more frequent school absence and tardiness, $r = .19, .14,$ and .09, respectively. 6) and 7) No support was found for a relationship between depression and frequency of television viewing, $r = .04$, and an unexpected relationship was found with weight gain, $r = .07$ ($p < .05$). 8) An inverse relationship was identified between family income and depression, $r = -.19$.

In a multiple regression analysis, scores on the PNID were predicted consistently by the variables of teacher-rated depression, social achievement, and self-rated depression in both the standardization and cross-validation samples. In general, the validity variables accounted for approximately 20% of the variance in the PNID scores. In addition, a varimax factor analysis with the collapsed validity variables and the PNID scale scores revealed a separate factor of other-rated depression.

The discriminant validity of the PNID is supported by the score pattern of children who were identified as overly active by their mothers. These "hyperactive" children were not found to be significantly more often nominated as depressed by their peers.

Critique

The PNID is an excellent instrument for assessing the symptoms of depression in longitudinal and epidemiological research with children. The test authors provide a superb example of scale construction, and the normative sample is both sizable and representative of children in metropolitan school settings, which enhances the generalizability of this research instrument. The greatest weakness of the PNID is the lack of substantive support for concurrent validity, and the consequent failure to support the instrument as a possible means to "mitigate inaccurate diagnosis" of depression. Simply stated, the PNID is not a practical clinical tool for everyday use.

Although the availability of norms for only third-, fourth-, and fifth-grade children is somewhat constraining, it is exactly the population to which the PNID ideally is suited. The use of peers as informants has a long history in sociometric research, and peer report provides a unique means to complete the assessment of depression in children. Administration problems with younger and older children suggest that the third-to-fifth grade age range is ideal for use of the PNID. One unanswered question with the PNID, and sociometric research in general, is what percentage of the peer group should participate in order to assure a valid and accurate assessment. Most sociometric research involves at least 70% of the peer group and many studies report significantly higher levels of participation. The user of the PNID should be careful to assure the highest participation possible.

Inasmuch as the individual version of the PNID is not yet available, a critique of this new instrument cannot be offered. However, in instances where peer report is not possible or in which clinical assessment is needed, the reader should be aware of a number of already established instruments that serve this purpose. For example, either Lang and Tisher's Children's Depression Scale (1978) or Kovacs's Children's Depression Inventory (1978) provides promising alternative self-report instruments. In each case, both the symptoms and severity of depression are assessed. The strength of the PNID is clearly in providing data from an alternative information source (e.g., the peer group) and in providing a promising research tool.

References

Kovacs, M. (1978). *Children's Depression Inventory (CDI)*. Unpublished manuscript, University of Pittsburgh.

Lang, M., & Tisher, M. (1978). *Children's Depression Scale*. Victoria, Australia: The Australian Council for Educational Research Limited.

Lefkowitz, M.M., & Tesiny, E.P. (1980). Assessment of childhood depression. *Journal of Consulting and Clinical Psychology, 48*, 43–50.

Lefkowitz, M.M., & Tesiny, E.P. (1981). *Manual for the Peer Nomination Inventory of Depression*. Unpublished manuscript, Long Island University.

Lefkowitz, M.M., & Tesiny, E.P. (1985). Depression in children: Prevalence and correlates. *Journal of Consulting and Clinical Psychology, 53*, 647–656.

Lefkowitz, M.M., Tesiny, E.P., & Solodow, E. (1988). *The Peer Nomination Inventory of Depression*. Unpublished manuscript, Long Island University.

Charles W. Stansfield, Ph.D.
Director, ERIC Clearinghouse for Languages and Linguistics, and Director, Division of Foreign Language Education and Testing, Center for Applied Linguistics, Washington, D.C.

PIMSLEUR LANGUAGE APTITUDE BATTERY

Paul Pimsleur. San Antonio, Texas: The Psychological Corporation.

Introduction

The Pimsleur Language Aptitude Battery (PLAB) is a 50-minute multiple-choice test designed to predict how well a student will do in foreign language study. The PLAB was designed to be administered to native English-speaking students in Grades 7 through 12 who are studying or planning to study a foreign language. It combines pure measures of foreign language aptitude with a measure of motivation and past grade point average (GPA) in order to obtain the maximum predictive power for this population of foreign language learners.

Dr. Paul Pimsleur, author of the PLAB, was (until his death at age 45 in 1972) one of the world's leading authorities on foreign language testing. After completing his Ph.D. in French, he earned a second master's degree in educational measurement at Teachers College, Columbia University in New York. In doing so, he became one of the first foreign language teachers to become trained in statistics, and subsequently carried out a number of important empirical studies with federal funding made available through the National Defense Education Act. Dr. Pimsleur taught French at the University of California at Los Angeles for 4 years and in 1961 joined the staff of the Ohio State University, where he taught a graduate course in foreign language testing and served as director of language laboratories until his death in 1972. In addition to publishing more than a dozen articles on foreign language testing, he developed the Pimsleur Modern Foreign Language Proficiency Tests in French (Pimsleur, 1967a), German (Pimsleur, 1967b), and Spanish (Pimsleur, 1967c), which received considerable use in American schools during the decade following their publication by Harcourt, Brace, Jovanovich in 1967.

The PLAB is the result of 8 years of interest in language aptitude by Pimsleur. In 1958, Pimsleur initiated a review of the literature on factors related to success in foreign language study. The review identified a number of variables that the author grouped under seven headings: 1) intelligence, 2) verbal ability, 3) pitch discrimination, 4) order of language study and bilingualism, 5) study habits, 6) attitudes and motivation, and 7) personality factors. Verbal intelligence and motivation were found to be the best predictors of successful foreign language study (Pimsleur, Mosberg, & Morrison, 1962). However, because the studies he reviewed were carried out mostly with learners studying under methods that emphasized the development of reading and translation skills, Pimsleur gathered additional data on students in classrooms emphasizing the acquisition of listening and speaking skills. In these two studies of over 20 factors believed to be related to the learn-

438

ing of French at the college level (Pimsleur, 1961; Pimsleur, Stockwell, & Comrey, 1962), verbal intelligence and motivation were again found to be the most important factors, while reasoning, word fluency, and pitch discrimination played a significant but lesser role.

Pimsleur (1962, 1963) performed similar studies involving students at the secondary level. Following these studies, he concluded that foreign language aptitude consisted of three main factors: verbal intelligence, motivation, and listening ability. His research identified seven item types that could measure these abilities, which he included in a revised experimental test battery. Following additional testing at the secondary level (Pimsleur, Sundland, & McIntyre, 1963) and an item analysis, certain items were deleted. In addition, the decision was made to drop two of the seven item types from the final version, but to add GPA to the test. Pimsleur found that his battery did have some predictive power, but that it was not as effective in predicting future performance as was past GPA. However when he included GPA, the battery was able to predict success with considerably greater accuracy than would GPA alone.

The final form of the test, and the only one ever developed, was administered to some 6,000 students in 13 states for norming purposes. Approximately half of these students took the test at the beginning of Grades 7, 8 or 9. The other half took the test after completing one level of high school French or Spanish. This administration produced separate norms tables for each of the junior high grades, and a single table for students in high school.

The PLAB is a multiple-choice test containing six parts. A complete set of materials includes the test tape, test booklets, answer sheets, scoring stencils, student performance charts, a class record, and a test manual.

In part 1, Grades in Major Subjects, examinees are given 4 minutes to list from memory on their answer sheet their most recent letter grades in English, social studies, mathematics, and science. The student is given 1 point for a D, 2 points for a C, 3 points for a B, and 4 points for an A. Thus a total of 16 points can be earned in this section.

In part 2, Interest, examinees are given 1½ minutes to rate their interest in studying a foreign language. The options and the points allotted for each are as follows: "Rather uninterested" (0 points), "More or less indifferent" (1 point), "Mildly interested" (2 points), "Rather interested" (3 points), and "Strongly interested" (4 points). In figuring the total raw score, the scorer doubles the number of points earned in this part. Thus, Part 2 is worth up to 8 points. Part 2 is intended to measure motivation, which Pimsleur considered a principal factor in language aptitude.

Parts 3 through 6 of the PLAB are pure aptitude measures, each of which employs a four-option format. They are administered through a test tape that presents both the directions and, in the case of parts 5 and 6, the items. Parts 3 and 4 measure verbal ability, while Parts 5 and 6 measure auditory ability.

Part 3, Vocabulary, is a 24-item measure of the student's vocabulary in English and lasts 5 minutes. The student reads a word and then chooses the appropriate synonym from among four choices printed in the test booklet. The assumption behind this is that the size of one's native language vocabulary indicates one's ability to learn vocabulary in a foreign language. The sample item ("prolonged") illustrates that the words included in this section would be fairly easy for an educated adult. For this reason the test is not suitable to differentiate language aptitude among educated adults, such as students enrolled at selective colleges, although it may have some application with nontraditional adult students, such as those enrolled in community colleges and in adult education programs.

In part 4, Language Analysis, the examinee is given 12 minutes to answer 15 items. The test booklet presents a number of words and sentences in Kabardian, a language of the Soviet Union, and their English equivalents. From these examples, the examinee must figure out how to say 15 new sentences in Kabardian. The items require the application of the examinee's sensitivity to grammatical systems.

In part 5, Sound Discrimination, the test tape teaches the examinee three words in Ewe, a language of Ghana and Togo, and their English translations. The examinee then hears 30 sentences in Ewe and must mark on the answer sheet which of the three words each sentence contains. The three words sound almost identical, and differ only in tone (level of pitch) and nasalization (whether they use nasal or nonnasal vowels). Recognition of these features is a real-life sound discrimination task encountered by foreign language learners. The only thing that varies from language to language are the specific features one may have to recognize. For example, an American secondary school student, who typically studies Spanish, French, or German, would encounter nasality that is common in French but is also found in Spanish and German before certain consonants.

In part 6, Sound-Symbol Association, the examinee hears a two- or three-syllable nonsense word made up of the sounds of English. He or she then marks on the answer sheet the one that appears to be what was said. For example, he hears *tarpdel* and chooses among "(a) trapled, (b) tarpled, (c) tarpdel, (d) trapdel." This part assesses the ability to associate a sound with its written representation. Such tasks are frequently encountered by foreign language students who may either learn or store a word in its printed form and then upon hearing it, must associate it with the printed form already learned or vice versa. Part 6 contains 24 items and lasts 9 minutes.

Practical Applications/Uses

The PLAB and the Modern Language Aptitude Test (MLAT) developed by Carroll and Sapon (1959) are the only commercially available foreign language aptitude tests that can be used with high school students. Of the two, only the PLAB was developed specifically for secondary school students and only the PLAB claims to be suitable for use with students at the junior high level. Perhaps for this reason, the PLAB is most often used at the junior high level.

The PLAB can be administered in a single class period. Fifteen to 20 minutes is required to distribute test materials, read the general directions, permit students to grid their name and other background information on the answer sheet, and complete parts 1 and 2. In preparing students to take part 1, it would be useful to advise them several days before the administration that they will have to list their most recent grades in English, social studies, mathematics, and science. This would produce more accurate information.

Directions and questions for Parts 3 through 6 are administered via the test tape, which lasts 36 minutes. The tape is recorded at 7½ inches per second and is only available on a 7-inch reel. After turning on the tape, the teacher circulates through the room to ensure that each student is completing the answer sheet in the correct manner. Thus, the PLAB is easy for a teacher or an aide to administer. Adequate instructions are provided in the manual (Pimsleur, 1966a). Although parts 1 and 2 should always be completed first, the taped portion can be administered on another occasion if necessary.

Student answer sheets are scored by hand using a scoring stencil made of a heavy manila paper. Holes are cut in the stencil to pinpoint the correct options. The scorer first positions the stencil over the answer sheet so that the holes display the correct option and then counts the number of marks visible to determine the raw score for each part. The score for each part is written in a box on the answer sheet. Then, the part scores are summed to obtain a verbal score, an auditory score, and a total score. Next, the scorer refers to the manual to determine the percentile rank and stanine associated with each raw score, and then writes this information in an appropriate box on the answer sheet and on the class record. The entire process takes 10 to 15 minutes per examinee, and no practice scoring is required. The total score is the number of correct or visible marks on the answer sheet. The one exception is part 2, Interest , where the scorer doubles the number of marks shown on the answer sheet. A total of 117 points may be obtained on the test.

The test requires a custom answer sheet containing printed options for several parts. Thus, it is not possible to substitute a standard scannable answer sheet in order to score the test locally by machine. For local scoring, the PLAB must be scored by hand. An optional scoring service is available from the publisher, The Psychological Corporation, at a cost of $1.20 per pupil with a minimum order of $50.00. This service provides a roster of raw scores followed by national and local percentile and stanine scores. Services available for an additional fee include lists of examinees ranked from high to low and labels for each student's permanent record. Two answer sheets are available, one IBM and one MRC. Although both may be hand scored, machine scoring is available only with the MRC answer sheet.

A one-page *Student Performance Chart and Report to Parents* may be filled out by the teacher and given to each student. It depicts the grades and interest level of the student and the stanine and percentile ranks for verbal ability, auditory ability, and the total battery. The reverse side of this score report describes the test for parents and explains how to read the performance chart.

The PLAB has never been widely used, and as it is now over 20 years old, few teachers are aware of its existence. This is because there is a strong feeling among foreign language educators that everyone can learn a foreign language and that everyone should be given an opportunity to do so. As aptitude tests are usually used to select or reject students for a program, there has traditionally been a fear that the test would be misused. This is unfortunate, because the PLAB can be quite helpful in counseling individual students. For instance, if a student does not perform well in class, but the teacher believes he or she has good potential, a high PLAB score can reinforce the teacher's expectations and the student can be encouraged to improve his or her performance. Similarly, a student who scores very high on the PLAB may be encouraged to take several foreign languages in high school or in college.

In addition to using the PLAB for selecting or grouping students according to their total score as described in the PLAB manual, test results can be used to diagnose individual strengths and weaknesses. By examining the part scores for verbal and auditory ability, one can use this information to place students in the most appropriate section according to the methods used by each teacher. Therefore, a student whose score is higher in auditory ability could be placed with a teacher who emphasizes listening and speaking, while one whose score is higher in verbal ability could be placed with a teacher who emphasizes reading and writing. Or in an individualized classroom, a teacher may use such information to determine the method of instruction most appropriate to each child. Similarly, a profile of an existing class can be constructed on the class record and examined for any salient strength in ability. Such information could be useful to the teacher in determining how to best present new material to the class or in knowing what material is likely to pose difficulty for the class as a whole.

Although not mentioned in the manual, it is also possible to compare raw scores on parts 3 through 6 in order to diagnose areas of weakness when a student exhibits problems while studying a foreign language. This involves subdividing the verbal ability factor into Vocabulary and Language Analysis. A student with a limited English vocabulary may also be a poor reader. In such a case, the student may be advised to receive remedial instruction in English. Students with a low Language Analysis score may require additional training in English grammar and they may need coaching on the idea of using grammar as a tool for listening and reading comprehension. Students with surprisingly poor scores on the auditory ability parts of the test should be recommended for a hearing test. Often, minor hearing problems can be identified in the foreign language classroom, where they usually explain poor performance. In some cases, analysis of the PLAB can indicate that a student should enroll in a different foreign language. For instance, some teachers have found that students who excel in Language Analysis perform better in Latin than in modern foreign languages (see Curtin, Avner, & Smith, 1983).

Technical Aspects

The PLAB offers norms showing the percentile rank corresponding to the raw score of students at the beginning of Grades 7 ($N = 1,201$), 8 ($N = 979$), and 9 ($N = 1,765$), and students who have completed one level of foreign language study in high school ($N = 3,117$). The average age and grade level of the high school group is not given. Separate norms are available for the verbal score (parts 3 and 4) and the auditory score (parts 5 and 6). In addition, means and standard deviations are reported for each of these groups for each part of the test.

The PLAB seems to be adequately reliable. Split-half reliabilities (comparing consistency of performance on different halves of the test) for the multiple-choice section (parts 3 through 6) for Grades 7, 8, and 9 showed correlations (an index of agreement) ranging from .85 to .89. No correlation between actual GPA and that reported in part 1 is given. Nor is the test-retest reliability (which indicates consistency of responses on two different administrations) of the Interest rating in part 2 reported. These correlations would probably lower the reliability of the total measure a little, although not seriously. The internal-consistency reliabilities (an alternate measure of parallel-form reliability) of parts 3, 4, 5, and 6 range between .57 and .82. No standard errors of measurement, which is an estimate of the probable extent of error in a test score due to imperfect reliability of the test, are reported.

The intercorrelations between the six parts vary between .14 and .50. Parts 3 and 4 and parts 5 and 6 show slightly higher correlations with each other than with other parts of the test, thus providing some support for the verbal and auditory ability constructs each purports to measure. Parts 3 through 6 are more highly correlated with each other than they are with parts 1 and 2, thereby indicating that these parts are either more reliable than parts 1 and 2 or that they are more similar in terms of the constructs that they measure. The second explanation is quite possible because parts 1 and 2 are not pure language aptitude measures, but simply other predictors of achievement.

The predictive validity of the PLAB is demonstrated through correlations with final grades and correlations with end of course achievement tests. Correlations with final grades for various groups comprising 500 students range from .44 to .79, with a median correlation of about .54. The correlation with the Listening Comprehension section of the Pimsleur French Proficiency Test (Pimsleur, 1967a) for some 3,186 students is about .54, while the correlation with the Reading Comprehension section is about .40. An additional predictive validity study (Fay, 1965) reported in the manual correlates the PLAB with the MIA Cooperative French Test. Multiple regression was used in this study as opposed to simple regression on the total score. The results generally support the predictive validity of the PLAB, with the highest multiple correlation being found with the Writing section ($r = .706$).

However, a more recent study involving high school students did not show correlations of this magnitude. Curtin, Avner, and Smith (1983) administered the PLAB to 311 first-year students and to 252 advanced (typically fourth-year) students of French, German, Russian, and Latin. They found a correlation with final grade of only .34 for the first-year group and .23 for the advanced group. On a multiple regression analysis, the optimal combination of part score weightings resulted in correlations of .43 and .33, which are considerably lower than the .706 obtained in the study by Fay cited in the manual (p. 17). Of the six parts of the test, the best predictor of final grade was part 1, GPA, which showed correlations of .33 for the beginning and .25 for the advanced group of students.

Critique

The PLAB is an interesting test that merits consideration by foreign language teachers who want to assess their students' aptitude for learning foreign languages. It may also be used to diagnose individual strengths and weaknesses in foreign language aptitude. The results of the test can provide useful information for counseling students.

The test was carefully constructed and field tested on an adequate number of students. It is easy to administer, score, and interpret. Interpretation is facilitated by tables of norms that include both percentile ranks and stanines, and the score report form explains scores to students and parents.

Clearly the weakest part of the PLAB is the manual. It was written before the basic background studies were completed. The predictive validity reported in the manual does not use the same weights for parts 1 and 2 that the final form uses. Thus, the information it provides is inadequate for judging the predictive validity of the final form. The results of a study involving the final form are promised in a revised version of the manual, but this revision has never appeared. The publisher did report on this study in an issue of its newsletter (Harcourt, Brace, Jovanovich, 1967), the *Pimsleur Language Test Forum,* but only an expectancy table was shown. No predictive validity coefficient was given. As the test continues to be marketed, the publisher should consider revising the manual based on the results of the study and other studies that have been conducted since.

Another weakness in the manual is found in the norms. Because the norms indicate a tendency for the test to become easier for students in each grade, it is unfortunate that separate norms for each high school grade were not reported. Similarly, very little information is reported on the sample of students on which the norms are based. Nonetheless, the norms reported in the manual are acceptably accurate for individual comparisons within an existing class of students.

In spite of the weaknesses of the manual, the PLAB is recommended to teachers who are interested in gaining a greater understanding of the cognitive abilities and preferences of their students. Although the test should not be used for selection, it may be useful for placement and for diagnosis.

The reader may wish to consult Hakstian (1972), Ryberg (1968), or an introductory article by Pimsleur (1966b) for additional information.

References

Carroll, J.B., & Sapon, S. (1959). *Modern Language Aptitude Test.* San Antonio: The Psychological Corporation.

Curtin, C., Avner, A., & Smith, L.A. (1983). The Pimsleur Battery as a predictor of student performance. *Modern Language Journal, 67*(1), 33–40.

Fay, B.L. (1965). *A study of the validity of the Pimsleur Language Aptitude Battery with beginning French students.* Unpublished master's thesis, The Ohio State University, Columbus.

Hakstian, A.R. (1972). Review of the Pimsleur Language Aptitude Battery. In O.K. Buros (Ed.), *The seventh mental measurements yearbook* (Review No. 256). Highland Park, NJ: Gryphon Press.

Harcourt, Brace, Jovanovich. (1967, November). *Pimsleur Language Test Forum No. 4.* New York: Author.

Ryberg, D.C. (1968). Review of the Pimsleur Language Aptitude Battery. *Journal of Counseling Psychology, 15*(3), 299–300.

Pimsleur, P. (1961). A study of foreign language learning ability: Parts I and II. In M. Zarechnak (Ed.), *Report of the Twelfth Annual Roundtable Meeting on Linguistics and Language Studies* (pp. 57–62). Washington, DC: Georgetown University Press.

Pimsleur, P. (1962). Predicting achievement in foreign language learning. *International Journal of American Linguistics, 29,* 129–136.

Pimsleur, P. (1963). Predicting success in high school foreign language courses. *Educational and Psychological Measurement, 23,* 349–357.

Pimsleur, P. (1966a). *Pimsleur Language Aptitude Battery: Manual for forms.* New York: Harcourt, Brace, Jovanovich.

Pimsleur, P. (1966b). Testing foreign language learning. In A. Valdman (Ed.), *Trends in language teaching* (pp. 175–186). New York: McGraw Hill.

Pimsleur, P. (1967a). *Pimsleur French Proficiency Test.* New York: Harcourt, Brace, Jovanovich.

Pimsleur, P. (1967b). *Pimsleur German Proficiency Test*. New York: Harcourt, Brace, Jovanovich.

Pimsleur, P. (1967c). *Pimsleur Spanish Proficiency Test*. New York: Harcourt, Brace, Jovanovich.

Pimsleur, P., Mosberg, L., & Morrison, A.V. (1962). Student factors in foreign language learning: A review of the literature. *Modern Language Journal, 46*, 160–170.

Pimsleur, P., Stockwell, R.P., & Comrey, A.L. (1962). Foreign language learning ability. *Journal of Educational Psychology, 53*, 15–26.

Pimsleur, P., Sundland, D.M., & McIntyre, R.D. (1963). *Underachievement in foreign language learning*. New York: Modern Language Association.

Lyn R. Haber, Ph.D., CCC-SP

Adjunct Associate Professor, Department of Psychology, University of Illinois at Chicago, Chicago, Illinois.

PORCH INDEX OF COMMUNICATIVE ABILITY

Bruce E. Porch. Palo Alto, California: Consulting Psychologists Press, Inc.

Introduction

The Porch Index of Communicative Ability (PICA) by Bruce E. Porch is designed to quantify communicative behavior in aphasic adults so that the clinician can measure changes due to time, surgery, drugs, or therapy. Such delicate comparisons of behavior are made possible by the complex and carefully refined scoring system, which is the PICA's greatest strength.

The scoring system assigns 1 to 15 (or 16) points per response, systematically reflecting the accuracy, responsiveness, completeness, promptness, and efficiency of each response. Although time-consuming to learn, the system has internal logic and is incredibly useful to the clinician: for an in-depth description of what the patient can do on each subtest, for communicating with other clinicians, for decisions about where (and even whether) to initiate therapy, and for documenting changes in ability. To their great credit, both the accompanying test manuals and the description of the PICA in the publisher's catalog stress the importance of extensive practice and training in the scoring of the PICA. A 40-hour workshop is highly recommended.

The PICA test is accompanied by two manuals. Volume 1, *Theory and Development* (1967), describes the background of the scoring system and validity and reliability measures. Volume 2, *Administration, Scoring, and Interpretation,* (revised in 1981) contains detailed directions for administrating, scoring, and interpretating the PICA. The test materials include one small bound booklet of the test format, two each of the 10 test objects, one set of plastic cards, and eight different preprinted sheets for recording responses, scores, and profiles. Three of these are for the patient to use in making responses to the graphic tests. There is, in addition, a Score Sheet for recording raw scores and initial computations, a Rating of Communicative Ability, on which the examiner can show test-retest changes, a Ranked Response Summary, showing how this patient's ordering of subtests from easy to hard compares with that of a large random sample, an Aphasia Recovery Curve Sheet, and a Predictive Data Sheet.

Each subtest, with the exception of the last one, refers to the same 10 objects, that are displayed or presented to the patient in a standardized order. The 18 subtests, with a precis of the task for each, are described as follows:

Subtest I. Describe the function of each test object;
Subtest II. Demonstrate the function of each object;
Subtest III. Demonstrate the function of each object as it is handed to the patient;
Subtest IV. Name each object;

446

Subtest V. Read each of 10 cards, and place it according to printed instructions in relation to the object whose function is stated on the card;

Subtest VI. Point to each object, whose function is given verbally by the examiner;

Subtest VII. Read each of 10 cards and place it according to printed instructions in relation to the object whose name is states on the card;

Subtest VIII. Match a picture of each object with the appropriate object;

Subtest IX. Say the name of each object, which completes a sentence about the object's function;

Subtest X. Point to each object, as it is named by the examiner;

Subtest XI. Match identical objects with each object;

Subtest XII. Imitate the (spoken) name of each object;

Subtest A. Write a sentence about the function of each object;

Subtest B. Write the name of each object;

Subtest C. Write each object's name spoken by the examiner;

Subtest D. Write each object's name spelled by the examiner;

Subtest E. Copy each object's name; and

Subtest F. Copy geometric forms.

Because each subtest contains 10 items, the patient gives 180 responses. Typically the test requires 1½ hours to administer (not 1 hour, as stated in the manual).

Directions for all 18 subtests are given verbally. In addition to understanding the verbal instructions, two of the subtests require the patient to read in order to respond, and five subtests elicit written language (the sixth subtest using a graphic response involves copying geometric forms). Because all 18 subtests must be administered for purposes of scoring, the PICA is not designed for the illiterate or for patients unfamiliar with English (these limitations are not mentioned in the manuals).

The 18 subtests are said to represent nine response modalities that the clinician uses to create the patient's profile: wirting (subtests A, B, C, D), copying (E, F), reading (V, VII), pantomime (II, III), verbal (I, IV, IX, XII), auditory (VI, X), visual (VIII, XI), gestural (II, III, V, VI, VII, VIII, X, XI), and graphic (A, B, C, D, E, F). These nine categories are based on early versions of the PICA, plus the more recent test developed for assessing communicative ability in children (Porch Index of Communicative Ability in Children) and are overlapping. They are collapsed into seven groups and then into three, for later profiles: verbal (four subtests: I, IV, IX, XII); gestural (eight subtests: II, III, V, VI, VII, VIII, X, XI); and graphic (six subtests: A, B, C, D, E, F).

Practical Applications/Uses

A clinician familiar with the PICA scoring system, reading a patient's performance on the PICA as assessed by another clinician, learns about the patient's communicative ability to an extent unmatched by other scoring systems. Furthermore, the clinician knows, before even seeing the patient, the extent of involvement, the prognosis, and to some degree the probable location of lesions, because patterns of behavior described by the performance scores reflect this information.

Great care was expanded in the development of the scoring system (See *Theory and Development,* Volume 1). The overriding concern in its design was the intent to describe a communicative response as fully as possible. A right/wrong judgment loses a great deal of information that could be of great value to the clinician. For example, if wrong, was the response almost right (Accuracy)? Did the patient require repetitions or additional cueing (Responsiveness)? Did he or she complete the task so that the response was complete (Completeness)? Was he or she quick to respond, or did he or she delay, or self-correct (Promptness)? To what extent is there motoric involvement (Efficiency)? These five dimensions of a response are included in the scoring of each response. They were selected primarily because each is of clinical significance. For example, the aphasic patient may be restricted to utterances of limited length, resulting in incomplete responses, or may show reduced ability to respond to stimulation, resulting in a need for repetitions or extra cues in order to respond.

The PICA scoring system divides responses across all modalities into 16 levels of goodness, ranging from Complex (16) to No Response (1). Each level assesses the response in relation to the five dimensions discussed previously. For example, a "13" response (Complete-Delayed) is accurate, responsive, complete, but significantly slow or delayed; whereas an "11" response (Incomplete-Delayed) differs on the dimension of completeness. The extreme power of this system is that it is applicable across modalities and is constructed to reflect precisely those aspects of behavior definitive of an aphasic patient.

The PICA avoids the extreme cumbersomeness of five dimensions times 16 levels of goodness through the internal logic of the scoring system. The system can be viewed as a series of binary decisions. The first decision concerns accuracy. If the response was accurate, then only levels 7–16 need to be differentiated. If it was not accurate, then only levels 1–6 are relevant and so on. The more one works with this system, the more impressive it becomes.

For all subtests, cues are detailed for the examiner if needed. For example, the cue for the first subtest is: "Have you ever used one of these (the tester points to test object)? What do you do with it?"

The average of the patient's score on each of the 10 items in each subtest indicates his or her ability to perform that task. When the PICA is readministered at a later time, the clinician looks for improvement in these subtest mean scores; the particular dimension(s) on which improvement has occurred (e.g., accuracy, responsivenes, etc.) can also be assessed.

Technical Aspects

Two general measures of reliability are described in the *Theory and Development* manual: scorer agreement and test-retest stability.

The complexity of the PICA scoring system makes it of critical importance to establish that independent scorers can agree. The manual reports scoring results from two clinicians who received the recommended 40 hours of training in scoring the PICA. They, in addition to the author, scored 30 aphasic patients. Reliability coefficients of .93 and above are reported across the 18 subtests among the three scorers: a most impressive result. There was statistically significant variation among the three scorers for only three of the subtests and for the Graphic and the Overall response levels.

These high reliability coefficients among scorers would be adequate had scorers trained by other than the author been compared with scorers trained by the author (as must be case in realistic clinical use of the PICA). Further, several factors in the PICA scoring system lead to artificially uniform scores that inflate the scorer agreement. First, although patients who are physically too involved to perform the test (e.g., totally paralyzed) are excluded, as are patients who refuse to perform the test, the sample did include both patients so severely impaired that their scores are unambiguously and uniformly low and patients only minimally impaired, so that their response scores are very high on all subtests. It is impossible to ascertain from the information provided on the patient sample how many fell into these extreme ranges.

Subtests V and VII require the patient to read the instructions in order to respond, and subtests A, B, C, D, and E require the patient to write sentences, words, or letters. Thus, 7 of the 18 subtests are clinically useful in aphasic patients only if they were previously literate. Irrespective of the degree of involvement, illiterate patients should perform extremely poorly on nearly half the subtests. All 18 subtests are included in the scoring. Of the 30 patients in the scorer reliability sample, education level was not available for 15 patients (half the sample); an additional 4 received a maximum of 3 years of schooling. This suggests that the low education level of a large segment of the sample, in combination with the heavy weight placed on literacy in the overall PICA, may well have led to seemingly high scorer agreement.

One frequent measure of the reliability of a test is to examine whether a subject consistently performs the same way. Forty subjects were tested twice within an interval of no longer than 2 weeks to minimize changes due to treatment, spontaneous recovery, or psychological factors. The subjects were drawn from a larger sample of patients used elsewhere in the research on the PICA.

Across each of the 18 subtests there was a very small but consistent improvement in score from first to second testing. However, the improvement was sufficiently consistent that the overall test-retest reliability was .99. Further, there was no significant correlation between the amount of improvement and weeks post onset, suggesting that even the small improvement was due to a minimal practice effect rather than to change in the patient. Overall, these are impressive results for a test-retest reliability measure.

Because the PICA is designed to be given repeatedly as a measure of change, it is unfortunate that there are no equivalent forms. This might remove even the small practice effect that was found. Furthermore, 30 of the 40 patients in the test-retest analysis were tested and scored both times by the same clinician. Consequently, one component of the high agreement may not be the subjects' consistency, but the scorer assigning the same score even when the patient's performance differed. There is no way to assess the magnitude of this effect.

Porch offers no experimental validation of the PICA. There are no results of comparisons showing that any of the subtest scores, combinations of scores, or variability or difference scores predict which patients recover, predict locus of brain lesion (as measured by CAT scans, post mortem, etc.), correlate with other language communication tests in general usage, or even correlate with independent clinical judgments of the patients. The only validity offered for the PICA is based on what Porch refers to as the face validity of the individual subtest and on reasonable deductions drawn from his own very substantial expertise.

Porch argues that it is unnecessary to demonstrate that the subtests test the modalities claimed for them. It is obvious that Subtest V involves reading and Subtest II involves gesturing. Although Porch is loosely right, three observations suggest that the face validity of the subtests is highly questionable and that an experimental analysis of validity (had one been attempted) might reveal fundamental problems with the subtests.

First, because all instructions are given verbally, a patient impaired in the verbal (input) modality will show depressed scores on all subtests, even those Porch labels as other than verbal. Second, Porch himself has changed the categorization of the modalities of the subtests across the three editions of the PICA and in the various test interpretations, even though he does not present any psychometric evidence for why one grouping of subtests is better than another. Third, some subtests explicitly require processing in two or more modalities, even though they are scored on only one modality. For example, Subtest V requires the patient to read a card in order to respond with a gesture. (This subtest is counted as a reading test in one grouping of modalities and as a gestural test in another, but never as a combination of both.)

If Porch's categorization of the subtests in the various modalities is correct, then a factor analysis of the intercorrelations among the subtests should reveal the appropriate orthogonal factors. Although Porch presents a table with the intercorrelations among the individual subtests from one sample of 150 patients, he does not report a factor analysis, or any statistical procedure designed to examine the underlying structure of the test. He does note, using a three-category classification (gestural, verbal, graphic), that the intercorrelations between subtests from within these categories tend to be higher than those between categories. Such comparison, while interesting, is inadequate for revealing other factors, and cannot assess whether his grouping is justified, let alone the best.

To the extent that the modality categorization is important for differential diagnosis, prognosis, and recommendations for treatment, a factor or other analysis of data already on hand is essential.

The best recommendation for the clinician concerning the validity of each of the subtests is to treat each separately at face value: this is what the patient can or cannot do. Making any combinations among the subtests to reveal dysfunction at a modality level is only a hypothesis.

Porch uses several related measures derived from the subtests to predict the patient's future performance, all of which involve the heterogeneity of current performance. One concerns variability within each subtest. Because the 10 items are assumed to be of equal difficulty, Porch suggests that the highest score obtained on any of the 10 items indicates the patient's probable potential for that subtest. Further, if the patient is highly variable, receiving very high and very low scores, Porch argues that the high variability will be a better predictor of eventual improvement than the current depressed mean of the entire subtest. Volume 2 of the manual provides two procedures for arriving at a variability score for each subtest, and for arriving at a combined variability score for each modality.

Although the assumption that the use of variability of current performance will predict future performance sounds plausible, Porch provides neither the rationale for that assumption nor, more importantly, any data to support it. Such data have already been available to Porch from his many samples of aphasic patients scored on the PICA; for example, is there a positive correlation between the variability score obtained at time 1 with a mean difference score between time 1 and time 2? In the absence of such evidence, the clinician should be wary of making prognoses based on this procedure.

The inclusion of these variability scores on the Scoring and Interpretation sheets for the patient can mislead the clinician into believing this undocumented procedure has proven validity.

The test interpretation procedure in Volume 2 of the manual instructs the examiner to convert the mean raw scores for each subtest into a percentile score for that subtest. All interpretation is based upon the percentile scores, which are given both separately for each subtest, combined across the subtest modalities, and displayed as profiles.

The percentile scores provided are based upon several large samples of aphasic patients who have been tested on the PICA. In the current editions of the two volumes of the manual, Porch reports that he computed percentile scores for the 18 subtests based on samples of 150, 375, 357, 190, 280, and 100 aphasic patients. Except for the sample of 150 collected in the 1960s, on whom the reliability studies were done, Porch does not provide any information either on how the samples were collected, or any patient biographic characteristics. The sample of 100 is labeled "bilateral damage," without evidence of how the diagnosis was determined; the sample of 357 is labeled "left hemisphere damage" (same proviso); the sample of 375 is simply called "a random sample of aphasic patients"; and the others are subcategorized. Percentile charts are presented in Volume 2 for the left-hemisphere and the bilateral samples, and a graph is presented for the random sample ($N = 375$), though reference is occasionally made to percentiles derived from the other samples (often without sufficient labeling, so that the careful reader cannot practice his or her skill at using the percentiles for interpretation, because he or she cannot locate the same percentile in the Appendix as Porch is using in the interpretation of a patient).

The PICA uses the conversion of raw subtest mean scores to percentile scores in two ways. The first allows the clinician to immediately remove all effects of unequal difficulty among the subtests, so he or she can compare performance directly among the subtests. The second, much more problematic use locates the patient in relation to a large body of aphasic patients on the basis of individual subtest scores, various modality scores, and overall score.

The problem the clinician faces in using the percentile scores to arrive at a diagnosis, prognosis, and therapy recommendation for a particular patient is that the clinician has no way of knowing whether this patient belongs to the population to which he or she is being compared. Even dividing the comparison groups into left and bilateral lesion is insufficient because neither of these are sufficiently differentiated in their communicative impairments. The label "aphasia" combines fundamentally different kinds of communication disorders. It makes no sense to compare an individual patient with a hodgepodge.

Even if there were a number of comparison groups on which percentiles were computed, each of which represented a unique kind of aphasia, Porch provides no mechanism for comparing the percentile profile of an individual patient with the percentile profile of each comparison group, to determine into which group the patient best belongs. While profile comparison methods do exist, they cannot be done by merely eyeballing the prominent similarities and differences, as Porch does.

Until these are both independent methods to classify the different kinds of communicative disorders distinctively and the proper profile-matching procedures to do the comparisons, trying to align the profile from an individual patient to that of a heterogeneous group profile is no more useful than what a skilled clinician does in studying the pattern of the individual patient's scores alone.

Critique

The PICA subtests, singly and in combination, raise a number of various problems for the clinician. Directions for all 18 subtests are given verbally. There are no purely visual or purely gestural instructions. If auditory input is impaired, the PICA does not permit the clinician to determine whether other input modalities are intact. For example, Subtests II and III, in which the patient is asked to pantomime the function of the test objects, are scored as the gestural modality, but the instructions are given verbally. The patient who responds inappropriately to these subtests may have an intact gestural system and be perfectly capable of miming the function of the objects, but hasn't a clue what is being asked of him or her. This problem could be solved in general by having the examiner give an example of the target behavior, using an additional object (the same extra object could be the example for every subtest).

Two factors that suggest the output modalities, as defined by the PICA, are confounded, have been described previously. 1) Several subtests, such as those involving reading, require several response modalities from the patient, although only one is counted, and 2) Porch himself changes the grouping of the subtests into modalities, so that he too cannot justify which subtests comprise which modalities. Therefore, the clinician, looking at the patient's score on some "modality," can retrieve the patient's behavior on the specific subtest. However, the clinician will not know, and not be able to know from the PICA subtests, singly or combined, whether single or multiple output channels are intact.

For example, one distinction tested in several modalities in the PICA is the patient's ability to produce and recognize the name of an object, in contrast to its function. Thus, in the verbal modality, the patient produces the name of the object in Subtest IV and describes its function in Subtest I. In the gestural modality, he or she points to the object named by the examiner in Subtest X and points to the object whose function is named by the examiner in subtest VI. In the graphic modality, the patient writes the name of each item in Subtest B and writes the function of each item in Subtest A. However, this regularity breaks down in the tests of reading, for Subtest VII is scored for the accuracy of the patient's ability to demonstrate knowledge of several prepositional phrases of place (e.g., to the right/left of, on, on top of, under, beneath) in which the target object is named, whereas Subtest V, scored similarly, identifies the target object by function. For symmetry, there should be no prepositional phrase, and the patient should be scored for ability to demonstrate reading comprehension of objects by name and by function.

Instead, in Subtest VII, one card might have just the written name, which the patient is to match to the corresponding object; in reading Subtest V, the printed card would describe the object's function. Had this symmetry been carried out in the reading tasks (with an example of the target behavior provided by the examiner to avoid confounding problems of input), the clinician could determine whether the patient could read object names, in contrast to recognizing his or her name (spoken input) or nonlinguistic visual forms (matching tasks).

The repeated distinction between name and function requires justification, experimental and theoretical: Can this distinction differentiate between specific impaired processes?

"Modality" normally refers to the five sensory input systems (and a less agreed upon set of output channels). These perceptual systems may be intact even when the language system is impaired.

"Can the patient hear?" is a very different question from "Can the patient hear and understand language?" A deaf person who uses sign language has the ability to communicate language, although he or she does not respond to auditory input. A brain-damaged person might have an intact peripheral auditory system, which responds to sounds, but be unable to interpret them. For this reason, copying, imitation, and matching might fall together as a "modality" for some patients, in that they do not require linguistic processing to perform. When Porch claims to test visual perception, defined as the ability to match pictures to objects (Subtest VIII) or objects to objects (Subtest XI), he intends to test the visual modality independent of language. However, because the instructions are verbally given and the examiner provides no example, the subtests are confounded for modality and the ability to hear and understand verbal language. This confounding plagues all modalities in the PICA, because all instructions are given verbally and without nonlinguistic demonstrations (e.g., gestural) in another modality from the one being tested.

Another significant weakness of the PICA concerns communicative abilities that are not tested: for example, auditory comprehension should be probed in phrases systematically varied for complexity (such as command forms), and no systematic phonemic analysis is included for patients with dysarthria.

The present ordering of subtests in the PICA is intended to present the patient with as little information as possible because the same 10 objects are used in all but the last subtest, and the patient is required to use the same information (i.e., name, function) repeatedly. Porch expects a familiarization effect from subtest to subtest. This suggests that the present order does not accomplish its purpose. Further, this provides a strong argument for finding alternative objects to use in succeeding subtests.

Another difficulty with the subtest order results because the clinician must attempt to administer all 18 subtests, even those he or she already knows the patient cannot perform. This causes the patient frustration and feelings of failure. For example, the patient who cannot produce an intelligible verbal response endures all four subtests that require such a response, even though the clinician may acquire on the first subtest all the relevant information about the patient's verbal response level. Conversely, for the patient who is only minimally impaired, ability to perform one subtest at a very high level predicts performance on several others, yet clinician and patient must play the tests through.

Considerable patient distress and clinician time could be avoided if the inability to perform one subtest predicted inability to perform on another, and the latter subtest could be omitted for that patient. "Inability to perform" would have to be empirically determined; it probably refers to a score of about 5 or lower. Volume 2 of the manual presents data on the relative difficulty among the subtests, but this analysis is not discussed there. If such a relationship among the subtests was obtained, then a preferable order of presentation would be to present the predictive subtest(s) first.

Another theoretically possible order would be to progress from easy to hard over all of the subtests (level of difficulty to be empirically determined), with cutoffs permitted at some established point. This may be impossible in practice. Porch emphasizes that modality difficulty changes with recovery and that bilaterally damaged patients show different modality strengths than those whose left hemisphere alone is damaged. The issue of the order of the subtests, and equivalent alternative objects, should be carefully reconsidered in subsequent versions of the PICA.

In the absence of any justification for the inclusion of individual subtests, the examiner turns to the explanations of purpose given in Volume 2 of the manual. The presentation of each subtest is accompanied by one section called Purpose and another called Factors Affecting Responses. It is this reviewer's opinion that the examples reflect extremely poor writing in Volume 2 of the manual. It seems more likely that these problems reflect the fundamental fuzziness concerning input and output, modality, and language.

The PICA is intended to test communicative ability, not to represent a theory or model of communication. This is reasonable: theories change rapidly, but a useful test can have a long life. Unfortunately, the lack of explicit rationale for inclusion, purpose, and underlying abilities assumed for each subtest, severely flaws the PICA.

The reviewer would offer the following pros and cons to a potential user of the PICA.

The *pros.* 1) The PICA has a remarkable scoring system, such that: a) it is highly reliable with sufficient training, b) data can be interpreted by someone other than the tester, c) much of the patient's performance, as well as its implications, can be retrieved by some one who has never seen the patient, d) it extracts meaningful variation in patient performance (e.g., accuracy, responsiveness), and e) it is appropriate for retesting to show changes. 2) Differences in retest performance can be interpreted as changes in the patient and therefore not due to measurement error or insensitivity. 3) The PICA includes a wide variety of communication tasks. 4) Precise test administration standards are given.

Prognosis and treatment of communicative disorders induced by insult to the brain are heavily dependent upon the patient's rate and kind of improvement post-trauma. This test measures both rate and kind of change in communication ability, accurately, reliably, and over a wide range of patient performance. Other tests simply do not permit the comparison of test-retest data with this refinement and confidence.

The *cons.* 1) The PICA is not suitable to administer to the illiterate, to non-English speakers, or to the severely motorically impaired. 2) The test fails to differentiate limitations in output from input impairment. 3) The test does not offer a convincing way to isolate which modalities are functional and which are dysfunctional. 4) There is no demonstrated validity to the modality distinctions used in the test. 5) Some important dimensions of communication abilities are missing, or inadequately represented. 6) The rigid requirement that every subtest be used makes the test frustrating for both patient and clinician. 7) The rigid administration procedure also generates a long test time, which wearies the patient and may depress scores. 8) The test is time-consuming for the clinician, both to administer and to score. 9) The test cannot and does not deliver on the promises of documented diagnostic and prognostic power.

The PICA is not designed for the clinician with limited time and a heavy caseload. Subtests on other aphasia tests succeed in isolating input/output; they also do better in isolating a limited number of modality abilities. The clinician might be perfectly comfortable with a coarser measure of change.

For all these reasons, this reviewer would not select the PICA to test aphasia patients but would invest in the intensive effort required to learn to use the PICA. As Porch observes, most aphasia tests include many of the same sorts of subtests. The clinician trained in the PICA scoring system can apply that same quantitative sensitivity to other patient communicative behaviors.

References

Porch, B.E. (1967). *Porch Index of Communicative Ability: Vol. 1. Theory and Development.* Palo Alto, CA: Consulting Psychologists Press.

Porch, B.E. (1981). *Porch Index of Communicative Ability: Vol. 2. Administration, Scoring, and Interpretation (rev. ed.).* Palo Alto, CA: Consulting Psychologists Press.

Sam F. Broughton, Ph.D.

'Developmental Program Administrator, South Carolina Department of Mental Retardation, Pee Dee Region, Florence, South Carolina.

PRE-MOD II

Joseph Kaplan and Sandy Kent. Portland, Oregon: ASIEP Education Company.

Introduction

PRE-MOD II is not a formal, standardized test. It is an informal, computerized behavior checklist which operates as an expert system to aid teachers and other educational personnel in the assessment, diagnosis, and remediation of classroom behavior problems with normal children and mildly to moderately handicapped children. It is based on the task-analytical model; the underlying premise of the model is that individuals fail to engage in a particular behavior because they lack one or more of the prerequisite behaviors necessary to engage in the desired behavior (Gagné, 1985; Kaplan & Kent, 1986). PRE-MOD II also relies heavily on the cognitive-behavioral approach to defining and intervening with classroom-behavior problems and is designed to be used in conjunction with the text, *Beyond Behavior Modification* (Kaplan, 1982).

PRE-MOD II was developed by Joseph Kaplan, Ed.D., and Sandy Kent, B.S., to allow school personnel to employ the task-analytical approach in remediating behavior problems. Readers familiar with this model may recognize some of its logistical difficulties. When applied to behavior problems, it requires the teacher to a) specifically identify an unwanted, maladaptive behavior and a wanted, desirable, replacement behavior; b) identify and list all of the prerequisite behaviors required to engage in the wanted replacement behavior; c) assess the student's mastery status in regard to each prerequisite behavior; d) write a performance objective which identifies and sets target mastery criteria for each deficient prerequisite behavior; and e) provide appropriate intervention for mastery of the identified, deficient prerequisite behaviors. This process can be so overwhelming that even highly motivated teachers may not adhere to it. PRE-MOD II was devised to assist teachers with the first four steps of the process.

PRE-MOD was initially published in 1982 by ASIEP Education Company. At that time it consisted of a 14-item behavior problem checklist which was contained on two computer diskettes. The current revision, PRE-MOD II, published in 1986, consists of 10 items and is contained on a single diskette. It runs on both the Apple II series and IBM-PC computers. The revision was undertaken to streamline the program and eliminate disk-swapping during use. The reduction in items was accomplished by a combination of consolidation and elimination. For example, four items rating provoked or unprovoked abusive language or physical aggres-

---

Specific items from PRE-MOD II are quoted with permission of the authors and publisher.

sion were consolidated into three items and a hyperactivity item was dropped (J. S. Kaplan, personal communication, November 2, 1987).

The 10 maladaptive behaviors currently represented in PRE-MOD II were selected following approximately 12 years of surveys of students enrolled in graduate behavior management courses at Arizona State University or Portland State University. These students (the majority of whom were presumed to be practicing teachers) completed questionnaires containing approximately 50 maladaptive behaviors observed in schools. Their task was to choose those behaviors which produced the most anxiety, anger, and frustration in themselves as teachers. The 10 behaviors ultimately selected for PRE-MOD II were those most frequently chosen as the most difficult with which to deal. The exact methods by which the original 50 or the final 10 behaviors were selected are not specified (Kaplan & Kent, 1986).

The list of 10 maladaptive behaviors is provided in the user's manual with a fairly detailed behavioral description and definition of each behavior. Also provided in the manual are suggested alternative target behaviors, referred to as target fair-pair behavior. For example, the maladaptive behavior, "Student directs abusive/provocative language (e.g., profanity, threats, and/or disparaging remarks) without provocation" is paired with the more desirable target fair-pair behavior "communicates with other in socially acceptable manner" (Kaplan & Kent, 1986, p. 6). "Student acts physically aggressive towards peers without provocation" is paired with "interacts with others without initiating physically aggressive act" (Kaplan & Kent, 1986, p. 6). The 10 items cover the following categories of maladaptive behavior: unprovoked abusive language, unprovoked physical aggression, provoked physical or verbal aggression, property destruction, noncompliance, off-task/inattentive behavior, disruptive behavior, withdrawn/uncommunicative behavior, inability to accept criticism, and stealing. The respective target fair-pair behaviors consist of socially acceptable communicating, nonaggressive interacting, provocation ignoring/assertive responding, property handling without harming, complying with directives, staying on-task, interacting without disruption, spontaneous/audible speaking, assertive responding to criticism, and acquiring items with permission only.

PRE-MOD II is not difficult to use. The user merely uses the diskette to load the computer and follows the instructions presented on the computer screen. Although it is possible to operate PRE-MOD II without reference to the user's manual, this practice is strongly discouraged. Those using PRE-MOD II should read carefully and understand thoroughly the material in the manual prior to using it. Additionally, the user should give consideration to the behaviors exhibited by the child to be rated, and note which of the 10 maladaptive behaviors are present. This last suggestion is especially important because the 10 target fair-pair behaviors appear on the computer terminal rather than the 10 maladaptive behaviors potentially exhibited by the child.

After loading the program, a title message and other information appear. No response is required of the user until the main menu appears. The main menu contains three items: a) behaviors 1 through 5, b) behaviors 6 through 10, and c) exit the program. Menu items are accessed by use of arrow keys to locate and the return/enter key to choose the items. Choosing either a or b produces five of the target fair-pair behaviors, and using the arrow keys highlights each of the behaviors in turn. After reading the list of target fair-pair behaviors, the user has three options: a) to choose the highlighted behavior by pressing the return/enter key, b) to select a different behavior by using the arrow keys, or c) to return to the main menu by pressing the escape key (which allows inspection of the other set of five behaviors, or exit from the program).

After choosing the target behavior applicable to the child being rated, PRE-MOD II requires the user to rate the child in regard to mastery of prerequisite behaviors for the chosen target behavior. The cognitive-behavioral orientation of PRE-MOD II is most evident at this point. Seven generic prerequisites are presented one-at-a-time for rating on a 3-point scale: Y (for yes) indicates mastery of the prerequisite, N (for no) indicates nonmastery, and ? indicates that the rater is uncertain of the child's status regarding the particular prerequisite. The seven generic prerequisite behaviors, although worded appropriately in each case for the chosen target behavior, can be summarized: 1) The student must understand what behavior is expected; 2) The student must be aware of his or her behavior; 3) The student must know how to engage in the target behavior; 4) The student must be able to control his or her behavior; 5) The student must know what happens when he or she engages in the target behavior as well as the maladaptive behavior; 6) The student must consider the consequences of engaging in the target behavior more rewarding than the consequences of engaging in the maladaptive behavior; and 7) The student should only endorse beliefs that are compatible with the target behavior. In addition to the seven generic prerequisites for each of the 10 target behaviors, unique prerequisites are given in an appendix of the manual for 3 (i.e., #3, student acts physically and/or verbally aggressive towards peers only in response to provocation; #5, student is noncompliant; #6, student is off- task/inattentive) of the 10 target behaviors. Suggested performance objectives, assessments, and interventions for students who have not mastered prerequisites also are provided.

The prerequisites can be rated either with or without assessments. The authors assume that most of the decisions regarding a student's mastery of a particular prerequisite behavior will be made without assessments. They assume that the rater is familiar with the student's behavior so that a brief review of recent observations and of interactions with the student is sufficient information to produce a Y or N decision. Prerequisite behaviors rated Y will be dropped from further consideration because they have been rated as mastered. Prerequisites rated as N will result in PRE-MOD II's presentation of a performance objective for the remediation of that behavior and a note referring the rater to the exact location of intervention suggestions found in the user's manual.

If the rater is uncertain of the student's mastery of a prerequisite (i.e., rates it ?), then specific suggestions for assessing each prerequisite behavior are provided in the manual. Some of these suggestions are similar regardless of the target behavior to which they are paired; others are specific to a particular target behavior. For example, suggested assessments for prerequisite 3 (student must know how to engage in the target behavior) include a) observing the child to determine if he or she engages in the behavior, b) asking the child to model the behavior, or c) asking the student to explain how to do the task. For prerequisite 7 (student only should endorse beliefs that are compatible with the target behavior), a separate beliefs inventory is provided in the manual for each of the 10 target behaviors.

The user is instructed to exit PRE-MOD II only after appropriate assessments allow all ?s to be converted to Ys or Ns. Users who complete the entire process are given a list of performance objectives to guide the development of remediation programs for the nonmastered behaviors and suggestions (from the manual) concerning possible interventions.

PRE-MOD II is more extensive than a behavior-problem checklist, although the initial routing device is a 10-item checklist. Rather than rating the student on severity or frequency of maladaptive behaviors, the user rates the student on the presence or absence of alternative adaptive behaviors. Rather than being compared to a norm group's response to the instrument, the student is assessed by the presence of deficits in prerequisite behaviors that might be preventing his or her display of more appropriate behavior. Rather than receiving a diagnostic classification of the child from a factor structure or cutoff score, the user is provided with *prescriptive* performance objectives to guide remediation.

Practical Applications/Uses

PRE-MOD II is most appropriate for use by classroom teachers or school psychologists and counselors who consult with teachers regarding classroom behavior problems. In fact, PRE-MOD II can best be regarded as a behavior management consulting system. It can provide potentially helpful information for teachers who wish to remediate one or more of the 10 sampled classroom behavior problems in their own classroom. It is not appropriate for teachers who wish to obtain either a diagnostic classification or a basis for referring a student to another classroom.

Neither the user's manual nor ASIEP catalog information mentions a particular age group to which the PRE-MOD II is directed. This lack of information is not as critical as it may be with other instruments, because no norms are involved. Ultimately, the individual teacher or the behavior management consultant will decide subjectively whether PRE-MOD II is an appropriate assessment system for a given student, based on the student's age, cognitive ability, social maturity, and type of behavior problem. As a general guide, PRE-MOD II appears most appropriate for children from kindergarten through middle school (assuming average cognitive ability). Variations in cognitive ability of individual cases could alter the appropriate age or grade range slightly and the methods by which recommended assessments are administered.

In regard to diagnostic groups or types of behavior problems appropriate for assessment with PRE-MOD, ASIEP (1987) describes it as suitable for children who are mildly to moderately handicapped and for normal and slow learners in the regular classroom. Within these broad guidelines, however, potential users should be aware that PRE-MOD II only assesses and makes remedial suggestions for children exhibiting a set of 10 specific behaviors. PRE-MOD II provides little assistance to teachers of children whose primary difficulty is not one of the selected 10 behaviors (e.g., psychosomatic complaints, hyperactivity, anxiety, self-stimulatory behavior, depression, lying, etc.).

Despite the above limitations, PRE-MOD II is applicable to all students who can function in regular classrooms and in some special classrooms, and the authors encourage adaptions and modifications to meet the needs of individual cases. Making the suggested modifications, additions, and adaptations, however, requires considerable familiarity with behavioral assessment procedures and the task-analysis model.

To administer the PRE-MOD II, the user must have familiarity with the classroom behavior of the child to be rated, the PRE-MOD II diskette, access to an Apple- or IBM-compatible computer system, and the ability to load a program from diskette. The instrument itself can be administered by any level of educational professional, but it is most economically used by the subject child's teacher. The time required to administer PRE-MOD II varies with the speed of the computer system employed, the number of target behaviors selected for the student, the level of the user's familiarity with the rated child, and the number of prerequisite behaviors about which the user is uncertain. In fact, if the user indicates uncertainty regarding mastery of a prerequisite behavior, he or she will be asked to exit the program to obtain further assessments of the child.

Scoring PRE-MOD II items requires rather simple decisions for anyone familiar with the child's classroom behavior. Prior to loading the program, the user must decide which of the 10 maladaptive behaviors are exhibited by the child. The choice of target behaviors follows from these initial decisions. Scoring the initial 10-item target behavior checklist is a yes-no process. The child simply is rated as exhibiting or not exhibiting each of the 10 target behaviors. For each target behavior rated as not exhibited, ratings of the seven target-behavior prerequisites will be required. This is where a 3-point rating (Y, N, or ?) of each prerequisite is prompted. Thus, a maximum of 80 ratings is required to administer and score the PRE-MOD II—10 yes-no ratings of the target behaviors and 70 3-point ratings of the prerequisites for each target behavior.

Once the results are obtained, preferably by using a computer printer to print the results, virtually no "interpretation" is required because the relevant performance objectives are generated by PRE-MOD II. The printout consists of 1) a listing of nonmastered prerequisite behaviors for each nonexhibited target behavior and 2) a listing of performance objectives to use in remediating the indicated deficits. At this point, the teacher is free to develop his or her own intervention, use or modify an intervention suggested in the user's manual, or obtain additional consultation.

Technical Aspects

No section of the user's manual addresses the psychometric properties of PRE-MOD II. Studies examining validity or reliability are not cited in the manual nor were they located in other sources, although reliability studies are planned as part of the further development of PRE-MOD II (J. S. Kaplan, personal communication, November 2, 1987).

PRE-MOD II is an informal evaluation procedure based on a task-analysis model rather than a formal test. Therefore, PRE-MOD II relies on content and face validity and its adherence to the task-analytical model to demonstrate its validity (J.S.

Kaplan, personal communication, August 14, 1987). Kaplan and others have expanded this model to include social behavior problems as well as academic behaviors (Howell & Kaplan, 1980; Kaplan, 1982; Kaplan, Howell, & McCollum-Gahley, in press), and PRE-MOD II is one outcome of this further development of the task-analysis model. Because the 10 target behaviors were chosen on the basis of teacher feedback over a number of years, a certain amount of face and content validity are present (Kaplan & Kent, 1986). No further item-analysis procedures are reported.

The seven prerequisite behaviors provided are more important than the particular behaviors sampled in assessing PRE-MOD II's validity because the prerequisites purport to identify and remediate the reasons for student misbehavior. These prerequisite behaviors appear to have been developed logically from the learning/cognitive-behavioral literature and from educational/clinical practice rather than from empirical investigation. They are described as "high probability explanations for student failure" (Kaplan et al., in press), but direct, supporting empirical evaluation of the seven specific prerequisite behaviors is not provided. Kaplan and his associates have spent more time justifying the model on the basis of research by others than on demonstrating the validity or reliability of PRE-MOD II itself. However, the prerequisites have a degree of face validity when regarded within the context of the task analysis and cognitive-behavioral literature (Cartledge & Milburn, 1986; Gagné, 1985; Kaplan, 1982; Meichenbaum, 1977).

The most important validity assessment of PRE-MOD II would be criterion and social validity. Do the suggested performance objectives and interventions actually produce the desired change in the target child? Do teachers perceive PRE-MOD II as a helpful assessment device which leads to meaningful interventions and behavior change in their students? These questions have yet to be researched.

Critique

PRE-MOD II is a useful example of how computer programs can serve as expert systems in helping educational and human service workers solve practical problems and operationalize models of human behavior. As noted earlier, the task-analytical model can be so overwhelming in its application that it is not employed by teachers. PRE-MOD II has made this useful model practical. The PRE-MOD II has successfully fulfilled this purpose. Unfortunately, the extent to which PRE-MOD II succeeds in diagnosing and remediating behavior problems is largely unknown due to a lack of published field trials and reliability and validity research.

Among PRE-MOD II's strengths are its face validity, ease of use and practicality, prescriptive/treatment orientation, ability to be used directly by classroom teachers rather than consultants, and helpful user's manual. Its weaknesses include a limited list of initial target behaviors, no reliability or validity research, and a tendency for the program to seem limited, redundant, or repetitive after multiple uses.

Areas for needed research on the PRE-MOD II include 1) interrater reliability for the 10 target behavior ratings and the 70 prerequisite behavior ratings, 2) test-retest reliability for the 10 target behaviors and 70 prerequisite behavior ratings, 3) experimental analysis of treatment outcomes generated by PRE-MOD II, 4) social validation through teacher ratings of efficacy and utility, 5) reliability and validity research on the suggested assessments for prerequisite behaviors, and 6) reliability and validity research on the provided beliefs inventories. The available information leaves a number of questions unanswered regarding PRE-MOD II's usefulness and effectiveness. However, it allows teachers to identify problem behaviors, specify target behaviors, and develop performance objectives and interventions that are systematic, defensible (by the model and literature), and might not have occurred otherwise.

References

ASIEP Education Company. (1987). *Educational materials*. Portland, OR: Author.

Cartledge, G., & Milburn, J.F. (Eds.). (1986). *Teaching social skills to children: Innovative approaches* (2nd ed.). New York: Pergamon Press.

Gagné, R.M. (1985). *The conditions of learning and theory of instruction* (4th ed.). New York: Holt, Rinehart, and Winston.

Howell, K.W., & Kaplan, J.S. (1980). *Diagnosing basic skills: A handbook for deciding what to teach*. Columbus, OH: Charles Merrill.

Kaplan, J.S. (1982). *Beyond behavior modification: A cognitive-behavioral approach to behavior management in the school*. Portland, OR: ASIEP Education Co.

Kaplan, J.S., Howell, K.W., & McCollum-Gahley, J.M. (in press). Direct assessment of social behavior. *Severe Behavior Disorders of Children and Youth*.

Kaplan, J.S., & Kent, S. (1986). *Prerequisite modification: A computer-assisted program in behavioral analysis*. Portland, OR: ASIEP Education Co.

Meichenbaum, D.H. (1977). *Cognitive behavior-modification: An integrative approach*. New York: Plenum Press.

Allan L. LaVoie, Ph.D.
Professor of Psychology, Davis & Elkins College, Elkins, West Virginia.

Eugene H. Foster, Ed.D.
Director, Tygart Valley Counseling Center, and Visiting Professor, Davis & Elkins College, Elkins, West Virginia.

QUICKSCREEN

Janet B. Fudala. Los Angeles, California: Western Psychological Services.

Introduction

Quickscreen is a prescreening test designed to be used at the kindergarten through second-grade levels. It purports to screen for auditory-vocal problems, auditory comprehension problems, visual-motor problems, and cognitive problems during a 15- to 25-minute classroom session (Fudala, 1980a). Students whose scores fall below recommended cutoffs would be candidates for more intensive screening or prediagnostic tests (Fudala, 1980a). The manual recommends that the test be administered by speech and communications specialists; reliability data support this suggestion because interrater agreement scores are lower among classroom teachers (Fudala, 1980a).

The test was in development from 1968 to 1980. Since it has been made commercially available, no published reports of its use have appeared in the educational or psychological literature. Perhaps its use is limited because it fills a very small niche in the public school system; many teachers have experience in detecting learning problems and can informally describe possible causes of the problem. In addition, standardized achievement testing helps to identify any students whose learning problems were overlooked by teachers. Clearly, the existing system obviates the Quickscreen.

Although the test is divided into four categories, it produces only a single cutoff score. Component scores are intended to help guide subsequent testing. The test forms are used by the children during the group administration. They perform various tasks, including copying words or figures and writing their names. While some of the tasks are being performed as a group, the examiner attends to each child briefly to read a sentence and ask the child to repeat it exactly. Scoring should not take more than a minute or two for each child; score sheets have space available for the examiner's comments regarding each child's strengths and weaknesses.

The cutoff scores have been arrived at empirically, based on more than 10,000 children's scores (Fudala, 1980a, p. 19). Two cutoffs are presented: high-risk, corresponding to scores in the bottom 15% of the norm samples, and possible-risk, corresponding to the bottom 35% of the norm samples. With the risk criterion constituting the bottom 35%, in a typical classroom many children will be labeled at risk.

Quickscreen's manual is professionally prepared and very useful. It contains ample instructions, sample forms, scoring examples, guides for interpreting scores, and even, somewhat inappropriately in our judgment, suggestions regarding follow-up tests and remediation techniques. These suggestions are not ordinarily the responsibility of the classroom teacher or of anyone but a properly trained school professional (e.g., a speech specialist or educational psychologist).

Parallel forms are available, though there is enough item overlap among them that one could expect retest facilitation. The manual (Fudala, 1980a, p. 30) indicates that forms for preschool, 3rd through 5th grades, 6th though 8th grades, and 9th through 12th grades are being developed. The manual contains data on Grades K-6.

Practical Applications/Uses

The value of Quickscreen is found in its ability to collect a large amount of information in a systematic way in a relatively brief period of time. The information it provides will very likely be useful to whomever does the follow-up testing, especially regarding the types of error the child makes. It will possibly enable subsequent testing to proceed more efficiently and can guide the selection of diagnostic tests. The manual appropriately cautions the user to employ the results only for the purpose of guiding referral and more detailed testing. Indeed, in order to be consistent with legislative mandates, Quickscreen's use should be restricted to the prereferral stage. It may also be useful for teacher assistance teams in targeting students for educational support services in the regular classroom before referring them for special education services. Such use would be consistent with the recommendation that, before acceptance into a learning disabilities program, concrete evidence of prereferral services should exist (see Geraldi & Coolidge, 1983).

Technical Aspects

The only data regarding reliability and validity are pubilished in the manual (Fudala, 1980a). Generally, it is desirable to have several independent sources of information to corroborate initial findings. The Quickscreen apparently has excellent test-retest reliability; with a sample of nearly 1,500 students in Kindergarten through Grade 6, a 1-week interval produced a stability coefficient of .96. A longitudinal study of students who took the Quickscreen in kindergarten showed high retest correlations each year for the next 6 years, with an average coefficient of .79. Parallel forms reliability, as reported in the supplement (Fudala, 1980b), ranged from .97 to .99 for the four kindergarten forms. Additional data on reliability come from studies of interrater reliability. Specialists obtained very high agreement coefficients (above .90) while classroom teachers obtained consistently lower ones (as low as .51). In summary, Quickscreen exhibits no problem with reliability.

Validity typically involves much more work to be demonstrated convincingly. Users must consider whether the Quickscreen (through its cutoff scores) actually predicts which children will have serious learning problems and whether it does so efficiently, relative to the alternatives (i.e., teacher referrals). The first question is answered in the manual (Fudala, 1980a, pp. 32–33); Quickscreen results accurately predict reading scores on the Metropolitan Achievement Tests at the first- through sixth-grade levels. Even more impressive are the correlations of Quickscreen scores obtained in the first grade with reading scores at Grades 2 through 6: the average predictive validity coefficient is nearly .75 for more than 500 children. Obviously the Quickscreen is able to measure and predict school performance.

However, proper question to ask is whether the test measures what it is supposed to measure; that is, what the test author claims it measures. Does the Quickscreen serve well as a screening test for children with auditory comprehension problems, with visual-motor problems, and so on? The manual is silent on these points. A related question on the classificatory efficiency of the cutoff scores is not addressed in the manual. The manual also overlooks the question of the utility of the test relative to alternatives, such as classroom-teacher referral. In summary, validity remains very much an open issue.

Critique

The Quickscreen has been professionally developed, and the manual and test forms have been prepared in the same quality fashion. Very large numbers of students have been tested, and norms based on more than 10,000 children are available. The test currently is limited to kindergarten through second grade, but the manual promises other levels are in development. Impressive data indicate that the test is reliable and stable, and can predict reading test scores several years later. The test cannot effectively screen for auditory, visual-motor, or cognitive problems as far as can be determined by the manual and the published literature. No data even address the question. Cutoff scores select about 35% of all children who need additional services; no follow-up data confirm the accuracy of this figure, but it would obviously exceed the limits imposed by staff and budget to deal with such a large proportion of a school's population. Classroom teachers are likely to do at least as good a job of prescreening as the Quickscreen, but again, no comparative data are available. The manual and test were copyrighted in 1980; now, 8 years later, additional information still is unavailable. The author should have done more in the intervening period if the Quickscreen is to meet contemporary standards for commercial tests.

References

Fudala, J.B. (1980a). *Quickscreen*. Los Angeles: Western Psychological Services.

Fudala, J.B. (1980b). *Quickscreen: Supplementary instructions for kindergarten level*. Los Angeles: Western Psychological Services.

Geraldi, R., & Coolidge, P. (1983). Steps before the referral. *Journal of Learning Disabilities, 16*, 534–536.

Priscilla A. Drum, Ph.D.

Professor of Educational Psychology, Graduate School of Education, University of California—Santa Barbara, Santa Barbara, California.

Carol N. Dixon, Ph.D.

Lecturer and Director of the Reading Clinic, Graduate School of Education, University of California—Santa Barbara, Santa Barbara, California.

READING/EVERYDAY ACTIVITIES IN LIFE

Marilyn Lichtman. New York, New York: Westwood Press, Inc.

Introduction

The Reading/Everyday Activities in Life (R/EAL) test assesses the ability of adults to read signs, ads, and other written information in the environment. The test was initially developed in 1972 and revised in 1977–78, although the manual does not indicate the purposes for or the extent of this revision. The term "adults" seems to refer to adolescents on up through any age, although children as young as 10 were tested in the first phase of the test's development. The purpose of the R/EAL is to determine whether examinees can read well enough to protect themselves and their families and to function in daily life.

At the time the R/EAL was developed, the author of the test, Dr. Marilyn Lichtman, had experience as a reading clinician and consultant and as coordinator of the doctoral program in Research and Evaluation at the Virginia Polytechnic Institute and State University. During 1972, she directed a study for the Job Corps, U.S. Department of Labor. The purpose for the study was to develop a means of assessing the literacy level of new enrollees in the Job Corps. The outcome of the Job Corps study was the R/EAL, which was used during 1973 and 1974 by the Office of Education in an evaluation of "Community Based Right-To-Read Programs" and in New York state in connection with their external high school diploma.

Having been developed in 1972, the original R/EAL predated most minimum competency tests by several years, being one of the first tests to focus on the semi-literate. Enrollees in the Job Corps were supposed to be trained so that they could function in the economic community, and some degree of literacy has been required for most forms of employment during the last quarter of the 20th century. Thus, a means of assessing who needs what kind of training was imperative. Subsequent subject samples have come from adult literacy programs of various types.

The manual indicates that The R/EAL has two forms, A and B; however, only Form A is reviewed here as only partial information and no specific test statistics were provided for Form B. Because the original R/EAL was developed in 1972, these reviewers' assumption is that the description of test development in the manual refers to Form A. The need for the 1978 revisions is not explained, nor is it clear exactly what changes were made. Alternate forms of the test would, of course, be useful in evaluating adult literacy programs of many kinds. During the last 10 years, a number of states have developed their own minimum competency tests for high-school graduation, and it may be that expressed need for the R/EAL has declined.

From a collection of printed materials that commonly occur in the environment, the test author subdivided these materials into nine general categories: 1) Signs and Labels; 2) Schedules and Tables; 3) Sets of Directions for Doing Something; 4) High Interest, Factual Articles; 5) Illustrated Advertisements; 6) Legal Documents; 7) Maps; 8) Print Advertisements; and 9) Fill-in-the-Blank Forms. These nine general categories are represented in actual test tasks by 1) road signs, 2) a television schedule, 3) directions for making pizza, 4) an informative article on drugs, 5) a grocery advertisement, 6) a lease agreement, 7) a road map, 8) a page of want ads, and 9) a job application. Each type is intended to represent a broad category of print (i.e., television schedules are similar to bus, train, plane, and radio schedules, and directions for making pizza are similar to any recipe or any assemblage instructions). The materials selected for inclusion in the test were chosen for "their importance, interest, and frequency of use" (Lichtman, 1972, p. 2). Details for substantiating these criteria are not provided, but for the most part both the categories and the selections appear reasonable. From a task analysis of what people do with each type of material, "terminal and enabling objectives" were outlined (Lichtman, 1972, p. 2). Again, the manual neither describes the task analysis procedures nor the objectives. However, from these procedures, five questions for each of the nine types of materials were developed for a total of 45 questions in Form A.

After an illustrative sample on a movie advertisement, the examinees can be tested either individually via an audiocassette and test booklet or orally by the examiner reading the cassette portion. Similar procedures can be used in groups depending upon the availability of cassette players and headphones. The cassette method is recommended by Lichtman (1972) because the examinees can control the pace by starting and stopping the cassette players as often as they wish. The cassette also is recommended because it "more closely resembled the process an individual might face in dealing with the selections" (Lichtman, 1972, p. 5). Although the cassette procedure appears to have a positive motivational effect, both the self-paced condition and the normative process description diminish the validity of the test as a measure of functional literacy. Safe driving requires rapid reading of road signs. Some recipes require the addition and mixing of ingredients in a timely fashion. Many personnel agents will not wait a lengthy period for a job application, or if they will, an overlong length of time is likely to receive unfavorable notice. Time is an essential performance requirement for many functional reading tasks. Also, the audio presentation mode does not simulate environmental conditions. In most employment situations, it is rare for instructions to be read aloud, at least for the kinds of materials that are represented by this test.

The answers are scored as right (1 point) or wrong (0 points), and the raw score is the total correct. Most item responses are open-ended in that the examinee has to write out the desired information fo each question after finding the information in the printed material. The one exception is the first test task, the road signs, where the examinee answers the question by selecting a number coded to each sign. As a set, the road signs were the easiest for the norming group, with an average of 79% correct for these five items. The recognition task of the road signs and the acceptance of almost any answer to questions concerning name and age for the last task, a job application with a correct response average of 76%, made these two types of materials the easiest for the norming group. The two hardest sets were the television schedule task (with an average of 51% correct) and the want-ad task (with an average of 55% correct). In both cases, the questions require that the examinee read unfamiliar, small-print material to find specific answers. The oral questions do not provide hints to the answers; thus, the tests that require the most reading ability are those that were hardest for the norm group.

An 80% correct criterion is indicated by the author as being representative of functional literacy, and scores between 51% and 80% correct are labeled marginal literacy, although reasons for these cutoff points are not provided. Supposedly, the examiner also can look at the subtest scores or the five items in each of the nine categories and, using the same 80% criterion (no more than one wrong per subtest), decide in which of the areas the examinee needs special help. Both the small number of items per subtest and the fact that only two errors on a subtest indicates poor performance make the raw scores inadequate criteria upon which to make reliable decisions. These reliability requirements are corroborated by the fact that the average performance of the norming group on all nine subtests indicates that they were functionally illiterate.

Practical Applications/Uses

The Reading/Everyday Activities in Life is intended to assess whether an individual is functionally literate, which is defined operationally in a general sense as capable of the reading tasks necessary for daily life. At one point the manual refers to the test as measuring minimum competencies, and at another point it makes reference to mastery of basic literacy skills, apparently equating competencies and basic skills with functional literacy. The test is intended to provide both a general evaluation of functional literacy/illiteracy and diagnostic information about specific strengths and weaknesses for each type of reading material. Within each of the types of material used, the R/EAL purports to measure such abilities as identification of categories of information, decoding names, locating specific numbers or symbols, and defining relevant vocabulary.

The R/EAL is designed for use with adults in basic educational settings (e.g., community college or adult literacy essential skills programs, or vocational counseling or training programs). Although the manual indicates that the test has not been used widely with individuals under high-school age, it might also be used in junior-high or senior-high remedial reading programs, learning disability programs, or by guidance counselors or resource specialists in public school settings.

The manual suggests that the R/EAL is "particularly suitable for minority populations, such as Blacks, Puerto Ricans, Mexican Americans, rural groups, and all others who have traditionally been singled out by the bias of standardized reading achievement tests" (Lichtman, 1972, p. 7). However, there is no specific evidence provided indicating that all of these groups were included in the test development or in the norming population. The R/EAL is clearly not appropriate for those who are severely visually or hearing impaired. Students for whom English is a second language may be unduly handicapped by the audio administration of the test directions and questions if their oral English skills are inferior to their written English abilities. For such ESL students, the audio condition might interfere with demonstration of their functional literacy.

An audiocassette tape is included with the test and the manual. The tape is the preferred method for administration of the test directions and questions. The manual recommends that students be allowed to take the test individually, so that they can control the presentation. Group administration is also feasible, particularly when each student has a cassette player and headphones. The manual also provides a script for administering the test without the use of the cassette tape, although the directions are incomplete. Pauses are noted in the script but not the length of the pauses. In addition, the manual does not mention whether scores from an examiner's oral administration of the test should be expected to differ from those obtained from student-controlled cassette tapes.

The R/EAL can be administered in any reasonably quiet setting that allows cassette use, sufficient lighting for the reading task, adequate writing space, and a chair. The manual indicates that the "R/EAL does not require a trained examiner for effective administration" (Lichtman, 1972, p. 10). However, even with cassette administration the examiner needs to be able to motivate students and to clarify directions appropriately if questions arise. When the test is examiner administered, the examiner's reading and pronunciation skills and his or her judgment about the pacing of questions and the duration of pauses become crucial.

Although the procedures outlined in the manual for tape administration of the R/EAL are easy to follow and fairly clear, several crucial issues, such as time limits, are not adequately addressed. Only one of four representative adults in a community college essential skills program who took the test for these reviewers was able to finish it in 1½ hours. The manual does not provide any indication of average testing time or whether students should be allowed or encouraged to rewind the tape as desired to repeat instructions or questions. All four individuals taking the test for these reviewers repeatedly rewound the tape. The manual cautions the examiner to be alert to irregularities during testing, warning that they may invalidate test results. The order for listening to the instructions, reading the test materials, and listening to and answering the questions needs to be clearly established in the manual.

The R/EAL is hand scored. Test responses are written out by the subject and evaluated on a 1 point/acceptable or 0 points/unacceptable basis. Each of the nine subtests has five questions, so the maximum correct test score is 45. An "acceptable response key" (Lichtman, 1972) is provided, and all the questions are relatively easy to score. Incorrect spelling and poor grammatical construction are not penalized; at least, not as long as the scorer is able to decipher the response. The manual does not give any estimate of scoring time, but once the scorer is familiar with the test most subjects' tests should be easily scorable in 10 to 20 minutes, including the time required for conversion to a criterion-referenced score (percent of items passed) and norm-referenced scores (percentiles and standard scores). Criterion-referenced conversions of raw scores to percent passed are provided for both Forms A and B; norm-referenced conversions are available only for Form A.

A gross estimate of functional literacy is obtainable from the 80% criterion-referenced standard. Beyond this, the interpretation of test responses for diagnostic purposes (i.e., what a subject can or cannot do in real life) is quite questionable. Although the test purportedly identifies literacy/illiteracy for different types of reading material, five short answer questions per type does not suffice for such judgments. It is possible that knowledgeable diagnosticians could identify patterns of difficulty across types of reading tasks (e.g., difficulty in locating numbers or in decoding names), but that type of analysis is not adequately developed in the manual. Some very general materials and activities are suggested as prescriptions for remediating identified areas of weakness, but, again, actual implementation would demand considerable expertise on the part of the instructor.

Technical Aspects

No test-retest or alternate forms (A to B) reliability information is supplied in the manual. The absence of test-retest information is a major omission because the Job Corps training pilot would have allowed for such testing. However, a statement in the 1978 Examiner's Manual indicates that reliability data on Form B and equivalent form reliability are currently being compiled. These reviewers did not receive any of this information. The only reliability information in the manual refers to Kuder-Richardson 20 (KR20), an estimate of item variance by total test variance (Kuder & Richardson, 1937). The KR20 estimate (.93) is quite high, based on a single sample of 434 subjects ages 16 to 21 (169 males, 265 females). The sample was obtained from a residential manpower training program. The manual states "Blacks, Spanish-surnamed, and rural whites comprised the majority of those tested" (Lichtman, 1972, p. 53), although no proportions are provided. Most had not completed high school, although, again, no proportions are provided. The norm sample did have an average of 9 years schooling and a reading grade equivalent on the Stanford Achievement Test of 5.2. The mean raw score for this group was 28.09 with a standard deviation of 10.36 and a standard error of measurement of 2.75. The nine subtest scores are obviously too brief (5 items) for a reliable estimate of reading comprehension of print within the particular category.

Face validity of the R/EAL is evidenced in several ways: the norm sample used, those in a residential manpower training program; the types of written material used, such as want ads and television schedules; the audiocassette, self-paced format that simplifies the task; and the item information requested. Many of these aspects of the R/EAL also confirm, to a degree, the content validity of the test. However, no procedures for content validity judgments are described in the manual. Also, the issue of the representativeness of the materials is not addressed. The materials used in the R/EAL seem valid, but whether they are sufficient in scope or the most valuable types of materials is moot. Construct validity for functional literacy is, indeed, a difficult problem because there is little agreement historically or currently on the definition of this ability. Lichtman does not address the question of construct validity, but assumes at least a vague definition of it in her statement that "functional literacy relates to reading experiences encountered in daily living" (1972, p. 2).

The four adult literacy students who took the task so their procedures and statements could be used in these reviewers' test evaluation liked the test. They particularly liked the audio component and the self-paced format. On the other hand, the only one to finish the test took 1½ hours, and the other three each spent at least 1 hour attempting to finish it. If a reader is that slow in performing any such reading tasks as those simulated in this test, he or she is not capable of functioning in everyday life. Road signs, recipe directions, and filling out many job applications cannot take this much time. Also, most of these tasks in real life are not accompanied by an audiotape to assist in performing them. Thus, the conditions that are most motivating for the subjects are those conditions that invalidate the results for functioning in real life.

Critique

A functional literacy test would be a useful addition to the testing literature. There are many community adult literacy programs and job training programs in businesses and in the military. Immigrants need to be able to function in our cities. Those who do not complete public schooling must understand written communications to maintain themselves. It is necessary to be able to assess minimal skills, to decide both who needs special help and how much the assistance has improved their functional literacy.

A test similar to the R/EAL is needed; the minimum competency tests for high-school graduation used by the various states, even if they survive the judicial investigations of their legality, will not suffice. The tests vary too much from state to state, and dropouts, immigrants, and older adults who may require new literacy skills to change jobs are not adequately dealt with by using the minimum competency tests. The tests that are developed must have more content validity than the R/EAL, and they must meet current testing reliability standards (American Educational Research Association, American Psychological Association, & National Council on Measurement in Education, 1985). Perhaps the R/EAL can be developed into such an instrument.

References

This list includes text citations and suggested additional reading.

American Educational Research Association, American Psychological Association, & National Council on Measurement in Education. (1985). *Standards for educational and psychological testing*. Washington, DC: American Psychological Association.

Cervero, R.M. (1985). Is a common definition of adult literacy possible? *Adult Education Quarterly, 36*(1), 50–54.

Chall, J.S. (1983). Literacy: Trends and explanations. *Educational Researcher, 12*(9), 3–8.

Diehl, W.A., & Mikulecky, L. (1980). The nature of reading at work. *Journal of Reading, 24,* 221–227.

Fisher, D.L. (1981). Functional literacy tests: A model of question-answering and an analysis of errors. *Reading Research Quarterly, 16,* 418–448.

Hunter, C., & Harman, D. (1979). *Adult illiteracy in the United States: A report to the Ford Foundation*. New York: McGraw-Hill.

Keefe, D., & Meyer, V. (1980). Adult disabled readers: Their perceived models of the reading process. *Adult Literacy and Basic Education, 4,* 120–124.

Kirsch, I.S., & Guthrie, J.T. (1977–78). The concept of measurement of functional literacy. *Reading Research Quarterly, 13,* 485–507.

Kirsch, I.S., & Jungeblut, A. (1986). *Literacy: Profiles of America's young adults: Final report.* Princeton, NJ: National Assessment of Educational Progress.

Kozol, J. (1985). *Illiterate America.* New York: Doubleday and Company.

Kuder, G.F., & Richardson, M.W. (1937). The theory of the estimation of test reliability. *Psychometrika, 2,* 151–160.

Lichtman, M. (1972). *Manual for Reading/Everyday Activities In Life (R/EAL).* New York, NY: Westwood Press, Inc.

Mikulecky, L. (1981). The mismatch between school training and job literacy demands. *The Vocational Guidance Quarterly, 30,* 174–180.

Stedman, L.C., & Kaestle, C.F. (1987). Literacy and reading performance in the United States, from 1880 to the present. *Reading Research Quarterly, 22*(1), 8–46.

Sticht, T.G., & Zapf, D.W. (1976). *Reading and readability research in the armed services.* Alexandria, VA: HumRRO.

Phyllis Anne Teeter, Ed.D.
Associate Professor of Educational Psychology, University of Wisconsin-Milwaukee, Milwaukee, Wisconsin.

RECOGNITION MEMORY TEST
Elizabeth K. Warrington. Windsor, Great Britain: NFER-Nelson Publishing Company Ltd.

Introduction

The Recognition Memory Test (RMT) was constructed by Elizabeth K. Warrington and published in 1984 by NFER-Nelson Publishing Company. Dr. Warrington is a Top Grade Clinical Psychologist at the National Hospital in London and a professor of Clinical Neurology at the Institute of Neurology. The RMT was devised as a measure of visual and verbal memory abilities for subjects and patients with neurological impairment resulting from the normal aging process or as a result of insult or injury to the brain. The author developed the test to fill a void in the clinical arena, in which many of the available memory tests for the 18 to 78 year age range lacked construct or discriminant validity. The author attempted to avoid some of the weaknesses of other instruments by developing a test in which memory was minimally related to cognitive abilities, task demands produced maximal discriminating power, and adequate age norms were available.

The RMT is an outgrowth and combination of two tests previously developed by the author. Warrington originally began using a Recognition Memory Test for Words (RMW) and a Recognition Memory Test for Faces (RMF) in 1974 to assess adults with global amnesia. Warrington employed Milner's (1966) findings that memory deficits are lateralized (i.e., patients with left-hemisphere dysfunction showed selective memory deficits for words, and patients with right-hemisphere damage showed selective memory deficits for nonverbal material). The author indicates that material-selective memory deficits are often found in patients with brain damage. She cites Smith (1974) who found memory disturbances to be associated with other neurological impairments, including head injury.

Due to the findings that unilateral hemispheric damage results in specific memory losses, Warrington designed the RMT to measure both verbal and nonverbal memory. Based on previous research, she incorporated the RMF in order to assess nonverbal deficits associated with right hemisphere dysfunction. The RMW was incorporated into the test because of previous findings (Coughlan, 1979) indicating that patients with left hemisphere damage had difficulty remembering single words from memory. Thus, Warrington has incorporated several theories and research findings into the development of the RMT.

The test manual also provides comparative norms for the RMT, the Advanced Progressive Matrices, and the Mill Hill Vocabulary Test. The manual provides two validity studies, one with patients having unilateral brain lesions and the other with subjects having generalized brain atrophy, which individual test scores can be compared.

The standardization sample was comprised of 310 volunteer subjects from 18 to 70 years of age. The sample was drawn from inpatients at three separate hospitals in England. Subjects from the inpatient sample were hospitalized for extracerebral diseases, and an unknown number of subjects were drawn from families and friends of the inpatient sample. All individuals with a history of cerebral insult, injury, or disease were excluded from the normative group. All subjects had been educated in the "normal English system." Warrington attempted to test a cross-section of people from London hospitals, and the RMT manual describes the "social class" of subjects. The table showing the distribution of subjects by sex and social class reveals that there were more females (174) than males (136), and the greatest percentage of females were housewives. The greatest number of males fell into categories of "intermediate occupation" (20), "skilled occupation (non-manual)" (18), "skilled occupation (manual)" (42), and "not known" (24). Very few males (9) or females (1) were described as "professional." There was no information concerning the intellectual functioning level of these subjects.

Although the norm sample was of adequate size (310), the manual shows that the number of subjects varied across age ranges, with 98 subjects between 18 and 39, 107 between the ages of 40 and 54, and 105 between the ages of 55 and 70. A further breakdown of ages reveals that fewer subjects were included in the lower ages (96 from 17 to 39), with 214 subjects between the ages of 40 and 70 years.

The manual indicates that age is correlated with recognition memory for words ($r = -.35$, $p. < .001$) and with recognition memory for faces ($r = -.13$, $p. < .05$). Mean scores for the RMW subtest show a gradual decline with age, from a mean score of 46.39 for the 17 to 25 year range to one of 42.63 for the 65 to 70 year range. The decline in the recognition memory for faces across ages is smaller, from a mean score of 43.1 (17 to 25 year range) to one of 42.26 (65 to 70 year range). Warrington did not provide significance tests for mean score comparisons across age ranges; however, based on correlational data, she indicated that the effect of age on memory test was negligible before the age of 40 years.

In the manual, the author provides the reader with a short review of several memory tests. Warrington indicates that the Wechsler Memory Scale is the most widely used instrument for assessment of memory. The strength of this scale lies in its standardization sample, but Warrington believes the scale is weakened by the cognitive demands of many of the items. Additionally, Wechsler scores are averaged across subtests, which Warrington believes "dilutes the memory component of the test" (1984, p. 1). Although other shortcomings of available memory tests are only briefly discussed, the author provides the reader with a reference for a more in-depth review of memory tests for clinical use.

The RMT is conveniently packaged in a plastic folder that includes the manual, stimulus materials for the memory for words subtest (one booklet) and the memory for faces subtest (two booklets), a list of 50 word pair distractor items for the memory for words section, and test protocols. The stimuli for the RMW subtest were selected from the Thorndike-Lorge list. Although the manual indicates that the words are 4 to 6 letters in length, there are several 3-letter words as well. Warrington found in pilot studies that "commonplace" words minimized ceiling effects; the words selected fit this category (e.g., *bake, cast, less, mile*, etc.). The word stimulus materials are bound in booklet format and are presented in uppercase letters on white 3" × 5" cards. The distractor list is comprised of 50 word-pairs printed in uppercase letters on an 8" × 11" card. The list of distractor words is not presented in the same order as the words in the booklet.

The manual is comprised of the "standardization of the original recognition memory tests for words (RMW) and faces (RMF) (subsequently combined and presented as the present Recognition Memory Test) in a normal sample" (Warrington, 1984, p.1). The manual also includes two validity studies investigating the effects of unilateral and diffuse brain damage on memory abilities and a comparative discussion of the RMT and other memory tests.

The RMF subtest stimuli consist of 50 photographs presented on 4" × 6" cards; the retention stimuli are presented in 50 pairs of faces on 5" × 8" cards. Both sets of stimulus materials are presented in booklet format. The face stimuli photographs are of males who depict a variety of facial features. As in the RMW subtest, the paired faces in the retention booklet are not presented in the same order as the single photographs.

The manual is 14 pages long and contains a description of the test items, the procedures and directions for administration, information on the standardization sample, descriptions of two validity studies, and norm tables. The manual is clearly written and easy to understand. The test protocols are succinct, and responses are easy to record.

Practical Applications/Uses

The Recognition Memory Test (RMT) is comprised of a verbal, word memory test (RMW) and a nonverbal, memory for faces test (RMF). The major purpose of the RMT is to "detect minor degrees of memory deficit across a wide age range of the adult population" (Warrington, 1984, p. 1). While the standardization sample was comprised of in-patient adults hospitalized for extracerebral diseases, Warrington also provides RMT data for patients with lateralized cerebal lesions and patients with diffuse brain disease.

The RMT is easy to administer and score. The directions generally are presented in a clear and concise manner. First, the RMW subtest is administered. The patient is told that this is a memory test and is instructed to look at a series of words and indicate whether the words generate pleasant or unpleasant associations. The manual does not explain why the patient is asked to judge the words on the dimension of "pleasantness." The subject is presented with 50 individual words and is then given the paired word list and asked to indicate which of the two words on each card has been read previously. Subjects are encouraged to guess if they are unsure. The word pairs are not in the same order as the individual words, so separate words have different interference times for retention.

The RMF subtest is presented in a similar manner. The subject is told that this is a test for memory of faces and is asked to indicate whether each face is pleasant or not. After the 50 pictures have been shown individually, the subject is asked to determine which of the paired faces has been seen before. Again, the author does not state why the patient is asked to rate the photographs on the "pleasantness" dimension. The interference times vary for each picture as the paired photographs are not presented in the same order as the single pictures.

The scoring procedures are simple, and the test can be quickly scored. The number of correct answers are converted to percentile scores for each test. Discrepancy scores are calculated when raw scores on the RMW subtest differ from scores on the RMF subtest. Percentiles are available, however, the manual indicates that scores from the RMT should be analyzed in context with other test findings and that the interpreter should have a working knowledge of lateralized dysfunction.

Technical Aspects

The manual does not provide the reader with any information concerning the reliability of the Recognition Memory Test. A test-retest reliability measure would be useful to determine individual changes in memory across time. Test-retest measures seem to be particularly critical to further understanding the long-term effects of brain injury on memory abilities in a clinical population.

Information concerning the construct validity of the RMT is presented in two studies using brain-injured subjects. The sample for the first study was drawn from 5,000 patients entering the National Hospital (from 1974 to 1979) and others from St. Bartholomew's Hospital (London, England) and Brook Hospital (Greenwich, England), who were referred for neuropsychological evaluation. Right-handed patients were selected who were diagnosed as having unilateral lesions using CAT scans and "other radiological investigations." The RMT was administered to 134 individuals with right-hemisphere lesions and 145 with left-hemisphere lesions. The right- and left-hemisphere groups were further divided according to the localization of the lesions: frontal, temporal, parietal, and occipital sites. When lesions covered the temporal and parietal lobes, subjects were included in both groups. However, when lesions covered frontal-parietal-temporal lobes, individuals were excluded from the study. There were sufficient numbers across each group to allow for subtype analysis. In fact, this is one the strengths of this study.

Although in some ways this study was carefully designed, there is a lack of information concerning subject variables that may affect memory abilities. Of particular interest would be whether these patients had been surgically treated for the lesions. If surgery had been performed, how long after the operation was the memory test administered? Did the subjects undergo other treatments like radiation or chemotherapy? What were the age and sex of the subjects?

When compared to the RMT normative sample, the left hemisphere group showed impairment on both the RMW and RMF subtests. The right hemisphere group showed significant impairment on the RMF subtest, with normal scores on the RMW subtest. When compared to the right-hemisphere group, the left hemisphere group was significantly impaired on the RMW subtest. The converse was also found, with the right-hemisphere group showing more impairment than the left-hemisphere group on the RMF subtest.

Interesting patterns also emerged for the subgroups, with the left temporal group showing more impairment than the right temporal group on the RMW subtest, and the right parietal group showing more impairment than the left parietal group on the RMF subtest. The left frontal group also was more impaired than the right frontal group for the RMW subtest.

The findings of this study provide strong evidence for the construct validity of the RMT. The left hemisphere group indeed showed memory impairments related to verbal material in all subgroups (frontal, temporal, parietal), with the left temporal group obtaining the lowest scores. The findings for the right hemisphere subgroups were less clear-cut, but the right lesion group as a whole was more impaired than the left lesion group on memory for faces.

The second validity study was comprised of 112 patients with known diffuse brain dysfunction. Their diagnoses were based on neurological evaluations and CAT scans. Subjects with brain atrophy resulting in significant language and perceptual deficits were excluded. Patients were further screened by a neurologist and classified into mild (little or no changes in sulci and ventricle size) or moderate (moderate, severe, and very severe changes in sulci and ventricle size) atrophy subgroups based on width of the sulci and ventricles. As in the first study, there was insufficient information reported about critical subject variables, including intellectual potential, sex, age, and treatment approaches.

The results of this study showed that the mild atrophy subgroup was more impaired than the normative sample on the RMW and RMF subtests. The author did not report differences between the moderate atrophy subgroup and the norm groups. The differences between the mild and the moderate atrophy subgroups were not great, with only one significant finding on the RMF subtest (for the ventricle dimension). The author states that the selection process may have affected these outcomes for the mild to moderate comparisons, and she suggests that the results "should not be interpreted as indicating that the test fails to discriminate between mild and moderate degrees of atrophy or that the degree of atrophy is not correlated with degree of memory loss" (Warrington, 1984, p. 5).

Although these two studies support the differential validity of this instrument, the author did not study the relationship between the RMT and other frequently used memory tests. Also, validity information for the standardization group is weak. The author presents information concerning the relationship between the RMT and the Advanced Progressive Matrices ($r = .45$ for RMW; $r = .33$ for RMF) and the Mill Hill Vocabulary Scale ($r = .38$ for RMW; $r = .26$ for RMF). Again, there is no measure of how the RMT is related to other memory tests for the standardization group.

Critique

The Recognition Memory Test appears to be a well-designed instrument for measuring memory deficits in adults. The RMT results seem to support other research and clinical findings showing that individuals with left-hemisphere damage display specific memory loss for verbal material (Milner, 1967) and that individuals with right-hemisphere damage show specific memory loss for recognition of faces (Milner, 1968; Warrington & James, 1967). The RMT is easy and quick to administer and score, and the standardization sample is of adequate size. For these reasons, the RMT can be considered to be an instrument with potential but in need of further study to determine how effective it is for the brain-damaged population. There are several reasons why more research is needed.

First, the RMT was standardized on a population living in England. Although it is possible that a sample from the United States would not differ significantly from the original standardization group, further study is needed to verify this. The standardization sample was also selected from a group of inpatients. These individuals may differ in meaningful ways from a group chosen at random outside a hospital. The extent to which hospitalization affects anxiety or other states that negatively impact on memory has not been established. The author should warn users that the RMT may lack generalizability and that it should not be used to determine memory scores for nonhospitalized individuals. Second, measures of test-retest reliability are needed to determine whether subject factors across repeated measures affect RMT scores. It would also be interesting to note whether stability measures differ on the RMW or RMF subtests. Third, other validity studies are needed to determine the nature and extent of memory loss in clinical populations with brain injury or disease. These studies need to define the sample carefully, providing details about treatment (e.g., type of injury or tumor, surgery, radiation, chemotherapy, postoperation time, postradiation time, measures used before and after medical intervention, etc.). The effects of other subject variables on memory abilities, such as age and sex, also need further investigation in brain-injured groups. Fourth, the author needs to explain further why certain procedures are used in the administration of the RMT. Of specific interest is the procedure in which subjects are asked to rate the stimuli on the dimension of "pleasantness." Does this particular task add another cognitive or emotional element that facilitates or inhibits memory abilities? Would scores differ considerably if subjects were simply told to study the words or faces because they will be asked to indicate whether they have seen the word or face before? Fifth, the exposure time for each stimulus does not appear to be uniform. In the test administration procedures, the author indicates that stimuli are presented "at the rate of approximately 1 item every 3 seconds" (Warrington, 1984, p. 11). Does this mean that some stimuli are exposed for longer periods? If so, this would be a major shortcoming of this test. Sixth, the interference times for the retention of separate stimuli are not equal. How did this affect test results? Were subjects less able to remember stimuli with longer interference times? These effects need further study. Finally, research is needed to determine how the RMT is related to other memory tests presently in use.

Generally, the RMT appears to be a fairly well designed instrument with potential for clinical use with brain-injured populations. It would be interesting to norm this test on children and young adults. The RMT also has research value for investigating the effects of psychological problems, such as depression and schizophrenia, on memory skills.

References

Coughlan, A.K. (1979). Effects of localized cerebal lesions and dysphasia on verbal memory. *Journal of Neurology, Neurosurgery, and Psychiatry, 42,* 914–923.

Milner, B. (1966). Amnesia following operation on the temporal lobes. In C.W. Whitty & O.L. Zangwill (Eds.), *Amnesia.* London: Butterworths.

Milner, B. (1967). Brain mechanisms suggested by studies of temporal lobes. In F.L. Darly (Ed.), *Brain mechanisms underlying speech and language.* New York: Grune & Stratton.

Milner, B. (1968). Visual recognition and recall after right temporal-lobe excision in man. *Neuropsychologia, 6,* 191–209.

Smith, E. (1974). Influence of site of impact on cognitive impairment persisting long after closed head injury. *Journal of Neurology, Neurosurgery, and Psychiatry, 37,* 719–726.

Warrington, E., & James, M. (1967). An experimental investigation of facial recognition in patients with unilateral cerebral lesions. *Cortex, 3,* 317–326.

Warrington, E. (1984). *Recognition memory test: manual.* Windsor, Berkshire: NFER-Nelson Publishing Co.

Alice G. Friedman, Ph.D.
Assistant Professor of Psychology, State University of New York at Binghamton, Binghamton, New York.

C. Eugene Walker, Ph.D.
Professor of Pediatric Psychology, Department of Psychiatry and Behavioral Sciences, University of Oklahoma Health Sciences Center, Oklahoma City, Oklahoma.

REVISED CHILDREN'S MANIFEST ANXIETY SCALE

Cecil R. Reynolds and Bert O. Richmond. Los Angeles, California: Western Psychological Services.

Introduction

The Revised Children's Manifest Anxiety Scale (RCMAS) is a self-report instrument that was developed to assess the nature and level of anxiety in children and adolescents. The questionnaire, which is labeled "What I Think and Feel," consists of 37 statements to which the child responds by circling "yes" or "no," depending on whether the item is descriptive of the child. Results yield a score for Total Anxiety and scores for four empirically derived subscales: Physiological Anxiety, Worry/Oversensitivity, Social Concern/Concentration, and Lie. The Total Anxiety scale includes 28 items (all items except those in the Lie subscale) and is designed to provide an objective measure of the child's overall level of anxiety. The Physiological Anxiety subscale consists of 10 items designed to assess the physical manifestations of anxiety, such as those related to breathing, sleeping, and hand sweating. The Worry/Oversensitivity subscale is comprised of 11 items related to the tendency to be afraid, nervous, or oversensitive to pressure. The Social Concern/Concentration subscale consists of seven items related either to concerns of a primarily social/interpersonal nature or to problems of concentration or attention. The Lie subscale is comprised of nine items that provide a measure of the child's unwillingness to admit minor common faults (e.g., "I never get angry").

The RCMAS is a recently revised version of the Children's Manifest Anxiety Scale (Castaneda, McCandless, & Palermo, 1956). The original scale was a 72-item, self-report measure based on the Manifest Anxiety Scale for adults (MAS; Taylor, 1951) and was comprised of items from the MAS that were reworded to make them appropriate for children. The earlier Children's Manifest Anxiety Scale had been standardized on 386 children from Grades 4 through 6 (Castaneda et al., 1956). In the 20 years that followed, the Children's Manifest Anxiety Scale was widely used to assess childhood anxiety in clinical and research settings (Reynolds & Richmond, 1985). Reynolds and Richmond (1978) revised the Children's Manifest Anxiety Scale in an effort to improve "the theoretical, psychometric, and practical aspects of the scale" (Reynolds, 1982, p. 1205). Their goal included 1) expanding the scope of the instrument to include a broader range of ages and indicators of anxiety and 2) improving readability of the questionnaire. They also sought to improve the internal validity of the instrument and develop additional normative data (Reynolds, 1982).

The manual (Reynolds & Richmond, 1985) for the RCMAS is comprehensive and well organized. Detailed information about test construction, standardization, and the psychometric properties of the instrument are included. Six brief case histories are presented to aid in the clinical interpretation of the instrument. A transparent scoring key is included with the test materials to ease scoring. Scoring is accomplished by simply counting the number of "yes" responses for the Total Anxiety scale and for each of the subscales. Raw scores are converted to scaled scores and percentiles. The Total Anxiety scale has a mean of 50 and a standard deviation of 10. The subscales each have a mean of 10 and a standard deviation of 3. Percentile equivalents and scaled scores of the scales are provided for each age/race/gender combination. According to the manual, scores falling beyond two standard deviations from the mean (> 70) are suggestive of problems and indicate the need for further evaluation. Scores two deviations below the mean (< 30) may indicate the child's unwillingness to respond truthfully to the questions.

Practical Applications/Uses

The Revised Children's Manifest Anxiety Scale was designed to be used by "psychologists or individuals with similar levels of training" (Reynolds & Richmond, 1985, p. 6) to assess the nature and level of anxiety of children aged 6 to 19 years. The authors recommend that a measure of anxiety be included as part of all routine psychoeducational evaluations of children experiencing academic problems because anxiety may influence the child's performance on measures of academic and intellectual ability. According to Reynolds and Richmond (1985), children and adolescents frequently experience anxiety related to peer and family relationships. The anxiety may have a negative impact on school performance without the child recognizing the extent or source of the anxiety. The RCMAS provides an objective method of facilitating quantification of anxiety and identifying its source.

The RCMAS can be administered individually or to groups. The instrument should be read aloud to children below third grade. Older children should be able to complete the instrument with a minimum of assistance from the examiner. The examiner may define words for children who are having difficulty, but the authors warn against giving specific frequencies when asked about words like "often." Individual administration is recommended for children with disabilities or reading problems.

The RCMAS is primarily a screening instrument rather than a diagnostic tool. When used for clinical purposes, the RCMAS should be used in conjunction with information gathered from behavioral observations, interviews, teacher and parental reports, and other measures of anxiety to provide an adequate assessment of the child's functioning. Because the scale is a self-report instrument, it is subject to distortion by children who are reluctant to respond accurately to the statements. A child who wishes to present a very positive or negative picture of him- or herself may deliberately provide false information.

Technical Aspects

Test construction of the Revised Children's Manifest Anxiety Scale was accomplished in a systematic manner that is described in detail in the test manual. Twenty items, derived from recommendations of a panel of teachers and clinicians, were added to the original Children's Manifest Anxiety Scale. The items were reworded to be understandable at a first-grade level and readable at a third-grade level. This early version of the instrument was administered to 329 children in Grades 1 through 12. Results were subjected to item analysis. Test items for the anxiety scales that did not meet a difficulty index of $.3 \leq p \leq .7$ and a biserial correlation with the total test score of $r_{bis} \geq .4$ were eliminated. Items in the Lie scale that correlated $\geq .30$ with the Total Anxiety scale or which did not correlate with other Lie scale items were also eliminated. The resultant questionnaire was cross-validated on a sample of 167 children. Results yielded a KR_{20} reliability estimate of .83 for the Total Anxiety scale for the first sample and .85 for the cross-validation sample.

The final 37-item RCMAS was standardized on a sample of 4,972 children between the ages of 6 and 19 years representing 13 states throughout the United States. The sample was 88% white and 12% black. Specific information about the socioeconomic status of the sample is not available, but the authors estimate that "an excellent cross section of school children was obtained" (Reynolds & Richmond, 1985, p. 19). A representative sample of mentally retarded, intellectually gifted, and learning disabled children (approximately 600) were included in the sample. Normative data for an additional 97 kindergarten children was also obtained. Coefficient alpha reliability estimates for the Total Anxiety scale across all age ranges were .85 for white females, .78 for black females, .84 for white males, and .85 for black males (Reynolds & Richmond, 1985). Reliability coefficients for black females at ages 6, 8, 10, and 11 were significantly below those for white females of the same age. Reliability estimates of the Total Anxiety scale for samples of Nigerian children (Pela & Reynolds, 1982) and Hispanic children (see Reynolds & Richmond, 1985) have equaled or exceeded .80. Reliability estimates for the subscales, as presented in the manual, are generally in the .60s and .70s; reliability estimates for the Lie scale are somewhat higher.

Factor analytic studies (Reynolds & Richmond, 1985) have supported the construct validity of the RCMAS subscales (Cowart, 1987). Factor analysis of the standardization sample (Reynolds & Paget, 1981), using a varimax rotation, revealed a five-factor solution that included three anxiety factors and two Lie scale factors. The resultant anxiety factors were similar to those obtained in a previous study of the RCMAS (Reynolds & Richmond, 1979), in the original MAS (Finch, Kendall, & Montgomery, 1974), and in subsequent studies (e.g., Reynolds & Harding, 1983). The Lie subscale items were divided into two distinct factors, those that contained double negatives and those that did not.

The RCMAS appears to reflect chronic rather than acute anxiety. Reynolds (1980) administered the State-Trait Anxiety Inventory for Children (STAIC; Spielberger, 1973), the RCMAS, and other measures to 42 middle-class white children (aged 6 to 16) referred for psychological evaluation. As expected, the RCMAS was strongly correlated ($r = .85$, $p < .001$) with the STAIC Trait scale and not so ($r = .24$,

$p > .05$) with the STAIC State scale. None of the anxiety measures correlated with scores on the Wechsler Intelligence Scale for Children-Revised (WISC-R).

Reynolds (1982) obtained similar results in a study of the convergent and divergent validity of the RCMAS. In this study he administered the RCMAS, the Goodenough-Harris Drawing Test IQ (Goodenough & Harris, 1963), and the STAIC (Spielberger, 1973) to 86 third-and fourth-grade middle- to upper-middle-class children. In addition, the children's teachers completed the Walker Problem Identification Checklist (Walker, 1971) to provide an external criterion of anxiety and behavior. The Walker is an observational checklist that yields scores for five scales: Acting-Out, Withdrawal, Distractability, Disturbed Peer Relations, and Immaturity. As expected, the RCMAS Total Anxiety Score correlated strongly (.65 for males, .67 for females) with the STAIC Trait scale but not with the STAIC State or with IQ. Positive correlations were obtained between the RCMAS subscales and most of the five behavior scales of the Walker; however, these correlations were, for the most part, modest. The Behavior Rating of the Walker correlated highest with the Concentration Anxiety subscale of the RCMAS (.47) for females and the Physiological Anxiety subscale of the RCMAS (.35) for males.

Research on the test-retest reliability of the RCMAS has been limited to studies involving elementary-school children (Reynolds & Richmond, 1985). Pela and Reynolds (1982) reported a test-retest reliability coefficient of .98 for Total Anxiety for 99 Nigerian children across a 3-week interval. Reynolds (1981) tested 534 children 9 months apart and obtained a coefficient of .68 for Total Anxiety.

Critique

The Revised Children's Manifest Anxiety Scale is a brief instrument that appears to provide a measure of chronic anxiety in children and adolescents. The instrument has a number of strengths, including ease of administration, scoring, and interpretation. The construction and standardization of the instrument are impressive compared to that of similar instruments. The weaknesses of the RCMAS are related more to the "newness" of the instrument than to deficits of the instrument itself. The RCMAS was published in 1985 and, to date, most of the studies of the psychometric properties of the instrument have been conducted by Reynolds and his colleagues. Replication of these results by other researchers and in other settings is needed.

There is limited information to date about the reliability and validity of the instrument. The internal consistency of the RCMAS appears to be adequate, as does the test-retest reliability. However, there has been limited investigation of the concurrent validity of the RCMAS. The few such studies that appear in the literature have, for the most part, compared the RCMAS to other paper-and-pencil self-report measures, thus introducing a mono-operational bias (Cowart, 1987). Further study of the relationship between the RCMAS and other indices of anxiety (e.g., behavioral measures) is needed before the RCMAS can be recommended for use as an outcome measure.

Lastly, caution should be taken when administering the RCMAS to certain populations. The internal consistency of the test was substantially lower for black females, particularly those who were 6, 8, and 14 years of age. Cowart (1987) notes that minorities were underrepresented in the standardization sample, as were children living in public institutions and those from low SES populations in rural areas.

Although further validity studies of the RCMAS are clearly warranted, studies to date suggest that the instrument has adequate psychometric properties for use as a screening instrument, and does, indeed, represent a substantial improvement over the original Children's Manifest Anxiety Scale.

References

This list includes text citations and suggested additional reading.

Castaneda, A., McCandless, B., & Palermo, D. (1956). The Children's Form of the Manifest Anxiety Scale. *Child Development, 27*, 317–326.

Cowart, C. (1987). Test review of the Revised Children's Manifest Anxiety Scale (RCMAS). *Journal of Psychoeducational Assessment, 5*, 77–80.

Finch, A.J., Kendall, P.C., & Montgomery, L.E. (1974). Multidimensionality of anxiety in children: Factor structure of the Children's Manifest Anxiety Scale. *Journal of Abnormal Child Psychology, 2*, 331–336.

Goodenough, F.L., & Harris, D.B. (1963). *Goodenough-Harris Drawing Test.* New York: Harcourt Brace Jovanovich.

Pela, O.A., & Reynolds, C.R. (1982). Cross-cultural application of the Revised Children's Manifest Anxiety Scale: Normative and reliability data for Nigerian primary school children. *Psychological Reports, 51*, 1135–1138.

Reynolds, C.R. (1980). Concurrent validity of What I Think and Feel: The Revised Children's Manifest Anxiety Scale. *Journal of Consulting and Clinical Psychology, 48*(6), 774–775.

Reynolds, C.R. (1981). Long-term stability of scores on the Revised Children's Manifest Anxiety Scale. *Perceptual and Motor Skills, 53*, 702.

Reynolds, C.R. (1982). Convergent and divergent validity of the Revised Children's Manifest Anxiety Scale. *Educational and Psychological Measurement, 4*, 1205–1212.

Reynolds, C.R., & Harding, R.E. (1983). Outcome in two large sample studies of factorial similarity under six methods of comparison. *Educational and Psychological Measurement, 43*, 723–728.

Reynolds, C.R., & Paget, K.D. (1981). Factor analysis of the Revised Children's Manifest Anxiety Scale for blacks, whites, males and females with a national normative sample. *Journal of Consulting and Clinical Psychology, 49*, 352–359.

Reynolds, C.R., & Paget, K.D. (1983). National normative and reliability data for the Revised Children's Manifest Anxiety Scale. *School Psychology Review, 12*(3), 324–336.

Reynolds, C.R., & Richmond, B.O. (1978). What I Think and Feel: A revised measure of children's manifest anxiety. *Journal of Abnormal Child Psychology, 6*, 271–280.

Reynolds, C.R., & Richmond, B.O. (1979). Factor structure and construct validity of "What I Think and Feel: The Revised Children's Manifest Anxiety Scale." *Journal of Personality Assessment, 43*, 281–283.

Reynolds, C.R., & Richmond, B.O. (1985). *Manual for the Revised Children's Manifest Anxiety Scale* (RCMAS). Los Angeles: Western Psychological Services.

Spielberger, C.D. (1973). *Manual for the State-Trait Anxiety Inventory for Children.* Palo Alto, CA: Consulting Psychologists Press.

Taylor, J.A. (1951). The relationship of anxiety to the conditioned eyelid response. *Journal of Experimental Psychology, 41*(2), 81–92.

Walker, H.M. (1971). *Walker Problem Identificaton Checklist.* Los Angeles: Western Psychological Services.

Ellis D. Evans, Ed.D.

Professor of Educational Psychology, University of Washington, Seattle, Washington.

REYNOLDS ADOLESCENT DEPRESSION SCALE

William M. Reynolds. Odessa, Florida: Psychological Assessment Resources, Inc.

Introduction

The Reynolds Adolescent Depression Scale (RADS; Reynolds, 1987) is a brief paper-and-pencil, self-report measure intended to assess the severity of depressive symptomatology in adolescents ages 13–18. Although similar in assessment focus to most measures of this type, the RADS is claimed (Reynolds, 1987) as the only measure of depressive symptomatology designed expressly for use with adolescents and that explicitly excludes any provision for a formal diagnosis of depressive disorder according to any specific and definitive criteria.

The RADS was developed over a 6-year period beginning in 1981 by William M. Reynolds, who holds a doctoral degree in school psychology from the University of Oregon (1976). Reynolds currently serves on the educational psychology faculty at the University of Wisconsin-Madison, where developmental work on the RADS has been coordinated. This work has been predicated on the dual assumption that depression is a serious and widespread form of psychological distress during adolescence and that most depressed teenagers go unidentified, courting the risk of even more serious pathology.

Initial field testing of the RADS took place early in 1981 with a suburban/rural high school population (ages 13–18) located in the Midwest region of the United States. The original version of this measure consisted of 32 items derived from symptomatology described by DSM-III (American Psychiatric Association, 1980) for major depression and dysthymic disorder as well as further symptoms represented on the adult and child version of the Schedule for Affective Disorders and Schizophrenia (Endicott & Spitzer, 1978; Puig-Antich, Orvaschel, Tabrizi, & Chambers, 1980). Field testing resulted in the elimination of two items, one concerning classroom concentration difficulty and one on social isolation tendency, because of insufficient item-total scale correlation. Thus, 30 items compose the published version of the RADS. Since 1981, this version has undergone a series of validity studies and tests of clinical application involving over 10,000 adolescents. Norms for RADS score interpretation are based upon a defined sample of 2,460 adolescents from one high school (Grades 10–12) and two junior high schools (Grades 7–9) in Reynolds's geographic region. The RADS is presented only in standard English for use with literate subjects.

To enable flexible use, the RADS is published in three forms: JS, O, and G. Forms HS and I are designed for individual and small-group administration. They differ only in that Form HS is designed for hand scoring, while Form I has optical character recognition sheets for machine scoring. Form G is intended for large-group

485

administration, screening programs, and research projects. This form is also set up for machine scoring. Item content and sequence are identical for all three forms. Thus, the forms differ primarily in their response scoring formats and print color of the answer sheets.

Form HS of the RADS consists of a single-page subject-response form entitled "About Myself." The front side of Form HS provides a section for identifying information from a subject such as subject's name, age, grade in school, sex, and date of RADS administration, together with a three-sentence paragraph of directions. The reverse side of this form begins with a brief paragraph of more detailed directions under which is listed the series of 30 items. The items are short declarative sentences intended to describe various feelings (i.e., symptoms). The items are listed vertically on the left side of the page. Parallel to these items on the right side of the page is a list of uniform response options designed to pull a subject's report of the frequency with which each feeling (symptom) is presently experienced. Frequency options are provided in a four-column, Likert-type format. Options range from "almost never" to "hardly ever" and "sometimes" to "most of the time," under which are printed corresponding rows of circles or bubbles for marking. Subjects respond by blackening the circle for each item according to their subjective sense of symptom frequency.

The extent of examiner participation depends upon the RADS form selected. Because of scoring procedures and logistics of administration, Forms I and G require more examiner attention to planning and directions for subjects. Even so, examiner preparation and participation is relatively simple and straightforward. Because the RADS manual is sufficiently clear and specific to guide a responsible administrator, no special training is mandated. RADS items are written simply and clearly in the present tense for ease of comprehension by adolescents in the intended age range of 13–18. Stated response time for the RADS is normally 5 to 10 minutes, although somewhat longer administration time may be required if an extremely large group of adolescents is involved. The RADS yields a score that serves to index the extent of severity of an adolescent's depressive symptom endorsement. Severity is measured in terms of increasingly high scores.

Practical Applications/Uses

The RADS was developed as a means to accomplish four objectives in working to benefit adolescents (Reynolds, 1987): 1) assess "clinically relevant" levels of depressive tendencies in individual adolescents, 2) screen for depression symptomatology in school-based or clinical populations of adolescents, 3) enable research on depression and associated constructs, and 4) evaluate the outcomes of treatment programs for depression-prone youths. The first two objectives are especially emphasized by Reynolds (1987) because of contemporary trends in adolescent drug abuse and suicidal ideation, both of which present a strong relationship to depression. Thus far, objective 3, research enablement, is illustrated primarily by the accumulation of validity studies for the RADS. This measure has any number of research applications because of its comparative ease of administration. Objective 4, using the RADS to assess the efficacy of depression treatment intervention, is noteworthy, although certain limitations (e.g., measurement reactivity) inhere in self-report measures for this purpose. The target population is male and female adolescents in Grades 7 to 12 who represent a broad spectrum of racial-ethnic and socioeconomic statuses.

Caveats appear insofar as the use of the RADS with exceptional adolescents is concerned, especially the mentally retarded and behavior disordered, for whom preliminary study has revealed significantly higher RADS scores as compared to adolescents in general. This finding is a concern for test administration and inter-pretation and not a reflection of inherent weakness in the measure. It appears that the RADS is best administered orally to mentally retarded youths, a variation whose relation to measurement validity is not yet clear. No mention is made of using the sacle with other groups of exceptional youths, such as the physically impaired or the intellectually gifted.

As previously mentioned, alternative RADS scoring forms are provided for the purpose of optional administrations—individual and small-group placements as well as large-group settings. Accordingly, the RADS is suited for use in a variety of settings including clinics and classrooms. Throughout the RADS manual, Reynolds (1987) repeatedly emphasizes that secure knowledge about depression is essential for "proper utilization" of the RADS. This emphasis seems mostly to concern score interpretation and use by trained psychologists or counselors, not RADS administration per se. Administration procedures are stated in explicit detail in the RADS manual (Reynolds, 1987). These procedures, embellished by separate appendixes, accommodate the classroom teacher as well as coordinators of large-scale school screening programs. As for most self-report measures of this type, respondents should be informed in advance that the RADS is a question-naire for the assessment of personal feelings, and that no right or wrong answers exist. Any pressure to elicit a positive or negative self-evaluation from the subject under assessment should be avoided. Adolescents can be assured that the RADS has been taken by thousands of individuals similar to themselves.

Scoring procedures may vary according to the RADS form selected. Forms I and G involve procedures for a mail-in scoring service (provided by the publisher), which are described in information sheets supplied with the questionnaires. These two forms require the use of a No. 2 pencil. The mail-in service provides complete scoring and a report of highlights for interpretation in relation to normative data and descriptive statistics. No fee is quoted for this service in the RADS manual (Reynolds, 1987). In contrast, hand scoring of Form HS is performed with a sepa-rate scoring key, a transparent plastic template (the use of which is essential be-cause six items are reverse-scored and quick scoring could otherwise be problem-atical). The template fits directly over the items on a respondent's answer sheet at the bottom of which is a coded space for the RADS score (RS), percentile rankings based upon an equivalent score from the total standardization sample (total per-cent) and specific norm groupings (e.g., ninth-grade girls), and a listing of "critical items" (CI). The latter six items, are proposed by Reynolds (1987) as special har-bingers of depression. Their empirical justification is based upon each item's power to differentiate between clinically depressed and nondepressed adoles-cents. A respondent's full endorsement of four or more critical items is claimed to indicate serious risk for depression, irrespective of the total RADS score. Other-wise, Form HS scoring is simply a matter of assigning a score of 1 to 4 for each of the 30 RADS items, then summarizing these scores for a total score (RS). The RS ranges from 30 to 120 on all three RADS forms. Form HS scoring should require less than a minute for each protocol; the template is sturdy and well designed for ease and clarity of scoring.

Score interpretation is based upon the principal that increasing scores represent increasing severity of depressive symptomatology and distress. Reynolds's (1987) disclaimers about diagnosis from RADS scores notwithstanding, a major feature of score interpretation involves a cutoff score to evaluate the severity of item endorsement. Adolescents who score at or above this point on the RADS are identified as candidates for further evaluation to determine potentially significant psychopathology. This score point was derived from RADS score frequency distribution and scatterplots that covaried the RADS with an independent measure, the Hamilton Depression Rating Scale (Hamilton, 1960, 1967). Two subsequent clinical investigations were conducted for validity checks, the results of which support the use of the cutoff score for distinguishing depressed from nondepressed adolescents.

In addition to the cutoff score criterion, the aforementioned critical items figure strongly in RADS score interpretations, along with extensive normative data from the standardization sample. This sample of 2,460 adolescents was composed of 75.8% white, 20.6% black, and 3.6% unspecified minority group subjects nearly equally distributed by gender. The sample provides a basis for descriptive statistics (means and standard deviation) as well as percentile ranks that correspond to the full range of possible raw scores by gender, Grades 7–12, and the total. Thus, individual scores can be compared to the average score and percentile ranks of adolescents in general (e.g., males and females at specific grade levels, etc.).

Tables for descriptive statistics and percentiles do not include race differentials, presumably because mean total RADS scores for whites and blacks were nearly identical. Moreover, the results of a three-way analysis of variance (grade x sex x race) revealed significant main effects for grade and sex only. Although small normative sex differences are suggested as "potentially meaningful" for interpretation, significant grade differences are dismissed as small in the "practical sense" (Reynolds, 1987, p. 14). Socioeconomic status does not figure into any formal score interpretation on the grounds that the Midwestern urban/suburban normative sample was heterogeneous and well stratified along socioeconomic lines. Score interpretation guidelines for special populations of adolescents are phrased only in terms of a separate study by Reynolds and Miller (1985) in which the RADS scores of small groups of educable mentally retarded (EMR) and nonmentally retarded adolescents from the same high school (matched for age, race, and sex) were compared. As a group, EMR subjects scored significantly higher than their nonretarded school mates, indicating more severe levels of depressive symptomatology. In sum, tables for data and their accompanying prose are clearly and succinctly presented. Proper score interpretation, however, requires basic skill in the comprehension and application of descriptive statistics, percentile rank equivalents, and standard errors of measurement.

Technical Aspects

The RADS manual (Reynolds, 1987) provides separate chapters for reliability and validity. Accordingly, this section of the review considers each technical quality in turn. First, consider reliability. Internal consistency coefficients based upon both the standardization sample and additional samples of adolescents provide the bulk of reliability data for the RADS. All reliability studies conducted by Reynolds (1987) have resulted in internal consistency estimates from computations of Cronbach's (1951) alpha. This method, justified as most appropriate for measures such as the RADS where item content is not randomly distributed, has generated a number of uniformly high coefficients for grade level, ranging from .89 to .93, with a total sample alpha of .93. Similarly, the split-half reliability coefficient for the total sample (corrected for attenuation) was .91. An independent study of RADS performance by ninth- and eleventh-grade subjects also yielded a split-half internal consistency coefficient of .91.

Reliability data are presented in three separate tables to illustrate homogeneity across subdivisions of the normative sample, as well as reliability estimates for 11 additional samples of adolescents from separate studies. These latter studies, with their collective N of 6,485 subjects, show a mean alpha of .92. Standard errors of measurement, clustering around four raw score points across studies, accompany these estimates as well. Two tables containing item-total scale correlations for the standardization sample are offered as still further evidence of item content homogeneity.

Considering a state construct such as depressive symptomatology, a coefficient of stability is perhaps less meaningful for reliability estimation, particularly if the test-retest interval is extensive. However, Reynolds (1987) anticipates the stability question by including results in table form from three more separate studies. These studies varied time intervals from 6 weeks to 3 months to 1 year, with stability coefficients of .80, .79, and .63, respectively. Mean RADS scores for subjects in these three studies changed very little across the two administrations for each group and were also similar to the standardization sample means. From the overall pattern of reliability evidence Reynolds (1987) concludes that the RADS is a reliable measure.

As for validity of the RADS, multiple forms of evidence are provided in the manual (Reynolds, 1987). These include content validity, concurrent validity (as an estimate of criterion-related validity), several variations of construct validity, and an attempt to establish "clinical validity" in terms of the relevance of RADS scores to issues of diagnosis and treatment efficacy.

The case for content validity rests upon two classes of evidence: 1) the degree of fit between item content with depressive symptomatology specified in clinical diagnosis and research activities and 2) item-total scale correlations that show item consistency with the sum of all other items. Reynolds (1987) claims that the 30 items relate to specific symptoms of depression stated in DSM-III (APA, 1980), and still others derived from the research diagnostic criteria as utilized in Carlson and Strober's (1979) study of adolescent depression. Reynolds (1987) acknowledges that these items are descriptive only and do not encompass all possible depression symptoms. Item-total scale correlations range from .16 to .69, with a majority falling in the .50s and .60s range and a median correlation of .53 for the total standardization sample.

A reasoned argument for concurrent validity as the most pertinent type of criterion-related validity underlies Reynolds's (1987) choice to validate the RADS in terms of independent scores from the Hamilton Rating Scale (HRS; Hamilton, 1982). The HRS was designed for use by trained examiners who apply the interview method to assess depression. According to Reynolds (1987), the HRS ranks among the most frequently used measures in psychiatric studies of depression and has demonstrated applicability to the adolescent population. For the RADS validity studies, a 17-item version of the HRS was used by five trained interviewers with 111 adolescents selected to include both depressed and normal subjects. Both the RADS and the HRS were administered to each subject in a counterbalanced and blind administrative procedure, with a resultant score correlation of .83 ($p < .001$). Additional steps taken to replicate this relationship have produced consistent findings. Thus the RADS and the HRS apparently share a large proportion of score variance, with the RADS having an advantage of administrative economy, especially if depression assessment is intended to screen adolescents at risk.

Support for construct validity of the RADS comes from a variety of studies conducted by Reynolds (1987) and his colleagues involving over 11,000 adolescents from diverse geographic locations, socioeconomic backgrounds, and racial-ethnic groups. Four types of evidence compose this aspect of RADS validity: 1) the relationship of the RADS to other self-report measures of depression and related constructs (convergent validity), 2) the correlations of RADS scores to potential confounding variables (discriminant validity), 3) the inferences from the factor analysis of RADS scores, and 4) the clinical efficacy data.

Concerning convergent validity, RADS scores show correlation clusters in the low to mid .70s with four other self-report measures of depression: the Beck Depression Inventory (Beck, Ward, Mendelson, Mock, & Erbaugh, 1961); the Center for Epidemiological Studies Depression Scale (Radloff, 1977); the Self-rating Depression Scale (Zung, 1965); and the Children's Depression Inventory (Kovacs, 1979, 1981). Additional relationships are reported for the RADS and certain related constructs such as self-esteem, learned helplessness, anxiety, loneliness, hopelessness, suicidal ideation, and perception of negative life events and social support, all of which were manifest in various self-report scales. The resulting patterns of correlations show a consistent convergence in predicted directions with magnitudes that reach statistical significance. For example, RADS scores are correlated negatively with self-esteem across several studies (-.65 to -.75) and positively with anxiety (.73 to .80) across several others.

As reinforcement for these convergent validity data, the argument for discrimination validity is built upon relationships of the RADS to social desirability, in the tradition of Crowne and Marlowe (1960), and academic achievement. Reynolds (1987) argues that because strong evidence of a social desirability relationship to RADS performance could confound any meaningful interpretation of RADS data, a demonstration of weak correlations between these two variables is necessary to allay suspicion about contamination. Reynolds (1987) also argues that, while depression may interfere with an adolescent's academic performance to some degree, the relationship between school grades and RADS scores will be low and negative. Both points of the foregoing argument are confirmed by correlational data consistent with prediction. That is, correlations between RADS scores and social acceptability response tendencies, as measured by a short form of the Crowne-Marlowe Social Desirability Scale, were low and negative, showing a .06

coefficient of determination. Correlations between RADS scores and academic achievement, as measured by grade point average, were equally low and negative, indicating a very small amount of shared variance between the two variables.

Factor analytic explorations of the RADS, summarized in the RADS manual (Reynolds, 1987), were performed to examine any underlying factor structure and item relationships on a purely statistical basis, not to claim construct validity on an a priori theoretical basis. Results are instructive in at least three ways: 1) describing five rotated factor loadings and various RADS item factor loadings, 2) revealing an important lack of sex differences in RADS factor structure, and 3) supporting RADS reliability analyses, as described earlier in this review. Because the RADS was developed as a unitary measure of depression (with homogeneous item content), Reynolds (1987) has chosen not to force any subscale definition from the factor analytic studies. This decision is apparently justified in terms of a dominant first factor loading, termed "generalized demoralization." Instead, resultant factors are taken to uphold "realistic domains" of depression in the descriptive sense—namely, cognition, internalized despondency, externalized somatic-vegetative complaint, and mood-anhedonia. Consequently, Reynolds (1987) interprets his empirically derived factors as consistent with broad categories of depressive symptomatology identified in related depression research (e.g., Rehm, 1981).

The clinical efficacy aspect of RADS validity has been scrutinized in two related ways: first, by testing the power of the aforementioned RADS cutoff score to corroborate independent assessment and diagnosis of depression among adolescents of both sexes; and, second, by documenting differential endorsements of RADS items by clinically diagnosed depressed and nondepressed youths. Clinical diagnoses in this segment of the RADS validation process were performed via interviews, using the Hamilton Rating Scale (HRS) and the Schedule for Affective Disorders and Schizophrenia (SADS; Endicott & Spitzer, 1978), the latter a central technique for the formal classification of depressive disorders. Results of these investigations have disclosed a high rate of accuracy in using the RADS cutoff score for its intended purposes. Specifically, convergent diagnosis results for the RADS in conjunction with the HRS and SADS were 89% and 85% agreement, respectively.

Finally, in addition to these tests of cutoff score power, clinical utility of the RADS has been demonstrated by its use as an outcome measure of treatment for depression among 30 moderately to severely depressed youths in relation to a waiting list control group of comparable depression levels (Reynolds & Coats, 1968). This study involved a pre-RADS and a post-RADS (follow-up) assessment strategy to show significant improvement in depressive symptomatology for subjects who received therapy. In contrast, controls maintained stable levels of depression throughout the approximately 12-week period of the study. From this evidence, Reynolds (1987) heralds the RADS as an instrument valuable for its utility and sensitivity to treatment effects.

Critique

Thus far in its development, the RADS is an encouraging measure of the self-report type for studies of adolescent depression. Potential users will find an unusually well-written and detailed professional manual from which to base their decisions. The general rationale for this instrument is reasoned and consistent generally with educated thinking about depression as reflected in the current scholarly literature (e.g., Dean, 1986; Gotlib & Colby, 1987). Even so, the atheoretical nature of the RADS in combination with other conceptual features provoke issues about which users should be mindful. Reynolds (1987) builds the interpretation of depression severity upon the frequency with which respondents endorse symptoms across a broad scope of affect descriptors. Oddly, this severity claim excludes any direct profession of symptom intensity by the RADS respondent. Because adolescents seemingly are not wont to admit self-failings and may more typically mask their depression by overt activity (Weiner, 1980), there is some question about the power of items drawn largely from the adult depressive symptomatology to accomplish adolescent depression measurement objectives. The RADS does not fully confront episodic or transitory versus chronic depression or other dimensions of depression (e.g., presence or absence of manic behavior) together with indications about the presence of life stress. It must be emphasized that the RADS focus on subjective feeling states with no accompanying self-reports of motor or verbal behavior necessarily delimits the working conception of depression implicit in the RADS.

These issues lead, naturally enough, to the matter of RADS validity. On the one hand, Reynolds (1987) merits kudos for his efforts to achieve acceptable levels of validity. The results of validity studies are exceedingly well presented, particularly as compared to most professional manuals for self-report measures known to this reviewer. On the other hand, the RADS validity strategy presents some puzzlements. Nowhere in the professional manual is a reader informed about who determined item content, including the degree of item fit with DSM-III, or who actually wrote the symptom descriptors. Normally, a panel of expert judges will be involved in the process of establishing content validity with acceptable agreement percentage figures as a measure of their success. This issue seems all the more important in view of an acknowledged lack of consensus about depression symptoms, most notably in terms of what symptoms are both necessary and sufficient to define depression (Rehm, 1981).

Among the more salient puzzlements, however, is Reynolds's (1987) limited choice of measures for concurrent and convergent validity. For these purposes, the RADS depends heavily upon measures such as the Hamilton Rating Scale and the Children's Depression Scale, both of which have been criticized as psychometrically weak (Glazer, Clarkin, & Hunt, 1981; Knoff, 1985; Sterling, 1985). Without rejecting these two instruments for validation study, Reynolds (1987) conceivably could have strengthened his stand by certain other scales suited to adolescent depression measurement that present reasonably adequate credentials. These include the adolescent version of the MMPI Depression Scale (see Mezzich & Mezzich, 1979) and the Depression Adjective Check List (Lubin, 1967). Other glaring puzzlements include a total lack of independent and overt behavioral criteria against which RADS scores might be validated, any study of an epidemiological type that might establish some predictive validity of the RADS in the proactive sense, and correlations between RADS scores and any concurrent informant measures. For example, it could be helpful for the reader to know the extent of correspondence between adolescents' self-reported RADS symptom endorsement and ratings on these items by their parents. In fairness, however, the RADS is a young measure and these validity shortcomings indicate a need for further authentication.

Validity issues aside, few will quarrel with the remarkably high reliability coefficients reported in the RADS manual (Reynolds, 1987). Because of the extent of these data, potential users should expect consistent results with the RADS in their work with adolescents. Reynolds (1987) is correct in his emphasis upon the value of internal consistency as the most telling indicator of reliability for measures of the RADS type. Yet the stability factor also looms as important in relation to the apparent elusiveness of mild, transitory depression among adolescents. This factor figures most strongly in the interpretation of individual scores as opposed to aggregate group data. Stability coefficient data are limited to three studies whose testing intervals ranged from 6 weeks to 1 year in duration. Reynolds (1987) argues that depression scores are expected to remain moderately stable over short time periods (e.g., 6 weeks), but are also expected to change after such periods. This leaves a score interpreter with a dilemma. With a 6-week stability coefficient of .80 as a benchmark, one should expect that test-retest reliability for shorter periods of time will be that high or higher. The stability of RADS scores drops precipitously, however, for retest periods beyond 3 months. Fully rigorous reliability study would involve estimates from more graduated time duration increases, perhaps beginning as early as 2 weeks and including 6- to 9-month intervals. In this way, a more complete picture of stability-reliability could be obtained, the results of which should increase the technical credibility of the RADS.

Regardless, Reynolds (1987) has generally provided a wealth of interpretation guidelines for a potential RADS user. The professional manual, buttressed by an extensive bibliography, is a convenient and scholarly introduction to adolescent depression and its measurement. The scale also stands as an impassioned effort to enjoin educators, counselors, psychologists, and researchers to the task of seeking better mental health for today's youth. Norm tables are clear and based upon a respectable number of adolescents. RADS users should be mindful, however, that the norm group has a provincial background and that Reynolds (1987) does not address the problem of percentile norm extrapolations for extreme scores.

To conclude, it is important to remember ourselves that the field of depression assessment is vulnerable to several major problems (Rehm, 1981). One problem is that measures typically result in a single severity score, despite the acknowledged heterogeneity of depression as a clinical syndrome. A related problem is that different content coverage is often encompassed by various instruments, thus reducing their comparability. Still another problem inheres in format differences. Such formats include response requirements such as true/false versus extent of agreement; symptom present or absent versus frequency of occurrence; and time references (recent past or present) that may introduce unknown sources of variation or amounts of error variance into the measurement process. The RADS adds to the existing potpourri of depression measures with a format involving frequency of present symptom occurrence, and should be used accordingly. Purists may object to still another measure without a definitive theoretical base, one that relies (like so many others) solely upon a phenomenological response orientation. Convergent validity data are comparatively stronger than are data in support of discriminant validity. The capacity of the RADS to differentiate closely related affect states (e.g., alienation) is yet unknown. As Reynolds (1987) himself admonishes, RADS users should not use the RADS as a diagnostic measure.

Despite these limitations, the RADS emerges as a strongly reliable measure with exceptional value as a research tool. Furthermore, the RADS shows good promise as an economical feature in a multiple screening methodology for adolescents at risk for depression. Use of the RADS as one measure in a multiple-method assessment strategy for therapy efficacy can also be recommended. This reviewer considers the RADS an exemplar of patient, careful psychometric study in the preparation of a self-report measure.

References

American Psychiatric Association. (1980). *Diagnostic and statistical manual of mental disorders* (3rd ed.). Washington, DC: Author.

Beck, A.T., Ward, C., Mendelson, M., Mock, J., & Erbaugh, J. (1961). An inventory for measuring depression. *Archives of General Psychiatry, 4,* 561–571.

Carlson, G.A., & Strober, M. (1979). Affective disorders in adolescents. *Psychiatric Clinics of North America, 2,* 511–526.

Cronbach, L.J. (1951). Coefficient alpha and the internal structure of tests. *Psychometrika, 16,* 297–334.

Crowne, D.P., & Marlowe, D. (1960). A new scale of social desirability independent of psychopathology. *Journal of Consulting Psychology, 34,* 349–354.

Dean, A. (1986). *Depression in multidisciplinary perspective.* New York: Brunner/Mazel.

Endicott, J., & Spitzer, R.L. (1978). A diagnostic interview: The Schedule for Affective Disorders and Schizophrenia. *Archives of General Psychiatry, 35,* 837–844.

Glazer, H.I., Clarkin, J.F., & Hunt, H.F. (1981). Assessment of depression. In J.F. Clarkin & H.I. Glazer (Eds.), *Depression: Behavioral and directive intervention strategies* (pp. 3–30). New York: Garland STPM Press.

Gotlib, I.H., & Colby, C.A. (1987). *Treatment of depression: An interpersonal systems approach.* New York: Pergamon.

Hamilton, M. (1960). A rating scale for depression. *Journal of Neurology, Neurosurgery, and Psychiatry, 23,* 56–62.

Hamilton, M. (1967). Development of a rating scale for primary depressive illness. *British Journal of Social and Clinical Psychology, 6,* 278–296.

Hamilton, M. (1982). Symptoms and assessment of depression. In E. S. Paykel (Ed.), *Handbook of affective disorders* (pp. 3–11). New York: Guilford.

Knoff, H.M. (1985). Review of Children's Depression Scale. In J.V. Mitchell, Jr. (Ed.), *The ninth mental measurements yearbook* (Vol. 1., pp. 317–318). Lincoln, NE: Buros Institute of Mental Measurement.

Kovacs, M. (1979). *Children's Depression Inventory.* Pittsburgh, PA: University of Pittsburgh School of Medicine.

Kovacs, M. (1981). Rating scales to assess depression in school-aged children. *ACTA Paedopsychiatrica, 46,* 305–315.

Lubin, B. (1967). *Manual for Depression Adjective Check List.* San Diego: Educational and Industrial Testing Service.

Mezzich, A.C., & Mezzich, J.E. (1979). Symptomatology of depression in adolescence. *Journal of Personality Assessment, 43,* 267–275.

Puig-Antich, J., Orvaschel, H., Tabrizi, M. A., & Chambers, W. (1980). *The Schedule for Affec-*

tive Disorders and Schizophrenia for School-age Children—Epidemiologic Version (3rd ed.). New York: New York State Psychiatric Institute.

Radloff, L.S. (1977). The CES-D Scale: A self-report scale for research in the general population. *Applied Psychological Measurement, 1,* 385–401.

Rehm, L.P. (1981). Assessment of depression. In M. Hersen & A.S. Bellack (Eds.), *Behavioral assessment: A practical handbook* (2nd ed.) (pp. 246–295). New York: Pergamon.

Reynolds, W.M. (1987). *Reynolds Adolescent Depression Scale: Professional manual.* Odessa, FL: Psychological Assessment Resources.

Reynolds, W.M., & Coats, K.I. (1986). A comparison of cognitive-behavioral therapy and relaxation training for the treatment of depression in adolescents. *Journal of Consulting and Clinical Psychology, 54,* 653–660.

Reynolds, W.M., G. Miller, K.L. (1985). Depression and learned helplessness in mentally retarded and nonmentally retarded adolescents: An initial investigation. *Applied Research in Mental Retardation, 6,* 195–306.

Sterling, F.E. (1985). Review of Children's Depression Scale. In J.V. Mitchell, Jr. (Ed.), *The ninth mental measurement yearbook* (Vol. 1, pp. 317–318). Lincoln, NE: Buros Institute of Mental Measurement.

Weiner, I.B. (1980). Psychopathology in adolescence. In J. Adelson (Ed.), *Handbook of adolescent psychology* (pp. 447–471). New York: John Wiley & Sons.

Zung, W.W.K. (1965). A self-rating depression scale. *Archives of General Psychiatry, 12,* 63–70.

Michael D. Franzen, Ph.D.

Associate Professor of Behavioral Medicine and Psychiatry, West Virginia University School of Medicine, Morgantown, West Virginia.

ROSS INFORMATION PROCESSING ASSESSMENT

Deborah G. Ross. Austin, Texas: PRO-ED.

Introduction

The Ross Information Processing Assessment (RIPA) is designed to evaluate symptoms following a closed head injury. In recent years, there has been a phenomenal clinical interest patients with closed head injuries. Previously, neuropsychological and speech pathology assessment instruments concentrated on individuals with discrete impairments secondary to localized tumor lesions or infarct lesions. Certainly, localized lesions offered the most dramatic dissociations among neurobehavioral skills with demonstrable deficits and sparing. However, the rich diversity of closed head injured patients is now well recognized, and broader spectrum assessment instruments have been developed to facilitate the profiling of strengths and weaknesses in this class of patients. Many of the broad spectrum instruments are time-consuming by necessity. Adequate sampling of different skill areas requires that a fair amount of time be spent with the patient. Deborah Ross developed the RIPA in order to allow a quick survey of different skill areas in the head-injured patient.

The RIPA is divided into 10 subtests. Each of the subtests involves asking the patient questions to which he or she generally is required to provide verbal responses.

Subtest I (Immediate Memory) asks the patient to repeat a series of items ranging from numbers to unrelated words to complete sentences.

Subtest II (Recent Memory) asks the patient a set of questions that involves the date, time, and place, the identity of the patient's care providers, and the recent activities of the patient.

Subtest III (Temporal Orientation-Recent Memory) asks the patient to answer questions related to previous and future times and the length of hospitalization.

Subtest IV (Temporal Orientation-Remote Memory) requires the patient to name the days of the week, months of the year, and the months related to various seasons or holidays.

Subtest V (Spatial Orientation) requires the examiner to ask the patient which state, city, and the name of the building in which he or she is at the moment, the place of his or her birth, and the location of different states and countries.

Subtest VI (Orientation to Environment) requires the patient to identify various people and to remember recent activities.

Subtest VII (Recall of General Information) asks the patient to name people holding current political offices and to identify a few historical figures.

Subtest VIII (Problem Solving and Abstract Reasoning) requires the examiner to present a few situations to the patient and to ask him or her to describe a reasonable course of action, to interpret proverbs, and to offer hypothetical reasons why a person might engage in a described course of action.

Subtest IX (Organization) asks the patient to name members of verbal classes such as animals, and to provide the classes for small lists of objects.

Subtest X (Auditory Processing and Retention) requires the patient to answer either "yes" or "no" to questions such as "Does it take longer to put on a hat than shoes?"

The numerical scoring system for each of the items is set on a scale of 0 to 3 (0 = unintelligible or no response and 3 = correct response). In addition, there is a set of 10 diacritical scores that are ways of describing qualitative aspects of the responses. These scores include confabulation, repetition, and self-correction. There are no guides provided for deciding among the numerical scores, but there are single sentence descriptions of diacritical scores with examples of responses to certain items.

The results of the RIPA are summed into the 10 subscale raw scores, transformed into percentile rankings, and plotted on two separate graphs, one for the raw scores and one for the percentile rankings. The profile sheet has space for two sets of scores (initial testing and retest scores). Additionally, the protocol profile sheet has room to sum the diacritical scores and compute the percentage of responses with each of the diacritical scores.

Practical Applications/Uses

The manual (Ross, 1986) suggests several uses for the RIPA: 1) to identify and quantify information processing deficits, 2) to determine the specific area of information processing breakdown, 3) to record associated qualitative behaviors through the use of the diacritical scores, and 4) to document progress in recovery. Specific treatment interventions are suggested for individuals scoring low on each of the 10 subtests.

Technical Aspects

The RIPA was first given to a sample of 100 normal adults between the ages of 16 and 57 years (average = 29 years). Most of the subjects had completed high school and a few were college graduates. Both blue-collar workers and professionals were included in the sample. However, the manual does not contain systematic descriptions of the sample characteristics beyond that which is mentioned above. Most of the normal subjects could accurately perform all of the items except Items 7 and 8 of Subtest VIII.

One hundred two clinical subjects with either closed head injuries or right-hemisphere lesions were given the RIPA, for a total of 247 administrations. These subjects were between the ages of 15 and 77 years. All of the subjects had objective neurodiagnostic evidence of either diffuse or right-hemisphere lesions. There were no subjects with dementing processes. All of the subjects had a Rancho Los Amigos scale score of at least Level V. These clinical subjects provided the sample from which the percentile transformations were derived. However, the entire test apparently was not given to each subject, as the number of subjects stated for the subtests varied from 84 for Subtest VI to 100 for Subtest VIII. There was no explanation given in the manual as to why different sized samples were used.

A test-retest study was conducted using 38 of the clinical subjects. The intertest interval ranged from 4 to 6 weeks. A repeated measures analysis of variance indicated that there was a significant interaction between the subtests and the trials. Examination of the simple main effects indicated that on the second trial there were more differences among subtest scores than there were at the original test occasion. The increase from occasion one to occasion two was different by subtest. It should also be pointed out that there was a significant effect of occasion on each of the subtests, indicating practice effects on each of the subtests.

There is no validity study reported.

Critique

The RIPA appears to be a good beginning towards producing an instrument capable of profiling the different areas of information processing that might be affected by diffuse or right-hemisphere injury. However, the instrument would benefit from a more rigorous evaluation of its psychometric properties. For example, although the retest study indicated significant practice effects, the standard error of prediction is not computed, limiting the interpretation of retest gains to guesses. Although the manual recommends that interpretation be based upon differences in subtest scores, there is no evaluation of the degree of unique variance contributed by each scale. There is some reason to suspect that the scales are highly intercorrelated because some of the subtests (e.g., II and VI, II and IV) share common procedures. Subtests II and III share 30% of their items.

There is also a need to compute and publish the standard error of differences for the various pairwise comparisons of subtest scores as suggested in the manual. Further, the RIPA does not measure accurately into the average or superior range. This is not a problem when the patient is highly impaired, but is a problem if the patient had a high level of premorbid functioning and is now relatively impaired or when the RIPA is used to document recovery. Finally, there is a need to provide empirical evidence regarding the relationship of scores to extratest variables that might be conducted in validity studies.

References

Ross, D.G. (1986). *RIPA—Ross Information Processing Assessment—Manual*. Austin, TX: PRO-ED.

Delwyn L. Harnisch, Ph.D.
Associate Professor of Educational Psychology, Institute for Research on Human Development, University of Illinois at Urbana-Champaign, Champaign, Illinois.

Sheila W. Valencia, Ph.D.
Assistant Professor of Curriculum and Instruction, University of Washington, Seattle, Washington.

SCAN-TRON READING TEST

SCAN-TRON Corporation. Rancho Dominguez, California: SCAN-TRON Corporation.

Introduction

The SCAN-TRON Reading Test was designed to provide normative information regarding reading achievement. When used in conjunction with the SCAN-TRON Optical Mark Reader Test Scorer, a minimum amount of time and effort is required in the administration. Two subtests were designed to measure distinct aspects of reading: vocabulary development and reading comprehension (with the addition of a third subtest, Word Attack, on Level 8). For Level 8, which corresponds to Grade 3, each student is administered 95 items, 30 items for Word Attack, 30 Vocabulary items, and 35 items for Reading Comprehension. For Levels 9 through 12, which are designed for use with Grades 4 through 8, each student is administered 80 items, 30 items for Vocabulary and 50 items for Reading Comprehension. The items for all subtests and levels are presented using a four-option, multiple-choice format. For Level 8, the subtests themselves are timed and require 55 minutes to take after the required 25 minutes for instructions. For Levels 9 through 12, 60 minutes of test-taking time is required along with approximately 20 minutes for instructions.

The following benefits of using the test are offered in the Teacher's Manual (Wick, Smith, Spiegel, & Stevens, 1985): 1) results are available for instructional use in a matter of minutes when scored by the SCAN-TRON Optical Mark Reader Test Scorer; 2) results can be used for assessment in Chapter 1 programs; 3) the option exists for out-of-level testing and associated norms; and 4) interpolation of scores to week of testing is possible. The teacher's manual was prepared in 1985 by John W. Wick, Professor of Educational Measurement at Northwestern University, and Jeffrey K. Smith, Associate Professor Educational Measurement at Rutgers University, with the assistance of Loyce D. Braun, Madelyn R. Smith, Dixie Lee Spiegel, and Jo Ann Stevens.

The SCAN-TRON Reading Test was developed as a part of the Comprehensive Assessment Program Achievement Series. Standardization for this test took place during the 1979-80 school year involving over 129,000 students from 157 school districts and 16 Catholic school systems with 2,763 classrooms in 423 schools participating in the fall standardization and 1,414 classrooms in 211 schools participating in the spring. The shorter SCAN-TRON Reading Test was then equated to this test with a sample of over 10,000 students using the equipercentile equating procedure.

There are five test booklets in the SCAN-TRON Reading Test, each of which ranges from 14 to 16 pages and contains items used in measuring vocabulary development and reading comprehension. The Word Attack subtest covers single consonants, consonant groups, vowels, and word formation. Areas measured in the Reading Comprehension subtest include literal comprehension, inferential comprehension, main idea of passage (both implied and stated), and context clues (using the context to define difficult or multiple-meaning words).

In addition to the subtest booklets, the required materials for testing include student answer sheets, which are color coded by subtest; a teacher's manual containing information on administering, scoring, and interpreting the subtests; and a norms booklet containing national percentile ranks, grade equivalents, and normal curve equivalents. Optional materials include the SCAN-TRON Optical Mark Reader Test Scorer (available at no cost to qualifying schools with a minimum purchase of materials); an out-of-level norms booklet for those students tested outside of grade level; Scan-Norms, a computer program designed to compute national percentile ranks, grade equivalents, and normal curve equivalents (available for the IBM PC, Apple IIe, or TRS 80 Models I and IV); and large bubble forms for special needs students. Three reporting formats are available from the SCAN-TRON Corporation: a Class List for score organization and ease of reference, a Parent Letter used to share test results and interpretations, and a Chart of Student Growth in Reading for monitoring progress throughout the school year.

For a given testing session in Level 8, students take subtests consisting of 30 Word Attack, 30 Vocabulary, and 35 Reading Comprehension items and transfer answers to answer sheets. For Levels 9 through 12, students take subtests consisting of 30 Vocabulary and 50 Reading Comprehension items. The raw scores are determined from the number of items answered correctly. Grade equivalent scores, normal curve equivalent scores, and percentile ranks can be determined from the raw scores by using the norms booklet or the optional Scan-Norms computer program.

Practical Applications/Uses

The SCAN-TRON Reading Test, when used in conjunction with the SCAN-TRON Optical Mark Reader Test Scorer, rapidly provides normative information regarding reading comprehension and vocabulary for students from Grades 3 to 8. Because information from this test is site processed, analysis and corrective actions may be taken without undue time delays.

In administering the SCAN-TRON Reading Test suggested materials include a test booklet and answer sheet for each student, for the test administrator, and also for any proctors; extra booklets and answer sheets in event of damage; an administration manual for the test administrator and proctors; and a timepiece that is accurate to the second. Although not required, it is suggested that the following items be available: an extra supply of No. 2 pencils, a Test In Session sign, and seatwork for students finishing early. To aid in the administration of the test, the examiner's manual suggests that one proctor be available for every 15 students tested.

Student answer sheets should be marked with the student's name, class, date of test, and grade number prior to beginning the testing. Once the answer sheets have been labeled, the examiner then completes the instructions for administering the test, giving special caution that answers be marked in their correct position on the student answer sheets. Total time required for the administration of Level 8 consists of 55 minutes student time and 25 minutes for instructions; for Levels 9 to 12, 60 minutes student time and 20 minutes for instructions is required.

In most cases the SCAN-TRON Reading Test will be scored with the SCAN-TRON Optical Mark Reader Test Scorer. For those cases in which hand scoring is desirable, answers to all test questions are provided in the Teacher's Manual. Following the scoring of the answer sheet, the raw scores are printed on the answer sheet and errors marked on the margin. Norms, grade equivalents, normal curve equivalents, and percentile ranks are then determined from the raw scores using the norms booklet. For those cases in which the test is given at a time different from the empirical norming dates, an interpolation procedure is outlined in the norms booklet. The Teacher's Manual provides a discussion of raw scores, normal curve equivalents, percentiles, and the recording and reporting of results.

Technical Aspects

The question of validity for the SCAN-TRON Reading Test is addressed solely through a discussion of face validity with no mention of predictive, concurrent, or construct validity. The objectives for each subtest are presented and should be carefully matched against the curriculum of any classroom or school district considering the use of this test. In the area of comprehension, these objectives represent a reasonable set of goals for most schools. The objectives in Word Attack are weakened by the isolation of decoding skills (i.e., the decoding section does not require application of skills to real words). It is unclear why there are no listed objectives for vocabulary, yet a vocabulary subtest score is reported for each grade level. Although it seems reasonable to select vocabulary items from *The Living Word Vocabulary* (Dale & O'Rourke, 1976) word list, more information is needed concerning exactly why these words are designated for a particular grade level of the test.

Reliability information is provided for each subtest using the Spearman-Brown prophecy formula and ranges from a low of .83 to a high of. 94 with a mean of .90. No subtest intercorrelations are provided; therefore, it is difficult to determine if reporting of information according to these subtest areas is appropriate or interpretable.

Critique

As described in the SCAN-TRON Reading Test Teacher's Manual, the Word Attack subtest is included in Level 8 only and is intended to measure a student's ability to "sound out words by using the graphic attributes of print" (Wick et al., 1985, p. 7). However, this statement is inconsistent with both the stated objectives of this section and with many of the items. For example, the objectives focus on the identification of isolated sounds and formation/identification of words with suffixes and compound words. A close examination of the Word Attack items reveals that of 30 items, 21 require students to identify isolated consonant or vowel sounds without referring to real words for their responses. The remaining 9 items test silent letters, suffixes, consonant substitutions, and compound words. Based upon a review of research in phonics, The National Academy of Education (Anderson, Hiebert, Scott, & Wilkinson, 1985) points out that the goal of phonics instruction is to teach the principle of systematic relationships between letters and sounds. To achieve this goal, they suggest that instruction focus on the most important relationships to enable phonics to help children approximate the pronunciation of words as checked against spoken language and context. Many of the Word Attack items fail to meet this goal.

The vocabulary sections present words in "non-informative" sentences. Although similar to approaches taken by most norm-referenced tests, evaluation of vocabulary within meaningful reading contexts (e.g., "informative" sentences, short paragraphs, longer texts as used in the comprehension section, etc.) would be more consistent with current reading theory. The importance of a student's knowledge of word meanings is that it helps them read and learn from text. Knowledge of word definitions alone is not the desired outcome of a reading program, but rather that students are able to use word meanings for the purpose of text comprehension.

Word selection for this test is an additional area of concern. Little information is provided concerning criteria for word selection and concerning the correlation of this subtest with other subtests in the instrument or other measures of vocabulary and comprehension.

The comprehension passages represent a variety of genres and, beginning at Level 9, are somewhat longer and more complete than those found in most reading comprehension tests of this type. This is an important improvement if reading tests are to reflect the actual school reading experiences of students. The majority of passages at Level 8, however, are not as well structured or interesting as they might be and would benefit from revision. All levels include seven reading passages with the proportion of narrative and expository selections approximately equal across levels. An exception occurs in Level 9, where a few of the selections are difficult to categorize, lacking structure and presenting a difficult text from which to construct comprehension questions. This balance of genres is a positive improvement over many existing measures.

The comprehension questions for the most part are well constructed, representing an emphasis on the important elements of each passage with balance of literal and inferential items at each level. Again, this represents a positive change from many existing measures. Because of the previously mentioned lack of structure and content of several of the passages, it is difficult to maintain this quality of questioning throughout the test. With some revisions, the Level 8 passages and these problem passages could be made consistent with the rest of the tests. The attention given to summarizing is important; however, selecting the best title might not be the most appropriate means of assessing this skill. Some alternative questions might better tap the ability to summarize. Beginning with Level 10, Vocabulary items are included as part of the comprehension items (using context).

This is an appropriate way to assess the ability to use vocabulary consistent with the emphasis on comprehension stressed earlier, and is an approach that should also be included in Levels 8 and 9.

The Teacher's Manual is quite easy to follow and presents very important information if one is considering using this test. Some questions concerning test development and norming are not addressed in the Teacher's Manual; they should be covered in a future Technical Manual which does not exist at present.

It is particularly notable that the publisher has provided out of level norms for testing students reading above or below grade. This represents clear support for matching students with testing level, promoting maximum student performance, and obtaining the most accurate test data possible. There is a problem, however, in that there are no out-of-grade norms provided for students reading below a third-grade level. Although the publisher may correctly believe the use of this test to be inappropriate for students reading below a third-grade level, many students in third grade read at a second-grade level or below. Should this be the rationale for this omission, the point should have been made in the manual that the test should not be administered to children reading below the third grade level.

The section of the Teacher's Manual entitled "Test Scores and What They Mean" provides a good discussion of raw scores, normal curve equivalents, and percentiles, but is problematic in the area of grade equivalents. The manual does not discuss the problems of interpretation of extrapolated grade equivalent scores (e.g., a fourth-grade student with a GE of 10.4; a seventh-grade student with a GE of 3.1) and the relation of grade equivalent scores obtained on the test with appropriate instructional level. These are two critical issues often misunderstood by teachers, parents, and administrators that result in serious misuse of test results. Because of concern over the misuse and misunderstanding of grade equivalent scores, the International Reading Association passed a resolution (1981) urging that "those who administer standardized reading tests abandon the practice of using grade equivalents to report performance of either individuals or groups of test takers" and that test publishers "eliminate grade equivalents from their tests." Although this may represent an ideal situation, it does signal the need for a more informative discussion of the use and interpretation of grade equivalents in the Teacher's Manual.

Recording and reporting of results is fully explained, and it is encouraging to observe that the parent letter does not include the use of grade equivalents. However, additional explanation of percentiles would be helpful for parents. The manual suggests placing information on the Chart of Student Growth in Reading at three points in the school year; however, it is not made clear if parallel forms of the tests are available. Even though 6 weeks would pass between testing if this approach is adopted, there is a legitimate concern in using the same test three times in a school year.

Recommendations for grouping are a welcome addition to any reading test manual. Although space is too limited to provide an in-depth discussion of grouping, the publisher makes a good effort in presenting some options and cautions regarding ability grouping. In particular, however, the rationale and advantages of heterogeneous grouping in some situations should also be introduced. It is surprising and discouraging that teachers are instructed to use grade equivalent scores for grouping as there are no explanations of the problems and misinterpretations of using such scores, and the test materials provide other standard scores that would serve this purpose equally well, if not better.

The recommended teaching strategies are broad but suggest some areas of emphasis for teachers. The suggestions for comprehension activities seem sound and practical. The recommendations for students experiencing difficulty in vocabulary focus on isolated word drill and a definitional approach to vocabulary development. This is inconsistent with current research on vocabulary growth, which suggests the need for many rich and varied experiences with words to foster word learning and reading comprehension.

The discussion of vision problems for below-level students is somewhat puzzling, as it is no more likely to cause a problem than any one of a number of other factors. Another assumption, that below level students in Grades 6 to 8 experience difficulty because they have not learned to decode, is an overgeneralization and misrepresentation of the possible problems. A better discussion of potential explanations is needed at this point. Additionally, the need for increased reading experiences discussed for above-level students should be included for students at all levels.

The SCAN-TRON Reading Test offers a good integration of scoring technology and testing. By providing a mechanism for on-site processing of tests, shorter turnaround time between testing and utilization of results is promoted. Unfortunately, there are some important concerns that must be addressed prior to recommending the use of this test. The test almost seems to be a marketing device designed to promote the sale of forms for the SCAN-TRON Optical Mark Reader Test Scorer. In reviewing the test, these reviewers received the impression that higher consideration was given to the eventual forms market and less to quality control and design of the test itself. This is demonstrated by marked inconsistencies within the stated goals of the test and measured objectives, lack of consistency between the test and current reading theory, lack of detail provided concerning the demographics of the norming populations, and lack of a technical manual for critical review. There is need for significant work to be done in preparation of a technical manual, a problem confounded by the fact that the norms utilized in the test are expiring and should be re-established.

References

This list includes text citations and suggested additional reading.

Anastasi, A. (1982). *Psychological testing*, (5th Ed.). New York: Macmillan Publishing Co.
Anderson, R.C., Hiebert, E.H., Scott, J.A., & Wilkinson, I.A. (1985). *Becoming a nation of readers*. Urbana, IL: University of Illinois, Center for the Study of Reading.
Dale, E., & O'Rourke, J. (1976). *The living word vocabulary*. Chicago: Field Enterprises Educational Corporation.
International Reading Association. (1981). *Resolution of the delegates assembly of the International Reading Association*. Newark, DE: International Reading Association.
Valencia, S., & Pearson, P.D. (1986). *New models for reading assessment* (Reading Education Report No. 71). Champaign, IL: Center for the Study of Reading.
Wick, J.D., Smith, J.K., Braun, L.D., Smith, M.R., Spiegel, D.L., & Stevens, J. (1985). *The SCAN-TRON Reading Test: Teacher's manual*. Rancho Dominguez, CA: SCAN-TRON Corporation.

Robert E. Shafer, Ph.D.
Professor of English, Arizona State University, Tempe, Arizona.

SCHOOL LIBRARY/MEDIA SKILLS TEST

Anne M.Hyland. Littleton, Colorado: Libraries Unlimited.

Introduction

The School Library/Media Skills Test (Hyland, 1986) is designed to measure students' knowledge about the school library/media center and skills in gathering and using information. More specifically, the 53-item test measures students' knowledge of the organization of the library/media center, understanding of how to select materials, skills in using print and nonprint resources, comprehension, and production/communication. The test, which has been normed for students in Grades 4-6, 7-9, and 10-12, is designed to determine the effectiveness of library instruction and to identify general trends in student library/media ability. Test results can be used in funding applications, in studies correlating library/media skills and general academic achievement, and in determining which library/media instructional techniques best suit the needs of students.

The test author, Anne M. Hyland, is Director of Curriculum and Instruction in Springfield, Ohio. She received a Master of Arts degree in Education (1968) and a Ph.D. in education (1978) both from the University of Toledo, Toledo, Ohio. She is a recipient of the American Library Association's John Cotton Dana, National Library's Public Relations Award, Education Division.

Test development was divided into two phases: 1) development of content validity and 2) development of construct validity and reliability. To determine content validity, a table of specifications for library/media skills was developed by 1) consulting a collection of approximately 60 national, regional, and state standards, 2) soliciting professional judgments from respected authors in the field of school library media, and 3) consulting elementary, secondary, and college curriculum guides. The standards and curriculum guides were examined to determine what general and specific skill areas library/media professionals thought were important for students to learn. All possible skills cited were noted and tallied. Total tallies for each category were adjusted to percentages of the total category so that each would carry equal weight in the final analysis. The skills fell logically into five broad areas: organization, selection, utilization, comprehension, and production. These were arranged in hierarchical order from skills requiring the least cognitive ability to those requiring the most cognitive ability. Benjamin Bloom's taxonomy of the cognitive domain, which divides the learning process into six steps, provided a guide both to the organization of the test, particularly in the hierarchical ranking of the five skill areas, and for the construction of pilot test items in the early stages of development.

The steps in Bloom's well-known taxonomy progress in sequence from lower level to higher level learning. Those at the lower levels are knowledge, comprehension, and application. The three higher level steps are analysis, synthesis, and evaluation. According to Bloom, the latter three require higher levels of thinking than the three at the lower level. Bloom also assumes that lower level knowledge is needed in order to accomplish the higher level tasks successfully. Accordingly, the successful completion of a higher level assignment would assure that all associated lower level skills have been mastered. The five broad areas of skills in the School Library/Media Skills Test, as collected from the 60 national, regional, and state standards and from the professional judgments of the respective authors in the field of school library/media, equated hierarchically with the cognitive abilities in Bloom's construct as shown in Table 1.

Grouping these five specific library/media skills according to the six logical thought processes of Bloom's taxonomy provided a structure and showed relationships between the skills. It also clarified the abilities students must master in order to move to higher levels of information use. For example, regarding *organization*, test developer was concerned with skills students must have in order to know how library/media materials are organized, thus enabling the students to find the materials they need. Once students are familiar with how materials are arranged, they must employ the skills needed to *select* appropriate resources. Progressing to the next level, once students select several resources, different, more advanced skills are required in order to *use* those resources. Both print and non-print resources were indicated. Following Bloom's taxonomy still further, the specification of abilities next concerned the skills students need in order to *comprehend* the given information. The specification of abilities then concentrated on the skills needed to enjoy or *appreciate* the artistic qualities of the various media productions. In the final step, *production/communication*, the specifications dealt with the skills necessary for understanding concepts and ideas and for presenting information in a meaningful way to others. At this point, the developer of the School Library/Media Skills Test had extended herself well beyond the point that usually concerns developers of media tests. Generally, the other developers focus only on examining how and why librarians organize information and how students learn about those organizing processes. For example, other tests center almost exclusively on such areas

Table 1

**Hierarchical Equation of Cognitive Abilities
in Bloom's Taxonomy and Skill Areas of School Library/Media Skills Test**

Cognitive Ability	Skill Area
Knowledge	Organization
Comprehension	Selection
Application	Use
Analysis	Comprehension and Appreciation
Synthesis	Production/Communication
Evaluation	

as dictionary skills and library use competence; all the previously published tests are book/print oriented.

The content validity of the instrument was assessed by a panel of 68 officers or chairpersons of the Ohio Professional School Library Media Association whom the association had identified to assist with regional accreditation inspections. The pilot instrument also was administered to 135 students. A difficulty index, a discrimination index, a co-efficient of internal consistency, and a correlation co-efficient were obtained from the pilot testing.

The second phase of the test concerned construct validity and reliability. The results of the pilot study were not available to this reviewer. The specific aspects of the test's construct validity and reliability will be discussed in the section on technical aspects.

The test is designed for administration by a teacher and/or media specialist to students in Grades 4–12. In order to take the test, students need a pencil, a test booklet, and an answer sheet. The answer sheet is not copyrighted and may be reproduced from a sample in the teacher's manual. Each test booklet contains directions the examiner is to read to the students before they begin to take the test. Students are to write their names and any other information needed at the top of the answer sheet and mark their answers directly on the answer sheet. The correct answers to the 53 test questions are provided in the teacher's manual. It is possible to consider scores for each of the five subsections or for each individual skill depending on the examiner's purpose(s) for testing.

A profile of test results emerges for the specific skills tested in the general area of organization. The specific skills profiled in this area are library citizenship, other information agencies, organization of the library, the Dewey decimal system, the Dewey arrangement, and alphabetical order. The second area, selection, tests knowledge and skills involving 1) kinds of media available for use, 2) parts of a card catalogue, 3) use of a card catalogue, 4) choosing a type and level of materials, and 5) using periodical guides. Again, results are profiled for each skill tested. A third category, utilization, breaks down into knowledge and skills involving the use of 1) reference books, 2) parts of books, 3) government documents, 4) equipment, and 5) other sources. Comprehension, the fourth category, profiles responses according to 1) self-direction in reading, 2) reading skills, 3) listening and viewing, 4) study and work skills involving research processes (classifying and synthesizing information), and 5) judgment in the use of newspapers, including periodicals and indexes. A fifth major category, production, involves 1) bibliographic form, 2) speaking and writing to communication, and 3) reproduction of graphics and other media.

Practical Applications/Uses

The test is designed to be used
1. to identify areas where students do or do not need additional library instruction.
2. as a pretest/posttest.
3. to verify areas of need when applying for grants or specialized funding.

4. for correlational studies among libraries/media skills, general academic achievement, or specific subject area achievement.
5. to determine whether special funding, such as chapter 1 or impacted funds, has an effect on student skills.
6. to identify general trends in student library/media abilities.
7. to evaluate various library instructional techniques to determine which are most effective.
8. to supply information to district administrators and supervisors in order to correlate unique building or area factors in order to determine those that most affect achievement.

The test can be used in a school library, in a subject matter classroom (e.g., an English classroom to test the effectiveness of a unit on library use), and in other settings within a school program. Because library instruction is at the heart of the school curriculum, all faculty members and administrators within a school district are potential users of the test. The test can be used with students from Grades 4–12. It also could be used with adults taking courses in the school (e.g., GED courses) and with senior citizens studying in literacy programs or general education programs.

As stated previously, this test can be administered by a teacher, school psychologist, librarian, or media specialist. Although the instrument is most appropriately used in a group situation within a library or classroom setting, it can be administered individually. The directions to the student are inside the test booklet in simple and direct form and also can be read easily by the person administering the test. The sequence of the test items can be altered if deemed appropriate for certain examinees, and in this reviewer's opinion the test clearly can be administered with a minimum of difficulty. The students need only a pencil, a test booklet, and an answer sheet to take the test. The test manual does not mention time specifications for administration.

In this reviewer's opinion, instructions for scoring are presented clearly in the test manual. The user should be able to learn to score the test in a relatively short period of time—not exceeding more than an hour or two. Scoring is accomplished by giving students credit for answers they have answered correctly (correct answers are provided in the test manual). A total score can be calculated for each of the five subsections, for the total test, or for each individual skill (skills are noted in a table in the test manual). The scores then, reflect the most effective place to focus instruction and to develop information about the instructional program. Although machine scoring apparently is not available, this reviewer finds the scoring procedure to be described carefully and fairly simple in comparison to many other tests.

Because the questions on the test are grouped according to the skill areas measured, test interpretation should involve an analysis of these skill area clusters. Such an analysis, which can be broken down according to groups or classes of students, shows the student skills that are strongest and weakest in each area. Results of the analysis will demonstrate patterns in the scores achieved by groups or classes of students or by individual students. As the test manual states, "Often a pattern is apparent and there are logical explanations for weaknesses and strengths; sometimes no pattern is noticeable." (Hyland, 1986b, p. 8) In this reviewer's opinion, teachers, media specialists, and school administrators should have no problem adequately and properly interpreting the results of the test. There is a short chapter titled, "Using Test Results to Direct Program Development," which, combined with the table, "Skill Areas of SCHOOL LIBRARY/MEDIA SKILLS Test" (p. 5) and the section on "Suggestions for Use," (p. 6) provides a useful guide to the interpretation of test results (Hyland, 1986b).

Technical Aspects

As mentioned previously in this review, the content validity for the School Library/Media Skills Test was established by consulting a collection of about 60 national, regional, and state standards; professional judgments by respected authors in the field of school library/media; and elementary and secondary college curriculum guides. Skill areas were isolated and all possible skills cited within these areas were noted and tallied. This is a fairly traditional way of establishing content validity. An assessment of the content validity was made by a panel of 68 officers or chairpersons of the Ohio Professional School Library/Media Association whom the association had identified to assist with regional accreditation inspections. A pilot instrument was developed and administered to 135 students. A difficulty index, a discrimination index, a coefficient of internal consistency, and a correlation coefficient were obtained from the pilot testing but were not described in the test manual.

Construct validity was measured in the pilot study by comparing scores of students with previous library/media training against scores of students without previous training. Evidence supporting construct validity on the final testing was measured by comparing various student and school district factors against students' scores, by item analysis, and by an analysis of internal consistency. The item analysis of the questions yielded a discrimination index and a difficulty index for each item. Discrimination index scores of .30 or greater indicated a moderate to high correlation with a person's overall test score. Difficulty index scores between .30 and .70 indicated test questions in the middle range of difficulty; therefore, a discrimination index of .30 or greater and a difficulty index of between .30 and .70 indicated support for the construct validity for the test. Eight of the questions had discrimination index scores below .30; all others were greater than .30. Difficulty index scores for Grades 4–9 and combined grades were between .30 and .70. Scores for Grades 10–12 were only slightly above .70. The item analysis discrimination index and the difficulty index using the Pearson Product Moment Coefficient of Correlation supported the construct validity of the test. The Kuder-Richardson 20 formula was used to evaluate the test developers' expectation that the test items would correlate with the total test at a level of .70 or above. The correlations were the strongest (.85 to .89) for the total test. Individual subsections did not correlate as well (.47 to .42).

The norming population comprised 2,670 students, equitably distributed between rural and suburban settings, representing 33 school districts across Ohio. Such factors as the cost per pupil expenditures and the overall wealth of the districts in which the pupils were registered were additional factors considered in choosing the norming population. The school district and student factors compared were designed to identify both group and external differences. Analysis of variance techniques was used to determine what effect each had upon student scores.

Student scores were analyzed according to five groups: sex, grade, relative cost per pupil, wealth per pupil, and type of library assistance available to students. The analysis yielded the following results:

1. *Sex*. In the final analysis, females scored higher than males, a result that correlates with research findings in the field of sex differences.
2. *Grade level*. Higher grade levels scored highest on the test. This was in keeping with the test's basic assumption that skills are learned and perfected through time and practice.
3. *Cost per pupil*. Students from districts that spent more per pupil for education scored higher. This supports generally held assumptions of the relationships between school finance and school achievement.
4. *Wealth per pupil*. Students from the least wealthy and the most wealthy districts scored highest. Taking into consideration the Ohio school financial structure, the wealth of the district was not as important as a community's desire to provide a quality education for its students. Results of the analysis supported that notion.
5. *Available assistance*. All combinations that included a full-time professional media/specialist scored higher than any combination with a part-time library/media specialist. It is logical to expect that full-time assistance would be more effective than part-time assistance.

The test manual provides tables that examiners may use to compare the test scores of their students to the mean scores of the 2,670 sample students. If the student population being tested is similar to the students representing the norming population, then the students being tested would be expected to score in a comparable range. If the students are different, the scores will be different. The test developers are confident that any differences can be attributed to the students' school library/media ability.

Critique

The School Library/Media Skills Test was constructed over a period of more than 10 years with a considerable amount of time and effort spent developing a table of specifications that represents the specific skills taught in library/media courses in various schools. For professionals attempting to find tests in the area of library/media skills, it is clear that the School Library/Media Skills Test is probably one of the most recent and comprehensive developed in that it deals with areas of media study such as the production of graphics and other media, as well as the comprehension and utilization of media other than books. Most tests on the market today are limited to books. Research done by the test author analyzed 31 tests developed between 1932 and 1978 found that three deal exclusively with dictionary skills, six are work-study skill subtests of general achievement tests; the 22 remaining tests measure only library skills competence and do not deal with media use (Hyland, 1986b).

Another unique feature of this test is the test developer's attempt to equate the skills necessary in organizing, selecting, utilizing, comprehending, and producing books and media with Bloom's analysis of thought processes, which assumes that learning moves in sequence from lower levels (knowledge, comprehension, and application) to higher levels (analysis, synthesis, and evaluation). Unfortunately, the test developer did not provide research to substantiate the assertion that the paradigm constructed equating skills specifications and categories actually equates with the hierarchy of skills specified in Bloom's taxonomy. Nevertheless, the test does seem to be a valuable tool since it is important for school districts to know how successfully students have been trained in various areas of research, including the uses of the library and media center.

The test can be administered easily by a teacher or a media specialist, and the compilation and analysis of results does not require a great deal of technical skill. The norming population seems to be representative of American school populations generally, with the exception of areas that have large numbers of bilingual students.

Another important point concerning the use of test results should not be overlooked here. It is quite possible to examine students' results in each specific skills area in each of the five general skill categories and apply them to student performance in other classes. For example, results in the general area of comprehension might be of interest not only to library/media specialists but also to faculty members in fields such as English, social studies, and reading.

The test manual is well written and easily understood by teachers, media specialists, and administrators. Although more specific examples concerning the tests use could probably have been included, Chapter III, "Using Test Results to Direct Program Development," provides to school faculties and administrators a considerable amount of assistance for developing programs that will point the way to improving the research skills of students in all areas.

References

This list includes text citations and suggested additional reading.

Davies, R.A. (1979). *The school library/media program: Instructional force for excellence.* (3rd ed.). New York: Bowker

Devine, T. (1972). *Listening in Schools Schoolwide: Activities and Programs,* Urbana, IL: National Council of Teachers of English.

Hackman, M.H. (1985). *Library/media skills and the senior high school English program.* Paula K. Montgomery, Editor. Littleton, Colorado. Libraries Unlimited.

Hart, T. (Ed.). (1985). *Instruction in school media center use.* (2nd ed.). Chicago: American Library Association.

Hyland, A.M. (1986a). *School Library Media/Skills Test.* Littleton, CO: Libraries Unlimited.

Hyland, A.M. (1986b). *School Library Media/Skills Test manual. Littleton, CO: Libraries Unlimited.*

Karpisek, M.E. (1983). *Making self-teaching kits for library skills.* Chicago: American Library Association. (3–6)

Kirkendall, C. (Ed.). (1982). *Teaching library use confidence: Bridging the gap from high school to college.* Ann Arbor: Pierian Press.

Laybourne, K., & Cianciolo, P. (Eds.) (1978). *Doing the media: A portfolio of activities, ideas and resources.* (rev. ed.). New York: McGraw-Hill.

Ploghoft, M.E., & Anderson, J.A. (1982). *Teaching critical television viewing skills: An integrated approach.* Springfield, IL: Charles C. Thomas.

Rice, J., Jr. (1981). *Teaching library use: A guide for library instruction.* Westport, MA: Greenwood Press.

Schapiro, L.L. (1976). *Teaching yourself in libraries: A guide to the high school media center and other libraries*. New York: H.W. Wilson.

Spirit, D.L. (1979). *Library/media manual*. New York: H.W. Wilson.

Taylor, A. (1977). *Hands on: A media resource book for teachers*. Ottawa, Ontario: National Film Board of Canada. (K-8)

Wehmeyer, L.B. (1984). *The school librarian as educator*. (2nd ed.). Littleton, CO: Libraries Unlimited.

Allan L. LaVoie, Ph.D.
Professor of Psychology, Davis & Elkins College, Elkins, West Virginia.

Eugene H. Foster, Ed.D.
Director, Tygart Valley Counseling Center, and Visiting Professor, Davis & Elkins College, Elkins, West Virginia.

SCHOOL PROBLEM SCREENING INVENTORY, FIFTH EDITION

Thomas D. Gnagey. East Aurora, New York: Slosson Educational Publications, Inc.

Introduction

The fifth edition of the School Problem Screening Inventory (SPSI; Gnagey, 1974) represents an ambitious attempt to assess much with one brief test. The SPSI provides scores for students from nursery school through high school. The intent of each score is to guide school professionals to make judgments about possible problems in their students. Scores fall into four general diagnostic categories: Learning Disabilities, General Learning Skill Deficits, Behavior Disorder (general, nonspecific) and General Maladjustment. There are also six specific scores: Learning Disabilities (visual-motor), Learning Disabilities (auditory-verbal), Mental Retardation, Behavior Disorder (undercontrolled), Behavior Disorder (overcontrolled), and Educational Handicap (socio-cultural).

Ratings of the students are performed by the classroom teacher using 37 descriptive items. The items are contained in a two-page test booklet that unfolds into a single long page. The teacher simply crosses out the line that applies to the child being rated; scoring can be done by the teacher or psychologist, as it is a mechanical process. Scores are transferred to the back page of the booklet, where they are compared to the various cutoff scores. Total time for the rating and scoring might be as little as 10 minutes if the teacher knows the student very well. Scoring is done prior to more intensive diagnostic testing. The results should guide the user in selecting appropriate assessment procedures. The manual indicates that teachers find the descriptive items immediately sensible, and that teachers have virtually universal understanding of the item intent (Gnagey, 1974, p. 2). On the face of it this seems an unlikely claim. For example, one item asks about typical IQ performance (or whether mental age is typically 20% or more below chronological age), and another asks about cross-dominance (do teachers really know which eye is dominant in each child in a classroom?). Teachers may consult student records to answer questions they are unsure of, but that naturally increases the administration time. Other items are more easily answered, as, for example, whether the student is clumsy, argumentative, or fearful. The teacher is urged to leave no item blank.

Practical Applications/Uses

The relatively short time that it takes to adminster the SPSI presents a tempting instrument for presorting or classifying students who have special needs. A considerable risk exists, however, that the user may overinterpret the results or prematurely label a student. Indeed, a question exists regarding the generalizability of the test norms to specific populations outside of the Midwest, and a very real risk exists that cultural differences could be ignored altogether.

Even when the SPSI is used conservatively by the seasoned psychologist, problems in interpretation and labeling remain. Gnagey fails to define the categorical terminology he has used. The terms *learning disabilities, mental retardation,* and *behavior disorders* are used freely but are not tied to federal- or state-legislative definitions nor to theoretical frameworks for understanding children with special needs. Widely different classification systems are used from state to state, and several states use noncategorical systems. The sole purpose of the classification of students at the local level is to select those students who will benefit best from existing instructional programs. The lack of appropriate definitions of the category labels precludes this local use. When used as a guide to individual assessment at the next level (of administration), broad, poorly defined categories make the selection of appropriate tests problematical.

Technical Aspects

The 37 items for the SPSI were chosen from 126 descriptive items based on their strong correlation with in-depth diagnostic findings. These items are weighted according to how well they discriminated among the categories of children as actually diagnosed. The weights are used in the scoring procedure.

Item selection was based on the same sample of data that guided the fourth revision (Gnagey, 1974, p. 8). Further, this same Midwest sample apparently constituted the cross-validation sample, which raises a serious question about the independence of the corroboration. The manual is too sketchy to permit any exploration of the characteristics of the sample or of the procedures used in the fifth revision.

In a similar way, the manual provides no details about reliability. There is no mention of internal consistency of the categories or of test-retest stability. Gnagey (1974) reports the intercorrelations of the six specific scales, but fails to mention the sample size or composition. Presumably it was based on some part of the sample used in the fourth and fifth revisions.

An important part of the documentation of a screening test is a classificatory accuracy table. Gnagey does not include one, and refers only to the cross-validation study (Gnagey, 1974). This is a serious omission, especially in light of the fact that the test, for the most part, is quite competently developed.

Critique

The SPSI was last revised almost 15 years ago. Major changes in the understanding of the characteristics of students with learning disability and mental retardation have taken place since that time. Hence, its diagnostic categories may not match well with those presently used, especially at the local level. A thorough literature search by these reviewers revealed no published literature that used the SPSI; therefore no independent information about its validity as a screening instrument is available. In fact, the manual contains no reference to the published literature either. The manual itself is much too small for serious use and contains several typographical errors and ambiguous statements.

In summary, while the SPSI seems to have strong potential as a guide for individual assessment of school-related problems, independent information regarding its utility is lacking. Until such facts are established, it would be better to use a screening instrument with stronger credentials.

References

Gnagey, T. D. (1974). *School Problem Screening Inventory* (5th ed). Ottawa, IL: Facilitation House.

Ann H. Stoddard, Ed.D.

Professor of Education, University of North Florida, Jacksonville, Florida.

SCREENING ASSESSMENT FOR GIFTED ELEMENTARY STUDENTS

Susan K. Johnsen and Anne Corn. Austin, Texas: PRO-ED.

Introduction

The Screening Assessment for Gifted Elementary Students (SAGES) is an instrument designed to identify gifted children, ages 7–0 to 12–11, and to assess their aptitude, achievement, and creativity. The test consists of three subtests: Reasoning, School Acquired Information, and Divergent Production. More specifically, the SAGES measures two categories of reasoning, three content areas of school acquired information, and divergent production using pictures and figures.

Both test authors, Susan K. Johnsen and Anne Corn, are professors of education at the University of Texas at Austin. Dr. Johnsen teaches courses in gifted education and has published widely in that field. Also, she co-authored and published the Test of Nonverbal Intelligence with Linda Brown. Dr. Corn teaches special education, specializing in the visually handicapped. She, too, has enjoyed a prolific publication record in this domain.

The SAGES, first published in 1987, was developed between January, 1985 and April, 1986. Two separate samples were selected. A sample of 1,567 normal children were selected from 16 states while a sample of 1,595 gifted children were selected from 21 states. According to the test authors, the SAGES was developed to address some of the needs of gifted identification procedures and their effects, such as limiting placement in gifted programs to academically achieving gifted children, using IQ tests and achievement tests interchangeably, as well as using IQ tests to identify creativity and leadership ability, using diagnostic tests as a screening device, preventing recognition of potential gifted performance through the use of multiple test scores criteria, and the underrepresentation of minority students in gifted programs.

Prior to item construction of the SAGES, standardized tests in the areas of achievement, creative thinking, and intelligence were examined. Basic elementary and middle school textbooks were examined for mathematics, science, and social studies content. In addition, types of activities in gifted classrooms were investigated.

The first 221 items representing reasoning, achievement, and divergent production were evaluated by university professors, teachers of the gifted, and gifted children. The selected 200 items were administered to 52 gifted children and to 28 normal children in Grades 1, 3, and 6. The initial items did not discriminate between the two groups. Therefore, a second set of 300 items was constructed and similarly critically evaluated. These items were administered to 440 gifted children

516

in Grades 2 through 6, specifically for item analysis. A third random sampling of 600 children, 300 gifted and 300 normal, were administered the items. Items were retained if they fell inside the .30–.80 range for discrimination and inside the 17% to 85% range for difficulty. Because item analysis was not applicable to divergent production, items retained were those that stimulated the greatest response from the standardization population.

The SAGES has not been revised since its first publication. Presently, there is only one version of the test, and it has been printed only in English. The pictures are large enough to accommodate the visually impaired for a group test, but Subtest II (School Acquired Information) might not accommodate this handicap. If the test is administered individually, the examiner can use Spanish or another language with children who do not speak English.

Subtest I, Reasoning, measures general intellectual ability, and the scores estimate a child's ability to learn new tasks necessary to achieve in gifted programs. The two sections, 29 classification items and 23 analogies items, use pictures and figures to designate relationships that may vary in one or more traits, associations, or meanings. The child must determine the initial relationship of three pictures or figures, then select a related picture or figure from five options. If a child does not know the name of a picture, telling the child is recommended. The analogies section is similar. A child determines how the first two pictures or figures on the page go together, and then selects from five choices the option that correctly completes the three picture or figure series.

Subtest II, School Acquired Information, requires students to read 41 multiple-choice items on mathematics, science, and social studies. The items are written on the cognitive levels of recall, comprehension, and application. The 41 items are weighted more in mathematics than in the other two areas. There are 23 math items, including word problems, that require the four computations and knowledge about fractions. The 10 social studies items include 2 items on map reading and 8 items on science.

Subtest III, Divergent Production, measures only one area of creative thinking—fluency. Two pages of the test are devoted to this section. The first page uses pictures, the second page, figures. Again, if the child does not recognize a picture, the examiner tells the child the name of the picture. An example of a child's response might be, "Trees, flowers, grass, and swings go together because they all belong in a park." A similar response, "Trees, flowers, grass, and swings go together because they are in a backyard," is also correct because an acceptable rationale for the grouping is provided.

The answer forms for group administration are only for Subtests I and II. Students mark one of the five bubbles for each item, including the trial items.

The profile sheet serves two purposes. The back of the sheet contains space for the listed grouping for Subtest III. Because this portion of the test is individually administered, the examiner fills in the child's response. Also on the back sheet is the item performance for Subtest I and II where the examiner records the responses if the SAGES is individually administered.

The front of the profile sheet is divided into six sections: 1) general information that includes name, age, sex, and date tested, 2) record of the subtest scores that comprises the child's raw scores and a standard score for both the normal and gifted population, 3) computation of program-related composites, which provide quotients, 4) other test scores, 5) a profile of sections II, III, and IV that includes a relative position with both the normal and gifted sample, and 6) a section for comments and recommendations.

Practical Applications/Uses

The SAGES was designed specifically to help identify "children for gifted classes that emphasize aptitude, achievement, and creativity" (Johnsen & Corn, 1987, p. 7). It can also be used to identify borderline children or those children who tend to "fall between the cracks" when traditional identifications procedures are used. The test authors state that the instrument should not be used to identify talent in leadership ability, in visual or performing arts, or in psychomotor areas. The SAGES can also be used to examine a child's relative strengths and weaknesses in the area of the constructs embodied in the test, as well as being used as a research tool to study and test theories of gifted behavior.

The test would be useful to teachers, counselors, and school psychologists who generally work closely together to identify a gifted pool at the elementary school level. Because the test claims to reduce cultural bias commonly found in traditional methods of identification, it can be used to identify minorities, especially blacks and Hispanics, who are sorely underrepresented in gifted programs.

Two separate samples were used to develop normative data, a normal sample and a gifted sample. Subjects were restricted to elementary school children, ages 7 to 12. These ages correspond generally to grade levels 2 through 7. Additional information about the sample included race, sex, ethnicity, residence, geographic area, and parent educational level. There is a gap in minority representation in relation to the total population. This is not surprising because the gifted sample was selected from children enrolled in gifted classes. Research has shown that fewer children from most minority groups are identified for selection to gifted programs.

The SAGES can be easily administered by classroom teachers who have familiarized themselves with the testing procedures in the manual. Subtests I and II can be administered in either a small group situation or individually. Subtest III must be administered individually because student responses are timed. The directions in the manual are very clear for both individual and group administration. Specific directions and questions are given, as well as correct and incorrect student responses (Subtest III).

Because each section of the test is complete within itself and addresses three separate features of giftedness, the SAGES can be administered in one sitting or divided into two to three sittings. Testing time varies for Subtest I and II. Thirty to 50 minutes are needed if the SAGES is administered individually, and 60–90 minutes if it is group administered. Because Subtest III is always individually administered, approximately 7 minutes are required for individual administration, .4 minutes for directions, and 3 minutes for actual test taking.

The use of basals and ceilings can be used to reduce individual testing time. The examiner may begin, using the entry level that has the child's chronological age next to it. The ceiling is reached when the child misses five consecutive items. The basal is established by testing downward (toward Item 1) until five items are answered correctly. Caution is suggested, however, if little is known about the child being tested. It is recommended that lower beginning levels should be used for normal children and higher entry levels for suspected gifted children.

No special training is needed to score the SAGES. The raw scores for the first two subtests are obtained by summing the correct answers. For classification and analogies, one point is received when the child points to a picture and figure that goes with the other three pictures or figures and shows the same relationship as the trial item. For the School Acquired Information, one point is received for each correct answer. For Divergent Production, samples of correct and incorrect responses are provided to assist the scorer. Repetitions and associations are scored 0. A score of 1 is given when a name for a class is generated.

Scoring the test is easy, and scoring time is minimal. If the test is individually administered, the scoring can occur as questions are asked. If the test is group administered, hand scoring will take no more than 2 to 3 minutes per individual sheet. The SAGES is hand scored for group testing. A template can be prepared for use with Subtests I and II. However, it is possible to use SCAN-TRON-type computer scored sheets for Subtest I and II with older elementary children.

Four types of scores are recorded on the Profile Sheet: raw scores, percentiles, standard scores, and quotients for the composites. Standard scores and percentiles are used to construct a profile of the test results. Age is the factor that is used to transform the raw scores into standard scores and percentiles. Tables are provided for both the normal and gifted samples. For example, Sara, who is age 8 years, 6 months, makes a raw score of 31 on the Reasoning test. The raw score is changed into 98% and 16 (standard score) for the normal group and 95% and 15 (standard score) for the gifted sample.

The program-related quotients are attained using the total of the standard scores of two or three subtests and using a conversion table. For instance, if Sara's total score is 46, then the corresponding quotient is 134 for the normal sample with a percentile rank of 99, while a raw score of 38 for the gifted sample equals a quotient of 117 and a percentile rank of 87.

The profile sheet includes space to report other test scores and comments. The test scores can be converted to the SAGES equivalent scores, if the tests measure the same three components measured by the SAGES. Using the "Other Information" section allows the examiner to write in comments and recommendations about the child's performance and interaction with school experiences. On the back sheet of the Profile Sheet, Section VII is provided for the examiner to record and tabulate the item performance.

·Four types of scores are provided by the SAGES: raw, standard, percentiles, and quotients. For the standard scores, the mean is 10 and the standard deviation is 3. A table for standard score interpretation (1–20) includes the descriptions "very poor" to "very superior." The table also reveals the "% included" for both the gifted and normal sample. This table permits an evaluator to determine the overall or partial giftedness of the examinee. If discrepancies are suspected, further evaluations can be recommended.

The composite quotient is similarly interpreted with quotients ranging from 70 to 130 with identical descriptions and "% included." The accompanying recommendation is that caution should be used when interpreting the SAGES test scores "since all behaviors associated with giftedness are not measured. The SAGES results should be treated as hypotheses and validated . . . through direct observation" (Johnsen & Corn, 1987, p. 22).

Interpretation of the SAGES scores is relatively simple and requires only that the examiner read and use the tables in the manual. The test authors state that the SAGES's most reliable score is the program-related quotient (PR-A) quotient, but that potential ability can be derived from a combination of other quotients. Borderline gifted performance may call for the examiner to determine whether the examinee is functioning at the upper limits of the normal range or at the lower limits of the gifted range. To assist the examiner in making a decision, other information, such as teacher-assigned grades, other test scores, observation, and clinical data, should be considered. When severe discrepancies in abilities occur, it is further suggested that consideration be given to testing and environmental conditions and similar factors.

Suggested oral questions to discover the reasons for a student's response and performance are listed, with the understanding that the answers to the questions are to be used for clarification and treated as clinical data, and not to change the original scores.

Once again, the test authors warn that when interpreting the test results the standard of error should be taken into consideration. They also remind users that the results are only samples of behaviors. Poor performance may be caused by several features, especially those traits generally exhibited by minority students, such as lack of equal opportunity to acquire necessary skills and the lack of motivation.

Technical Aspects

Two types of reliability are reported: internal consistency for Reasoning and School Acquired Information, and interscorer for Divergent Production. The Cronbach coefficient alpha was used to determine reliability for consistency. Alphas range from .85 to .94 for the normal sample, alphas range from .85 to .94 and from .82 to .92 for the gifted sample. The average alpha may be considered moderate but acceptable for both groups on both subtests.

Sixteen teachers were used to judge the reliability of Divergent Production. Interscorer reliability was considered in this section to be of high consistency, with .94 agreement on the pictures used and 1.00 agreement on the figures.

The standard error of measurement for the SAGES is 1, indicating a small degree of error for both the gifted and normal samples.

Test validity was determined using three areas: content validity, criterion-related validity, and construct validity. Content validity was reported by stating that SAGES content is similar to content used in different schools' identification procedures and is similar to currently used tests that screen for gifted children.

The criterion-related validity was divided into two sections, aptitude and school acquired information. Three aptitude tests were used: Wechsler Intelligence Scale for Children-Revised ($N = 43$), Short Form Test of Academic Aptitude ($N = 686$), and Ross Test of Higher Cognitive Processes ($N = 152$). Two separate achievement test scores were correlated with the SAGES: Iowa Tests of Basic Skills ($N = 120$) and the California Achievement Test, Forms C and D ($N = 151$). Correlations show a moderate relationship between the SAGES and the three aptitude tests, .42 to .51. Correlations between the SAGES and the achievement tests revealed coefficients in the range of .49 to .82 in the areas of math, reading, and language. These coefficients show a moderate relationship between the SAGES and the standardized tests. However, the correlations were adequate enough to support the claim that each of the two subtests measures what they profess to measure.

There is no evidence that the section on Divergent Production was correlated with any test of creativity or tests that purport to measure divergent thinking.

Critique

It has long been a contention that early identification of gifted children is important and practical, basically because it provides an opportunity for early intervention. Gifted children have skills beyond those usually attributed to their chronological age. Consequently, challenging educational programs can be tailored to fit them.

The SAGES is a new instrument for identifying gifted children in the elementary grades. It is easy to use and can be administered in a reasonable time limit. It is also consolidated and inexpensive. With comparative information on both normal and gifted samples, it is easier to use the scores to recommend children as candidates for gifted programs, especially borderline children from minority groups. Even with children who have been nominated for a gifted pool, the SAGES certainly would be useful as a follow-up assessment in conjunction with other standard instruments. If SAGES periodically identifies a child inaccurately, systematic evaluation of gifted programs can determine if a child remains there. The other side is that the SAGES may save children who generally "fall between the cracks" with traditional procedures. If the SAGES does no more than identify the potential of these children, it will be considered worthwhile.

Given the rigor during the SAGES development, it is surprising that the criterion-related validity of Divergent Production was not measured using a recognized creativity test, such as the Torrance Tests of Creative Thinking, which measures fluency. In addition, to suggest that fluency is the major construct in productive thinking is misleading. Originality, elaboration, synthesis, and richness and colorfulness in imagery are a few of the other characteristics that creative and gifted children possess and should be observed. These qualities were not measured by the SAGES.

Granted, the SAGES has not been around long enough to generate a multiplicity of comments on its use and its effect. However, the moderate correlations reported for construct validity indicate that the test developers should revisit this section. Furthermore, mean scores were reported for both the normal and the gifted sample, but no measures of variability were provided. Standard deviations might indicate a clearer difference between the two samples, and the degree of overlap in performance.

Additionally, no comparative research has been reported to determine the SAGES's worth as a screening device, even for borderline children. Before research is conducted, the test authors may want to consider a revision of two of the multiple-choice items. The stem of number 2 could be made clearer, and the options for number 4 should be consistent. The key for this item is a "giveaway."

Overall, the SAGES can be useful as a part of the screening process for gifted children, but, in this reviewer's opinion, it cannot be totally substituted for the more traditional procedures being presently used. If it is able to identify borderline children, especially from underrepresented groups, the SAGES will be of great benefit. More research should assure users of the SAGES's sensitivity to gifted behavior and its ability to screen for this behavior effectively through a validity update.

Users would be wise to regard all of the cautions recommended by the test developers, especially the caveat for the interpretation of scores because all measures of gifted behavior are not assessed by the SAGES.

References

This list includes text citations and suggested additional reading.

Cicirelli, V.G. (1965). Form of the relationship between creativity, IQ, and academic achievement. *Journal of Educational Psychology, 56*, 303–308.

Johnsen, S.K., & Corn, A. L. (1987). *Screening Assessment for Gifted Elementary Students.* Austin, TX: PRO-ED.

Karnes, F., & Koch, S.F. (1985). State definitions of the gifted and talented: An update and analysis. *Journal for the Education of the Gifted, 4*, 285–306.

Meeker, M. (1985). Toward a psychology of giftedness: A concept in search of measurement. In B.B. Wolman (Ed.), *Handbook of intelligence* (pp. 787–799). New York: John Wiley.

Renzulli, J.S. (1978). What makes giftedness? Reexamining a definition. *Phi Delta Kappan, 60*, 180–184, 261.

Richert, E.S. (1985). Identification of gifted students: An update. *Roeper Review, 8*, 68–72.

Richert, E.S., Alvino, J.J., & McDonnell, R.C. (1982). *National report on identification: Assessment and recommendations for comprehensive identification of gifted and talented youth* (Educational Information Resource Center). Washington, DC: Government Printing Office.

Runco, M. (1986). The discriminant validity of gifted children's divergent thinking test scores. *Gifted Child Quarterly, 30*, 78–82.

Sternberg, R.J. (1982). Nonentrenchment in the assessment of intellectual giftedness. *Gifted Child Quarterly, 26*, 53–67.

Sternberg, R.J. (1985). Cognitive approaches to intelligence. In B.B. Wolman (Ed.), *Handbook of intelligence* (pp. 59–118). New York: John Wiley.

Sternberg, R.J. (1986). Identifying the gifted through IQ: Why a little bit of knowledge is a dangerous thing. *Roeper Review, 8*, 143–146.

Tannenbaum, A. (1983). *Gifted children: Psychological and educational perspectives.* New York: Macmillan.

Torrance, E.P. (1984). The role of creativity in identification of the gifted and talented. *Gifted Child Quarterly, 28*, 153–162.

Trentham, L.L., & Hall, E.G. (1987). Relationship between scores on the Gifted Student Screening Scale and scores on IQ tests. *Roeper Review, 9*, 261–271.

Richard Colwell, Ph.D.

*Professor of Music and Secondary Education, University of Illinois at
Urbana-Champaign, Urbana, Illinois.*

SEASHORE MEASURES OF MUSICAL TALENTS, SERIES A

*Carl E. Seashore. San Antonio, Texas: The Psychological
Corporation.*

Introduction

The Seashore Measures of Musical Talents are designed to measure a student's
potential in music. The present measures are not all that different from Seashore's
1912 efforts to measure musical capacity. Carl E. Seashore, a respected psychologist,
began to investigate the possibility of measuring a student's musical aptitude around
1909. He was influenced at that time by the phenomenal interest in intelligence testing that occurred at the turn of the century, his own interest in learning to sing, and
the differences in the sound of professional singers. By 1902, Seashore had devised a
tonoscope, an instrument that provided him with a visual image of song. With this
instrument he charted many of the great singers of his day as they sang folk songs
and arias from well-known oratorios. Noting differences and being aware of other
trait differences in individuals, he hypothesized that there was likely a musical intelligence distinct from the verbal intelligence being measured by Binet and others.

Seashore's idea of musical intelligence predates the recent hypotheses of psychologist Howard Gardner. Seashore believed that musical intelligence was inborn
as he had no other explanation for why some individuals were 400 times better at
perceiving differences in aural stimuli. A child's ear was well developed by the age
of 5 and did not become more sensitive with age or training; thus, a degree of
inborn talent was his only plausible explanation. Arguing for native talent put him
at odds with behaviorists such as Lundin (1985) and gestalt psychologists such as
Mursell (1932). Thus, the battle was joined, data notwithstanding.

Seashore also formulated his musical intelligence hypothesis in response to
Horatio Parker, who claimed that great musicians were not born but were primarily
great technicians. Seashore, who had been working in his laboratory on the perception of aural stimuli, had concluded by this time that musical talent was not
one, but a hierarchy of talents. Given a "musical mind," which Seashore believed
was also a normal mind, musicians, by definition, had "in a serviceable degree,
those capabilities which are essential for the hearing, the feeling, the understanding, and, ordinarily, for some form of expression of music, with a resulting drive or
urge toward music" (Seashore, 1938, p. 2).

Seashore gathered data from 1912 until 1919, at which time the test was published. It contained five tests: Sense of Pitch, Intensity Discrimination, Sense of
Time, Sense of Consonance, and Tonal Memory. The Sense of Rhythm test was
added in 1925. In the one major revision of the test (Seashore, 1939) consonance

was dropped and a timbre discrimination test substituted. The 1960 version of the test is the one familiar to us today and it is essentially the 1939 edition recorded in 1960 on a 33¹/₃ rpm record. The sections of the present test are labeled Pitch, Rhythm, Loudness, Time, Timbre, and Tonal Memory.

The original (1919) Pitch test contained 100 pairs of pure tones; the examinee was required to judge whether the second tone of each pair was higher or lower in pitch than the first. The present version consists of 50 pairs of pure tones, the difference ranging from 9 to 59 cents.

The Loudness test is based on 50 pairs of pure tones with differences ranging from .5 to 4 decibels. The Rhythm test has short pulses of pure tones comprising 10 pairs of five note patterns in ²/₄ meter, 10 six note patterns in ³/₄ meter, and 10 pairs of seven note patterns in ⁴/₄ meter.

The Time test requires the subject to judge whether the second tone is longer or shorter than the first. Differences range from .05 to .30 seconds. Changing the 3rd and 4th partials of a pure tone allowed Seashore to construct the Timbre test. 50 pairs are given and the student determines whether the tone color is the same or different.

Tonal Memory, perhaps the most discriminating subtest, consists of 10 pairs of three note patterns, 10 pairs of four note patterns, and 10 pairs of five note patterns. Although comparing two tones requires musical memory, the need to remember five patterns and to determine which note is changed requires the most sophisticated musical memory task in the entire battery. Musical memory was considered of major significance by Seashore. Révész (1954) states that he and Seashore agreed that musicality consisted of a sense of rhythm, a musical ear, and musical memory. The student of music testing has already learned that musical memory, tonal and rhythmic, is the one unifying concept of all music aptitude tests.

It appears that Seashore was partial to the Pitch test; his first published research in that area, in 1910, was on the measurement of pitch discrimination. He wrote a few articles on the importance of the sense of rhythm, the first article appearing in the *Musical Quarterly* in 1918. Yet, he did not include Rhythm in the 1919 version of the test, and it was 7 years before his publisher acceded to a revision of the instrument. A similar delay occurred with timbre. Seashore discussed its importance in *The Psychology of Musical Talent* (Seashore, 1919), but it was not added as a section of the Talent test until after his death.

A potential user of the test would need to purchase a record or tape, answer sheets, scoring key, and the manual.

Practical Applications/Uses

The uses for the test are given as educational and vocational counseling, admission to musical instruction in schools, and selection for membership in bands and other musical organizations. Many of these purposes were not suggested by Seashore; they stem from a publisher who was quick to learn that most music aptitude testing is accomplished for the purpose of recruiting students for the school instrumental music program. At the time of his death, Seashore remained opposed to deriving a single score of music intelligence, a score that could be cited as evidence that a student should begin the study of piano, violin, or trumpet. Seashore's admonition that one needed to possess his six abilities to a "serviceable degree" stemmed from research results indicating that some successful musicians possessed high levels of ability on only five of the six submeasures, a passable level on the sixth (Seashore, Lewis & Saetzeit, 1960).

In the Pitch test, 50 pairs of tones are presented; the student determines whether the second tone is higher or lower than the first. The same number and type of task are required on the Loudness, Rhythm, and Timbre tests. In the Rhythm and Tonal Sequence tests there are 30 pairs of patterns. In the Tonal Sequence test, the student determines which note is changed.

Norms are presented for three levels. Levels were chosen rather than single grades because differences among the adjacent grades generally were too small to warrant norms for each grade. The levels are Grades 4 and 5, Grades 6 through 8, and Grades 9 through 16. Sex differences were too small and inconsistent from one level to another to report. Norms are not given for the total test; each section is evaluated separately.

The Seashore measures continue to be useful for school teachers. Doing well on the Seashore test is a positive reinforcer of musical potential and ability. The test draws attention to discriminatory skills that may have been ignored. Being aware of the need to make fine distinctions likely sets the stage for improvement of those students with the ability to improve. Improvement is possible for many students, but the data are compelling that there is a sizable number of individuals who have so little background or talent that education does not result in a marked improvement with considerable training and experience.

The major problem with the measures continues to be the format. Item numbers are not announced on the recording and it is possible for a student to get behind and never catch up. There are pauses after each 10 questions but these are not lengthy pauses and serve primarily as reassurance for those who are "keeping up" with the test or an opportunity for those who are fairly mature and/or "test-wise" to adjust their marking to conform to the auditory stimulus. The test would be considerably longer with complete directions and item numbers on the recording. Presently, the advertised length is 30 minutes for the recording, but the test administrator is to allow another 30 minutes for test administration directions. That recommendation seems appropriate and reasonable. As the test was designed for fourth-grade students and older, the problems of navigating one's way through the test are manageable. If one gives a different "talent" test at an earlier age, administration of the Seashore measures at fifth grade or later can provide important diagnostic information. The Seashore information might also serve as a warning for those who should not be advised to make a career of music. This reviewer has observed many college conducting teachers use the Seashore measures as a means of sectioning these classes. Its validity for predicting those who will be successful in conducting class is amazingly good. The Seashore measures have a major advantage over other measures in that sections can be given and often two sections may be adequate for the teacher's need. The Pitch, Rhythm, and Tonal Memory tests are recommended by this reviewer.

Technical Aspects

With as many questions as there are in each of the Seasore measures, one would expect the measures to be rather reliable. The KR 21 formula applied to Grades 4 and 5 are pitch .82, loudness .85, rhythm .87, time .72, timbre .55, and tonal memory .81. For Grades 6 through 8, the respective coefficients are .84, .82, .69, .63, .63, and .64. For high school students, pitch is .84, loudness .74, rhythm .64, time .71, timbre .68, and tonal memory .83. Twelve public schools were involved in providing these data for the manual (Seashore, Lewis, & Saetzeit, 1960) and many competent researchers have reported higher reliabilities (i.e., Tilson, 1941; Mc-Creey, 1937; Leblanc, 1954; and Olds, n.d.). Seashore's basic concept of music talent has been accepted by the profession with most of the talent tests constructed for promotion by band instrument manufacturing companies following his basic outline.

Validity, always the crucial issue in "talent" tests, remains a fuzzy issue. Seashore took a reasonable stance that there was no question about what he was measuring with each of his tests in the series. Taking a pure tone, playing two of these tones that differed in frequency (pitch), and requiring the examinee to render a judgment as to which one was higher was clearly a test of pitch discrimination. No one has questioned the content validity of each of the separate tests. Seashore's argument, hinted at earlier in this review, was that making discriminations about higher and lower, louder and softer, and so on were clearly daily tasks of every musician, and one had to be reasonably good at these tasks or one's musicianship suffered. The criticism made of Seashore's position was that the sum of the parts does not constitute the whole, a fact that Seashore also admitted in his first publication. Adequate performance on acoustical measures (the six tests) could never equal the complex tasks required of musicians who must interpret music with feeling and line. Seventy years of research has not settled the argument of what is musicality because those individuals who sit for a talent test are usually those who are interested in music and those who do well on the Seashore measures tend to do well in music. A negative argument can be constructed that doing well on the Seashore measures may not be a guarantee of musicality but not doing well may be an indicator that the examinee will have problems in the study and performance of music.

Critique

Seashore did publish a Form B of his measures that required even finer discrimination in the same six areas. Perhaps he felt the "looseness" in the scores, especially in the Time and Timbre sections, were due to the lack of rigor in the test items. Although Form B has not been available for years, an effort was made by this reviewer to administer the test to grade school students. Confirmation was quickly made that the difficulty of the test was a factor, but not a positive factor, that contributed to the validity of the instrument. The discriminations required in Form B are too fine to be discerned in the traditional classroom. Sergeant (1973) had earlier raised concerns that the discriminations required in Form A were also too fine for valid measurement. Any disturbance or extraneous noise that intrudes upon the testing situation are factors that must be taken seriously in assessing the validity of the Seashore measures. Student interest is of concern, as is student fatigue. Without mental effort to stay with the recording and physical and mental alertness, scores can be affected. As the measures are constructed to become increasingly more difficult, there is a tendency to quit after a question that was difficult. Sometimes the question is difficult only because of temporary mental fatigue. Scores of the students tested in 1988 tend to confirm the published norms for Grades 4–5 and 6–8. How Seashore established his norms remains questionable, as he cites 2,555 students for the Pitch test of Grades 6–8, but only 951 for the Timbre and 952 for the Time tests. His "favorite" tests, Rhythm, Pitch, and Tonal Memory, were taken by twice as many students. The difference in sample size is even greater in Grades 4–5. The three "favorite" tests had a sample in excess of 3,000, but Loudness norms are based on 380, Time 377, and Timbre on 377 students.

Seashore reports norms for over 4,000 students on each of the tests at the secondary school level, indicating that his primary interest may have been at this level, thus explaining his retention of a testing format that is somewhat difficult for elementary age students to manipulate.

One criticism of the test has always been the use of electronically generated sound (pure tones) rather than real music (see Beck & Shaw, 1962; Lundin, 1985; and Mursell, 1937). As some of those critics are now advocates of computer-assisted instructional programs that also rely on electronically generated sounds, one has to guess, then, that one of the criticisms of the Seashore test has now disappeared.

These measures have been translated into other languages (e.g., Seashore-Test Fur Musikalische Begabung Testanweisung, 1966). The test results appear to be comparable in most countries, the discrimination tasks are not culturally dependent. Reliability figures in 1988 range from .78 to .91 with positive student attitudes. Support for the validity of Seashore's ideas is provided by the research of Horn and Stanov (1982), who found pitch imagery loading on pitch and tonal memory portions of Seashore and the kinaesthetic factor for development of pitch perception loading on rhythm and tonal memory.

References

This list includes text citations and suggested additional reading.

Beck, J., & Shaw, W.A. (1962). Magnitude estimation of pitch. *Journal of the Acoustical Society, 34,* 92–98.
Bentley, A. (1975). *Musical ability in children and its measurement.* London: Harrap.
Colwell, R. (1970). *The evaluation of music teaching and learning.* Englewood Cliffs, NJ: Prentice Hall.
Davies, J. (1978). *The psychology of music.* Stanford: Stanford University Press.
Dowling, W.J., & Harwood, D.L. (1986). *Music cognition.* Orlando: Academic Press.
Edmundson, H.S. (1954). *The Seashore Measures of Musical Talents as a prognostic guide in language rehabilitation for persons with aphasia.* Unpublished doctoral dissertation, University of Michigan, Ann Arbor.
Farnsworth, P.R. (1931). An historical, critical, and experimental study of the Seashore-Kwalwasser Test Battery. *Genetic Psychology Monographs, 9,* 291–393.
Horn, J.L., & Stanov, L. (1982). Auditory and visual factors of intelligence. *Intelligence, 6,* 165–185.
Larson, W.S. (1938). Practical experience with music tests. *Music Educators Journal, 24*(31), 68–74.

Leblanc, G. (1954). *Music talent quiz* (E.C. Moore, Ed.). Kenosha, WI: G. Leblanc Corporation.

Lehman, P. (1968). *Tests and measurements in music.* Englewood Cliffs, NJ: Prentice Hall.

Lundin, R.W. (1949). Development and evaluation of a set of musical ability tests. *Psychological Monographs, 63*(10), 13.

Lundin, R.W. (1985). *An objective psychology of music* (3rd ed.). Malibar, FL: Robert E. Krieger.

McCreey, C.L. (1937). *Advanced Rhythm and Pitch Test.* Chicago: Lyons Band Instrument Co.

McLeish, J. (1950). The validation of Seashore's Measures of Musical Talent by factorial methods. *British Journal of Psychology, 3,* 129–140.

Michel, P. (1971). *Musikalische fahigkeiten und fertigkeiten.* Leipzig: Breitkoph and Hartel.

Mursell, J.L. (1932). Measuring musical ability and achievement. *Journal of Educational Research, 25,* 116–126.

Mursell, J. (1937). *The psychology of music.* New York: Norton Publishers.

Olds, F.E. (n.d.) *Music Talent Test.* Chicago, IL: Olds and Sons, Inc.

Radocy, R., & Boyle, J.D. (1979). *Psychological foundations of musical behavior.* Springfield, IL: Charles C. Thomas.

Révész, G. (1954). *Introduction to the psychology of music.* Norman: University of Oklahoma Press.

Seashore, C.E. (1919). *The psychology of musical talent.* Boston: Silver Burdett.

Seashore, C.E. (1935). Improvability in pitch discrimination. *Psychological Bulletin, 32,* 545.

Seashore, C., Lewis, D., & Saetzeit, J. (1960). *Manual-Seashore Measures of Musical Talents.* New York: The Psychological Corporation.

Serafine, M.L. (1988). *Music as cognition: The development of thought as sound.* New York: Columbia University Press.

Shuter-Dyson, R. & Gabriel, C. (1981). *The psychology of musical ability* (2nd ed.). London: Methuen.

Stanton, H.M. (1953). *Musical capacity measures of children repeated after musical training* (University of Iowa Studies: Series on Aims and Progress of Research, No. 259). Iowa City: University of Iowa.

Stanton, H.M. (1935). The measurement of musical talent. *University of Iowa Studies in the Psychology of Music, 2.*

Super, D.E. (1949). *Appraising vocational fitness by means of psychological tests.* New York: Harper & Brothers.

Tilson, L.M. (1941). *Tilson-Gretsch Musical Aptitude Test.* Chicago, IL: The Fred Gretsch Mfg. Company.

Tilson, L.M. (1940–41). A study of the prognostic value of the Tilson-Gretsch Tests for Musical Aptitude. *Teachers College Journal, 12,* 110–112.

Whybrew, W.E. (1971). *Measurement and evaluation in music.* Dubuque, IA: William C. Brown.

Wilson, W.E. (1950). *Use of the Seashore Measures of Musical Talent in the prediction of certain academic grades for music students at the Pennsylvania State College.* Unpublished master's thesis, Pennsylvania State University, College Park.

Wyatt, R.F. (1945). Improvability of pitch discrimination. *Psychological Monographs, 58,* 1–58.

Kenneth D. Hopkins, Ph.D.

Professor of Research and Evaluation Methodology, University of Colorado, Boulder, Colorado.

SRA ACHIEVEMENT SERIES, FORMS 1-2

Robert A. Naslund, Louis P. Thorpe, and D. Welty Lefever. Chicago, Illinois: Science Research Associates, Inc.

Introduction

The SRA Achievement Series (SRAAS) Forms 1–2 is designed to assess a student's general scholastic achievement in reading, math, language, science, and social studies. The SRAAS, like several other achievement batteries, requires more than 100 separate tests (and composites) because it consists of all core curricular content areas for all grade (K-12) levels. In addition, an optional academic ability test, the Educational Ability Series (EAS) that was co-normed with the SRAAS, compounds the task. Naturally in such an array of tests there will be considerable differences in quality.

Forms 1 and 2 of the SRAAS represent the fourth edition of one of several long-standing batteries of standardized achievement tests. The SRAAS tests are organized into eight grade level combinations: 1) A (K.5–1.5); 2) B (1.5–2.5); 3) C (2.5–3.5); 4) D (3.5–4.5); 5) E (4.5–6.5); 6) F (6.0–8.5); 7) G (8.0–10.5); and 8) H (9.0–12.9). The current edition of the SRAAS introduces two new levels, one at each grade level extreme: Level A is a readiness test and level H extends the scope to include Grades 9–12, thus making the SRAAS parallel with its major standardized achievement test battery competitors. The SRAAS test materials consist of a User's Guide, a norms booklet, and four technical reports, as well as an "examiner's manual" for each of the eight levels.

Reading and Mathematics tests appear at all levels of the SRAAS; Language Arts tests are introduced at level C; Reference Materials, Social Studies, Science tests start with level E; and Applied Skills (an additional composite score based on 60 items drawn from five of the other achievement tests) is a new composite score available only for the high school level (H). The number of items and the required testing time for administering all the available achievement tests at levels A-H varies from 140 items and 2 hours (level A) to 410 items and 3.6 hours (levels E-G). If the EAS, the optional companion scholastic ability test, is included an additional 30 minutes of testing time is required.

Unlike the new editions of many standardized achievement batteries, the current edition of the SRAAS represents a major revision. All of the approximately 5,000 items for the two forms of various achievement areas for the eight levels are new; they were selected after extensive field testing of students in almost 1,000 classes in 38 states using approximately 12,000 items.

The items appear to have been developed with appropriate attention to common United States curricula subject-matter specifications. As with other achievement batteries, the lack of uniformity in the science and social studies curricula among districts and states attenuates the content validity for these tests compared with measures of reading, math, and language arts (Hopkins, George, & Williams, 1985). Likewise, the lack of communality in the high school curricula in the United States causes the achievement tests in standardized test batteries, like level H of the SRAAS, to require virtually nothing that is unique to the high school curriculum (e.g., no algebra is required for any math item); only middle school language arts, general science, and social studies courses are needed. Clearly, standardized achievement tests must be based on the core curriculum and common objectives, which currently do not exist in American high schools. Consequently, as with other standardized achievement test batteries (Hopkins, Stanley, & Hopkins, in press), the content validity of the high school level of the SRAAS is quite limited. One can hardly be surprised that most high school principals and teachers have little enthusiasm (especially if they actually examine the items) for tests that really only represent the pre-high school curriculum.

The content validity of the SRAAS for levels A-G appears to be excellent in Reading and Mathematics. The content validity of the Language Arts tests has limited scope (i.e., mechanics, grammar, and spelling) but otherwise appears to be very good (unfortunately, it is not practical to have a direct measure of the second "R" in standardized test batteries). Nevertheless, potential test users need to know which of the important core objectives are not assessed by the SRAAS to be fully aware of what the SRAAS does, and does not, assess. Unlike several of its competitors, at the early test levels (A-C), the SRAAS does include a measure of the important curricular objective of Listen Comprehension (even if it is with limited success).

Like most of its competitors, the promotional literature for the SRAAS seems excessive in some of its claims. The SRAAS is clearly norm-referenced in design, yet claims to have "criterion-referenced features" (which are really only item clusters that vary greatly in difficulty; some item subsets have a national mean of less than 40%, while the average for others is more than 80%). Objectives-referenced or domain-referenced are more appropriate descriptors. In some of the publisher's promotional materials, other ambitious and unfounded claims include "bias free . . . test content is fair to all students" and "test levels correspond to the actual sequence of skill development in your classroom."

Practical Applications/Uses

The SRAAS has exceptionally useful feedback forms for communicating the performance of an individual or group. The *Individual Skills Profile* gives the student's performance at several different levels of aggregation, from item clusters within each of the various content areas, to the Composite score for the entire test (e.g., in Reading Vocabulary there are item subsets for "Literal Meanings" and "Nonliteral Meanings"). For each of these item clusters, the performance of the student (percent correct) is given, along with the percent of questions answered correctly by the national norm group. Although the number of items in some of the clusters is too small to yield reliable inferences (no reliability data are given at this level of reporting specificity), the item clusters do provide clues for a more diagnostic appraisal. Strangely, the conventional standard error of measurement is *not* employed for confidence bands, but rather the archaic probable error of measurement (PE $\approx .67\sigma_\epsilon$); the use of PE gives the illusion of greater precision, especially when one is accustomed to using .68 confidence bands for true scores. The fact that the PE is employed is easily missed in the SRAAS literature (clarified only in Technical Report #2). Users are told that if the confidence bands do not overlap, that a true difference is likely, yet the actual probability of a type-I based on non-overlapping .50 confidence intervals is greater than .3 (and approximately double what it is when the conventional standard error bands are used).

The Group Skills Profile can be especially useful, providing the same information as the Individual Skills Profile, but for the class, school, or district as a whole. Naturally the diagnostic profile for a group has much greater measurement precision than that for an individual. Even greater specificity is allowed by the Group Item Analysis report, which gives the proportion of correct answers for the group on each item, together with the national proportions. The Group Item Analysis has its greatest usefulness at the district level.

To illustrate the various levels of reporting performance, suppose for example a district's performance is below expectation in mathematics: 1) the performance can be examined at a less global level—Math Concept, Math Computation, and Math Problem Solving; 2) the results can be examined within Math Computation (or the other subtests) on each of the 3–7 item clusters, and 3) the local versus national performance could be examined on the individual items to see if the deficit is evident on all items within a cluster.

A noteworthy feature of the SRAAS is that both clinical and statistical procedures were used to minimize sex and ethnic item bias. Items ("outliers") with large differences in normalized z-scores (normalized z-scores obtained by transforming within-group item difficulties) were considered biased. The particular items that met the statistical bias criterion varied greatly depending on whether the contrasting groups were male-female, majority-black, or majority-Hispanic. Almost all items meeting the bias criterion were eliminated. On the final forms fewer than 1% of the item were biased; the retained items were needed to prevent loss of content validity ("no other items were acceptable in terms of statistical or content criteria"; Technical Report No. 3, p. 45).

Technical Aspects

Unfortunately the technical information for the SRAAS is scattered among four separate technical reports (plus a fifth booklet that contains norm and conversions tables); it is often a time-consuming and frustrating task to locate the particular information that is needed.

The reliability data for the SRAAS are impressive. Internal consistency estimates rarely fall below .80 (except for Listening Comprehension, which obviously needs more items and developmental work, especially for students in Grades 2 and above where four of the reliability estimates fall below .60).

The SRAAS makes the common error of viewing the reliability of raw scores as the same as for scores that are nonlinear transformations of raw scores (e.g., Growth Scale Values and Grade Equivalents). The assessment of reliability should always be in the metric to be used in interpretation (or a linear transformation thereof), which is almost never raw scores for norm-referenced tests. The reliability estimates provided are not seriously in error because of this incongruity (raw scores typically correlate in the .90s with GSV or GE scores); nevertheless the method of estimating reliability employed was slightly off-target (as is common).

Internal-consistency reliability estimates can be seriously inflated if tests are speeded; commendably, the SRAAS (unlike most of its competitors) provides data on the extent of speededness (the percent of examinees who attempt at least 90% of the items) for the various tests at each of the levels to be evaluated. With few exceptions, the tests appear to be primarily power tests, and in this reviewer's best professional judgment probably more so than most other standardized achievement batteries. Even so, those students who are extremely slow-working and not inclined to guess at will obtain scores much below their "ability twins" who work quickly and have the gambling response style. Such irrelevant discrepancies could be reduced by making the correction-for-chance formula standard; the SRAAS (like most of its competitors) ignores the problems caused by unattempted items.

The SRAAS is to be commended for including some alternate form reliability estimates, even though these data are limited. The data are based on samples from 72 to 246 students depending on the A-H level represented. In spite of their limitations, the data are sufficient to confirm that the internal-consistency estimates are not seriously inflated (Listening Comprehension measures continues to be outliers, with reliability estimates ranging from only .45 to .66).

One-year stability coefficients (spring-to-spring, using alternate forms) are also provided for Grades 3–10 for various SRAAS tests (levels D-H). The coefficients are extremely high for the Composite (.88 and above) and for total scores in Reading, Math, and Language Arts (above .78). The stability coefficients for the Reference Materials, Social Studies, and Science measures are lower, but still substantial.

Data are provided that demonstrate that the SRAAS tests have substantial criterion-related validity when course grades are used as criteria, although there is much variation in the coefficients from sample to sample. Very high correlations are also found for SRAAS tests with various other related standardized tests (Iowa Tests of Basic Skills [ITBS], Metropolitan Achievement Tests [MAT], Comprehensive Tests of Basic Skills [CTBS], etc.), although the samples are often very small and of uncertain representativeness.

Of more fundamental importance, however, is one of the criteria that the SRAAS (and other standardized achievement tests) use for item selection—the correlation of item difficulty with grade level (grade differentiation). When the purpose of an achievement test is to proportionately represent the curricular content and objectives, how can grade differentiation per se be justified for item selection? Why should discriminating (among students) items be excluded just because their success rate does not change substantially for adjacent grades? Suppose for example, the ability to use the metric system is an instructional objective at Grades 4, 5, and 6, but due to lack of time or judged importance is either ignored or ineffectively taught at the three grade levels; the criterion of grade-differentiation might exclude these items because there was little correlation between performance on these items with grade level. If these items are eliminated, the resulting tests not only have a nonrepresentative set of objectives represented, but fail in one of their purposes of identifying topic/areas/skills in need of improvement. The important suggestions of Buros (1977) have not been heeded, not only by the SRAAS, but its competitors as well. Naturally it is very tempting for commercial test publishers to include items that exaggerate the amount of growth between grade levels. Unfortunately, the proportion of items that were eliminated because of this criterion is not reported.

Like its competitors, the SRAAS provides several alternative scales in which test performance can be expressed: 1) Growth Scale Value (GSV); 2) Grade Equivalents (GE); 3) Stanines, National Percentiles (for first and seventh months of the school year); and 4) NCE (from percentiles). The rationale and procedures for the GSV are wholly inadequate and the GSV scores are virtually uninterpretable. For example, the median GSV at Grade 4.1 varies from 240 to 300 depending on the test; at Grade 5.1 the median GSV scores vary from 259 to 304. Unfortunately, test users are not told that it is not their fault if they cannot make sense of the GSV scores.

The national percentile for reading and other curricular areas for a given GSV or GE score is the same regardless of the test level taken. The reader is told that if content shifts dramatically between levels, this (equivalence) assumption becomes questionable, which often appears to be the case. For example, a GE score for Total Reading as high as 5.3 can be obtained on the readiness test (level A) and as low as 2.2 on level H! Data to support this implicit claim of equivalence of GE (and GSV) scores across grades and levels is not provided.

Percentiles are converted to normalized NCEs without any discussion about the rationale for this procrustean normalization, or any consideration of the shapes of the empirical distributions. Because the percentiles are available only for the first and seventh school months, error will be increased if the SRAAS is given at other times.

Unfortunately, skewness and kurtosis indices for the various distribution are absent, an unnecessary lacuna in the computer era. This information is especially relevant when normalization procedures are involved.

Although not presented as norms per se, distribution information (10th, 25th, 50th, 75th, and 90th percentiles) is given on each test and level separately for males and females, and for Hispanics, blacks, and whites. The small number of Hispanic students indicates that in several instances these values can be viewed only as rough estimates of corresponding parameters. Unfortunately the reader is not informed as to whether these percentiles are for fall or spring norms.

The SRAAS was standardized in both the fall and spring 1978—a very desirable strategy that reduces interpolation error. Although a three-stage sampling design was employed (geographical region, district, and school within district), many serious questions remain about the representativeness of the norms. The proportions of districts/schools refusing to participate is not reported, nor is the reader told how they were replaced. It is not clear how schools within a district were selected. These omissions are significant impediments to making judgments about the representativeness of the norms. Norms are also provided for subgroups of schools or districts that lack clear definition; for example, "large districts" are districts with 50,000 or more students and "low SES schools" are even more ambiguous (who knows whether a given school has 25% or more of its students below the poverty line as defined by the "Orshansky Poverty Indicator?"). These special norms are not given in any of the technical booklets. The User's Guide makes appropriate suggestions for out-of-level testing for very low-achieving classes, but the empirical consequences in terms of the validity of normative data are uncertain.

A comprehensive analysis of the 1978 SRAAS norms, however, seems of uncertain value because a single-sheet promotional piece that includes this classic understatement accompanies current materials:

> We have made two major improvements to the Achievement test since this booklet was written; one was an update of the norms. . . . In the fall of 1983 and spring of 1984, we standardized a new norm-referenced test entitled SRA Survey of Basic Skills. This test also measures achievement in kindergarten through 12th grade. During the fall standardization, we equated the SRA Achievement series test to the SRA Survey of Basic Skills, so that the norms you are now receiving are based on the norm group of fall of 1983 and spring of 1984 rather than the previous standardization of 1978.

Thus, it appears that all of the normative information from the 1978 standardization and all of the technical normative information presented in the five booklets has been superceded by equating (equipercentile?) with the SRA Survey of Basic Skills. Consequently, the already considerable uncertainly about the representativeness of the SRAAS norms (especially the "large district," non-public schools, and low SES schools) is magnified.

Although not a integral part of the SRAAS, the Educational Ability Series (EAS) is a coordinated set of eight difficulty levels (A-H) of a general ability tests that "provides an estimate of general learning ability for students in grades K-12." (Users Guide, p. 24) Its purpose is to allow a comparison of an examinee's academic performance with his or her performance on the EAS, the items of which "are far more independent of curriculum content than are the achievement test items." (User's Guide, p. 24). The administration time of the EAS is very short (30 minutes) and composed of both verbal and nonverbal components. The technical reports are lacking in information about the development of the EAS. Its content and construct validity appear quite limited (e.g., as many as 25% of the items could just as well have appeared in a reading vocabulary test). The "jingle" fallacy is alive and well.

The EAS yields an EAS quotient which "is a standard-score scale with a mean of 100 at kindergarten level and increases by 0.5 each grade level year until the end of grade 10 when it is 105.0. Then it increases to 107.0 by the end of grade 11 and 108.0 by the end of grade 12. The standard deviation is 16" (User's Guide, p. 24). Any supporting rationale for this bizarre scale is missing. Notice that it is grade-based rather than age-based (like other similar measures) and has a constant standard deviation but a rising mean. Parents and teachers will likely be quite confused when they see dramatic increases in a nonpromoted pupil's EAS quotient and associated percentile rank. A pupil's age is not a factor in defining the EAS quotient.

The EAS is not used to obtain statistically based expectancy scores for the SRAAS test, but only as a backdrop for interpretation. Unfortunately, non-overlapping PE (probably error) percentile bands (previously discussed) are the recommended criterion for a significance difference, a procedure that does not take the regression effect into account. Its chief virtue appears that it only requires 30 minutes of testing time.

Critique

The construct validity of the EAS is very limited, and inferior to the companion measures of most other standardized achievement tests. With an improved EAS and better norming, the SRAAS could stand with the very best of the current standardized achievement test batteries.

References

Buros, O.K. (1977). Fifty years in testing: Some reminiscences, criticisms, and suggestions. *Educational Researcher, 6,* 9–15.

Hopkins, K.D., Stanley, J.D., & Hopkins, B.R. (in press). *Educational and psychological measurement and evaluation* (7th ed.). Englewood Cliffs, NJ: Prentice-Hall.

Hopkins, K.D., George, C.A., & Williams, D.D. (1985). The concurrent validity of standardized achievement tests by content area using teachers' ratings as criteria. *Journal of Educational Measurement, 22,* 177–182.

Robertson, G.J. (1985). Review of the SRA Achievement Series. In J.V. Mitchell, Jr. (Ed.), *The ninth mental measurements yearbook* (pp. 1430–1434). Lincoln, NE: Buros Institute.

Michael Ayers, Ph.D.
Clinical Psychologist, Section of Neuropsychology, Department of Neurosurgery, HCA-Presbyterian Hospital, Oklahoma City, Oklahoma.

Neil H. Pliskin, Ph.D.
Postdoctoral Fellow in Clinical Neuropsychology, University of Oklahoma Health Sciences Center, Oklahoma City, Oklahoma.

STIMULUS RECOGNITION TEST

T. L. Brink, James Bryant, Mary Lou Catalano, Connie Janakes, and Charmaine Oliveira. San Carlos, California: T. L. Brink, Ph.D.

Introduction

The Stimulus Recognition Test (SRT) was developed by T. L. Brink, James Bryant, Mary Lou Catalano, Connie Janakes, and Charmaine Oliveira in 1979 as a rapid and convenient assessment instrument to test aged senile confusion due to Organic Brain Syndrome (OBS). The authors base the SRT on the assumption that deficiencies in auditory and visual recognition memory have potential as screening factors for the presence and severity of dementia.

The primary researcher involved in the development of the SRT is T. L. Brink, editor of the *Clinical Gerontologist*. The *Clinical Gerontologist* is a psychological journal designed to meet the needs of mental health professionals and practitioners who deal with the geriatric or aged population. Dr. Brink is on the faculty of the Western Graduate School of Psychology and the clinical faculty of the Psychiatric Department of Stanford University School of Medicine. His long list of credits includes the authorship of over 200 reviews and articles for medical and psychological journals. Most notable is his expertise and specialization in geriatric, gerontology, dementia, and delirium. He is the author of *Geriatric Psychotherapy* published by Human Science Press in 1979.

The SRT consists of 29 cards that the purchaser of the test prepares. Each card should be 4" × 6", with the letters and numbers written in a ¼" black line approximately 3" high. In essence, the SRT consists of one page that provides directions for preparing the 29 test cards, directions for administration, scoring, and a brief list of references.

Practical Applications/Uses

Although the SRT was designed to be brief and easy to administer in screening elderly individuals for dementia, this test could also be easily administered to the brain-injured population and may have utility for blind and deaf individuals as well.

The SRT consists of 10 trials involving auditory and visual stimuli. The first seven trials involve the presentation of between three to five cards, each with a different combination of letters or numbers. Test items for the first seven cards range from a single letter (e.g., *s*), to strings of four digits (e.g., *1146*). The last three trials use auditory stimuli only and range from three to five words per trial. The simplest items on the auditory recognition section consist of three-letter words (e.g., *hat*) and the most complex item involves recognition of larger words (e.g., *honeycomb*).

The SRT may be administered in a large number of settings, the essential re quirement being an individual testing format that is free from distractibility. The simplicity of the SRT allows for a potentially wide range of professionals to admin- ister this test. The authors note that even a layperson "with minimal knowledge of test administration" could easily administer the SRT. Allowing time for repeat instructions, the total time of the SRT should be no longer than 10 minutes.

The SRT is administered in one session with all 10 trials given in succession. The examiner shows the patient the first card and asks the name of the letter/number on the card, establishing whether the patient can clearly see/hear the letter. The exam- iner then explains that other cards with letters/numbers will be shown, but the patient must remember the first card and must stop the examiner either by saying "stop" or "that's the one" or by touching the card. After selecting one of the signals, the examiner practices the procedure with the patient on the first card. The exam- iner then explains that the card will appear again and when it does the patient is to give the signal of recognition, but must not give the signal for any other card dis- played. Each card is shown for approximately 2 seconds before going on to the next one. If no signal is given when the initial card is presented or if an incorrect identi- fication is made, the trial is scored as a fail. A trial is scored correct only if the patient correctly identifies the initial "target" card and no other. The instructions are to be given only once at the beginning of the trial; the examiner should not give any response to the patient's questions during the testing procedure. All trials pro- ceed in this manner, with a *complete repetition of the instruction* at the beginning of each trial.

As with other aspects of the SRT, scoring is quite simple and involves a 1–10 point range. The authors suggest that when 8–10 trials are passed, the examiner should "assume" the patient is lucid and alert. When 5–7 trials are passed, "assume mild dementia." When 3–4 trials are passed, "assume moderate dementia," and finally, when 2 or less are passed, "assume severe dementia." False positives are more likely to be observed in individuals with limited formal education as well as individuals who are deaf, blind, or severely depressed.

Technical Aspects

In attempting to validate the SRT, the authors thought it was important to dis- tinguish between two different measures of retention-recall that related to normal aging as opposed to recognition related to organic brain syndrome (OBS). Thus, the authors felt a valid test assessing the symptoms of OBS in geriatric patients should focus on short-term information processing rather than on sensory or long- term memory. Therefore, the SRT is designed to assess what the authors consider current short-term memory. The examiner presents a stimulus on which the patient will be tested shortly after, but not before several seconds have erased the original sensory memory trace.

In developing the SRT, the authors (Brink, Bryant, Catalano, Janakes, & Oliveira, 1979) visited four extended care facilities. They assembled the staff at these facilities and requested that the staff rate patients in one of two categories, being "consistently lucid and alert" or "consistently confused." The staff members were asked to take "a mental walk" around their facility and rate any of the patients fitting these categories. Classifications that were not unanimous were not utilized. Of the 273 total patients from all four facilities, a final sample of 62 cases was derived, of which 18 patients were rated as lucid and alert and 33 were rated as confused. In addition to staff ratings, patients in both categories were administered the Face-Hand Test (FHT) and the Mental Status Questionnaire (MSQ), both being scored on a 0–10 range.

Each patient then was given 17 trials in stimulus recognition. Each trial consisted of a new group of stimuli. Whereas some groups had numbers (e.g., 3,7,5), other groups were administered shapes, colors, objects, words, letters, digits, and questions from the MSQ. All stimuli involved either a verbal or visual presentation. The administration procedures were essentially identical to the current Stimulus Recognition Test.

Of the 17 trials of the initial Stimulus Recognition Test, 10 were selected to form the current test. Items selected to establish the SRT were based on ability to distinguish between the lucid and alert patients and those who had been designated as confused. Each test selected was based on its ability to discriminate below the .001 level. The same process was repeated for the FHT scores and the MSQ scores. A t-test was used to compute statistical significance on each item for both the MSQ and FHT ($p < .005$). A score range of 1–10 was possible for all three tests.

T-test analysis was performed to demonstrate the capabilities of the MSQ, FHT, and SRT in separating patients rated as lucid and alert from those rated as confused. Finally, each patient's score on any one test was compared to his scores on the other two tests. Using Pearson product moment correlation coefficient and a rank difference correlation coefficients, correlational statistical analysis reveals the SRT correlates .8 with staff ratings, the Face-Hand Test, and the Mental Status Questionnaire. The authors interpret these results as encouraging evidence for the utility of the SRT in differentiating between dementia and confusion in elderly institutionalized patients. Although the SRT may have some face validity, research addressing other aspects of validity and reliability is lacking. In essence, the SRT provides no scientifically sound research addressing reliability or validity.

Critique

The test authors designed the SRT to serve as an easily administered, brief screening instrument to detect the presence of senile confusion and mental deterioration in elderly populations. The SRT is based on the premise that cognitive deficits associated with organic brain syndromes can be differentiated from normal age decrements through examination of recognition as opposed to recall procedures, a paradigm considered by some as resistant to age-related changes in mental abilities (Schoenfeld & Robertson, 1966). The authors propose using a similar recognition memory format for differentiating of clinically significant confusional states brought on by OBS from normal aging. Senile confusional states are thought to represent a deficit in short-term information processing, which other screening measures cited by the authors as widely used in geriatric populations do not adequately assess. However, significant problems exist in test conceptualization, construction, and diagnostic validity that call into question the usefulness of the SRT as a screening tool.

The construct validity of the SRT is based on a 1966 finding that recognition memory procedures are resistant to normal age-related changes and can, therefore, distinguish abnormal OBS-related states. This viewpoint is not representative of contemporary thought regarding memory dysfunction in pathological populations. A distinction has been made between effortful and automatic processing as an explanation for recall/recognition performance differences; recall requires more effortful processing and retrieval. It is important to note, however, that patients with Alzheimer's disease tend to show deficits in both types of processing (Weingartner, Grafman, Boulette, Kaye, & Martin, 1983), suggesting that the SRT may not measure what it purports to. In fact, the SRT requires adequate sustained attention for successful performance that patients experiencing senile confusion may lack.

There are several problems with the test structure itself. Identification of the target stimulus card through both verbal and gestural means places a special emphasis on the card not present for distractor stimuli. This allows the target stimulus to be encoded through multiple modalities (i.e., special emphasis). Some form of nonverbal designation should be employed after the initial trial. Further, the fact that the first item in each array is designated as the target allows for temporal encoding of the stimuli after several trials; that is, the subject may indirectly learn that the first item repeated will always be the designated item. Another problem related to test structure involves the simplistic and gross nature of the SRT. In some respects, the SRT is analogous to the Trails A test from Halstead's (1947) Trail Making Test, in that the easiness of the task allows for a definitive opinion regarding organicity, although one trades off the ability to detect more subtle organic impairments. On a more positive note, the current strategy does eliminate the problem of false alarms, shown to be a critical factor in recognition memory tasks (Miller, 1975).

The SRT provides no normative information, and research addressing reliability and validity are minimal. Comparison of the SRT to the MSQ and FHT was conducted in an extended care population as detailed in the Technical Aspects section of this review (Brink et al, 1979). However, there are significant problems pertaining to group membership that must be considered questionable. The investigators report that based on staff consensus, test differences were analyzed between patients designated as "lucid and alert" ($n = 18$) and "consistently confused" ($n = 33$) in nursing care settings. One must question the nature of lucid and alert patients residing in extended care facilities. Given the ease of the current test format, the reviewers believe that the SRT will have poor discriminative validity beyond serving as a gross measure of confusion. If a patient fails one item on the test, it should almost be considered pathognomic. Yet, the "lucid and alert" group had a mean of only 7.6 trials correct (out of 10). Further, the high intercorrelations reported between the SRT, MSQ, and FHT could also be interpreted to reflect the attentional factor required with these tasks.

In conclusion, the authors of the SRT attempt to screen for senile confusion related to OBS in the elderly. The SRT does not reliably accomplish this task beyond providing a gross discrimination that would be apparent through any brief contact with the patient by a trained professional. Brief cognitive screening can be administered easily and accomplished reliably through measures such as the Mini-Mental State Exam (Folstein, Folstein, & McHugh, 1975), which assesses the areas of orientation, attention, abstraction, short-term memory, and visuo-construction in a short period of time. Furthermore, it is unclear why the authors of the SRT selected the MSQ and FHT for correlational analysis. Correlation analysis utilizing well-documented and normed tests for dementia such as the Fuld Object Memory Evaluation (Fuld, 1984) and WAIS-R (Wechsler, 1981) profile analysis would be good alternatives. The pattern of WAIS-R subtest scores and the discrepancy between the right hemisphere performance scores and left hemisphere verbal scores provided good information in differentiating normal decline associated with aging and pseudodementia. Although the authors are to be commended for their efforts and desires to create a simple and easy-to-administer screening instrument for dementia, clearly more research addressing reliability and validity is warranted. Ideally, such research would utilize other well-normed tests of dementia as well as provide a sound scientific approach.

References

Brink, T.L. (1979). *Geriatric psychotherapy.* New York: Human Science Press.

Brink, T.L., Bryant, J., Catalano, M.L., Janakes, C., & Oliveira, C. (1979). Senile confusion: Assessment with a new stimulus recognition test. *Journal of the American Geriatrics Society, 27,* (3), 126–129.

Folstein, M.F., Folstein, S.E., & McHugh, P.R. (1975). Mini-Mental State: A practical method for grading the cognitive state of patients for the clinician. *Journal of Psychiatric Research, 12,* 189–198.

Fuld, P.A. (1984). Test profile of cholinergic dysfunction and of Alzheimer-type dementia. *Journal of Clinical Neuropsychology, 6,* 380–392.

Halstead, W.C. (1947). *Brain and intelligence.* Chicago: University of Chicago Press.

Miller, E. (1975). Impaired recall in the memory disturbance of presenile dementia. *British Journal of Social and Clinical Psychology, 14*(1), 73–79.

Schoenfeld, D., & Robertson, E.H. (1966). Memory storage and aging. *Canadian Journal of Psychology, 20,* 228.

Wechsler, D. (1981). *Wechsler Adult Intelligence Scale-Revised.* San Antonio, TX: The Psychological Corporation.

Weingartner, H., Grafman, J., Boulette, W., Kaye, W., & Martin, P.R. (1983). Forms of memory failure. *Science, 221,* 380–382.

Victor S. Alpher, Ph.D.

Assistant Professor of Psychology, University of Tennessee-Knoxville, Knoxville, Tennessee.

STRUCTURAL ANALYSIS OF SOCIAL BEHAVIOR

Lorna Smith Benjamin. Madison, Wisconsin: Intrex Interpersonal Institute.

Introduction

The Structural Analysis of Social Behavior (SASB) is designed to measure interpersonal and intraspychic domains. Comprehensive attempts to integrate understanding of social and interpersonal behavior with these domains could be expected to be complex. Certainly any system that affords the possibility of measurement is worth a close look, for there have been relatively few to make the attempt. The SASB emerges as one comprehensive system that is parsimonious without sacrificing understanding of complexities.

Lorna Smith Benjamin began developing SASB during the early 1960s at the University of Wisconsin Medical School with "only books, paper, pencil, ideas, and about $300 a year in computer time" (Benjamin, 1974, p. 123). As a clinical psychologist with a strong background in psychometrics and mathematics, she was interested in developing a model of interpersonal and intrapsychic space that would "be concrete enough to be tested and proven wrong, yet abstract enough to have broad and meaningful applications" (Benjamin, 1974, p. 123). In January, 1988, Dr. Benjamin assumed a new position as Professor of Psychology at the University of Utah in Salt Lake City.

Interpersonal theory traces its roots back to propositions of Harry Stack Sullivan (1953). A fundamental tenet involves the notion that the self-concept is grounded in the appraisals of significant others during development. Benjamin has taken this rather static concept and developed a coherent and dynamic model of interpersonal behavior and intrapsychic functioning, along with a sensitive and usable measurement technology.

Benjamin also incorporates some of the personological ideas of Henry A. Murray (1938). Specifically, this involves the distinction between alpha press and beta press, that is, between how the world "really is" versus how the subject perceives it. Murray believed that prediction of behavior would be more accurate if beta press, or "how the person sees the world," is taken into account. SASB attempts to measure interpersonal and intrapsychic aspects of the beta press.

Interpersonal measurement models have been developed by Timothy Leary and his colleagues (see Leary, 1957) as well as Lorr and McNair (1963), Schaefer (1965), and Kiesler (1983). Wiggins (1982) has provided a detailed comparison of these models. However, none of the previous models attempts to encompass the range of phenomena that can be integrated by SASB.

SASB is not simply one test. Rather, it is a system for conceptualizing and analyzing interpersonal relations and for relating these phenomena to the development and maintenance of the self-concept. It can be used rigorously as a research tool at a fine-grained level of analysis (e.g., the analogue coding method) and can also be used with somewhat greater degrees of freedom as a tool to support exploration of the interpersonal and intrapsychic domains in the clinical setting.

SASB reduces the interpersonal and intrapsychic domains to three essential variables: Focus, Affiliation, and Interdependence (see Figure 1).

Focus involves three circumplex "surfaces" involving either transitive action directed from the other to the subject (Other surface), an intransitive state of the subject (Self surface), or transitive action directed at the self by the subject (Introject surface). Theoretically, any transaction between two interactants can be classified on one of these surfaces.

Each surface is comprised of two bipolar orthogonal axes, Affiliation-Disaffiliation (abscissa) and Independence-Interdependence (ordinate). The vertical (ordinate) axis has different anchor points depending on the nature of the focus. Enmeshed or highly interdependent transactions are placed in the lower half of each surface; autonomous or independent transactions are placed in the upper half.

Coding on the three dimensions makes it possible to generate 108 transaction codes (36 for each surface) from three ratings in the full SASB model. In addition, Benjamin has developed empirically derived clusters, resulting in 24 categories (8 for each surface). Short descriptors of the 108 category codes are depicted in Figure 2 (see Benjamin, 1984, for full descriptors). The cluster model is shown in Figure 3.

Prior to 1986, SASB was available in a long form (SASB-LF) that required up to several hours to complete one battery (Intrex Interpersonal Institute, 1983). The SASB-LF was used in research and in clinical practice by Dr. Benjamin and her associates. During the mid-1980s Dr. Benjamin began introducing SASB to larger clinical audiences through workshops sponsored by The Psychological Associates (P.O. Box 53592, Fayetteville, North Carolina, 29305). A series of videotapes of seminars on the use of the self-report instruments, as well as the research coding procedures based on the structural model, are available from Intrex Interpersonal Institute (P.O. Box 55218, Madison, Wisconsin, 53705).

As of October, 1987, clinical users of the Intrex Report from an administration of SASB-SF or SASB-LF must attend one of Dr. Benjamin's one-day workshops. Potential users qualified to take these courses to satisfy the requirement include 1) licensed psychologists; 2) psychiatrists; 3) physicians with one year of postgraduate training in psychiatry; and 4) individuals permitted by law in their respective states to practice psychotherapy. Also, the user must have some familiarity and documented formal clinical training in some form of psychoanalytic object relations theory. This is necessary to provide an appropriate developmental context for interpreting the Intrex Report and developing sound SASB-based clinical interventions. Further information, including the *SASB Short Form User's Manual* (Intrex Interpersonal Institute, 1987), can be obtained directly from Intrex Interpersonal Institute, and users who plan to use the SASB self-report questionnaires clinically should write directly to the institute.

The SASB Short Form (SASB-SF) was introduced by Dr. Benjamin through

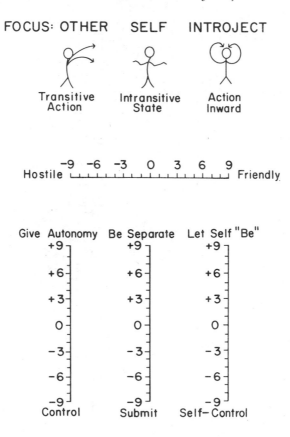

Fig. 1. The three dimensions of interpersonal space as hypothesized by the SASB model are Focus (stick figures), Affiliation (horizontal 18-point scale), and Interdependence (vertical 18-point scales). Anchor points on the interdependence scales differ depending on focus, and are shown in the figure aligned underneath the respective three types of focus. After just three judgments are made about Focus, Affiliation, and Interdependence, the SASB model automatically generates the 108 qualitatively different categories shown in Figure 2. From L.S. Benjamin, "Adding social and intrapsychic descriptors to Axis I of DSM-III" in T. Millon and G. Klerman (Eds.), *Contemporary issues in psychopathology*. Reprinted by permission. Copyright 1986, The Guilford Press.

Intrex Interpersonal Institute in late 1987. As of mid-1988 two parallel versions of the SASB-SF are available for clinical use. SASB-LF and SASB-SF were developed to generate classifications of transactions *from the rater's point of view* through the method of self-report. Test items on the SASB-LF generate classifications of transactions on the full 108-category model. Test items on the SASB-SF generate classifications on the 24-category cluster model.

A subject completing the SASB-SF may complete what is called the Standard Series of ratings. This involves a sequence of ratings about one's relationship to the

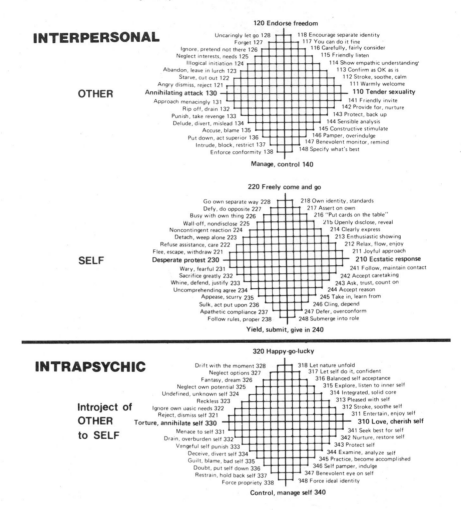

Fig. 2. Full version of the SASB model. A total of 108 classifications of interpersonal and intrapsychic behavior can be made on the basis of only three decisions: Focus, amount of Affiliation, and amount of Interdependence (see Figure 1 and text). Identifying the three underlying dimensions and arranging them according to the structure shown in this figure also permits a number of inferences. Examples include predictions of what will go with what (complementary), what will draw out the opposite of what you have now (antitheses), and the connection between the social milieu and the self-concept (introjection). From L.S. Benjamin, "Structural analysis of differentiation failure," *Psychiatry,* 1979, 42, 1–23. Reprinted by permission.

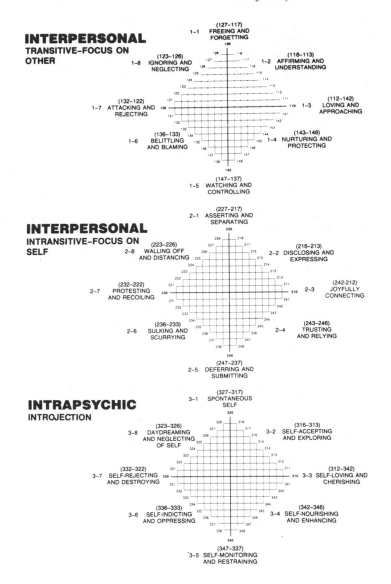

Fig. 3. The 1986 Cluster version of the SASB model. Items from the full model (Figure 2) are grouped to form clusters. On each surface, cluster numbers begin with a 1 at 12 o'clock and proceed clockwise. Each cluster number is preceded by the number of the model surface. For example, Cluster 1-6, Belittling and Blaming, is the sixth cluster on the first surface and Cluster 2-6, Sulking and Scurrying, is the sixth cluster on the second surface. Clusters 1-6 and 2-6 are complementary. (See text for details.) From L.S. Benjamin, "Use of the SASB model to develop treatment plans for personality disorders. I: Narcissism." *Journal of Personality Disorders, 1,* 43–70. Copyright 1986, The Guilford Press. Reprinted by permission.

self (the "Introject") during states described as "Best" and "Worst." Then, ratings are made about one's relationship to a significant other, also at "Best" and "Worst" (there are separate test booklets for male and female significant others). Next, ratings are made about one's relationship with mother and then with father and finally about the relationship between parents. These latter ratings are ordinarily made with the instructional set of describing relationships with parents and between parents when the rater was 5–10 years of age. For special purposes such as research or atypical relationship patterns, nonstandard administrations can be accommodated by Intrex Interpersonal Institute in providing specially constructed test and answer booklets and computer scoring. The Standard Series involves 792 ratings for the long form and 176 ratings for the short form.

SASB-SF is a self-report instrument that is structured basically in a true/false format. It allows the rater to indicate degrees of agreement or disagreement on an interval scale ranging from 0–100 in 10-point increments. Anchor points are 0-Never, Not at All and 100-Always, Perfectly; a rating of 50 or above indicates "True." An identical answer booklet is used for the parallel forms.

The Intrex Report provides graphic representations or "maps" of relationships as the rater sees them. In addition, it will describe possible connections between the rater's self-concept, or Introject, and significant present and past interpersonal relationships. In order to utilize the Intrex Report fully, the clinical user must also understand SASB-based concepts of *complementarity, antithesis, similarity, opposition,* and *introjection* (see Technical Aspects section). In addition to the user's manual, the clinician considering SASB should read Benjamin (1974, 1979, 1984, 1986a, 1986b, 1987) to increase familiarity with the use of the concepts.

In addition to providing maps of different relationships, the Intrex Report contains useful numerical indices for summarizing the data. Correlations between obtained ratings and 63 theoretically/mathematically ideal configurations (21 per surface) allows for precision in describing each relationship pattern. In addition, three Pattern Coefficients quantitate the degrees of Affiliation-Disaffiliation (the Attack or ATK coefficient) and Interdependence-Autonomy (the Control or CON coefficient) present. The Conflict coefficient (CFL) indicates patterns in which both high degrees of Affiliation *and* Disaffiliation or of Interdependence *and* Autonomy are endorsed.

The Attack coefficient, positive or negative, indicates the overall friendliness of the data set, taking into account all item ratings, not just the poles of the horizontal axis. The Control coefficient, likewise, takes all ratings into account: the overall separateness or enmeshment, autonomy-taking or submitting, self-liberation or self-control in quantitating the data set. The actual extremes of the horizontal and vertical dimensions may be thought of as the most primitive, unmodulated behaviors (e.g., murderous attack and tender sexuality on the horizontal dimension). These *points* are measured only with the full 108-category SASB-LF. So, if an investigator were working with a population for whom such extremes would be relevant and wanted to maximize statistical power, use of the more lengthy long form could be justified.

It may be useful for clinicians who use the SASB to consider odd-numbered clusters as representing somewhat more intense, undersocialized, or primitive behaviors. Even-numbered clusters may be viewed as representing "mixed" behaviors that are more socialized, less intense, and "civilized."

Practical Applications/Uses

Benjamin (Intrex Interpersonal Institute, 1987) asserts that SASB can be used by clinicians of diverse theoretical persuasions, assuming there is some basis in object relations theory. She states:

> Intrex reports are particularly helpful to psychotherapies in which it is presumed that the main therapy task is for the patient to learn about his or her interactive patterns, where they came from, and what purposes they have had. At some point in therapy the patient has the opportunity to decide whether to change those patterns and goals, and can have support in changing to more appropriate patterns. . . . The Intrex report which connects perceptions of early significant social experiences to current problems in relationship and in self concept is very helpful in identifying patterns needing change, and in providing hypotheses about the interpersonal roots of those patterns. (Intrex Interpersonal Institute, 1987, p. 6)

Thus, clinicians involved in treating individuals for whom relationships with and perceptions of others are important in the development and maintenance of "mental illness," broadly defined (cf. McLemore & Benjamin, 1979), would find SASB a potentially useful tool. This would include adolescents and adults involved in individual psychotherapy as well as families and groups. For example, discrepancies in how different family members view one another can be clarified by examining Intrex Reports for ratings by each family member of one another. Intrex Reports can also open the door for exploration of transference, by suggesting hypotheses about how a patient would view parental/authority figures based on past experience (e.g., ratings of relationship with mother and father in childhood).

Most practitioners would be interested primarily in learning to use the SASB-SF. The instructions are simple and the test can be self-administered once the basic instructions are explained. The reading level required is similar to that of the Minnesota Multiphasic Personality Inventory (approximately sixth grade). With an appropriate background, a competent interpersonally oriented clinician could employ SASB with adolescent and adult clients of diverse cultural and socioeconomic backgrounds.

Unlike many other self-report instruments, it is recommended that the SASB-SF be administered *after* a comprehensive clinical intake assessment interview has been conducted (i.e., factors potentially affecting interpretation of relationship patterns should be thoroughly explored). The optimal use of SASB-SF involves a collaborative exploration of the Intrex Report findings by the clinician and the patient/rater. Thus, it is imperative that the patient/rater and the clinician be amenable to and prepared for such an intense interpersonal involvement. This could exclude severely decompensated patients or patients with low premorbid ego resources. On the clinician side, this would exclude clinicians who do not accept the value of a developmental/historical analysis of relationship patterns (see

Schacht, Binder, & Strupp, 1984). Clinical use of SASB necessitates *at minimum* intake and follow-up sessions of 45 minutes each. However, the integration of Intrex Report findings into assessment and treatment planning will probably involve more substantial time commitments.

Computer technology is required to generate Intrex Reports. At present, processing of Standard and Nonstandard Series SASB-SF ratings is conducted by Intrex Interpersonal Institute. The user's manual (Intrex Interpersonal Institute, 1987) provides a method for graphically depicting maps based on the Cluster model, because each SASB-SF item corresponds to one cluster on the 24 Cluster model categories. However, owing to the fact that much of the utility of SASB derives from the correlations with theoretical profiles (best fit curves) and pattern coefficients (ATK, CON, CFL), processing and standardized computer interpretation with the Intrex Report are important. Standard Series pattern coefficient norms for college students for the short form and the long form are reproduced in the short form manual (Intrex Interpersonal Institute, 1987).

Norms can be expected to differ for each type of rating across diverse populations. Stringent criteria have been promulgated by Benjamin for accepting the "significance" of correlations within the individual case. For SASB-LF, the criterion is .71, indicating over 50% shared variance; for the SASB-SF, the criterion is .81. The SASB self-rating method assumes a cooperative and collaborative patient-clinician relationship; to whatever extent "socially desirable" ratings occur, they are considered "valid" in the sense that they accurately reflect the patient's view of his or her interactions with the world and the self (see Benjamin, 1974).

Technical Aspects

The major exposition of the development and construct validation of the SASB assessment method is presented in Benjamin (1974). In this paper, she described the rationale for the expansion of the circumplex model of interpersonal behavior to three "surfaces," which were described briefly in the previous section. The "Other" surface was described originally as "Parentlike." It involved behaviors that were prototypically characteristic of a parent and were "active in nature and concerned with *what is going to be done to or for the other person*" (p. 395). The "Self" surface was originally described as "Childlike" and involved behaviors that were prototypically characteristic of children and were "reactive and concerned with *what is going to be done to or for the self*" (p. 395).

The psychological concepts defining the first two SASB surfaces have evolved. Benjamin (1987) has renamed the former parentlike surface the Transitive Focus and the former childlike surface the Intransitive Focus. Transitive Focus involves "what is to be done to, for, or about the other person," and Intransitive Focus "what is going to be done to, for, or about the self" (Benjamin, 1987, p. 50). The concept of Intransitive Focus is a particularly difficult one to express in the English language for it involves a differentiated expression of the *state* of the self (Benjamin, 1987; Benjamin, personal communication, July, 8, 1988).

By incorporating into the SASB model the active-passive (actually active-reactive) dimensions of interpersonal behavior, Benjamin was able to resolve a particularly difficult psychometric problem. This involves the structure of a circumplex model. Briefly, in a circumplex ordering of variables, contiguous variables should have high positive correlations. Variables 90 degrees apart should have no correlation (orthogonality), and variables 180 degrees apart should have high negative correlations. In previous models, such as the Leary interpersonal system, *submission* was considered the opposite of *dominance*. In such models, the single surface tends not to manifest true circumplex structure in the correlation matrix (see Wiggins, 1982). Benjamin introduced with the active-reactive distinction the idea that the opposite of *dominate* or *control* is *give autonomy* or *emancipate*, rather than *submit*. In other words, to have dominate and submit on the same circumplex is to confound the active and reactive dimensions of interpersonal behavior (see Wiggins, 1982).

The splitting of the interpersonal surfaces into active and reactive planes makes it possible to develop additional hypotheses about interpersonal behavior. Benjamin developed the application of the concepts of *opposition, similarity, complementarity,* and *antithesis* to the SASB model.

By incorporating the notion that the opposite of dominate is autonomy-giving, the axes of the circumplex were relabeled Affiliation and Interdependence. Submitting, a *reactive* state involving concern about what is being done to the self, now occupies a *topographically* identical position on the Self surface as dominate occupies on the Other surface. Active and reactive behaviors occupying the same topographic points on the respective surfaces are defined as *complementary.*

Complementarity is an important aspect of the construct validity of the SASB model, in addition to the affiliation-interdependence axes and the circumplex ordering of variables in which opposites should be highly negatively correlated. The principle of similarity posits the idea that stable important interpersonal relationships will tend to be characterized by patterns involving identical points or regions on the two interpersonal surfaces. The principle of antithesis posits that a stable, complementary relationship pattern can be "broken up" or destabilized by introducing either a transitive action (Other Focus) or intransitive reaction (Self Focus) that is the *opposite* of the *complement* for the immediately antecedent behavior.

Using the Cluster model, for example (Figure 3), the complement of Cluster 1–5 *(Watching and Controlling)* is Cluster 2–5 *(Deferring and Submitting).* Cluster 1–5 involves a high degree of interdependent transitive action directed at another, and Cluster 2–5 involved a high degree of interdependent intransitive reaction, permitting a stable behavior sequence. The antithesis of Cluster 2–5, or opposite of the complement for Cluster 1–5, is Cluster 2–1 *(Asserting and Separating).* An asserting and separating reaction involves *taking autonomy* and therefore will destabilize a transaction involving another's interdependent/enmeshed *Watching and Controlling* (Cluster 1–5).

The concept of introjection was described previously. In topographic terms, the introjection of the attitudes of significant others about the self involves points on the Introject surface and the Other surface. Repeated transitive actions perceived by the individual from the significant other are internalized in such a way that the individual treats the self with the same transitive action. So, if the significant other is experienced as *Ignoring and Neglecting* (Cluster 1–8), the person learns to treat the self with *Daydreaming and Neglecting of Self* (Cluster 3–8). If the other is experienced as consistently *Affirming and Understanding* (Cluster 1–2), the person learns to treat the self in a *Self-accepting and Exploring* (Cluster 3–2) manner.

Introjection, complementarity, opposition, similarity, and antithesis are the dynamic concepts that make it possible to use the structural model of social behavior in a clinically relevant way (see Benjamin, 1986b).

The item content of the SASB model on which the SASB-LF and SASB-SF self-report questionnaires are based has been developed in a multistep iterative process involving item generation and selection guided by the underlying rationale described previously. Several clinical and normal samples have taken the evolving versions and provided data that were subjected to autocorrelation, circumplex analysis, and factor analysis (Benjamin, 1974).

Autocorrelational analysis was employed as a within-subjects procedure. This demonstrated that for a given subject, adjacent data points along the circumplex tended to be endorsed in a similar fashion; this led to high correlations among adjacent points and negative correlations between opposite points. The circumplex analysis approach tested this logic on a between-subjects correlation matrix. Finally, the axes Affiliation and Interdependence were tested using a factor-analytic procedure with a transformation allowing graphic representation of the factor loadings in a two-space (Guttman, 1966).

Results of the autocorrelations, circumplex analysis, and two-space (affiliation by interdependence) factor representations were highly consistent across samples and individuals. The two-space representation of the affiliation-interdependence axes was weak for the third surface, the Introject focus. Subsequent item revision leading to the final SASB-LF (Intrex Interpersonal Institute, 1983) seems to have resolved this minor deviation.

Additional approaches to the validity question are reported by Benjamin (in press). Using the full 108-category model, she compared the pattern of factor loadings with the actual theoretical values for each point on the three circumplex surfaces. This amounts to a test of the theoretical structure of the SASB factors. Canonical correlations between theoretical values and factor loadings were quite high. For the Affiliation axis, all correlations were at .93 or better. For the Interdependence axis, 14 of 22 correlations were .85 or better. The lowest correlations involved ratings of the early relationship with father on the Interdependence (power) dimension. However, rather than indicating a failure of the structure of the model, this may point to an interesting phenomenon revealed by the model when applied through actual ratings by persons of their relationships. That is, in retrospect, relationships with father are seen as deviating from the theoretical model itself.

Another test involved having judges rate the items on SASB-LF on the three dimensions (Focus, Affiliation, Interdependence). On the Affiliation axis, canonical correlations with the theoretical values were at .99. On the Interdependence (vertical) dimensions, ratings for Other Focus correlated .96, for Self Focus correlated .98, and for Introject correlated .95. These results demonstrate that the test items conform to test structure in the opinion of external judges.

The construct validity of the *model* for the Structural Analysis of Social Behavior appears well supported by a preponderance of the evidence (cf. Landy, 1986). The resulting SASB-LF was characterized by consistent circumplex ordering of variables, with coefficients of internal consistency in the .90 range. Test-retest reliability for SASB-LF was .87. In the clinical setting, where interpersonal relationships and self-concept tend to destabilize, test-retest reliability can be expected to be lower.

Benjamin (personal communication, July 8, 1988) has recently completed reliability studies for the two forms of SASB-SF. Average reliabilities for the pattern coefficients for the same form was .790 (range .667 to .898), and for equivalent forms was .655 (range .408 to .832). These test-retest coefficients are comparable to reported test-retest coefficients for subscales of the Wechsler Adult Intelligence Scale-Revised and Wechsler Intelligence Scale for Children Revised. However, the somewhat lower reliabilities for "Worst" ratings of Significant Other and Introject suggest that the use of these pattern coefficients for research purposes will necessitate increasing statistical power, for example through increasing sample sizes. Clinical users will want to explore fully the meanings of these variables for the individual patient in a collaborative way.

A review of the numerous studies that pertain to other types of validity of the underlying SASB model is beyond the scope of the present article. These studies employ the SASB analogue coding procedure, which can be applied to behavior ratings and ratings of verbal dialogue, with some latitude in the definition of units of analysis. A selected bibliography of relevant major papers is included in the reference section of this review.

Instead, the results of studies involving the SASB self-report questionnaires will be considered. These studies have employed the previously mentioned long form that requires 792 ratings for the Standard Series. For specific research questions, subsets of ratings may be used. This reduces the amount of time required, which for the full SASB-LF standard series is extensive. At present, there are no validity studies per se for the short form. However, because of the psychometric properties of the SASB-SF, the reliability of the summary indices, such as the pattern coefficients, is comparable to the long form.

Essex, Klein, Lohr, and Benjamin (1985) employed the long form in a large-scale study of depression and intimacy in relationships for a nonclinical population of women over 50. In the first study, conducted in 1978, the relationship between the SCL-90-R scale for depression (Derogatis, 1977; Derogatis, Lipman, & Covi, 1973) and SASB-LF ratings of a relationship with a significant other identified by the subject (usually spouse) was examined. The four relevant SASB-LF ratings were 1) how the subject saw herself acting on the significant other (Other Focus); 2) how the subject saw the other reacting to her (Self Focus); 3) how she saw the other acting on her (Other Focus); 4) how she saw herself reacting to the significant other (Self Focus). For each set of ratings, the researchers regressed the depression measure onto three SASB variables for each rating: 1) friendliness (ATK coefficient); 2) control (CON); and a coefficient of consistency (a lag correlation coefficient that reflects the concordance of adjacent ratings around the circumplex).

In the first study, the consistency measure was found to be related to depression for each of the four rated transactions. Greater levels of depression were associated with less consistency, for ratings of both active and reactive states for self and significant other. In addition, depression was negatively associated with friendliness (high negative ATK coefficient) in ratings of the significant other's approach (active/transitive focus) and the rater's own approach to the significant other.

In the second phase of this study, the subjects who participated in the rating study were recontacted approximately 1 year later. The depression measure and the SASB measures were readministered. However, this time the SASB ratings were made using the "Best State" and "Worst State" instructional sets, in order to tap the possible relationship of person by situation interaction to depression. The major significant finding was that depression was found to be associated with ratings of the significant other as less submissive (CON coefficient for other's reaction). Also, depressed women rated themselves as spending significantly less time than less depressed women with their significant others in the "Best" situation. A "friendliness difference" score, reflecting mismatch between ratings of action and reaction (ATK coefficients), was computed that showed greater mismatch in the more depressed women. This can be interpreted as suggesting that complementarity may be associated with affective symptomatology.

Swift, Bushnell, Hanson, and Logemann (1986) investigated the use of the SASB-LF Introject surface measure in characterizing adolescents meeting modified DSM-III (American Psychiatric Association, 1980) criteria for anorexia nervosa. Compared to a control sample, their 30 inpatient subjects were significantly more self-attacking, which corresponds to psychological suicidality (3–8 on the Cluster model). Surprisingly, the Control and Conflict coefficients did not differ from normals, despite the fact that self-restraint is seemingly associated with anorexia. On the other hand, correlations of SASB Introject measures and the Offer Self-Image Questionnaire for Adolescents (Offer, Ostrov, & Howard, 1977) revealed a negative association between most Offer scales, which indicate good adjustment, and self-attack on SASB. High scores on achievement- and mastery-oriented Offer scales were associated with self-restraint measured by the Introject CON (Control) coefficient.

Humphrey (1986) studied a sample of eating-disordered patients from a psychiatric inpatient service. Three patient groups were included, based on DSM-III criteria—Bulimic, Anorexic, and Combined. Patients and controls were all females aged 15–23. The Bulimic and Combined groups perceived their parents as both less *Nurturing and Comforting* (Cluster 1–3) and less *Affirming and Understanding* (Cluster 1–2) than the control group. Other findings distinguished eating-disordered patients from controls, but not bulimics from anorexics. Humphrey concluded that the findings partially supported the hypothesis that bulimia is related to deficits in affective and tension regulation resulting from poor nurturance and soothing from the parent. However, the overall pattern of findings more strongly supported the conclusion that no pattern of deficits specific to bulimia versus anorexia had been identified.

Rudy, McLemore, and Gorsuch (1985) investigated the use of the SASB questionnaires in a study of psychotherapy. Forty-two outpatients and their therapists completed SASB ratings of each other. The Hopkins Symptom Checklist (Derogatis, Lipman, Rickels, Uhlenhuth, & Covi, 1974) was used as a measure of symptomatic status. Therapeutic progress was rated by patients and therapists on questionnaires adapted from Strupp, Fox, and Lessler (1969) and Rogers and Dymond (1954). Ratings were made after completion of at least six therapy sessions.

Rudy et al. (1985) found that SASB relationship scores were highly predictive of reported progress, accounting for (at minimum) 65% of reported progress variance in canonical correlational analysis. Patients who reported greater progress rated their therapists on the Other surface (i.e., therapist's active focus on/initiative toward the patient) as more affiliative and autonomy-giving than those reporting lesser progress. In fact, therapist Other surface ratings by patients accounted for 60% of patient-rated progress variance. A surprising finding was that the therapist's own ratings of their Introjects (Introject Focus) were associated with symptom improvement; that is, more affiliative and self-accepting therapist introjects were associated with symptom reduction, but not with patient-rated progress. Overall, the analyses supported the concept that the patient's perception of the therapeutic relationship was the most important predictor of improvement.

Benjamin (1986a) used variables from the SASB-LF to examine the utility of the SASB in differentiating nine psychiatric diagnostic groups. An overall accuracy rate of 48.8% based on discriminant function analysis with a subset of SASB questionnaire ratings was obtained. For certain groups, the correct classification rate was quite high: Major Depression Uncomplicated (86.7%); Bipolar Manic (60.0%); Borderline (58.3%); Major Depression with Psychosis (57.1%); Bipolar Depressed (50.0%).

The overall rate of 48.8% based on so-called "Meet the World" SASB ratings (i.e., those dealing with the rater's reported actions and reactions) was quite comparable to or better than other traditional measures: SCL-90-R (26.1%) and the Minnesota Multiphasic Personality Inventory (40.9%). Interestingly, nurse/observer-generated SASB questionnaire ratings led to a 63.3% overall classification rate that approached the accuracy of the best measure (nurse-generated symptom ratings [70.9%]). Numerous additional findings for the many potentially important SASB variables are reported in this study, which are far more extensive than can be conveyed here. As with some of the research presented previously, the utility of the ATK, CON, and CFL coefficients is explored empirically.

Benjamin (1974) discusses the 3-dimensional (Autonomy by Affiliation by Conflict) representation of group data on these pattern coefficients for different diagnostic groups. Clearly, social-interpersonal-intrapsychic descriptors afforded by SASB reveal different patterns. And "there is no reason to believe that these social and intrapsychic differences are secondary to the psychiatric presentation" (Benjamin, 1986a, p. 627).

Critique

The studies discussed previously exemplify some of the directions that concurrent and predictive validity assessments of the SASB-LF have proceeded. Results so far suggest that the measures of the interpersonal and intrapsychic domains are not only sensitive and reliable, but also will demonstrate broad validity. Obviously, much more research can be conceived and the SASB self-report approach lends itself to the generation of a plethora of hypotheses about clinical phenomena, including psychotherapy process and outcome (e.g., Alpher, Henry, & Strupp, 1988), interpersonal and intrapsychic characteristics of diagnostic groups (see Benjamin, 1986a), as well as social-interpersonal perceptions and behavior in different situations (Connors & Alpher, 1987). As mentioned above, the ultimate arbiter concerning a psychometric device such as SASB will likely be the "preponderance of the evidence" (Landy, 1986).

Fortunately, the extensive instrument development for the long form and now the short form has been carefully and thoughtfully conducted by the originator of SASB. These early studies are most encouraging. More extensive concurrent validity studies with SASB-SF can be expected in the near future (Intrex Interpersonal Institute, 1987). Predictive studies involving process and outcome with the long form in short-term dynamic psychotherapy are under way at the Center for Psychotherapy Research at Vanderbilt University under the direction of Dr. Hans H. Strupp (see Strupp & Binder, 1984, pp. 312–313).

Wiggins (1982) recently reviewed existing circumplex models of interpersonal behavior. He stated: "The recent circumplex model of interpersonal behavior presented by Benjamin . . . *is the most detailed, clinically rich, ambitious, and conceptually demanding of all contemporary models*" (italics added, p. 193). Hopefully this brief review has given some sense of these four aspects of the Structural Analysis of Social Behavior model.

The SASB self-report questionnaires are at the leading edge of interpersonal measurement technology and perform well. Evidence for their utility as adjuncts to psychotherapy is yet to be systematically demonstrated. However, the language of SASB is close to the phenomenology of patient's experience. Because it affords a person by situation (Best-Worst) measurement approach, patients find that it encompasses the variability within relationships (e.g., I'm different with Y in this situation and that one), in action-reaction patterns, and across relationships (e.g., With Y I invite friendly submission, but with Z I invite hostile abandonment). Talking with patients in the language of SASB is highly likely to lead to feelings in the patient of being understood and respected, because it facilitates discourse close to the way the patient sees the interpersonal world. In other words, clinically SASB can be as much a tool of empathy as it is a theory of interpersonal behavior or development of the self-concept.

Structural Analysis of Social Behavior is a dynamic and engaging tool in the hands of both researcher and practitioner. Because of this, it is the opinion of this reviewer that SASB is on the forefront of efforts to forge a bridge between clinical research and clinical practice.

Furthermore, SASB has added new rigor and precision to concepts that have previously been regarded as "psychodynamic" and therefore untestable (Benjamin, 1986a). Parloff (1984) recently assessed the status of psychotherapy research and concluded that the gap between research and practice was largely due to the lack of attention to research in the dynamic therapies. It is likely that SASB will be intricately involved in the "new wave" of research on these therapies. Thus for the researcher or clinician, as well as graduate student or clinical trainee, investment in learning to use SASB as a method for case conceptualization is likely to be rewarding.

Finally, training in the use of the SASB questionnaires, currently required for clinical applications, is likely to of most value if one has spent some time learning the model and familiarizing oneself with Benjamin's writings (especially Benjamin, 1974, 1979, 1984, 1986a, 1986b, 1987), as well as with object relations theory (e.g., Greenberg & Mitchell, 1983). A full volume on SASB by Dr. Benjamin is in preparation (Benjamin, in press) and will make her ideas about therapy based on SASB and related empirical work more accessible.

References

Alpher, V.S., Henry, W.P., & Strupp, H.H. (1988, June). *Developmental level of object representation, capacity for dynamic process and intrapsychic change in short-term psychodynamic psychotherapy.* Paper presented at the meeting of the Society for Psychotherapy Research, Santa Fe, NM.

American Psychiatric Association. (1980). *Diagnostic and statistical manual of mental disorders* (3rd ed.). Washington, DC: Author.

Benjamin, L.S. (1974). Structural analysis of social behavior. *Psychological Review, 81,* 392–425.

Benjamin, L.S. (1979). Structural analysis of differentiation failure. *Psychiatry: Journal for the Study of Interpersonal Processes, 42,* 1–23.

Benjamin, L.S. (1984). Principles of prediction using Structural Analysis of Social Behavior. In R.A. Zucker, J. Aronoff, & A.J. Rabin (Eds.), *Personality and the prediction of behavior* (pp. 121–174). New York: Academic.

Benjamin, L.S. (1986a). Adding social and intrapsychic descriptors to Axis I of DSM-III. In T. Millon & G.R. Klerman (Eds.), *Contemporary directions in psychopathology* (pp. 599–638). New York: Guilford.

Benjamin, L.S. (1986b). Operational definition and measurement of dynamics shown in the stream of free associations. *Psychiatry: Interpersonal and Biological Processes, 49,* 104–129.

Benjamin, L.S. (1987). Use of the SASB dimensional model to develop treatment plans for personality disorders. I: Narcissism. *Journal of Personality Disorders, 1,* 43–70.

Benjamin, L.S. (in press). *Interpersonal diagnosis and treatment: The SASB approach.* New York: Guilford.

Connors, G.J., & Alpher, V.S. (1987). Toward a reconceptualization of person-environment interactions: Applications to research on drinking behavior. *Drugs & Society, 2,* 99–146.

Derogatis, L.R. (1977). *SCL-90-R. Administration, scoring & procedures manual-II for the R(evised) version.* Towson, MD: Clinical Psychometric Research.

Derogatis, L.R., Lipman, R.S., & Covi, L. (1973) SCL-90: An outpatient psychiatric rating scale—preliminary report. *Psychopharmacology Bulletin, 9,* 13–27.

Derogatis, L.S., Lipman, R.S., Rickels, K., Uhlenhuth, E.H., & Covi, L. (1974). The Hopkins Symptom Checklist (HSCL): A measure of primary symptom dimensions. In P. Pichot (Ed.), *Psychological measurements in psychopharmacology* (pp. 79–110). Basel: S. Karger.

Essex, M.J., Klein, M.H., Lohr, M.J., & Benjamin, L.S. (1985). Intimacy and depression in older women. *Psychiatry: Interpersonal and Biological Processes, 48,* 159–178.

Greenberg, J.R., & Mitchell, S.A. (1983). *Object relations in psychoanalytic theory.* Cambridge, MA: Harvard University Press.

Guttman, L. (1966). Order analysis of correlation matrices. In R.B. Cattell (Ed.), *Handbook of multivariate experimental psychology* (pp. 438–458). Chicago: Rand-McNally.

Humphrey, L.L. (1986). Structural analysis of parent-child relationships in eating disorders. *Journal of Abnormal Psychology, 95,* 295–402.

Intrex Interpersonal Institute. (1983). *Intrex user's manual parts I and II.* Madison, WI: Author.

Intrex Interpersonal Institute. (1987). *SASB Short Form user's manual.* Madison, WI: Author.

Kiesler, D.J. (1983). The 1982 interpersonal circle: A taxonomy for complementarity in human transactions. *Psychological Review, 90,* 195–214.

Landy, F.J. (1986). Stamp collecting versus science: Validation as hypothesis testing. *American Psychologist, 41,* 1183–1192.

Leary, T.F. (1957). *Interpersonal diagnosis of personality.* New York: Ronald.

Lorr, M., & McNair, D.M. (1963). An interpersonal behavior circle. *Journal of Abnormal and Social Psychology, 67,* 68–75.

McLemore, C.W., & Benjamin, L.S. (1979). Whatever happened to interpersonal diagnosis? A psychosocial alternative to DSM-III. *American Psychologist, 34,* 17–34.

Murray, H.A. (1938). *Explorations in personality.* New York: Oxford.

Offer, D., Ostrov, E., & Howard, K.I. (1977). *The Offer Self-Image Questionnaire for Adolescents: A manual.* Chicago: Michael Reese Hospital.

Parloff, M.B. (1984). Psychotherapy research and its incredible credibility crisis. *Clinical Psychology Review, 4,* 95–109.

Rogers, C.R., & Dymond, R. (1954). *Psychotherapy and personality change.* Chicago: University of Chicago.

Rudy, J.P., McLemore, C.W., & Gorsuch, R.L. (1985). Interpersonal behavior and therapeutic progress: Therapists and clients rate themselves and each other. *Psychiatry: Interpersonal and Biological Processes, 48,* 264–281.

Schacht, T.E., Binder, J., & Strupp, H.H. (1984). The dynamic focus. In H. H. Strupp and J. L. Binder, *Psychotherapy in a new key: A guide to time-limited dynamic psychotherapy* (pp. 65–109). New York: Basic.

Schaefer, E.S. (1965). A configurational analysis of children's reports of parental behavior. *Journal of Consulting Psychology, 29,* 552–557.

Strupp, H.H., & Binder, J.L. (1984). *Psychotherapy in a new key: A guide to time-limited dynamic psychotherapy.* New York: Basic.

Strupp, H.H., Fox, R.E., & Lessler, K. (1969). *Patients view their psychotherapy.* Baltimore, MD: Johns Hopkins University.

Sullivan, H.S. (1953). *The interpersonal theory of psychiatry.* New York: Norton.

Swift, W.J., Bushnell, N.J., Hanson, P., & Logemann, T. (1986). Self-concept in adolescent anorexics. *Journal of the American Academy of Child Psychiatry, 25,* 826–835.

Wiggins, J.S. (1982). Circumplex models of interpersonal behavior in clinical psychology. In P. C. Kendall & J. N. Butcher (Eds.), *Handbook of research methods in clinical psychology* (pp. 183–221). New York: Wiley.

Researches Based on SASB Coding Method

Benjamin, L.S. (1979). Structural analysis of differentiation failure. *Psychiatry: Journal for the Study of Interpersonal Processes, 42,* 1–23.

Benjamin, L.S. (1982). Use of Structural Analysis of Social Behavior (SASB) to guide intervention in psychotherapy. In J.C. Anchin & D.J. Kiesler (Eds.), *Handbook of interpersonal psychotherapy* (pp. 190–212). New York: Pergamon.

Benjamin, L.S. (1987). Use of the SASB dimensional model to develop treatment plans for personality disorders: I. Narcissism. *Journal of Personality Disorders, 1,* 43–70.

Benjamin, L.S., Foster, S.W., Giat-Roberto, L., & Estroff, S.E. (1986). Breaking the family code: Analyzing videotapes of family interactions by SASB. In L.S. Greenberg & W.M. Pinsoff (Eds.), *The psychotherapeutic process* (pp. 391–438). New York: Guilford.

Greenberg, L.S., & Webster, M.C. (1982). Resolving decisional conflict by gestalt two-chair dialogue: Relating process to outcome. *Journal of Counseling Psychology, 29,* 468–477.

Henry, W.P., Schacht, T.E., & Strupp, H.H. (1986). Structural Analysis of Social Behavior: Application to a study of interpersonal process in differential psychotherapeutic outcome. *Journal of Consulting and Clinical Psychology, 54,* 27–31.

Humphrey, L.L., Apple, R.F., & Kirschenbaum, D.S. (1986). Differentiating bulimic-anorexic from normal families using interpersonal and behavioral observation systems. *Journal of Consulting and Clinical Psychology, 54,* 190–195.

Humphrey, L.L., & Benjamin, L.S. (1986). Using Structural Analysis of Social Behavior to assess critical but elusive family processes. A new solution to an old problem. *American Psychologist, 41,* 979–989.

Kenneth T. Wilburn, Ph.D.

Associate Professor of Education, University of North Florida, Jacksonville, Florida.

STUDENT OPINION INVENTORY

National Study of School Evaluation Staff. Falls Church, Virginia: National Study of School Evaluation.

Introduction

The Student Opinion Inventory (SOI) is a paper-and-pencil questionnaire that can be self- or group-administered. The SOI is designed to be used either by itself to measure students' attitudes and morale or as part of an overall school evaluation program. Items covered by the instrument include students' attitude toward faculty, administration, counselors, curriculum, co-curricular activities, facilities, and the overall satisfaction with the school. The instrument is one of four in a series that includes the Teacher Opinion Inventory, Parent Opinion Inventory, and the Community Opinion Inventory. These instruments are used primarily in school evaluation and accreditation faculty self-studies.

The SOI was developed by the National Study of School Evaluation (NSSE) to be a part of a complete school evaluation program. Like the other forms of the inventory, the SOI follows a three-phase design. In phase one, NSSE utilized a design team that included university professors, practicing school administrators, and public school teachers that were familiar with the goals and objectives of school evaluation. The initial instrument was reviewed by the Administrative Committee of the NSSE and other educators with pertinent expertise. In phase two, the instrument was pilot tested at three different types of schools in different regional areas of the Association of Colleges and Schools. The opinions of the students, teachers, and administrators participating in the field testing were used to make final revisions of the instrument. Phase three consisted of an extensive field test of the instrument that was conducted in 1979 and involved 10,120 secondary school students, at 27 schools located in 20 states representing all geographic regions of the country. After a statistical analysis of the field-test data, final revisions of the instrument were completed.

The SOI has two parts: Part A and Part B. There are 34 multiple-choice items in Part A, which assesses student's opinions on various aspects of their school (e.g., In how many activities of your school would you feel that you are "welcome" to participate? (A) All (B) Most (C) About half (D) Few, or (E) None). Part B consists of 12 open-ended questions that allow students to make recommendations for school improvement (e.g., If you could change one thing about the activities provided by your school, what would you like to change?)

In the manual for administration the purpose of the SOI is discussed clearly. Information about the National Study of School Evaluation (NSSE), how the SOI was developed, how to administer the SOI, scoring and interpreting results, instrument reliability and validity, and a sample copy of the instrument are all provided in the manual.

Of particular importance is the identification of SOI items that are also included on the Teacher Opinion Inventory and Parent Opinion Inventory and how to group specific items from the SOI to produce six subscales. Items from the three different opinionnaires (i.e., parent, teacher, and student) allow for the examination of general issues from the perspective of the three survey populations. For the more specific program-related items the manual provides detailed instructions for the interpretation of subscale scores for six subscales: Student-Teacher, Student-Counselor, Student-Administrator, Student Curriculum and Instruction, Student-Participation, and Student-School Image.

The manual also includes directions for selection and notification of students, materials needed for administration, tips toward ensuring accuracy of results and the interpretation of both single items and subscale scores.

The format of the manual facilitates its use and the content is presented in a writing style appropriate for most school administrators and teachers.

Practical Applications/Uses

The SOI was developed for use in faculty self-studies and program reviews traditionally required by accreditation agencies. The inventory is an appropriate instrument for evaluation and research studies looking at student opinion and school climate. There are three parallel forms for parents, teachers, and community members that allow the perceptions for all four groups to be compiled and discussed. If administered anonymously, as suggested, the results of the SOI should provide the faculty and staff with insight into the students' perceptions of their school.

The SOI (1981a) was developed to accomplish the following: 1) to assess student opinion toward many facets of the school and to provide students with the opportunity for input into the school assessment and improvement process. The SOI was designed to be used alone or with the other inventories as part of a complete school evaluation program. The SOI itself is designed specifically for use with students.

The test administrator is cautioned as to how this instrument should be used to get the best results. The manual states that the attitude of the test administrator as perceived by the students has an influence on how important students perceive their task to be. In addition, students must feel that their responses are truly anonymous. It is also suggested that there be no discussion of the items until students complete the questionnaire.

The directions for administration are not complicated and are easy to follow. The test is simple to administer. However, students below the fourth grade may have difficulty with the instrument's reading level. In addition, some students may need clarification concerning which specific persons in the school are referred to as "administrator" or "counselor." The SOI is untimed; most often Part A can be completed in 25 minutes and Part B in 20 minutes.

The SOI can be self- or group-administered. Students may record their responses directly in the test booklet or on common machine optical scan sheets. It is suggested that the frequencies for each item be tallied, with A=5, B=4, C=3, D=2, and E=1. Information is provided in the administrator's manual on the items that are common between the inventories and which items on the SOI may be grouped together in order to produce scores for six subscales. The manual also cautions the interpretation of certain items on the test for elementary students (e.g., items dealing with course selection) because the item content is not appropriate for that level. There are no separate answer sheets for Part A, but the 5-point scale lends itself to the use of standard machine scan answer sheets.

The interpretation of Part A is made from the frequency distribution of how the student responds to each item. The interpretation of the written comments in Part B would be subjective and demand content analysis. There are no norms provided for different types or levels of schools and no case studies are cited in the manual on how results could be used. There is, however, a detailed discussion of how to calculate item and/or subscale means.

Technical Aspects

The instrument was field tested using a national sample of 10,120 students during November 1979, from 27 secondary schools in 20 states representing all geographical sections of the United States. Results from the entire population were used in determining reliability and a subpopulation of seven schools was selected to conduct the validity study.

The validation study conducted at the seven selected secondary schools, a subpopulation of the national sample of 27 schools, provided a total of 367 student responses for the validity study. To provide an external measure of validity six semantic differential subscales were developed to use as a comparison with the six subscales of the SOI. It was predicted that there would be a positive correlation between the independently developed subscales and the six subscales of the SOI as well as the overall correlations between the seven schools participating in the validity portion of the study and the other 20 schools participating in the reliability study. Results indicate that the Student-Participation and Student-Curriculum and Instruction subscale correlations with the corresponding semantic differential subscales were positive and significant. The Student-Counselor, Student-Teacher, and Student-Administrator correlations with the corresponding semantic differential subscales were positive but moderately so.

Coefficient alpha reliability coefficients of internal consistency are given for the seven subscales. No test-retest reliability coefficients have been established. The reliability coefficients for the seven subscales range from .68 to .93 with a median coefficient alpha of .87.

Critique

The SOI appears to have face validity, adequate measures of construct validity, and general reliability. The content of the questions relate to the evaluation standards used by accreditation organizations. The field-test data produced by the inventory indicate very good consistency of scores for the SOI when used with secondary school students. The SOI meets a need for an instrument to address students' opinions of the school and to provide students with an avenue for input into the school assessment and evaluation process. The SOI is not, however, based upon any research base related to effective teaching, effective schooling, or positive school climate. As a result of its research void, the instrument has limited value and generalizability. Because the items were designed for both elementary and secondary students, they are very broad and many items are particularly inappropriate for elementary school students. The areas of student concerns are very generic (i.e., student activities, selection of vocation, schoolwork, homework, personal problems, etc.). This does not give the student an opportunity to react to the programs and services of their particular school and/or to their own personal areas of concern.

The Student Opinion Inventory provides a global accounting of student opinion and addresses many of the areas typically identified for review as part of a school evaluation or accreditation process. The correlation of topics between the instrument's, student, parent, and faculty test forms do provide for an opportunity to cross check perceptions of different populations concerning common aspects of the school. As part of this review, the reviewer informally contacted administrators, counselors, and teachers in the N.E. Florida school district of Duval County. The overall reaction of those contacted was overwhelmingly positive. The most negative comments were from elementary school personnel concerning the use of secondary school terms and the reading level required for some items. These professionals felt that the inventory provided them with good demographic information about the general concerns of their pupils.

The National Study of School Evaluation needs to review the instruments thoroughly with the aim of including items supported by research on school effectiveness, school climate, and pupil attitudes that foster positive pupil growth. Studies where the SOI was used need to be conducted and reported in the manual. Consideration needs to be given to the development of instruments suited particularly for elementary, middle-grades, and secondary level students. The recording of answers should be taken out of the test booklet and placed on a separate answer sheet. The SOI should be revised so as to provide each school with the opportunity to insert individualized questions in Part A, possibly as a separate subscale, or in Part B. The NSSE should consider upgrading the manual and the instrument so that it conforms to standards for good tests.

References

National Study of School Evaluation. (1981a). *Parent Opinion Inventory.* Falls Church, VA: Author.

National Study of School Evaluation. (1981b). *Student Opinion Inventory.* Falls Church, VA: Author.

National Study of School Evaluation. (1981c). *Teacher Opinion Inventory.* Falls Church, VA: Author.

Randall M. Jones, Ph.D.
Assistant Research Professor, Smith Substance Abuse Education Project, The University of Arizona, Tucson, Arizona.

SUBSTANCE ABUSE PROBLEM CHECKLIST

Jerome F. X. Carroll. Eagleville, Pennsylvania: Eagleville Hospital.

Introduction

The Substance Abuse Problem Checklist (SAPC; Carroll, 1983a) is a paper-and-pencil questionnaire developed to assist practitioners in obtaining information from clients entering treatment for substance abuse. According to Carroll (1984), the self-administered questionnaire 1) addresses both environmental and individual issues, 2) assesses generic problems related to substance use and abuse, 3) involves the client in the treatment process, 4) saves staff time, and 5) can be used to evaluate treatment effectiveness.

The author of the checklist, Jerome Carroll, Ph.D., has worked as an administrator, clinician, and researcher in substance abuse centers for almost two decades. Carroll's employment experience and familiarity with Alcoholics Anonymous' (AA) emphasis on personal inventories, combined with growing pressures to involve clients in the planning of treatment, were primary motivations for his development of the SAPC.

In conceptualizing the SAPC, Carroll and his colleagues identified eight problem categories reflecting broad-based treatment concerns: 1) Motivation for Treatment, 2) Physical and Sexual Health, 3) Personality Problems, 4) Social Relationships, 5) Job Related Problems, 6) Leisure Time, 7) Religious Problems, and 8) Legal Problems. Specific problem statements were developed for each category. A "large pool" (number unknown) of items was generated; subsequent attempts to shorten the list focused primarily on eliminating redundancy and reducing completion time. Next, a pilot test was administered to the first 100 patients entering Eagleville Hospital, Eagleville, Pennsylvania, for treatment of substance-related problems. The results of the pilot study were used to eliminate items that were seldom selected and to revise items to "make them less severe or absolute in their meaning" (Carroll, 1983b, p. 4). However, because the manual fails to present information concerning the revision, many questions remain unanswered. How many items were eliminated? Which items were eliminated? What criteria facilitated this process? And, which items were rewritten? Nevertheless, the SAPC currently consists of 377 "problems" associated with the eight categories identified by Carroll and his colleagues.

The Motivation for Treatment section contains 17 items consisting of "relatively short phrases describing patient problems typically encountered by clinical staff treating adult drug/alcohol abusers" (Carroll, 1983b, p. 2) and embracing issues related to the program, the staff, and the patient's motivation for entering treatment. The Physical and Sexual Health section (75 items) is composed of 50 items dealing with eating and sleeping patterns, known health problems (pain, ulcers, blackouts, headaches, eyesight, etc.), and energy levels. The remaining 25 items in this section query the respondent about sexual functioning (drive, performance, inhibitions, and experience). The Personality Problems section contains 97 statements about the patient's life philosophy, emotional status, self-esteem, stress, and ambition. Many of these items garner the respondent's opinions about how others perceive him or her on dimensions such as trust, social skill, and values. The 50 statements contained in the Social Relationship section are geared primarily toward the patient's family history, friends and acquaintances, and environmental aspects of his or her neighborhood (safety, availability of drugs, acceptance). The Job Related Problems section contains 52 statements describing current employment status, employment opportunities, education, qualifications, previous employment problems, employment relationships, and specific skills (reading, math, etc.). The Leisure Time issues tap the respondent's hobbies and recreation, physical and mental liabilities, and recreational preferences. Additionally, several items assess economic and time constraints that hinder the respondent's ability to participate in preferred leisurely activities. The Religious Problems section consists of 26 statements about moral beliefs and practices, spiritual experiences, and guilt. Finally, the section of Legal Problems contains 18 items addressing such issues as pending arrests, divorce, bankruptcy, property seizure, and parole/probation.

The cover of the SAPC contains demographic questions dealing with the respondent's age and sex as well as directions for completing the checklist. Pages 2–8 of the booklet contain the 377 problem statements, arranged by category, and three open-ended questions concerning treatment.

According to the instructions, the SAPC may be administered individually or in a group setting. Carroll (1983b) recommends that initial detoxification efforts precede completion of the questionnaire. The instrument is self-explanatory: clients are informed that the test booklet contains "different kinds of problems which alcoholics and addicts typically have when they enter treatment" (Carroll, 1983a, p. 1). To complete the instrument, the respondent must underline statements that describe his or her current status, circle statements that are particularly problematic, and ignore statements that are not relevant. Additionally, the three open-ended questions in the last section relate acknowledged problems to substance use, identify particularly relevant issues, and facilitate planning of treatment.

Purportedly, clients with a reading grade equivalence of 5.6 as measured by the Gates-MacGinitie Reading Tests (Gates & MacGinitie, 1965) require no assistance when completing the SAPC, but Carroll (1983b) reports that respondents who obtain reading equivalency scores of 4.1 and below typically request assistance. Projected completion time ranges from 30–40 minutes. Once the questionnaire has been completed, "the clinician need merely introduce himself to the patient and explain that he wishes to get to know the patient better by reviewing the responses" (Carroll, 1984, p. 33).

Practical Applications/Uses

Although Carroll (1983b) maintains that the SAPC has potential for research—longitudinal designs to monitor treatment effectiveness, cross-sectional designs to examine interindividual differences, and prospective designs to predict treatment outcome—he undermines this claim by noting that "the SAPC is not a test; therefore, the usual approaches to demonstrate the test reliability do not pertain" (Carroll, 1984, p. 34). Regarding any efforts to establish reliability, he emphasizes possible distortion of self-presentation due to the client's "clarity of cognitive functioning, trust that information will not be used against him/her and willingness to report personal problems, awareness of problems, especially how these problems relate to addiction, and, progress realized in treatment" (Carroll, 1983b, pp. 5-6). Attempts to establish reliability and validity for this instrument do exist (Carroll, 1983b, 1984), although these efforts fall short (see Technical Aspects) of providing the convincing psychometric evidence needed for the previously mentioned types of research purposes. Furthermore, because the instrument fails to "yield a single, overall score of general maladjustment and/or scaled scores for its eight categories," Carroll's claim that "it does offer a number of interesting research possibilities" is unsubstantiated (Carroll, 1983b, p. 5).

As such, the utility of the SAPC is necessarily limited to its ability to quantify self-reported problems, a process that may or may not facilitate the interview. According to Gynther and Green (1982), self-report inventories fail to 1) take situational variation into account, 2) control distortion of responses, 3) capitalize on a personality theory in the development of the item pool, and 4) make accurate predictions of descriptions of individual clients (p. 358).

At best, the SAPC represents a method for eliciting perceptions of problems in a nonconfrontive and, presumably, nonthreatening fashion that may enhance rapport between client and therapist. On the positive side, the SAPC does provide a wealth of information regarding the patient and his or her perceptions of past and present life circumstances, although much of the information may be suspect due to the self-report format. Additionally, a number of problems presented in the checklist are so general that their link to substance abuse appears weak. For example, while reviewing the SAPC, this reviewer found that 67 of the problem statements were personally descriptive (completion time was under 30 minutes). Of these, 5 dealt with motivation for treatment, 24 with physical and sexual health, 18 with personality, 1 with social relationships, 4 with job-related problems, 10 with leisure time, and 5 with religion. None of these 67 items dealt with legal issues.

Technical Aspects

Immediately following his "not a test" disclaimer regarding the reliability issue, Carroll (1984) describes a test-retest effort to establish temporal stability. The average interval between assessment was 3.9 days. All patients ($N = 46$) who entered treatment at Eagleville Hospital during early January 1983 participated in the reliability study. "Response consistency was computed for each of the eight categories of problems comprising the SAPC. A patient's response was considered consistent if a particular problem was selected (or ignored) on both administrations of the SAPC" (Carroll, 1984, pp. 34-35). Needless too say, these estimates were quite impressive, ranging from 84.9% (personality) to 94.9% (sexual problems), with a median consistency coefficient of 91.7% (social relationships and religion). Unfortunately, without more information, it remains unclear as to whether problems were checked consistently on both occasions or whether statements that were ignored on the first administration also were ignored on the second. By clumping the estimates of reliability by category, interested readers cannot possibly interpret the meaning of these coefficients. Similarly, if only a few problems were noted at intake, and a few different problems emerge on the follow up, the reliability estimates provided by Carroll will necessarily be impressive given the large number of items within each of the categories.

In that the SAPC was developed in 1983 and subsequently "adopted by 90 different treatment centers throughout the United States" (Carroll, 1985), these crude estimates of reliability are surprising indeed. A quick review of individual items reveals a great deal of overlap within and between categories (e.g., Section 1—"I don't think the treatment staff really understands me or my problems." Section 3— "No one knows what's good for me, but me." Section 4—"My family doesn't understand me.") There *are* techniques to examine internal consistency for checklist inventories. Essentially this format yields dichotomous data that are converted easily to binary variables for each problem statement. Thus, KR-20 coefficients could be calculated to estimate internal consistency within each of the eight problem categories, confirmatory factor analyses could be performed to establish factorial validity across the eight categories, and construct validity could be estimated by summing items within each of the eight categories and correlating scale scores to obtain convergent-discriminant estimates.

Regarding validity, Carroll implies in the following statement that the entire population of substance-related problems is represented within the eight sections of the SAPC:

> Since the SAPC is not a test, many procedures normally performed to demonstrate validity would not pertain. The developer can confidently state that the SAPC has content validity. (Carroll, 1984, p. 35)

At the same time, Carroll must recognize that selected staff members from a single hospital in one Eastern city collaborated to generate the list of 377 items. No doubt, participating staff members were exposed to a very select group of addicts: those who sought treatment, those who could afford treatment, and those who were willing to complete the SAPC. The question remains: How representative are these patients (and likewise their problems) of the substance-abusing population?

Carroll (1984) notes that "in a study of 114 Eagleville patients, 20 SAPC items were selected by 50 or more respondents" (p. 35). In other words, among clients seeking treatment for substance abuse, less than half identified more than 5% of the items on the SAPC problematic, or from another perspective, less than 4% of the SAPC items were selected by a majority of clients seeking treatment. With estimates such as these, it is difficult to argue that the SAPC is valid.

Carroll's "not a test" explanation for avoiding a rigorous examination of reliability and validity is weak. How difficult could it be to examine criterion, construct, and convergent-discriminant validity, given access to a population of patients in treatment? Why haven't these efforts been initiated? How does one justify using the SAPC for research and evaluation given these deficiencies?

Critique

Purportedly, everyone benefits from the SAPC: treatment personnel are relieved of the hassles involved with probing and guessing about the client; rapport and trust is enhanced because treatment begins with information the client has chosen to share; and, by sharing select information, the client assumes an active role in planning the treatment program. Perhaps the SAPC is useful as an initial icebreaker, but empirical support for this contention is elusive to this reviewer.

Speculation regarding the utility of the SAPC for evaluating treatment also is suspect. Aside from the fact that this instrument fails to yield interpretable scores and has yet to demonstrate acceptable levels of reliability and validity, many of the "problem statements" in the checklist are not likely to change as a function of treatment (e.g., "missing parts of my body," "scars," "hearing, vision, dental problems," etc.). Individuals attempting to evaluate treatment programs and/or to initiate research in the substance use/abuse arena are advised to look elsewhere. The SAPC is not an acceptable research instrument by this reviewer's criteria. Likewise, the utility of the Substance Abuse Problem Checklist as a clinical aid has not yet been established empirically.

References

Carroll, J.F.X. (1983a). *Substance Abuse Problem Checklist.* Eagleville PA: Eagleville Hospital.

Carroll, J.F.X. (1983b). *Substance Abuse Problem Checklist manual.* Eagleville, PA: Eagleville Hospital.

Carroll, J.F.X. (1984). The Substance Abuse Problem Checklist: A new clinical aid for drug and/or alcohol treatment dependency. *Journal of Substance Abuse Treatment, 1,* 31–36.

Carroll, J.F.X. (1985). The Substance Abuse Problem Checklist: A clinical timesaver. (Source unknown)

Gates, A.I., & MacGinitie, W.H. (1965). *Teachers manual, Gates-MacGinitie Reading Test (Survey E),* Boston: Houghton Mifflin Co.

Gynther, M.D., & Green, S.B. (1982). Methodological problems in research with self-report inventories. In P.C. Kendall & J.N. Butcher (Eds.), *Handbook of research methods in clinical psychology* (pp. 355–386). New York: John Wiley & Sons.

Brian W. McNeill, Ph.D.
Assistant Professor and Counselor, University Counseling Center and Department of Counseling Psychology, University of Kansas, Lawrence, Kansas.

SUICIDE INTERVENTION RESPONSE INVENTORY

Robert A. Neimeyer and William MacInnes. Memphis, Tennessee: Robert A. Neimeyer, Ph.D.

Introduction

The Suicide Intervention Response Inventory (SIRI) is a brief screening instrument designed to assess a respondent's ability to choose an appropriate therapeutic response to a suicidal individual. The SIRI was developed and introduced in 1981 by Robert A. Neimeyer of Memphis State University and William MacInnes of the University of Nebraska. Given the growing number of suicide and crisis intervention centers throughout the country, the test authors perceived a need to evaluate the appropriate-response skills necessary in crisis situations by the various types of caregivers involved in suicide intervention.

The SIRI consists of 25 items, each of which includes an initial "client" remark followed by two possible "helper" replies. Utilizing a forced-choice response format, the respondent is required to discriminate between what is considered a facilitative reply from the standpoint of crisis theory and a reply that is considered deleterious to effective intervention (Neimeyer & MacInnes, 1981). Respondents simply are instructed to select the reply they feel to be the most appropriate.

The content of the items for the SIRI was rationally derived from the test authors' personal experience in crisis counseling, from case reports, and from anecdotal accounts of professional and paraprofessional counselors (Neimeyer & MacInnes, 1981). Item content focuses on difficulties typically encountered in responding to the suicidal client. These include problems in attending to implicit or explicit suicide threats, avoiding simple reassurance or minimization of problems, and securing a verbal contract from the client not to consider self-injury before making further contact. The SIRI items have been constructed to cover a range of problem situations presented to the suicide interventionist (i.e., depressed, angry, or confused clients), and they require a variety of responses (i.e., reassurance, direct inquiry regarding suicidality and empathic responding).

Practical Applications/Uses

Dr. Neimeyer (personal communication, May 6, 1988) suggests that the SIRI provides an economical and straightforward "screening" device for sophistication in selecting appropriate responses to clients experiencing a suicidal crisis. As a result, he views the instrument as most appropriate as part of a battery of procedures designed to select and to evaluate the potential abilities of crisis or suicide "hotline" paraprofessionals. However, the SIRI also appears to be useful in assessing the suicide intervention skills of the broad range of mental health professionals, including counselors, social workers, nurses, and other groups. In every study to date, there have been subsets of respondents (usually 15-20%) who are markedly deficient in intervention skills with suicidal populations. Thus, at a minimum, the SIRI can identify these potentially destructive "helpers" so they can be screened out or referred for special training or supervision prior to assuming a crisis counseling role (R. A. Neimeyer, personal communication, May 6, 1988).

The SIRI also can be applied to program evaluation. For example, Neimeyer and Diamond (1983) importantly point out that many times suicide victims consult physicians within 4 months of taking their lives, often communicating their intent through a variety of direct or indirect means. Thus they have applied the SIRI in the evaluation of physicians' suicide intervention skills in medical school training programs. Similarly, the SIRI might be applied in the training and evaluation of students in social work, counseling, and professional psychology programs. Administration of the instrument and examination of responses to individual items in training courses may stimulate group discussion and serve as examples of appropriate responses to suicidal clients.

Scores for the SIRI are derived simply by summing the number of correct responses. A higher number of correct options is suggestive of the greater level of intervention skill on the part of a respondent. At this point in the instrument's development, a test manual is not available and there are no normative guidelines or cutoff scores indicating what might be considered a low versus a high level of performance by different groups of respondents. Instructions for the SIRI are simple and clear, and the presence of an examiner is only necessary to provide clarification regarding instructions.

Technical Aspects

The test authors have paid close attention to issues of reliability and validity in the initial development of the SIRI. In regards to issues of reliability, Neimeyer and MacInnes (1981) report a Kuder Richardson Formula 20 coefficient alpha (a measure of internal consistency) of .845. A similarly high test-retest reliability coefficient of .864 is reported over a 3-month period.

In terms of validity considerations, the SIRI has been demonstrated to discriminate between groups differing in level of expertise in suicide intervention. For example, scores of crisis volunteers in training were found to be significantly higher than untrained psychology students. Also, veteran crisis counselors evidenced higher scores than less experienced volunteers (Neimeyer & MacInnes, 1981). These effects of training and experience also have been replicated in groups of beginning versus advanced medical students (Neimeyer & Diamond, 1983). Additionally, the SIRI has been found to be sensitive to the effects of specific training in crisis intervention. Scores increased over 3 months of training for new paraprofessionals in crisis services as compared with groups of control subjects who received no training (Neimeyer & MacInnes, 1981). The SIRI demonstrates a moderate correlation with global therapeutic skills as measured by the Counseling Skills Evaluation film (Wolf & Wolf, 1974; $r = .66$). This moderate correlation also suggests that the SIRI taps some domain specific skills other than global counseling ability (Neimeyer & MacInnes, 1981).

In reference to the SIRIs predictive ability, Neimeyer and Oppenheimer (1983) demonstrated that scores on the SIRI were unrelated to individual interview ratings obtained from a crisis hotline staff member assessing "potential as a counselor." However, in this study, CSE scores were also found to be unrelated to staff ratings. Thus, one might question the rating skills of staff members regarding "potential as a counselor" that have no relationship to global counseling skills. Later studies have shown that SIRI scores were not related to factors that might influence a suicide interventionist's ability to respond in a facilitative manner, such as death anxiety (Neimeyer & Neimeyer, 1984) and belief that suicide is ethically acceptable under certain circumstances (Neimeyer & Diamond, 1983). Preliminary work on the underlying factor structure of the SIRI indicates that the instrument may not reflect just a unitary skill of recognizing facilitative replies to the suicidal client, but may be more multidimensional in nature, tapping such skills areas as elaboration of the complaint, exploration of suicidality, involvement, and reflection of negative feelings (Neimeyer & Hartley, 1986).

Critique

Overall, the SIRI appears to be a carefully developed instrument with application to an area where screening and evaluation of potential workers has all too often relied on global, nonobjective procedures. Neimeyer and Hartley (1986) report that the SIRI has been incorporated into counselor education programs and program evaluation efforts in over 100 crisis intervention, medical, and academic settings.

However, the instrument could use some interpretive guidelines for users in the form of cutoff points or normative reference groups that might be included in a future test manual. As the test authors acknowledge, the forced-choice-item format makes the SIRI susceptible to ceiling effects when used as a measure of improvement over training and evaluation of more advanced trainees. Dr. Neimeyer (personal communication, May 6, 1988) reports, however, that current work includes experimentation with a Likert-type response format that may alleviate problems associated with ceiling effects in more sophisticated trainees. Also, more predictive studies are needed for the SIRI focusing on relating SIRI scores (i.e., ability to recognize an appropriate response in a crisis situation) to effectiveness (i.e., ability to produce an appropriate response) as a crisis counselor.

Additional current work (R.A. Neimeyer, personal communication, May 6, 1988) with the SIRI includes the application of confirmatory factor-analytic procedures in order to identify possible subscales, subsequent need for item addition or deletion, and perhaps clarification of the results of Neimeyer and Hartley (1986), whose findings are limited in applicability to novice counselors. In sum, Dr. Neimeyer and his colleagues are to be commended for their ongoing work in developing and addressing the current limitations of the SIRI. Further work can only build and improve upon what is currently an extremely useful and practical instrument.

References

Neimeyer, R.A., & Diamond, R. (1983). Suicide management skills and the medical student. *Journal of Medical Education, 28,* 562–567.

Neimeyer, R.A., & Hartley, R.E. (1986). Factorial structure of the suicide intervention response inventory. *Suicide and Life-Threatening Behavior, 16,* 434–447.

Neimeyer, R.A., & MacInnes, W.D. (1981). Assessing paraprofessional competence with the Suicide Intervention Response Inventory *Journal of Counseling Psychology, 28,* 176–179.

Neimeyer, R.A., & Neimeyer, G.J. (1984). Death anxiety and counseling skill in the suicide interventionist. *Suicide and Life-Threatening Behavior, 14,* 126–131.

Neimeyer, R.A., & Oppenheimer, B. (1983). Concurrent and predictive validity of the suicide intervention response inventory. *Psychological Reports, 52,* 594.

Wolf, S., & Wolf, C.M. (1974). *Counseling Skills Evaluation (manual).* Poway, CA: Psychological Skills Development Corporation.

Gregory H. Dobbins, Ph.D.
Associate Professor of Management, University of Tennessee, Knoxville, Tennessee.

Dirk D. Steiner, Ph.D.
Assistant Professor of Psychology, Louisiana State University, Baton Rouge, Louisiana.

SYSTEM FOR TESTING AND EVALUATION OF POTENTIAL

Melany E. Baehr. Park Ridge, Illinois: London House Press.

Introduction

The System for Testing and Evaluation of Potential (STEP) provides estimates of potential for successful performance (PSP) and assessment of job-linked skills for higher level positions. Potential is defined as the fit between important job responsibilities of a position and the skills, abilities, personality characteristics, and background characteristics of the job candidate (Baehr, 1987). STEP was developed specifically for higher level jobs (e.g., vice presidents, middle managers, first- and second-line supervisors).

STEP was developed by Dr. Melany E. Baehr through her work at the Human Resources Center of the University of Chicago and at London House Press. The first validity study was conducted in 1963 and the research is continuing today. Most of the validity work is summarized in *The Development and Validation of Estimates of Potential for Successful Performance of Higher Level Personnel* (Baehr, 1984) and "A Review of Employee Evaluation Procedures and a Description of High Potential Executives and Professionals" (Baehr, 1987).

STEP is broken into three major parts. 1) The demands of the job are assessed with the Managerial and Professional Job Functions Inventory (MP-JFI). The MP-JFI was developed to provide job analysis information for a variety of uses. 2) The manual suggests using the information for job descriptions, clarification of job duties, diagnosing training and development needs, and, potentially, administering wages and salaries. 3) In addition to the *Interpretation and Research Manual* (Baehr, Wallace, & Hunt, 1986), Baehr (1988) has written a chapter on research relevant to the MP-JFI.

The inventory consists of 140 items, each describing a function performed in managerial and professional jobs. The items are further classified into 16 dimensions, each represented by 6 to 10 items. Financial Planning and Review, Coping with Difficulties and Emergencies, and Personnel Practices are three examples of the 16 dimensions. The respondent rates the importance of each function on a four-point scale with the constraint that approximately equal numbers of functions should be assigned to each of the four importance rating categories (ranging in importance from "little or none" to "outstanding").

570

Administration procedures of the MP-JFI are flexible. Individual or large groups may take the test at any one time, and supervision is not required. The inventory is untimed and is generally completed in approximately 30 to 60 minutes.

The items were tested on 893 employees in a "vocationally heterogeneous sample" (Baehr, Wallace, & Hunt, 1986, p. 13), although the sex and race composition of the group is never mentioned. A factor analysis identified the 16 dimensions. Most of the dimension intercorrelations are low, suggesting that the dimensions are independent.

The technical manual reports on the development of occupational profiles using the importance ratings of the MP-JFI. The test authors state that the inventory was "administered to representative samples of employees" (Baehr, Wallace, & Hunt, 1986, p. 6) in 12 occupational groups defined by crossing 3 occupational levels (from vice presidents to line supervisors) with 4 functional areas (line, professional, sales, and financial). The profiles were compared for the 12 occupational groups, and the manual reports the number of dimension differences between various occupational levels and functional areas. Most of the 16 dimensions successfully distinguish between levels within the functional areas. They also successfully distinguish between functional areas within Levels II and III, but not within Level I, the executive positions. Thus, individuals at the executive level perform similar tasks irrespective of functional area.

The profiles for occupational groups provide a standard against which to compare responses of individuals. The manual suggests that individuals whose responses are very discrepant from the norm for their level and functional area probably have an inappropriate concept of their position.

Once the job has been analyzed with the MP-JFI, it is classified into the four managerial hierarchies (Line, Professional, Sales, or Financial). The potential of the applicant then is assessed with the Managerial and Professional Test Battery. This instrument consists of nine paper-and-pencil tests that assess background and experience, mental abilities, creativity, personality characteristics, and personal and emotional adjustment. The predictors are weighted differentially depending upon whether the job has been classified into the line, professional, sales, or financial hierarchy. Potential estimates are provided for each occupational level within the relevant managerial hierarchy. The nine tests in the Managerial and Professional Test Battery are as follows:

1) The *Experience and Background Inventory* (EBI) is a biodata survey developed in 1980 by Baehr and Froemel that measures past performance and experience. It was designed to be used in selection and placement decisions and for counseling at higher level positions. The current instrument was constructed by revising the Personal History Index developed by Baehr, Burns, and McMurry in 1965. Initial instruments were developed for each sex separately, but finding similar dimensions, one form was written and items were stated in a nonsexist way. For example, sex is likely to have an influence on responses, particularly on questions regarding the spouse's occupation.

The EBI contains 107 items that cover family, education, and work histories. It is an untimed test, can be administered individually or in groups, and takes approximately 15 to 20 minutes to complete. Although some items have nearly continuous response choices (e.g., "How many years in all have you been employed?"), all are scored as contributing or not contributing to one or more of the 16 factors and many responses do not contribute to any factor.

The 16 scored factors were derived from factor-analysis studies. The factors include such things as school achievement, aspiration level, drive, general family responsibility, professional-successful parents, and active relaxation pursuits. The factors appear to be fairly independent; only 10 of the 120 of the intercorrelations exceed .40. Norms are based on a sample of 500 higher level professionals, including at least 283 men and 208 women. Norms are presented by age group, but not by sex.

2) The *Nonverbal Reasoning Test* was developed by R. J. Corsini in 1943 and was revised in 1947 and 1957. The test is designed to measure a person's capacity to think logically through pictorial problems. The test contains 44 multiple-choice items and can be administered individually or in groups. Items require the applicant to determine the logical relationship between a series of pictures. The test is untimed and takes about 15 minutes to complete. Clear instructions are provided in the test manual.

The norms for the Nonverbal Reasoning Test are based on more than 4,500 responses "from a wide variety of occupational groups" (Baehr, 1985, p. 8). Unfortunately, the sex and race of the norm group are not provided.

3) The *Bruce Vocabulary Inventory* (Bruce, 1959) is a 100-item multiple-choice test designed to assess the applicant's vocabulary. Each item asks the respondent to circle the word that means the same or almost the same as an identified word. The items were selected at random from the even number pages of the *Oxford Universal Dictionary.*

4) The *Word Fluency Test* was developed by Melany Baehr at the Human Resources Center at the University of Chicago in 1961. It is a measure of the extent that an individual can think of isolated words at a rapid rate. Applicants are asked to generate words from a specified category (e.g., types of food) that begin with 16 different letters. Applicants have 10 minutes to complete the test. The Word Fluency Test is scored by counting up the number of answers that fit the prescribed features of the category.

Norms are provided based upon the responses of 6,113 individuals from a wide variety of occupational groups. Once again, little detail is presented about the characteristics of the norm group.

5) The *Closure Flexibility Test* assesses the applicant's ability to see a figure that is embedded in a large and more complex diagram. The test is timed, and applicants have 10 minutes to complete 49 items. It is based upon the original Gottschaldt Figures Test that was constructed by Thurstone in 1944. The test has undergone three revisions, and the current version was constructed by Thurstone and Jeffrey in 1984.

Norms for the Closure Flexibility Test are based upon the responses of 5,200 individuals from a wide variety of occupational groups. No other information is presented about the norm group.

6) The *Cree Questionnaire* is designed to assess an individual's creative-innovative potential. Creativity is defined as the intellectual capacity and personality characteristics that are necessary to formulate problems and delineate original solutions (Thurstone, 1950). The questionnaire consists of 145 items that ask respondents

whether a behavior is typical of them. Applicants respond to each question by indicating Yes, No, or ? (uncertain). The test is untimed and can be administered either individually or in a group. The Cree Questionnaire is typically completed in 15–20 minutes.

The test was developed under the guidance of T. G. Thurstone and John Mellinger at the Psychometric Laboratory at the University of North Carolina in 1957. Three hundred seventy-seven items were administered to 142 engineers who had been identified as creative inventors and 141 who had been identified as having little creativity. One hundred forty-five items were found to differentiate significantly between the creative and noncreative engineers. These items were retained on the Cree Questionnaire.

Furcon (1965) administered the 145-item Cree Questionnaire to 1,016 male subjects. Responses to these items were factor analyzed and revealed a 13-factor solution. The subfactors assessed by the Cree Questionnaire are 1) Dominance (11 items); 2) Indifference (8 items); 3) Independence (12 items); 4) Autonomous Work Environment (10 items); 5) Selective Activity (10 items); 6) Work Involvement (10 items); 7) Work Under Pressure (5 items); 8) High Energy Level (10 items); 9) Fast Reaction Time (8 items); 10) High Ideation Rate (8 items); 11) High Theoretical Interests (9 items); 12) High Artistic Interests (6 items); and 13) High Mechanical Interests (5 items). Correlations among the 13 subfactors are fairly small.

7) The *Press Test* (Baehr & Corsini, 1957) is described as a test of the ability to perform a task under stress. Stress is defined as interference from distracting stimuli. A cognitive test is repeated with and without interfering background stimuli, and the degree of performance decrement when adding the interference is assessed. The test is based on the work of Stroop (1935).

The Press Test takes about 10 minutes and can be administered individually or in small groups. The test consists of three parts, and each part is timed to allow 90 seconds of work. Part I assesses reaction time to verbal stimuli. Part II is a test of reaction time to colored stimuli. Part III contains the distraction. Four columns of color names are printed in a color other than the color name. Subjects are asked to put the first letter of the color of the ink in the appropriate circle, ignoring the printed word. The score in Part III is compared to performance on Parts I and II to obtain a measure of the effect of distraction.

Norms are based "on a sample of more than 4,000 derived from various occupational groups" (Baehr & Corsini, 1959b, p. 11). No more detail about the norm group is provided.

8) The *Temperament Comparator* (Baehr, 1957) is designed to "assess the relatively permanent and basic temperament traits which characterize an individual's behavior" (Baehr, 1981, p. 1). Its intended use is for selection, placement, and development in organizational positions where "behavioral requirements" are important.

The test covers 18 traits and samples from 511 items in the Guilford (1940) and Guilford-Martin (1943a, 1943b) inventories. The Temperament Comparator contains 153 paired-comparison items and provides a profile of 18 traits and 5 behavior dimensions. The behavior dimensions, which are combinations of traits determined through factor analysis, are Extroversive/Impulsive versus Reserved/Cautious; Emotionally Responsive versus Emotionally Controlled; Self-Reliant/Individually-Oriented versus Dependent/Group-Oriented; Excitable/High Energy versus Placid/Low Energy; and Socially-Oriented versus Not Socially-Oriented. In addition to the 18 traits, one scale measures Consistency of Response, which is thought to measure personal insight and emotional health status.

Test completion generally takes about 20 minutes and can be administered to any size group. Trait scores represent the number of times a trait was chosen as the more representative of the respondent's behavior. Scores can range from 0 to 17. The Consistency of Response score is determined by the number of times transitivity is exhibited.

Norms are given for 5,000 individuals in a wide variety of occupational groups. No mention is made of the sex, race, or age composition of the norm group.

8) The *EMO (Emotional Health) Questionnaire* was designed to assess personal, emotional adjustment. The instrument is purported to reflect internal psychodynamics and the relationship with the external environment. The questionnaire was developed in clinical settings to provide checks on emotional health status during treatment. In 1957, it was revised by Drs. George and Melany Baehr so that it would be appropriate for industrial and occupational settings. In these settings, it is intended for personality diagnosis or to gauge the individual's present level of adjustment.

There are several levels of interpretation of EMO scores. At the most thorough level, the manual suggests that results of the questionnaire be used as an adjunct to the interview in placement of managerial and specialized personnel. At less-complex levels, the manual suggests the usefulness of the EMO for screening individuals with certain emotional states. The manual also concludes that variables on the EMO "are most useful in the prediction of job performance, especially where resistance to pressure and stress are an important aspect of the job" (Baehr, 1959, p. 2).

The EMO contains 140 items describing different experiences. Respondents indicate whether or not they have had the experience at least once during the past month. If an individual responds positively to this question, he or she is asked to indicate whether they were "pleased," "not affected," "troubled a little," or "troubled very much" by the experience. The purpose of this response format is to measure frequency and intensity of experiences.

Scores are provided on 10 psychodiagnostic dimensions. Thirty of the items are buffer items that deal with nondisturbing everyday events. These items are also included in scoring. The 10 dimensions are 1) Rationalization (defined as blaming others for own failure); 2) Inferiority Feelings; 3) Hostility; 4) Depression; 5) Fear and Anxiety; 6) Organic Reaction (referring to physical symptoms); 7) Projection (defined as experiencing one's own hostile desires as intentions of others); 8) Unreality; 9) Sex; and 10) Withdrawal (from contacts and activities). An eleventh scale is Buffer Items, which is diagnostic when people are disturbed by daily events. The subscales of the EMO are rather highly correlated.

A factor analysis was conducted on a sample of 1,193 male subjects, 1,030 of which were employed and the remainder being hospitalized for emotional disorders, primarily schizophrenia. The analysis produced 21 factors that, for practicality, were subjected to a second-order factor analysis. The four resulting factors differentiated between the employed and hospitalized samples and are recommended for use in the rapid screening procedure. The factors are Internal Adjustment (dealing with insecurity, fear, and anxiety); External Adjustment (dealing with depression, projection, and unreality); Somatic Adjustment (dealing with organic symptoms and sex adjustment problems); and General Adjustment (dealing with tension concerning everyday experiences).

The third major part of the STEP is the Managerial and Professional Skills Functions Inventory (MP-SFI). The MP-SFI is identical to the previously described MP-JFI except for the responses requested. This form requests ratings of the respondent's own ability to perform each function, not the importance of the function to the job as was the case in the MP-JFI. The major use of the ability form is to determine an individual's readiness for a new position and for career counseling and guidance. Baehr (1988) suggests that when using both the MP-JFI and MP-SFI, the MP-SFI should be administered first, approximately one week before the MP-JFI.

Research on the MP-SFI is apparently scant, as no information is reported in the technical manual. The manual recommends training when differences between self-rated abilities and importance ratings are substantial (more than five normalized standard score units), but again, validity data are needed to evaluate both the ability responses and their relation to the importance ratings and other criteria.

Practical Applications/Uses

London House recommends three major uses for the STEP. First, the battery can be used as a selection device (STEP-S). Candidates are administered the MP-JFI and the Managerial and Professional Test Battery. A potential score is determined for Levels I, II, and III in the appropriate managerial hierarchy. The STEP-S takes about 2 hours to administer. London House recommends the STEP-S program for selecting applicants into entry-level managerial positions. In addition, STEP-S identifies applicants who have outstanding potential and should be groomed for promotion into higher level management positions.

The STEP can also be used for selection and training (STEP-ST). Applicants are administered the MP-JFI, the Managerial and Professional Test Battery, and the MP-SFI. The STEP-ST provides an estimate of potential for all levels in the appropriate managerial hierarchy and also describes the specific skills of the applicant. Thus, training programs can be provided for applicants who have great potential but are deficient in certain skills areas. The STEP-ST requires approximately 2½ hours to administer.

The final use of the STEP is for selection, training, and counseling (STEP-STC). The STEP-STC provides an estimate of potential, an evaluation of current skills, and detailed information on each of the predictors. London House recommends that career counseling be conducted based upon the results to help each employee understand their strengths and weaknesses. Specifically, job candidates should discuss ways of improving their weaknesses and of fully utilizing their strengths. The STEP-STC requires approximately 4 hours to administer.

All parts of the STEP can be administered individually or in groups. The physical setting should be pleasant and quiet. The administration procedure is clearly described in the *Administrator's Guide* (Moretti & Baehr, 1986) and in the individual manuals that accompany each test. STEP is administered on the company's site.

The STEP can be scored through two mechanisms. First, the user can return the test batteries to London House. Second, the company can use London House's Immediate Test Analysis by Computer (ITAC) system. This system requires that the applicant's responses be read to an operator at London House. The operator enters the data directly into a computer, and the user will receive a potential score for each applicant the same day. Although adequate instructions are provided for hand scoring the individual tests, potential estimates cannot be obtained without using London House's scoring services.

The feedback provided by the STEP is very clear. The employer receives a potential estimate for each of the three occupational levels within the appropriate hierarchy. In addition, these scores are interpreted with a verbal label of "Highly Questionable," "Questionable," "Marginal," "Acceptable," "Desirable," "Very Desirable," or "Outstanding." If the STEP-ST is administered, the employer also receives an evaluation of the extent to which the applicant's job skills are desirable for the three levels in the hierarchy. Finally, if the STEP-STC is administered, the employer receives potential estimates plus a score for each of the predictors that contribute to the potential estimate and the job skills assessment.

Although London House maintains that the STEP can be interpreted by managers without specialized knowledge in testing, the reviewers feel that a professional with testing expertise should be consulted to ensure that the limitations of the test are clearly understood. In addition, testing expertise is needed with the STEP-STC because individual feedback will be provided to the candidate.

Technical Aspects

Fifty-three concurrent validity studies have been conducted to examine the validity of STEP. Forty-seven of these studies have used supervisory evaluations on a paired-comparison scale as the criterion. Paired-comparison evaluation techniques avoid leniency errors that can deflate validity coefficients. Of the 47 studies using supervisory evaluations, 24 also included objective measures of performance (e.g., average sales, tenure, salary). The remaining six studies used only objective indices.

Ten of the 53 validity studies have extremely small sample sizes ($N < 26$). The remaining 43 studies have sample sizes ranging from 26 to 240 with a mean sample size of 111. The results of the 43 studies are very impressive, with validity coefficients ranging from .31 to .90 and a mean validity coefficient of .62.

A second validity study used the STEP to demonstrate that the individual tests in the Managerial and Professional Test Battery differentiate between managers employed in Level I, Level II, and Level III positions and differentiate between Line, Professional, Sales, and Financial functions within levels. The results of these analyses are also very impressive. For example, Levels I, II, and III in the line managerial hierarchy significantly differ on 88% of the 26 predictors in the Managerial and Professional Test Battery. For the professional, sales, and financial hierarchies, the percentage of tests that differentiate between Level I, Level II, and Level III are 65%, 73%, and 50%, respectively. In addition, the predictors differentiate extremely well between the line, professional, sales, and financial hierarchies within Levels II and III, but not within Level I. Thus, the skills and abilities needed to perform Level III and Level II jobs differ as a function of the hierarchy, while Level I (top executive) jobs require the same skills, abilities, and attributes across the four functional areas.

A third validity study focused on examining the intercorrelations between the predictors in the Managerial and Professional Test Battery. In general, the intercorrelations between the predictors are very low. For example, only 6 of 960 correlations between factors in the Experience and Background Inventory and the other predictors were significant at $p < .001$. Similarly, when the Press Test was correlated with the other predictors, the only correlations in the .30s were with the cognitive tests of Nonverbal Reasoning, Word Fluency, Bruce Vocabulary, and Closure Flexibility. Furthermore, Word Fluency is correlated .41 with the Bruce Vocabulary, and Closure Flexibility is correlated .50 with Nonverbal Reasoning.

A couple of problems with these validity studies should be noted. First, all of the criterion-related studies have used a concurrent design. Thus, it is possible that the validity of the STEP would decrease when administered to actual applicants due to differences in motivation, experiences, training, and so on.

Second, almost all of the validity studies have been conducted at the lower level of each managerial hierarchy. For example, only 3 studies have used executives from Level I while 44 studies have used employees from Level III, the lowest level of the hierarchy. In response to this problem, recent validation efforts (Baehr, in press) have taken a synthetic validity approach. This research has attempted to determine which of the 24 predictors from the Managerial and Professional Test Battery predict importance ratings for each of the 16 job functions assessed with the MP-JFI. Stepwise regression analyses indicate that all but one of the 16 dimensions can be predicted by the 24 measures with an average multiple correlation of .41. This line of research is continuing with the expectation of developing a matrix that links job requirements (assessed with the MP-JFI) to personal skills and attributes (assessed with the Managerial and Professional Test Battery). Once this work is complete, the weighting of predictors could be tailored to the specific profile that is identified with the MP-JFI.

The reviewers are also concerned about the large number of predictors that are included in the STEP. Forty-one predictors can be derived from the STEP and 24 are included in the calculation of potential scores. In several validity studies, stepwise regression analyses were used to predict job performance. Such a procedure will overfit the regression equation, thus resulting in a multiple correlation that is larger than it should be. Although some of the multiple correlations have been "shrunk," the researchers should cross-validate their results in an independent sample. In addition, Baehr and her associates need to present the unique contribution of each predictor and discuss whether the contribution of each predictor changes from study to study. The reviewers would expect that the number of predictors could be reduced dramatically without significantly affecting the validity of the STEP.

The manner in which studies that found differences between Level I, Level II, and Level III positions were interpreted is also of concern. Although such differences are consistent with the hypothesis that the skills, abilities, and attributes assessed in the Managerial and Professional Test Battery are necessary for successful performance at higher level positions, the results could also be produced by any factor that is confounded with level, including age, socioeconomic status, formal training, etc.

For example, sex of employee would probably differ across the three levels (with a larger percentage of men occupying top level positions). However, such findings do not indicate that "maleness" is essential for success at higher level positions.

There are numerous questions about the validity studies that could not be answered in the technical manuals. For example, more information is needed about sample characteristics. In addition, the relative contribution of the individual predictors should be presented, or, at a minimum, the manual should at least indicate which predictors were significant. Furthermore, while the difficulty in finding sample sizes that are large enough to validate the instrument for minority groups is recognized, it is disappointing that research has not compared the potential scores of blacks, whites, and Hispanics and that only one study has investigated the effects of age and sex on potential scores. Although this study suggests that sex and age do not affect potential scores, the lack of statistical power may explain these null results. The reviewers strongly encourage future research to examine test performance for all minority groups.

A large number of studies have also been conducted to investigate the reliabilities of individual tests in the Managerial and Professional Test Battery. Several major findings are revealed in these studies. First, the reliabilities of the cognitive measures are adequate. For example, the Nonverbal Reasoning Test has KR_{20}s that range from .72-.80, the Word Fluency Test has a test-retest reliability over 1 month of .78, and Closure Flexibility has a split-half reliability of .94. In addition, test-retest reliabilities over 1 week were .72, .82, and .80 for Parts I, II, and III of the Press Test and ranged from .78 to .90 for the Temperament Comparator. Internal consistency reliability (KR_{20}) averaged .78 for the second-order factors of the EMO.

The reliabilities of some of the other tests are clearly unacceptable. For example, one scale of the MP-JFI has a coefficient alpha less than .50 and six more have alpha coefficients less than .80. Similarly, alpha coefficients range from .55 to .89 for the factors of the Experience and Background Inventory. Coefficient alpha for the dimensions of the Cree test range from .11-.78, with nine of the dimensions having alphas less than .50.

Some research has also examined the validity of the individual tests in the STEP. An earlier form of the Background and Experience Inventory produced an r of .42 using six dimensions to predict paired comparison ratings and an r of .50 using five dimensions to predict mean sales volume rank with 210 sales representatives. In a validity study for police samples, white and black officers took the earlier form and some of the dimensions were retained. The technical manual does not give details of the results of this study (Baehr, Furcon, & Froemel, 1968) other than to say that there were "some differences but also considerable overlap, in the predictive dimensions for Black and for White police officers" (p. 16).

Validity evidence is also provided for the Press Test. The manual reports that the Press Test is a significant predictor of success for occupations including clerks, accountants, engineers, and sales representatives. No information is provided, however, on the level of the validity nor on the nature of the criteria of success. In addition, the manual states that the test is valid for blacks and whites, although sample sizes of black employees did not exceed 32. Furthermore, the similarity of the validity coefficients for the different races was not presented or discussed. No information is given with regard to sex differences on this test.

The Temperament Comparator has also been used in 62 criterion-related validity studies, although the manual is rather vague about details of the studies. For example, one of the studies (Baehr & Burns, 1972) involved 141 supermarket managers. The extent of information the manual provides is "Three of the five *TC* factor scores . . . survived validation and made sizable positive weight contributions to the prediction equation" (Baehr, 1981, p. 11). The ambiguity about members of the group and the size of the weights is typical of this manual (and others in the STEP).

The EMO has been validated using various minority groups, and this manual is rather complete, relative to the others, in giving technical information, including sample sizes of the minority groups. In a criterion-related validity study of bus operators, a test battery was validated that included the EMO. Of 11 tests in the validation, the EMO was one of three to survive. Concurrent validities were .46, .43, and .47 for white, black, and Spanish samples. Unfortunately, no further detail is given regarding which scales were predictive and how predictive they were, or whether the same variables were predictive for each of the different samples. Similarly, little detail is given for a validation study of police patrolmen. The EMO was included in a battery that yielded multiple correlations of .56 for whites and .61 for blacks.

When using the suggested normalized standard score of 40 to reject, the EMO results in disparate rejection rates for various groups (e.g., 14.22% of whites would be rejected, 25.83% of blacks, and 24.56% of Spanish-surnamed individuals). The technical manual's conclusion with regard to adverse impact is that differences exist but they are "not likely to be as severe as disparities demonstrated on ability and aptitude tests" (Baehr, 1981, p. 86). As usual, no information is provided regarding sex differences.

Unfortunately, with the exception of the cognitive ability tests and EMO, little evidence of construct validity is presented for instruments in the STEP. The reviewers were especially concerned about the construct validity of the Cree Questionnaire and Temperament Comparator. These instruments should be related to comparable measures that exist in the literature. Baehr and her associates appear satisfied to demonstrate that STEP predicts performance, but, due to inadequate attention to construct validity, are unable to delineate the specific constructs that are predictive. Furthermore, personal counseling and training are impossible if the individual measures do not possess construct validity. Thus, the value of STEP-ST and STEP-STC seems questionable.

The rationale behind the Managerial and Professional Skills Functions Inventory also seems problematic. As was noted earlier, this instrument asks the respondent to rate his or her own ability on each of the items contained in the MP-JFI. Unfortunately, no validity evidence is available. Given the research that has been conducted on self-evaluation of abilities (e.g., Mabe & West, 1982), it seems unlikely that job candidates would accurately rate their own skills, especially when low ratings may prevent them from advancing into upper levels in the organization.

Critique

The importance of an instrument like the STEP cannot be overemphasized. Identifying managerial talent is critical for the long-term effectiveness of any organization. The validities reported for the STEP indicate that it may be a useful instrument for this purpose. Unfortunately, several issues must be resolved before the reviewers can endorse the instrument.

First, more validity work needs to be conducted on the instrument. It is critical that this research use a predictive rather than a concurrent design and include samples from Level I within the managerial hierarchies. Furthermore, specific attention needs to be focused on the construct validity of the predictors. For example, intercorrelations between the predictors and other measures of similar constructs should be determined. In addition, correlations between scores on the Managerial and Professional Skills Function Inventory and an applicant's actual strengths and weaknesses as measured with an assessment center need to be determined. Finally, more validity studies are needed for the tests that have little data available on the current as opposed to a previous form (e.g., the Experience and Background Inventory and the Emotional Health Questionnaire).

Although the reviewers espouse the notions of validity generalization, more evidence about the fairness of the tests for various protected groups would be desirable. The tests simply have not been used on large numbers of women, blacks, or other racial minorities. London House is encouraged to engage in such research.

Although the manuals cover most of the general issues necessary to understand and use the tests, they often lack some crucial information, as discussed previously. It would be useful to have more information on the demographic characteristics of the norm groups and the individual b-weights for the predictors. Such information would allow users to determine the manner in which each predictor affects potential scores and whether their applicant pool is similar to the norm group used for the STEP. Similarly, the incremental validity of each predictor should be presented and discussed. The reviewers would like to be convinced that it is necessary to administer 11 tests to predict job success adequately. This concern is exacerbated because research indicates that a single measure of cognitive ability can predict performance in managerial jobs fairly well (Hunter, 1986).

Despite the above concerns, the validity coefficients obtained with the STEP are impressive and slightly larger than other techniques that are available for selecting managerial personnel. London House is encouraged to continue their research on the instrument, paying particular attention to the issues that have been raised in this review. If these issues can be adequately addressed, then the STEP will offer organizations an excellent method for selecting managerial employees.

References

This list includes text citations and suggested additional reading.

Baehr, G. O. (1959). *EMO Questionnaire: Interpretation and research manual*. Park Ridge, IL: London House.

Baehr, G.O., & Baehr, M.E. (1957). *EMO Questionnaire*. Park Ridge, IL: London House.

Baehr, M.E. (1957). *The Temperament Comparator*. Park Ridge, IL: London House.

Baehr, M.E. (1961). *Word Fluency*. Park Ridge, IL: London House.

Baehr, M. E. (1981). *Temperament Comparator: Interpretation and research manual*. Park Ridge, IL: London House.

Baehr, M.E. (1984). *The development and validation of the estimates of potential for successful performance of higher-level personnel.* Chicago, IL: University of Chicago.

Baehr, M.E. (1985). *Nonverbal Reasoning: Interpretation and Research manual.* Park Ridge, IL: London House Press.

Baehr, M.E. (1987). A review of employee evaluation procedures and a description of "high potential" executives and professionals. *Journal of Business and Psychology, 1,* 172–202.

Baehr, M. E. (1988). The Managerial and Professional Job Functions Inventory (MP-JFI). In S. Gael (Ed.), *Job analysis handbook* (pp.1072–1085). New York: John Wiley & Sons.

Baehr, M.E. (in press). *A human resource management system for testing and the evaluation of potential.* Park Ridge, IL: London House.

Baehr, M. E., & Burns, F. M. (1972). *The improvement of selection and utilization procedures for personnel in the supermarket industry.* Chicago: The University of Chicago, Industrial Relations Center.

Baehr, M.E., Burns, R.K., & McMurry, R.N. (1965). *Personal History Index.* Park Ridge, IL: London House.

Baehr, M.E., & Corsini, R.J. (1959a). *The Press Test.* Park Ridge, IL: London House.

Baehr, M.E., & Corsini, R.J. (1959b). *The Press Test: Interpretation and research manual.* Park Ridge, IL: London House.

Baehr, M.E., & Froemel, E.C. (1980). *Experience and Background Inventory.* Park Ridge, IL: London House.

Baehr, M.E., & Froemel, E.C. (1986). *Experience and Background Inventory: Interpretation and research manual.* Park Ridge, IL: London House.

Baehr, M.E., Furcon, J.E., & Froemel, E.C. (1968). *Psychological assessment of patrolman qualifications in relation to field performance.* Washington, DC: U.S. Government Printing Office.

Baehr, M.E., Wallace, G.L., & Hunt, B.A. (1986). *Managerial and Professional Job Functions Inventory: Interpretation and research manual.* Park Ridge, IL: London House.

Bruce, M.M. (1959). *Bruce Vocabulary Inventory.* New Rochelle, NY: Author.

Corsini, R.J. (1957). *Non-Verbal Reasoning Test.* Park Ridge, IL: London House.

Furcon, J.E. (1965). *Creative personality: A factor analytic study.* Unpublished master's thesis, Depaul University, Chicago.

Guilford, J.P. (1940). *Inventory of Factors STDCR.* Beverly Hills, CA: Sheridan Supply Co.

Guilford, J.P., & Martin, H.G. (1943a). *Guilford-Martin Inventory of Factors GAMIN.* Beverly Hills, CA: Sheridan Supply Co.

Guilford, J.P., & Martin, H.G. (1943b). *Guilford-Martin Personnel Inventory O AG Co.* Beverly Hills, CA: Sheridan Supply Co.

Hunter, J.E. (1986), Cognitive ability, cognitive aptitudes, and job performance. *Journal of Vocational Behavior, 29,* 340–362.

Mabe, P.A., & West, S.G. (1982). Validity of self-evaluations of ability: A review in meta-analysis. *Journal of Applied Psychology, 67,* 280–296.

Moretti, D.M., & Baehr, M.E. (1986). *System for Testing and Evaluation of Potential-STEP.* Park Ridge, IL: London House.

Stroop, J.R. (1935). Studies of interference in serial verbal reactions. *Journal of Experimental Psychology, 18,* 643–667.

Thurstone, L.L. (1950). *Creative talent* (Research Rep. No. 61). Chicago: The University of Chicago.

Thurstone, L.L., & Jeffrey, T.E. (1984). *Closure Flexibility.* Park Ridge, IL: London House.

Thurstone, T.G., & Mellinger, J. (1957). *Cree Questionnaire.* Park Ridge, IL: London House.

Joyce A. Eckart, Ed.D.
Assistant Professor of Education, Oakland University, Rochester, Michigan.

TEACHER FEEDBACK QUESTIONNAIRE

Office of Public and Professional Services. Kalamazoo, Michigan: Office of Public and Professional Services, Western Michigan University.

Introduction

The Teacher Feedback Questionnaire (TFQ), based on the 1968 Teacher Image Questionnaire (The Evaluation Center, Western Michigan University, personal communication, July 26, 1988), is a 27-item, self-administered assessment designed to record students' perception of teacher performance. Information from the TFQ is intended to help teachers gain insight into teaching performance as perceived by the students they teach. The first 25 items of the TFQ call for Likert-type responses using six categories: 1) Strongly Disagree, 2) Disagree, 3) Neutral, 4) Agree, 5) Strongly Agree, 6) Don't Know. For each statement, a teacher behavior is presented, followed by a short description of that behavior (e.g., *Noise Control*. The teacher keeps the classroom from being too noisy so that students can get their work done). The 25 teacher behaviors are 1) knowledge of subject, 2) clarity of presentation, 3) variety of methods, 4) variety of materials, 5) student interest, 6) instructional pace, 7) teacher interest, 8) teacher disposition, 9) attitude toward students, 10) fair treatment, 11) orderly procedures, 12) noise control, 13) classroom control, 14) helping students, 15) praise, 16) homework, 17) expectations for students, 18) return of students work, 19) tests, 20) emphasis on learning, 21) class rules, 22) use of class time, 23) grading in assignments, 24) sense of humor, and 25) grading for class. On the final two items respondents are asked to identify any teacher behaviors that are especially liked and to make suggestion for teacher improvement. The TFQ is published through the Office of Public and Professional Services, College of Education, Western Michigan University, Kalamazoo, Michigan. No information is provided about individual authorship.

The instrument consists of a 4-page, $8^{1}/_{2}"\times 11"$ consumable booklet and an optical scanning sheet. Directions for administration are given on the first page of the questionnaire. First, students are asked to respond to each statement by telling whether or not it describes *"your teacher."* Students are advised that information from the class will be used to make a group report and that individual students' answers will not be shown to the teacher. Next, students are asked to code school and demographic information on the optical scanning sheet. Neither the teacher's name nor the student's name appears on the form. Confidentiality of individual responses is emphasized, and students are asked to be fair and honest in answering each item. Finally, the directions conclude with the statement, "Your answers can help your teacher do the best possible job for you and your class" (Office of Public and Professional Services [OPPS], 1986a, p. 1).

Pages 2 and 3 contain the 25 teacher-behavior statements. For ease in marking, the code to be used reappears on page 2. For each statement, one of the 25 teacher behaviors appears in capital letters followed by an explanation of the teacher behavior. Students are to blacken in the circle on the answer sheet that corresponds to their opinion on how that statement describes their teacher.

On page 4, students are asked to respond to two questions. The first question asks for information about the perceived strengths of the teacher. The second question asks for suggestion for improvement to make the teacher more effective in the classroom.

An administration instruction sheet and a packet for reading and interpreting the report are included with the questionnaire. It is suggested that someone other than the teacher being rated administer and collect the questionnaires so that the anonymity of each student will be ensured. There is no grade or age level suggested. Respondents are instructed to code their grade level as elementary, middle, or high school. A time limit of 30 minutes is suggested. The completed answer sheets are sent to The Evaluation Center at Western Michigan University to be scored. A report is returned to the teacher with directions for interpreting the information and for developing a plan of action. If that teacher wishes others to receive the report, a release form must be included. The report contains two components: an item-response data summary and a report of written comments.

(1) *Item-response data summary.* For each item the following information is given: responses (1–5) number of responses, responses (1–5) item mean score, responses (1–5) standard deviation and a frequency distribution, responses (1–6). A basic explanation of these statistical concepts is presented in the report. For clarity of interpretation, an example is given in the report in which the mean score and the cumulative frequencies ($N = 4$) for each of the items, A, B, and C, are the same. However, the distribution of responses over the six choices, 1) Strongly Disagree, 2) Disagree, 3) Neutral, 4) Agree, 5) Strongly Agree, and 6) Don't Know, is different. The difference in response distribution leads to a different interpretation of the score for each item.

Item A: three respondents selected disagree, one respondent selected strongly agree. For Item A, 75% of those who answered that item disagreed with it. Perceptions of the group were consistent. The one response of 5 (strongly agree), an outlier, could have been due to reading the coding wrong. Item B: one respondent strongly disagree, two respondents selected neutral, and one respondent selected agree. For Item B, however, 50% of the respondents were neutral (i.e., neither agreed nor disagreed), 25% agreed, and 25% strongly disagreed. Half of the class surveyed had no opinion on how their teacher performed, yet the mean for this item is also 2.75. There was a place to mark "don't know," response 6. Students do think that this item applies to their teacher; nevertheless, they are undecided if their teacher practices this teacher behavior. The teacher could make a deliberate attempt to stress this behavior so that students are aware of it. Item C: one respondent selected strongly disagree, one respondent selected disagree, and two respondents selected agree. Interpreting the results for Item C are less clear than either Item A or B. 50% of those responding agree, 50% disagree, and of those 25% disagree strongly. Implications and a plan for action are not clear from the responses for this item. Although no action plan should be formed based on just these scores, it is especially true in the case of Item C where the distribution appears to be bimodal. Other information on the makeup of this class would be necessary in order to set up a plan for self-development (Office of Public and Professional Services, 1986b).

2) *Report of written comments*. Responses to the last two questions are copied verbatim. No attempt is made to summarize or reword these comments. The only changes are mechanical. The meaning of responses have been guarded to ensure that the meaning conveyed is the meaning intended.

Teachers have the option of requesting a total score for all respondents or scores for each section of respondents. Thus a teacher in middle school or high school who teaches multiple sections might compare results from different sections. Information about factors such as class makeup, content area, reason for taking the course, and time of day could make interpretation of the report more meaningful. Instructions for interpreting the results of the TFQ are clear. A distinction is made between actual teaching behavior and how that behavior is perceived by the students. If a teacher is dissatisfied with the score on a particular item, three considerations may help with the decision of how much attention to give it: Does it appear that the distribution of responses could be significantly changed? Are the resources for change available? Is this item an important one to focus attention on? (OPPS, 1986b). A low response to an item might be interpreted in at least three ways. The behavior is not practiced because the teacher does not know how to do it, does not value it, or is not perceived as sincerely practicing it. There will be a different plan of action depending on the interpretation of the score by the teacher and the attention given to each item.

Practical Applications/Uses

The TFQ was designed to help the classroom teacher gain insight into teaching performance as perceived by students in the class. It was not designed to evaluate teachers for tenure, merit, or promotion. It is a formative evaluation tool that the teacher can use to aid in his or her professional development. The teacher behaviors that are identified in the instrument have been shown to have significant implications for effective teaching. The questionnaire is easy to administer. The resulting confidential report is a representation of how the teacher is perceived by the students. The information is for the teacher's use in professional development.

Technical Aspects

Little technical information is available about the TFQ. No information about how items were chosen for inclusion in the questionnaire is provided. No reasons are given for the ordering of the teacher behaviors nor is the process described for how the sentences were formed describing the behaviors. No validation studies are described. No measures of reliability are furnished. No reference to a norming population is provided. The statistics offered to the teacher are descriptive and based on his or her class(es). No attempt has been made to compare findings to a larger pool of respondents. Apparently the TFQ is being used for research purpose, as information is required that is not used in reporting scores to the classroom teachers. It is unfortunate that this information has not been shared.

Critique

In light of the current emphasis on accountability, instruments are needed to help teachers measure their teaching effectiveness and develop strategies to strengthen their teaching skills. Team teaching, peer coaching, and mentoring have been identified as ways to aid teachers in professional growth. It appears logical that data about perceptions from students would provide more valuable information for teachers. An instrument that is nonthreatening and solely designed for self-improvement is a wise inclusion for a program of professional development. Unfortunately, although the TFQ hints at such an instrument, it falls short of expectations. Further work needs to be done on norming, validity, and reliability. If the instrument is for development, suggestions should be given about when the instrument should be administered so that it truly is a formative tool. If this is the case, an alternate form should be created so that in a retest situation the teacher could see if those items that he or she had decided to focus on had indeed changed. The questionnaire could be reused if the optical scanning sheet had space on it for answers to the essay responses. The instrument also would be more useful if it were a part of a larger inservice program that offered further suggestions and strategies for development of effective teacher behaviors.

In conclusion, the Teacher Feedback Questionnaire is relevant and could be useful to the classroom teacher. However, the potential user needs to be aware that the instrument lacks measures of validity or reliability. As it is, the TFQ should not become a part of inservice programs for self-development and more importantly should not be used by administrators for summative evaluation of teachers for tenure, promotion, or merit.

References

Educator Feedback Center. (1968). *Teacher-Image Questionnaire*. Kalamazoo, MI: Author.

Office of Public and Professional Services. (1986a). *Teacher Feedback Questionnaire*. Kalamazoo, MI: Author.

Office of Public and Professional Services. (1986b). *Teacher Feedback Questionnaire: Reading and interpreting your report*. Kalamazoo, MI: Author.

Robert J. Drummond, Ed.D.
Program Director, Counselor Education, University of North Florida, Jacksonville, Florida.

TEACHER OPINION INVENTORY

National Study of School Evaluation Staff. Falls Church, Virginia: National Study of School Evaluation.

Introduction

The Teacher Opinion Inventory (TOI) is a questionnaire that measures teachers' opinions of the organization and administration of their school, curriculum and instruction, student discipline, counseling and advisement program, school and community relations, and job satisfaction. The instrument is one of three instruments in a series, which includes the Parent Opinion Inventory and the Student Opinion Inventory, used primarily in school evaluation and accreditation studies.

The Teacher Opinion Inventory was developed by the National Study of School Evaluation to be a part of a complete school evaluation program. The development of the TOI followed a three-phase design. In phase one, the organization utilized a group of experts that included professors of curriculum and instruction, professors of school administration, and doctoral-level students to suggest the initial set of items. The initial instrument was developed and reviewed by the Administrative Committee of the National Study of School Evaluation and other educators with pertinent expertise. In phase two, the instrument was field tested in eight locations representing different types of schools and geographical areas. The opinions of the teachers participating in the field testing were used to make the final revisions of the instrument. In phase three, the reliability of the instrument and the internal consistency were computed.

The TOI was revised in 1980 after a statistical analysis based upon the responses from 1,435 teachers in 26 schools from 20 states representing all geographic sections of the United States (TOI, 1981c, p. 2).

The TOI has two parts: Part A and Part B. There are 64 multiple-choice items in Part A, which assesses teacher opinion on various aspects of the school (e.g., When you need to talk with the principal, can you do so with relative ease? A) Always, B) Usually, C) About half the time, D) Seldom, or E) Never. Part B consists of eight open-ended questions that allow a teacher to make recommendations for school improvement (e.g., If you had to change one thing about your school curriculum, what would you like to see changed?).

The examiner role in administering the TOI is discussed clearly, but the survey can be self- or group-administered. There are no separate answer sheets. Teachers record their opinions and comments in the test booklet. The manual for the TOI is a 12-page booklet containing information on the development, administration, scoring, interpretation, and reliability and validity of the instrument. The booklet also contains a copy of the questionnaire.

Practical Applications/Uses

The TOI is a valuable instrument to use in self-studies required by accreditation agencies. The survey is an appropriate instrument for evaluation and research studies looking at teacher opinion and school climate. There are companion forms for parents and students and the perceptions of all three groups can be compared. If the form is administered anonymously, as suggested, and the answers compiled and discussed, the results may stimulate a healthy dialogue between teachers and administrators.

The TOI (1981c) was developed to accomplish three goals:

1. To assess teacher opinion toward many facets of the school.
2. To provide teacher recommendations for improvement.
3. To provide valuable data for the school administration to guide in decision making relative to program development, policy formation, administrative organization, faculty development, and community relations. (p. 2)

The TOI (1981c) was designed to be used alone or with the Student Opinion Inventory, the Parent Opinion Inventory, or as part of a complete school evaluation program (p. 2). The TOI itself is designed specifically for use with teachers.

The test administrator is cautioned as to how this instrument should be used to get the best results. The manual states that the attitude of the administrator as perceived by teachers has an influence on how important teachers perceive the task to be. If they feel that their responses are valuable and that their responses are anonymous, the test authors feel that teachers will take the task seriously and the results will be valuable. It is also suggested that there be no discussion of the items until the teachers complete the questionnaire, and that all teachers complete the inventory at the same time.

The directions are not complicated and are easy to follow. The test is simple to administer. The TOI is untimed and most often will be completed in 15 to 25 minutes by teachers.

The TOI may be either hand scored or computer scored, if optical scan sheets are available and used. It is suggested that the frequencies for each item be tallied, with $A=5$, $B=4$, $C=3$, $D=2$, and $E=1$. Information is given in the manual on the items that are common across the three inventories (teacher, student, and parent). The manual also cautions the interpretation of certain items on the test for elementary teachers because the item content is usually not appropriate for that level.

The interpretation of Part A is made from the frequency distribution of how the teachers responded to each item. The interpretation of the written comments would be subjective and demand content analysis. There are no norms for different types or levels of schools, and no case studies are given in the manual on how the results could be used.

Technical Aspects

The instrument appears to have face validity. The content of the questions relate to evaluative standards used by accreditation organizations. The consensus of expert, teachers, and administrators was used as validity criteria.

The TOI (1981c) reports an alpha reliability coefficient for Part A. The coefficient of .91 was computed from the responses of 1,435 elementary and secondary teachers from selected schools in seven states during the 1978-79 school year. No test-retest reliability coefficients were reported.

Although the scale is used widely in school evaluation studies and primarily when schools are accredited by regional accreditation agencies, little research has been conducted on the scale. None is reported in the test manual.

Critique

The TOI fills a need for an instrument to assess teachers' opinions of their school. The root of the items come from school evaluation and accreditation criteria. The TOI, however, has limited value because it is not based upon the research on effective schools and effective teaching. The items are very broad because they are designed for both elementary and secondary teachers. Some of the items are not really appropriate for primary and elementary school teachers. The areas of the curriculum are very global (i.e., business, English, language arts, science, etc.) This classification does not really give teachers an opportunity to react to more specific deficiencies or assets in the courses offered by the school. The TOI could be packaged better to make it an easier instrument to use and score as well as attractive to take. If teachers recorded their answers to the multiple-choice items in the booklet, it would be tedious to do an analysis. The teachers are left limited space to write their comments to the open-ended questions. Probably because the inventory presents problems for administrators and committee members in scoring and interpretation, many schools (when going through the evaluation and accreditation process) tend not to use it. NSSE needs to thoroughly review the instrument and present more evidence on its validity and reliability. No concurrent validity is reported and no studies are cited that have used the TOI. NSSE should consider upgrading the manual and instrument so that it conforms to standards for good tests and is more attractively packaged and usable.

References

National Study of School Evaluation. (1981a). *Parent Opinion Inventory.* Falls Church, VA: Author.

National Study of School Evaluation. (1981b). *Student Opinion Inventory.* Falls Church, VA: Author.

National Study of School Evaluation. (1981c). *Teacher Opinion Inventory.* Falls Church, VA: Author.

Geoffrey F. Schultz, Ed.D.
Associate Professor of Educational Psychology, Indiana University-Northwest, Gary, Indiana.

Harvey N. Switzky, Ph.D.
Professor of Educational Psychology, Northern Illinois University, DeKalb, Illinois.

TEACHING STYLE INVENTORY

Harvey F. Silver and J. Robert Hanson. Moorestown, New Jersey: Hanson, Silver, Strong and Associates, Inc.

Introduction

Based on a Jungian psychological typology, the Teaching Style Inventory (TSI) is a personality assessment designed to identify individual preferred teaching styles. The instrument is used in the classroom on a case-by-case basis as a way for teachers to recognize fully their own teaching assets and to become conscious of their teaching liabilities when making instructional decisions. The authors of the Teaching Style Inventory are Harvey F. Silver, Ed.D., and J. Robert Hanson, Ed.D.

This inventory is a self-descriptive test based on Carl Jung's theory of psychological types (1921). Jung's empirical research in the phenomenology of the psyche led him to formulate a structural theory of character, in which he posited the perceptual functions of *sensation* and *intuition* and the judgment functions of *thinking* and *feeling*. These four functions—used in understanding how people characteristically learn, communicate, solve problems, and make decisions— provide the theoretical construct upon which this personality inventory is based.

Jung defined the perceptual functions, *sensation* and *intuition*, as irrational processes; they are receivers of information, but they do not evaluate, interpret, or judge that information. The sensation function operates through the five senses, so that the focus is on the concrete, tangible reality of the present. Individuals in whom this function predominates tend to distrust any information or ideas for which they cannot clearly perceive a concrete basis; they demand that things "make sense." Conversely, the perceptual function of intuition is defined by Jung as perception through the unconscious; that is, a person using intuition can arrive at a perception without being aware of the concrete basis for that perception. Thus, intuitive individuals jump from the concrete present to the unknown future or to the abstract and complex interrelationships of events, whereas individuals receptive to sensation focus their energies on the present.

The judgment functions, thinking and feeling, are rational processes; they evaluate the information acquired through the perceptual functions of sensation and/or intuition. Evaluation using the thinking function entails an impersonal, logical appraisal of perceptions. The criteria for the thinking person are whether or not a thought or an action is valid or invalid, reasonable or unreasonable. Individuals who favor the thinking function appear to others as impersonal, analytical, and

589

lacking in concern for others. By contrast, the criteria for feeling judgments are not whether a thought or an action is valid or invalid, but whether it is important or unimportant, valuable or worthless, particularly in relation to human values and their effect on people. The feeling judgment is made with concern not for logic and truth, but for consequences, especially those that benefit or cause misfortune to humanity. Jung intended the judgment function of feeling to indicate a value judgment rather than an emotional one.

The functions are dichotomous in nature. Each member of a pair is in essential opposition to the other and therefore the members cannot be used simultaneously. For example, the use of sensation rules out the concurrent use of intuition, and one cannot have a thinking and a feeling judgment at the same time. The functions can, however, be exercised consecutively: a person can arrive at a logical conclusion about a thought or an action and then evaluate its good and bad consequences before deciding what action to take.

The Teaching Style Inventory is modeled on the premise that characteristic and consistent modes of thought develop through training and experience and that these modes can be differentiated within the two functions of perception and judgment. The TSI integrates a perception mode (sensation or intuition) with a judgment mode (thinking or feeling) to conceptualize the domains of behavior that characterize an individual's teaching style. As a result, four distinct behavior styles are possible: 1) sensation-thinkers; 2) sensation-feelers; 3) intuitive-thinkers; 4) and intuitive-feelers.

According to the test authors, teaching styles are based on the different ways teachers prefer to use their information-gathering perceptions and evaluative judgments to instruct students in classroom environments (H.F. Silver, personal communication, November 1987). The preference for either type of perception function (sensing and intuition) is independent of the preference for either type of judgment function (thinking and feeling). The TSI is designed to help identify and develop a personal teaching profile based on the preferences for particular behaviors (i.e., teaching approaches in classroom).

The behaviors are defined within the following 10 evaluation areas: 1) classroom atmosphere; 2) teaching techniques; 3) planning; 4) what one values in students; 5) teacher-student interactions; 6) classroom management; 7) student behaviors; 8) teaching behaviors; 9) student evaluation; and 10) student goals. In each of the 10 categories, four possible teaching approaches are described. These are sensing-thinking; sensing-feeling; intuitive-thinking; and intuitive-feeling. Each behavior description is professionally appropriate and pedagogically sound; correspondingly, each choice reflects a constellation of teaching behaviors that in a classroom context define a particular perceptive-judgmental teaching style.

Based upon the individual's conscious preferences and pertinent to the way he or she teaches in each of the 10 categorical areas, the teacher is asked to weight the behavioral descriptions in each category by assigning a 5 to the behavior that best characterizes his or her teaching style, a 3 to the behavior that next best characterizes his or her teaching style, a 1 to the next most characteristic behavior, and a 0 to the behavior that least characterizes the individual's teaching style. The weighted scoring enables the test user to rank the order of teacher-preferred behavior (based upon which perceptual-judgmental functional style is being used) in each of the classroom areas and also to identify an overall composite teaching style by totaling the various weights by each perceptual-judgmental function.

The composite perceptual-judgmental styles of teaching as defined by the test authors (from the test materials) are as follows:

1) *Sensing-thinking* teachers are primarily outcomes-oriented (skills learned, projects completed). They maintain highly structured, well-organized classroom environments. Work is purposeful, emphasizing the acquisition of skills and information. Plans are clear and concise. Discipline is firm but fair. Teachers serve as the primary information source and give detailed directions for student learning.

2) *Sensing-feeling* teachers are empathic and people-oriented. Emphasis is placed on the students' feelings of positive self-worth. These teachers share personal dealings and experiences with students and attempt to become personally involved in students' learning. This type of teacher believes that school should be fun and introduces much learning through games and activities that involve the students actively and physically. Plans are changed frequently to meet the mood of the class.

3) *Intuitive-thinking* teachers are intellectually oriented, placing primary importance on students' intellectual developments. These teachers provide the time and the intellectual challenges to encourage students to develop skills in critical thinking, problem solving, logic, research techniques, and independent study. Curriculum planning is developed around concepts frequently centering on a series of questions or themes. Evaluation is often based on open-ended questions, debates, essays, or position papers.

4) *Intuitive-feeling* teachers are innovatively oriented. They encourage students to explore their creative abilities. Insights and innovative ideas are highly valued. Discussions revolve around generating possibilities and new relationships. The classroom environment is often full of creative clutter, and this type of teacher encourages students to develop their own unique styles. Curriculum emphases focus on creative thinking, moral development, values, and flexible, imaginative approaches to learning. Curiosity, insight, and artistic self-expression are encouraged.

The test authors state that "no one teaching style adequately represents the totality of one's teaching behavior" (Silver & Hanson, 1981). The TSI is designed to profile the teacher's style in terms of preference: 1) a dominant style, which is the most preferred and most often used; 2) an auxiliary style, which is next most likely to be used; 3) a back-up style; and 4) the least used style (Silver & Hanson, 1981). A profile may be plotted where scores from the highest number (dominant) to the lowest (least used) are charted, providing a visual estimate of the relative strengths of each style.

Practical Applications/Uses

The application of the Jungian model of psychological type offers a valid format for defining different teaching styles. The use of this model to explain the development of individual teaching styles is well documented (Von Fange, 1961; Carlyn, 1976; DeNovellis & Lawrence, 1983; Lawrence, 1982). Professional educators and researchers have been able to identify typological style differences in both teachers and student learners. Their findings have noted the importance of teacher instructional approach to improve learning (Lawrence, 1984; Yokomoto & Ware, 1981; & McCaulley, 1977).

The test authors state that the TSI is designed primarily to analyze the variance between instructor learning style and instructor-adopted teaching style. The test authors of the TSI postulate that when a teacher enters the classroom he or she will practice a particular style of teaching that is a projection of his or her own learning style; in other words, a teacher will naturally instruct students to learn in the mode or fashion in which he or she learns. Variance between the teacher's instructional style and the teacher's personal learning style is an indication of the degree to which the teacher expands his or her preferred teaching style (and learning style) to meet the needs of different student learning patterns and different kinds of content. For teacher training and other professional development programs that may find practical value in applying the TSI in this manner, the test authors provide a Learning Style Inventory (LSI) to identify an individual teacher's learning style as it compares to the teacher's identified teaching style (Silver & Hanson, 1981). The LSI identifies the learning style in the same typological format as the TSI, allowing for easy comparison.

In summary, the TSI enables the user to assess and gain insight into the strength and differentiation of the individual's conscious attitudes and behaviors as they relate to an adopted teaching style and to establish an operational analysis of instructor teaching style as it relates to the instructor's own learning style.

Technical Aspects

Before a psychological test is deemed ready for operational use, it must provide evidence of technical adequacy by way of a manual or other technical publication that gives evidence to support any and all claims for its use. Regrettably, the test authors (Silver & Hanson, 1981) of the TSI have not yet complied with this requirement. The inventory is reported to be still in the validation-research phase and therefore lacks the research foundation that is necessary to be of valid use to classroom teachers. Because the test was marketed in 1981, the reviewers are surprised that no validity or reliability data are yet available. For an inventory such as the TSI to be usable, construct and criterion-related validity and internal consistency reliability need to be minimally established.

Critique

What appears to be a potentially useful and practical instrument for teachers is still in need of construct validation. Because the TSI was designed to implement Jung's theory of psychological types, its validity is determined by its ability to demonstrate relationships and outcomes predicted by theory. The theory suggests that persons are, or become, different types, and the TSI attempts to classify persons according to true type or "style." The theory postulates that basic preferences for sensing or intuitive perception lead to different interests and that basic preferences for thinking or feeling judgment lead to differences in acting on those interests. The test authors believe that teaching behaviors are surface indicators of the effects of perception-judgment preferences. If the TSI adequately reflects those preferences, then actual classroom behaviors should be in the direction predicted by the theory, allowing for measurement error, state of development, and environmental pressures that interfere with expression of style preferences.

Criterion-related validity also needs to be investigated. A number of "type" inventories, such as the Myers-Briggs Type Indicator (MBTI), tap the same construct; therefore, continuous scores correlated in the expected directions with other instruments would satisfy this psychometric requirement.

Internal consistency and replicability over time are also important to establish. To permit reliability comparisons with other instruments, continuous score reliability estimates for the four style preferences need to be established. Also, the TSI scores are assumed to reflect underlying dichotomies, and the major interest of the test user is in maintaining a consistency of style. Therefore, reliabilities that reflect these hypothesized dichotomies need to be reported.

Once the TSI psychometric development is completed, the instrument may become a very efficient format to examine teaching styles in the context of Jung's psychological typology. The length of the inventory allows for quick and easy administration. The content of each inventory is specific to the classroom behavior of teachers, whereas similar formats such as the more lengthy MBTI examines behavior across a variety of experiential domains.

Another area of concern is that the abbreviated format may be a problem for some users. The TSI is designed only to identify style differences within the functions of perception and judgment. The more comprehensive MBTI expands the definition of type in the context of the attitudinal constructs of introversion and extraversion, constructive information that this reviewer thinks essential to understanding teaching styles.

Overall, the Teaching Style Inventory appears to offer a typological inventory that is specific to classroom situations and very efficient to use. The evaluation of individual teaching styles using an instrument based on the concept of psychological typology is very practical. A teacher who is aware of his or her dominant, auxiliary, and least-used (perceptual and judgmental) functions, and who is skilled and experienced in teaching within the various styles, has at his or her disposal an important tool in increasing classroom efficacy. The importance of motivating and positively affecting students is often viewed as an essential ingredient to successful teaching and learning, but rarely is any information offered or available as to how to achieve and maintain this goal.

References

Carlyn, M. (1976). The relationship between Myers-Briggs personality characteristics and teaching preferences of prospective teachers. *Dissertation Abstracts International, 37,* 3493A. (University Microfilms No. 76–27, 081)

DeNoveallis, R., & Lawrence, G. (1983). Correlates of teacher personality variables (Myers-Briggs) and classroom observation data. *Research in Psychological Type, 6,* 37–46.

Jung, C.G. (1971). Psychological types. In H.G. Baynes (Trans; revised by R. Hull). *The collected works of C.G. Jung* (Vol. 6). Princeton, NJ: Princeton University Press. (Original work published in 1921)

Lawrence, G. (1982). *People types and tiger stripes* (2nd ed.). Gainesville, FL: Center for Applications of Psychological Type.

Lawrence, G. (1984). A synthesis of learning style research involving the MBTI. *Journal of Psychological Type, 8,* 2–15.

McCaulley, M.H. (1977). *Myers Longitudinal Medical Study (Monograph II).* Gainsville, FL: Center for Applications of Psychological Type, Inc.

Silver, H.F., & Hanson, J.R. (1981). *The TLC: Teaching Style Inventory/Learning Style Inventory.* Moorestown, NJ: Hanson, Silver and Associates, Inc.

Von Fange, E.A. (1961). *Implications for school administration of the personality structure of educational personnel.* Unpublished doctoral dissertation, University of Alberta, Canada.

Yokomoto, C.F., & Ware, J.R. (1982). Improving problem solving performance using the MBTI. *Proceedings of the 1982 American Society of Engineering Education Annual Conference* (pp. 163–167).

Michael Ayers, Ph.D.
Clinical Psychologist, Section of Neuropsychology, HCA-Presbyterian Hospital, Oklahoma City, Oklahoma.

Robert L. Heilbronner, Ph.D.
Clinical Psychologist, Section of Neuropsychology, HCA-Presbyterian Hospital, Oklahoma City, Oklahoma.

TEST OF LATERAL AWARENESS AND DIRECTIONALITY

Joseph F. Lockavitch and August J. Mauser. East Aurora, New York: United Educational Services, Inc.

Introduction

The Test of Lateral Awareness and Directionality (LAD) is a short test that measures right and left labeling abilities at two levels: lateral awareness, which requires the ability to relate persons or objects to the right or left side of space with the person being examined as the point of reference, and directionality, which requires the examiner mentally to assume the position or reference point of another person or object before an orientation relationship can be determined. Both lateral awareness and directionality require the accurate use and comprehension of the language labels *right* and *left*. Research indicates that laterality and directionality are independent constructs (Lockavitch, 1977).

The LAD is based on research and clinical observations of various educators, neurologists, and neuropsychologists. Lateral discrimination was originally part of Binet and Simon's intelligence battery (Laurendeau & Pinard, 1970); deficits in lateral awareness and directionality have been noted in children and adults who exhibit learning disabilities or who have central nervous system disorders. Other research indicates that children and adults with decrements in reading, mathematics, and arithmetic also have impaired lateralization abilities. Belmont and Birch (1965) demonstrated that developmentally retarded subjects showed more impairment with right and left awareness than normal controls.

Neuropsychological research has documented the relationship between lateral awareness and directionality of individuals who have lesions to the parietal-occipital region and to the right or left cerebral hemisphere. The majority of research indicates that the left hemisphere is more sensitive to tasks involving lateralization, whereas directionality or disturbances in spatial attention are more marked in individuals with right-hemisphere lesions (Luria, 1973). In the 1920s, Gerstmann documented lateralization disturbance as a common deficit in individuals with left-hemisphere parietal-occipital lesions. This disturbance was one of the four features of Gerstmann's syndrome. The other three features included the inability to identify fingers on tactual stimulation (finger agnosia), loss of the ability to write (agraphia), and loss of the ability to perform mathematical operations (acalculia).

The LAD was developed in 1980 by Joseph Lockavitch, Ed.D., at Sacred Heart College in North Carolina, and August Mauser, Ed.D., at Northern Illinois University. The LAD was developed in four phases. Phase I involved a pilot study conducted on a group of first-, second-, third-, fourth-, and fifth-grade students to determine the empirical feasibility of the LAD. Phase II involved steps taken to determine the validity and reliability of the LAD. In Phase III, factor analyses were performed on the responses of the pilot sample. Internal consistency and reliability were derived in Phase IV.

The components of the complete LAD test package include a 28-page test manual, 36 test plates, 25 recording forms, and a scoring template. The examiner has the option of administering the test individually or to a small group of no more than 5 subjects. The examiner can participate or engage in the test with the subject(s), or allow the subject(s) to work independently recording their own answers. When given individually, caution must be taken to score the responses according to the subject's orientation. During the course of testing, the examiner must be alert to notable body contortions or reliance on external cues by the subject. For example, subject(s) may attempt physically to orient themselves in relation the person or object on the test template.

The examiner is seated in front of the subject and the following instructions are read:

> I am going to ask you some questions that will show how well you know right from left. You are not expected to answer all the questions correctly, so relax, pay attention, and try to do the best you can. I will show you a picture and ask you a question. I want you to look carefully at the drawings and decide which one shows the correct answer. When you have decided, point to (or mark) your answer. If you would like the question repeated, let me know and I will repeat it for you. (Lockavitch & Mauser, 1980)

For younger children, who will indicate their responses by pointing, the examiner turns to Plate A and says: "This picture shows different shapes. Point to the square please." Finally, for students who mark their own answers, the examiner turns to Plate A and says: "On each card that I will show you, there are 2 or 4 drawings. The drawings are numbered." The examiner then points to each drawing and says the number and asks: "Which one is the square?" The subject is to respond out loud and point. The examiner then points to the square and says: "That's correct. This is #3. On your answer sheet put a mark in column 3." The examiner reviews this procedure until the subject understands the directions with certainty. When presenting each item, the examiner also says the number aloud so the subject will not lose the correct place on the answer sheet. Each scoring sheet yields a total of three scores. Each of the lateral awareness and directionality items are worth 1 point. The lateral awareness subtest contains 15 items and the directionality subtest contains 20 items. Thus, the maximum score for the entire test is 35. Scoring is simple and involves one clear template.

The recording form sheet is quite simple. At the top of the form are spaces for name, age, and date. Listed vertically are the 15 lateral awareness items on the left side of the form and the 20 directionality items on the right side of the form. Within each lateral awareness and directionality test item are boxes labeled 1 through 4 that are used to record the subject's answer, as well as a box to record the points scored for each item. At the bottom of the form is a box to score the total lateral awareness score, total directionality score, and total LAD score. The stimulus instructions for each item are printed on the back of the previous recording form for easy administration.

Practical Applications/Uses

The LAD is designed for children in Grades 1 through 12, as well as adults. The authors posit that lateral awareness is usually fully developed by age 8, whereas directionality is usually developed by age 10. They suggest that the LAD is a relatively simple test for children and adult subjects who have reached the developmental age, and who have no deficiencies or organicity. The test reportedly becomes simpler with progression in age and development.

Scores on the LAD fall within one of three categories (underdeveloped, moderately developed, or fully developed) that purportedly define the level of development of lateral awareness and directionality skills. The theory is based on clinical observations that individuals scoring within the underdeveloped or moderately developed category are likely to experience difficulty in specific academic areas, particularly those involving symbol and form interpretation such as mathematics, arithmetic, and reading. The classification of an individual in the underdeveloped or moderately developed category, however, does not necessarily imply that the individual is functioning below the developmental level; the classification merely shows that the risk for academic-related deficiency or organicity is higher when the subject has passed the developmental age and has poor performance. The manual provides scoring ranges for the classification of individuals into underdeveloped, moderately developed, and fully developed.

Technical Aspects

In order to determine empirically the feasibility of the LAD, a pilot study was conducted with a group of first-, second-, third-, fourth-, and fifth-grade students. Two hundred eighty-eight students were selected on a random basis. Selection of items for the initial testing was based on three primary sources: 1) test items that were present in the existing body of literature, 2) empirical data collected during a 9-year period on children who exhibited difficulty with lateral awareness and directionality, and 3) the advice given by a panel of experts in the field.

The initial testing instrument attemped to measure both the basic and the complex levels of lateral awareness and directionality. Items were developed to measure the following constructs: same direction, 180° rotation, 90° rotation, 180° inversion, 180° inversion with a 180° rotation, and persons and objects in relation to the examinee. The preceding six constructs constituted what was believed to be the lateral awareness component of the initial LAD test. The directionality section of the initial LAD test consisted of six constructs. Items were presented in the same direction, with a 180° rotation and with a 90° rotation wherever possible. The initial constructs measured were person-to-person, object-to-person, person-to-object, person-to-person with an intervening variable, three persons, and three objects.

Results of the pilot study reduced the number of items on the LAD test to 35. The sixth construct in the lateral awareness subtest (persons and objects in relation to the examinee) was transferred from the lateral awareness subtest to the directionality subtest because it did not measure knowledge of left and right within self as much as it measured the relation of both persons and objects to self. The pilot study also indicated that a change in the test format was needed. The test was still presented by order of the constructs contained within each subtest, but the items within each construct were randomly presented. Items were also randomly placed on the page in order to eliminate the subject receiving help from external cues.

A test is declared valid to the degree that it measures what it purports to measure. To determine content validity, a factor analysis of the responses made by the 288 students in the pilot study was performed. Ten factors were extracted; only those factors with a factor loading of .40 and above were retained. One factor was eliminated and the remainder accounted for 58.3% of the variance. A second-order factor analysis was performed on the nine factors and a factor loading of .30 or above was the criterion. The nine factors were reduced to three, which accounted for 52.3% of the variance. Because one of the nine original factors loaded on both second-order factor 2 and second-order factor 3, second-order factor 3 was collapsed into second-order factor 2 and eliminated. Each of the two remaining factors was labeled directionality and lateral awareness.

To establish concurrent validity, the manual (Lockavitch & Mauser, 1986) states that, the LAD total score and its two subtests were compared to a three-dimensional, individually administered, assessment instrument, the Piaget-Elkind Test of Right-Left Judgment. The results revealed a correlation of .46 between directionality and the Piaget-Elkind score, .39 between lateral awareness and the Piaget-Elkind score, and .58 between the total LAD score and the Piaget-Elkind score. All the correlations were significant at the .01 level. To the extent that the LAD measures the constructs lateral awareness and directionality, then construct validity is demonstrated or assumed. The LAD manual provides no evidence for the construct validity of this test. To establish the usefulness of the LAD to measure deficits in lateral awareness and directionality, failure to use a group of patients with impairments in these abilities would limit the claim for criterion or predictive validity.

Reliability of a test refers to its sensitivity, accuracy, and repeatability in measurement. Reliability of the LAD was determined by performing item analysis on the items within each factor. Tables are included in the manual that contain information on reliability of the initial nine factor items, the second-order nine factor items, the complete LAD, plus the directionality and lateral awareness subtests. Reliabilities on the initial nine factors range from .53 to .91. The overall reliability coefficient was .95 for the directionality subtest, .88 for the lateral awareness subtest, and .93 for the LAD total score. The authors suggest that the results of the reliability studies indicate that the LAD test and its subtest are reliable for use in both group and individual assessment.

Critique

The Test of Lateral Awareness and Directionality was primarily designed to be used as a screening instrument for early identification of students with potential academic problems. However, it also appears to have the potential to address organicity in children over 9 years of age and in adults. The lateral awareness subtest appears to have utility in addressing left-hemisphere lateralization deficits commonly seen in individuals with left parietal-occipital lobe dysfunction. The directionality subtest, on the other hand, appears to have utility in addressing deficits in right-hemisphere visual-spatial orientation tasks. Thus, the directionality subtest may be potentially helpful in screening degenerative disorders in which visual-spatial and orientation disturbances are early symptoms. Given the fact that subjects can point instead of verbalize their responses, the LAD may also be useful with deaf or hearing-impaired subjects.

As a face valid test of lateral awareness and directionality, the LAD lacks supportive research demonstrating its efficacy in a clinical population. Furthermore, the test manual provides no information on predictive or criterion validity. In interpreting the results of this test, one cannot be completely sure whether a deficient performance on this test reflects deficits in lateral awareness and directionality, or some other ability compromised by brain impairment. As in the case in a number of assessment instruments in clinical neuropsychology, minimal attention has been devoted to the validity of the LAD as a measure of cognitive functioning. Although the LAD appears to have adequate utility in assessing lateral awareness and directionality, it may not be the most parsimonious means for the assessment of these abilities.

The test results of the LAD have neuropsychological significance; however, their relevance in the area of visual-spatial processing and lateralized brain dysfunction remains unclear. Furthermore, the impact of impaired lateral awareness and directionality on an individual's psychosocial and interpersonal functioning has yet to be determined. Use of the test results would be maximized within the context of a comprehensive neuropsychological test battery. Clearly, the LAD requires further research incorporating both normative and brain-impaired populations.

References

Bilmont, L., & Birch, H. (1965). Lateral dominance, lateral awareness, and reading disability. *Child Development, 36*, 57–71.

Laurendeau, M., & Pinard, A. (1970). *The development of the concept of space in the child.* New York: International Press.

Lockavitch, J.F., (1970). *The development and validation of a measuring instrument designed to measure lateral awareness and directionality in elementary school children.* Unpublished doctoral dissertation, Boston University, Boston.

Lockavitch, J.F., & Mauser, A.F. (1980). *The relationship of lateral awareness and directionality to academic and intellectual ability.* Unpublished manuscript.

Lockavitch, J.F., & Mauser, A.J. (1986). *Test of Lateral Awareness and Directionality.* East Aurora, NY: United Educational Services, Inc.

Luria, A.R (1973). *The working brain* (pp. 151–155). New York: Basic Books.

Nancy J. Spekman, Ph.D.
Director of Training and Research Projects, Marianne Frostig Center of Educational Therapy, Pasadena, California.

Nora Slaff, Ph.D.
Educational Diagnostician, Marianne Frostig Center of Educational Therapy, Pasadena, California.

TEST OF PROBLEM SOLVING

Linda Zachman, Carol Jorgensen, Rosemary Huisingh, and Mark Barrett. Moline, Illinois: LinguiSystems, Inc.

Introduction

The Test of Problem Solving (TOPS) is an appealing, individually administered, standardized measure of expressive problem-solving abilities in school-aged children. The integration of linguistic knowledge with reasoning ability is measured by utilizing real-life situational contexts presented both auditorially (oral questions) and visually (picture stimuli). Performance on the test is thought to reflect the ability to verbalize logical thought processes. Five areas of reasoning or problem-solving skills are examined: 1) *Explaining Inferences*—the ability to utilize picture clues to explain orally presented inferences; 2) *Determining Causes*—the ability to explain why a situation or event occurred; 3) *Negative Why Questions*—the ability to explain why a given situation or event might not occur; 4) *Determining Solutions*—the ability to generate logical and appropriate solutions to problem situations; and 5) *Avoiding Problems*—the ability to explain what might have been done to avert a problem situation. The authors believe that these skills are among those needed by school-aged children for academic and social success.

The TOPS authors, Linda Zachman, M.A., CCC, Carol Jorgensen, M.A., CCC, Rosemary Huisingh, M.A., CCC, and Mark Barrett, M.A., CCC, are speech-language pathologists with clinical experience working with preschool and school-aged children and adults. They also have co-authored, with M.K. Snedden, a manual of exercises for expressive reasoning (Zachman, Jorgensen, Barrett, Huisingh, & Snedden, 1982).

Development of the TOPS took place over a 3-year period and was stimulated by the absence of a standardized measure of expressive problem solving. The authors began with an extensive review of tests and literature in the areas of problem solving, cognition, and intelligence. Based on this review, they selected six skill areas "recognized by experts" as important to problem solving, cognition, and expressive language (Zachman, Jorgensen, Huisingh, & Barrett, 1984, p. 63). The authors do not identify the body of literature and test instruments they reviewed, however, nor do they present criteria by which they selected the particular skill areas. Given the vast literature base that addresses theoretical models and underlying constructs of intelligence, problem solving, reasoning, and expressive language, Zachman et al. should position their test and present users with a detailed discussion of the model or constructs the TOPS purports to measure and of the framework utilized in test construction.

An initial item pool of 96 items (16 items measuring each of six thinking tasks) was generated. Everyday situational contexts were selected and illustrated, but no information is given regarding the procedures or the criteria utilized in selecting the contexts or in developing the picture stimuli. The initial form of the test was administered by 75 speech-language pathologists to 456 children between the ages of 6.0 and 11.11. Children were selected randomly within the categories of race, sex, and age from 52 schools located in Pittsburgh, Pennsylvania, and Downey, California. Scoring criteria associated with response ratings of 2, 1, or 0 points were established after examining the actual responses given by children in this sample.

Item retention was based on difficulty and discrimination indexes. First, the percentage of children passing each item had to increase at successive age levels. Second, each item had to discriminate significantly at each age level between high and low scorers on the total test. Accordingly, five subskill areas and the 50 items that best met the criteria were retained for the final version. The manual does not present the percent-passing data, but the results of the chi square analyses used to test for high and low performance differences are reported. An examination of these data reveals that 9 of the 50 items retained do not discriminate at the .05 level at one and sometimes two age levels.

Normative data for the TOPS are based on the 1983 assessment of 842 normal children randomly selected at six age levels (6.0-6.11, 7.0-7.11, 8.0-8.11, 9.0-9.11, 10.0-10.11, and 11.0-11.11) from the same schools and districts that participated in the item selection phase of test development. Children receiving special services because of cognitive and language/learning disabilities and those with known hearing loss were excluded. The number of subjects at each age level ranged from 136 to 144, and females represented 51-57% of the subjects at each age level.

The authors state that "no attempt was made to obtain a representative national sampling" except with respect to racial participation (Zachman et al., 1984, p. 60). The percentages of Caucasians, blacks, and Hispanics/others represented at each age level are listed in the manual and reportedly parallel the 1980 U.S. census data; however, because the census data are not provided in the manual, direct comparisons are not possible. By limiting subject selection to the criterion of race, other important demographic factors such as geographical location, size of community, economic level, acculturation of parents, and intelligence were not considered during the subject selection process. Thus, the authors have limited the usefulness or applicability of their test on a national level.

In addition, the generalizability of the test norms is limited by the authors' exclusion of children receiving special services due to cognitive or language/learning disabilities. As Salvia and Ysseldyke (1985) note, tests designed to identify children with particular problems should include such children in their standardization samples (p. 101). Thus, the authors have excluded children the test might have been designed to identify and/or evaluate, and the norms actually represent performance levels associated with school success rather than reasoning and linguistic difficulties.

TOPS examinees are presented with a series of 15 black-and-white line drawings that represent common experiences and events thought to be familiar to most children. No time limits are placed on performance and the test is always administered in entirety. Most illustrations are quite clear, with minimal detail; however, some require the interpretation of visual stimuli not seen in reality (e.g., musical notes coming out of a stereo speaker, cross-hatching to indicate darkness in a room). Each illustration is accompanied by three to five open-ended questions that the examiner presents orally. The 50 questions are divided into five subskill areas with different question forms associated with each area (see Figure 1). Some questions require accurate interpretation of the visual stimuli (e.g., all Explaining Inferences questions), whereas others use the given situation and may build on preceding questions, but do not actually necessitate using the pictures (e.g., 90% of the items in Avoiding Problems). All responses are generated and formulated by the child and expressed orally.

Fig. 1. A Description of the Five Areas of Problem Solving Included in the TOPS

Subtest	Question type	Example*	Expected Content of Responses
Explaining Inferences	How do we know . . . ? How can you tell . . . ?	How do we know these two people are at a restaurant?	Explanations underlying the inference
Determining Causes	Why . . . ? What caused . . . ?	Why did they decide to go to a restaurant?	Explanations of the events leading up to the illustrated event
Negative Why Questions	Why wouldn't (aren't, shouldn't) . . . ?	Why won't they wash dishes after they eat?	Explanations as to why something might not, or should not, be done
Determining Solutions	What could (should, will) they do . . . ?	The waitress brought them hamburgers and french fries, but they ordered spaghetti. What could they do?	Logical ideas as to what will be done next and how a particular problem might be solved
Avoiding Problems	What could have been done . . . ?	What could the waitress have done to keep from making this mistake?	Logical ideas as to how individuals might have avoided the problem situation in which they find themselves

*Actual test items have been reproduced here with the permission of the publisher, LinguiSystems, Inc.

The examiner plays a critical role throughout the testing process. He or she asks all the questions, probes when appropriate, and must record all responses verbatim. The examiner also is responsible for establishing a comfortable level of rapport, considered essential for trying to elicit a child's responses in a natural interactive manner. The implication here is that a normal conversational mode is desired; however, the task is structured and the examiner cannot interject information or ask additional relevant questions. Thus, the expectation for true dialogue and conversation is probably unrealistic.

The test protocol is well organized and presented. A reduced copy of each picture stimulus is provided as well as the associated questions and the subskill area into which each question is categorized. Unfortunately, the allotted space for recording responses is quite limited and may be inadequate in many instances. Adequate space is provided to record all scores and to graph profiles based on both age equivalents and standard scores.

Practical Applications/Uses

Zachman et al. describe the TOPS as a measure of expressive problem solving. They state that the designated population is between 6.0 and 11.11 years of age and that clinical use may be appropriate with older children. They do not, however, indicate more specifically whether the test is meant for "normal" children only or for groups such as the language/learning disabled or mentally retarded. The manual actually contains no sections on test purpose or intended use. It is unclear whether the TOPS was intended for screening or diagnostic decisions, for placement decisions or program planning, for predicting school/social success and/or to explaining school/social failure, for research purposes, or for measuring individual student progress. Further, there are no guidelines stating when administration of the TOPS would be indicated (such as when children have been referred for particular types of learning problems) or not indicated (such as when children present with certain expressive language disorders). The authors also do not suggest that the TOPS be given as part of a battery, and thus there are no guidelines on how TOPS performance can be interpreted with respect to performance on other measures. These reviewers, however, would recommend its use only as part of a battery of instruments measuring both a) verbal and nonverbal problem-solving abilities, b) intelligence, and c) specific receptive and expressive language skills.

The TOPS must be given in a quiet and comfortable environment with appropriately sized furniture. The authors recommend that the test be administered only by trained professionals familiar with language and cognitive development. To these reviewers, an in-depth knowledge of the development and disorders of cognitive and language abilities would appear essential. Speech-language pathologists, educational diagnosticians, and psychologists are likely candidates.

The test manual indicates that approximately 20 minutes are required for test administration. However, the clinical experience of these reviewers in giving the TOPS to learning disabled students shows that 30-40 minutes are usually necessary. Given the open-ended format of the questions, the authors felt no need for demonstration items. However, most other tests with a similar open-ended format do provide training items, both to make sure the child understands the task and to demonstrate an appropriate response. Because there are no basals or ceilings, the entire TOPS is always given. It is possible for the test to be administered over more than one session, but a break should occur at the end of the questions associated with a particular picture.

Test administration is relatively straightforward. The child is shown the series of illustrations and the examiner asks several proscribed questions associated with each. The questions must be presented exactly as written and can be repeated only once. Although the examiner is allowed to probe (e.g., "Tell me more," "Explain it to me better," "What do you mean?"), the manual does not specify how many times a probe can be used for any question or when it is acceptable to do so other than "when a child appears confused" or a more complete response is desired. It is unclear whether the authors mean to imply that a probe might be appropriate whenever a child's initial response would be scored with less than full credit. This requires the examiner to be highly familiar with the scoring criteria and examples for each item.

It is critical that the examiner record all responses verbatim; many aspects of linguistic quality are considered during scoring, and all linguistic elements must be present. Verbatim recording may be very difficult when testing children who speak a lot, speak quickly, reformulate their responses frequently, circumlocute, or have articulation difficulties. Recording difficulties may be compounded by the limited space available on the test protocol. Audiotape recording may need to be considered in some instances.

Scoring criteria for the TOPS reflect an attempt to consider the factors of both language proficiency and problem-solving (reasoning) abilities simultaneously. As noted previously, each response is scored as either 2, 1, or 0. A 2-point response contains all of the essential or most relevant information *and* is expressed in a linguistically appropriate fashion. A 1-point response contains acceptable (but not the most important or concise) information *or* contains all the important information but is "linguistically or semantically imprecise, reflecting vagueness, ambiguity, confusion, incompleteness, or immaturity" (Zachman et al., 1984, p. 15). Zero points are awarded when the information is irrelevant *or* the information is acceptable but expressed poorly. The manual provides guidelines and examples for each level of response for each question. These are indeed helpful, but the rationale used for assigning some responses to a particular level is not always clear, and in some instances these reviewers felt that 1-point responses were actually superior to, or at least equivalent to, some 2-point responses. Further, our experience has been that examinees often generate responses that go beyond the manual guidelines.

Overall, these reviewers find the discussion on scoring quite vague. Zachman et al. rarely define their terms, and some are applied imprecisely. For example, *syntax, grammar,* and *sentence structure* appear to be independent skill areas rather than terms that typically are used interchangeably to refer to the morphology and word order of language. By referring to "linguistic and semantic" factors, the authors imply that the area of semantics is separate from linguistics, in contrast to a more widely found usage that places *semantics* (along with *syntax, phonology,* and *pragmatics)* under the umbrella term of *linguistics.*

Further, the criterion for penalizing a response based on linguistic and semantic imprecision is itself vague and would seem to leave considerable room for judgment calls and subjectivity (i.e., what one administrator scores as ambiguous or immature may be considered appropriate and correct by another). The scoring examples given typically reflect content and vocabulary factors rather than linguistic factors such as grammar; however, it would appear that minor and major syntax errors, reformulations, circumlocutions, and vague or immature vocabulary selections would be penalized equally. It is unclear whether the examiner is to consider phonological (articulation) errors.

The test authors recommend both quantitative and qualitative interpretation of test performances. Three norm-referenced scores are provided: age equivalents, percentiles, and standard scores (mean$=50$; SD$=5$). The manual provides an acceptable general discussion of each type of score, but offers no guidance on how to interpret them (i.e., what level of score constitutes an area of concern that might require additional testing or follow-up). Further, standard error of measurement (SE_m) information is provided in the section on reliability, but the authors make no mention of how it should be used when interpreting scores.

Zachman et al. present a brief discussion of each subskill area and attempt to consider the skills underlying each task. For example, children must understand the questions (some are particularly long and syntactically complex), sort relevant from irrelevant information, call on related past experiences, take the perspective of others, understand the concept of cause and effect, sift through possible explanations and select the most important, and then verbalize their responses. Unfortunately, however, the way the TOPS is scored does not permit the separation of linguistic from reasoning skills; that is, children with receptive and expressive language disorders are not distinguished from those with reasoning problems, nor are those with syntactic disorders distinguished from others with semantic difficulties.

Other possible confounding or explanatory factors must be considered as well when interpreting a child's score. First, the authors make no mention of the nonverbal reasoning and picture interpretation skills that are required to respond successfully to many questions. Although most pictures are relatively clear, some contain too little information, some require very fine attention to visual detail, and others utilize more abstract representations and require interpretation beyond what is seen in reality. A verbal description accompanies these pictures, but still the visual representations could create confusion. Children with generalized deficits in interpreting meaningful nonverbal information might experience difficulties processing these and other aspects of the pictures (e.g., facial expressions, gestures, body postures) that are essential for understanding and performing the tasks. (See, for example, Johnson and Myklebust's [1967] discussion of nonverbal disorders in learning disabled children.) There is also one instance in (Picture 4, Question 13) in which the verbal description does not seem entirely consistent with the illustration and confusion could be created.

In addition, the authors make no mention of social appropriateness. It is obvious from the scoring examples that socially inappropriate responses are scored as 0. Coming from children with social/emotional problems, however, such responses may be more reflective of their emotional status than either their linguistic or problem-solving abilities.

Zachman et al. suggest that test interpretation should include qualitative analyses and these reviewers agree, feeling that this is the only way to obtain the most interesting and relevant information. However, given all of the possible confounding factors, this could be a very time-consuming process, requiring considerable sophistication on the part of the test user. Further, it is not clear as yet that such qualitative analyses would really allow for separation of all the underlying skills discussed earlier. As a beginning, the authors could consider developing separate criteria and scoring systems for evaluating reasoning and language. Further, using the TOPS as part of a battery could facilitate interpretation, as would a variety of informal, follow-up testing procedures that the authors might recommend.

Finally, Zachman et al. provide a few, very vague (and sometimes overlapping) ideas regarding the social or academic problems possibly associated with low scores in the subskill areas. For example, a child with a low score on Determining Solutions might have problems with reading comprehension and math story problems. Some of these associations make a degree of intuitive sense, whereas others are less clear (e.g., a child who scores low on Negative Why Questions might appear impulsive or be a "poor problem solver"; a child with a low score on Avoiding Problems may repeat mistakes; a child with a low score on Determining Causes might have problems understanding "certain" math processes). Within their discussion, Zachman et al. do not attempt to separate the confounds of language, reasoning, or other factors when considering difficulties (i.e., regardless of the possible difficulty underlying a low score, school manifestations are assumed to be the same), nor do they provide any data to support these hypothesized relationships. Furthermore, the authors do not allude to possible differences in practical reasoning and logical reasoning (à la Piaget). The TOPS attempts to measure reasoning within practical, real-life situations only; thus, performance on this test should not be equated with other forms of reasoning.

Technical Aspects

The manual presents two types of reliability information on the TOPS. Although not specified, one assumes that the group on which the reliability data were established was the standardization sample. The first set of reliability data provide a measure of the test's internal consistency. Correlation coefficients presented for each subskill area and for the total test at each age level were calculated using a split-half procedure corrected by the Spearman-Brown prophecy formula. It is not clear, however, which score (raw score, percentile, age equivalent, or standard score) was used to calculate these data. Total test reliability coefficients range from below .80 at the 9- and 10-year levels (.78 and .67, respectively) to .80 at the 8- and 11-year levels and .90 at the 6- and 7-year levels. Although the authors indicate that these are all "very satisfactory levels" (Zachman et al., 1984, p. 62), the frequently set criterion of .80 for individual tests to be considered appropriate for screening decisions (Salvia & Ysseldyke, 1985; Sattler, 1982) is not met at the 9- and 10-year levels. Further the criterion level of .90 for diagnostic decisions is met only at the 6- and 7-year levels.

Even greater variability is found when looking at the five different tasks at each age level. The range extends from .15 (Determining Solutions, age 9) to .82 (Explaining Inferences, age 6). Only one correlation coefficient (out of 30) reaches the criterion level of .80 necessary for screening decisions. Generally, the tasks are somewhat more reliable at the younger age levels than the older ones, but it would appear to these reviewers that none of the tasks can be considered a reliable measure of problem solving and reasoning. As the authors indicate, subtest reliability may be lowered because of the small number of items on each subtest (10), a reduced range of scores due to group homogeneity, or variation in growth rates, and Zachman et al. recommend caution in the use of some subtests at some age levels. However, the reader is left with a more optimistic picture of the subtests than the data support.

Zachman et al. do not provide data regarding the stability of test scores over time (i.e., test-retest reliability). They do present a standard error of measurement (SE_m) for subtests and the total test at each age level. As a measure of the amount of variation that might be expected in any individual's test score given repeated measurement of that individual, SE_m is based on hypothetical repeated test administrations and should not be considered an acceptable substitute for actually testing the same children on two separate occasions (test-retest). Subtest SE_m ranges from 1.65 to 2.51 raw score points; total test SE_m ranges from 4.6 to 5.23 raw score points. When SE_m is applied to subtest and total test scores, it can be seen that a child's score must be interpreted as falling within a rather wide band or range.

Finally, there is no indication that interrater reliability was measured. Given the potential for individual interpretation in scoring TOPS responses, this would appear to be a serious omission.

The authors' claim of the TOPS's content validity is based on the care taken during the development phase to select underlying skill areas recognized and agreed upon by "experts"; however, they provide no data regarding the experts consulted or the procedures followed to obtain such a level of consensus. These reviewers find it hard to believe that experts in the area of cognition could actually agree on a reduction of this large area to the five underlying subskills examined in the TOPS. Although we agree that these are relevant subskills, considerably more information should have been provided to support their selection.

Zachman et. al. present internal consistency data in defense of the the TOPS's validity; however, such data (i.e., subtest-total correlations) constitute reliability information and offer nothing about whether the subtests or the total test measure the constructs claimed. The authors also claim that item-selection criteria (difficulty and discrimination indexes) provide support for validity, but again this says nothing about the actual constructs being measured.

Thus, insufficient data are provided regarding either construct or criterion-related validity. Zachman et al. state that such information should be established in future studies. Evidence for a test's validity, of course, accumulates over time, but not to attempt to establish any of this prior to publication is a serious omission. For example, construct validity could have been tested by correlating performance on the TOPS with other tests or subtests claiming to measure similar, but not necessarily identical, skills. The Comprehension subtest of the WISC-R comes to mind as a measure of expressive problem solving that utilizes real-life situations and some similar question forms, but it does not utilize pictures; the Picture Arrangement subtest requires attention to visual detail, picture interpretation skills, and understanding of causal and consequent events, but does not require receptive or expressive language. Other measures of language and verbal/nonverbal reasoning should be considered. To support the claim that the TOPS measures a skill thought to improve with age, Zachman et al. could have tested for significant group differences in performance across the age range tested or correlated test scores with chronological age. Their intersubtest correlations (most between .40 and .60) indicate some overlap across subtests with respect to the trait being measured, but also that some unique aspect is measured by each. These data, though, cannot be used as the basis for concluding, as the authors do, that the TOPS measures proficiency in expressive problem solving. To support the claim that the test measures skills related to school and social success, performance on the TOPS could be correlated with a variety of achievement tests and measures of a child's interaction skills and peer acceptance. Further, the prediction that TOPS scores can be used to distinguish between high and low achievers in selected areas could be tested. Finally, factor analysis could help to establish the claim that five different factors are measured.

Critique

Clinicians and diagnosticians will be attracted to the TOPS for several reasons. It promises to provide a standardized measure of expressive problem solving that 1) evaluates different subskills of problem solving; 2) utilizes familiar, real-life situations, presented visually and auditorially; and 3) offers a convenient, easy-to-administer format. These reviewers agree that the TOPS is unique in this regard. Unfortunately, however, we feel it is premature to recommend its use as a standardized instrument.

To facilitate use of the TOPS as a norm-referenced measure, the authors and publishers would be well advised to consider the following modifications. First, Zachman et al. need to address more clearly the underlying skills required for adequate performance on the TOPS. Their discussion should include more in-depth attention to the general area of problem solving and to the five subskill areas that are purportedly measured; further, they need to better address the complex interactions between and among verbal and nonverbal skills, visual and auditory skills, practical and logical reasoning, and problem-solving and social skills. Second, significant revisions in the manual should address a) the test's purpose and intended use(s), b) the population(s) for whom it is intended, c) expanded test development information, d) clarification of scoring criteria, e) clarification and consistent usage of terminology, and f) improved guidelines for both quantitative and qualitative analysis of test results. Third, consideration should be given to renorming the test on a group of students that is more representative demographically and that includes individuals with both cognitive and linguistic deficits. Fourth, greater attention needs to be devoted to the collection and presentation of data that substantiate the technical adequacy of the TOPS.

Our clinical experience giving the TOPS has shown that examinees are attentive and interested, the pictures are appealing, and the illustrated situations are generally familiar. Further, we have found that the pictures and questions elicit very good language samples from students, and their responses frequently reflect levels of reasoning ranging from concrete to abstract. At this time we can recommend use of the TOPS as an informal tool only. It should be included in a complete diagnostic battery of formal and informal measures. When interpreted by a skilled clinician, inclusion of the TOPS in such a battery could provide additional insight into the cognitive and linguistic processing skills of children.

References

Johnson, D.J., & Myklebust, H. (1967). *Learning disabilities: Educational principles and practices*. New York: Grune & Stratton.

Salvia, J., & Ysseldyke, J.E. (1985). *Assessment in special and remedial education* (3rd ed.). Boston: Houghton Mifflin.

Sattler, J.M. (1982). *Assessment of children's intelligence and special abilities* (2nd ed.). Boston: Allyn & Bacon.

Zachman, L., Jorgensen, C., Barrett, M., Huisingh, R., & Snedden, M.K. (1982). *Manual for exercises for expressive reasoning*. Moline, IL: LinguiSystems.

Zachman, L., Jorgensen, C., Huisingh, R., & Barrett, M. (1984). *Test of Problem Solving examiner's manual*. Moline, IL: LinguiSystems.

Frances Lawrenz, Ph.D.
Associate Professor of Science Education, University of Minnesota, Minneapolis, Minnesota.

TESTS OF ACHIEVEMENT AND PROFICIENCY

Dale P. Scannell. Chicago, Illinois: Riverside Publishing Company.

Introduction

The Tests of Achievement and Proficiency (TAP) Form G and parallel Form H (Levels 15–18) are a Grades 9–12 extension of the Iowa Tests of Basic Skills. The TAP for each grade level is a set of instruments designed to assess student basic skills and abilities in six curricular areas: Reading Comprehension, Mathematics, Written Expression, Using Sources of Information, Social Studies, and Science. All of the instruments have a multiple-choice format and are designed to be answered on separate answer sheets. Each curricular area test takes 40 minutes to complete and has approximately 60 items. The test battery also contains an optional 15-item questionnaire that elicits information about a student's previous course work, attitudes toward school subjects, use of leisure time, and post-high school plans among other factors. In addition to these traditional paper-and-pencil tests in the six curricular areas, there are two optional supplementary tests, one in writing and one in listening for each grade level 9–12.

The Tests of Achievement and Proficiency were developed by a team of scholars at the University of Kansas headed by Dale P. Scannell. Dr. Scannell was Dean of the University of Kansas, School of Education, while the TAP was developed, and is now Dean of the College of Education at the University of Maryland. He began his work in education as a high school chemistry teacher and obtained his Ph.D. in educational psychology, measurement, and statistics from the University of Iowa in 1958. Since then, he has published a variety of papers on assessing student performance as well as several books on educational measurement. He has also been involved in the development of the other forms of the TAP both with the Houghton Mifflin Company and with Riverside Publishing Company (Form T).

The other three members of the TAP Form G development team were members of the Curriculum and Instruction Department at the University of Kansas during the development process, but have since retired. Dr. Oscar Haugh specialized in secondary English and reading; Dr. Alvin Schild specialized in secondary social studies, and Dr. Gilbert Ulmer specialized in secondary mathematics.

The TAP Form G went through an extensive development procedure. Earlier editions of the tests (TAP Form T) were updated to facilitate a match of test items with current curricular goals. Form G development began with the writing and selection of appropriate test items in the early 1980s. The test developers state in their *Preliminary Technical Summary* that the "items for these tests were written to meet rigid content specifications . . . influenced by current trends and emphases in instructional curricula" (p. 7). More specific topic criteria were listed as place-

610

ment and emphasis in current instructional material, recommendations of "authority" (e.g., national curriculum committees, methods textbook authors), frequency of need or occurrence, frequency of error, and importance. Also mentioned in conjunction with item development was continuous interaction with users about the items.

After the initial item development, two qualitative reviews were conducted: one by a panel selected by Dr. Scannell and one by the Riverside Publishing Company's editorial staff (see the *Preliminary Technical Summary,* 1986, and the *Manual for School Administrators,* 1986). Additionally, in February and in November of 1982, two large TAP item tryout studies were conducted with a total of more than 11,000 students in 25 high schools in 17 states. The feedback from these reviews and tryouts was used to modify and refine the items.

A third national item tryout was conducted in the fall of 1983 along with the tryout of the Iowa Tests of Basic Skills items. The sample was specifically designed to oversample minority students to provide sufficient data for analyzing group differences. In addition, a third qualitative review of the items was conducted by a panel of independent experts selected on the basis of geographic region, gender, and ethnicity. This 17-member panel consisted of 9 women and 8 men; further, its ethnic composition was 1 white, 9 black, 3 Hispanic, 2 American Indian, and 2 Oriental. Each panel member conducted an independent review of the items, and their comments along with the quantitative results from the national tryout were used to delete or modify items for the final version of the TAP Form G.

The TAP Form G was standardized in October/November 1984 and April/May 1985 by administering it to a national sample of students. The sample averaged more than 14,000 pupils per grade. Students in the spring sample were those who had taken the tests in the fall. The sample was selected to ensure adequate representation of all reporting categories. To accomplish this task, a stratified, random sample of school districts was selected. The sample was stratified on three variables: 1) size of enrollment, 2) geographic region (New England/Midwest, Southeast, Great Lakes/Plains and West/Far West), and 3) socioeconomic status (high, high average, average, low average, and low). Once a school district was selected, one of three sampling plans was used to select buildings within multibuilding districts. The obtained sample was weighted to match actual population percents. Representative random samples were also selected for Catholic and private, non-Catholic schools. In addition 1,000 high school students were administered both the original TAP Form T and the new TAP Form G to provide data to equate these forms.

The TAP Form G test battery is available as a Basic Battery (Scannell, Haugh, Schild, & Ulmer, 1986a), which includes the Reading Comprehension, Mathematics, Written Expression, and Using Sources of Information tests, or as a Complete Battery (Scannell, Haugh, Schild, & Ulmer, 1986b), which includes these four tests, plus the Social Studies and Science tests. The instruments for each grade level within the various curricular areas contain items from the instruments for the previous levels as well as new items. The Complete and Basic Batteries are available in separate grade-level booklets or in a multilevel booklet. Because there is overlap on the items within each curricular area, the multilevel booklet (94 pages) is *not* four times larger than the separate level booklets (52 pages). Tests for all curricular areas are included in either the single or multilevel booklets and all items, numbers, and pages are identical. The multilevel booklet is spiral-bound with tagboard covers, while the separate level booklets are paper covered and stapled. Both are printed on off-white paper with blue and green ink. The print size for both the items and the response options is about 9 points (1/8 inch), but the items are printed in boldface type to make them more prominent. The Frye readability formula applied to a random sample of items in the Level 15 (Grade 9) booklet showed the items to be at about an eighth-grade reading level. All items are multiple choice with four or five response options. An "I don't know" option is not available.

The test booklets begin with student directions for marking names and answers on the answer sheet. In the multilevel booklet a description of where to start for each level is also included. This general descriptive information is followed by the directions for the first test. Each subsequent test also has its own separate page for directions.

The items for each curricular area test can be grouped by content and skill areas. In the first test of the battery, Reading Comprehension, the 120 total items for the four levels are grouped into two content areas, textbook and everyday, and three skill areas: facts, inferences, and generalizations.

The Mathematics test is next in the booklet, and the 96 items for the four levels of this test are grouped into seven content areas: 1) operations; 2) equivalent forms and order; 3) common applications; 4) algebra; 5) geometry and measurement; 6) statistics, graphs, and tables; and 7) basic mathematical principles. These seven content areas are crossed with three skill areas: computation, concepts, and problem solving.

The 129 total items on the four levels of the Written Expression test are grouped into six content areas: 1) spelling; 2) capitalization and punctuation; 3) grammar and usage; 4) sentence/paragraph structure; 5) organizing ideas; and 6) writing conventions. There are also four skill areas: 1) knowledge/information, 2) comprehension, 3) application/analysis, and 4) synthesis/evaluation.

The next test, Using Sources of Information, has 129 items for the four levels grouped into three content areas: 1) map reading; 2) reading graphs, tables, and diagrams; and 3) knowledge and use of reference materials. The test contains the same four skill areas as the Written Expression test.

The 123 Social Studies test items for the four levels are grouped into two content areas, historical perspective and patterns and systems; and the same four skill areas as the Written Expression test.

The final test in the TAP battery is Science. The 108 science items for the four levels are grouped into four content areas: 1) nature of science; 2) life science; 3) earth and space science; and 4) chemistry and physics. The science test contains five skill areas, four of which are those used for the Written Expression test and the fifth being experimental methods/techniques.

The optional Listening and Writing tests for each level are not part of the Basic or Complete Battery Test Booklets and must be requested separately. The Listening test covers a wide spectrum of listening situations from immediate recall of isolated details to inferential skills that require synthesis and evaluation. Each test contains six parts: 1) remembering exactly what is heard; 2) identifying word meanings in context; 3) remembering main points and details; 4) distinguishing between fact and opinion; 5) listening to a lecture; and 6) detecting bias. The Writing test is designed to assess a student's ability to develop, organize, and express ideas in four writing modes of ascending difficulty: narration (Level 15, Grade 9); explanation (Level 16, Grade 10); analysis (Level 17, Grade 11); and argumentation (Level 18, Grade 12). For each mode, students are offered a choice of writing an essay on one of two topics of comparable difficulty and specificity.

Practical Applications/Uses

The stated purpose of the TAP Form G is to provide efficient and comprehensive appraisal of high school (Grades 9–12) student progress toward widely accepted academic goals in the basic skill areas (*Manual for School Administrators*, 1986). It is designed to be used by school districts to analyze individual, class, building, and district strengths and weaknesses; to study a student's progress through high school; to plan instruction; to select remedial and enrichment activities; and to revise courses and instructional activities. To accomplish these goals the TAP Form G is comprised of a battery of tests, each assessing a different high school subject matter area. The individual and aggregated results of the tests would be useful to teachers, counselors, principals, school district personnel, parents, and students.

The TAP is designed to be used by typical students in Grades 9–12, but probably would be appropriate for advanced eighth graders or young adults as well. The norming group, however, would not directly apply to these cases. The TAP for a specific grade level may not be appropriate for students who are significantly above or below that grade level in academic achievement, nor would it be appropriate for students who have difficulty reading or marking answer sheets. As an alternative, it would be possible to read the tests to students or to mark answer sheets for them, but the time constraints would probably have to be changed and then the relationship to the norming group would be weakened. Large print versions of the test battery can be printed by individual states or districts, as they are required. Braille editions were developed for the Colorado testing program and are on file at the American Printing House for the Blind (APHB) in Lexington, Kentucky.

Both the TAP Basic and Complete Batteries are designed to be administered to intact groups of Grade 9–12 students. The students could be all from one grade level or, if the multilevel booklet is used, from a variety of different grade levels. Whether the Basic Battery or the Complete Battery is being given, it is recommended that the administrator divide the testing into two sessions. Completion of the Basic Battery requires 2 hours and 40 minutes while the Complete Battery requires 4 hours. In addition to the 40 minutes required for each curricular area test, 10 minutes should be allowed for distribution and collection of materials, 10 minutes for directions and answer sheet orientation, and 10 minutes for completing the 15-item questionnaire.

The TAP is designed to be administered by high school teachers although anyone familiar with standardized tests, answer sheets, and high school content would be an appropriate administrator. Detailed explanations of how to administer the TAP are provided by Riverside Publishing Company in both the *Manual for School Administrators* and the *Preliminary Teacher's Guide*. The explanations include general advance preparations, descriptions of how to care for materials, and specific written protocols for the examiner to read at the beginning of the entire test battery and before each subject matter test. The *Preliminary Teacher's Guide* (1986) is quite detailed and very easy to understand. It appears that giving the individual curricular area tests in an alternate order might also be possible, but somewhat inconvenient because the curricular area tests are prearranged in the battery booklet.

Three different types of answer sheets are available for each of Levels 15–18. (All answer sheets have separate areas for each of the six tests and for names, etc.). Individual items are numbered and bubble response areas are lettered. The MRC (Measurement Research Center) answer sheets must be used if scoring services are to be requested from Riverside or if the hand-scoring answer guides are to be used. There are two types of MRC answer sheets, one for the TAP alone and one for the TAP and the Cognitive Abilities tests (another set of tests from the Riverside Publishing Company) combined. The combined answer sheets must be used if combined score reports are required. Districts can score the third type, NCS (National Computer System) answer sheets, with their own machines. Separate answer sheets are required for each of the four levels of the tests. As is always the case with answer sheets, they must be marked carefully to ensure accurate scoring.

Although it is possible to hand score the instruments, it certainly would be more efficient to use optical scan machines. In addition, if the Riverside scoring service is not used, the local machine would have to be programmed to produce the summary scores for individuals and subject matter areas as well as for any class, building, or district aggregates. Unless the user administers only a small number of tests or has existing machine scoring and aggregation capabilities, it seems most efficient to use the Riverside scoring service.

The Riverside scoring service provides a comprehensive set of scores. Standard scores (within grade percentile ranks and stanines), grade equivalents, and normal curve equivalents are available for all tests, as well as the Basic Composite (an average of the first four tests) and the Battery Composite (an average of all of the tests). In addition, an Applied Proficiency Skills, score can be determined by adding the results from specific items designed to measure such skills from the Reading Comprehension, Mathematics, Written Expression, and Using Sources of Information tests. Two Minimum Competency ratings can be obtained from degree of success on the Reading Comprehension and Mathematics tests. The Minimum Competency score is "yes" if the student exceeded the median level for Grade 8 students, "no" if not, and "may" if a student would reach this level by making average progress from the present grade through Grade 12.

These scores can be used to produce a variety of reports useful for different purposes. One of the most common is the List Reports, which report the scores for each student for individual tests, composites, competency, applied proficiency skills, and the results of the questionnaire. Another common report is the Ranked Lists by Skill which groups the individual student data by content area. For school or district information, Group Item Performance, Building Criterion-Referenced Skills Analysis, and Class/Building/System Averages reports are available. There is also a narrative report available that provides a graph of the individual student's national percentage rank scores and a personalized letter to the student's parents describing the results and how to interpret them.

The reports tend to be quite dense because of the amount of information they contain, but they are arranged carefully and annotated well. In addition, the Riverside Publishing Company provides a detailed and understandable description of all of the scores they provide in their *Preliminary Teacher's Guide Levels 15–18* (1986) and in the *Manual for School Administrators Levels 15–18* (1986). The TAP scores should be understandable to anyone with a minimal background in measurement. Of particular importance is the care taken in the manuals to point out what the scores do *not* mean and that all scores should be interpreted with care.

Technical Aspects

Several different types of technical information are available for the TAP and they are presented in the *Manual for School Administrators Levels 15–18* (1986). Included are data on the validity and reliability of the tests as well as item fairness, difficulty, and discrimination. The raw mean scores for each test by level are usually slightly over half of the total number of items (about 40 correct from the approximately 60-item tests). The standard deviations for all tests and levels average about 10 points and the standard errors of measurement average about 3.2. The TAP was scaled using Thurstone's discriminate model for scaling applied to the responses of many individuals tested on one occasion (Nunnally, 1978). Reliability estimates for each test for each grade level were computed using the Kuder-Richardson Formula 20 on the norming sample data. The reliabilities range from .85 to .98, demonstrating a high degree of internal consistency. Kuder-Richardson reliabilities were also computed for the individual content and skill areas within each test at each level (e.g., "Maps" on the Using Sources of Information Test).

As would be expected from the smaller number of items included in these subscales, the reliabilities are lower than those for the total tests (Borg & Gall, 1983) and range from .12 to .93, with most in the .50 to .80 range and with a median value of .68. A 6-month test-retest reliability calculated on the students in both the fall and spring standardization samples is reported. Pearson product-moment correlations range from .75 to .92 and average .82. The reliabilities of the differences between pairs of tests in the battery are also reported (e.g., difference between Level 15 and Level 16 scores on the Reading Comprehension Test), as are the reliability of difference between the TAP tests and the scores on the Cognitive Abilities Test. These reliabilities are lower than those for the individual tests because of accumulated errors of measurement but still in an acceptable range (Nunnally, 1978).

The TAP developers provide a variety of information about the validity of the test battery (Cook & Campbell, 1979). First, content validity is addressed. The developers point out in their *Preliminary Technical Summary* (1986) that the issue of content validity is difficult and that the major responsibility lies with the user of the test to guarantee that the test is valid for the type of interpretations needed in the local situation. Conversely, the developers did employ a variety of techniques to guarantee as much content validity as possible. As mentioned in the description of the test development, the developers used a variety of sources to determine what content to include on the tests. Further, both quantitative and qualitative techniques were used to eliminate test item bias and to ensure that the retained items were functioning as desired in terms of difficulty and discrimination.

Construct validity (i.e., how well the TAP measures general notions like achievement or educational development [Borg & Gall, 1983]) was assessed by determining the intercorrelations among the subtests of the battery within each level. The intercorrelations among the six tests of the TAP Form G by each level were conducted on the data from the standardization sample and range from .55 to .83, indicating that high scores on one test in the battery are indeed related to high scores in other tests.

In addition, the correlations between the TAP battery scores and the scores on the Cognitive Abilities Test, high school course grades, high school grade point averages, and scores on the SAT (Scholastic Aptitude Test) or the ACT (American College Testing Program) were determined. The correlations among the TAP tests and the Cognitive Abilities Test were conducted on the approximately 12,000 students per grade who took both tests during the fall standardization. These range from .57 to .83 and show a reasonable pattern of relationships, with the Cognitive Abilities Test Quantitative score correlating more highly with the TAP Mathematics Test and the Cognitive Abilities Test Verbal score correlating more highly with the more verbally oriented TAP tests. The correlations of end-of-year course grade and GPAs with the TAP tests were obtained from a sample of approximately 2,000 students per grade from four high schools in four states. The ACT and SAT data were obtained from 11th-graders in these same four schools. The correlations of TAP tests with course grade and GPA are about .5. The TAP composite score correlated .87 with the ACT composite scores, .78 with the SAT verbal score, and .69 with the SAT mathematics score. The TAP composite/SAT/ACT correlations can be used to predict SAT or ACT scores from a student's score on the TAP.

An analysis of the student self-report data from the 15-item questionnaire in light of student scores on the TAP is also provided. The relationships appear to be consistent with general expectations and the data may provide an interesting basis for local comparisons.

Critique

As certainly could be expected from a group that has been involved in norm-referenced tests for so many years, the TAP battery appears to be an excellent update to the field of standardized tests. The development was carefully implemented and followed all of the procedures necessary to produce accurate assessment instruments. The qualitative reviews attest to the item fairness and validity, and the results of the quantitative analyses of the tests and individual items show that the instruments are of very high quality and should discriminate among students in a valid and reliable fashion.

The only apparent flaws in the assessment battery are those inherent in any standardized test. The most serious consideration is content validity, (i.e., the degree to which the sample of test items represents the content that the test is designed to measure [Anderson, Ball, & Murphy, 1975]). Content validity was addressed by the TAP developers by their selecting items through perusal of existing curricular materials, national curriculum organization statements, and so on, as well as through the three qualitative reviews of the potential items and through feedback from users. The team of authors also had academic expertise in the curricular areas assessed. Although this reviewer believes the tests are, indeed, content valid for the domain decided upon by the test developers, a very strong case for this is not presented in manuals. Content validity should be determined by systematically conducting a set of operations, such as defining in precise terms the specific content universe to be sampled, specifying objectives, and describing how the content universe will be sampled to develop test items (Borg & Gall, 1983). There is no documentation of how the test developers accomplished these operations other than the general guidelines provided in the manuals. A second consideration is that the tests may not be content valid for a particular local situation. The authors of TAP also point out this potential difficulty to users, suggesting that the individual items be examined and objectively matched with the local curriculum to ensure accurate inferences.

Other validity difficulties in the use of the TAP involve over- or misinterpretation of the various scores. For example, the data must be used with caution in conducting evaluations of local curriculum programs. Or, as another example, the percentage scores say nothing about the number of items answered correctly. The TAP developers, however, do an excellent job of cautioning the user about these potential problems in all of their manuals. Each individual type of score is carefully explained and examples of what it means and does not mean are provided. This is a great service to TAP test users in an era of overreliance on test scores.

The test manuals are excellent. All are very clearly written and explicit. Every possible contingency (i.e., timing, administration instruction, test score interpretation, etc.) seems to have been accounted for and the step-by-step procedures make it easy for anyone to use the tests correctly. The manuals even provide instructions on how to improve teaching based on test results. One minor problem with the present manuals is that not all of the information is available in one place. The *Manual for School Administrators* is the most complete, and although all have the same copyright dates, it seems the most recent in that the results of more data analyses are presented. Some other technical information, however, is only available in the *Preliminary Technical Summary* (1986). It is this reviewer's recommendation that a potential user should obtain copies of all the manuals to obtain the maximum benefit of the Tests of Achievement and Proficiency.

References

This list includes text citations and suggested additional reading.

Anderson, S.B., Ball, S., & Murphy, R.T. (1975). *Encyclopedia of educational evaluation.* San Francisco: Jossey-Bass.
Borg, W.R., & Gall, M.D. (1983). *Educational research.* New York: Longman.
Cook, T.D., & Campbell, D.T. (1979). *Quasi-experimentation design and analysis issues for field settings.* Boston: Houghton Mifflin.
Fry, E. (1972). Selecting books. *Reading instruction for classroom and clinic* (p. 249). New York: McGraw-Hill.
Hays, W.L. (1973). *Statistics for the social sciences.* New York: Holt, Rinehart & Winston. *Manual for school administrators levels 15–18.* (1986). Chicago: Riverside Publishing Co.
Nunnally, J.C. (1978). *Psychometric theory.* New York: McGraw-Hill.
Preliminary teacher's guide levels 15–18 (1986). Chicago: Riverside Publishing Company.

Preliminary Technical Summary (1986). Chicago: Riverside Publishing Company.

Rossi, P.H., & Freeman, H. E. (1987). *Evaluation: A Systematic Approach*. Beverly Hills: Sage.

Scannell, D.P., Haugh, O.M., Schild, A.H., & Ulmer, G. (1986a). *Tests of Achievement and Proficiency Multilevel Booklet for Levels 15–18 Form G Basic Battery.* Chicago, IL: Riverside Publishing Company.

Scannell, D.P., Haugh, O.M., Schild, A.H., & Ulmer, G. (1986b). *Tests of Achievement and Proficiency Multilevel Booklet for Levels 15–18 Form G Complete Battery.* Chicago, IL: Riverside Publishing Company.

Worthen, B.R., & Sanders, J.R. (1987). *Educational evaluation: Alternative approaches and practical guidelines*. New York: Longman.

Jon D. Swartz, Ph.D.
*Associate Dean and Professor of Education and Psychology,
Southwestern University, Georgetown, Texas.*

TORRANCE TESTS OF CREATIVE THINKING

*E. Paul Torrance. Bensenville, Illinois: Scholastic Testing Service,
Inc.*

Introduction

The Torrance Tests of Creative Thinking (TTCT), used to identify gifted and creative individuals, are multiple-task paper-and-pencil measures of four aspects of "creative thinking"—fluency, flexibility, originality, and elaboration. Available in two equivalent forms, A and B, the Verbal test consists of seven word-based subtests: Asking, Guessing Causes, Guessing Consequences, Product Improvement, Unusual Uses, Unusual Questions, and Just Suppose. The Figural test has three picture-based subtests: Picture Construction (from a marked cue), Picture Completion (also with cues), and Parallel Lines.

The Torrance tests were created as part of a long-term research program that emphasized classroom experiences that stimulate creativity. Developed within an educational environment, some of the tests are adaptations of techniques used in the Aptitudes Research Project; scores are based on factors originally identified by Guilford (Torrance, 1962, 1963, 1965). The research edition of the TTCT was published in 1966, after 9 years of work by Torrance and his colleagues on the nature of creative behavior and its assessment.

E. Paul Torrance (Ph.D., University of Michigan, 1951), an educational psychologist, has been Alumni Foundation Distinguished Professor Emeritus at the University of Georgia since 1974. He has been head of the Department of Educational Psychology at the University of Georgia, director of the Bureau of Educational Research at the University of Minnesota, and director of a program of research in support of Air Force survival training. Author or editor of several books on creativity, he and his colleagues have developed a variety of instructional materials designed to encourage creativity in children. In addition to the TTCT, Torrance is author or coauthor of the Human Information Processing Survey, an instrument for assessing processing preference in brain functioning; the Khatena-Torrance Creative Perception Inventory, two separate tests of creative self-perceptions; Thinking Creatively in Action and Movement, an observational measure of improvisational behavior for studying creativity in very young children; Thinking Creatively with Sounds and Words, a test of imagination imagery that was developed to complement the TTCT; and, in 1987, Your Style of Learning and Thinking, a measure of learning strategy and brain hemisphere preference in problem solving.

The TTCT has changed significantly over the years. A revision was published in 1974, and since 1984 a "streamlined" scoring of the figural forms has been available (Torrance & Ball, 1984). (Streamlined scoring for the verbal forms will be available soon.) This alternative scoring procedure yields norm-referenced measures for

619

fluency, originality, abstractness of titles, elaboration, and resistance to premature closure. In addition, an overall Creativity Index and criterion-referenced scores for several creativity indicators are provided.

In the current version of the TTCT, means and standard deviations are presented separately for fluency, flexibility, originality, and elaboration for Figural Forms A and B for 11 different educational levels from kindergarten through graduate school ($N = 19,111$). Means and standard deviations also are presented separately for fluency, flexibility, and originality for Verbal Forms A and B for 15 different educational levels from first grade through graduate school ($N = 13,663$). In addition, two sets of data are provided for converting raw scores to standard scores, one on a fifth-grade equivalency sample and one on a combined sample of college graduates and undergraduates.

The manuals, worksheets, and other test materials provided by Scholastic Testing Service are clear, usable, and engaging. Most of the tasks are "game-like" and children seem to enjoy them.

Practical Applications/Uses

As noted previously, the TTCT is a paper-and-pencil measure of individual creativity in which four mental characteristics are measured: fluency, flexibility, originality, and elaboration. The TTCT is used appropriately with kindergartners through graduate students, is easily administered and scored, and is suitable for group use. An examiner is required, and the total test takes about 75 minutes of administration time. Although the tasks can be administered by anyone who can read and follow directions, and scoring can be done with a minimum of training, results should be interpreted by persons with psychometric training.

Torrance's definition of creativity is concerned with assessing problem solving in a general sense, with "effective dealing with the environment" at the core of his construct of creative thinking. Rather than a test of all aspects of creativity, therefore, the TTCT should be used as follows: 1) in basic studies that will yield a more complete understanding of the human mind and its functioning and development; 2) in studies designed to discover effective bases for individualizing instruction; 3) as a source of clues for remedial and psychotherapeutic programs; 4) for assessing the differential effects of various kinds of experimental programs, new curricular arrangements or materials, organizational arrangements, teaching procedures, and the like; and 5) as a means of becoming aware of potentialities that might otherwise go unnoticed (Torrance, 1974).

The TTCT materials are reasonably priced, and a scoring service is available through the publisher. The current cost of this service is $2.67 per test booklet; a specimen set is $10.00 postpaid.

The manual and administration guide provide clear directions for administering and scoring the TTCT, although scoring is somewhat tedious. The TTCT can be administered individually or in groups, but individual oral administration is recommended below the fourth grade. The Figural TTCT (three picture-based exercises) requires 30 minutes of testing time, the Verbal TTCT (seven word-based exercises) 45 minutes. Speed is important—with 5- to 10-minute time limits for the subtests—but the artistic quality of the responses does not affect scoring.

Treffinger, Torrance, and Ball (1980) have provided guidelines and instructions for training test administrators and scorers. Because variations in testing procedures can influence test scores significantly, it is imperative that users follow the standard procedures carefully.

Technical Aspects

Several studies of reliability and validity are reported in the TTCT *Norms-Technical Manual*. Inter- and intrascorer reliability is high, with coefficients generally above .90. Classroom teachers who had only studied the *Scoring Guide* showed mean reliability coefficients that ranged from .88 to .96 for the figural tests and from .94 to .99 for the verbal tests. Originality was the most difficult characteristic to score and Fluency the easiest. Test-retest reliabilities, using alternate forms, were somewhat lower, ranging from .50 for Figural fluency to .93 for Verbal fluency. Most test-retest reliabilities over short periods are in the .60s and .70s. Given the varying grade levels and sample sizes, the TTCT appears to have adequate reliability, especially for use with groups. In general, the verbal scores show higher reliability than the figural scores.

"Since a person can behave creatively in an almost infinite number of ways and since there is a diversity of definitions of creativity, it is impossible to provide all researchers and potential users of tests of creative thinking satisfactory evidences of validity" (Torrance, 1974, p. 21). After this disclaimer, Torrance discusses content validity as it applies to the TTCT and summarizes more than 50 studies on construct, concurrent, and predictive validity. The validation studies suggest that the TTCT does measure behaviors consistent with the literature on creative behavior. The question of predictive validity is one of the most complex and controversial, as it revolves around the difficulty in defining the construct of creativity. Obviously, the TTCT does not assess every dimension of creativity. The data on predictive validity presented by Torrance seem to indicate that the TTCT scores are predictors of later creative accomplishment (Treffinger, 1985). On the other hand, in his evaluation of the TTCT, Chase (1985) concludes that the TTCT does not have a firm base in construct validation.

The scoring system currently employed presents some problems as well. An often-cited study by Yamamoto and Frengel (1966), in which the results of 800 fifth-graders were factor analyzed, gave no support to the interpretation of the TTCT scores in terms of simple constructs. Indeed, several reviewers (Anastasi, 1982; Baird, 1972; Chase, 1985; & Treffinger, 1985) have warned against interpretating the scores as if they were independent factors. Anastasi (1982), for example, in reviewing the TTCT, concluded: "It would thus seem inadvisable to derive more than one score from any one test or to treat similarly labeled scores from different tests as measures of a single trait" (p. 391).

Critique

Critical evaluations of the TTCT have not varied much in the years since it was first published. Fifteen years ago Baird (1972) concluded: "The TTCT seems to be useful as a basis for further research into the nature and nurture of creativity. The work already done with the TTCT has made a considerable contribution to the literature on creative behavior [but] . . . the TTCT should probably be used for assessment of an individual's creative potential only with great caution" (p. 838). Recently, in the same series, Treffinger (1985) concluded: "In the complex and still-evolving domain of creativity assessment, the TTCT can be recommended as sound examples of instruments useful for research, evaluation, and general instructional planning decisions. . . . No test of creative thinking can purport to represent a comprehensive assessment of the many forms and expressions of creativity, but the TTCT offers useful insights into several relevant dimensions" (p. 1634).

In conclusion, the Torrance Tests of Creative Thinking are still evolving. Themselves a revision of the Minnesota Tests of Creative Thinking, the Torrance tests have undergone significant changes since first introduced in 1966. Despite the shortcomings, this reviewer is not aware of a better set of tests for assessing creativity in children and adults.

References

This list includes text citations and suggested additional reading.

Anastasi, A. (1982). *Psychological testing* (5th ed.). New York: Macmillan.

Baird, L.L. (1972). Torrance Tests of Creative Thinking. In O. K. Buros (Ed.), *The seventh mental measurements yearbook* (pp. 836–838). Highland Park, NJ: Gryphon Press.

Chase, E.I. (1985). Torrance Tests of Creative Thinking. In J.V. Mitchell, Jr. (Ed.), *The ninth mental measurements yearbook* (pp. 1631–1632). Lincoln, NE: Buros Institute of Mental Measurements.

Torrance, E.P. (1962). *Guiding creative talent.* Englewood Cliffs, NJ: Prentice-Hall.

Torrance, E.P. (1963). *Education and the creative potential.* Minneapolis: University of Minnesota Press.

Torrance, E.P. (1965). *Rewarding creative behavior.* Englewood Cliffs, NJ: Prentice-Hall.

Torrance, E.P. (1967). The Minnesota studies of creative behavior: National and international extensions. *Journal of Creative Behavior, 1,* 137–154.

Torrance, E.P. (1972a). Predictive validity of "bonus" scoring for combinations on repeated figures tests of creative thinking. *Journal of Psychology, 81,* 167–171.

Torrance, E.P. (1972b). Predictive validity of the Torrance Tests of Creative Thinking. *Journal of Creative Behavior, 6*(4), 114–143.

Torrance, E.P. (1972c). Tendency to produce unusual visual perspective as a predictor of creative achievement. *Perceptual and Motor Skills, 34,* 911–915.

Torrance, E.P. (1974). *Norms-technical manual, Torrance Tests of Creative Thinking.* Bensenville, IL: Scholastic Testing Service.

Torrance, E.P., & Ball, O.E. (1984). *TTCT streamlined (revised) manual including norms and directions for administering and scoring Figural A and B.* Bensenville, IL: Scholastic Testing Service.

Treffinger, D.J. (1985). Torrance Tests of Creative Thinking. In J.V. Mitchell, Jr. (Ed.), *The ninth mental measurements yearbook* (pp. 1632–1634). Lincoln, NE: Buros Institute of Mental Measurements.

Treffinger, D.J., Torrance, E.P., & Ball, O.E. (1980). Guidelines for training creativity test administrators and scorers. *Journal of Creative Behavior, 14,* 47–55.

Yamamoto, K., & Frengel, B.A. (1966). An exploratory component analysis of the Minnesota Tests of Creative Thinking. *California Journal of Educational Research, 17,* 220–229.

Dwight R. Kauppi, Ph.D.

Associate Professor and Director, Rehabilitation Counseling Program, Department of Counseling and Educational Psychology, State University of New York at Buffalo, Buffalo, New York.

VOCATIONAL INTEREST, TEMPERAMENT, AND APTITUDE SYSTEM

Jewish Employment and Vocational System. Philadelphia, Pennsylvania: Vocational Research Institute.

Introduction

The Vocational Interest, Temperament, and Aptitude System (VITAS) is an evaluation system that uses 21 work samples to assess a client's vocational interests, temperaments, and aptitudes. It was designed for use with educationally and culturally disadvantaged clients, whose characteristics might not be fairly reflected by commonly used vocational tests. For such client groups, work samples can have many advantages over standardized tests. The activities involved are likely to be familiar, so the anxieties associated with standardized test administration are not as likely to occur. The assessment situation is more similar to a work situation, allowing a more comprehensive observation and evaluation of client work-related behaviors, including the client's interpersonal skill, ability to follow instructions, expressed interest in various activities, and work temperaments. Work evaluation procedures usually are spread out over days rather than hours, thus allowing for longer periods of observation. Client interest is likely to be high for the concrete, face valid activities of work samples. The advantages of work samples for assessing persons with disabilities have been known for many years. VITAS brings the technique to the larger group of persons who are disadvantaged.

The VITAS is part of the Jewish Employment and Vocational Service (JEVS) work-sample systems and is distributed by JEVS's Vocational Research Institute. The VITAS was completed in 1979 by the Vocational Research Institute under a contract with the U.S. Department of Labor. The VITAS is based on the earlier JEVS work-sample system that had been developed for use with persons who have disabilities. The VITAS was modified to take less time than the earlier system and to be suitable for males and females with less than a 12th-grade education. The groups targeted for the VITAS were the clients of employment programs for the disadvantaged, such as CETA.

The VITAS was field tested and normed on CETA and State Employment Service clients in several sites across the U.S. to give a cross-section of race, urban and rural dwellers, and geographic area. Two sets of norms are currently available. The 1980 norming population was 63% female, 63% Caucasian, with 84% having 12th-grade education or less. The median age of this group was 25 years. The number of subjects per work-sample norm ranged from 242 to 329.

During 1980 to 1981, secondary-school norms were collected from three school systems, located in New Jersey, Texas, and Georgia. The students in this norm group were 68% male, 78% Caucasian, and had a mean grade level of 8.7 years. They were all considered disabled students under P.L. 94-142, with 67% in the Learning Disabled category. The number of students in the norm for each work sample varied from 175 to 229.

The VITAS was originally keyed to 18 of the 114 Worker Trait Group Arrangements (WTGAs) in the 1965 *Dictionary of Occupational Titles (DOT;* U.S. Department of Labor [DOL], 1965.). Each of the 21 work samples was weighted on one to four of the WTGAs, based on how each work sample represented one of the significant aptitudes for a WTGA, and whether the activity of the work sample looked like the work conducted by incumbents in the WTGA. After the VITAS was developed, the U.S. Department of Labor published the 1977 revision of the *DOT* (U.S. DOL, 1977), and an accompanying *Guide for Occupational Exploration* (U.S. DOL, 1979). In the *Guide,* 66 Work Groups are described, with estimates of the aptitudes, temperaments, and interests appropriate for each group. The VITAS work samples have been keyed to 16 of these Work Groups, with each work sample identified as significant for one to four of the groups listed. The results of the VITAS work samples can be reported in terms of both the WTGAs and the Work Groups.

The VITAS is carefully standardized, going so far as to provide a recommended floor plan for the assessment area. The content of each work sample can be readily inferred from its title. Sorting, assembling, and collating samples include Nuts, Bolts, and Washers Assembly, Packing Matchbooks, Nail and Screw Sorting, Collating Material Samples, and Pipe Assembly. The use of a variety of tools is included in Tile Sorting and Weighing, Pressing Linens, Budget Book Assembly, Lock Assembly, Calculating, Message Taking, Bank Teller, Payroll Computation, Census Interviewing, Laboratory Assistant, Drafting, and Spot Welding. Additional samples from office work include Verifying Numbers and Filing by Letters. Inspection tasks include Circuit Board Inspection and Proofreading.

Work samples are administered individually, with clearly standardized directions, including photographs of materials as they should be arranged at the beginning of each test. Instructions are given orally, with demonstration by the examiner and, on some work samples, a practice trial for the client. The amount of assistance to be provided beyond the brief standardized instruction is limited.

The amount of time spent on each work sample can vary greatly. The average amount of time taken by the school norm group varied from 6 minutes on the Circuit Board Inspection task to just over 46 minutes on the Calculating task. Most of the tasks take from 20 to 40 minutes for the average client to complete. A client should be able to complete the evaluation in 2½ days. Work samples can be completed in any order, although usually the easier tasks are administered first.

The testing environment is similar to a work situation, with the client punching in and out of tasks and having behavioral expectations imposed. The evaluator instructs the clients about the work evaluation process and allows opportunities for questions and clarification at a motivational group session at the end of the first day.

The maximum client to evaluator ratio is 5:1, though smaller numbers are recommended for inexperienced evaluators; with five clients, however, an assistant is recommended, to help in scoring and disassembling the work samples. The evaluator observes the client throughout the testing process, to report on the client's general work habits, infer information about the client's temperament, and to supplement the aptitude evaluations based on the work-samples scores.

Each work sample is scored by the amount of time taken to complete the sample and the number of errors made. Templates, standards, and keys ease scoring for errors, and the client punches a time clock at the completion of each task, thus recording the time. Each work sample has been examined to determine which of the nine aptitudes assessed by VITAS applies to which parts of each sample. For example, the instructions suggest that the Nuts, Bolts, and Washers Assembly work sample assesses F (finger dexterity) in picking up parts and threading nuts on bolts, K (motor coordination) in placing washers and nuts on bolts, and P (form perception) in selecting the proper size of parts. All work samples include at least two aptitudes and several assess as many as seven aptitudes. Spot Welding, for example, lists E (eye-hand-foot coordination) in pressing foot pedal, F in scribing and positioning the metal, K in aligning the metal and positioning tools, M (manual dexterity) in holding and using tools, N (numerical) in measuring metal, and P and S (spatial) in using diagrams and sample to assemble squares. The other two aptitudes assessed by VITAS are C (color discrimination) and Q (clerical perception). General intelligence and verbal aptitude are not included in the list of aptitudes assessed by the work samples because of the difficulties in culture-free measurement of those aptitudes.

The reporting and synthesis of client performance is done through several records. The administrator completes a General Observations sheet for each client, with headings of Physical Description, Attendance and Punctuality, Verbal Ability, Interpersonal Behavior, and General Worker Characteristics. Each work sample has a Work Sample Record for recording aptitude and behavior observations, types of errors, and time. At the end of the work-samples administration, the evaluator conducts a review of the evaluation with the client, including the elicitation of client likes and dislikes through the completion of a Vocational Interest Interview form.

The Work Sample Records and the Vocational Interest Interview form are used to complete the Evaluation Report. This report synthesizes the evaluator's observations about work behavior, appearance, interpersonal skills, and verbal ability, and the description of the client's manipulative skills, perceptual abilities, and numerical ability. Specific recommendations are made for employment or training and appropriate supportive services. The client's time and quality performance in each work sample is rated 1, 2, or 3 if it would fall in the lower, middle, or upper third, respectively, of the norming sample. These ratings can then be related to WTGAs or the more recent Work Groups. The VITAS manual suggests that to recommend Work Group, the client must have earned a 2 or 3 rating for Time and Quality for all the work samples representative of that Work Group, have expressed interest in that group, and have demonstrated suitable temperament for that group. The aptitudes for each group are measured at the lowest levels required, so as not to exclude those with potential for performance.

Practical Applications/Uses

The VITAS would be most useful in a setting where additional support services are available. The value of the procedure for the clients will depend in part on the opportunity for vocational counseling, training, and support, because the kinds of disadvantaged persons for whom the VITAS is designed are likely to need more than just information about their aptitudes, interests, and temperaments. The quality of the final evaluation report will depend on the ability of the examiner, as much of the report depends on careful observation and inference on his or her part. Examiners train for 1 week at the Vocational Research Institute before they can administer the VITAS; however, because the judgment of the examiner is crucial in evaluation, users of VITAS should be careful in their selection of examiners.

The system also requires a commitment of space (25' x 25') and money (about $10,000), for which the purchaser receives a carefully packaged set of durable work samples. The VITAS will serve persons with low reading ability and little test sophistication; although not designed for use with disabled adults, it could be used in many settings that have clients with disabilities.

Technical Aspects

The VITAS shares with most work sample systems a lack of technical development. No data are given for reliability or validity, or for any evaluation of psychometric characteristics. Much of the report is based on observations rather than scores, and the relationship between client performance and subsequent outcomes has not been established. The norm groups are limited and not likely to be representative of describable larger groups. This lack of data is common to work-sample systems, which generally rely on face validity and clinical satisfaction for the evaluation of their performance.

Critique

The VITAS has the advantage of being part of a well-developed JEVS system, so the samples and procedures will be familiar to many who work in rehabilitation. The instructions are standardized and careful observation of the client is stressed. The significance of interests and temperaments in vocational adjustment needs to be recognized for clients who are culturally or educationally disadvantaged as it has been recognized for the college-bound. However, the assessments of interests and temperaments in the VITAS are largely clinical and unstandardized, and their validity is unknown.

The vocational guidance of persons who are disabled or disadvantaged should not be stereotyped or limited. The VITAS moves in the right direction by including a variety of tasks as work samples and in stressing the importance of interests and temperaments as well as abilities. However, only 4 of the 12 interest areas included in the *Guide to Occupational Exploration* (U.S. DOL, 1979) are included in the VITAS, so many jobs will be overlooked if the VITAS is used in isolation. As with any test, work sample, or assessment device, the VITAS should be used as part of a program of professional services, not as the only tool.

References

This list includes text citations and suggested additional readings.

Abrams, M. (1979). A new work sample battery for vocational assessment of the disadvantaged: VITAS. *Vocational Guidance Quarterly, 28*(1), 35-43.

Botterbusch, K. F. (1987). *Vocational assessment and evaluation systems: A comparison.* Menomonie, WI: Materials Development Center.

U.S. Department of Labor. (1965). *Dictionary of occupational titles* (3rd ed.). Washington, DC: U.S. Government Printing Office.

U.S. Department of Labor. (1977). *Dictionary of occupational titles* (4th ed.). Washington, DC: U.S. Government Printing Office.

U.S. Department of Labor. (1979). *Guide for occupational exploration.* Washington, DC: U.S. Government Printing Office.

Zimmerman, B. (1979). VITAS. *Evaluation and Work Adjustment Bulletin, 12*(1), 29-31.

Roger D. Carlson, Ph.D.
Visiting Associate Professor of Psychology, Whitman College, Walla Walla, Washington.

WALKER-MCCONNELL SCALE OF SOCIAL COMPETENCE AND SCHOOL ADJUSTMENT

Hill M. Walker and Scott R. McConnell. Austin, Texas: PRO-ED.

Introduction

The Walker-McConnell Scale of Social Competence and School Adjustment (WM) is a 43-item teacher rating scale of social skills for students at the elementary school level. It was specifically designed for the screening and identification of social skills deficits in students from kindergarten to sixth grade. It is designed to measure overall social skills as well as skills that are specifically regarded as teacher-preferred social behavior, peer-preferred social behavior, and school adjustment behavior.

The senior author of the WM, Hill M. Walker, is Professor and Associate Dean of the College of Education at the University of Oregon. Dr. Walker received his B.A. in 1962 from Eastern Oregon State College, and both his M.A. and Ph.D. from the University of Oregon (in 1964 and 1967, respectively). He has been in Special Education and Rehabilitation at the University of Oregon since 1966. Scott R. McConnell received his Ph.D. in school psychology at the University of Oregon in 1982. Currently he is on the faculty of the Psychology in the Schools program at the University of Minnesota.

The scale was developed out of a concern for the correlations that have been found between social incompetence (i.e., social skills deficits) and the later development of various behaviors that are regarded by schools and community as inappropriate. Because the mental health movement has shifted its concern from remediation to prevention, it was felt that an instrument was needed that would detect such social skills deficits in the early elementary school years. The move toward the mainstreaming of handicapped children made it important that an instrument be devised that would facilitate specific social skill interventions in such contexts.

Sociometric techniques like those developed by Moreno (1934, 1953) have been used for many years in the assessment of social status and peer popularity. However, Walker and McConnell (1988) point out that besides the practical difficulties with the attainment of sociogrammatic portrayals, knowledge of one's social status provides little information about the specific skills underlying that status. The WM was developed in order to provide a more cost-effective means of ascertaining specific behavioral deficits in the social skills area of one's school experience.

The development of the scale involved more than 5 years of research and development. The 43-item scale was derived from an item pool of 100 items thought to

628

be important because of issues raised in the professional literature, as well as some that were selected or adapted from other scales that are in use. After reviewing the items for relative independence and face validity, 83 items remained as the first tryout pool. Those items were used on 134 students enrolled in Grades K- 5 in Eugene-Springfield, Oregon, public schools and were rated by their nine teachers. A number of selection criteria were developed for deleting of items that were not effectively contributing to the scale. The items then were factor-analyzed, which ultimately yielded 43 items contributing to three factors—teacher-preferred social behavior, peer-preferred social behavior, and school adjustment behavior. The WM was normed on a sample of 1,812 cases from four major U.S. census zones— West, North Central, Northeast, and South. Normative data were collected from teacher ratings of students in each grade-level K-6 at 15 normative sites.

The scale consists of 43 Likert-type items on four pages. Responses are made directly on the Profile/Rating Form. Five response choices ranging from 1 ("Never") to 5 ("Always") allow the respondent to choose a frequency of occurrence to behaviors such as "Shows sympathy for others" (an item on the Teacher-Preferred Social Behavior subscale), "Shares laughter with peers" (an item on the Peer-Preferred Social Behavior subscale), and "Uses free time appropriately" (an item on the School Adjustment Behavior subscale). Instructions are included on the form as well as spaces for demographic data, scores, and narrative comments.

Three of the four chapters of the 50-page softcover manual (Walker & McConnell, 1988) are devoted to a highly technical discussion of the development and psychometric adequacy of the WM, as well as an extensive review of empirical research that has been done with the WM. One chapter gives instructions concerning administration, scoring, and interpretation.

The test authors caution that teachers who rate children on the WM should have observed the children for at least 2 months prior to rating. The scale takes approximately 5 minutes per pupil to complete. Scores yielded are for each of the three subscales as well as a total score. Tables are given for both standard score and percentile rank conversion for each subscale as well as total score.

Practical Applications/Uses

The WM was designed for screening and identification of social skills deficits. It can be used to facilitate certification as handicapped, program planning, and writing of Individual Education Programs (IEPs) for the handicapped, as well as to measure change in teachers' perceptions of student social behavior over time. It was not designed as either a diagnostic or classification instrument.

The WM is intended for teacher use in a school setting, although the questions are answerable by parents as well as professionals who have observed the child. The limiting factor for the person using the WM is only the appropriateness of the items to the child's actual environment. The test authors suggest that when social skills screening is conducted individually, a same-sexed peer from the class should be nominated by the teacher to represent the class norm in terms of social skills. Because the WM is a passive device that is not dependent upon student input, students can be rated independent of their handicapping conditions.

Scoring can be done by the teacher responding and is easily accomplished using simple addition within 5 minutes. Subscale designations for each item are printed in the Profile/Rating Form. The interpreter's level of psychometric sophistication needs only to be at the level of understanding standard scores or percentiles because tables of each based upon the norming study are given in the manual.

Prescriptively, the test authors recommend that a student who scores in excess of one standard deviation below the mean for the norming sample on the Peer-Preferred Social Behavior subscale receive social competence interventions designed to improve peer-related social skills. The authors also suggest that low scorers on the Teacher-Preferred Social Behavior and the School Adjustment Behavior subscales obtain social skills interventions designed to improve adult-related social behavior and adjustment to school. Finally, the authors recommend that any social skills that are rated as infrequently or never observed be targeted for instruction or remediation.

Technical Aspects

Many studies attesting to the validity of the WM are contained in the manual. Types of validity discussed are content validity, item validity, factorial validity, discriminant validity, criterion-related validity, and construct validity. For the purposes of the present discussion, the most salient features of the latter three types of validity in the administration of the WM will be discussed. The reader is referred to the manual (Walker & McConnell, 1988) for a more detailed discussion, as well as an extensive bibliography.

In the development of the WM, the authors found that the three factors identified accounted for 67.6% of the variance of the responses; specifically, the Teacher-Preferred Social Behavior factor accounted for 53.6%, the Peer-Preferred Social Behavior factor accounted for 8.5%, and the School Adjustment Behavior factor accounted in 5.5% of the common variance. Thus, one should keep in mind that the factor structure of the WM is dominated by items that are directed at teacher-preferred social behavior directed toward peers.

Discriminant validity was investigated by means of several studies that made use of the WM for the identification of students of varying groups (including those derived through sociometry). Generally, the WM is very sensitive in discriminating students who by their membership in particular groups would be expected to vary predictably in terms of their social behavior.

Several studies are also described by the test authors that demonstrate the scale's criterion-related validity. The WM fares well when comparisons are made to several other instruments measuring social competence, as well as discriminating between students who have been independently classified (e.g., boys who are described as antisocial vs. normal). The authors report that to date, no studies have been completed that demonstrate predictive validity.

Construct validity of the WM is demonstrated through correlations with peer nomination that remained high over a 2-year period. WM ratings also discriminated well between boys who were designated antisocial versus normal.

Test-retest reliability studies were done that showed the WM to be most stable for short intervals and less stable for long periods of time. Internal consistency was investigated by means of coefficient alpha. The total scale as well as all three subscales at all grade levels yielded alphas in excess of .90. Thus, the authors conclude that the scale had a very high degree of internal consistency.

Interrater reliability studies reported in the manual report correlations between raters ranging from low to moderate. The authors suggest that discrepancies between raters might be due to differing teacher demand characteristics.

Estimates of standard error of measurement for the norming sample are reported by the authors in the manual and are judged to be quite small.

Critique

For what it intends to do, the WM is a good instrument that is based on a good foundation of empirical research. It is important to remember, however, that there are a number of parameters that qualify its use. First, the results are based upon the judgments of teachers. The data are therefore secondary source data. Second, the behaviors rated are value laden in terms of those that are best for the purposes of the school or the student *within* the context of the school. Therefore, its scope of inquiry is narrow. For that reason it should not be used as if it measures enduring psychosocial traits. Until the necessity of the social values implicit in the schools and the WM are demonstrated to be somehow essential to human conduct through, for example, cross-cultural studies, one would do well to keep in mind that behavioral prescription based upon a student's outcomes is done for the purposes of the social context of the school rather than essential for human social conduct. One serious yet overriding question has to do with whether the public schools as instruments of the state have the legal or moral right to regulate the types of social behaviors that the WM measures.

In using the WM, the reviewer has encountered teachers who object to rating students on the WM because they believe it violates a student's right to privacy with respect to social conduct. Those teachers note that the behavior might be public for all to observe, but question whether it is right and correct to document that behavior. Nowhere in the WM manual are precautions spelled out for the storage, security, and release of test results. To date, the practical effects of releasing data of this sort to school teachers or officials remains unexplored.

Because the scale is not measuring necessarily enduring psychological traits, it is hard to know how to interpret data about its reliability. One does not know whether the lower reliability coefficients for longer periods of time reflect actual changes in patterns of student behavior over time, decay in teacher recollection or halo effect, or instability of the scale itself. In that sense, it is more akin to an "achievement" test rather than to an "aptitude" test. Over time, changes in scores associated with an achievement test presumably represent changes in student knowledge, whereas changes in scores associated with an aptitude test are presumed to represent test unreliability or practice effects. Where one draws the line between the unreliability of an instrument and changes inherent in the subject becomes a difficult question to answer with measures like the WM.

With respect to interrater reliability, the test authors make the following statement:

> Across these studies, these correlations suggest low to moderate levels of inter-rater agreement of the WM for teachers and their aides. These relatively

modest agreement levels are not uncommon for adult rating measures of child social-behavioral attributes. Students perform divergently in the presence of difference persons and situations, thus highlighting the importance of carefully considering the situational specificity of noncognitive forms of behavior in assessment contexts of this nature and their effects on both child behavior and adult perceptions of it. (Walker & McConnell, 1988, p. 33)

In light of this truism, it is remarkable that the WM has a relatively high degree of validity; one also might expect more pessimistic results of any studies done on the scale's predictive validity. With such a qualification in mind, one should be cautious about making predictions about the student's social behavior that might result in important psychosocial effects for the child.

In this reviewer's use of the WM (Carlson, 1988), a problem arose that could have potential psychometric side effects. Many teachers questioned the appropriateness of particular items to the particular environment in which they saw the student. For example, if a teacher had ample opportunity to observe a student exhibiting leadership behavior among peers yet the student never did, this teacher would mark the same response ("Never") as a teacher who never saw leadership behavior because he or she never saw the student playing among peers. However, a pilot study done by the reviewer in which teachers' ratings were weighted by their rating of the confidence of their response yielded no significant differences.

In terms of interpretation, the reviewer also found that teachers sometimes fail to grasp the significance of two factor labels: teacher-preferred social behavior and school adjustment behavior. Although factorially independent, the definitions are not inherent in the labels. Thus, it is sometimes necessary to define each. Teacher-preferred social behavior refers to "peer- related social behavior that is highly valued or preferred by teachers" (Walker & McConnell, 1988, p. 2). School adjustment behavior refers to "adaptive social-behavioral competencies highly valued by teachers within classroom instructional contexts" (Walker & McConnell, 1988, p. 3).

Technically, the WM has been carefully developed and is unusually well documented. When properly used and interpreted, the WM can be a source of valuable observational information given by teachers about elementary school student social behavior.

References

Carlson, R.D. (1988, April). *"At risk" in kindergarten: A study selection, retention, promotion, and transition.* Paper presented at the annual meeting of the American Educational Research Association, New Orleans.

Moreno, J. (1934). *Who shall survive? A new approach to the problem of human interrelations.* Washington, DC: Nervous and Mental Disease Publishing Co.

Moreno, J. (1953). *Who shall survive? Foundations of sociometry, group psychotherapy, and sociodrama.* Beacon, NY: Beacon House.

Walker, H.M. and McConnell, S.R. (1988). *The Walker-McConnell Scale of Social Competence and School Adjustment: A social skills rating scale for teachers.* Austin, TX: PRO-ED.

Raymond H. Holden, Ed.D.
Chief Psychologist, Vocational Resources, Inc., Providence, Rhode Island.

WECHSLER MEMORY SCALE-REVISED

David Wechsler. San Antonio, Texas: The Psychological Corporation.

Introduction

The Wechsler Memory Scale-Revised (WMS-R) is an individually administered clinical instrument for appraising major dimensions of memory functions in adolescents and adults. The scale is intended to be used as a diagnostic and screening device in conjunction with a general neuropsychological examination or any other clinical examination requiring the assessment of memory functions. The functions assessed include memory for verbal and figural (visual) stimuli, meaningful and abstract material, and delayed as well as immediate recall. The WMS-R represents an extensive revision of the original Wechsler Memory Scale (WMS; Wechsler, 1945) and is expected to better address those aspects of memory functioning that are considered clinically significant. The changes incorporated into the new revision include 1) provision of norms stratified at nine age levels, 2) replacement of a single global summary score (the original Memory quotient) with five composite scores, 3) addition of new subtests measuring figural and spatial memory, 4) addition of measures of delayed recall, and 5) revision of scoring procedures for several subtests to improve scoring accuracy.

In the new WMS-R, 12 subtests are grouped under five separate memory scores: Subtest I, Verbal Memory (includes subtests Logical Memory I and Verbal Paired Associates I); Subtest II, Visual Memory (Figural Memory, Visual Paired Associates I, Visual Reproduction I); Subtest III, General Memory (Verbal Memory plus Visual Memory); Subtest IV, Attention/Concentration (Digit Span, Visual Memory Span); and Subtest V, Delayed Recall (Logical Memory II, Verbal Paired Associates II, Visual Paired Associates II, and Visual Reproduction II). A preliminary subtest, Information and Orientation questions, is scored independently but does not contribute to any of the Memory Indexes above.

The complete WMS-R test kit contains a test manual (a very extensive 150-page manual, including a general introduction to the test, directions for administration and scoring, discussion of reliability and validity, factor analyses, and clinical studies with the new WMS-R), record forms, copying sheets for Visual Reproduction I and II (included in the record form), Figural Memory and Visual Paired Associates stimulus booklets, Visual Paired Associates, Folders A and B, four Visual Reproduction cards, and two Visual Memory span cards. The examiner will also need a stopwatch and two black lead pencils with erasers for each WMS-R administration.

Administration time for the total test (including all the tests listed above) is estimated at 45 minutes to 1 hour. If time is limited, a short form of the test can be administered by omitting the tests in Subtest V, Delayed Recall, which is estimated to be approximately 30 minutes.

Although David Wechsler died in 1981, the publishers wisely decided to continue to use his name as author of the revised scale. Dr. Aurelio Prifitera was the project director for the WMS revision.

Practical Applications/Uses

The WMS-R is designed to investigate memory or memory loss in populations between the ages of 16 to 69. The new expanded format allows more equal testing of visual and verbal memory. The need for such an instrument has long been desired, and it is surprising that so few tests have been developed specifically for this purpose, given the clinician's common referral question: What is the status of this patient's memory? In a comprehensive review of the topic of memory loss in psychopathology, Russell (1981) states "the area of clinical memory testing is still woefully underdeveloped" (p. 287). However, two current neuropsychological batteries include sampling of memory, both short term and long term. These are the Halstead-Reitan Neuropsychological Test Battery (Boll, 1981) and Luria's Neuropsychological Tests (Golden, 1981).

The WMS-R manual (Wechsler, 1987) provides specific directions for administration of the subtests and scoring directions with examples of more difficult scoring decisions for Logical Memory and Visual Reproduction (see Wechsler, 1987, Appendices A and B). Some subtests have specific time limits, and these should be strictly adhered to.

Besides the WMS-R kit, as noted the examiner needs a record form, two black lead pencils with erasers, and a stopwatch. Tests are to be given in the order recommended in the manual, beginning with Information and Orientation questions (e.g., "When were you born?" and "What month is it now?"). Exact verbal directions should be utilized as spelled out in the manual. Verbal and visual subtests are alternated, beginning with Mental Control (counting backwards from 20 to 1, repeating the alphabet, counting by 3's), followed by Figural Memory, a new test requiring the subject to recall three designs just previously presented implanted in a group of nine designs. Logical Memory I involves repeating details of a short paragraph just previously read by the examiner. Story A is almost identical to that in the WMS; Story B is new and has been substituted because it is thought to be more current than the original. Visual Paired Associates I, a new test, requires the subject to indicate the correct color associated with each of six abstract figures. Verbal Paired Associates I is the same test as in the WMS, presenting eight word pairs (e.g., Metal-Iron, School-Grocery) and requires the subject to respond with the second word when the examiner names the first word of each pair. Visual Reproduction I is the same test as in the WMS, but with a fourth more complex drawing added to be drawn by the subject. Digit Span is the traditional WAIS-R subtest. Visual Memory Span requires the subject to tap small squares in the same sequence as the examiner demonstrates, increasing in difficulty from two to seven taps.

If the complete WMS-R is administered, the Delayed Recall trials are presented approximately 30 minutes after the original administration. These repeated tests are labeled Logical Memory II, Visual Paired Associates II, Verbal Paired Associates II, and Visual Reproduction II. After the raw scores have been tabulated on the front page of the Record Form, the examiner must convert these sums into Indexes by use of Appendix C in the manual. Each index (Verbal Memory, Visual Memory, General Memory, Attention/Concentration, and Delayed Recall) has a mean of 100 and a standard deviation of 15. Although not specifically stated, the index is reminiscent of the previous Memory Quotient of the WMS, and is easily comparable to the WAIS-R IQ, because on that instrument each age group also has a mean of 100 and a standard deviation of 15 (index values range from 50 to 140; WAIS-R IQ scores range from 45 to 150). No separate male or female norms are needed.

And what individuals with psychopathology could be evaluated with WMS-R? Anyone age 16 to 75 with a diagnosis of functional psychosis, depression, or any of a multitude of organically based conditions. Small samples from 14 clinically diagnosed groups were administered the WMS-R and their memory scores were compared with the normative sample. Tests of significance are shown in Table 1. In all groups, significant differences were obtained despite the small sample sizes.

Table 1

**Significance of Differences in Index Scores of Clinical Groups
from the Normative Sample (N = 333)**

Diagnosis	N	p
Depression	30	**
Schizophrenia	14	**
Post-traumatic Stress	19	**
Alcoholism	62	**
Alzheimer's Disease	24	**
Dementia	18	**
Huntington's Disease	13	**
Closed Head Injury	20	**
Stroke	15	*
Brain Cancer	13	*
Seizure Disorder	58	**
Multiple Sclerosis	29	*
Worksite Neurotoxins	18	**

*Significant beyond .01
**Significant beyond .001

Technical Aspects

Like other test productions of The Psychological Corporation (e.g., WAIS-R, WISC-R), the standardization, reliability, and validity studies of the WMS-R are impressive. The standardization sample for the WMS-R was a stratified sample designed to represent the normal population of the United States between the ages of 16 years, 0 months and 74 years, 11 months. Using data from the 1980 U.S. Census, desired proportions of individuals in various demographic categories were computed. Approximately 50 cases in each of six age groups (16–17, 20–24, 35–44, 55–64, 65–69, and 70–74) were selected with approximately equal numbers of males and females (although females begin to outnumber males after age 50 with a steadily increasing ratio of women to men up to age 74 and beyond). Whites and non-whites were included in the same proportions as in the 1980 U.S. Census, and geographic regions (i.e., Northeast, North Central, South, and West) were represented as in the census data.

Complete WAIS-R tests were administered to age groups 35–44 and 65–69, and a four-subtest short form of the WAIS-R to all members of the other age groups. For the total sample, the mean IQ was 103.9 with a standard deviation of 14.2. Each case in the standardized sample was prespecified according to age, sex, race, and geographic region. Only nonimpaired individuals were included in the sample. Excessive use of alcohol or a neurological or psychiatric disorder disqualified subjects from the sample. To partially indicate the fit of the sample to U.S. population figures, in the 20- to 24-year age bracket the sample included 80% white, 20% non-white (U.S. census: 81.1% white, 18.9% non-white). For the 65- to 69-year age bracket, the sample included 90.9% white, 9.1% non-white (U.S. Census: 89% white, 11% non-white).

Reliability was established by test-retest coefficients of correlation for five of the subtests and internal consistency estimates for the remaining seven subtests. The average reliability coefficients across age groups for subtests ranged from .41 to .90 with a median value of .74. (Several subtests have restricted score ranges, which has the effect of lowering reliability coefficients for these subtests.) The overall average coefficients for subtests across all age groups ($N = 306$) range from .70 for Visual Memory to .90 for Attention/Concentration. Interscorer reliability coefficients for Logical Memory and Visual Reproduction I were .99 and .97, respectively. In the oldest age group tested (age 70–74, $N = 50$), stability coefficients were the highest, ranging from .80 to .93. In fact, with increasing age, reliabilities continue to rise on all composite indexes. This is indeed fortunate that in the older, more possibly memory-impaired groups, reliability is high.

Factor analysis of the WMS-R was performed on the entire standardization sample using age corrected raw scores on eight subtests. The orthogonally rotated factor matrix yielded a two-factor solution. Factor I (with high loadings on Logical Memory I, Verbal Paired Associates I, Visual Paired Associates I, Visual Reproduction I, and Figural Memory) appears to be a general memory and learning factor. This corresponds exactly with the General Memory Index. Factor II (with high loadings on Mental Control, Digit Span, and Visual Memory Span) resembles an attention-concentration factor, and corresponds exactly with the Attention/Concentration Index. These factors are similar to those found in earlier factor analyses of the WMS.

Critique

Reviews of the original WMS were positive from the beginning. Kogan (1949), in Buros's *Third Mental Measurements Yearbook*, declared "This simple, concise measure of memory function has already proved to be a valuable addition to the available clinical techniques. Administration time is brief, directions are clear, and scoring criteria are objective" (p. 302). No mention was made of the rather limited standardization (200 normal adults, ages 25–50). Newman (1953), in his WMS review in the *Fourth Mental Measurements Yearbook*, criticized the inadequate standardization, as well as lack of reliability data. He noted that there were no studies then extant to justify the conclusion that the test could detect specific memory defects in individuals with specific organic brain injuries. Present studies of specific pathological groups, noted in the Practical Applications/ Uses section of this reveiw, scotch his criticism, as highly significant differences occur in all functional and organically impaired groups studied.

It is notable that the focus of interpretation of the WMS has changed significantly over time, from the earliest 1949 review to the present. The earlier reviews stressed the importance of correlating the WMS with Wechsler's Deterioration Index on the WAIS; the present view emphasizes the WMS role in neuropsychological assessment. The Deterioration Index is no longer considered a viable construct. The new concept of Memory "Index," with its mean, range, and standard deviation comparable to WAIS-R IQ scores, provides a possible comparison of any differences between intellectual functioning in general and specific memory intactness or loss.

In summary, The Psychological Corporation has produced a revised test of immediate and short-term memory that has noted reliability and adequate validity, to say nothing of the excellent nationwide standardization that is typical of the high scientific quality of all Wechsler intelligence scales. The record form is compact, the scoring system is relatively simple, and the manual comprehensive and informative. One caveat: the 1945 WMS cost $1.50; the 1988 WMS-R kit costs $189.00 at the time of this writing. Not all memory functions are tapped. Long-term memory is not included, but some indication of long-term memory is elicited from the Information subtest of WAIS-R. Olfactory memory, tactile memory, and memory for previously learned skills (e.g., bicycling, typing) are omitted. However, for the major domains of verbal and visual memory, the WMS-R will be a hard test to beat.

References

This list includes text citations and suggested additional reading.

Boll, T.J. (1981). The Halstead-Reitan Neuropsychological Battery. In S.B. Filskov & T.J. Boll (Eds.), *Handbook of clinical neuropsychology* (pp. 577–607). New York: Wiley-Interscience.

Golden, C.J. (1981). A standardized version of Luria's Neuropsychological Tests: A quantitative and qualitative approach to the neuropsychological evaluation. In S.B. Filskov & T.J. Boll (Eds.), *Handbook of clinical neuropsychology* (pp. 608–642). New York: Wiley-Interscience.

Kogan, K.L. (1949). A review of the Wechsler Memory Scale. In O.K. Buros (Ed.), *The third mental measurements yearbook* (pp. 302–303). Highland Park, NJ: Gryphon Press.

Mensch, I.N. (1953). A review of the Wechsler Memory Scale. In O.K. Buros (Ed.), *The fourth mental measurements yearbook* (p. 364). Highland Park, NJ: Gryphon Press.

Newman, J. (1953). A review of the Wechsler Memory Scale. In O.K. Buros (Ed.), *The fourth mental measurements yearbook* (pp. 364–365). Highland Park, NJ: Gryphon Press.

Russell, E.W. (1981). The pathology and clinical examination of memory. In S.B. Filskov & T.J. Boll (Eds.), *Handbook of clinical neuropsychology* (pp. 287–319). New York: Wiley-Interscience.

Wechsler, D. (1945) A standardized memory scale for clinical use. *Journal of Psychology, 19*, 87–95.

Wechsler, D. (1987) *A manual for the Wechsler Memory Scale-Revised*. San Antonio: The Psychological Corporation.

Leonard J. West, Ph.D.
Professor of Education, Baruch College, The City University of New York, New York, New York.

WORD PROCESSING TEST

The Psychological Corporation. San Antonio, Texas: The Psychological Corporation.

Introduction

The Word Processing Test (WPT) is designed to measure competence at "inputting and editing . . . manuscript and numerical copy . . . in text and tabular form" (The Psychological Corporation, 1985, p. 2). The test can be used only with Wang OIS and VS systems, the Wang PC, and "selected" IBM systems (which IBM systems are not specified). Of two alternate forms of the test, Form A is available only to business and industrial personnel departments for testing job applicants and employees; Form B, to schools, vocational training programs, and employment agencies (but may also be purchased by industrial users). At the time of preparation of the test manual (March, 1985), norms and intercorrelations among the subtests of the WPT were available only for Form A, whereas reliability data are supplied for the alternate forms. At the time this review was prepared (mid-1987), normative data for Form B were not yet available.

The relative recency of the development of word processing technology accounts for the few published tests of word processing proficiency and for the absence to date of individuals with an established association with testing in that field, as contrasted, for example, with the state of affairs for clerical tests in general. In any event, the WPT materials do not provide the names of any individuals as authors or test developers.

Although, word processors have been increasingly replacing ordinary typewriters, the categories of inputting and editing in the WPT reflect what ordinary typewriters and word processors do and do not have in common. Both devices share a requirement for keyboarding or stroking skills, which the WPT designates as "inputting." Stroking skills are universally tested in 5-minute straight copy timings and are scored for speed, accuracy, or for a composite of those two criteria. The distinguishing feature of word processors is automatization of the editing and storing of text. Significant modifications of the text do not require—as contrasted with typewriters—complete retyping of a page or document. Accordingly, the WPT's editing component requires the examinee to use the device to execute editorial changes in the test materials.

The test packages consist of a manual, a Personal Scoring Record, and, for each of the two forms, a test booklet, scoring key, and edit disk. In both forms, testing begins with an untimed, unscored practice exercise, usually requiring about 5 minutes. That exercise is intended as warm-up and for familiarizing the examinee with the machine used for testing. Formal testing, consisting of 25 minutes of actual typing, follows and begins with inputting. In all tasks, 12-pitch type and an

86-character line are to be used, and the examinee is to follow as much as possible the formatting of the material in the test booklet.

Because, on keyboard devices, tasks with the same general label can vary greatly in internal features, the WPT tasks are described here in detail.

Inputting. Inputting consists of two 5-minute timed tasks (manuscript and table) that require exact, word-for-word, line-for-line copying of materials clearly printed in a font similar to that of a typewriter. In Form A, the manuscript consists of a two-page memorandum of 486 "standard" (i.e., 5-stroke) words; in Form B, of a two-page, 450-word business letter. The memorandum includes 10 instances of numbers and symbols, and the business letter, of none except in the inside address. Numbers and symbols excluded, the materials in both forms approximate the average difficulty level of the vocabulary of written business communications, as measured in recent studies reviewed by West (1983, pp. 369–372).

In both forms, the tables for inputting are cast in memorandum form, consisting of three pages of 4-digit random numbers that begin following a 1-sentence introduction on the first page. Each page contains 5 columns (without column headings) and 13 rows of numbers (260 digits per page). The memo labels consist of *To/From* lines (but no *Subject* line) and are to be repeated on each page, accompanied by a page number on pages 2 and 3. Examinees are to set tab positions for even spacing on the page before the timing begins.

For both the manuscript and table inputting, examinees who complete the work before time is up are to input the materials a second time. The volume of materials supplied is such that, according to the norms tables, it is likely that only a fraction of 1% of the most skilled of three norms groups can begin either of the tasks a second time.

Editing. Editing consists of two time-limit tasks: 10 minutes for a manuscript and 5 minutes for a table. The completion times of those who finish beforehand are to be recorded by the examiner in the Personal Scoring Records. As inferred from the manual's scoring table, completion times of early finishers are to be recorded to the nearest quarter-minute. The original documents are printed in a font similar to that of a typewriter, and the editorial corrections to be made are handwritten and consist of revisions, insertions, deletions, and relocations of portions of the text. The examiner is responsible for loading the Edit Test Disk into the system, and the manual contains directions for doing so. Examinees are to "supercopy" disk contents into their own document, and the examiner is to assist examinees to do so. The unedited document appears in the "workspace" (i.e., on the screen or CRT), and examinees are to make the corrections indicated in the test booklet on their copies, not to the original on the system.

In Form A, the manuscript consists of a report (including a 3-row, 3-column table with column headings) that, if completed within the 10 minutes, extends to about $2^{1}/_4$ pages of very widely spaced text of approximately 350 words. In Form B, the manuscript consists of a memorandum report (including a table like that of Form A) which, if completed, extends to three pages of very widely spaced text of nearly 700 words. The 38 corrections to be made in each test form are worth 72 points.

Both forms require the editing of a 2-page table that includes a table title and column headings. Examinees are to follow the formatting of the test materials and, before the 5-minute timing begins, are to set tabs for even spacing across the page.

In Form A, the table consists of 6 columns and 28 rows; the table in Form B consists of 5 columns and 11 rows (each of which requires a 3- to 4-line address in one of its 5 columns). In both forms, the tables include both spelled-out words and arabic numerals and call for revisions, insertions, deletions, and relocations of portions of the text. The 15 corrections to be made in each form are worth 26 points.

Test Scoring. The two input tasks are scored for "net words per minute," with "net" defined as total words typed minus number of errors. The editing tasks are scored for "net score per minute" — a composite of work time (10 or fewer minutes for the manuscript, 5 or fewer minutes for the table) and the points earned for making correctly as many of the specified corrections as possible. For example, with 72 points as the maximum for manuscript corrections, the examinee who earns 62 points would have an overall "net" score of 6.2 in 10 minutes of work, but of 8.0 if the work had been completed in $7^{3/4}$ minutes. The meaning of "net" differs between the input and edit tasks. The scores for the latter tasks are *not* measures of stroking skills; the volume of keystroking in them is far below that of the input tasks. Also, the input tasks' "net" is the typist's "correct" words per minute. The typist's traditional "net" words per minute deducts 10 words (not 1 word) for each error from total words typed before dividing by time in minutes. In typewriting classrooms, however, there has been a strong move toward separate scoring of speed and accuracy and the avoidance of composite scores.

Practical Applications/Uses

As previously stated, the Word Processing Test may be used only with Wang and selected IBM systems, and the two forms of the test are aimed at different examinees and examiners. Form A is intended for job applicants and employees tested by employers; Form B, primarily for students tested in their classrooms by their teachers and for job seekers tested by employment agencies.

The complete test (an unscored, 5-minute warm-up, plus 25 minutes of formal testing, made up of two inputting and two editing tasks) requires about 40 minutes to administer. The WPT manual provides explicit requirements and procedures for test administration and scoring. Together with the test booklets, scoring keys, and the form on which each examinee enters background information (and on which the examiner records scores), everything needed to administer and score the test is supplied. To facilitate scoring, the manual includes a table that displays the net score for each possible combination of work time and points earned on the edit tasks. The manual's appendices contain the rules for scoring typographical errors and the procedures for applying point scoring to the edit tasks. For the input tasks, overlays of heavyweight, transparent plastic make speed scoring and error identification convenient, fast, and more reliable than might otherwise be the case. Edit scoring keys vividly mark and number the corrections serially, corresponding to their numbering in the record form. As well, there are sample scored input and edit protocols that model the scoring procedures. The various tactics for maximizing the reliability of scoring are praiseworthy indeed. Likewise, the manual's instructions to examinees, which are to be read verbatim to them, are clear and with one exception complete, maximizing the chances of uniform administration conditions among examiners.

Among several minor reservations of this reviewer, one concerns the omission in the instructions to examinees that they are to correct their own errors in all tasks, which is self-evident for the edit tasks but not necessarily so for the input tasks. Correcting typographical errors is so simple and quick on word processors that it is routine for operators to make such corrections. Perhaps, therefore, WPT examinees do so without being so instructed. On the other hand, the instructions for the 5-minute input timings make apparent that those are tests intended as an analogue to straight copy testing among typists, in which error correction is forbidden. Conceivably, some WPT examinees might act accordingly. If so, outcomes are not consistently interpretable across all examinees. An explicit instruction to correct whatever errors were sensed during the timing would have been preferable. (Differences in interpreting measures of stroking skills among word processors versus typists are addressed in the Technical Aspects section of this review.)

A second minor matter concerns the handwritten editing of the editing tasks, primarily the manuscript (or text) task. The handwritten editing is big, bold, and sometimes redundant—no doubt to preclude any ambiguity about what corrections the examinee is to make. However, the appearance of the test materials lacks face validity. If, for example, an underlined side heading is inserted, would any editor arrow the insert and add in solid caps "insert heading and underline"?

Final minor reservations concern language usage and jargon in the WPT manual. The manual instructs the examiner to "retrieve the contents of the Edit Test Disk into [sic] the word processing system" (p. 6). Things are retrieved "from" rather than "into" something. The manual refers to the "workspace" (meaning the screen) and to making a "supercopy." Such Wang-specific terms, if they must be used, should be accompanied by equivalents more widely current across word processing systems. Another instance of awkward language occurs in a memo's introductory sentence that begins "Enclosed please find." For one thing, nothing had been lost. Additionally, the information contained in the memo is not "enclosed" (on separate sheets) but makes up the text of the memo, beginning immediately below the introductory sentence. The statement "Here is . . ." would be more accurate.

Technical Aspects

This section deals primarily with norms, reliability, and validity, and secondarily with omissions of ancillary information that could provide a more precise basis for interpreting the composite scoring of the editing tasks and the norms for those tasks.

Norms. As stated previously, normative data are confined to Form A of the Word Processing Test. For each of the two input tasks (text and table), separate norms are provided for each of three groups: 90 employed word processors (mean of 2.4 years of experience), 57 temporary word processors (mean of 1.4 years of part-time experience), and 85 business school students. For each of the two editing tasks, norms are reported for the same groups of full-time and part-time employees, but not for students. The full-time employees were from three companies; the part-time employees were registered with six different agencies; and the students were at four different institutions. Geographically, the East and Midwest were represented. No data on sex or ethnicity of examinees are supplied.

Reliability. Reliability coefficients, standard errors of measurement, means, and standard deviations are reported for 52 word processing temporaries tested on both forms (with Form A administered first). Alternate-form reliability coefficients of .92 (text input), .86 (table input), .91 (text edit), and .85 (table edit) were obtained. Practice effects from the administration of Form A first are evident in higher mean scores on Form B than on Form A. It would have been preferable to have counter balanced the order of administration of the two forms. Perhaps the two forms are equivalent in difficulty (at least among temporary employees), perhaps not.

Validity. The WPT manual (p. 16) maintains that the validity of the WPT "is inherent in its content," that its tasks are of the sort frequently assigned by employers, and that the "form and style of [its] materials are very similar to those often confronted by word processing employees." Text and numerical copy are certainly appropriate, and the function keys required for executing corrections in the edit tasks are "common to most types of word processing equipment" (p. 16). As well, their use is applied to a suitable variety of revisions, insertions, deletions, and relocations of portions of the contents.

This reviewer, however, strongly disagrees with the quoted contention about the form and style of its materials. The styling of the WPT's materials is, in a number of respects, so unlike realistic input and output materials that it seems likely to have puzzled examinees. That styling calls into question the validity of the test. Styling of the test materials seems to have been governed by ease of proofreading of outcomes and of scoring, rather than by realism. To date, word processors have a prior history as typists and have been taught in typewriting classes the conventions for formatting various tasks. Those formats for the most part also apply to word processing. Straight copy timings are double-spaced and use paragraph indention. But the WPT text input task blocks the paragraphs and uses quadruple spacing between them. Furthermore, cast in memo form, the paragraphs would be single-spaced as a usable job product. Regarding the table input-task, 4-digit random numbers are hardly realistic—money and percentage columns would be more to the point. Moreover, the columns are spread out too widely across the page. The formatting of the text edit task is equally unrealistic in several respects. A blank half-page should not separate the title of the report from the beginning of its text; a narrow 3-column table should not be spread across a width of 86-characters; report typing requires indention of the first line of each paragraph, not blocking. A 350-word report (Form A) requires two, not three, pages. In the table edit task the column headings, unwisely, are in solid rather than initial caps and, violating standards of layout among typists, are not centered in relation to the longest item in the rows below. Because the hardware accommodates an 86-character line, it is mandated for all tasks, although so long a line should rarely if ever to be used. The fastest way, however inelegant, prevails in the WPT test. The artificial, unrealistic, and inelegant formatting of the WPT tasks significantly reduces test validity.

Another unfortunate feature is the paging of the test booklets, which are spiral-bound at the top of the page (like typewriting textbooks, with which examinees are certainly familiar). The sequencing of the paging, however, is not standard. As one example that can stand for the entire booklet, the second page of a two-page task is upside down on the reverse side of page 1. Upon completing page 1, the examinee must flip the page over the spiral binding at the top and then rotate the entire test booklet 180°. To proceed to the next task, another 180° rotation is required. And for the next task, which takes several pages, one does not flip the page after completing page 1 but rotates the booklet 180°. The examinee must go back and forth between two different manipulations of the booklet from task to task and within tasks of more than two pages. Such manipulations are not only awkward and time-consuming; they also introduce an irrelevant factor in what should be an unconfounded measure of proficiency. One can readily imagine some examinees having to turn the pages and the booklet itself several times until the correct next page is found and the booklet is laid down on the desk. If it is in fact desirable for test booklets to be top-bound then the sequencing of pages as in typewriting textbooks would preclude irritation among examinees and reduce irrelevant variance in test scores.

On the plus side, intercorrelations among the subtests are of moderate size, supporting the inclusion of all of them. Input/input and edit/edit correlations (.56 and .59) are, understandably, higher than input/edit correlations (.23, .33, .37, .38)—with the latter correlations suggesting a modest role for stroking speed and accuracy in executing on-the-job tasks.

Omissions. The deficiencies noted here are ones of omission, the first of which concerns interpretation of scores on the 5-minute manuscript input timing (assuming correction by examinees of errors sensed during the timing). As contrasted with the prohibition against error correction in straight copy testing among typists, under error-correction in the WPT the count to be subtracted from total words is not of the number of misstrokes but of those misstrokes that were not sensed and corrected during the timing. On word processors, corrected errors leave no trace; error counts among typists and word processors do not mean the same thing. Mainly, however, the dependable kinesthetic feedback on which sensing of misstrokes rests is nominal among novices, increases gradually until word-per-minute (wpm) speeds in the 30s are reached, and levels off thereafter. Typists at gross speeds of 30–90 wpm sense their misstrokes kinesthetically 40% to 45% of the time (West, 1967; 1983, Chapter 4). That point is made because, according to the norms table for text input in the WPT manual, about 35% of one of the norms groups (students) and about 15% of the temporary part-time employees were at novice levels of speed. For them, the count of uncorrected errors in the text input task is partly a reflection of their stroking speed; novices do not sense as large a proportion of their errors as do faster typists.

Another pertinent phenomenon that affects interpretation of WPT text input scores is the essentially zero correlation between stroking speed and the number of errors in straight copy testing of typists across the range of skill from novice through through expert (5–100+ wpm), as revealed by a review of studies done over half a century (West, 1983, pp. 125–126). Would the same absence of relationship also be found between speed and number of uncorrected errors in straight copy testing of word processors? The outcome might have implications for scoring stroking skills among word processors but, regrettably, the WPT manual does not supply the desired information.

The interpretation of norms for the edit tasks would be much easier if information were provided on the *number* of examinees who in fact completed each of those tasks, the completion time of the fastest such examinee, and the number of persons who correctly made, all of the specified changes. As well, a tally of the percentage of persons who reached the point of, and then correctly made all of the 38 and 26 corrections specified in the test booklet would be informative and give the prospective test user a better sense of what the edit scores mean. Without the foregoing information, interpretation of edit scores is vague; almost any "net score per minute" can be derived from many different combinations of work time, corrections attempted, and corrections successfully made.

The general point addressed here is that for performance tests as complex as the WPT and its use of composite scores, the manual's routine supplying of nothing but norms, reliability, and validity data is not sufficiently helpful in interpreting outcomes.

Critique

The Word Processing Test is of practicable length (about 40 minutes) and is highly reliable for a test of its kind. Its measures of stroking skills and of the editing of text that primarily distinguishes word processing from typewriting are pertinent. In this reviewer's judgment, however, the formatting of materials and of models for scoring are substantially artificial and unrealistic, reducing validity. As well, the paging of the text booklets is nonstandard, irritating to the examinee, and a potential source of confusion and waste of time.

The accompaniments to the test materials, however, are admirable. The manual is clearly written, virtually guaranteeing uniformity in test administration among examiners. Similarly, the materials for proofreading and scoring the products of the examinees' work virtually guarantee highly reliable scoring.

Were the formatting of the test materials to be revised in realistic directions and the paging of the test booklet to be more convenient, the WPT would be judged a good test for its purposes.

References

The Psychological Corporation. (1985). *Word Processing Test manual.* San Antonio: Author.

West, L.J. (1967). Vision and kinesthesis in the acquisition of typewriting skill. *Journal of Applied Psychology, 51,* 161–166.

West, L.J. (1983). *Acquisition of typewriting skills: Methods and research in teaching typewriting and word processing* (2nd ed.). Mission Hills, CA: Glencoe/Bobbs-Merrill.

Patrick Groff, Ed. D.
Professor of Education, San Diego State University, San Diego, California.

WORD RECOGNITION TEST

Clifford Carver. London, England: Hodder and Stoughton Educational.

Introduction

The Word Recognition Test (WRT) is designed to assess young children's overall abilities in word recognition and to analyze the errors these children make when attempting to recognize words. The WRT is made up of 50 items, printed 10 per page in an eight-page test booklet. Each item consists of a horizontal row of five or six printed words or pseudowords (e.g., *pos*). Each of the 50 items contains at least one true word. The true words are common ones with the exception of *inkpot*, a word few modern children would recognize. Twenty of the 50 items contain six words or pseudowords; the remaining 30 items contain five each. Twenty of the total of 270 words or pseudowords in the WRT are disyllabic; the remaining 250 are monosyllabic. Five items contain no pseudowords; 104 of the 270 words in the WRT are pseudowords.

Published in 1970, the WRT apparently was created solely by Clifford Carver, a former associate professor of educational psychology at the University of Manitoba, Canada. The 1987 printing of the WRT is said by its publisher to be its twenty-fifth, which suggests that the test has some degree of popularity among test users. However, there is no information offered that the test has been revised since 1970.

Construction of the WRT began with the selection of 300 experimental test items designed to measure the knowledge of letters and written words and the ability to hear and analyze speech sounds in children aged 4 years, 0 months through 8 years, 6 months. The 300-item battery was reduced to its final 50 items after tests were made concerning the ability of the original 300 items to discriminate between children whose total score on the test was high or low and from intercorrelations obtained on their validity and reliability. The test author provides a chart of word recognition age norms for the final version of the test based on the scores children make on it. For example, a child's score of 29–30 (out of 50) indicates that the child's word recognition age is 6 years, 0 months. The range of scores possible, on the test are described as being in 10 "general stages of word recognition" (Carver, 1970, p. 16). The word recognition behavior of children at each of these stages is described. For instance, children who score 29–30 are in stage six. In this stage, "practically all [speech] sounds [are] heard and visually identified . . . ." Children at this stage are "more or less able to identify short vowel sounds and associate the visual letters" (Carver, 1970, p. 17).

Practical Applications/Uses

The *Manual of Instructions* provided for the administrators of the WRT gives very specific directions as to what these administrators should say and do. Several wise precautions about test administration are included here The front page of the test booklet for the WRT provides a trial item that the administrator of the test is instructed to use to introduce the format of the test to examinees. The administration of each item then is the same. The administrator reads aloud a key word (e.g., *toy*) and then reads a sentence or a sentence fragment in which the key word appears. Children taking the test attempt to find and underline this key word from a given array of words in their test booklet (e.g., *tay, try, toy, tuy, boy*). The child is credited with 1 point for each word correctly underlined. Children are encouraged to guess the answer of any item to which they cannot readily respond. The WRT takes about 15 to 30 minutes to administer. As a "relaxing reward" (Carver, 1970, p. 2) to children for completing the test, space is allowed in the test booklet for children to draw a man. This drawing supposedly "gives a rough approximation of the child's motor or visuo/motor ability" (Carver, 1970, p. 2).

As noted, the scores from the WRT are said to measure the child's overall abilities to recognize words. The WRT recommends that children who are 2 years behind their chronological age norms in the test be referred to remedial reading classes. The author of the WRT also claims that the test is designed so that errors reveal the interaction of a child's aural and visual abilities, the ability to organize a series of visual symbols, the ability to analyze speech sounds, and levels of comprehension of spoken language. Teachers administering the WRT are encouraged to examine the errors children make to determine if these errors involve initial phoneme-letter correspondences; the distortion of letters (e.g., *yam* for *jam*); mid-vowel correspondences (e.g., *mit* for *met*); serial distortions (e.g., *aws* or *was*); reversals (e.g., *giw* for *wig*); word endings (e.g., *cak* for *cake*) consonant clusters (e.g., *tap* for *trap*); *r*-controlled spellings (e.g., *port* for *part*); and predictably versus unpredictably spelled words (e.g., *red, who*). The author of the WRT claims such examinations will give the teacher insights into the child's aural and visual abilities, and into his or her abilities to analyze and comprehend speech sounds and spoken language. The author offers no suggestions offers as to what the teacher should do with such insights, however. No recommendations are made as to how to remedy the error made on the WRT.

There does not appear to be any special versions of the WRT written for children other than normal-learning, standard-English speaking children. The test is simple to administer and does not require any unique training on the part of its administrator. Ordinary classroom teachers could easily follow the directions given in its *Manual of Instructions*. The WRT is designed for group testing in regular classrooms. The test is hand scored, an uncomplicated process. However, it does not appear that the test is amenable to machine or computer scoring. Each child is given 1 point for each correct response in its 50 items. The test results are readily interpreted. As noted, its author provides sets of word recognition norms and general stages of word recognition for this purpose.

Taken at the values and functions for the WRT claimed by its author, the test would be useful for anyone, (e.g., parent, teacher, clinician, private remedial reading instructor, etc.), who needs to determine if a given child aged 4 to 8½ years recognizes written words at, below, or above his or her chronological age group. The child's general stage of word recognition is also provided by the WRT. The scores made on the WRT can be interpreted as a child's ability to recognize letters, to apply phonics information known, and to comprehend spoken language in general.

Technical Aspects

The author of the WRT claims that during and after construction of the test he carried out "intensive statistical studies" (Carver, 1970, p. 19) on the reliability and validity of the test and on ways to establish its age-level norms. Evidence is presented to confirm this assertion. High coefficients of correlation were obtained by the test author between WRT scores and scores on the Schonell Graded Word Reading Test ($r = .90$) and the Burt Word Reading Test ($r = .82$). The reliability of the WRT, is indicated by similar high r's obtained between its original and final versions. A split-half (odd-even items) r of .95 was obtained. As for the establishment of chronological age norms for the WRT the test author reports that there is "reasonably steady progression" of scores for children taking the test from ages 4 through 9 (Carver, 1970, p. 20). Although the author concedes that "the use of an exact age norm is very suspect at the early stages of word recognition" (Carver, 1970, p. 21), the steady linear growth of chronological age group scoring on the WRT gives support to the author's contention that the word recognition age norms established for the WRT are reasonably accurate ones. To support this assumption, Carver reports that his administration of the final version of the WRT to "fairly representative children" (Carver, 1970, p. 7) yielded average age scores that were very close to the WRT norms. These norms of the WRT range from a 10–14 (out of 50) score, which is the word recognition age norm for 4 years, 0 months, to a 49–50 score, which is the norm for 8 years, 6 months and beyond.

Carver gives a description of his attempts to analyze the relative difficulty of the separate items of the WRT. The degree to which an item differentiates more-able word-recognizers from the less-able was calculated. The items finally accepted for inclusion in the WRT had discrimination values that ranged from .60 to .94. Items that discriminated between able and less able children below the .60 level apparently were eliminated and not included in the final version of the test. The scores on this final version did not fall into a normal, bell-shaped curve of distribution, and it is noticeable. Instead, Carver notes, the items in the WRT were selected to reflect the word recognition ability of children at chronological age 6 to 6½ years. This decision was made because the test author felt that accurate information about word recognition is most needed at this age level.

Critique

The WRT appears to be an easily administered, quick test of young children's abilities to listen to spoken words and identify these in printed form. If such information is needed by schools or other the WRT agencies for that purpose, the WRT can be suggested. It is immediately apparent, however, that the WRT is an indirect examination of word recognition. Clearly, the reading behavior that it tests is not that normally practiced by young children. Beyond their reading of labels and signs, it is rare for young children to attempt to recognize all words as separate items. The evidence (Groff & Seymour, 1987) suggests that young children rely heavily on context as a cue for word recognition. It is only after they gain some degree of maturity in the application of phonics information do they decrease their dependence on context cues for this purpose. The format of WRT thus seems more applicable to the testing of older children's word recognition practices than it does young children's.

The criticism aside that the WRT is an expedient means of testing word recognition, and thus is not the most desirable mode of use for this objective the WRT appears to be as well thought through and carefully constructed as any of it competitors. Its construction, in fact, seems to utilize considerably more sophisticated techniques than do some other tests of its kind (Groff, 1987b). The WRT is commendable, as well, for its modesty in what it purports it actually can measure about word recognition. This is a characteristic not always seen in word recognition tests.

The least convincing part of the WRT is its claim concerning the errors children make on specific items that the test represents. It is doubtful, then, that "a very comprehensive set of inferences can often be made" (Carver, 1970, p. 15) from the manner in which the author of the WRT recommends that these inferences be arrived at. For example, all the words or pseudowords in some items begin with the same letters (e.g., *t, j, c, w, k,* and *b*) or end with the same letters (e.g., *y, g, t, ss, p, g, ce,* and *sh*). It is hypothesized that because these words all begin or end with the same letters, these letters are therefore eliminated as critical cues in children's recognition of the key word in these items. Why hypothesize about this matter? The WRT could have been constructed so as to determine children's letter recognition abilities in a more direct and reliable manner through the use of a simple letter recognition section of the test. Then, if children demonstrated they could not recognize *t,* for example, there would be dependable evidence that *t,* in fact, was for them a critical word recognition cue.

Objections can also be made to Carver's view that children's aural abilities are involved essentially in their acquisition of letter knowledge. It seems demonstrably wrong, however, for the test author to argue that with children both "visual and aural organization" is reflected as "letter knowledge" (Carver, 1970, p. 13). Children can distinguish (visualize) letters and even name letters before they have attained any phonics (aural) information or have learned how to apply it. One never knows for sure, then, whether an error in the WRT is due to lack of letter knowledge or to a lack of phonics information. The explanation the author gives concerning how to analyze an error in the WRT, (i.e., why a child who has heard *wing* would underline *weng, wung, wig,* or *wag*) thus is unconvincing. His belief that an erroneously chosen word will tell "whether the confusion is likely to be aural or visual" (Carver, 1970, p. 15) is not persuasive. The child who wrongly underlines *weng* in response to hearing *wing* may exhibit *both* aural and visual misperception, not one or the other.

Certain other technical questions one can raise about the WRT do not appear to be answered satisfactorily by its author. For example, the 50 items in the test are said to be arranged generally in an increasing order of difficulty. There is no way of knowing if this is so. For that matter, it is startling to find *ashes* the fifth most difficult word and *splashes* the forty-eighth most difficult. Why were the items in the WRT not arranged in their precise order of difficulty? Such an ordering would have helped to reveal answers to some critical word recognition questions, such as what phoneme-letter correspondences are more difficult for children to decode than are others? How much less difficult are predictably spelled words than unpredictably spelled ones? What is the relationship of the frequency of occurrence of written words and children's abilities to recognize them? Why were the items in the WRT at least not arranged to move from what are known to be the least difficult phoneme-letter correspondences for children to decode (i.e., those at the beginnings of words) on to those that are increasing more difficult (i.e., at the ends and middles of words)?

Other constructions of the WRT remain open to question. Why in different items did the author use different numbers of pseudowords and different numbers of total words (done randomly throughout the test)? Posing items with six rather than five choices adds a difficulty to the six-choice item that confuses what an error with the item implies. It obviously is more difficult, all other things being equal, for children to attain a correct score on a six-choice item than on one with five choices. Why are 7% of the total words or pseudowords of the WRT ones of two syllables (again, presented randomly)? Disyllabic words are significantly more difficult for children to recognize than are monosyllabic ones (Groff & Seymour, 1987). In this regard, why are there five items in the WRT with no pseudowords? These are items also scattered through the test: items number 8, 18, 20, 33, and 35. It is unclear, as well, what the subjective evidence that can be gained from analyses of children's drawings of a man has to do with any problems they may have with recognizing words.

Finally, one can argue with the author of the WRT's assumption that information about word recognition ability is most needed for children in the 6 to 6½ year age group. It appears more reasonable to conclude that this would be true for 8-year-old children. At 8 years American children have had at least 2 years of training in phonics. It is crucial at this point in their schooling to determine if they have attained sufficient phonics knowledge to decode words automatically and if they are ready to enter the independent reading programs that are, at present, so highly recommended by organizations like the National Council of Teachers of English. Thus, a test that concentrates on the word analysis abilities of 8-year-old children would be of greater value to today's teachers than would the WRT, which reflects the abilities of children entering first grade.

This criticism insists, as well, that the WRT does not present enough detail of a systematic, diagnostic nature about phonics that is useful for deciding what to teach first-graders. A more direct and effective way to measure their letter knowledge would be to expose letters and determine if they can name them. Then, while teachers using the WRT get a general idea of the categories of phonics errors children make, they get little or no help from its manual of instructions as to the scope of phoneme-letter correspondences the WRT for example, examines. It is true, for example, that the WRT tests mid-word vowel phoneme-letter correspondences. Teachers need more specific information than this, however. They need to know exactly how many of the vowel correspondences are tested if they are to use test results for a *diagnosis* of what individuals need to learn. The WRT gives only part of this needed information.

References

This list includes text citations and suggested additional reading.

Aukerman, R.C. (1984). *Approaches to beginning reading.* New York: John Wiley & Sons.
Carver, C. (1970). *Manual of Instructions, Word Recognition Test.* London: Hodder and Stoughton Educational.
Groff, P. (1987a). *Preventing reading failure.* Portland, OR: National Book. (1987).
Groff, P. (1987b). Review of Diagnostic and Achievement Reading Tests. In D.J. Keyser & R.C. Sweetland (Eds.), *Test critiques: Volume VI* (pp. 143–148). Kansas City, MO: Test Corporation of America.
Groff, P., & Seymour, D.Z. (1987). *Word recognition.* Springfield, IL: C.C. Thomas.
Henderson, L. (1982). *Orthography and word recognition in reading.* New York: Academic Press.
Johnson, D.D., & Baumann, J.F. (1984). Word identification. In P.D. Pearson (Ed.), *Handbook of reading research* (pp. 583–608). New York: Longman.
Perfetti, C.A. (1985). *Reading ability.* New York: Oxford.

INDEX OF TEST TITLES

653

INDEX OF TEST PUBLISHERS

business phone—[III:466]

Callier Center for Communication Disorders, The University of Texas at Dallas, 1966 Inwood Road, Dallas, Texas 75235; (214)905-3000—[IV:119]

Carney, Weedman and Associates, 4776 El Cajon Boulevard, Suite 203, San Diego, California 92115; (619)582-2005—[VII:173]

Center for Child Development and Education, College of Education, University of Arkansas at Little Rock, 33rd and University, Little Rock, Arkansas 72204; (501)569-3422—[II:337]

Center for Cognitive Therapy, 133 South 36th Street, Room 602, Philadelphia, Pennsylvania 19104; (215)898-4100—[II:83]

Center for Educational Assessment, College of Education, University of Missouri, 403 South 6th Street, Columbia, Missouri 65211; (314)882-4694—[VII:342]

Center for Epidimiologic Studies. *See* Epidemiology and Psychology, Research Branch, Division of Clinical Research, NIMH.]

Center for Psychological Service, 1511 K Street N.W., Suite 430, Washington, D.C. 20005; (202)347-4069—[VI:512]

Center for the Study of Adolescence, 2959 South Cottage Grove Avenue, Chicago, Illinois 60616; (312)791-4199—[V:297; VI:387]

Chandler, Louis A., Ph.D., 5D Forbes Quadrangle, Pittsburgh, Pennsylvania 15260; (412)624-1244—[VI:570]

Chapman, Brook & Kent, 1215 De La Vina, Suite F, Santa Barbara, California 93101; (805) 962-0055—[IV:183]

Childcraft Education Corporation, 20 Kilmer Road, Edison, New Jersey 08818; (800) 631-5652—[IV:220]

Clinical Psychology Publishing Company, Inc., 4 Conant Square, Brandon, Vermont 05733; (802)247-6871—[III:461]

Clinical Psychometric Research, P.O. Box 619, Riderwood, Maryland 21139; (301)321-6165—[II:32; III:583]

Coddington, R. Dean, P.O. Box 307, St. Clairsville, Ohio 43950; (614)695-4805—[III:383, 388]

College Board Publications, The, 45 Columbus Avenue, New York, New York 10023; (212)713-8000—[VI:120, 609; VII:10]

College Hill Press, Inc., 4284 41st Street, San Diego, California 92105; (619)563-8899—[III:293]

Communication Research Associates, Inc., P.O. Box 11012, Salt Lake City, Utah 84147; (801)295-8046; III:669; VII:290]

Communication Skill Builders, Inc., 3830 East Bellevue, P.O. Box 42050, Tucson, Arizona 85733; (602)323-7500—[II:191, 562; V:118; VII:202]

Consulting Psychologists Press, Inc., 577 College Avenue, P.O. Box 60070, Palo Alto, California 94306; (415)857-1444—[I:34, 41, 146, 226, 259, 284, 380, 482, 623, 626, 663, 673; II:23, 56, 113, 263, 293, 509, 594, 697, 729; III:35, 51, 125, 133, 349, 392, 419; IV:42, 58, 132, 162, 570; V:141, 189, 226, 303, 556; VI:29, 87, 97; VII:20, 55, 59, 66, 87, 446]

C.P.S., Inc., P.O. Box 83, Larchmont, New York 10538; no business phone—[I:185; III:604]

Creative Learning Press, Inc., P.O. Box 320, Mansfield Center, Connecticut 06250; (203) 423-8120—[II:402; VII:110]

Croft, Inc., 2936 Remington Avenue, Baltimore, Maryland 21211-2891; (301)235-1700—[III:198]

CTB/McGraw-Hill, Publishers Test Service, Del Monte Research Park, 2500 Garden Road, Monterey, California 93940; (800)538-9547, in California (800)682-9222 or (408)649-8400—[I:3, 164, 578; II:517, 584, 780; III:186; IV:79, 238; V:406, 494; VI:149, 615; VII:102, 144, 189]

Curriculum Associates, Inc., 5 Esquire Road, North Billerica, Massachusetts 01862-2589;

(800)225-0248, in Massachusetts (617)667-8000—[III:79]

Dean, Raymond S., Ph.D., Ball State University, TC 521, Muncie, Indiana 47306; (317) 285-8500—[VI:297]

Delis, Dean, Ph.D., 3753 Canyon Way, Martinez, California 94553—[I:158]

Denver Developmental Materials, Inc., P.O. Box 6919, Denver, Colorado 80206-0919; (303)355-4729—[VII:234]

Devereux Foundation Press, The, 19 South Waterloo Road, P.O. Box 400, Devon, Pennsylvania 19333; (215)296-6908—[II:231; III:221; V:104]

Diagnostic Specialists, Inc., 1170 North 660 West, Orem, Utah 84057; (801)224-8492—[II:95]

DLM Teaching Resources, One DLM Park, Allen, Texas 75002; (800)527-4747, in Texas (800)442-4711—[II:72; III:68, 521, 551, 726; IV:376, 493, 683; V:310; VI:80, 586; VII:49]

DMI Associates, 615 Clark Avenue, Owosso, Michigan 48867; (517)723-3523—[VI:115]

D.O.K. Publishers, Inc., P.O. Box 605, East Aurora, New York 14052; (800)458-7900—[II:211; VI:303, 582]

Eagleville Hospital, 100 Eagleville Road, Eagleville, Pennsylvania 19408; (215)539-6000—[VII:561]

Economy Company, The, P.O. Box 25308, 1901 North Walnut Street, Oklahoma City, Oklahoma 73125; (405)528-8444—[IV:458]

Educational Activities, Inc., 1937 Grand Avenue, Baldwin, New York 11520; (800)645-2796, in Alaska, Hawaii, and New York (516)223-4666—[V:290; VI: 249]

Educational and Industrial Testing Service (EdITS), P.O. Box 7234, San Diego, California 92107; (619)222-1666—[I:279, 522, 555; II:3, 104, 258; III:3, 215; IV:199, 387, 449; V:76]

Educational Assessment Service, Inc., 6050 Apple Road, Watertown, Wisconsin 53094; (414)261-1118—[II:332, VI:415]

Educational Development Corporation, 10302 East 55th Place, Tulsa, Oklahoma 74146; (800)331-4418, in Oklahoma (800)722-9113—[III:367;VI:244]

Educational Testing Service (ETS), Rosedale Road, Princeton, New Jersey 08541; (609) 921-9000—[III:655; VI:404]

Educators Publishing Service, Inc., 75 Moulton Street, Cambridge, Massachusetts 02238-9101; (800)225-5750, in Massachusetts (800)792-5166—[IV:195, 611; VI:188, 392]

Elbern Publications, P.O. Box 09497, Columbus, Ohio 43209; (614)235-2643—[II:627]

El Paso Rehabilitation Center, 1101 E. Schuster Avenue, El Paso, Texas 79902; (915)566-2956—[III:171, 628]

Elsevier Science Publishing Company, Inc., 52 Vanderbilt Avenue, New York, New York 10017; (212)867-9040—[III:358]

Epidemiology and Psychology, Research Branch, Division of Clinical Research, NIMH, 5600 Fishers Lane, Rockville, Maryland 20857; (301)443-4513—[II:144]

Essay Press, P.O. Box 2323, La Jolla, California 92307;(619)565-6603—[II:646; IV:553]

Evaluation Research Associates. *See* FAAX Corporation.]

FAAX Corporation, P.O. Box 545, Teall Station, Skaneateles, New York 13152; (315)685-5718—[II:551; III:158]

Family Social Science, University of Minnesota, 290 McNeal Hall, St. Paul, Minnesota 55108; (612)625-5289—[VII:209, 417]

Family Stress, Coping and Health Project, School of Family Resources and Consumer Sciences, University of Wisconsin, 1300 Linden Drive, Madison, Wisconsin 53706; (608)262-5712—[VI:10, 16]

Foreworks, P.O. Box 9747, North Hollywood, California 91609; (818)982-0467—[III:647]

Foundation for Knowledge in Development, The—[I:443 *See* Psychological Corporation, The]

G.I.A. Publications, 7404 South Mason Avenue, Chicago, Illinois 60638; (312)496-3800—[V:216, 351]

Grune & Stratton, Inc.—[I:189; II:819; III:447, 526; IV:523; V:537; VI:52, 431 *See* Psychological Corporation, The]

Guidance Centre, Faculty of Education, University of Toronto, 10 Alcorn Avenue, Toronto, Ontario, Canada M4V 2Z8; (416)978-3211/3210—[III:271]

Halgren Tests, 873 Persimmon Avenue, Sunnyvale, California 94087; (408)738-1342—[I:549]

Hanson, Silver, Strong and Associates, Inc., P.O. Box 402, Moorestown, New Jersey 08057; (609)234-2610—[VII:589]

Harding Tests, P.O. Box 5271, Rockhampton Mail Centre, Q. 4702, Australia; no business phone—[IV:334]

Harvard University Press, 79 Garden Street, Cambridge, Massachusetts 02138; (617) 495-2600—[II:799]

Hilson Research Inc., 82-28 Abingdon Road, P.O. Box 239, Kew Gardens, New York 11415; (718)805-0063—[VI:265]

Hiskey, Marshall S., 5640 Baldwin, Lincoln, Nebraska 68507; (402)466-6145—[III:331]

Hodder & Stoughton Educational, A Division of Hodder & Stoughton Ltd., P.O. Box 702, Mill Road, Dunton Green, Sevenoaks, Kent TN13 2YD, England; (0732)450111—[IV:256; VII:646]

Hodges, Kay, Ph.D., 801 Duluth Street, Durham, North Carolina 27710; (919)684-6691—[VI:91]

Humanics Limited, 1389 Peachtree Street, Suite 370, Atlanta, Georgia 30309; (404)874-2176—[II:161, 426]

Humanics Media—[V:522, 524; VI:76 *See* Western Psychological Services]

Industrial Psychology Incorporated (IPI), 515 Madison Avenue, Suite 1614, New York, New York 10022; (212)355-5330—[II:363]

Institute for Child Behavior Research, 4182 Adams Avenue, San Diego, California 92116; (619)281-7165—[VII:185]

Institute for Personality and Ability Testing, Inc. (IPAT), P.O. Box 188, 1602 Coronado Drive, Champaign, Illinois 61820; (217)352-4739—[I:195, 202, 214, 233, 377; II:357; III:139, 246, 251, 319, 567; IV:595; V:283; VI:21, 359, 560; VII:374]

Institute for Psycho-Imagination Therapy, c/o Joseph Shorr, Ph.D., 111 North La Cienega Boulevard, #108, Beverly Hills, California 90211; (213)652-2922—[I:593]

Institute for Psychosomatic & Psychiatric Research & Training/Daniel Offer. *See* Center for the Study of Adolescence]

Institute for the Advancement of Philosophy for Children, Montclair State College, Upper Montclair, New Jersey 07043; (201)893-4277—[VII:365]

Institute of Psychological Research, Inc., 34 Fleury Street West, Montreal, Quebec H3L 1S9, Canada; (514)382-3000—[II:530; VI:601]

Instructional Materials & Equipment Distributors (IMED), 1520 Cotner Avenue, Los Angeles, California 90025; (213)879-0377—[V:109]

International Universities Press, Inc., 315 Fifth Avenue, New York, New York 10016; (212) 684-7900—[III:736]

INTREX Interpersonal Institute, P.O. Box 55218, Madison, Wisconsin 53705; (801)363-6236—[VII:541]

Jamestown Publishers, P.O. Box 9168, 544 Douglass Avenue, Providence, Rhode Island 02940; (800)USA-READ or (401)351-1915—[V:212]

Jastak Associates, Inc., 1526 Gilpin, Wilmington, Delaware 19806; (800)221-9278 or (302) 652-4990—[I:758, 762; IV:673; VI:135]

Johnson, Suzanne Bennett, Ph.D., Childrens's Mental Health Unit, Box J-234, J. Hillis Miller Health Sciences Center, University of Florida, Gainesville, Florida 32610—[VI:594]

Jossey-Bass, Inc., Publishers, 433 California Street, San Francisco, California 94104; (415)433-1740—[III:395]

Kent Developmental Metrics, 126 W. College Avenue, P.O. Box 845, Kent, Ohio 44240-3178; (216)678-3589—[III:380]

Khavari, Khalil A., Ph.D., Midwest Institute on Drug Use, University of Wisconsin-Milwaukee, Vogel Hall, Milwaukee, Wisconsin 53201; (414)963-4747—[VII:193]

Kovacs, Maria, Ph.D., 3811 O'Hara Street, Pittsburgh, Pennsylvania 15213-2593; (412) 624-2043—[V:65]

Krieger, Robert E., Publishing Company, Inc., P.O. Box 9542, Melbourne, Florida 32901; (305)724-9542—[III:30]

Ladoca Publishing Foundation—[I:239 *See* Denver Developmental Materials, Inc.]

Lafayette Instrument Company, Inc., P.O. Box 5729, Lafayette, Indiana 47903; (317)423-1505—[V:534]

Lake, David S., Publishers, 19 Davis Drive, Belmont, California 94002; (415)592-7810—[II:241]

Lea and Febiger, 600 Washington Square, Philadelphia, Pennsylvania 19106; (215)922-1330]

Learning House, distributed exclusively by Guidance Centre, Faculty of Education, University of Toronto, 10 Alcorn Avenue, Ontario, Canada M4V 2Z8—[VI:66, 70, 73]

Lefkowitz, Monroe M., Ph.D., P.O. Box 1685, Lenox, Massachusetts 01240; (413)637-2113—[VII:432]

Lewis, H. K., & Co. Ltd., 136 Gower Street, London WC1E 6BS, England; (01)387-4282—[I:47, 206, 595; IV:408]

Libraries Unlimited, P.O. Box 263, Littleton, Colorado 80160-0263; (303)770-1220—[VII:505]

LinguiSystems, Inc., 716 17th Street, Moline, Illinois 61265; (800)ALL-TIME, in Illinois (309)762-5112—[II:831; V:221; VII:282, 600]

London House Press, 1550 North Northwest Highway, Park Ridge, Illinois 60068; (800) 323-5923, in Illinois (312)298-7311—[III:510; IV:463; V:565; VI:529; VII:570]

Macmillan Education, Houndmills, Basingstoke, Hampshire RG21 2XS, England; (0256) 29242—[VII:40]

Marathon Consulting and Press, P.O. Box 09189, Columbus, Ohio 43209-0189; (614)237-5267—[II:138, 535; VI:640; VII:159]

Martinus Nijhoff—[III:288 *See* SWETS and Zeitlinger, B.V.]

Medical Research Council, Department of Psychological Medicine, Royal Free Hospital, Pond Street, London NW3 2QG, England; (01)794-0500—[V:314]

Merrill, Charles E., Publishing Company, 1300 Alum Creek Drive, P.O. Box 508, Columbus, Ohio 43216; (614)258-8441—[I:125; II:35; IV:3, 176, 590; VII:34 [*Editors' note:* Most C. E. Merrill tests now published by The Psychological Corporation.]]

Modern Curriculum Press, Inc.—[IV:229; V:37; VI:143 *See* PRO-ED]

Monitor, P.O. Box 2337, Hollywood, California 90028; no business phone—[V:21, 113; VI:3]

National Business Education Association, 1914 Association Drive, Reston, Virginia 22091; (703)860-8300—[VI:373]

National Computer Systems/PAS Division, P.O. Box 1416, Minneapolis, Minnesota 55440; (800)328-6759, in Minnesota (612)933-2800—[I:455, 466, 660; II:128; III:454; IV:425; VI:216, 252]

National Institute on Mental Retardation, Kinsmen NIMR Building, York University Campus, 4700 Keele Street, Downsview, Ontario M3J 1P3, Canada; (416)661-9611—[VI:622]

National Study of School Evaluation, 5201 Leesburg Pike, Falls Church, Virginia 22041;

VII:119, 245, 485]

Psychological Corporation, The, A Subsidiary of Harcourt Brace Jovanovich, Inc., 555 Academic Court, San Antonio, Texas 78204; (800)228-0752—[I:47, 106, 117, 206, 252, 295, 328, 494, 499, 595, 608, 614, 648, 720, 728, 740, 750; II:16, 63, 175, 182, 319, 326, 436, 446, 463, 495, 579, 653; III:13, 58, 226, 296, 427, 434, 633, 682, 698, 711; IV:149, 320, 394, 414, 478; V:271, 287; VI:38, 56, 158, 226, 322, 336, 341, 476, 536 ; VII:44, 264, 338, 350, 389, 438, 523, 633, 639]

Psychological Publications, Inc., 5300 Hollywood Boulevard, Los Angeles, California 90027; (213)465-4163—[I:654; IV:294]

Psychological Services, Inc., Test Publication Division, 100 West Broadway, Suite 1100, Glendale, California 91210; (818)244-0033—[I:266]

Psychological Test Specialists, P.O. Box 9229, Missoula, Montana 59805; no business phone—[I:530; II:299, 376, 451, 603; III:375; V:128]

Psychologists and Educators, Inc., P.O. Box 513, St. Louis, Missouri 63006; (314)536-2366—[I:568; III:206; V:323, 483; VI:412; VII:381]

Psychometric Affiliates, P.O. Box 807, Murfreesboro, Tennessee 37133; (615)890-6296—[IV:519; V:367; VI:437, 486]

Psychonomic Society, Inc., *Psychonomic Science*, 2904 Guadalupe, Austin, Texas 78705; (512)476-9687—[V:513]

Psytec, Inc., P.O. Box 300, Webster, North Carolina 28788; (704)227-7361—[V:55]

Pumroy, Donald K., Ph.D., CAPS, College of Education, University of Maryland, College Park, Maryland 20742; (301)454-2026—[VII:328]

Purdue University Bookstore, P.O. Box 3028, Station 11, 360 State Street, West Lafayette, Indiana 47906; (317)743-9618—[V:326]

Quay, Herbert C., Ph.D., P.O. Box 248074, University of Miami, Coral Gables, Florida 33124; (305)284-5208—[V:371]

Reddin, W. J., and Associates, Station Road, Motspur Park, New Malden, Surrey KT3 6JH, England—[VII:321]

Reid Psychological Systems, 233 North Michigan Avenue, Chicago, Illinois 60601; (312) 938-9200—[I:631]

Reitan Neuropsychology Laboratory, 1338 East Edison Street, Tucson, Arizona 85719; (602)795-3717—[I:305, 536; II:637; III:640]

Research Psychologists Press, Inc., 1110 Military Street, P.O. Box 610984, Port Huron, Michigan 48061-0984; (800)265-1285, in Michigan (313)982-4556—[II:369, 501; III:499; IV:144, 509]

Riverside Publishing Company, The, 8420 Bryn Mawr Avenue, Chicago, Illinois 60631; (800)323-9540, in Alaska, Hawaii, or Illinois call collect (312)693-0040—[I:421, 603, 641; II:416, 674, 835; III:475; IV:11, 310, 453; V:517; VI:277, 397, 544; VII:228, 255, 610]

Rocky Mountain Behavioral Science Institute, Inc. (RMBSI), P.O. Box 1066, Fort Collins, Colorado 80522; (303)221-0602—[I:436, 682; V:266]

Roll, Samuel, Ph.D., 5712 Osuna N.E., Albuquerque, New Mexico 87109; (505)881-1464—[II:559]

SCAN-TRON Corporation, Reading Test Division, 2021 East Del Amo Boulevard, Rancho Dominguez, California 90220; (213)638-0520—[VII:499]

Scholastic Testing Service, Inc. (STS), 480 Meyer Road, P.O. Box 1056, Bensenville, Illinois 60106; (312)766-7150—[I:300; II:45; III:75, 344; IV:245, 264, 666; V:90, 505; VI:239; VII:427, 619]

Schubert, Herman J. P., & Schubert, Daniel S. P., 500 Klein Road, Buffalo, New York; no business phone—[III:579]

Science Research Associates, Inc. (SRA), 155 North Wacker Drive, Chicago, Illinois 60606; (312)984-7000—[I:29, 364, 406; II:198, 204, 275, 282, 395, 759, 773, 815; III:620; IV:635, 642; VII:529]

Sewall Rehabilitation Center, 1360 Vine Street, Denver, Colorado 80206; (303)399-1800—[VI:469]

Sheridan Psychological Services, Inc., P.O. Box 6101, Orange, California 92667; (714) 639-2595—[VII:149]

Slosson Educational Publications, Inc., P.O. Box 280, East Aurora, New York 14052, (000) 828-4800, in New York (716)652-0930—[II:40; III:152; IV:251, 578, 620, 623; VI:509; VII:97, 513]

Social and Behavioral Sciences Documents, American Psychological Association, 1200 17th Street N.W., Washington, D.C. 20036—[VI:167]

Sowa, Claudia J., Room 168 Russner Hall, University of Virginia, Charlottesville, Virginia 22901; no business phone—[VI:426]

Special Child Publications (SCP), P.O. Box 33548, Seattle, Washington 98133; (206)771-5711—[II:216]

Springer Publishing Company, 200 Park Avenue South, New York, New York 10003; (212)431-4370—[III:539, 564, 686]

Stanford University Press—[II:737 *See* Consulting Psychologists Press, Inc.]

Stanton Corporation, 5701 Executive Center Drive, Suite 300, Charlotte, North Carolina 28229; (800)528-5745, in North Carolina (704)535-0060—[V:451]

Stoelting Company, 1350 South Kostner Avenue, Chicago, Illinois 60623; (312)522-4500—[I:274, 288, 411; II:255, 347, 383, 392, 411, 457, 491, 751; III:43, 302, 310, 496; IV:103, 157, 307, 341, 354, 357, 585; V:203, 230; VI:183, 292; VII:220]

Stress Research Company. [*See* Coddington, R. Dean]

SWETS and Zeitlinger B.V., Heereweg 347b, 2161 CA Lisse, The Netherlands; 02521-19113—[VI:204]

Teachers College Press, Teachers College, Columbia University, 1234 Amsterdam Avenue, New York, New York 10027; (212)678-3929—[II:244, 303; VII:126]

The Test Agency Ltd., Cournswood House, North Dean, High Wycombe, Bucks HP14 4NW, England; (024)3384—[VI:313]

Test Analysis and Development Corporation, 2400 Park Lane Drive, Boulder, Colorado 80301; (303)666-8651—[II:707; IV:400]

T.O.T.A.L. Child, Inc., 244 Deerfield Road, Cranston, Rhode Island 02920; (401)942-9955—[IV:444]

Union College, Character Research Project. [*See* Personality Research Services Ltd.]

United Educational Services, Inc., P.O. Box 357, East Aurora, New York 14052; (800) 458-7900—[V:26; VII:595]

United States Department of Defense, Testing Directorate, Headquarters, Military Entrance Processing Command, Attn: MEPCT, 2500 Green Bay Road, North Chicago, IL 60064; (800)323-0513, in Illinois call collect (312)688-6908—[I:61]

United States Department of Labor, 200 Constitution Avenue N.W., Room N-4460, Washington, D.C. 20213; (202)535-0192—[I:83; III:673; V:150; VII:240]

University Associates, Inc., Learning Resources Corporation, 8517 Production Avenue, P.O. Box 26240, San Diego, California 92121; (619)578-5900—[I:559; II:765; VI:109]

University of Illinois Press, 54 East Gregory Drive, Champaign, Illinois 61820; (217)333-0950—[I:354; II:543; V:32]

University of Minnesota Press—[I:466 *See* National Computer Systems/PAS Division]

University of Vermont, College of Medicine, Department of Psychiatry, Section of Child, Adolescent, and Family Psychiatry, 1 South Prospect Street, Burlington, Vermont 05401; (802)656-4563—[I:168]

University of Washington Press, P.O. Box 50096, Seattle, Washington 98145; (206)543-4050, business department (206)543-8870—[II:661, 714]

Valett, Robert E., Department of Advanced Studies, California State University at Fresno, Fresno, California 93740; no business phone—[II:68]

Variety Pre-Schooler's Workshop, 47 Humphrey Drive, Syosset, New York 11791; (516) 921-7171—[III:261]

Vocational Psychology Research, University of Minnesota, N620 Elliott Hall, 75 East River Road, Minneapolis, Minnesota 55455; (612)625-1367—[II:481; IV:434; V:255; VI:350]

Vocational Research Institute, 2100 Arch Street, 6th Floor, Philadelphia, Pennsylvania 19103; (215)496-9674—[VII:623]

Walker Educational Book Corporation, 720 Fifth Avenue, New York, New York 10019; (212)265-3632—[II:689]

Western Psychological Services, A Division of Manson Western Corporation, 12031 Wilshire Boulevard, Los Angeles, California 90025; (213)478-2061—[I:315, 338, 511, 543, 663; II:108, 430, 570, 607, 723, 826; III:145, 255, 282, 340, 402, 415, 615, 714, 717; IV:15, 33, 39, 259, 274, 300, 351, 382, 440, 501, 565, 606, 649; V:9, 73, 83, 378, 382, 425, 458, 549; VI:60, 260, 505, 519, 576, 629; VII:277, 301, 313, 404, 463, 480]

Westwood Press, Inc., 251 Park Avenue South, 14th Floor, New York, New York 10010; (212)420-8008—[VII:466]

The Wilmington Press, 13315 Wilmington Drive, Dallas, Texas 75234; (214)620-8531—[VI:383]

Wonderlic, E. F., & Associates, Inc., Frontage Road, Northfield, Illinois 60093; (312)446-8900—[I:769]

World of Work, Inc., 2923 North 67th Place, Scottsdale, Arizona 85251; (602)946-1884—[VI:644]

Wyeth Laboratories, P.O. Box 8616, Philadelphia, Pennsylvania 19101; (215)688-4400—[V:499]

York Press, Inc., 2712 Mount Carmel Road, Parkton, Maryland 21120; (301)343-1417—[VII:163]

Zung, William W. K., M.D., Veterans Administration Medical Center, 508 Fulton Street, Durham, North Carolina 27705; (919)286-0411—[III:595]

INDEX OF TEST AUTHORS/REVIEWERS

SUBJECT INDEX

Marriage and Family: Family

Marriage and Family: Premarital and Marital Relations

Neuropsychology and Related

Personality: Adolescent and Adult

Personality: Child

Personality: Multi-level

Research

EDUCATION

Academic Subjects: Business Education

Academic Subjects: English and Related: Preschool, Elementary, and Junior High School

Academic Subjects: English and Related Multi-level

Academic Subjects: Fine Arts

Academic Subjects: Foreign Language & English as a Second Language

Academic Subjects: Industrial Arts

Academic Subjects: Mathematics Basic Math Skills

Academic Subjects: Mathematics-Upper Math Skills

Academic Achievement and Aptitude

Education Development and School Readiness

Intelligence and Related

Library and Media Skills

Miscellaneous

Management and Supervision

ABOUT THE EDITORS

Daniel J. Keyser, Ph.D. Since completing postgraduate work at the University of Kansas in 1974, Dr. Keyser has worked in drug and alcohol rehabilitation and psychiatric settings. In addition, he has taught undergraduate psychology at Rockhurst College for 15 years. Dr. Keyser specializes in behavioral medicine—biofeedback, pain control, stress management, terminal care support, habit management, and wellness maintenance—and maintains a private clinical practice in the Kansas City area. Dr. Keyser co-edited *Tests: First Edition, Tests: Supplement,* and *Tests: Second Edition* and has made significant contributions to computerized psychological testing. More recently, he has been involved in the development of Test Corporation's *Applied Testing Series.*

Richard C. Sweetland, Ph.D. After completing his doctorate at Utah State University in 1968, Dr. Sweetland completed postdoctoral training in psychoanalytically oriented clinical psychology at the Topeka State Hospital in conjunction with the training program of the Menninger Foundation. Following appointments in child psychology at the University of Kansas Medical Center and in neuropsychology at the Kansas City Veterans Administration Hospital, he entered the practice of psychotherapy in Kansas City. In addition to his clinical work in neuropsychology and psychoanalytic psychotherapy, Dr. Sweetland has been involved extensively in the development of computerized psychological testing. Dr. Sweetland co-edited *Tests: First Edition, Tests: Supplement,* and *Tests: Second Edition* and is currently involved in developing Test Corporation's new *Applied Testing Series.*